Gourmet's BEST DESSERTS

Gourmet's BEST DESSERTS

From the Editors of Gourmet

CONDÉ NAST BOOKS
RANDOM HOUSE • NEW YORK

Copyright © 1987 Condé Nast Books

All rights reserved under International and Pan-American copyright conventions. Published in the United States by Random House, Inc., New York, and simultaneously in Canada by Random House of Canada, Limited, Toronto.

Library of Congress Cataloging-in-Publication Data

Gourmet's best desserts.

Includes index.
1. Desserts. I. Gourmet.
TX773.G67 1987   641.8′6   87-15055
ISBN 0-394-56422-7

Most of the recipes in this book were previously published in *Gourmet*.

Manufactured in the United States of America

98765432   24689753   23456789

Book design: Barbara Marks
Instructional illustrations: Lauren Jarrett
Decorative illustrations: Patti Hefner

Frontispiece: Zabaglione with Raspberries (page 343)

PROJECT STAFF

For Condé Nast Books
Jill Cohen, Director
Jonathan E. Newhouse, Special Consultant
Ellen Maria Bruzelius, Project Manager
Kristine Smith, Project Assistant
Diane Pesce, Composition Manager
Serafino J. Cambareri, Quality Control Manager

For *Gourmet*
Jane Montant, Editor-in-Chief
Evie Righter, Editor
Kathleen Nilon, Assistant Editor
Romulo Yanes, Staff Photographer

For Random House, Inc.
Anet Sirna-Bruder, Production Manager
Sarah Timberman, Project Editor

Produced in association with Media Projects, Incorporated.
Carter Smith, Executive Editor
Judy Knipe, Project Editor
Charlotte McGuinn Freeman, Permissions Editor
Barbara Marks, Art Director
Maro Riofrancos, Indexer

Gourmet Books is indebted to Georgia Chan Downard for her superb professionalism and invaluable culinary knowledge in creating and testing recipes for this project.

Gourmet Books would like to thank Zanne E. Zakroff, Kemp M. Minifie and Sara Moulton, in particular, as well as the food department of *Gourmet* for their generous participation. Appreciation is due, too, to Marjorie H. Webb and Nancy Purdum for their meticulous attention to detail in the styling of *Gourmet* photographs.

Gourmet's Best Desserts would be a significantly different title were it not for the wonderful contributions of Luis Lemus, staff photographer from 1969 to 1984, and our current staff photographer, Romulo Yanes.

Media Projects and Gourmet Books would like to thank Joan Michel, Blair Brown Hoyt, and especially Donna Ryan for their assistance in the preparation of the manuscript.

The text of this book was set in Bembo by the Composition Department of Condé Nast Publications, Inc. The four-color separations were done by The Color Company. The book was printed and bound by R. R. Donnelley & Sons. Text paper is 80-pound Consoweb Brilliant Gloss.

CONTENTS

COLOR PHOTOGRAPHS

LINE ILLUSTRATIONS

Beating eggs and sugar over simmering water. Beaten eggs and sugar falling in a ribbon. 16

Slicing cake horizontally. Holding cake on outstretched palm. Positioning cake on cake pan. Positioning cake on cake stand. Rotating cake to frost. Using cake comb. 19

Filling and holding a pastry bag. Piping a rosette. Assorted pastry tips. Forming a parchment paper cone. Feathering sugar icing. 20

Rolling up a jelly roll. 41

Pouring warm glaze over cake. 66

Cutting in butter with fingertips/with two knives. Rolling pie dough over rolling pin. Rolling pie dough off rolling pin. 121

Crimping pie dough for decorative edge: fluted edge; scalloped edge; rope edge. Cutting lattice strips. Weaving lattice crust. A simple lattice crust, a decorative edge. 122

Cutting pastry leaf cutouts. 145

Rolling tart dough over rolling pin; rolling dough off rolling pin. Trimming crust with pin. Pricking bottom of shell; weighting lined shell with raw rice; lined and weighted shell on baking sheet. 163

Arranging apple slices, rounded side up, in tart shell. 172

Arranging papaya slices decoratively in tart shell. 174

Steps for making puff paste: Blending flour and butter with pastry blender; cutting deep cross in center of the dough; kneading butter and flour together. Rolling détrempe into rough square; rolling corners of dough into strips; folding strips of dough over butter to enclose butter completely. Rolling dough into rectangle; folding top third of dough rectangle over center and bottom third over the top (first turn); turning folded dough seam side down. 190

Forming free-form square puff paste shell. 192

Forming free-form round puff paste shell. 193

Forming free-form puff paste strip. 194

Cutting top layer of dough and assembling jalousie. 197

Forming and scoring gâteau Pithiviers. 200

Forming palmiers. 205

Rolling Danish pastry dough: Arranging butter on bottom half of dough rectangle; rolling out dough; rolling the first turn. 216

Forming Danish pastry bear claws and envelopes. 219

Steps for making pâte à chou: Adding flour all at once to butter mixture; beating flour mixture until it forms a ball; incorporating eggs. 220

Piping pâte à chou puffs with pastry bag. 223

Piping out éclairs with pastry bag. 226

Stretching strudel dough. 235

Egg whites at soft peak stage; egg whites and sugar at stiff peak stage. 238

Pouring hot sugar syrup into beaten egg whites. 240

Six stages of sugar syrup: Thread; soft ball; firm ball; hard ball; soft crack; hard crack. 241

Piping out a continuous spiral of meringue to form a layer. 251

Piping ladyfingers at angles across length of baking sheet. 287

Shaping cookie wafers in bowl, pinching in sides to make tulipe. 288

Curling cookie wafers around rolling pin. 290

Procedure for steaming a pudding. 326

Making caramel cage: Drizzling syrup with fork over ladle to form web. 363

Doubling piece of paper to form collar; fitting soufflé dish with collar. 417

Spinning sugar with whisk between spoon handles to form threads. 543

INTRODUCTION

When we began selecting *Gourmet's Best Desserts,* we looked first to the early 1960's. What we remember of those enchanted years was an exceptional state of hope. We whistled "Camelot," and life and style for several years, at least, were high and fashionable. France held great sway in the American mind, and its fashion and cuisine dominated American thinking. At that time, too, we witnessed an extraordinary interest in travel to Europe and were enriched with that great dividend of exploration—returning home with new ideas, recipes, and aspirations. Interest flourished in international cuisines and especially in French cooking, the wines of France, and the very country itself. In fact, it was in 1961 that Julia Child *et al.*'s Volume I of *Mastering the Art of French Cooking* was published.

The late James Beard, a dear friend and a former contributor to *Gourmet* from 1969 to 1971, and the person most responsible for changing how Americans think of food, continued his remarkable literary output during the 1970's and published in 1972 *American Cookery,* a loving history book of recipes and anecdotes on classic American combinations and their derivation. And even though trans-Atlantic flight had been reduced to just over three hours in a supersonic plane, Americans were rediscovering their native traditions. So that while the world rocked on its axis during the 1970's, the world of food and interest in all things culinary continued to gain momentum. It was a time of experimentation, and we would all gain.

Then, predictably, but long overdue, in the 1980's American cooking came full swing into its own. Our young Turks had gone to Europe to study and cook. They had come home with lots of culinary ideas, not the least of which celebrated all things American. Culinary curiosity bounced from one coast to the other with wonderful stopovers mid-country. We started to grow our own herbs at home, make our own cheeses and *crème fraîche,* applaud homemade doughnuts and those other indigenous American favorites—lemon meringue pie and vanilla ice cream and brownies—and the list could go on and on. Our elaborate dinner parties of the 1960's—and we did seem to have the time to prepare them then—were simplified. The demands of our busier life styles required fine food that was lighter and easier to make.

During those years *Gourmet* remained in the forefront of culinary think-

ing. Back issues of the magazine give testimony to how tastes did change and demonstrate *Gourmet*'s long-standing appreciation of American cuisine. *Gourmet* recipes also prove how timeless is the standard of excellence.

Gourmet's Best Desserts, then, presents the very best recipes from a twenty-five-year period. To say that there is at least one recipe for everyone is an understatement. There are the classics: from France, the fanciful Gâteau Saint-Honoré, heady Pineapple Savarin Chantilly, and beautiful Bavarois Rubané; from America, the incomparable Devil's Food Cake with Rhubarb Sauce, Old-Fashioned Lemon Hermits, and the ever-true Rice Pudding. There are more contemporary combinations like Rum-Marinated Mango Crêpes and White Chocolate Mousse with Dark Chocolate Sauce. We have even included some brand-new recipes—a glorious Chocolate Brioche Bread Pudding, for one—to render this compilation as complete and enticing as we possibly could.

Fifteen chapters are presented, starting with Cakes, continuing on to Pies and Tarts, and thirteen chapters later ending with Essential Preparations. Each chapter begins with a general introduction, and some, like Pastry and Meringues, to mention only two, contain detailed instructional text with illustrations on the basic techniques called for in those respective chapters. (Throughout we have annotated all recipes with cross references to illustrations in other chapters as well.) When a chapter has several sections, as does Pastry, for instance, each new grouping of recipes also begins with a short introduction.

As to the order of the recipes in each chapter, we have always begun with the most basic. In Puddings and Custards, for example, we start with vanilla cornstarch pudding. Simple, but dandy. In Pastry, we embark with a recipe and explanation for making classic puff paste, and then several recipes later we test your skills with the magnificent and challenging Gâteau Pithiviers. Throughout this volume are *Gourmet*'s splendid four-color photographs, which should be referred to as much for their handsomeness as for the pointers they provide on presentation. Finally, two indexes—a general index and a recipe title index—will assist you in finding the dessert of choice.

All recipes have been reformatted for this volume; each lists equipment that will be needed, and many are preceded by helpful notes explaining some aspect or even the history of the recipe.

Gourmet's Best Desserts chronicles the art of dessert-making. Simultaneously this book celebrates a remarkable tradition of American cooking—our readiness to embrace other cuisines and yet remain faithful to our own. It was an extraordinary opportunity to select what we consider to be *Gourmet*'s best desserts over the last twenty-five years, and whether you are making the splendid recipes within or reading them for their intrinsic pleasure, we hope you will enjoy this volume for an equal amount of time.

JANE MONTANT
Editor-in-Chief
July, 1987

Gourmet's BEST DESSERTS

CAKES

e celebrate with cake—birthdays, weddings, christenings, holidays. There is hardly an important event in our lives that goes unnoticed—without cake, we mean. And for good reason: Cake is a glorious concept.

To begin with, think of the number of different types of cake that exist, just awaiting delectation. There are spongecakes that can be filled and rolled or layered and iced. There are pound cakes, and loaf cakes, and Bundt cakes, and cheesecakes. There are two-layer cakes, three-layer cakes, seven-layer cakes, and tortes. There are fruitcakes and keeping cakes and cakes with fresh fruit. And those are just *some* of the types. Then there are the flavors. A chocolate cake is not a spice cake is not a vanilla cake is not a buttermilk cake. But then again, a chocolate cake is not a cocoa cake either. It is fair to say, when you come right down to it, no two cakes are alike.

Another aspect of the universal appeal of cakes has to do with the fact that no matter your level of expertise there is a cake for you to bake. Easiest to do are those one-bowl batters. Then there are the constructs—layer upon layer, with syrups and cream, and pale pink flowers on the top. You will reserve perhaps two days for that cake and regret not one minute.

History and culture are also part of cake-making. The great cuisines of the world—French, Italian, Austrian, and American—have all contributed to the repertoire. How a French cake differs from an Austrian cake is an interesting lesson in geography and government combined.

In the one hundred or so recipes that ensue we included numerous classic receipts, those that have stood the test of time—devil's food cake and strawberry shortcakes, as examples. We have also included some nonclassics, but wonderful combinations nonetheless. See Highland Molasses Ginger Cake with Glacéed Fruits (page 108). To maximize cake-making in general, information and illustrations follow on technique.

The natural sequence of events is to celebrate with cake. Let us instead celebrate the cake.

Cassata (page 27)

*B*aking a cake involves three separate but equally important processes: (1) preparation of the cake batter, (2) baking of that batter and cooling of the cake, and, (3) its decorating, or finishing. Without steps 1 and 2, there is no step 3, and without a reasonably executed step 3, steps 1 and 2 are sadly compromised. In truth, a glorious cake—and there are so many wonderful recipes for them—is the sum of its parts. Let us, therefore, address each of these steps individually.

PREPARING TO BAKE

Before making a batter you will want to prepare your cake pans, preheat the oven, and assemble your ingredients, probably in that order. Be sure to butter or grease your pans carefully as even the most perfectly executed batter will look woebegone if the layer won't drop easily from the pan. Also, allow your oven to preheat sufficiently. By all means rely upon an oven thermometer. And try to ascertain if there are hot spots in your oven. If so, you will need to rotate the cake pans front to back and vice versa once during baking to ensure an even bake. Unless otherwise indicated, most cakes bake on the middle rack of the oven and that rack should be in place before you start preheating the oven.

For baking in general, but especially for the baking of cakes and pastries, it is important to measure the ingredients accurately. There is no such thing as "a touch of this and a little of that" in baking. The chemistry of cake-making does not allow for it. Therefore, the proper measuring cups are needed, particularly for the dry ingredients. Metal or plastic nested cups tend to work best, and *Gourmet* has traditionally spooned flour into the cup and leveled off the top of the cup with a spatula or knife. Know that it is this manner of measuring flour that has been used throughout in the recipes in this book. To deviate from it is to alter the amount of flour called for. Remember, too, that certain ingredients, such as baking powder, lose their potency with time and should be periodically replaced on the shelf. Now you are ready to make the batter.

MAKING THE CAKE

While cake batters differ in specific ingredients, all batters have some things in common: butter, shortening or vegetable oil, eggs, sugar, flour, and flavorings. It is the proportion of these ingredients that determines the kind of batter and, consequently, the kind of cake you make. For example, we all know that a *génoise* layer does not resemble a pound cake in texture. We also recognize that an angel food cake and a chiffon cake are not the same. We also rightfully suspect that spongecake batters differ. What differentiates each of these is its batter, and it is the ingredients of that batter and how they are combined that will render the unique characteristics of that kind of cake.

There are three different types of cakes. There are those cakes that incorporate significantly little fat and rely on beaten eggs for leavening. We call these spongecakes. Among this grouping is the renowned *génoise*, base to many a glorious combination. How this type of cake is prepared is specific and for purposes of identification will be called the sponge, or foam, method.

On the other hand, there are those that have a high fat content, meaning they rely on butter mixed most frequently with sugar, with eggs, flavorings, and flour added. These cakes are rich and moist and require a certain method of preparation to achieve that crumb. Let us call it the creaming method.

Lastly, there are those cakes that do not rely on either the sponge or creaming method, but on an ingredient that is added to bring elevation about—baking powder or baking soda or both. These are called blended batters, and they are much easier to prepare than the two kinds of batter described above.

Because *génoise* layers are so multipurpose and can be employed as the base of so many combinations—see Cassata (page 27), for example, Hazelnut Génoise with Coffee Buttercream (page 23), and Petits Rouleaux (page 28), to name just a few—it is important to know what to look for when combining this batter of eggs, sugar, flour, salt, vanilla, and clarified butter. As mentioned, it is a foam batter dependent upon beaten eggs for leavening. You begin by combining the eggs with the sugar; you then place that bowl over a pan of simmering water and stir the mixture until warm and the sugar is thoroughly dissolved (see illustration page 16). Do not allow the bottom of the bowl to touch the hot water. It is primarily the combination of the heat and the stirring that expands the molecules in the eggs. You then remove the bowl from the pan and with an electric mixer beat the batter until it triples in volume. This is a very clear point in the stage of this batter and the signal to proceed with quickly folding in the dry ingredients, and lastly, the clarified butter. A *génoise* batter should then be poured into the prepared pan(s) and baked immediately.

For other foam method cakes, the batter is actually beaten with an

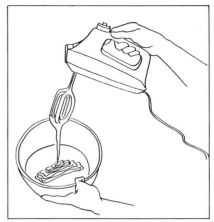

Beating over simmering water   Falling in a ribbon

electric mixer to a point where it falls in a ribbon back on itself (see illustration above). This is yet another way of incorporating as much air as possible into the batter, which in turn leavens the cake.

As specific as the preparation of a foam batter is, so is preparation of a creamed batter. You begin by beating air into softened butter and sugar and you continue to work air into that batter until it has achieved a creamy, full texture. When that batter has achieved that texture, it is ready to be baked, and, unless your eyes were deceiving you, you can expect a strong, healthy elevation from such a correctly air–filled prepared batter.

Blended batters are by far and away the easiest ones to combine and, as already noted, depend upon no specific stage of preparation for leavening. Baking powder and baking soda or both, and even yeast, will provide the chemical impetus.

With the batter made, you can proceed to the truly fascinating aspect of cake-baking, the transformation of batter that occurs in combination with heat.

BAKING THE CAKE

While some culinary combinations lend themselves to being made in advance, cake batters do not fall into this convenient category. Once made, a batter, especially one with baking powder or stiffly beaten egg whites, for that matter, should be baked.

As mentioned earlier, unless otherwise indicated, cakes bake on the middle rack of a preheated oven. Know, too, that baking times are not written in stone. They are indications. Your oven, or an environmental factor like altitude, will have a sizable effect on how long a cake bakes. Therefore, slightly before the end of the suggested baking time start testing your cake for doneness. You can use a wooden skewer, a toothpick, or a clean broom straw. Some sources might suggest inserting a knife into the center of the layer, but we believe the thinner the tester the better.

It is easy to tell when a tester inserted into a cake comes out "clean" or "with crumbs adhering to it." It is also obvious when the tester comes out wet—with batter on it—as is sometimes desired. In this specific instance, though, it is not necessarily obvious that the cake is actually baked through. Here is where the suggested time for a cake to remain in the pan on a rack becomes significant. During that period a cake continues to cook, and in its own way, set. We've all had experiences when, in a rush, we tried to unmold a cake almost straight from the oven. Without having had the opportunity to finish baking, or to cool and contract, as the case may be, the layer is far too fragile, to say nothing of hot, to unmold.

When the cake is ready to unmold, using one hand, bring the cooling rack right up to the rim of the cake pan, which you hold in your other hand with your palm stretched out along the bottom. Gently turn the cake pan upside down on the rack. To dump a cake is a most successful way of breaking it.

As important as it is to let a cake cool in the pan on a rack, allowing air to fully circulate, so it is important to let the cake cool completely out of the pan. Recognize, though, that certain cakes, if left to cool for too long, can develop a hard crust. You do not want to leave any cake to cool on the counter overnight.

FINISHING THE CAKE

With a cooled cake you can proceed to finishing it, or to putting the icing on the cake! This might be as simple as sifting confectioners' sugar on top, as we do with Sand Torte (page 72), or having a sugar or chocolate glaze ready and pouring it over the top of the cake. See Scripture Cake (page 74) and Armagnac Chocolate Cake with Prunes (page 63). And then again, it might mean pulling out all the stops as we do with Bride's Cake (page 104), where a buttercream, a seven-minute icing, and royal icing flowers all adorn the glorious fourteen-layer finished product. Needless to say, experience and nerve dictate the cakes one bakes and decorates.

Regardless of your level of experience, cake decorating requires practice. No one, not even the most adroit baker, has learned how to work a pastry bag overnight. Decorating cakes also necessitates equipment:
- several light-weight pastry bags with an assortment of decorative tips, which would initially include a plain, star, and fluted tip
- a cake stand
- a cake comb
- a collection of different sized spatulas

All of these will be available at better kitchenware stores.
More than anything else, though, you will need time and the opportunity to practice. Think of the splendid reasons you now have for baking cakes!

Let us assume you are decorating a layer cake such as Walnut Cake with Coffee Buttercream (page 56). You will have made your buttercream while the cake is cooling. Your layers are now on the counter; your equipment is assembled. Instead of what the recipe calls for, you decide you want to halve the layers, making not a two- but a four-layer cake. As illustrated opposite, place one hand on the top of one of the layers to gently anchor it. Then, using a long-bladed, serrated knife, cut the cake horizontally through the center into even layers. There is no reason to rotate the cake; with a simple sawing motion cut it apart. Transfer the bottom layer to a cake stand, if you are using one, and spread the cut side of it evenly with buttercream or another filling of choice—jam, for instance. Replace the top layer, cut side down, on top of the filling. Split, fill, and stack the remaining layer in the same manner.

There are several ways to position a cake to make it easier to apply the frosting. As shown on page 19, you can hold the cake in one hand on your outstretched palm. You can also place the cake on an inverted cake pan of the same size as the cake. Or you can place it on a cake stand. It is easier to frost a cake if the sides are free-standing, and in this regard we highly recommend a turntable, available at better kitchenware stores, if you are eager for a professionally finished appearance to your cake. If you opt to frost the cake on the platter on which you are going to serve it, cover the edge of the platter with strips of wax paper, which you can simply remove by pulling gently from under the cake when you have finished decorating it.

Using an appropriately sized spatula, spread the sides of the cake first, using a flicking downward motion of your wrist, and then the top evenly with buttercream. To achieve a very smooth final finish, then hold the spatula stationary in one hand against the buttercream on the sides of the cake and rotate the cake to even out the icing. This is a simultaneous action and a very consistent amount of gentle pressure should be applied to the spatula, otherwise the buttercream on one side of the cake will be thicker than on the other. To level out the buttercream on the top of the cake, lay the spatula flat against the buttercream and rotate the cake as before. When you are done, you should have a beautiful smooth surface that doesn't even suggest use of a spatula. Practice will make this easier to do as well.

You are now ready to finish the cake. The choice of how you want to do this is yours, despite what a recipe might dictate. There is the cake comb which, when drawn around the top or sides of the cake, renders a very, simple pretty, circular ridged pattern. It is also easy and fast to do. Press some toasted chopped nuts around the sides of the cake, and *c'est fini*, the cake is finished.

For a more elaborate presentation, you can decorate the cake with

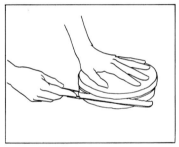

Slicing horizontally

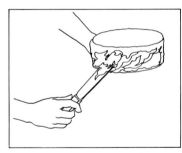

Holding on outstretched palm

Positioning on cake pan

Positioning on cake stand

Rotating cake to frost

Using cake comb

rosettes of buttercream, just one of many designs you will come to recognize. This will involve working with the pastry bag. You will first need to select the proper tip, a selection of which is shown in the illustrations on page 20. Each tip produces a different design, as you can tell from the names. The more proficient you become with a pastry bag, the larger your collection of decorative tips will grow.

To make rosettes you will be using a star, also known as a rosette, tip. Fit it onto the pastry bag; then using the spatula to transfer buttercream, fill the bag as shown on page 20. Use a manageable amount of buttercream to begin with. Twist the top of the bag closed and at the same time gently squeeze the buttercream in the bag down toward the tip. You are now ready to start forming rosettes, or swirls. Holding the top of the bag in one hand, put your other hand at the bottom near the tip and guide the bag in a circular motion, or spiral, as you gently apply pressure on the buttercream to extrude it onto the top of the cake. Finish the spiral by lifting the tip straight up and continue making rosettes in the same manner. The key to making rosettes, or any pattern, lies in the amount of pressure you use on the bag.

Should you want to finish the rosettes with, let us say, a touch of chocolate glaze or a different-colored buttercream, there is no need to utilize another pastry bag. Using parchment or wax paper you can form a cone that acts as a pastry bag. This improvisation is put to good use in bakeries and pastry shops, where each color of frosting requires yet another

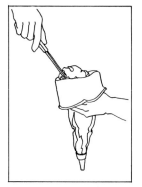

Filling and holding a pastry bag

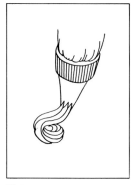

Piping a rosette

plain	large star	rose petal	fluted	rope

Assorted pastry tips

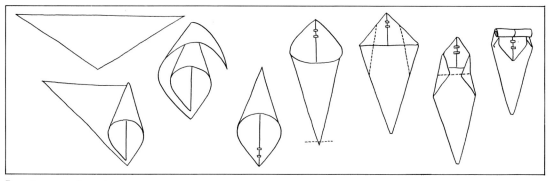

Forming a parchment paper cone

Feathering icing

clean pastry bag. You will find this paper cone comes in very handy when decorating Gingerbread Men (page 303) with Sugar Icing (page 540) or Spice Cookie Hearts (page 302) with royal icing (page 515). Following the illustrations opposite, simply cut a triangle of paper, form it into a tight cone, and fill it with a small amount of frosting.

Fine finishing also includes a technique called feathering, which requires no special equipment once you have applied the frosting that you are going to detail. Let us again assume you have applied a thin line of royal icing to the top of the cake as on Chocolate Mousse Dacquoise (page 248). As shown in the illustration opposite, gently draw a knife through the icing, pulling it in one direction, creating a feathery, fluted effect. Then pull the knife in the opposite direction. The pattern looks far more complicated than its execution dictates.

This short primer on cake decorating only hints at the wonders that can be created with frosting and a pastry bag. When you are up for a challenge, attempt Royal Icing Flowers (page 515). And then there are all those other marvelous devices, like Marzipan Decorations (page 545), that amuse the top of Carrot Cake with Cream Cheese Frosting (page 51).

With a cake the pleasures are endless. There is the fun of making and decorating it, and then the joy of eating it. No sooner is that done than the next cake calls.

GÉNOISE

We know *génoise* layers as those extraordinarily light French cakes made of eggs, sugar, flour, and clarified butter. In fact, the history books have it that *génoise*, as its name indicates, originated in Genoa, Italy, then traveled to France, where it found a permanent home.

What we also know about *génoise* is that it is not a simple batter. It needs to be beaten with an electric mixer to three times its original volume; in short, while you might contemplate trying to do something like this by hand, you are advised not to. But do not avoid making *génoise* on account of this. The cake acts as the foundation of any number of wonderful desserts. It is eminently adaptable and lends itself to being layered not only with buttercream but also with ice cream, and *crème anglaise*, and even pastry cream.

There is vanilla *génoise*, chocolate *génoise*. There are *génoise* layers and sheets. *Génoise* rolls, *génoise* slices. If you want to master one very basic batter, which *Gourmet* has relied upon for years with great success, *génoise* is the one to conquer. (For information on the combining of the batter and an illustration, see pages 15 and 16.)

VANILLA GÉNOISE BATTER

Yield:
two 9-inch layers

Equipment:
hand-held electric
mixer

6 large eggs
1 cup sugar
1 cup all-purpose flour
¾ teaspoon salt

1½ teaspoons vanilla
6 tablespoons clarified butter (page
536), melted and cooled to
lukewarm

In a metal bowl whisk together the eggs and the sugar, set the bowl over a pan of simmering water, and stir the mixture until warm and the sugar is dissolved (see illustration page 16). Remove the bowl from the pan and with the mixer beat the mixture at moderate speed for 10 to 15 minutes, or until it is triple in volume and cooled to room temperature. While the eggs are being beaten, sift the flour with the salt onto a sheet of wax paper and in a bowl combine the vanilla and the clarified butter. Sift and fold the flour mixture in batches into the egg mixture until the mixture is just combined, stir one fourth of the mixture into the butter mixture, and fold the butter mixture quickly into the batter.

Variation:

CHOCOLATE GÉNOISE BATTER: Reduce the amount of flour to ⅔ cup and add ⅓ cup unsweetened cocoa powder. Sift the flour and cocoa, one third at a time, into the beaten egg mixture. Proceed with the recipe as directed.

GÉNOISE SHEET CAKE

Yield:
jelly-roll, one 15½ by
10½ inches sheet
for 1

Equipment:
jelly-roll pan, 15½ by
10½ inches

1 recipe vanilla or chocolate génoise *batter (recipe above)*

Butter the jelly-roll pan, line it with wax paper, leaving a 2-inch overhang on both short ends, and butter the paper. Preheat the oven to 350° F.

Pour the *génoise* batter into the pan, spreading it evenly with a metal spatula. Bake the sheet in the middle of the oven for 20 minutes, or until the paper pulls away easily from the ends of the cake. Cover the cake with wax paper and a baking sheet, and invert the cake onto the baking sheet. Peel off the wax paper and trim away any rough edges from the sides of the the cake. Cover the cake with a fresh piece of wax paper, roll it up, and let cake cool completely.

Unroll, fill, and reroll the cake. Transfer the cake carefully with metal spatulas to a cake board.

HAZELNUT GÉNOISE WITH COFFEE BUTTERCREAM

Yield:
one 8-inch cake

1 recipe vanilla génoise *batter (recipe opposite)*

FOR THE COFFEE BUTTERCREAM

Equipment:
two 8-inch cake pans
upright electric mixer
pastry brush
candy thermometer
7-inch cardboard
 round

6 egg yolks
¾ cup sugar
⅓ cup water
2½ sticks (1¼ cups) unsalted butter,
 softened

2 tablespoons coffee extract, or to
 taste, made by mixing 2
 tablespoons instant freeze-dried
 coffee or espresso with 1 tablespoon
 boiling water
1 to 2 tablespoons Cognac or rum

½ recipe sugar syrup (page 542) with
 1 to 2 tablespoons Cognac or rum
 added when syrup cools to room
 temperature

1 cup finely ground hazelnut praline
 (page 544)

Butter the cake pans, line the bottoms with wax paper, and butter the paper. Dust the pans with flour, knocking out the excess. Preheat the oven to 350° F.

Pour the *génoise* batter into the pans, smoothing the tops, and bake the layers in the middle of the oven for 20 to 25 minutes, or until the tops are golden and a tester comes out clean. Let the layers cool in the pans on a rack for 5 minutes, invert the cakes onto racks, and carefully remove the wax paper. Let the cakes cool completely.

Make the buttercream:

In the bowl of the mixer beat the egg yolks until light and thick. In a small heavy saucepan combine the sugar and the water. Bring the syrup to a boil and boil it over moderate heat, stirring and washing down any sugar crystals clinging to the sides of the pan with the brush dipped in cold water until it reaches the soft-ball stage, or the candy thermometer registers 238° F. (For the stages of sugar syrup, see illustrations page 241.)

With the mixer running, pour the hot syrup into the yolks in a stream, beating, and continue to beat the mixture until it is completely cool. Beat in the butter, a little at a time, add coffee extract to taste, and beat well. Stir in the Cognac or rum. Chill the coffee buttercream, covered, until firm but still soft enough to spread.

The layers may be made up to 1 day in advance and kept wrapped in plastic wrap at room temperature. The cake may be assembled up to 2 days in advance, covered loosely with plastic wrap, and chilled. Let the cake come to room temperature before serving.

Put 1 teaspoon of the buttercream in the center of the cardboard round. Halve one of the layers horizontally with a serrated knife, arrange one half-layer, cut side up, on the cardboard round, and brush some of the sugar syrup over the cake. Cover the layer with a ¼-inch-thick layer of buttercream, smoothing it with a metal spatula, and sprinkle it with 2 tablespoons of the hazelnut praline.

Set the second half-layer, bottom side up, on the buttercream, pressing down slightly, and moisten the top of the cake with sugar syrup. Cover the top with a ¼-inch-thick layer of buttercream, smoothing it with a metal spatula, and sprinkle it with 2 tablespoons of the hazelnut praline. Halve the remaining cake horizontally and continue to layer the cake, ending with a fourth layer, bottom side up. Moisten the top of the cake with sugar syrup and cover the sides and top with the remaining buttercream, smoothing it with the spatula. Press the remaining hazelnut praline around the sides of the cake and chill the *génoise* until the buttercream is set.

ORANGE GÉNOISE WITH ORANGE BUTTERCREAM

Yield:
one 9-inch cake

Equipment:
two 9-inch round
  cake pans, 1½
  inches deep
upright electric mixer
pastry brush
candy thermometer

Here is the classic *génoise* combination. Two light layers are brushed with flavored syrup, then the whole is iced with buttercream and fancifully decorated. A splendid cake for the summer.

1 recipe vanilla génoise batter (page 22)

FOR THE ORANGE BUTTERCREAM

6 egg yolks	*¼ cup orange-flavored liqueur*
¾ cup sugar	*½ drop red food coloring*
⅓ cup water	*½ drop yellow food coloring*
2½ sticks (1¼ cups) unsalted butter,	
* very well softened*	

FOR THE SYRUP

½ cup sugar	*¼ cup orange-flavored liqueur*
½ cup water	

the rind of 3 navel oranges, cut into	*1 recipe apricot glaze (page 540) with*
* ¾-inch julienne strips and blanched*	* 2 to 3 tablespoons orange-flavored*
* in boiling water for 5 minutes*	* liqueur added*

thin slices of navel orange, peeled, for garnish

Butter the cake pans, sprinkle them with flour, and knock out the excess. Preheat the oven to 350° F.

Pour the *génoise* batter into the the cake pans and bake in the middle of the oven for 20 to 25 minutes, or until golden. Invert the layers onto a rack and let them cool completely.

Make the orange buttercream:

In the bowl of the mixer beat the egg yolks until light and thick. In a small heavy saucepan combine the sugar and water. Bring the syrup to a boil and boil it over moderate heat, stirring and washing down any sugar crystals clinging to the pan with the brush dipped in cold water until it reaches the soft-ball stage, or the candy thermometer registers 238° F. (For the stages of sugar syrup, see illustrations page 241.)

Orange Génoise with Orange Buttercream (opposite)

With the mixer running, pour the hot syrup into the yolks in a stream, beating, and continue to beat the mixture until it is completely cool. Beat in the butter, one tablespoon at a time, add the liqueur, and beat well. Stir in the food coloring. Chill the buttercream, covered, until firm, but still soft enough to spread.

Make the syrup: In a small heavy saucepan dissolve the sugar in the water over moderate heat and cook for 5 minutes. Remove the pan from the heat and stir in the liqueur.

Refresh the strips of orange rind under running cold water and pat them dry with paper towels. In a bowl combine them with the apricot glaze.

To assemble the cake: Invert one of the 9-inch cake pans and put 1 teaspoon of the orange buttercream in the center of the tin. Set a *génoise* layer on the tin and brush the top with syrup. Cover the layer with a ¼-inch-thick layer of the buttercream, smoothing it with a metal spatula. Chill the cake for 10 to 15 minutes, or until the buttercream is quite firm. Set the second *génoise* layer, bottom side up, on the buttercream, pressing down slightly, and moisten the top of the cake with orange-liqueur syrup. Cover the top and sides with the remaining buttercream, smoothing it with the spatula. Press the glazed strips of orange julienne onto the sides of the cake. Decorate the top with the peeled orange slices and brush the slices with some of the glaze. Arrange bunches of glazed strips of orange julienne in the center of each orange slice. Chill the cake until the buttercream is firm.

Photo above.

CREOLE CHEESE GÂTEAU

Yield:
one 6-inch cake

1 recipe vanilla génoise batter (page 22)

Equipment:
jelly-roll pan, 17¾ by
  11¾ by 1½ inches
upright electric mixer
6-inch springform
  pan, 3 inches deep
parchment paper
6-inch cake pan
pastry brush
pastry bag fitted with
  fluted tip

FOR THE CREOLE CHEESE
1 teaspoon unflavored gelatin
3 tablespoons cold water
1¼ cups well-chilled heavy cream
4 ounces cream cheese, well softened

⅓ cup superfine granulated sugar
1 teaspoon grated lemon rind
1 teaspoon vanilla

1 recipe brandy syrup (page 542)
1 cup seedless raspberry jam, melted
  and cooled

12 large whole strawberries
2 cups sweetened whipped cream

Line the jelly-roll pan with wax paper and butter the paper. Preheat the oven to 350° F.

Pour the *génoise* batter into the jelly roll pan, spreading it evenly with a spatula, and bake the cake in the middle of the oven for 20 minutes, or until lightly browned. Loosen the wax paper from the sides of the pan and invert the sponge sheet onto a baking sheet. Let the cake cool and peel off the paper.

Make the Creole cheese:

In a small bowl sprinkle the gelatin over the water and let it soften for 10 minutes. Set the bowl over simmering water and stir the gelatin until dissolved. Let cool. In a chilled bowl with the mixer beat the heavy cream until it holds soft peaks. In a large bowl combine the cream cheese, sugar, lemon rind, and vanilla. Stir in the cooled gelatin mixture and fold in the whipped cream.

To assemble the cake:

Line the bottom and sides of the springform pan with the parchment paper and extend the sides by tying a strip of parchment paper around the pan to form a collar. Using the 6-inch cake pan as a guide, cut 2 rounds from the sponge sheet, reserving the remaining cake for another use. Moisten one side of the sponge layers with the brandy syrup and fit one layer into the springform pan. Spread a thin layer of the raspberry jam on the sponge and top it with a ¾-inch layer of the Creole cheese. Top the cheese with the remaining sponge layer, moistened side down, and brush the top with the syrup. Fill the pan with the remaining Creole cheese. Chill the cake for at least 4 hours or overnight.

Remove the sides of the pan, remove the parchment paper, and transfer the cake to a cake stand. Spread a thin layer of jam in the center of the cake, then arrange decoratively several strawberries in the middle of the jam. Brush the berries with jam, pipe rosettes of whipped cream around the top of the cake, and chill the cake until ready to serve.

CASSATA
Ricotta and Ice-Cream Cake

Yield:
one 8- by 4-inch loaf
cake

This renowned Italian ice-cream cake has layers of *génoise* separated by ricotta filling and strawberry ice cream. While vanilla cake is the classic preparation, a chocolate sheet cake would make a lovely variation.

1 vanilla génoise *sheet cake (page 22), cooled but not rolled*

Equipment:
food processor fitted
  with steel blade
loaf pan, 8 by 4 by 4
  inches
hand-held electric
  mixer
pastry bag fitted with
  large star tip

FOR THE FILLING
1 pound ricotta
¼ cup superfine granulated sugar
¼ cup heavy cream

¼ cup orange-flavored liqueur
¼ cup chopped glacéed mixed fruits
2 ounces semisweet chocolate, chopped

2 pints Strawberry Ice Cream (page 350), softened
1½ cups well-chilled heavy cream

¼ cup confectioners' sugar, sifted
¼ cup orange-flavored liqueur
chopped glacéed fruits for garnish

Make the filling:

In the food processor combine the ricotta, the sugar, cream, and orange-flavored liqueur. Transfer the mixture to a bowl and fold in the glacéed fruits and the chocolate. Chill, covered, for 2 hours, or until the filling is firm, but still of spreading consistency.

Line the loaf pan with plastic wrap. Cut the *génoise* sheet crosswise into four 8- by 4-inch strips and fit one of the strips into the bottom of the loaf pan. Spread 1 pint of the strawberry ice cream over the cake and freeze the dessert for 30 minutes, or until the ice cream is firm.

Top the ice cream with a second layer of sponge sheet, pressing it down slightly, and spread the ricotta cheese filling over the cake. Top the filling with a third layer of sponge sheet, pressing it down slightly. Spread the remaining 1 pint strawberry ice cream over it and chill the layers until the ice cream is firm. Top the dessert with another layer of sponge sheet (the cake need not be in one piece), and chill the cake, covered, with plastic wrap, for 30 minutes, or until the ice cream is firm. Weight the cake lightly and freeze it overnight.

In a chilled bowl with the mixer beat the heavy cream with the confectioners' sugar and the orange-flavored liqueur until it holds soft peaks. Release the cake from the sides of the pan with a knife, invert it onto a chilled platter, and remove the plastic wrap. Spread the whipped cream smoothly over the sides and top of the cake with a spatula, reserving a small amount of it. Put the reserved whipped cream into the pastry bag and pipe it decoratively over the cake. Arrange the chopped glacéed fruits over the cream. Chill the cake for 2 hours before serving. To serve, cut the cake in thin slices.

Photo on page 12.

PETITS FOURS GLACÉS

Yield:
24 petits fours

Equipment:
upright electric mixer
rectangular cake pan,
　13 by 9 by 2 inches
pastry bag fitted with
　small fluted tip
　(optional)

*1 recipe vanilla or chocolate génoise
　batter (page 22)*
1 recipe fondant (page 540)

apricot jam
2 or 3 drops food coloring of choice

Line the bottom of the cake pan with wax paper, butter the paper, and dust the pan with flour, shaking out the excess. Preheat the oven to 350° F.

Pour the *génoise* batter into the cake pan, spreading it evenly, and bake in the middle of the oven for 15 to 20 minutes, or until a cake tester comes out clean. Let the cake cool in the pan on a rack for 10 minutes, turn it out onto the rack, and remove the paper. Let cool completely.

Divide the sheet cake into 2 cakes by cutting it in half lengthwise and cut each half horizontally into 2 layers. Spread three of the layers with a thin layer of apricot jam and stack the layers. Cut the cakes into 1½- by 2-inch rectangles with a serrated knife and arrange the rectangles on a large cake rack on a baking pan.

Place the fondant in the top of a double boiler over hot water and let it soften. Stir in the food coloring of choice. Do not let the fondant become too hot or it will lose its shine. Keep the fondant warm.

Pour the fondant over the petits fours, letting it drip down the sides. If desired, with the pastry bag decorate the cakes with fondant swirls.

PETITS ROULEAUX

Jelly-Roll Slices

Yield:
12 jelly-roll slices

Equipment:
jelly-roll pan, 11½ by
　7½ inches

*1 vanilla génoise sheet cake (page
　22) made with ½ recipe batter,
　cooled but not rolled*

½ cup confectioners' sugar
1½ cups red currant jelly

Spread the sheet cake with the currant jelly. Cut the cake crosswise into 3 pieces and beginning with a short side roll up each piece tightly. Cut each roll into 4 slices and transfer the slices to a platter.

Photo opposite.

Walnut Twists (page 206),
Fondant Brandied Cherries in Chocolate Cases (page 532),
Petits Rouleaux (above)

GÉNOISE WITH KIRSCH FONDANT AND FRESH STRAWBERRIES

Yield:
one 7½-inch cake

Equipment:
7½-inch fluted cake
  pan or *Kugelhupf*
  mold
candy thermometer

Enchanting to look at, this fluted *génoise* is iced with shiny fondant and decorated with fondant-dipped strawberries. A cake for an occasion.

½ recipe vanilla génoise *batter (page 22)*
2 recipes fondant (page 540)

¼ cup kirsch
3 or 4 drops red food coloring

20 large unblemished strawberries, with hulls on, for garnish

Butter the fluted cake pan well and preheat the oven to 350° F.

Pour the *génoise* batter into the prepared pan and bake the cake in the middle of the oven for 30 minutes, or until it is puffed and golden and pulls away easily from the sides of the pan. Turn the *génoise* out onto a rack and let it cool completely.

Place the fondant in the top of a double boiler and let it soften over hot water. Stir in the kirsch and the food coloring. Do not let the fondant become too hot or it will lose its shine. Should the fondant become too thick, thin it with a little unbeaten egg white or with small amount of sugar syrup (page 542) cooked until the candy thermometer registers 220° F.

To assemble the cake:
Line a jelly-roll pan with wax paper, set a rack on top of it, and place the *génoise* on the rack. Pour the fondant over the cake, letting it drip down the sides, leaving a smooth, thin coating. Transfer the cake to a serving plate.

With a metal spatula scrape up the fondant from the jelly-roll pan and put it in a small saucepan. Melt the fondant over very low heat and dip the tips of the strawberries into it, letting the excess run off. Lay the berries on a sheet of wax paper and let the fondant dry. Garnish the top of the cake and the serving plate, if desired, with the berries.

TORTES

Some people associate the word *torte* with a cake made of ground nuts, and they are not wrong. The definition of *torte*, however, also includes a cake of either German or Austrian descent that is layered with fillings or icings, jams, or whipped cream—the imporant part being that it is layered. The tortes that follow fall within this description and, as you can imagine, share layers in common, and great variety besides.

Three of the four tortes that follow derive from Austria, land of sophisticated *Konditorei* and bowls of whipped cream. Wachauer Torte (recipe opposite) is by comparison simple, a two-layer cocoa cake with cocoa buttercream. Kaisertorte (page 34), far more imperial sounding, stands higher, in three layers, and is made of and glazed with chocolate. Sugar Kirsch Torte (page 36) in true European splendor combines light *génoise* layers, meringue layers, and a delicately colored, pale pink buttercream. The remaining torte in this grouping is a glorious combination of white cake, drifty white buttercream made with only egg whites, and fresh raspberries. A perfect summer offering.

There is something Old World and wonderful about tortes. Perhaps it is because some of them, like the kirsch combination, are so lovely to look at and fanciful. Remember: Even that remarkable dessert started with a simple *génoise* layer.

WACHAUER TORTE

Cocoa Cake with Cocoa Buttercream

Yield:
one 9-inch layer cake

Equipment:
two 9-inch round
  cake pans
upright and hand-held
  electric mixers
pastry bag fitted with
  small decorative tip

Unlike Kaisertorte (page 34) this Austrian cake is made with cocoa powder and a considerable amount of ground walnuts. It is a simpler cake by comparison, but no less good.

FOR THE CAKE

*4 large eggs, separated, plus 1 egg
    white, at room temperature*
6 tablespoons granulated sugar
*2 tablespoons unsweetened cocoa
    powder*
pinch of salt

pinch of cream of tartar
⅓ cup sifted all-purpose flour
1 cup ground walnuts
*½ stick (¼ cup) unsalted butter,
    melted and cooled*

FOR THE COCOA BUTTERCREAM

1 cup confectioners' sugar, sifted
3 egg yolks
⅓ cup water
*3 tablespoons unsweetened cocoa
    powder*

*2 sticks (1 cup) unsalted butter,
    softened*

Make the cake:

Preheat the oven to 350° F. Butter and flour the cake pans.

In the bowl of the upright mixer beat the egg yolks with 3 tablespoons of the granulated sugar until light and lemon colored. Beat in the cocoa powder. In another bowl with the hand-held mixer beat the egg whites with the salt until frothy, add the cream of tartar, and beat until the whites hold soft peaks. Gradually add the remaining 3 tablespoons granulated sugar and beat the meringue until it holds stiff peaks (see illustrations page 238). Fold the meringue into the yolk mixture alternately with the flour and ground walnuts. Fold in the melted butter.

Divide the batter between the cake pans, smoothing the tops with a spatula, and bake the layers in the middle of the oven for 20 minutes, or until a cake tester inserted in the centers comes out clean. Let the layers cool in the pans for 5 minutes. Invert the layers onto racks and let cool completely.

Make the cocoa buttercream:

In a bowl combine the confectioners' sugar, egg yolks, water, and cocoa powder. Set the bowl over simmering water and with the hand-held mixer beat the mixture until thick and triple in volume. Set the bowl in a larger bowl of crushed ice and stir the mixture until cold. In another bowl cream the butter and beat it, 2 tablespoons at a time, into the egg mixture. Beat the buttercream until well combined and fluffy. Makes about 1½ cups.

Put one of the cake layers on a serving plate, spread it with some of the buttercream, and top it with the remaining cake layer. Spread the sides and top of the cake with the remaining buttercream. Using a pastry comb (see illustration page 19) or long serrated knife make ridges around the sides of the cake. With the knife score the cake into 12 pieces. Fill the pastry bag with the remaining buttercream and pipe a rosette onto each piece.

RASPBERRY TORTE

Yield:
one 8-inch layer cake

1 recipe vanilla génoise batter (page 22)

Equipment:
two 8-inch round
  cake pans
pastry brush
candy thermometer
upright electric mixer
7-inch cardboard
  round

FOR THE BUTTERCREAM

1¼ cups sugar
⅓ cup water
5 egg whites at room temperature
pinch of salt
⅛ teaspoon cream of tartar

3 sticks (1½ cups) unsalted butter,
* softened*
2 to 3 tablespoons eau-de-vie de
* framboise (raspberry brandy), or*
* to taste*

FOR THE SUGAR SYRUP

⅓ cup sugar
⅓ cup water

1 tablespoon eau-de-vie de
* framboise*

⅔ cup sieved raspberry preserves
2½ cups fresh raspberries

2 cups Raspberry Sauce (page 508) as
* an accompaniment*

Make the *génoise*:

Preheat the oven to 350° F. Butter the cake pans, line the bottoms with wax paper, and butter the paper. Dust the pans with flour, knocking out the excess.

Divide the *génoise* batter between the cake pans, smoothing the tops, and bake the layers in the middle of the oven for 20 to 25 minutes, or until the tops are golden and a cake tester inserted in the centers comes out clean. Let the cakes cool in the pans on a rack for 5 minutes, invert the layers onto a cake rack, remove the paper, and let the layers cool completely.

Make the buttercream: In a small heavy saucepan combine the sugar with the water. Bring the mixture to a boil and boil it over moderate heat, stirring and washing down any sugar crystals clinging to the sides of the pan with the brush dipped in cold water until it reaches the hard-ball stage, or the candy thermometer reaches 248° F.

In the bowl of the mixer beat the egg whites with the salt until frothy. Add the cream of tartar and beat the whites until they hold stiff but not dry peaks. With the mixer running, add the hot syrup to the whites in a stream, beating, and beat the mixture until completely cool. (For the stages of sugar syrup and how to pour it, see illustrations pages 240 and 241.) Beat in the butter, a little at a time, and add the *framboise*. Chill the buttercream, covered, until firm but still soft enough to spread.

Make the sugar syrup: In a small saucepan combine the sugar with the water. Bring the mixture to a boil, stirring, and simmer it until clear. Let the mixture cool to room temperature and stir in the *eau-de-vie de framboise*.

To assemble the torte: Put 1 teaspoon of the buttercream in the center of the cardboard round. With a serrated knife halve one of the cake layers horizontally (see illustration page 19). Place one half-layer, cut side up, on the cardboard round and brush some of the syrup over it. With a spatula smooth a thin layer of the raspberry preserves over the cake. Cover the preserves with a ¼-inch-thick layer of the buttercream, smoothing it with a spatula. Set aside 12 raspberries for the garnish and sprinkle one third of the remaining raspberries over the cake. Set the second half-layer, bottom side up, on the buttercream, pressing down slightly. Repeat layers of syrup, preserves, buttercream, and half the remaining raspberries. Halve the remaining cake layer horizontally and continue to layer the cake, ending with the last cake layer, bottom side up. Brush the top of the cake with the syrup and coat it with a thin layer of raspberry preserves. Cover the sides and top of the cake with the remaining buttercream, smoothing it with the spatula, and with the spatula or a long knife score 12 slices on the top of the torte.

The torte may be prepared up to 2 days in advance and kept chilled, covered loosely with plastic wrap. Let the torte come to room temperature before serving. Garnish the top of the torte with the reserved raspberries, transfer the torte carefully to a cake plate, and serve with the raspberry sauce.

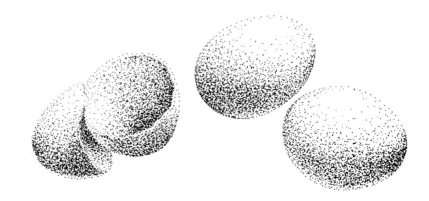

KAISERTORTE
Toasted Almond and Chocolate Torte

Yield:
one 8-inch cake

This Austrian specialty, with its distinctive decoration, combines chocolate almond layers, chocolate buttercream, and chocolate glaze.

Equipment:
8-inch springform pan
hand-held electric
  mixer
food processor fitted
  with steel blade
3-inch round cutter

FOR THE CAKE
2½ ounces dark sweet chocolate,
  chopped
½ stick (¼ cup) unsalted butter
5 large eggs, separated, at room
  temperature
3 tablespoons confectioners' sugar
1½ teaspoons vanilla

1½ teaspoons dark rum
1 cup whole blanched almonds (for
  procedure page 549), toasted
⅓ cup all-purpose flour
¼ teaspoon salt
¼ teaspoon cream of tartar
½ cup granulated sugar

FOR THE CHOCOLATE BUTTERCREAM
3 ounces dark sweet chocolate,
  chopped
3 sticks (1½ cups) unsalted butter,
  softened

1⅓ cups sifted confectioners' sugar
4 egg yolks
½ teaspoon vanilla

FOR THE GLAZE
1½ ounces dark sweet chocolate,
  chopped
3 ounces (⅔ cup) sugar cubes

2 tablespoons hot water
½ teaspoon flavorless vegetable oil

¾ cup sliced blanched almonds, toasted

Make the cake:

Preheat the oven to 350° F. Butter the springform pan, line the bottom with wax paper, and butter the paper. Dust the pan with flour and knock out the excess.

In the top of a double boiler set over simmering water melt the chocolate with the butter, stirring, and let the mixture cool.

In a large bowl with the mixer beat the egg yolks with the confectioners' sugar until the mixture is thick and lemon colored. Beat in the vanilla and rum. Add the melted chocolate mixture and combine well. In the food processor or in a blender grind the almonds with the flour to a powder. In a large bowl with the mixer beat the egg whites with the salt until frothy, add the cream of tartar, and beat the whites until they hold soft peaks. Add the granulated sugar, one tablespoon at a time, beating, and beat until the whites hold stiff peaks (see illustrations page 238). Stir one fourth of the whites into the chocolate mixture. Fold in the remaining whites and the almond flour mixture gently but thoroughly. Spoon the batter into the springform pan, smooth the top, and bake the cake in the middle of the oven for 35 to 40 minutes, or until a cake tester inserted in the center comes out clean. Let the cake cool in the pan on a rack.

Make the chocolate buttercream:

In the top of a double boiler set over simmering water melt the chocolate and let it cool. In a bowl with the mixer cream the butter. Add ⅓ cup of the confectioners' sugar and beat until light and fluffy. In another bowl with the mixer beat the egg yolks until thick and lemon colored. Gradually add the remaining 1 cup confectioners' sugar and the vanilla, beating, and beat the mixture well. Beat the butter mixture into the yolk mixture, a little at a time, and beat the mixture until smooth. Add the melted chocolate and combine the buttercream well.

Run a thin knife around the sides of the pan, remove the sides carefully, and with a serrated knife cut the cake horizontally into 3 layers (see illustration page 19). Place the bottom layer, cut side up, on a cake plate and spread it with 1 cup of the buttercream. Top with the middle cake layer. Spread the middle layer with 1 cup of the buttercream and top it with the remaining cake layer, cut side down.

Make the glaze:

In the top of a double boiler set over simmering water melt the chocolate, stirring. In a small heavy saucepan combine the sugar cubes and the hot water and cook the mixture over moderately low heat, stirring, until the sugar is dissolved. Bring the glaze to a boil over moderate heat, remove the pan from the heat, and, working quickly, add the chocolate and the oil, stirring until smooth.

Pour the glaze immediately onto the center of the torte and with a knife dipped in hot water spread it into a 6-inch round. Press the cutter lightly onto the center of the glaze and leave it in place. Spread the remaining buttercream around the sides of the torte and over the top, covering the edges of the glaze but leaving the area protected by the cutter untouched. Press the sliced almonds gently onto the buttercream, covering it almost completely, and remove the cutter.

Chill the torte for at least 2 hours. Let the torte stand at room temperature for 20 minutes before serving.

SUGAR KIRSCH TORTE

Yield:
one 7-inch cake

Equipment:
7-inch round cake
  pan, 2 inches deep
upright electric mixer
pastry brush
small pastry bag fitted
  with star tip

This culinary construction of *génoise* layers, meringue layers, and pale pink buttercream is as extraordinary to look at as it is to taste.

1 recipe vanilla génoise *batter (page 22)*

FOR THE MERINGUE LAYERS
4 egg whites at room temperature
pinch of salt
1 cup sugar

*½ cup blanched almonds (for
  procedure page 549), lightly
  toasted and ground*

FOR THE BUTTERCREAM
4 egg yolks
1 cup sugar
½ cup milk, scalded

*2½ sticks (1¼ cups) unsalted butter,
  softened*
¼ cup kirsch
a few drops of red food coloring

FOR THE SUGAR SYRUP
¼ cup sugar
¼ cup water

¼ cup kirsch

½ cup blanched almonds, lightly toasted and chopped coarse

Preheat the oven to 350° F. Butter and lightly flour the cake pan.

Pour the *génoise* batter into the pan and bake the cake in the middle of the oven for 25 minutes, or until it is golden and shrinks from the sides of the pan. Remove the cake from the pan and let it cool on a rack.

Make the meringue layers:

Reduce the oven temperature to 250° F.

In the bowl of the mixer beat the egg whites with the salt until frothy. Beat in the sugar, a little at a time, and continue beating the meringue until it is very stiff. Fold in the ground almonds.

Draw two 7-inch circles on a sheet of wax paper and lay the paper on a baking sheet. Spread the meringue ¼ inch thick within the circles and bake the layers in the middle of the oven for 45 minutes, or until hard and dry. Let the meringue layers cool on the baking sheet and carefully remove them from the paper.

Make the buttercream:

In the bowl of the mixer beat the egg yolks with the sugar until light and lemon colored. Pour in the scalded milk in a thin stream, stirring. Transfer the mixture to a saucepan and cook it over low heat without letting it boil, stirring, until it is thick enough to coat a spoon. Put the saucepan in a bowl of ice water and stir the custard until barely warm. Transfer the custard to the bowl of the mixer, turn the mixer to high, and beat in the butter, one tablespoon at a time. Continue to beat the buttercream until it holds stiff peaks. Beat in the kirsch and the food coloring. Chill the buttercream until firm but still of spreading consistency.

Sugar Kirsch Torte (opposite)

Make the sugar syrup: In a small saucepan dissolve the sugar in the water over moderate heat and cook for 5 minutes. Remove the pan from the heat and stir in the kirsch.

To assemble the torte: Using a serrated knife, cut the *génoise* in half horizontally (see illustration page 19) and brush the cut side of each layer with the warm kirsch syrup. Put 1 teaspoon of the buttercream in the center of one of the cake pans, inverted, and set one of the meringue layers, smooth side down, on the pan. Spread a thin layer of buttercream over the meringue. Top it with one of the *génoise* layers, cut side up, and spread the cake with some of the buttercream. Cover the buttercream with the remaining *génoise* layer, cut side down, and spread the cake with more of the buttercream. Put the second meringue layer, smooth side up, on top of the buttercream. Trim the sides of the cake. With a metal spatula smooth some of the buttercream on the sides and top of the cake, reserving about ⅓ cup. Fill the pastry bag with the reserved buttercream and pipe ribbons on top of the torte. Press some of the chopped almonds around the base of the torte and sprinkle a few almonds decoratively on the top. Transfer the torte to a serving plate and chill it for 2 hours.

Photo on page 37.

SPONGECAKES AND ROLLED CAKES

Earlier in this chapter we mentioned the versatility with which sponge-cakes can be made. Some depend solely upon beaten egg whites for their leavening. Others incorporate whole eggs, first the yolks and then the beaten whites, as well as baking powder and/or baking soda for an airy, light texture. No matter the variations of components, though, the crumb of a spongecake is delicate and fine.

The batters for spongecakes lend themselves to being baked in sheet pans, or jelly-roll pans, the first step to a rolled cake. And the variety of rolled cakes is endless and exceptionally pleasing. Think of it: There are beloved jelly rolls—see our Great American Jelly Roll (page 40). Then there is the roll as complex and grand as Bûche de Noël (page 114). Somewhere in between those two levels of expertise reside the rolls we have included in this grouping. There is a glorious Lemon Roll (page 42) that is filled with lemon cream, but might just as easily be filled with a judicious amount of orange buttercream. Ginger Walnut Roll (page 41) is filled with molasses-flavored whipped cream, and Double Chocolate Roll (page 44), a cake that contains no flour whatsoever and is described as soufflé-like in texture, is filled with chocolate cream, or *ganache*. Care is required to roll a sheet cake, but the process itself is very easy. For illustrations on how to guide the roll, see page 41, and then make rolled cakes part of your every-day baking repertoire.

BOSTON CREAM PIE

Yield:
one 9-inch cake

Equipment:
two 9-inch cake pans
upright electric mixer
8-inch cardboard
   round

Boston cream pie, not a pie at all, is often made with a batter to which hot milk is added. We've used sponge batter instead, with the layers separated by pastry cream and the whole topped with chocolate glaze. Boston cream pie is an American classic and rightfully so.

FOR THE CAKE

*6 large eggs, separated, at room
   temperature*
1 cup granulated sugar
1½ teaspoons vanilla

¼ teaspoon plus pinch of salt
¼ teaspoon cream of tartar
1 cup cake flour, sifted

*1 recipe pastry cream (page 537) combined with 1 tablespoon rum or Cognac
   if desired*

FOR THE CHOCOLATE GLAZE

2 tablespoons unsalted butter
*1 ounce semisweet chocolate, chopped
   coarse*

2 tablespoons heavy cream
½ cup confectioners' sugar
1 teaspoon vanilla

Make the cake:

Butter the cake pans, line the bottoms with wax paper, and butter the paper. Dust the pans with flour, knocking out the excess.

In the bowl of the mixer beat the egg yolks until combined. Add ¾ cup of the granulated sugar, a little at a time, and beat the mixture until it falls in a thick ribbon when the beater is lifted (see illustration page 16). Beat in the vanilla and transfer the mixture to a bowl.

Preheat the oven to 350° F.

In the bowl of the mixer beat the egg whites with the pinch of salt until frothy. Add the cream of tartar and beat the whites until they hold soft peaks. Add the remaining ¼ cup granulated sugar, a little at a time, and beat the whites until stiff (see illustrations page 238). Fold the whites into the batter gently but thoroughly. Sift the flour with the remaining ¼ teaspoon salt and fold it in batches into the egg mixture until just combined. Divide the batter between the cake pans and bake the layers in the middle of the oven for 20 to 25 minutes, or until a cake tester inserted in the centers comes out clean. Let the cakes cool in the pans on racks for 5 minutes. Invert them onto the racks, peel off the wax paper, and let cool.

Put 1 teaspoon of the pastry cream in the center of the cardboard round and arrange one of the cake layers on it. Spread the top of the layer with the pastry cream, smoothing it with a spatula, and set the second layer on top of it. Transfer the cake on the round to a cake plate.

Make the chocolate glaze:

In the top of a double boiler over simmering water melt the butter with the chocolate, stirring. Remove the pan from the heat and beat in the cream, confectioners' sugar, and vanilla and continue to beat until smooth.

Pour the glaze slowly and carefully over the top of the cake, smoothing it with a spatula and taking care not to let any of it drip down the sides of the cake. Serve the cake at room temperature.

GREAT AMERICAN JELLY ROLL

Yield:
one 15-inch rolled
  cake

Equipment:
jelly-roll pan, 15½ by
  10½ by 1 inches
upright and hand-held
  electric mixers

This jelly roll, a clever variation on strawberry shortcake, makes a lovely light summer dessert and a perfect ending to a July Fourth celebration.

4 large eggs, separated, at room temperature
½ cup granulated sugar
1 teaspoon vanilla
1 tablespoon grated orange rind
½ teaspoon plus pinch salt
⅛ teaspoon cream of tartar
½ cup all-purpose flour, sifted

½ cup strawberry jam
⅔ cup well-chilled heavy cream
3 tablespoons confectioners' sugar plus additional for dusting
1 tablespoons orange-flavored liqueur if desired
1 cup strawberries, hulled and sliced

Butter the jelly-roll pan and line it with wax paper, leaving a 2-inch overhang on each of the short sides. Butter the wax paper and dust it with flour, shaking out the excess. Preheat the oven to 400° F.

In the bowl of the upright mixer beat the egg yolks until combined. Add all but 2 tablespoons of the granulated sugar, a little at a time, and beat the mixture at medium speed for 3 to 4 minutes, or until light and creamy. Beat in the vanilla and 2 teaspoons of the orange rind and pour the batter into a large bowl.

In the bowl of the mixer beat the whites with the pinch of salt until frothy. Add the cream of tartar and beat the whites until they hold soft peaks. Add the reserved 2 tablespoons granulated sugar, a little at a time, and beat the whites until stiff (see illustrations page 238). Fold the whites into the batter, gently but thoroughly. Sift the flour with the remaining salt and fold it in batches into the batter until the mixture is just combined.

Pour the batter into the pan, spread it evenly with a spatula, and bake the cake in the middle of the oven for 10 to 12 minutes, or until it pulls away from the sides of the pan and a cake tester inserted in the center comes out clean. Sift confectioners' sugar lightly over the top of the cake, cover the cake with wax paper and a baking sheet, and invert the cake onto the baking sheet. Peel off the wax paper and trim any hardened edges from the sides of the cake. Cover the cake with a fresh piece of wax paper. Starting with a long side roll up the cake, lifting it with the wax paper and finishing with the seam side down (see illustrations opposite). Let the cake cool completely.

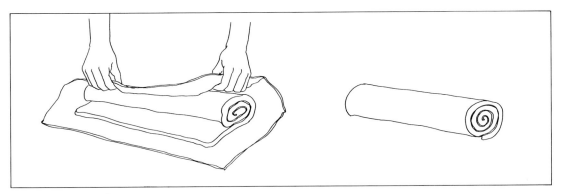

Rolling up a jelly roll

Unroll the cake, remove the paper, and spread the cake with the strawberry jam, leaving a ½-inch border at each of the short ends. In a chilled bowl with the hand-held mixer beat the cream with the remaining 3 tablespoons confectioners' sugar and the orange-flavored liqueur, if desired, until it holds soft peaks. With a spatula spread the cream on the cake, smoothing it into an even layer and leaving a 1-inch border on all sides. Scatter the strawberries over the cream, sprinkle them with the remaining orange rind, and roll up the cake. Transfer the jelly roll to a platter, seam side down, and trim the ends. Dust with sifted confectioners' sugar.

GINGER WALNUT ROLL WITH MOLASSES CREAM

Yield:
one 16-inch rolled cake

Equipment:
jelly-roll pan, 16 by 11 by 1 inches
upright and hand-held electric mixers
pastry bag fitted with star tip

Make the cake:

FOR THE CAKE
7 large eggs, separated, at room temperature
⅓ cup granulated sugar

pinch of salt
¾ cup ground walnuts
2 teaspoons ground ginger

FOR THE MOLASSES CREAM
1½ teaspoons unflavored gelatin
3 tablespoons cold water
1½ cups well-chilled heavy cream

½ cup molasses
3 large walnut halves brushed with honey for garnish

Preheat the oven to 350° F. Butter the jelly-roll pan, line it with wax paper, and butter the paper.

In the bowl of the upright mixer beat the egg yolks until frothy. Gradually add the granulated sugar and continue to beat the mixture for 3 to 4 minutes, or until it falls in a ribbon when the beater is lifted (see illustration page 16).

In a bowl with the hand-held mixer beat the egg whites with the salt until they hold stiff peaks. Gently but thoroughly fold one fourth of the whites into the yolk mixture and pour the mixture over the remaining whites. Combine the ground walnuts and the ground ginger. Sprinkle the nut mixture over the egg mixture and gently fold the batter until there are no traces of white. Pour the batter into the jelly-roll pan, spreading it evenly with a metal spatula, and bake the cake in the middle of the oven for about 25 minutes, or until it is lightly browned and springy to the touch. Let the cake cool in the pan on a rack.

Make the molasses cream:

In a small saucepan sprinkle the gelatin over the water and let it soften for 5 minutes. Heat the mixture over moderately low heat, stirring, until the gelatin is dissolved and the liquid is clear. In a chilled bowl with the mixer beat the heavy cream until it holds soft peaks, add the gelatin mixture in a stream and the molasses, beating, and beat the cream until it holds stiff peaks.

To assemble the roll:

Loosen the wax paper from the side of the jelly-roll pan with a knife and invert the cake onto a baking sheet covered with a sheet of wax paper. Peel off the paper on top and spread the cake with the molasses cream, reserving ½ cup of it for garnish and leaving a 1-inch border. Starting with a long side, roll up the cake, lifting it with the wax paper and finishing with the seam side down (see illustrations page 41). Transfer the roll carefully to a platter. Fill the pastry bag with the reserved molasses cream and pipe it decoratively on top of the roll. Position the walnut halves on the cake.

Photo on page 252.

LEMON ROLL

Yield:
one 15-inch rolled cake

Equipment:
jelly-roll pan, 15½ by 10½ by 1 inches
upright electric mixer

FOR THE LEMON CREAM
6 egg yolks
1 cup granulated sugar
½ cup fresh lemon juice, strained

1 tablespoon grated lemon rind
½ stick (¼ cup) unsalted butter, softened

FOR THE CAKE
4 large eggs, separated, at room temperature
1 tablespoon grated lemon rind
1 tablespoon fresh lemon juice, strained

1 stick (½ cup) unsalted butter, softened

1 cup granulated sugar
pinch of salt
pinch of cream of tartar
¼ cup cornstarch
¼ cup all-purpose flour

confectioners' sugar for dusting

Make the lemon cream:

In a small heavy saucepan combine the egg yolks, granulated sugar, lemon juice, and rind and cook over moderate heat, stirring until thick. Do not let it boil. Remove the pan from the heat and stir in the butter, one tablespoon at a time. Transfer the mixture to a bowl and let it cool, covered with a buttered round of wax paper.

Make the cake:

Preheat the oven to 350° F. Butter the jelly-roll pan, line it with wax paper, leaving a 2-inch overhang on both of the short ends, and butter the paper.

In a large bowl beat the egg yolks with the lemon rind, the lemon juice, and ½ cup of the granulated sugar until the mixture falls in a ribbon when the beater is lifted (see illustration page 16). In the bowl of the mixer beat the egg whites with the salt until frothy, add the cream of tartar and beat the whites until they hold soft peaks. Beat in the remaining ½ cup granulated sugar, one tablespoon at a time, and beat the meringue until it holds stiff peaks (see illustrations page 238).

Sift the cornstarch and flour together onto a sheet of wax paper. Fold one fourth of the meringue into the yolk mixture and fold in the remaining meringue alternately with the cornstarch mixture. Turn the batter into the jelly-roll pan, spreading it evenly, and bake the cake in the middle of the oven for 17 minutes, or until the paper pulls away easily from the ends of the cake. Leave the cake in the pan, cover it with a dampened dish towel, and let it cool on a rack.

In a bowl cream the butter. Beat in the lemon cream, a little at a time, and continue to beat the mixture until fluffy. Chill the filling, covered, for 30 minutes.

To assemble the lemon roll:

Dust a 16-inch length of wax paper with the confectioners' sugar. Remove the towel from the sheetcake and turn the cake out onto the wax paper. Peel the wax paper off the top of the cake and spread the cake with the lemon cream filling, leaving a 1-inch border on the long side farthest from you. Beginning with the long side nearest you, roll up the cake, lifting it with the wax paper (see illustrations page 41). Transfer the lemon roll, seam side down, to a serving board and dust it with the confectioners' sugar.

DOUBLE CHOCOLATE ROLL

Yield:
one 16-inch rolled
  cake

Equipment:
jelly-roll pan, 16 by 11
  inches
upright electric mixer

This is a flourless cake—indeed, its texture is more like a soufflé—and, therefore, it must be handled with care. This roll is filled with a chocolate cream, or *crème ganache,* a mixture of chocolate simmered with heavy cream. It can be used warm as a glaze or, when chilled and whipped, as a creamy filling or frosting.

FOR THE CAKE

8 ounces semisweet chocolate, broken
    into pieces
¼ cup cold strong brewed coffee
7 large eggs, separated, at room
    temperature

¾ cup granulated sugar
pinch of salt
¼ teaspoon cream of tartar

FOR THE FILLING

1½ cups heavy cream
8 ounces semisweet chocolate, broken
    into bits

1 to 2 tablespoons coffee-flavored
    liqueur or dark rum

sifted confectioners' sugar for garnish

Butter the jelly-roll pan, line it with wax paper, and butter the paper. Preheat the oven to 350° F.

Make the cake:

In the top of a double boiler set over hot water melt the chocolate with the coffee until the mixture is smooth and let cool.

In the bowl of the mixer beat the egg yolks until they are smooth. Beat in ⅔ cup of the granulated sugar, a little at a time, and beat the mixture until it falls in a ribbon when the beater is lifted (see illustration page 16). Pour the mixture into a large bowl.

In the bowl of the mixer beat the egg whites with the salt until they are frothy. Add the cream of tartar and beat the whites until they hold soft peaks. Add the remaining granulated sugar, a little at a time, and beat the whites until they hold stiff peaks (see illustrations page 238).

Combine the chocolate mixture with the egg yolk mixture. Stir in one fourth of the whites and fold in the remaining whites gently but thoroughly. Spoon the batter into the pan, spread it evenly with a spatula, and bake the cake in the middle of the oven for 15 minutes, or until a cake tester inserted into the center comes out clean. Turn off the oven, open the oven door, and let the cake stand for 5 minutes.

Transfer the pan to a rack, cover the cake with dampened paper towels, and let the cake cool just to room temperature, about 15 minutes. Remove the towels and run a knife around the sides of the pan to release the wax paper. Cover the top of the cake with wax paper and a baking sheet, invert the cake onto the baking sheet, and peel the wax paper off the top.

Make the filling:

In a saucepan combine the heavy cream with the chocolate and cook, stirring, until the chocolate is melted and the mixture is slightly thickened. Transfer the mixture to the bowl of the mixer and chill it, but do not let it solidify. With the mixer beat the chocolate cream until it forms soft peaks (do not overbeat or the mixture will become granular) and stir in the coffee-flavored liqueur or rum.

Spread the filling over the cake, leaving a 1-inch border. Starting with a long side, roll up the cake jelly-roll fashion, lifting it with the wax paper and finishing with the seam side down (see illustrations page 41). (The roll may crack.) Transfer the cake to a platter and chill it, loosely covered. Before serving, trim the ends of the roll and sprinkle the roll with the confectioners' sugar.

ANGEL FOOD AND CHIFFON CAKES

We all remember angel food cake for its extraordinary whiteness and chiffon cake for its exceptional lightness. How these qualities were arrived at wasn't important. The color of one and the texture of the other were what was memorable, and that both were brilliantly named.

We now know that the batter for angel food cake is based exclusively on egg whites that have been beaten to stiff, glossy peaks. Moreover, there is no fat or shortening in the mix. The cake is pristine and white because it started off that way. Angel food cake is a salient example of what can be achieved by the power of beaten whites, and all of the principles for whipping egg whites successfully (see the introduction to "Meringues," page 237) apply.

We have also discovered that chiffon cake attains its lightness because oil—not butter or shortening—is used in the batter. Unlike angel food cake, egg yolks are also incorporated. It is the oil, though, that renders this cake light yet rich.

Each of the three cakes that follow bakes in a tube pan and has a specific method of cooling, with the pan suspended upside down on the neck of a bottle. The cake must be allowed to cool completely in this manner. To try to cool any of these cakes in the conventional manner, on a rack, will undo most of what was achieved during baking with the uniqueness of these respective batters.

ANGEL FOOD CAKE

Yield:
one 10-inch tube cake

Equipment:
upright electric mixer
10-inch tube pan

A good angel food cake is light and airy. You want to be sure to beat the egg whites—on which so much of the texture depends—to stiff peaks, and to combine the batter well, but not to overmix it. This grand cake, served with chocolate whipped cream, is one of those old-time favorites.

1¼ cups egg whites at room
   temperature
¼ teaspoon salt
1 teaspoon cream of tartar
1½ cups sugar

1 teaspoon vanilla
¼ teaspoon almond extract
1 cup sifted cake flour
1 recipe Chocolate Whipped Cream
   (page 496) as an accompaniment

In the bowl of the mixer beat the egg whites with the salt until frothy. Add the cream of tartar and beat the whites until they hold soft peaks. Gently fold in the sugar, ¼ cup at a time, incorporating each addition before adding the next, and beat the whites until they hold stiff peaks (see illustrations page 238). Fold in the vanilla and the almond extract.

Preheat the oven to 375° F.

Sift the flour 3 more times. Sift ¼ cup of the flour over the batter and fold it in quickly and lightly. Sift another ¼ cup flour over the batter and fold it in. Continue sifting and folding in the flour ¼ cup at a time until it is all folded into the batter, but do not overmix.

Pour the batter into the ungreased tube pan and bake the cake in the middle of the oven for 35 to 40 minutes, or until it springs back when pressed lightly with a finger. Remove the cake from the oven and suspend it upside down on the neck of a bottle. Let the cake cool completely.

With a sharp knife carefully loosen the cake from the sides and center tube of the pan. Tap the bottom of the pan firmly on the work surface to loosen the cake, and turn the cake out of the pan. Invert the cake onto a cake platter and serve it with the chocolate whipped cream.

COCONUT ANGEL FOOD CAKE WITH ORANGE FROSTING

Yield:
one 9-inch tube cake

Equipment:
upright electric mixer
9-inch tube pan

This angel food cake, which is slightly dressier than the preceding recipe, is covered with a superb orange frosting that is actually a variation on the much-beloved and ever-reliable seven-minute frosting.

FOR THE CAKE

8 egg whites at room temperature
½ teaspoon salt
½ teaspoon cream of tartar
1 cup superfine granulated sugar
½ teaspoon almond extract

½ teaspoon vanilla
¾ cup cake flour
1½ cups shredded unsweetened coconut

FOR THE ORANGE FROSTING

1¼ cups granulated sugar
2 egg whites
¼ cup fresh orange juice

1 tablespoon light corn syrup
1 teaspoon grated orange rind
pinch of salt

Make the cake:

In the bowl of the mixer beat the egg whites with the salt until frothy. Add the cream of tartar and beat the whites until they hold soft peaks. Sprinkle ½ cup of the superfine sugar over the whites, 2 tablespoons at a time, and continue to beat the whites until they hold stiff peaks (see illustrations page 238). With a rubber spatula fold in the remaining ½ cup superfine sugar, 2 tablespoons at a time, the almond extract, and the vanilla.

Preheat the oven to 275° F.

Sift the cake flour 4 times onto a sheet of wax paper. Sift it over the egg whites, one fourth at a time, folding it lightly into the whites. Fold in ½ cup of the coconut. Pour the batter into the ungreased pan and bake the cake in the middle of the oven for 1½ hours. Remove the cake from the oven, suspend it upside down on the neck of a bottle, and let it hang for 1½ to 2 hours, or until cooled completely.

Increase the oven temperature to 350° F. Toast the remaining 1 cup coconut on a baking pan in the middle of the oven, shaking the pan occasionally, for 10 minutes. Let the coconut cool.

Make the orange frosting:

In the bowl of the mixer combine the granulated sugar, egg whites, orange juice, corn syrup, grated orange rind, and salt. Set the bowl over a saucepan containing 3 inches of boiling water and whisk the mixture until it is hot and foamy. Return the bowl to the mixer and beat the frosting at high speed for 7 minutes, or until it is cool and holds stiff peaks. Makes about 3 cups.

With a sharp knife release the cake from the sides and center tube of the pan and invert it onto a rack. Turn the cake right side up onto a cake plate and cover the sides and top with the orange frosting. Press the toasted coconut onto the sides of the cake.

CINNAMON WALNUT CHIFFON CAKE
WITH APPLE BUTTER FROSTING

Yield:
one 10-inch tube cake

Equipment:
upright electric mixer
10-inch tube pan
food processor fitted
  with steel blade

The chiffon cake is identifiable by the use of oil as opposed to butter in the batter. Because the oil is flavorless, you will note a lovely combination of spices and a fragrant apple butter frosting are used to give the cake its extraordinary flavor.

FOR THE CAKE

2¼ cups cake flour
1⅓ cups granulated sugar
1 tablespoon double-acting baking
  powder
1½ teaspoons cinnamon
1 teaspoon plus pinch of salt
¼ teaspoon freshly grated nutmeg
⅛ teaspoon ground cloves

6 egg yolks at room temperature
¾ cup apple juice
½ cup vegetable oil
1 teaspoon vanilla
½ teaspoon grated lemon rind
8 egg whites at room temperature
¼ teaspoon cream of tartar
⅔ cup finely chopped walnuts

FOR THE FROSTING

1½ sticks (¾ cup) unsalted butter,
  softened

1 cup confectioners' sugar, sifted
½ cup apple butter, or to taste

Make the cake:

Sift the flour, ¾ cup of the granulated sugar, the baking powder, cinnamon, 1 teaspoon of the salt, nutmeg, and cloves onto a sheet of wax paper. In a large bowl combine the egg yolks, apple juice, oil, vanilla, and lemon rind. Beat in the flour mixture until the batter is smooth.

Preheat the oven to 325° F.

In the bowl of the mixer beat the egg whites with the pinch of salt until frothy. Add the cream of tartar and beat the whites until they hold soft peaks. Add the remaining granulated sugar, a little at a time, and beat the whites until they hold stiff peaks (see illustrations page 238). Stir one fourth of the whites into the yolk mixture and fold in the remaining whites and the walnuts.

Pour the batter into the ungreased tube pan and bake the cake in the middle of the oven for 1 hour, or until a cake tester comes out clean. Suspend the cake upside down on the neck of a bottle and let it cool completely. With a thin knife loosen the cake from the sides and center of the tube pan and invert the cake onto a rack.

Make the frosting:

In the food processor or in a blender put the butter, confectioners' sugar, and apple butter, turn on the motor, and blend the ingredients scraping down the sides of the container with a rubber spatula two or three times, until the frosting is smooth.

Spread the sides and top of the cake with the frosting and transfer the cake carefully to a cake stand.

LAYER CAKES

Who will ever forget having laid eyes for the very first time on a seven-layer cake? It just wasn't possible, all those thin, thin layers. It had to be magic, done by something other than man. As we have all grown up to learn, layer cakes are made by men and women—even seven-layer cakes—and indeed the same principles apply whether you are making two or seven layers.

For many of us, though, the magic of the layer cake never disappeared even with all that adult knowledge. It probably has something to do with the transformation of components. You start with two or three cake pans, a bowl of batter, and another of frosting. And when you are done you have a high-standing, captivating construct just waiting to be sliced.

Layer cakes can be plain or fancy, as both our Lady Baltimore (page 53) and Robert E. Lee (page 54) cakes demonstrate. Each obviously hails from the South, each is deservedly an American classic, and each is a grand, elegant edifice. Other layer cakes are not nearly so highfalutin: Take Banana Cream Layer Cake (page 50), for example, its moist nutted layers are covered with simple whipped cream. With other layer cakes it is the layers themselves that are simple—carrot cake, for instance, does not compare in complexity with a *génoise* layer, nor does it require the technical know-how to produce well. Strawberry Cream Cake (page 58), which ends this short collection on layer cakes, requires the same expertise as a *génoise* layer but ends up looking like a splendid mosaic once you are done arranging the candied strawberries and trimming the sides.

What is so exceptional about the layer cake, aside from the pure pleasure it brings, is the obvious number of guises it takes. You will find other wonderful examples of layer cakes in the *génoise* grouping in this chapter and in the chocolate cake selections. We would also suggest you review the instructional text on cake-making at the beginning of this chapter to maximize the layer cake's full and singularly pleasing effect.

BANANA CREAM LAYER CAKE

Yield:
one 8-inch layer cake

Equipment:
two 8-inch round
  cake pans
food processor fitted
  with steel blade
hand-held electric
  mixer

A lovely moist banana cake, made with buttermilk, that is then spread with sweetened whipped cream. This is a good cake for children.

*3 very ripe bananas, or enough to
    measure 1 cup purée*
½ cup buttermilk
1¾ teaspoons vanilla
*1½ sticks (¾ cup) unsalted butter,
    softened*
*1½ cups plus 2 tablespoons and
    2 teaspoons sugar*

2 large eggs
2 cups sifted cake flour
1 teaspoon baking soda
*1 teaspoon double-acting baking
    powder*
½ teaspoon salt
⅔ cup finely chopped walnuts
1½ cups well-chilled heavy cream

Butter the cake pans, line them with wax paper, and butter the paper. Preheat the oven to 350° F.

In the food processor or in a blender purée the bananas. In a small bowl combine the purée with the buttermilk and 1 teaspoon of the vanilla.

In a bowl with the mixer cream the butter with 1½ cups of the sugar until light and fluffy. Beat in the eggs, one at a time, beating well after each addition. Into a bowl sift the cake flour, baking soda, baking powder, and salt. Beat into the egg mixture alternately with the banana mixture, beating well after each addition. Stir in the walnuts. Pour the batter into the cake pans and bake in the middle of the oven for 40 minutes, or until a cake tester inserted in the centers comes out clean. Let the layers cool in the pans for 10 minutes. Invert the cakes onto racks and let them cool completely. Remove the wax paper, wrap the layers in plastic wrap, and let the layers stand overnight.

In a chilled bowl with the mixer beat the cream with the remaining 2 tablespoons plus 2 teaspoons sugar and ¾ teaspoon vanilla until it holds stiff peaks. Put one cake layer on a serving plate, spread it with one third of the whipped cream, and top the cream with the remaining layer. Spread the remaining whipped cream on the sides and top of the cake.

CARROT CAKE WITH CREAM CHEESE FROSTING AND MARZIPAN RABBITS AND CARROTS

Yield:
one 8-inch layer cake

Equipment:
three 8-inch round
 cake pans
hand-held electric
 mixer

While slightly less fanciful when undecorated, this remains a wonderful carrot cake, moist and spicy.

marzipan decorations (page 545) if desired

FOR THE CAKE
2 cups all-purpose flour
2 cups granulated sugar
2 teaspoons baking soda
1 teaspoon salt
1 tablespoon cinnamon

pinch of ground allspice
4 large eggs
1 cup vegetable oil
4 cups finely grated carrots (about 1 pound)

FOR THE FROSTING
1 pound cream cheese, softened
1 stick (½ cup) unsalted butter, softened

4 cups confectioners' sugar, sifted
2 teaspoons vanilla

½ cup apricot jam

Make marzipan decorations the day before you intend to serve the cake and let them dry overnight.

Make the cake:

Line the cake pans with wax paper and butter the paper. Dust the pans with flour and knock out the excess. Preheat the oven to 350° F.

Into a bowl sift together the flour, granulated sugar, baking soda, salt, cinnamon, and allspice. In a large bowl with the mixer beat the eggs for 1 minute, or until frothy, and add the oil in a stream, beating. Gradually beat in the flour mixture and beat the batter until it is just smooth. Stir in the carrots. Divide the batter among the cake pans, smoothing the tops, and bake the layers in the middle of the oven for 25 to 30 minutes, or until a cake tester inserted in the centers comes out clean. Let the layers cool in the pans on racks for 10 minutes. Run a thin knife around the edges of the cake pans and invert the layers onto the racks. Let the layers cool completely and peel off the wax paper.

Make the frosting:

In a large bowl with the mixer cream together the cream cheese and the butter. Add the confectioners' sugar, a little at a time, beating, and beat in the vanilla.

The cake, undecorated, may be made up to 3 days ahead and chilled, covered. Let the cake come to room temperature before serving.

Set one cake layer on a serving plate, spread half the apricot jam over it, and top it with another cake layer. Spread the layer with the remaining jam and top it with the remaining cake layer. Spread the frosting over the sides and top of the cake and garnish the cake with the marzipan decorations if desired.

BUTTERMILK SPICE CAKE WITH CARAMEL FROSTING

Yield:
one 9-inch layer cake

Equipment:
two 9-inch round
  cake pans
hand-held electric
  mixer
candy thermometer

FOR THE CAKE
2¼ cups sifted cake flour
1 teaspoon double-acting baking
  powder
1 teaspoon salt
1 teaspoon cinnamon
¾ teaspoon baking soda
½ teaspoon ground cloves
1½ sticks (¾ cup) unsalted butter,
  softened

1 teaspoon vanilla
¾ cup firmly packed light brown
  sugar
1 cup granulated sugar
3 large eggs
1 cup buttermilk

FOR THE CARAMEL FROSTING
1½ cups firmly packed dark brown
  sugar
½ cup water

½ teaspoon cream of tartar
6 egg whites at room temperature
1½ teaspoons vanilla or coffee extract

Make the cake:

Butter the cake pans. Preheat the oven to 350° F.

Into a bowl sift together 3 times the flour, baking powder, salt, cinnamon, baking soda, and cloves. In a large bowl with the mixer cream the butter with the vanilla until light and fluffy and gradually beat in the brown sugar. Gradually beat in the granulated sugar and continue beating until light and smooth.

Add the eggs, one at a time, beating well after each addition. Sift about one third of the flour mixture over the batter and gently stir it in. Add ½ cup of the buttermilk and stir carefully to blend. Repeat, adding one more third of the flour, the remaining ½ cup buttermilk, and the last third of the flour. Divide the batter evenly between the cake pans and bake in the middle of the oven for 30 to 35 minutes, or until a cake tester inserted in the centers of the layers comes out clean and the cake has pulled away from the sides of the pans. Let the layers stand in the pans on racks for 5 minutes, then turn them out onto the racks to cool completely.

Make the caramel frosting:

In a small deep saucepan combine the brown sugar, water, and cream of tartar, stirring over low heat until the sugar is dissolved. Increase the heat to moderately high, cover the pan, and bring the syrup to a boil. Remove the cover and boil the syrup until the candy thermometer registers 228° F., or the syrup spins a long thread when dropped from a spoon.

In a bowl with the mixer beat the egg whites until they hold stiff peaks. Beating constantly, gradually pour the syrup in a thin stream into the egg whites until well combined and the frosting stands in very stiff peaks. (For the stages of sugar syrup and how to pour it, see illustrations pages 240 and 241.) Beat in the vanilla or coffee extract.

To assemble the cake:

Set one of the layers on a cake plate and spread the layer with one third of the caramel frosting. Top it with the second layer. Spread the remaining frosting over the sides and top of the cake.

LADY BALTIMORE CAKE

Yield:
one 9-inch layer cake

Equipment:
three 9-inch round
  cake pans, 1½
  inches deep
upright electric mixer
pastry brush
candy thermometer

Some say this classic American cake originated in Maryland, others in Charleston, South Carolina. No matter. Its three light layers are filled with meringue that is studded with dried fruits and nuts. This is a superb Southern-style extravaganza, perfect for a special occasion.

2 cups chopped raisins
2 cups chopped walnuts

½ cup chopped dried figs
1 cup medium-dry Sherry

FOR THE CAKE
3 cups sifted cake flour
1 tablespoon double-acting baking
  powder
⅛ teaspoon salt
1½ sticks (¾ cup) unsalted butter,
  softened

1¾ cups sugar
1 cup milk
1 teaspoon almond extract
½ teaspoon vanilla
6 egg whites at room temperature

FOR THE ITALIAN MERINGUE
2 cups sugar
⅔ cup water
½ teaspoon cream of tartar

4 egg whites at room temperature
1 teaspoon vanilla
1 teaspoon almond extract

In a bowl combine the raisins, walnuts, and figs. Pour in the Sherry and let the mixture macerate, covered, at room temperature overnight.

Make the cake:

Flour the cake pans, knock out the excess flour, and line them with buttered rounds of wax paper. Preheat the oven to 375° F.

Into a bowl sift together the cake flour, baking powder, and salt. Sift the mixture 2 more times and set it aside.

In the bowl of the mixer cream the butter until light. Beat in the sugar, ¼ cup at a time, and continue to beat until light and fluffy. Stir in the dry ingredients alternately with the milk and beat the batter until smooth. Stir in the almond extract and the vanilla. In the bowl with the mixer beat the 6 egg whites until they hold stiff peaks and fold them gently but thoroughly into the batter.

Divide the batter among the cake pans and bake the layers in the middle of the oven for 25 minutes, or until the cakes pull away from the sides of the pans. Turn the layers out onto racks to cool and peel off the wax paper.

Make the Italian meringue:

In a saucepan combine the sugar, water, and cream of tartar. Cook the mixture over moderately low heat until the sugar is dissolved, washing down any sugar crystals clinging to the sides of the pan with the brush dipped in cold water. Raise the heat to moderately high and bring the syrup to a boil. Cook the syrup, undisturbed, until it reaches the soft-ball stage, or the candy thermometer registers 240° F. In the bowl of the mixer beat the egg whites until they hold stiff peaks and, beating constantly, pour the hot syrup into the whites in a stream. (For the stages of sugar syrup and how to pour it, see illustrations pages 240 and 241.) Continue to beat the meringue until it is lukewarm. Add the vanilla and the almond extract.

To assemble the cake: Drain the macerated fruits and nuts and fold them into the meringue. Set one of the cake layers on a cake plate. With a metal spatula spread the layer with ¾ cup of the meringue and top it with the second layer. Spread the second layer with the meringue in the same manner and top it with the third layer. Spread the remaining meringue over the sides and top of the cake, making decorative peaks.

ROBERT E. LEE CAKE

Coconut Cake with Lemon Filling

Yield:
one 8-inch layer cake

Equipment:
three 8-inch round
   cake pans
hand-held electric
   mixer
pastry brush
candy thermometer

We don't know if Robert E. Lee was devoted to coconut cake, but if he was this one would have had to have been his most preferred. Three layers and lemon filled, it is decorated with pristine coconut and garnished with candied violets.

FOR THE CAKE

6 large eggs, separated, at room
   temperature
1 cup sugar
1 tablespoon grated orange rind
2 teaspoons grated lemon rind
2 teaspoons fresh orange juice

2 teaspoons fresh lemon juice
pinch of salt
¼ teaspoon cream of tartar
1 cup all-purpose flour sifted with ½
   teaspoon double-acting baking
   powder and ¼ teaspoon salt

FOR THE LEMON FILLING

4 egg yolks
⅓ cup sugar
½ stick (¼ cup) unsalted butter, cut
   into pieces

½ cup fresh lemon juice
2 teaspoons grated lemon rind

FOR THE FROSTING

¾ cup sugar
¼ cup water
4 egg whites at room temperature
pinch of salt
pinch of cream of tartar

1 tablespoon fresh lemon juice
1 tablespoon grated orange rind
2 teaspoons grated lemon rind
1 teaspoon vanilla

2 cups grated fresh coconut (for procedure page 549), or to taste

Make the cake: Line the cake pans with wax paper and butter the paper. Dust the pans with flour and knock out the excess. Preheat the oven to 350° F.

In a large bowl with the mixer beat the egg yolks with ½ cup of the sugar until the mixture is lemon colored and falls in a ribbon when the beater is lifted (see illustration page 16). Stir in the orange rind, lemon rind, orange juice, and lemon juice. In a bowl with the mixer beat the egg whites with the pinch of salt until frothy, add the cream of tartar, and beat the whites until they hold soft peaks. Add the remaining ½ cup sugar, a little at a time, beating, and beat the meringue until it holds stiff peaks (see illustrations page 238). Fold the meringue into the yolk mixture alternately with the flour mixture.

Divide the batter among the cake pans and bake the layers in the middle of the oven for 25 minutes, or until a cake tester inserted in the centers comes out clean. Let the layers cool in the pans on racks for 5 minutes, invert them onto the racks, and let them cool completely.

Make the lemon filling: In a heavy stainless steel or enameled saucepan combine the egg yolks, sugar, butter, and lemon juice. Cook the mixture over moderate heat, without letting it boil, whisking vigorously, until it thickens. Stir in the lemon rind, pour the mixture into a bowl, and let it cool. Chill the filling, covered with buttered wax paper, for at least 1 hour.

Make the frosting: In a small heavy saucepan combine the sugar with the water, bring the liquid to a boil, and boil it over moderate heat, stirring and washing down any sugar crystals clinging to the sides of the pan with the brush dipped in cold water, until it reaches the soft-ball stage, or the candy thermometer registers 234° F. In a bowl with the mixer beat the egg whites with the salt until frothy, add the cream of tartar, and beat the whites until they hold soft peaks. With the mixer running add the hot syrup in a stream and beat the meringue until it is completely cool. (For the stages of sugar syrup and how to pour it, see illustrations pages 240 and 241.) Beat in the lemon juice, orange rind, lemon rind, and the vanilla.

To assemble the cake: Set one of the layers on a cake plate and spread it with half the lemon filling. Top it with a second layer and spread it with the remaining filling. Top with the remaining cake layer. Spread the frosting on the top and sides of the cake, then press grated fresh coconut all over the frosting.

WALNUT CAKE WITH COFFEE BUTTERCREAM

Yield:
one 9-inch layer cake

This elegant cake combines a nutted batter with coffee buttercream—an unusually fine, sophisticated marriage of flavors.

Equipment:
pastry brush
two 9-inch round
  cake pans
upright electric mixer

FOR THE CAKE

2½ sticks (1¼ cups) unsalted butter, softened

1½ cups sugar

4 large eggs, separated, at room temperature

1 cup walnuts, finely ground

2 teaspoons light rum

1 teaspoon vanilla

pinch of cream of tartar

1¼ cups all-purpose flour sifted with 2 teaspoons double-acting baking powder

1 recipe coffee buttercream (page 23)

Make the cake:

Brush the cake pans with oil, line them with wax paper, and brush the paper with oil. Preheat the oven to 350° F.

In the bowl of the mixer cream together the butter and 1¼ cups of the sugar until light and fluffy. Beat in the egg yolks, one at a time, beating well after each addition. Add the walnuts, rum, and vanilla and continue to beat the mixture until it is well combined.

In the bowl of the mixer beat the egg whites with the cream of tartar until they hold soft peaks. Beat in the remaining ¼ cup sugar, one tablespoon at a time, and continue to beat the meringue until it holds stiff peaks (see illustrations page 238). Fold the meringue into the walnut mixture alternately with the flour mixture. Divide the batter between the cake pans and bake the layers in the middle of the oven for 45 minutes, or until a cake tester inserted in the centers comes out clean. Let the layers cool in the pans on racks for 5 minutes and invert them onto the racks.

Set one of the cake layers on a serving plate and spread one third of the buttercream over it. Top it with the remaining cake layer. Spread the remaining buttercream over the sides and top of the cake.

Strawberry Cream Cake (page 58), Ananas en Surprise (page 370), Orange Spiced Rhubarb (page 468)

STRAWBERRY CREAM CAKE

Yield:
one 9-inch layer cake

Equipment:
9-inch square baking
   pan, 2 inches deep
upright electric mixer
pastry brush
candy thermometer

This magnificent-looking and -tasting cake, with its mosaic-like motif of berries around the sides and its candied berries on top, is best made in stages, preferably on an early summer day.

FOR THE CAKE

3 large eggs
1½ cups granulated sugar
1¾ cups all-purpose flour
*2 teaspoons double-acting baking
   powder*

pinch of salt
¾ cup milk, scalded
*¾ stick (6 tablespoons) unsalted
   butter, cut into bits and softened*
1 teaspoon vanilla

FOR THE FILLING

*3 large eggs, separated, at room
   temperature*
*1 cup plus 2 tablespoons granulated
   sugar*
⅓ cup plus ½ cup water

*1½ sticks (¾ cup) unsalted butter, cut
   into bits*
1 tablespoon orange-flavored liqueur
pinch of salt
pinch of cream of tartar

FOR THE SUGAR SYRUP

⅓ cup granulated sugar
⅓ cup water

1 tablespoon orange-flavored liqueur

FOR THE MACERATED STRAWBERRIES

about 2 pints strawberries, hulled
*3 tablespoons orange-flavored liqueur,
   kirsch, or Cognac*

1 tablespoon fresh lemon juice
*1 tablespoon granulated sugar, or to
   taste*

*¼ cup sliced blanched almonds,
   toasted lightly*
½ cup red currant jelly, melted
confectioners' sugar for dusting

*1 pint Candied Strawberries (page
   523) with the stems intact*
*lightly whipped cream as an
   accompaniment if desired*

Make the cake:

Butter the cake pan well and dust it with flour. Preheat the oven to 350° F.
   In the bowl of the mixer beat the eggs with the granulated sugar until combined well. Sift in the flour, baking powder, and salt and beat until smooth. Add the scalded milk in a stream, beating, then beat in the butter and the vanilla until the batter is combined well. Pour the batter into the baking pan and bake the cake in the middle of the oven for 50 minutes to 1 hour, or until a cake tester inserted in the center comes out clean. Let the cake cool in the pan on a rack for 10 minutes, invert it onto the rack, and let it cool completely.

Make the filling:

In the bowl of the mixer beat the egg yolks at medium speed until light and thick. In a small saucepan combine ⅓ cup of the granulated sugar with the ⅓ cup water, bring the syrup to a boil, and boil it, stirring and washing down any sugar crystals clinging to the sides of the pan with the brush dipped in cold water until the candy thermometer registers 238° F. (For the stages of sugar syrup, see illustrations page 241.) With the mixer running add the hot syrup to the yolks in a stream and beat until completely cool. With the mixer running add the butter, one piece at a time. Add the liqueur and continue to beat the mixture until just combined.

In a saucepan combine the remaining ⅔ cup plus 2 tablespoons sugar with the remaining ½ cup water and bring the mixture to a boil over moderate heat. Boil the syrup, stirring and washing down any sugar crystals clinging to the sides with the brush dipped in cold water until the candy thermometer registers 248° F. and keep the syrup at that temperature.

In the bowl of the mixer beat the egg whites with the salt until frothy, add the cream of tartar, and beat the whites until they hold soft peaks. With the mixer running add the hot syrup in a stream and beat the meringue until completely cool. (For the stages of sugar syrup and how to pour it, see illustrations pages 240 and 241.) Fold the meringue gently but thoroughly into the butter mixture and chill the filling, covered, for at least 30 minutes, or until firm but still spreadable.

Make the sugar syrup: In a small saucepan combine the sugar with the water and cook the mixture over moderate heat until the sugar is dissolved. Remove the pan from the heat, stir in the liqueur, and let the syrup cool.

Make the macerated strawberries: In a ceramic or glass bowl toss the strawberries with the liqueur, lemon juice, and sugar and chill, covered, for at least 2 hours or overnight.

To assemble the cake: With a serrated knife halve the cake horizontally. Put the bottom layer, cut side up, on a serving plate, brush it with some of the syrup, and spread half the filling over it. Arrange the macerated strawberries hulled side down in the filling, making sure that there are even lines of strawberries along all four sides of the cake. Spread the remaining filling evenly over the berries and sprinkle the almonds over the filling. Brush the cut side of the remaining cake layer with the remaining syrup and set it on the filling, cut side down. Chill the cake, covered with plastic wrap, for 1 hour, or until the filling is slightly firm.

With the serrated knife cut ¼ inch off the sides of the cake to expose the strawberries along the sides. Brush the top and sides of the cake with the melted currant jelly and let the glaze cool for 15 minutes. Sift the confectioners' sugar lightly over the cake, garnish the cake with the candied strawberries, and serve it with the whipped cream if desired.

Photo on page 57.

CHOCOLATE CAKES

What distinguishes chocolate cake, aside from its popularity, which ranks it right up there with Coca-Cola as one of America's favorite sweets, is its many glorious interpretations. In fact, it is infrequent that two chocolate cakes are exactly the same. Chocolate itself has character, comes in different colors, and tastes unlike anything else in the world. It follows that chocolate cakes should have commensurate variety.

Our collection of chocolate cakes gives testimony to that depth. We offer the American classic devil's food layer cake with billowy white frosting and an unexpected but wonderful rhubarb sauce as an accompaniment. We've a flourless and confection-like Queen of Sheba Soul Cake (page 66) that is made with two different chocolates and ounces of butter. We include *Rehrücken* (page 68), an Austrian molded cake, glazed with chocolate. We've Chocolate Almond Cupcakes (page 69), which might well be the best cupcakes you will ever taste. We've a chocolate mousse cake, a chocolate marbled cake, and, last but not least, a chocolate Armagnac cake with pecans and prunes.

Baking succesfully with chocolate means melting it correctly. This can be done in several ways, but the most foolproof method melts it in the top of a double boiler over barely simmering, or hot, water. When melted, chocolate should be smooth and glossy. If heated to too high a temperature or over direct heat, chocolate seizes up and turns identifiably clumpy and granular. For all intents and purposes, chocolate is unusable if it has seized up. Don't embark upon such a reckless course. The well-being of a chocolate cake—not to mention the well-being of those who are going to enjoy it—is far too valuable to be tampered with like that.

DEVIL'S FOOD CAKE WITH RHUBARB SAUCE

Yield:
one 8-inch layer cake

Equipment:
three 8-inch round
  cake pans
hand-held electric
  mixer
pastry brush
candy thermometer

Some devil's food cakes are made with cocoa, others with vegetable shortening, and still others with both baking soda and baking powder. This one, made with melted chocolate *and* buttermilk, is particularly memorable. It stands three layers tall and when frosted and served with rhubarb sauce is incomparable as chocolate layer cakes go.

FOR THE CAKE

3 ounces unsweetened chocolate,
  chopped coarse
1½ sticks (¾ cup) unsalted butter,
  softened
1½ cups sugar
1½ teaspoons vanilla

3 large eggs, beaten well
2⅔ cups all-purpose flour
1½ teaspoons baking soda
½ teaspoon salt
1½ cups buttermilk
2 tablespoons heavy cream

FOR THE BOILED WHITE FROSTING
2½ cups sugar
¾ cup milk
2 tablespoons light corn syrup
2 tablespoons unsalted butter

2 tablespoons light cream or half-and-half
1 teaspoon vanilla

1 recipe Rhubarb Sauce (page 508) as an accompaniment

Make the cake:

Butter the cake pans, line them with wax paper, and butter the paper. Preheat the oven to 350° F.

In the top of a double boiler set over simmering water melt the chocolate and let it cool. In a bowl with the mixer cream the butter, beat in the sugar, a little at a time, and the vanilla, and beat the mixture until light and fluffy. Add the eggs and the melted chocolate and combine the mixture well. Into another bowl sift the flour with the baking soda and salt. Add the flour mixture to the batter alternately with the buttermilk and combine the batter until smooth. Add the heavy cream and stir the batter 3 or 4 times, or until just combined (the batter will be thick). Divide the batter evenly among the pans, smooth the tops, and bake the layers in the middle of the oven for 25 to 30 minutes, or until a cake tester inserted in the centers comes out clean. Let the layers cool in the pans on racks for 10 minutes and turn them out onto the racks. Peel off the paper and let the layers cool completely.

Make the boiled white frosting:

In a deep heavy saucepan combine the sugar with the milk, corn syrup, and butter. Cook the mixture over moderately low heat, stirring and washing down any sugar crystals clinging to the sides of the pan with the brush dipped in cold water until the sugar is dissolved. Bring the mixture to a rolling boil and boil it, covered, for 1 minute. Uncover and boil it undisturbed until the candy thermometer registers 238° F. (For the stages of sugar syrup, see illustrations page 241.) Remove the pan from the heat and beat the mixture with a wooden spoon until it begins to stiffen and has lost its gloss. Beat in the light cream, one teaspoon at a time, and the vanilla and beat the frosting until it is lukewarm and of spreading consistency (the frosting will appear grainy). Use while still warm.

Arrange one cake layer on a serving plate and using a metal spatula or a long knife dipped in hot water spread a thin layer of frosting over it. Top the frosting with another cake layer, spread the cake with a thin layer of the frosting, and top the cake with the remaining layer. Spread the remaining frosting over the sides and top of the cake and let the cake stand in a cool place for 1 hour, or until the frosting is set. Serve the rhubarb sauce with the cake.

CHOCOLATE ORANGE MARBLE CAKE

Yield:
1 cake

Equipment:
deep 1½-quart baking
  pan
hand-held and upright
  electric mixers

The combination of chocolate and orange is a classic one.

2 sticks (1 cup) unsalted butter,
  softened
1¼ cups sugar
2 large eggs, separated, plus 1 egg
  yolk, at room temperature
1¾ cups all-purpose flour
¾ teaspoon baking soda
¾ teaspoon double-acting baking
  powder

1 cup sour cream
the grated rind of 1 orange
2 ounces unsweetened chocolate,
  melted and cooled
pinch of cream of tartar
½ cup fresh orange juice

Butter the baking pan and line it with buttered wax paper. Preheat the oven to 350° F.

In the bowl of the upright mixer cream together the butter and 1 cup of the sugar until light. Add the egg yolks, one at a time, beating well after each addition. Into a bowl sift together the flour, baking soda, and baking powder. Add the flour mixture to the butter mixture alternately with the sour cream and beat until smooth.

Divide the cake batter between 2 bowls and into one stir the grated orange rind. Into the other bowl stir the melted chocolate. In a third bowl with the hand-held mixer beat the egg whites with the cream of tartar until they hold stiff peaks. Fold half the whites into the orange batter and half into the chocolate. Transfer the chocolate batter to the bowl with the orange batter and lightly swirl a spatula through the batters to marbleize the mixture. Pour into the baking pan and bake the cake in the middle of the oven for 1 hour and 10 minutes, or until a cake tester inserted in the center comes out clean. Transfer the cake to a rack and let it cool in the pan for 5 minutes.

In a bowl combine the orange juice with the remaining ¼ cup sugar and while the cake is still warm slowly pour the glaze over it. Let the cake cool completely, invert it onto a rack, and remove the wax paper. Invert the cake onto a board and serve it sliced.

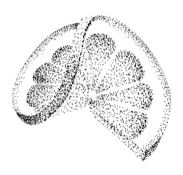

ARMAGNAC CHOCOLATE CAKE WITH PRUNES

Yield:
one 8½-inch cake

Equipment:
8½-inch round cake
   pan, 2 inches deep
hand-held electric
   mixer

You will note that there is no flour called for in this recipe. The leavening that does occur is triggered by the stiffly beaten egg whites. What you have, then, is a sensational combination of complex flavors and textures—chocolate, prunes, Armagnac, and pecans—in a single rich layer. This cake should be sliced thin and savored.

FOR THE CAKE

⅓ cup chopped pitted prunes
¼ cup Armagnac
6 ounces German sweet chocolate or
   semisweet chocolate, chopped
   coarse
3 tablespoons strong brewed coffee
1 stick (½ cup) unsalted butter, cut
   into bits and softened

3 large eggs, separated, at
   room temperature
½ cup plus 2 tablespoons granulated
   sugar
pinch of salt
pinch of cream of tartar
1 cup ground pecans
¼ cup cornstarch, sifted

FOR THE ICING

4 ounces German sweet chocolate or
   semisweet chocolate, chopped
   coarse
1 tablespoon Armagnac

3 tablespoons confectioners' sugar
½ stick (¼ cup) unsalted butter, cut
   into bits and softened

whole pecans for garnish

Make the cake:

In a small ceramic or glass bowl let the prunes macerate in the Armagnac for 30 minutes. Line the cake pan with wax paper and butter and flour the paper. Preheat the oven to 350° F.

In the top of a double boiler set over hot water melt the chocolate with the coffee. Remove the pan from the heat and beat in the butter, by bits, making sure that each piece is incorporated before adding the next.

In a large bowl with the mixer beat the egg yolks until smooth, add ½ cup of the granulated sugar, a little at a time, and beat the mixture until it falls in a ribbon when the beater is lifted (see illustration page 16). In a bowl with the mixer beat the egg whites with the salt until frothy, add the cream of tartar, and beat until they hold soft peaks. Gradually beat in the remaining 2 tablespoons granulated sugar and beat the whites until they hold stiff peaks (see illustrations page 238).

Stir the chocolate mixture into the yolk mixture and add the pecans, the prunes and the Armagnac in which they macerated, and the cornstarch. Stir one third of the whites into the chocolate mixture and fold in the remaining whites until there are no traces of white. Spoon the batter into the pan and bake the cake in the middle of the oven for 40 minutes, or until a cake tester inserted 2 inches from the rim of the cake comes out clean (the center of the cake will remain moist). Transfer the cake in the pan to a rack and let it cool completely. Turn the cake out onto the rack, peel off the paper, and transfer the cake to a plate. Chill the cake for 1 hour, or until it is well chilled.

Make the icing: In the top of the double boiler set over hot water heat the chocolate with the Armagnac until it is just melted. Remove the pan from the heat and stir in the confectioners' sugar. Stir in the butter, making sure that each piece is incorporated before adding the next.

Spread the sides and top of the cake with the chocolate icing and chill the cake until the icing is set. To serve, let the cake come to room temperature and decorate the top with the whole pecans.

CHOCOLATE MOUSSE CAKE WITH GANACHE ICING

Yield:
one 9-inch layer cake

Equipment:
two 9-inch round
   cake pans
upright mixer
pastry brush
candy thermometer
pastry bag fitted with
   medium fluted tip
8-inch cardboard
   round

This wonderful chocolate cake is layered with chocolate mousse and glazed with chocolate cream, or *crème ganache*. There is a subtle taste of orange to the whole and orange slices are employed as garnish. The cake is elegant and exciting and would befit any special occasion.

FOR THE CAKE

8 ounces semisweet chocolate, chopped
   coarse
¾ stick (6 tablespoons) unsalted
   butter, cut into tablespoons and
   softened
8 large eggs, separated, at room
   temperature

1 cup sugar
2 tablespoons orange-flavored liqueur
1 tablespoon grated orange rind
¼ teaspoon plus pinch of salt
pinch of cream of tartar
⅔ cup sifted cake flour

FOR THE CHOCOLATE MOUSSE

9 ounces semisweet chocolate, chopped
   coarse
6 egg yolks at room temperature
¾ cup plus 1 tablespoon sugar
2 tablespoons water

1¼ sticks (10 tablespoons) unsalted
   butter, cut into tablespoons and
   softened
2 tablespoons orange-flavored liqueur
4 egg whites at room temperature

FOR THE GANACHE ICING

1 cup heavy cream
8 ounces semisweet chocolate, chopped
   coarse

1 to 2 tablespoons orange-flavored
   liqueur

about 14 halved orange slices for garnish

Make the cake: Butter the cake pans, line the bottoms with wax paper, and butter the paper. Dust the pans with flour and knock out the excess. Preheat the oven to 350° F.

In the top of a double boiler heat the chocolate over hot water, stirring, until just melted. Remove the pan from the heat and stir in the butter, one tablespoon at a time. Continue to stir the mixture until smooth.

In the bowl of the mixer beat the egg yolks until combined. Add ¾ cup of the sugar, a little at a time, and continue to beat the mixture until it falls in a ribbon when the beater is lifted (see illustration page 16). Beat in the melted chocolate mixture, the liqueur, and the orange rind. Transfer the mixture to a large bowl.

In the bowl of the mixer beat the egg whites with the pinch of salt until frothy. Add the cream of tartar and beat the whites until they hold soft peaks. Add the remaining ¼ cup sugar, a little at a time, and beat the whites until they are stiff (see illustrations page 238). Sift the flour with the remaining ¼ teaspoon salt onto a sheet of wax paper. Stir one fourth of the whites into the batter. Fold in the remaining whites and sift and fold the flour mixture in batches into the egg mixture until just combined.

Pour the batter into the cake pans, smoothing the tops, and bake the layers in the middle of the oven for 30 to 35 minutes, or until a cake tester inserted into the centers comes out clean. Let the cakes cool in the pans on racks for 5 minutes, invert the cakes onto the racks, and remove the wax paper carefully. Let the cakes cool completely. (The cakes form a thin crust that will flake off.)

Make the chocolate mousse: In the top of the double boiler heat the chocolate over hot water, stirring until just melted.

In the bowl of the mixer beat the egg yolks until light and thick. In a small heavy saucepan combine the sugar with the water. Bring the mixture to a boil and boil it over moderate heat, stirring and washing down any sugar crystals clinging to the sides of the pan with the brush dipped in cold water until the syrup reaches the soft-ball stage, or the candy thermometer registers 238° F. (For the stages of sugar syrup, see illustrations page 241.) With the mixer running add the hot syrup to the yolks in a stream, beating, and beat the mixture until it is completely cool. Beat in the butter, a little at a time, the melted chocolate, and the liqueur. Reserve one third of the mixture in a small bowl, covered. Chill the remaining mixture, covered, until firm.

In a large bowl with the mixer beat the egg whites with the salt until they hold soft peaks. Add the remaining 1 tablespoon sugar and beat the mixture until it just holds stiff peaks. Stir one fourth of the whites into the remaining chocolate mixture, fold in the remaining whites gently but thoroughly and chill the mousse, covered, until firm.

Make the *ganache* icing: In a small heavy saucepan bring the cream just to a simmer. Remove the pan from the heat, add the chocolate, and let the mixture stand, covered, for 5 minutes. Stir in the liqueur and continue to stir the *ganache* until smooth and tepid. Strain through a fine sieve into a small pitcher or a bowl with a lip.

To assemble the cake: Put 1 teaspoon of the mousse in the center of the 8-inch cardboard round and set one of the cake layers, bottom side up, on the cardboard.

Cover the cake with some of the mousse, smoothing it into an even layer, and top it with the remaining cake layer, bottom side up. Cover the top and sides of the cake with the remaining mousse, smoothing it with a spatula, and chill the cake until it is cold.

Set the cake on a rack over a jelly-roll pan and pour the *crème ganache* over it, smoothing it with a spatula to completely cover the top and sides of the cake. Let the cake stand at room temperature for 10 minutes and scrape any excess chocolate glaze from the jelly-roll pan back into the saucepan. Heat the excess *ganache*, stirring, until smooth, cool it to tepid, and pour it over the cake, smoothing it with a spatula over the top and sides of the cake. Chill the cake until the glaze is set.

Transfer the reserved chocolate mixture to the pastry bag. Arrange orange slices, rounded sides up, on the top of the cake, piping the buttercream along the base on each side of the slices. Arrange the remaining slices, rounded sides up, against the side of the cake and pipe the buttercream decoratively around the bottom edge of the cake.

The cake may be prepared up to 2 days in advance and kept covered loosely with plastic wrap and chilled.

Let the cake stand at room temperature for at least 15 minutes before serving.

Photo on front jacket and page 510.

Pouring warm glaze

QUEEN OF SHEBA SOUL CAKE

Rich Chocolate Cake

Yield:
one 9-inch cake

For all intents and purposes, this cake, made with unsweetened chocolate but glazed with semisweet, is flourless. Dense and luxurious, almost creamy, it is a cake to remember when only the best of chocolate "confections" will do.

Equipment:
9-inch round cake pan, 2 inches deep
hand-held electric mixer

FOR THE CAKE
9 ounces unsweetened chocolate, cut into pieces
1 stick (½ cup) unsalted butter, softened
¾ cup sugar

6 large eggs, separated, at room temperature
1 tablespoon all-purpose flour
pinch of salt
pinch of cream of tartar

FOR THE ICING
6 ounces semisweet chocolate, cut into pieces
2 large eggs

1 stick (½ cup) unsalted butter, softened

lightly whipped cream as an accompaniment if desired

Make the cake: Butter the bottom and sides of the cake pan. Line the bottom of the pan with wax paper, butter the paper, and dust the pan with flour, shaking out the excess.

In the top of a double boiler set over hot water melt the chocolate, stirring. In a bowl with the mixer beat the butter with the sugar until the mixture is pale and fluffy. Add the chocolate and beat the mixture until combined well. Add the egg yolks, one at a time, beating well after each addition. Beat in the flour and chill the mixture, covered, until barely firm.

Preheat the oven to 450° F.

In a large bowl with the mixer beat the egg whites with the salt until frothy, add the cream of tartar, and beat until they hold stiff peaks. Stir one third of the whites into the chilled batter and fold in the remaining whites gently but thoroughly. Spoon the batter into the pan and bake the cake in the middle of the oven for 5 minutes. Reduce the oven temperature to 300° F. and bake the cake for 25 to 30 minutes more, or until a cake tester inserted 2 inches from the rim of the pan comes out clean (the center of the cake will remain moist). Transfer the cake in the pan to a rack and let it cool for 10 minutes. Turn the cake out onto the rack, peel off the paper carefully, and let the cake cool completely.

Make the icing: In the top of the double boiler set over hot water melt the chocolate, stirring. In a bowl with the mixer beat the eggs and the butter until well combined. Add the chocolate, beat the icing until it is fluffy, and chill it, covered, for 15 to 30 minutes, or until it is cool but still of spreading consistency. Spread the sides and top of the cake with the icing. Transfer the cake to a serving plate and serve it with the whipped cream if desired.

REHRÜCKEN

Almond Chocolate Log

Yield:
1 loaf cake, 10½ by
  4½ by 2½ inches

Equipment:
food processor fitted
  with steel blade
Rehrücken pan
  (available at
  specialty
  kitchenware stores)
  or loaf pan, 10½ by
  4½ by 2½ inches
hand-held electric
  mixer
pastry brush

Rehrücken means saddle or haunch of venison in Austrian. This chocolate cake, baked in a special pan to resemble the haunch, contains no flour—only rusk or cake crumbs—and requires at least one day to mellow. It is an especially appropriate cake to prepare for the Christmas holidays.

FOR THE CAKE

2 ounces semisweet chocolate, cut into
  pieces
1 cup whole blanched almonds (for
  procedure page 549)
½ cup stale cake crumbs or rusk
  crumbs
¾ stick (6 tablespoons) unsalted
  butter, softened

⅓ cup sugar
4 large eggs, separated, at room
  temperature
pinch of salt
1 generous tablespoon strained
  strawberry jam

FOR THE DECORATION

3 ounces semisweet chocolate, cut into
  pieces
3 tablespoons hot water

1½ teaspoons unsalted butter
¼ cup slivered blanched almonds

sweetened whipped cream as an accompaniment

Make the cake:

In the top of a double boiler set over hot water melt the chocolate, stirring until smooth. Let cool.

In the food processor or in a blender pulverize the almonds. In a bowl combine the almonds with the cake or rusk crumbs.

Butter the *Rehrücken* pan or loaf pan. Dust the pan with flour and knock out the excess. Preheat the oven to 350° F.

In a bowl with the mixer cream together the butter and sugar until light and fluffy. Add the egg yolks, one at a time, beating well after each addition. Stir in the melted chocolate and two thirds of the nut mixture. In a large bowl with the mixer beat the egg whites with the salt until they hold stiff peaks and fold them gently but thoroughly into the butter mixture alternately with the remaining nut mixture. Pour the batter into the cake pan and bake the *Rehrücken* in the middle of the oven for 40 to 45 minutes, or until a cake tester inserted in the center comes out clean. Let the cake cool in the pan on a rack for 30 minutes, invert it onto the rack, and let it cool completely. Brush the cake with the strawberry jam and let dry.

Finish the cake:

In the top of the double boiler set over hot water melt the chocolate with the hot water and butter, stirring until the mixture is smooth. Pour the chocolate along the center of the cake and tilt the cake so that the icing spreads over the sides. With a spatula dipped in hot water spread the chocolate over both ends of the cake and the sides where necessary and let the chocolate set. Stud the cake with the slivered almonds and let it stand, covered loosely, for at least 1 day to mellow. Serve with the whipped cream. Photo on page 275.

CHOCOLATE ALMOND CUPCAKES

Yield:
8 cupcakes

Equipment:
hand-held electric mixer
8 half-cup brioche tins or other molds

Just as with certain brownies, the tops of these cupcakes may crack when baked, due in large part to the leavening power of the egg whites. The insides of the cupcakes remain fantastically moist and delicious, however.

4 ounces semisweet chocolate, cut into pieces
1 stick (½ cup) unsalted butter, cut into bits and softened
¾ cup plus 2 tablespoons granulated sugar
4 large eggs, separated, at room temperature
pinch of salt
pinch of cream of tartar
1 teaspoon grated orange rind
1 cup finely ground blanched almonds
⅓ cup sifted cornstarch
sifted confectioners' sugar for sprinkling

In the top of a double boiler set over hot water melt the chocolate. In a large bowl with the mixer beat the butter with the ¾ cup granulated sugar until the mixture is light and fluffy. Add the egg yolks, one at a time, beating well after each addition, and beat the mixture until well combined.

Generously butter the brioche tins. Preheat the oven to 350° F.

In a bowl with the mixer beat the egg whites with the salt until frothy, add the cream of tartar, and beat the whites until they hold soft peaks. Gradually beat in the remaining 2 tablespoons granulated sugar and beat the whites until they hold stiff peaks (see illustrations page 238). In a large bowl combine the egg yolk mixture, the chocolate, and the grated orange rind. Stir one fourth of the whites into the chocolate mixture and fold in the ground almonds and the cornstarch alternately with the remaining whites until there are no traces of white remaining.

Spoon the batter into the brioche tins, filling each mold three-fourths full. Put the tins on a baking sheet and bake the cupcakes in the middle of the oven for 25 to 30 minutes, or until a cake tester inserted in the centers comes out almost clean. (The center of the cupcakes should be moist. The tops may crack.) Let the cupcakes cool in the tins on a rack for 15 minutes, turn them out onto the rack, and let them cool completely. Before serving, sprinkle the cupcakes with the confectioners' sugar.

POUND AND BUNDT CAKES

We have grouped together pound and Bundt cakes for the simple reason that with the solitary exception of Sand Torte (page 72) all the batters incorporate considerable amounts of butter which, when properly creamed with sugar, will render an extraordinary crumb. Sand Torte, on the other hand, relies upon eggs and lots of air for its marvelous texture.

These kindred kinds of cake are curiously versatile. They easily grace a tea table and are equally at home in a picnic hamper. They tend to keep well, particularly so the recipe for Orange Pecan Cake (page 73), an actual, old-fashioned keeping cake. Keeping cakes, traditionally made with the addition of buttermilk, reach their peaks about two days to a week after being baked, when the cake's flavors and texture have fully developed. Save this cake for a rainy day.

CREAM CHEESE AND NUT POUND CAKE

Yield:
one 9-inch loaf cake

Equipment:
loaf pan, 9 by 5 by 3 inches
hand-held electric mixer

2 sticks (1 cup) unsalted butter, softened
1¼ cups sugar
3 ounces cream cheese, softened
4 large eggs at room temperature, beaten lightly
1½ teaspoons vanilla

2 cups cake flour, sifted
¼ teaspoon salt
1 teaspoon double-acting baking powder
1 cup finely chopped pecans, toasted and skins removed hazelnuts (for procedure page 549), or other nuts

Butter the loaf pan and dust it with flour, knocking out the excess. Preheat the oven to 350° F.

In a bowl with the mixer cream the butter. Gradually beat in the sugar and then the cream cheese, a little at a time, and continue to beat the mixture until fluffy. Add the eggs, one tablespoon at a time, and the vanilla and beat the mixture until well combined.

Sift the flour with the salt and baking powder and beat into the egg mixture, a little at a time, until smooth. Fold in the nuts. Pour the batter into the pan and smooth the top with a spatula. Bake the cake in the middle of the oven for 1 to 1¼ hours, or until a cake tester inserted in the center comes out clean. Let the cake cool in the pan on a rack for 5 minutes, turn it out onto the rack, and let it cool completely.

BLUEBERRY LEMON POUND CAKE

Yield:
1 tube cake

Equipment:
4-quart tube pan, 4
  inches deep
hand-held electric
  mixer

2 sticks (1 cup) unsalted butter,
  softened
2 cups granulated sugar
6 large eggs, separated, at room
  temperature
2 tablespoons fresh lemon juice
4 teaspoons grated lemon rind
3 cups cake flour

1 teaspoon baking soda
1/4 teaspoon plus pinch of salt
1 cup plain yogurt
pinch of cream of tartar
1 1/2 cups blueberries, picked over
1 tablespoon all-purpose flour
1 tablespoon confectioners' sugar

Butter the tube pan and dust it with flour, shaking out the excess. Preheat the oven to 375° F.

In a large bowl with the mixer cream the butter. Beat in 1 1/2 cups of the granulated sugar, a little at a time, and beat the mixture until light and fluffy. Beat in the egg yolks, one at a time, beating well after each addition, and add the lemon juice and rind. Sift together the cake flour, baking soda, and the 1/4 teaspoon salt and add to the egg yolk mixture alternately with the yogurt.

In a bowl with the mixer beat the egg whites with the pinch of salt until frothy, add the cream of tartar, and beat the whites until they hold soft peaks. Gradually beat in the remaining 1/2 cup granulated sugar and beat the meringue until it holds stiff peaks (see illustrations page 238). Stir one fourth of the meringue into the batter and fold in the remaining meringue gently but thoroughly.

Toss the blueberries with the all-purpose flour and stir into the batter. Spoon the batter into the tube pan and smooth the top. Bake the cake in the middle of the oven for 1 hour, or until a cake tester inserted halfway between the center and the edge comes out clean. Let the cake cool in the pan on a rack for 10 minutes, invert it onto the rack, and let it cool completely.

Before serving, sift the confectioners' sugar over the cake and transfer the cake to a platter. Or serve the cake sliced, toasted lightly, and buttered.

ORANGE POPPY SEED CAKE

Yield:
1 Bundt cake

Equipment:
1-quart decorative ring mold
hand-held electric mixer

1 stick (½ cup) unsalted butter, softened
¾ cup granulated sugar
2 large eggs
½ cup sour cream
⅓ cup poppy seeds plus seeds for garnish
¼ cup fresh orange juice

1 tablespoon grated orange rind
1 teaspoon vanilla
1¼ cups all-purpose flour
½ teaspoon double-acting baking powder
¼ teaspoon baking soda
pinch of salt
sifted confectioners' sugar for dusting

Butter the ring mold, dust it with flour, and shake out the excess flour. Preheat the oven to 350° F.

In a bowl with the mixer cream together the butter and granulated sugar until light and fluffy. Beat in the eggs, one at a time, beating well after each addition. Beat in the sour cream, the ⅓ cup poppy seeds, the orange juice, orange rind, and vanilla. Sift together the flour, baking powder, baking soda, and salt. Add to the egg mixture and combine the batter well. Pour into the ring mold and bake the cake in the middle of the oven for 40 minutes, or until a cake tester inserted halfway between the center and the rim comes out clean. Let the cake stand in the pan on a rack for 5 minutes, invert it onto the rack, and let it cool completely. Stand the cake upright, dust it with the sifted confectioners' sugar, and garnish it with the remaining poppy seeds.

SAND TORTE

Yield:
1 *Kugelhupf* cake

Equipment:
1½-quart *Kugelhupf* mold
upright electric mixer

Wonderful in texture due to the extraordinary amount of air beaten into the batter, this cake is the perfect accompaniment to fruit or ice cream.

¾ cup all-purpose flour
½ cup blanched almonds (for procedure page 549), toasted lightly and very finely ground
4 large eggs plus 2 egg yolks
½ cup granulated sugar

6 tablespoons clarified butter (page 536), cooled
1 teaspoon vanilla
½ teaspoon grated lemon rind
sifted confectioners' sugar for dusting

Butter the *Kugelhupf* mold, dust it with flour, and shake out the excess. Preheat the oven to 350° F.

Into a bowl sift together the flour and the ground almonds. In the bowl of the mixer combine the eggs, egg yolks, and the granulated sugar. Set the bowl over a saucepan containing 2 inches of hot but not boiling water and heat the mixture over low heat, stirring occasionally, until lukewarm (see illustration page 16). Transfer the bowl to the mixer and beat the mixture at high speed for 10 minutes, or until very light and triple in volume. Sift in the flour mixture, about ¼ cup at a time, folding in each portion lightly but thoroughly. Combine the clarified butter with the vanilla and the lemon rind and stir into the batter, about one tablespoon at a time. Pour the batter into the mold and bake the cake in the middle of the oven for 35 to 40 minutes, or until golden. Turn the cake out onto a rack and let it cool completely. Sift the confectioners' sugar over the top of the cake.

ORANGE PECAN CAKE

Keeping Cake

Yield:
1 *Kugelhupf* cake

Equipment:
1 ½-quart *Kugelhupf* pan or round tube pan
hand-held electric mixer

While we do not have to stoke fires and heat ovens to uneven temperatures these days, then bake in large quantities, there is still much good to be said about the cake that keeps and actually improves with flavor as it stands. Here is a wonderful example of one.

FOR THE CAKE

¾ stick (6 tablespoons) unsalted butter, softened
½ cup granulated sugar
1 large egg
1 cup sifted all-purpose flour, plus 2 tablespoons
½ teaspoon double-acting baking powder

½ teaspoon baking soda
⅛ teaspoon salt
½ cup buttermilk
the grated rind of 1 orange
½ cup finely chopped pecans
⅓ cup finely chopped dates

FOR THE GLAZE

⅓ cup fresh orange juice
¼ cup superfine granulated sugar

2 tablespoons orange-flavored liqueur
sifted confectioners' sugar for dusting

Make the cake:

Butter the *Kugelhupf* pan. Preheat the oven to 350° F.

In a bowl with the mixer cream together the butter and granulated sugar until fluffy. Add the egg and beat until light. Into a bowl sift together the 1 cup sifted flour, the baking powder, baking soda, and salt. Beat into the butter mixture alternately with the buttermilk. Stir in the orange rind. In another bowl toss the pecans and dates with the remaining 2 tablespoons flour. Fold into the batter and turn the batter into the pan. Bake the cake in the middle of the oven for 50 minutes, or until a cake tester inserted halfway between the center and the edge comes out clean. Remove the cake from the oven but do not unmold it.

Make the glaze:

In a bowl combine the orange juice, sugar, and liqueur. While the cake is still hot and still in the pan prick it with a skewer at ½-inch intervals and slowly pour the glaze over it. Let the cake cool in the pan on a rack. Turn the cooled cake out of the pan, wrap it tightly in plastic wrap and foil, and let it stand at room temperature for 2 or 3 days. Before serving, transfer it to a platter and dust it with the confectioners' sugar.

SCRIPTURE CAKE WITH MILK AND HONEY GLAZE

Yield:
1 Bundt cake

Equipment:
1½-quart ring mold
hand-held electric
    mixer
candy thermometer

All the ingredients in scripture cake, save the baking powder, of course, have references in the Bible. This spice cake, which is studded with dried fruits, has also been considered a fruitcake. Like fruitcake, it keeps well, carefully wrapped.

FOR THE CAKE

1 cup golden raisins
1 stick (½ cup) unsalted butter,
    softened
1 cup sugar
3 large eggs
3 tablespoons honey
1¾ cups all-purpose flour
2 teaspoons double-acting baking
    powder

½ teaspoon cinnamon
½ teaspoon ground allspice
¼ teaspoon freshly grated nutmeg
¼ teaspoon salt
a pinch of ground cloves
½ cup milk
1 cup chopped dried figs
½ cup sliced blanched almonds, lightly
    toasted

FOR THE GLAZE

1 cup sugar
¼ cup milk
1 tablespoon light corn syrup

1 tablespoon unsalted butter
¼ cup honey

Make the cake:

Put the raisins in a small bowl, cover them with hot water, and let them soak for 15 minutes.

Butter the ring mold, dust it with flour, and shake out the excess. Preheat the oven to 325° F.

In a large bowl with the mixer cream the butter. Add the sugar, a little at a time, beating, and beat until light and fluffy. Add the eggs, one at a time, beating well after each addition. Add the honey and combine the mixture well. Into a bowl sift together 1½ cups of the flour, the baking powder, cinnamon, allspice, nutmeg, salt, and cloves. Stir into the butter mixture alternately with the milk and combine the batter well.

Drain the raisins, pat them dry, and combine them with the figs, almonds, and the remaining ¼ cup flour. Toss the mixture well and fold it into the batter. Stir the batter well to incorporate the fruit mixture and spoon it into the ring mold. Smooth the top and rap the mold on a hard surface once or twice to expel any air bubbles. Bake the cake in the middle of the oven for 55 to 60 minutes, or until a cake tester inserted halfway between the edge and the center comes out clean. Transfer the cake to a rack and let it cool in the mold for 10 minutes. Invert the cake onto the rack and let it cool completely.

Make the glaze:

In a small heavy saucepan combine the sugar with the milk, corn syrup, and butter and bring the mixture to a boil over moderate heat, stirring until the sugar is dissolved. Boil the mixture, covered, for 1 minute. Uncover and boil it until the candy thermometer registers 238° F. Stir in the honey, bring the mixture to a boil, and boil it until the candy thermometer returns to 238° F. (For the stages of sugar syrup, see illustrations page 241.) Remove from the heat and let the glaze cool, stirring constantly with a wooden spoon, until thickened slightly but still thin enough to drizzle over the cake (the glaze will turn opaque as it cools). If necessary, reheat the glaze over low heat, stirring, to thin it to the desired consistency. Makes about 1 cup.

Wrap the cake tightly in plastic wrap and store it in an airtight container for up to 4 days.

Put the cake on the rack over wax paper and drizzle the glaze evenly over it, letting it run down the sides. Let the cake stand until the glaze has set and transfer it with metal spatulas to a cake plate.

COFFEECAKES AND YEAST CAKES

For organizational purposes, we have grouped coffeecakes and yeast cakes together. That they are entirely different in composition is obvious. That there are coffeecakes much better suited for tea than for breakfast is less obvious, and that there are yeast cakes much better suited for dessert even less so. What constitutes a good morning cake? What, on the other hand, constitutes a good tea cake? Something simple and subtle in flavor we would suspect. And while yeast cakes, and particularly bread, are expected at breakfast, not all yeast cakes are appropriate at that early morning hour.

Our collection of coffeecakes, all leavened with baking powder or baking soda or both is short; the cakes are simple, and the flavors are subtle and pleasing. An easy-to-make cake such as Cinnamon Cake (page 76) would readily enhance a tea cart. So would Blueberry Pecan Crumb Cake (page 77), with its brown sugar-nut topping. Pumpkin Sour Cream Coffeecake (page 78) would not only accompany a cup of tea well, but it might also be a wonderful offering at a fall tailgate picnic. So even though these are called coffeecakes and we associate coffee and cake in the morning, they should not be relegated to breakfast any more than "quick" bread should be thought of as bread.

At the mention of yeast, some people quake in their boots. It is complicated and alive and has to be proofed, they mumble. And anyway, how can you tell when it's ready? they ask. Yeast takes too long, someone else chimes in. There is some truth to all of this. Yeast is alive and, for precautionary reasons—for the simple purpose of finding out if it is going to work—should be proofed. To proof is to dissolve the yeast in warm water, checking for bubbles and foam as "proof" that the yeast is active and alive. And yes, a cake made with yeast does take longer to make, because the dough must be left to rise. That happens to be part of the great appeal of working with a yeast dough, however. With that said, why is each of the yeast cakes that follow appropriate as a dessert?

Streusel Plum Cake (page 79), small purple plums atop a slightly sweetened dough, is simply a different kind of fruited cake, not unlike Cherry Kuchen (page 86), if you will. Moravian Sugar Coffeecake (page 80), with the depressions in that dough filled with brown sugar and butter, in a way resembles a clever bar cookie and would be superb with poached fruit as an accompaniment. The final two recipes in this section are both *Stollen,* traditional holiday offerings, and should have no constraints whatsoever on when they are served. During the holidays, anything goes.

Were we asked the question, What is in a name as regards the recipes that follow? we would reply adaptability.

CINNAMON CAKE

Yield:
one 9-inch square
  cake

Equipment:
9-inch square cake
  pan, 2 inches deep
hand-held electric
  mixer

1¼ cups sugar
½ teaspoon cinnamon
2 sticks (1 cup) unsalted butter, cut
  into pieces and softened
2 large eggs, beaten lightly
2½ cups all-purpose flour

4 teaspoons double-acting baking
  powder
½ teaspoon salt
1¼ cups milk
⅓ cup cinnamon sugar (page 541)

Butter and flour the cake pan, knocking out the excess flour. Preheat the oven to 350° F.

In a bowl combine the 1¼ cups sugar with the cinnamon. Add the butter and cream the mixture with the mixer until very light. Beat in the eggs. In another bowl sift together the flour, baking powder, and salt. Add ½ cup of the dry ingredients at a time to the egg mixture alternately with the milk and combine until smooth. Pour the batter into the cake pan, spread it evenly with a metal spatula, and bake the cake in the middle of the oven for 45 minutes, or until well browned and a cake tester inserted in the center comes out clean. Let the cake cool on a rack for 5 minutes.

Sprinkle the cinnamon sugar over the still-warm cake. Cut the cake into squares and serve it warm.

BLUEBERRY PECAN CRUMB CAKE

Yield:
1 cake, 13 by 9 inches

Equipment:
baking pan, 13 by 9 inches
hand-held electric mixer

FOR THE CAKE

½ stick (¼ cup) unsalted butter, softened
¼ cup vegetable shortening at room temperature
1 cup sugar
3 large eggs, beaten lightly
1¾ cups plus 1 tablespoon all-purpose flour
1 teaspoon double-acting baking powder
1 teaspoon baking soda
¼ teaspoon salt
1 cup sour cream
1 tablespoon grated lemon rind
3 cups blueberries, picked-over

FOR THE TOPPING

1 cup firmly packed light brown sugar
¼ cup all-purpose flour
½ cup finely chopped pecans
½ stick (¼ cup) unsalted butter, cut into bits

Make the cake: Butter the baking pan, dust it with flour, and knock out the excess flour. Preheat the oven to 350° F.

In a large bowl with the mixer cream the butter and the shortening. Add the sugar, a little at a time, beating, and beat until light and fluffy. Beat in the eggs, one at a time, beating well after each addition. Into another bowl sift together the 1¾ cups flour, the baking powder, baking soda, and salt. Add the dry ingredients to the egg mixture alternately with the sour cream, stirring until the batter is just combined. Fold in the lemon rind. Toss the blueberries with the remaining 1 tablespoon flour and add to the batter. Spread the batter in the baking pan.

Make the topping: In a small bowl combine the brown sugar with the flour and pecans and blend in the butter until the mixture resembles coarse meal.

Sprinkle the topping evenly over the batter and bake the cake in the middle of the oven for 50 minutes, or until a cake tester inserted in the center comes out clean. Let the cake cool in the pan on a rack for 10 minutes, cut it into squares, and transfer it to a platter.

PUMPKIN SOUR CREAM COFFEECAKE

Yield:
one 8-inch cake

Equipment:
8-inch square baking
  pan
hand-held electric
  mixer

A splendid offering for the fall, this cake combines pumpkin, sour cream, and spices, plus a nutted brown sugar topping.

FOR THE CAKE
1/3 cup granulated sugar
1/2 stick (1/4 cup) unsalted butter,
  softened
1/3 cup fresh or canned pumpkin purée
1/4 cup sour cream
1 large egg, beaten lightly
1 1/2 tablespoons grated orange rind

1 1/4 cups sifted all-purpose flour
1 tablespoon double-acting baking
  powder
1/2 teaspoon baking soda
1/4 teaspoon freshly grated nutmeg
1/2 teaspoon salt
1/3 cup milk

FOR THE STREUSEL TOPPING
1/4 cup firmly packed light brown
  sugar
3 tablespoons cold unsalted butter, cut
  into bits

2 tablespoons granulated sugar
2 tablespoons all-purpose flour
1/2 teaspoon cinnamon
1/3 cup chopped walnuts

Make the cake:

Butter the baking pan. Preheat the oven to 375° F.

In a large bowl with the mixer cream together the sugar and the butter. Add the pumpkin purée, sour cream, egg, and orange rind and beat until well combined. Into another bowl sift together the flour, baking powder, baking soda, nutmeg, and salt. Stir the flour mixture into the pumpkin mixture alternately with the milk and blend until just combined. Pour the batter into the pan.

Make the streusel topping:

In a small bowl combine the brown sugar, butter, granulated sugar, flour, and cinnamon and blend the mixture until it resembles coarse meal. Sprinkle the streusel evenly over the batter and top it with the walnuts.

Bake the coffeecake in the middle of the oven for 45 minutes, or until a cake tester inserted in the center comes out clean. Let the cake cool in the pan on a rack for 10 minutes and cut it into squares. Serve the cake warm or at room temperature.

STREUSEL PLUM CAKE

Yield:
one 10-inch cake

Purple plums with a sugar topping on a sweetened yeast dough base—an unusually good combination of textures and flavors.

Equipment:
upright electric mixer
  fitted with the
  dough hook
  (optional)
one 10-inch round
  cake pan or piece of
  cardboard
pastry brush

FOR THE CAKE

1½ teaspoons active dry yeast
2 tablespoons lukewarm water
¼ cup plus pinch of granulated sugar
2 cups all-purpose flour

½ teaspoon salt
½ cup milk
½ stick (¼ cup) unsalted butter
1 egg yolk

FOR THE TOPPING

*1 pound small purple plums, pitted
  and quartered*
⅓ cup all-purpose flour
¼ cup granulated sugar

3 tablespoons unsalted butter, softened
⅛ teaspoon cinnamon
*1 egg white, beaten lightly, for egg
  wash*

sifted confectioners' sugar for dusting

Make the cake:

In a small bowl proof the yeast in the water with the pinch of sugar for 15 minutes, or until foamy.

Into a large bowl sift together the flour, the remaining ¼ cup sugar, and the salt. In a saucepan combine the milk with the butter, heat the mixture over moderate heat until the butter is melted, and let it cool to lukewarm. Lightly beat the egg yolk with a little of the milk mixture and add it and the yeast to the flour mixture. Gradually add the remaining milk mixture and blend to form a dough. With the dough hook of the electric mixer, or with a wooden spoon, beat the dough until smooth and elastic and no longer sticky. Put the dough into a lightly buttered bowl, turn to coat it with the butter, and let it rise in a warm place, loosely covered, for 1½ hours, or until double in bulk.

Butter a baking sheet well and on it, using the cake pan, trace a 10-inch circle. Punch down the dough, roll it on a floured surface into a 10-inch circle, and arrange it on the baking sheet, stretching it to fit the outline and making a 1-inch rim. Let the dough rise, loosely covered, for 30 minutes.

Preheat the oven to 400° F.

Arrange the plums, skin side down, in concentric circles on the dough.

Make the topping:

In a bowl blend the flour, granulated sugar, butter, and cinnamon with a fork until the mixture forms crumbs. Sprinkle the streusel over the plums. Brush the edge of the dough with the lightly beaten egg white and bake the cake in the middle of the oven for 10 minutes. Reduce the oven temperature to 375° F. and bake the cake for 30 minutes more, or until the edge is golden. Let the cake cool on the baking sheet for 10 minutes, remove it carefully to a rack, and let it cool completely. Just before serving, sprinkle the cake with the confectioners' sugar.

MORAVIAN SUGAR COFFEECAKE

Yield:
one 15- by 10-inch
   cake

Equipment:
food mill
15- by 10-inch jelly-
   roll pan
pastry brush

This unique cake combines mashed potatoes and lard in the yeast dough. Left to rise, it is then punched down and into indentations in the dough go butter, brown sugar, and cinnamon—an unbeatable mix.

*¾ pound baking potatoes, peeled and
   cubed
1 cup cold water
¼ cup plus 1 teaspoon granulated
   sugar
½ stick (¼ cup) unsalted butter, cut
   into bits, plus 3 tablespoons, plus
   additional melted butter for
   brushing the dough*

*3 tablespoons lard
½ teaspoon salt
1 tablespoon active dry yeast
1 large egg
3½ cups unbleached flour
1½ tablespoons cinnamon
1 cup firmly packed light brown sugar
¼ cup heavy cream*

Put the potatoes in a saucepan. Add the water and bring it to a boil. Cook the potatoes, covered, over moderate heat for 15 minutes, or until tender. Drain the potatoes and reserve the water. Purée the potatoes through the food mill or a ricer into a large bowl (there should be about 1 cup purée), add ½ cup of the reserved water, the ¼ cup granulated sugar, 3 tablespoons butter, the lard, and the salt and combine the mixture well.

In a small bowl proof the yeast in ¼ cup of the reserved lukewarm potato-to water with the remaining 1 teaspoon granulated sugar for 15 minutes, or until foamy. Add the yeast mixture and the egg to the potato mixture and combine well. Stir in the flour, one cup at a time, and combine the dough well.

Turn the dough out onto a floured surface and knead it, incorporating more flour if necessary to keep it from sticking, for 10 minutes, or until smooth and elastic. Form the dough into a ball, transfer it to a buttered bowl, and turn it to coat with the butter. Let the dough rise, covered loosely with a towel, in a warm place for 1½ hours, or until double in bulk.

Punch down the dough, transfer it to a floured surface, and let it rest for 10 minutes. Roll out the dough ½ inch thick and fit it into the jelly-roll pan. Brush the dough lightly with the melted butter and let it rise, covered with the towel, in a warm place for 30 minutes, or until puffy.

Preheat the oven to 400° F.

Punch indentations in the dough with your thumb and fill them with the remaining ½ stick cut-up butter. Sprinkle the dough with the cinnamon and brown sugar and drizzle the cream over it. Bake the cake in the middle of the oven for 20 minutes, or until browned and bubbly. Let the cake cool in the pan on a rack for 5 minutes and cut it into squares.

BAYRISCHER NUSS STOLLEN

Bavarian Nut Stollen

Yield:
1 *Stollen*

Equipment:
pastry brush

Simpler ingredients than the following recipe for Dresden *Stollen*. This German Christmas yeast bread is cleverly shaped to bake into a lovely braid.

FOR THE *STOLLEN*

1 envelope active dry yeast
¼ cup lukewarm milk, plus 1 cup scalded
1 cup plus 1 teaspoon granulated sugar
½ stick (¼ cup) unsalted butter, cut into bits
1 large egg, separated, white beaten lightly

grated rind of ½ lemon
4½ cups all-purpose flour
1 teaspoon plus pinch of salt
⅓ cup water
2½ cups ground walnuts
½ teaspoon cinnamon

FOR THE GLAZE

1 cup confectioners' sugar
2 tablespoons hot water

½ cup chopped walnuts

Make the *Stollen*:

In a small bowl proof the yeast in the lukewarm milk with the 1 teaspoon sugar for 10 minutes. In a large bowl pour the scalded milk over the butter, stir until the butter is melted, and let it cool to lukewarm. Beat in the egg yolk and the lemon rind. Into another bowl sift together the flour, ⅓ cup of the remaining sugar, and the 1 teaspoon salt. Add the flour mixture and the yeast mixture to the butter mixture and beat the dough until very smooth. Transfer the dough to a buttered bowl, turn it to coat with the butter, and let it rise in a warm place, covered with a dish towel, for 1½ hours, or until double in bulk.

In a saucepan combine the remaining ⅔ cup sugar with the ⅓ cup water. Bring the mixture to a boil over moderate heat, washing down any sugar crystals clinging to the sides of the pan with the brush dipped in cold water until the sugar is dissolved, and boil the syrup for 5 minutes. Stir in the ground walnuts, cinnamon, and the pinch of salt and off the heat let cool to lukewarm. Stir in the egg white and let cool completely.

Butter and flour a baking sheet.

Punch down the dough, roll it on a floured surface into a 19- by 14-inch rectangle on a floured surface, and spread it with the nut mixture, leaving a ½-inch border. Beginning with a long side roll the dough tightly jelly-roll fashion and pinch the edges and ends to seal. Put the roll seam side down on a cutting board and with a sharp knife halve it lengthwise. Twist the halves together, keeping the cut edges up, pinch the ends, and push the twist together lightly. Arrange the *Stollen* on the baking sheet and let it rise in a warm place, covered with the towel, for 30 minutes, or until it has increased one and a half times in bulk.

Preheat the oven to 375° F.

The *Stollen* will keep, wrapped in plastic wrap and foil, in a cool, dry place for up to 2 weeks.

Bake the *Stollen* in the middle of the oven for 15 minutes, reduce the heat to 350° F., and bake the *Stollen* for 25 to 30 minutes more, or until golden, covering it lightly with foil if it browns too quickly. Let the *Stollen* cool on the baking sheet.

Make the glaze: Into a small bowl sift the confectioners' sugar, add the hot water, and stir the mixture until smooth and glossy.

Drizzle the glaze over the *Stollen* in a zigzag pattern, sprinkle it with the chopped walnuts while still moist, and let it dry.

Photo on page 275.

DRESDEN STOLLEN

Yield:
2 *Stollen*

Equipment:
pastry brush

This German holiday yeast bread contains dried fruits, candied fruits, and nuts. Unlike the preceding recipe in which the dough is twisted, this dough is folded in the traditional manner. When dusted with confectioners' sugar, a *Stollen*'s shape symbolizes the infant Jesus wrapped in swaddling clothes.

*½ cup diced glacéed mixed fruits or
    diced mixed fruit peel*
¼ cup raisins
¼ cup dried currants
¼ cup halved glacéed cherries
2 tablespoons diced glacéed angelica
¼ cup dark rum
1 envelope active dry yeast
¼ cup warm milk plus ½ cup milk
*½ cup plus ½ teaspoon granulated
    sugar*
½ teaspoon salt
½ teaspoon almond extract

½ teaspoon grated lemon rind
*2 cups plus 2 tablespoons all-purpose
    flour*
*1 cup almond flour (available at
    specialty foods shops)*
1 large egg, beaten lightly
*¾ stick (6 tablespoons) unsalted
    butter, softened, plus melted butter
    for brushing*
*½ cup slivered blanched almonds,
    lightly toasted*
¼ teaspoon cinnamon
confectioners' sugar for dredging

In a bowl combine the mixed glacéed fruits, raisins, currants, cherries, and angelica, stir in the rum, and let the mixture macerate overnight.

In a small bowl proof the yeast in the warm milk with the ½ teaspoon of granulated sugar for 10 minutes. In a saucepan combine the remaining ½ cup milk, ¼ cup granulated sugar, and the salt. Cook the mixture over low heat, stirring, until it is warm and transfer it to a bowl. Drain the fruit mixture through a sieve set over the warm milk mixture and stir the juices, the almond extract, lemon rind, and yeast mixture into the milk. Add ½ cup all-purpose flour and ½ cup almond flour, stir the mixture until it is well combined, and let the sponge rise in a warm place, covered with a dish towel, for 1 hour.

Stir the dough and add the egg, ½ cup of the remaining all-purpose flour, and the remaining ½ cup almond flour. Blend in the softened butter and turn the dough out on a floured surface. Knead the dough, adding ¾ to 1 cup more of the remaining all-purpose flour, or enough to keep the dough from being sticky, for 10 to 15 minutes, or until smooth and elastic.

Spread the fruits on paper towels, pat them dry, and in a large sieve toss them with the almonds and 2 tablespoons all-purpose flour. Halve the dough, form each half into a rough rectangle, and press half the fruit mixture into each rectangle, folding and turning the rectangles several times to incorporate the fruit. Form the dough into two balls, put each ball in a lightly buttered bowl, turning the balls to coat with the butter, and let the balls rise in a warm place, covered, for 3 hours, or until triple in bulk.

Butter a baking sheet.

Press down the dough and roll each piece on a well-floured surface into a 9- by 5-inch rectangle. Brush the top of each rectangle well with the melted butter. In a small dish mix the remaining ¼ cup granulated sugar with the cinnamon and sprinkle half the mixture on each rectangle. Fold a long side of each rectangle over the top so that the fold extends a little past the center and press up the folds, forming a lip, but do not press the center edges down.

Transfer the rolls, seam side up, to the baking sheet, leaving 4 inches between them, and let them rise in a warm place, lightly covered, for 1 hour, or until almost double in bulk.

Preheat the oven to 375° F.

The *Stollen* will keep, wrapped in plastic wrap and foil, for 2 to 3 weeks.

Brush the tops of the *Stollen* well with the melted butter and bake them in the middle of the oven for 30 minutes, or until golden. Dredge the warm *Stollen* with the confectioners' sugar, transfer them to a rack, and let them cool.

CAKES WITH FRUITS

There are cakes that we have known about and liked ever since childhood—certain birthday cakes, for example, and other favorite layer cakes, like carrot, perhaps. Included among this nostalgic category are several of our cakes made with fruit: Strawberry Shortcakes (page 91), Pineapple Upside-Down Cake (page 88), and batter cake, made with frozen peaches and fresh red raspberries, but which many of us who grew up in the country remember being made with red raspberries only and for just a few weeks in the year. What these classic cakes have in common that renders them so satisfying is in large part their simplicity. One is made with biscuits and berries in fresh fruit syrup. Another is the very sweet concept of fruit on the bottom and cake on the top that someone was then clever enough to reverse. The ideas are very simple and straightforward and honest. These cakes, like the others in this grouping, are easy to like.

GLAZED APPLE CAKE

Yield:
one 9-inch cake

Equipment:
food mill fitted with
  fine disk
9-inch springform pan

*3 large McIntosh apples (about 1½
  pounds), cored and quartered
¼ cup water
2-inch strip of lemon peel
1 stick (½ cup) unsalted butter,
  softened
1 cup sugar
1 large egg
2¼ cups all-purpose flour*

*2 teaspoons baking soda
1 teaspoon cinnamon
½ teaspoon freshly grated nutmeg
¼ teaspoon ground cloves
¼ teaspoon salt
½ cup finely chopped pecans, toasted
2 Granny Smith apples
¼ cup apricot jam, strained
whipped cream as an accompaniment*

In a stainless steel or enameled saucepan combine the McIntosh apples with the water and lemon peel, bring the water to a boil, and simmer the apples, covered, for 20 minutes, or until tender. Cook the mixture, uncovered, over moderately high heat, stirring, until the water is almost evaporated. Force the mixture through the food mill into a bowl and let the purée cool.

Generously butter the springform pan and preheat the oven to 350° F.

In a large bowl cream the butter, beat in the sugar, and beat the mixture until light and fluffy. Beat in the egg and the apple purée. Into a bowl sift together the flour, baking soda, cinnamon, nutmeg, cloves, and salt. Stir the flour mixture and the pecans gently into the apple mixture and pour the batter into the springform pan.

Peel and core the Granny Smiths, halve them lengthwise, and cut them crosswise into thin slices. Arrange the apple slices decoratively in bunches on the batter, pressing them slightly into the batter. Bake the cake in the middle of the oven for 1¼ hours, or until a cake tester inserted in the center comes out clean. Remove the cake to a rack.

In a small saucepan melt the jam over low heat, brush it over the cake, and let the cake cool in the pan on a rack for 20 minutes. Run a sharp knife around the edge of the pan to loosen the cake and remove the sides of the pan. Serve the cake warm or at room temperature with the whipped cream.

Photo opposite.

Variation:

GLAZED PEAR CAKE: Substitute 3 large firm but ripe pears to make the fruit purée. Use 2 firm but ripe unpeeled pears, halved lengthwise, cored, and cut into thin slices for the top of the cake.

Glazed Apple Cake (opposite)

MARILLENKUCHEN

Apricot Cake

Yield:
1 cake, 15½ by 10½
  by 1 inches

Equipment:
jelly-roll pan, 15½ by
  10½ by 1 inches
hand-held electric
  mixer

2 sticks (1 cup) unsalted butter,
  softened
1 cup granulated sugar
2 teaspoons grated lemon rind
1 teaspoon vanilla
2 pinches of salt
5 large eggs, separated, at room
  temperature

⅓ cup sifted cornstarch
pinch of cream of tartar
2 cups sifted all-purpose flour
2½ pounds apricots, peeled, pitted,
  and quartered
confectioners' sugar for dusting

Butter the jelly-roll pan and sprinkle it with flour, knocking out the excess. Preheat the oven to 350° F.

In a bowl with the mixer beat the butter with ½ cup of the granulated sugar, the lemon rind, vanilla, and one pinch of salt until the mixture is very light and fluffy. Gradually beat in the egg yolks alternately with the cornstarch. In a large bowl with the mixer beat the egg whites with the salt until frothy, add the cream of tartar, and beat until the whites hold soft peaks. Gradually add the remaining ½ cup granulated sugar and beat the meringue until it holds stiff peaks (see illustrations page 238). Fold the meringue into the yolk mixture alternately with the flour, pour the batter into the jelly-roll pan, and smooth the top with a spatula.

Arrange the apricot quarters, cut side up, in straight rows on the batter and bake the cake in the middle of the oven for 30 minutes, or until golden and a cake tester inserted in the center comes out clean. Let the cake cool in the pan on a rack, sift the confectioners' sugar over it, and cut the cake into squares.

CHERRY KUCHEN

Yield:
one 8-inch square
  cake

Equipment:
8-inch square baking
  pan
pastry blender
  (optional)

2 cups all-purpose flour
¾ cup plus 2 tablespoons sugar
¼ teaspoon double-acting baking
  powder
¼ teaspoon salt
1 stick (½ cup) unsalted butter

1 teaspoon cinnamon
1½ pounds sweet cherries, stemmed
  and pitted
2 egg yolks
1 cup sour cream

Preheat the oven to 400° F.

Into a bowl sift together the flour, the 2 tablespoons sugar, baking powder, and salt. Cut in the butter with the pastry blender or with two knives until the mixture is mealy. Press the dough on the bottom and halfway up the sides of the baking pan.

In a bowl combine the cinnamon and the remaining ¾ cup sugar. Arrange the cherries on the dough, sprinkle the cinnamon sugar over them, and bake the kuchen in the middle of the oven for 15 minutes. In a bowl combine the egg yolks with the sour cream, pour the mixture over the cherries, and bake the kuchen for 30 minutes more. Transfer the cake in the pan to a rack and let it cool for 10 minutes. Cut the cake into squares and serve it while still warm.

PEACH RASPBERRY BATTER CAKE

Yield:
one 9-inch square
  cake

Equipment:
9-inch square baking
  dish
hand-held electric
  mixer

FOR THE FRUIT LAYER
½ cup sugar
1½ teaspoons cornstarch
one 10-ounce package frozen sliced
  peaches, thawed and drained well,
  reserving ⅓ cup of the syrup

1 tablespoon fresh lemon juice, or to
  taste
2 cups red raspberries, picked over

FOR THE BATTER
1 stick (½ cup) unsalted butter,
  softened
½ cup sugar
1 large egg, beaten lightly
1 teaspoon vanilla
1 cup all-purpose flour

1½ teaspoons double-acting baking
  powder
pinch of salt
½ cup milk
1 teaspoon grated lemon rind

Make the fruit layer:

In a heavy stainless steel or enameled saucepan combine the sugar and the cornstarch, add the reserved peach syrup and the lemon juice, and combine the mixture well. Add the peaches and the red raspberries, bring the liquid to a boil over moderate heat, stirring constantly, and simmer the mixture for 5 minutes. Remove the pan from the heat.

Make the batter:

Lightly butter the baking dish and preheat the oven to 350° F.

In a large bowl with the mixer cream the butter, beat in the sugar, a little at a time, and beat until light and fluffy. Add the egg and the vanilla and beat the mixture until smooth. Sift together the flour, baking powder, and salt. Add the flour mixture to the egg mixture in batches alternately with the milk, beating well after each addition, stir in the lemon rind, and blend the batter until smooth.

Spread the batter evenly in the baking dish, spoon the peach-berry mixture over it, and bake the dessert in the middle of the oven for 20 minutes. Reduce the heat to 325° F. and bake the cake for 20 to 25 minutes more, or until puffed and golden. Let the cake cool in the pan on a rack for 10 minutes and cut it in squares.

PINEAPPLE UPSIDE-DOWN CAKE

Yield:
one 9-inch cake

Equipment:
9-inch ovenproof
  stainless steel or
  enameled skillet,
  1½ inches deep
upright electric mixer

Especially sweet with its brown sugar and fruit topping, pineapple up-side-down cake is an American classic. Any fruit can be substituted for the pineapple provided it does not render undue moisture when baked. Unlike other cakes, pineapple upside-down cake unmolds marvelously from the skillet in which it is baked. A cake pan can be used if your skillet is not ovenproof.

¾ stick (6 tablespoons) unsalted butter
½ cup firmly packed dark brown sugar

one 3-pound pineapple, peeled, cored, and sliced into ⅓-inch-thick rings

FOR THE CAKE
⅔ cup milk
1 large egg, beaten lightly
1 teaspoon vanilla
1 teaspoon grated lemon rind
1½ cups all-purpose flour
½ cup granulated sugar

2 teaspoons double-acting baking powder
½ teaspoon salt
¾ stick (6 tablespoons) unsalted butter, cut into bits and softened

1 tablespoon dark rum
pecan halves for decoration

glacéed cherries for decoration

1½ cups whipped cream flavored with rum as an accompaniment if desired

In the ovenproof skillet melt the butter, add the brown sugar, and cook the syrup over moderate heat, stirring, until golden. Arrange the pineapple rings in the skillet and cook them over moderate heat, shaking the pan occasionally, for 5 to 7 minutes, or until the syrup is golden brown. Let cool for 5 minutes, pour ½ cup of the syrup carefully into a small bowl, and reserve.

Make the cake:
Preheat the oven to 350° F.

In a bowl combine the milk, egg, vanilla, and lemon rind. Into the bowl of the mixer sift together the flour, granulated sugar, baking powder, and salt. With the mixer running add the milk mixture in a stream and beat the batter until well combined. Add the butter, one piece at a time, beating, and beat the batter until smooth. Pour the batter over the pineapple, set the skillet on a baking sheet, and bake the cake in the middle of the oven for 30 to 35 minutes, or until a cake tester inserted in the center comes out clean. Let the cake cool in the skillet for 5 minutes, invert a serving plate over the skillet, and invert the cake carefully onto it.

In a small stainless steel or enameled saucepan combine the reserved syrup and the rum and boil the mixture for 1 minute, or until thick. Spoon the glaze over the cake, smoothing it around the sides, and decorate the cake with the pecans and cherries. Serve the cake warm or at room temperature with the rum-flavored whipped cream if desired.

Cranberry Upside-Down Cake (page 90), Pumpkin Ginger Caramel Custards (page 337)

PLUM AND NECTARINE UPSIDE-DOWN CAKE

Yield:
one 9-inch cake

Equipment:
hand-held electric
　mixer
non-stick 9-inch
　round cake pan or
　non-stick 10-inch
　ovenproof skillet

1 stick (½ cup) unsalted butter,
　softened
¾ cup sugar
1 large egg, beaten lightly
1 cup all-purpose flour
1 teaspoon double-acting baking
　powder
¼ teaspoon salt

⅓ cup milk
2 tablespoons brandy
1 teaspoon vanilla
2 plums, pitted and sliced thin
1 nectarine, pitted and sliced thin
lightly whipped cream as an
　accompaniment if desired

Preheat the oven to 350° F.

In a bowl with the mixer cream 6 tablespoons of the butter, add ½ cup of the sugar, and beat the mixture until light and fluffy. Beat in the egg. In another bowl sift together the flour, baking powder, and salt. Add the flour mixture to the butter mixture alternately with the milk, beating until the batter is smooth, and beat in the brandy and vanilla.

In the cake pan or skillet melt the remaining 2 tablespoons butter over moderately low heat, stir in the remaining ¼ cup sugar, and cook the mixture, stirring gently, for 2 minutes. Remove the pan from the heat and in the bottom of the pan arrange the plum and nectarine slices decoratively, overlapping them slightly. Return the pan to the heat and cook the mixture, undisturbed, for 2 to 3 minutes, or until the fruit begins to give up its juices. Remove the pan from the heat, spoon the batter carefully and evenly over the fruit, and bake the cake in the middle of the oven for 30 to 40 minutes, or until a cake tester inserted in the center comes out clean.

Let the cake cool in the pan on a rack for 10 minutes, invert a serving plate over the pan, and invert the cake onto it. Serve the cake warm or at room temperature with the whipped cream if desired.

CRANBERRY UPSIDE-DOWN CAKE

Yield:
one 9-inch cake

Equipment:
9-inch round cake
　pan, 1½ inches deep
hand-held electric
　mixer
pastry brush

Here is a wonderful finale to the Thanksgiving Day dinner.

¾ stick (6 tablespoons) plus 3
　tablespoons unsalted butter,
　softened
1 cup sugar
1 pound cranberries, rinsed, picked
　over, and patted dry
1 large egg
1 teaspoon vanilla
1 teaspoon minced orange rind

1¼ cups all-purpose flour
1½ teaspoons double-acting baking
　powder
¼ teaspoon salt
½ cup milk
⅓ cup red currant jelly
sweetened whipped cream as an
　accompaniment if desired

Preheat the oven to 350° F.

Butter the bottom and sides of the cake pan with the 3 tablespoons butter, sprinkle ½ cup of the sugar evenly over the bottom, and arrange the cranberries in the pan.

In a bowl with the mixer cream together the remaining ¾ stick butter and ½ cup sugar. Add the egg, vanilla, and orange rind and beat the mixture until well combined.

Into another bowl sift together the flour, baking powder, and salt. Stir the dry ingredients into the butter mixture, ½ cup at a time, alternately with the milk and stir the batter until it is just combined. Pour the batter over the cranberries and smooth the top. Bake the cake on a baking sheet in the middle of the oven for 1 hour, or until well browned. Transfer the cake to a rack and let it cool in the pan for 20 minutes. Run a thin knife around the inside of the pan and invert the cake onto a cake stand.

In a small saucepan melt the currant jelly over low heat, stirring, and brush it over the cake. Serve the cake warm or at room temperature with the whipped cream if desired.

Photo on page 89.

STRAWBERRY SHORTCAKES

Yield:
8 servings

Equipment:
3-inch round cutter
pastry brush

Cream biscuits with just a touch of lemon are split, lightly buttered, then filled with a splendid strawberry syrup. These shortcakes are marvelous and very easy to make.

*3 pints strawberries, hulled, plus 8
    small unhulled berries for garnish*
½ cup plus 2 tablespoons sugar
*¼ cup fresh lemon juice plus
    additional to taste*
2 cups all-purpose flour
*1 tablespoon double-acting baking
    powder*

½ teaspoon salt
*2 tablespoons unsalted butter, cut into
    bits, plus butter for spreading*
1½ teaspoons minced lemon rind
¾ to 1 cup heavy cream
milk for brushing the biscuits
*lightly whipped cream as an
    accompaniment*

Chop 1 pint of the strawberries. In a stainless steel or enameled saucepan combine them with the ½ cup sugar and the ¼ cup lemon juice. Bring the liquid to a boil and cook the mixture over moderately high heat, stirring, for 10 minutes, or until it is thickened and reduced to about 1¼ cups. Pour the mixture into a bowl and let it cool completely. Slice the remaining 2 pints strawberries, stir them into the cooked strawberries, and add lemon juice to taste. Let the mixture stand for 1 hour.

Butter a baking sheet and preheat the oven to 400° F.

Into a bowl sift together the flour, the remaining 2 tablespoons sugar, baking powder, and salt. Blend in the 2 tablespoons butter and the lemon rind with your fingertips until the mixture resembles coarse meal. Stir in enough of the heavy cream to make a soft dough. Form the dough into a ball and roll or pat it out ½ inch thick on a floured surface. Cut out rounds with the cutter dipped in flour and arrange them on the baking sheet 2 inches apart. Form the dough scraps gently into a ball, repeat the procedure, and arrange the rounds on the baking sheet. Brush the tops of the rounds lightly with the milk. Bake the biscuits in the middle of the oven for 15 to 20 minutes, or until puffed and golden.

Split the biscuits horizontally with a fork and while they are still warm spread the halves with the remaining butter. Mound the bottom halves of the biscuits with the strawberry mixture and top the berries with the biscuit tops. Arrange the shortcakes on a platter, garnish them with whole berries, and serve them with the whipped cream.

Variation:

BLUEBERRY SHORTCAKES: In a saucepan combine 1 pint blueberries, picked over, with ½ cup sugar and 1 tablespoon fresh lemon juice. Cook the berries, covered, over low heat for 5 minutes. Remove the cover and reduce the juices over high heat until thickened. Transfer the syrup to a bowl, let cool, and stir in 2 cups fresh blueberries.

Make biscuits as described above and form shortcakes with the blueberry syrup. Serve with whipped cream.

CHEESECAKES

Cheesecakes—a subject dear to many people's hearts. It seems we love them, or we don't. And those of us who do love them know exactly why. It is either the ratio of sour cream to cream cheese in the batter, or the crust, or that hint of lemon, or all that glistening fruit on top. It is never because it is vaguely, unidentifiably, good.

There are other reasons to love cheesecake—its richness, for one; its silky, heavenly, texture, for another. Or, to be more level-headed about it, at least an appreciation is due for the sheer variety with which cheesecakes are made. Some are baked (see New York Cheesecake, recipe below); others are not (see Refrigerator Cheesecake, page 95). Some have fruit on top (see Kiwi Ricotta Cheesecake, page 96). Some have crumb crusts (see Chocolate Cheesecake, page 94), while others have pastry crusts. Each type is distinct and eminently likable in its own way. The following selection of cheesecakes should convert those cheesecake naysayers yet.

NEW YORK CHEESECAKE

Yield:
one 9-inch
  cheesecake

This cheesecake, made with cream cheese, ricotta, and sour cream, bakes—like all good cheesecakes—slowly and needs to cool for the suggested amount of time to achieve its incomparable texture.

Equipment:
hand-held or upright
  electric mixer
9-inch springform pan

1 pound cream cheese, softened
1 pound ricotta
1½ cups sugar
4 large eggs at room temperature
½ stick (¼ cup) unsalted butter,
  melted and cooled

3 tablespoons all-purpose flour
3 tablespoons cornstarch
2½ teaspoons vanilla
2 cups sour cream

Preheat the oven to 325° F.

In a large bowl with the mixer cream together the cream cheese, ricotta, and sugar. Beat in the eggs, one at a time, beating well after each addition. Add the butter, flour, cornstarch, and vanilla and beat the mixture until well combined. Fold in the sour cream. Pour the batter into the ungreased springform pan and bake the cheesecake in the middle of the oven for 1 hour (the cake will be soft in the center). Turn off the heat (do not open the oven door) and let the cake stand in the oven for 2 hours. Remove the cake from the oven, set it on a rack, and let it cool completely in the pan. Chill the cheesecake, loosely wrapped, for at least 2 hours. Remove the sides of the pan and transfer the cake to a cake stand or plate.

Variation:

MARBLED NEW YORK CHEESECAKE: Prepare the batter as above and pour half of it into the springform pan. To the remaining batter add 4 ounces semisweet chocolate, melted and cooled, and beat the mixture until well combined. Pour the chocolate batter onto the white batter in the pan and swirl a spatula lightly through the mixture to create a marbled pattern. Bake the marbled cheesecake and cool it as directed above.

CHOCOLATE CHEESECAKE

Yield:
one 9-inch cake

Equipment:
9-inch springform pan
hand-held electric
  mixer
food processor fitted
  with steel blade

While this splendid chocolate cheesecake is baked, and slowly, you will note that its crumb crust, unlike the one on page 95, is not. There are endless variations on the way cheesecakes are prepared. The results, especially of this combination, can be unforgettable.

1⅓ cups chocolate wafer crumbs
½ stick (¼ cup) unsalted butter,
  melted

¾ cup plus 2 tablespoons sugar

FOR THE FILLING
1 cup heavy cream
8 ounces semisweet chocolate, cut into
  bits
4 large eggs, separated, at room
  temperature
1½ pounds cream cheese, softened

1 cup sour cream
2 tablespoons cornstarch
1 teaspoon almond extract
pinch of salt
pinch of cream of tartar

whipped cream for garnish

chocolate curls (page 545) for garnish

Generously butter the springform pan.

In a bowl combine the chocolate wafer crumbs, the melted butter, and 2 tablespoons of the sugar. Press the mixture onto the bottom and sides of the springform pan and chill the shell until it is to be filled.

Make the filling: In a saucepan scald the heavy cream, remove the pan from the heat, and let the cream cool for 5 minutes. Add the semisweet chocolate and stir it until melted. In a bowl with the mixer beat the chocolate cream until cooled and light in texture.

In a large bowl with the mixer beat the egg yolks with ½ cup of the remaining sugar until the mixture is thick and lemon colored and falls in a ribbon when the beater is lifted (see illustration page 16). Add the chocolate cream and beat the mixture until well combined. In the food processor blend the cream cheese, sour cream, cornstarch, and almond extract until smooth. Add the cream cheese mixture to the chocolate mixture and stir the batter until well combined.

Preheat the oven to 300° F.

In a bowl with the mixer beat the egg whites with the salt until frothy, add the cream of tartar, and beat until the whites hold soft peaks. Add the remaining ¼ cup sugar and beat the whites until they hold stiff peaks (see illustrations page 238). Fold the whites into the chocolate mixture. Pour the batter into the shell, put the springform pan in a baking pan, and add enough hot water to the baking pan to reach halfway up the sides of the springform pan. Bake the cheesecake in the middle of the oven for 1½ hours. Turn off the heat (do not open the oven door) and let the cake stand in the oven for 1 hour. Set the cake in the pan on a rack and let it cool completely. Chill the cheesecake, loosely covered, for at least 2 hours.

Remove the sides of the pan and transfer the cake to a cake stand or plate. Garnish the cake with the whipped cream and the chocolate curls.

REFRIGERATOR CHEESECAKE

Yield:
one 10-inch cake

Equipment:
10-inch springform pan
hand-held electric mixer

Unlike the preceding recipe, this cheesecake is not baked, relying instead on gelatin and a good chill to achieve its luscious texture.

1 Graham Cracker Crust (page 125), made with 2 additional tablespoons unsalted butter and ½ teaspoon cinnamon added
4 large eggs, separated, at room temperature
1 cup sugar
1 cup heavy cream, scalded
1½ pounds cream cheese, softened

1½ teaspoons grated lemon rind
1½ teaspoons vanilla
1 tablespoon unflavored gelatin
¼ cup fresh lemon juice
pinch of salt
⅛ teaspoon cream of tartar
1 cup sour cream
fresh fruit for garnish if desired

Preheat the oven to 350° F. Generously butter the springform pan.

Press the graham cracker crumb crust mixture onto the bottom and sides of the springform pan and bake in the lower third of the oven for 10 minutes. Let the crust cool.

In a bowl with the mixer beat the egg yolks until smooth, add ¾ cup of the sugar, and beat the mixture until it falls in a ribbon when the beater is lifted (see illustration page 16). Add the hot cream in a stream and beat until combined. Transfer the yolk mixture to a heavy saucepan and cook it over moderately low heat without lettting it boil, stirring until it is thick enough to coat a spoon. Pour the yolk mixture into a bowl and let it cool.

In a large bowl with the mixer beat the cream cheese until smooth. Add the yolk mixture, lemon rind, and vanilla and beat until combined.

In a small bowl let the gelatin soften in the lemon juice for 5 minutes. Set the bowl in a larger bowl of hot water and stir the gelatin until dissolved. Add the gelatin mixture to the cream cheese mixture and chill the filling, covered loosely, until cold, but do not let it set.

In a bowl with the mixer beat the egg whites with the salt until frothy, add the cream of tartar, and beat the whites until they hold soft peaks. Add the remaining ¼ cup sugar, a little at a time, and beat the whites until stiff (see illustrations page 238). Stir one fourth of the whites into the cream cheese mixture and fold in the remaining whites. Fold in the sour cream. Pour the filling into the crust. Chill the cheesecake, covered loosely, for at least 3 hours or overnight.

Garnish the cheesecake with fresh fruit if desired.

KIWI RICOTTA CHEESECAKE

Yield:
one 9-inch cake

Equipment:
9-inch springform pan
food mill fitted with
  fine disk
pastry brush

A more complex cheesecake than those that have preceded it, this one has a sugary, short crust, a high-standing, rich cream filling, and a crown of sliced kiwi fruits. This is cheesecake at its elegant, sophisticated best.

1 recipe pâte sucrée *(page 165)*   *raw rice for weighting the shell*

FOR THE FILLING
2 cups whole-milk ricotta   *2 tablespoons dark rum*
2 cups skim-milk ricotta   *3 tablespoons fresh lemon juice*
1 cup heavy cream   *1 tablespoon all-purpose flour*
3 egg yolks plus 1 large egg   *2 teaspoons vanilla*
½ cup sugar   *2 teaspoons grated lemon rind*
¼ cup toasted and skins removed (for   *pinch of salt*
  procedure page 549) ground
  hazelnuts

½ cup honey   *4 kiwis*

On a floured surface roll out the *pâte sucrée* ⅛ inch thick. Fit the dough into the springform pan set on a baking sheet, pressing it 2 inches up the sides of the pan, and crimp the edge of the crust decoratively. Prick the bottom of the shell with a fork and chill the shell for 1 hour.

Preheat the oven to 425° F.

Line the shell with wax paper, fill the paper with the rice, and bake the shell in the lower third of the oven for 10 minutes. Remove the rice and the paper carefully. Bake the shell for 10 to 15 minutes more, or until golden, and let it cool on a rack.

Reduce the oven temperature to 350° F.

Make the filling:
Purée the whole-milk and skim-milk ricotta through the food mill into a large bowl. Add the heavy cream, egg yolks, whole egg, sugar, hazelnuts, rum, 2 tablespoons of the lemon juice, flour, vanilla, lemon rind, and salt and combine the mixture well. Pour the filling into the shell and bake the cake in the middle of the oven for 1 hour, or until the top is golden. Let the cake cool in the pan on a rack and chill it, loosely covered, for at least 2 hours. Remove the sides of the pan and transfer the cake to a cake stand.

In a small bowl combine the honey and the remaining 1 tablespoon lemon juice. Peel the kiwis, halve them lengthwise, and cut them crosswise into ¼-inch slices. Arrange the kiwis decoratively on top of the cake and, just before serving, brush them with the honey glaze.

Variation:
FRUIT TOPPINGS FOR CHEESECAKE: Whole strawberries or peeled sliced peaches or nectarines may be substituted for the kiwis. Brush with apricot glaze (page 540).

EASTER CHEESE TORTE

Yield:
one 9-inch cake

Equipment:
9-inch springform
  pan, 2 inches deep
hand-held electric
  mixer

An unusual combination, the ricotta filling of this cheesecake is made with cream of farina and is studded with candied fruits. We suspect this cake to be of Italian origin, specifically designed to end the Lenten period.

FOR THE SHELL

2 recipes pâte brisée *(page 164) substituting 2 tablespoons granulated sugar for the salt and adding 1 teaspoon grated lemon rind*

FOR THE FILLING

½ cup cream of farina
2⅔ cups boiling salted water
1⅓ cups milk, scalded
4 large eggs, separated, at room temperature
⅓ cup granulated sugar
1¼ pounds ricotta, sieved

¾ cup in all diced Candied Orange Peel (page 522) and diced glacéed citron combined
¼ cup honey
1 teaspoon vanilla
½ teaspoon grated lemon rind
confectioners' sugar for sprinkling

Make the shell:

Cut off and roll into a ball one third of the dough, sprinkle it lightly with flour, and chill it, wrapped in wax paper. On a lightly floured surface roll out the remaining dough a bit thicker than ⅛ inch. Drape the dough over the rolling pin and press it firmly into the springform pan, cutting off any excess dough with the floured rolling pin (see illustrations page 121). Prick the bottom of the shell with a fork and chill the shell for 1 hour.

Preheat the oven to 400° F.

Line the shell with foil, put a cake pan the diameter of the shell on the shell, and bake the shell in the lower third of the oven for 10 minutes. Remove the cake pan and the foil and bake the shell for 10 minutes more, or until lightly colored. Transfer the pan to a rack and let the shell cool.

Make the filling:

Reduce the oven temperature to 375° F.

In a saucepan sprinkle the cream of farina over the boiling salted water, stirring, and simmer the mixture, stirring, for 4 minutes. Stir in the scalded milk, cook the mixture, stirring, for 5 minutes, and let it cool. In a bowl with the mixer beat the egg yolks with the granulated sugar until the mixture falls in a ribbon when the beater is lifted (see illustration page 16). Add the ricotta, the candied orange peel and citron, honey, vanilla, and lemon rind and stir in the farina mixture. In a bowl with the mixer beat the egg whites until they hold stiff peaks and fold them into the ricotta mixture.

Roll out the remaining dough a bit thicker than ⅛ inch and cut it into long strips 1 inch wide. Fill the shell with the ricotta filling. Arrange the dough strips lattice-fashion over the top (see illustrations page 122). Bake the torte on a baking sheet in the middle of the oven for 1 hour and 10 minutes, or until the filling is set. Let the torte cool completely in the oven with the door slightly open.

Before serving, sprinkle the confectioners' sugar over the top.

CAKES FOR SPECIAL OCCASIONS

The cakes that have preceded these for special occasions are hardly everyday cakes. There is nothing whatsoever usual or commonplace about Cassata (page 27), or Kaisertorte (page 34), or Chocolate Mousse Cake with Ganache Icing (page 64). Each is an extraordinary combination, and the only thing everyday about any of them might be that we would probably like to have a little of each of them every day.

With that said, this selection of cakes for special occasions follows the calendar year, starting in January and ending with the holidays. We've chosen recipes appropriate for either a religious holiday, Orange Almond Sponge Cake (page 100), for Passover, for example, a national holiday like Thanksgiving, or a special event, such as a June wedding. Our grouping is admittedly arbitrary, and there is no reason why, with the obvious exceptions of bride's and groom's cake and the highly traditional and seasonal Bûche de Noël, you could not serve any of these cakes anytime you desired. The Epiphany cake, Galette des Rois (page 100), is most fitting, of course, in January. It is no less delicious in June, perhaps accompanied by a lovely fruit compote.

This small collection ends with several fruitcake recipes—a white fruitcake, a dark, rich, many-fruited combination, and a dried fruits—only cake, which has neither flour nor sugar added. You will also find a recipe for Panforte (page 109), that splendid dense fruit and nut Italian cake, which like many fruitcakes improves in flavor with time. If you are thinking of preparing these fruitcakes as Christmas gifts, be sure to build into your own calendar the number of weeks each cake will need to mellow.

ZUPPA INGLESE

Yield:
6 to 9 servings

Equipment:
one 9-inch cake pan
hand-held or upright
   mixer
2-quart serving bowl

Zuppa Inglese, a marvelous Italian creation, is not an English soup at all, but a layered dessert of liqueur-soaked cake and custard. A true *zuppa Inglese* contains the red liqueur *alkermes*, the same red of the British flag (one explanation of the dessert's name). Because *alkermes* is not allowed in the United States, Peter Herring, the easily obtainable, red, cherry-flavored liqueur, is substituted with excellent results.

½ recipe vanilla génoise *batter (page 22) with 1½ teaspoons grated lemon rind added*

FOR THE CUSTARD
6 egg yolks
½ cup sugar
2 tablespoons all-purpose flour

2 cups milk, scalded
1 teaspoon grated lemon rind

¼ cup Peter Herring
2 tablespoons Cognac

2 tablespoons sliced blanched almonds, toasted

Butter the cake pan, sprinkle it with flour, and knock out the excess. Preheat the oven to 350° F.

Pour the *génoise* batter into the pan and bake the cake in the middle of the oven for 20 minutes, or until a cake tester inserted in the center comes out clean. Let the layer cool in the pan for 10 minutes, turn it out on the rack, and let it cool completely. Slice the *génoise* into 3 layers.

Make the custard: In a bowl with the mixer beat the yolks until combined. Add the sugar, a little at a time, and beat the mixture until light and creamy. Beat in the flour. Add the milk in a stream and beat the mixture until combined. Pour the custard into a saucepan and cook it over moderately low heat without letting it boil, stirring, until it is thick enough to coat a spoon. Pour the custard into a bowl and stir in the lemon rind.

In a small bowl combine the Peter Herring and the Cognac.

Ladle about ½ cup of the custard into the serving bowl and cover it with a cake layer, cut side down. Sprinkle the cake with one third of the liqueur mixture and pour one third of the remaining custard over it. Add another cake layer, sprinkle it with half of the remaining liqueur mixture, and top the liqueur with half of the remaining custard. Top the custard with the remaining cake layer, cut side down, sprinkle the cake with the remaining liqueur mixture, and cover it with the remaining custard. Chill the dessert for 3 hours or overnight. Before serving, sprinkle the top of the dessert with the toasted almonds.

GALETTE DES ROIS

French Butter Cake

Yield:
one 8-inch cake

Equipment:
8-inch round cake pan
pastry brush

Epiphany, beginning January 6th, commemorates Christ's baptism. This French butter cake is made to celebrate that day. Inside the cake a small porcelain figure or bean, representing Christ, is placed. A party is made; the cake is cut, and the child who finds the figure or bean becomes *le roi*, the king, or *la reine*, the queen, for that day.

2½ cups all-purpose flour	1¾ sticks (¾ cup plus 2 tablespoons)
1 cup sugar	unsalted butter, cut into bits
1 tablespoon grated lemon rind	1 dried bean if desired
pinch of salt	1 tablespoon water
6 egg yolks	

Preheat the oven to 400° F. Butter the cake pan.

In a bowl combine the flour, sugar, lemon rind, and salt and form a well in the center. Lightly beat 5 of the egg yolks, stir them into the dry ingredients, and blend the mixture until it resembles coarse meal. Add the butter and knead the dough until blended. Press the bean into the dough if desired and press the dough into the cake pan.

Beat the remaining egg yolk with the water and brush the egg wash over the dough. Score the cake several times with the tines of a fork to form a diamond pattern and bake the *galette* in the middle of the oven for 50 to 55 minutes, or until golden brown. Let the *galette* cool in the pan for 10 minutes, run a knife around the edge, and turn the *galette* out onto a rack. Let cool completely.

ORANGE ALMOND SPONGE CAKE

Passover Cake

Yield:
one 10-inch tube cake

Equipment:
hand-held electric
  mixer
10-inch tube pan
pastry brush

The batter for this Passover cake incorporates potato starch, matzoh meal, and ground nuts in place of flour and is leavened by the considerable number of egg whites. It is a marvelously light cake, with a haunting flavor of citrus.

FOR THE CAKE

12 large eggs, separated, at room temperature	½ cup potato starch
1½ cups granulated sugar	½ cup matzoh cake meal
⅓ cup fresh orange juice	1 teaspoon cinnamon
2 tablespoons fresh lemon juice	¼ teaspoon plus pinch of salt
1 tablespoon grated orange rind	½ cup finely ground almonds
1 teaspoon grated lemon rind	¼ teaspoon cream of tartar

FOR THE GLAZE

²/₃ cup granulated sugar

¹/₃ cup water

the rind of 1 orange, pith removed and
   cut into julienne strips

1 tablespoon fresh orange juice

1 tablespoon fresh lemon juice

¹/₄ cup sliced blanched almonds,
   toasted

confectioners' sugar for sifting

Make the cake: In a bowl with the mixer beat the egg yolks until smooth. Gradually add 1 cup of the granulated sugar and beat the mixture until it falls in a ribbon when the beater is lifted (see illustration page 16). Beat in the orange juice, lemon juice, orange rind, and lemon rind. Into another bowl sift the potato starch, matzoh cake meal, cinnamon, and the ¹/₄ teaspoon salt. Gradually add the dry ingredients to the yolk mixture, beat the batter until it is well combined, and stir in the ground almonds.

Preheat the oven to 325° F.

In a bowl with the mixer beat the egg whites with the pinch of salt until frothy. Add the cream of tartar and beat the whites until they hold soft peaks. Add the remaining ¹/₂ cup sugar, a little at a time, and beat the whites until they hold stiff peaks (see illustrations page 238). Stir one fourth of the whites into the batter and fold in the remaining whites gently but thoroughly.

Pour the batter into the ungreased tube pan, smooth the top with a spatula, and bake the cake in the middle of the oven for 1¹/₄ hours, or until a cake tester inserted halfway between the center and the edge of the pan comes out clean. Remove the cake from the oven and suspend it upside down on the neck of a bottle. Let the cake cool completely. Run a thin knife around the inside of the pan and invert the cake onto the rack.

Make the glaze: In a small heavy saucepan combine the sugar and the water, bring the mixture to a boil, stirring, and cook it until it is translucent. Add the orange rind and cook the syrup for 5 minutes, or until the rind is translucent and the syrup forms a thread when pressed between two fingers. (For the stages of sugar syrup, see illustrations page 241.) Stir in the orange juice and lemon juice, let the glaze cool for 5 minutes, and brush it over the cake.

Garnish the cake with the toasted almonds and sift the confectioners' sugar over it.

SIMNEL CAKE

Yield:
one 8-inch cake

Equipment:
8-inch springform pan
hand-held electric
  mixer
pastry bag fitted with
  medium plain tip
pastry brush

Simnel cake, an English fruitcake filled with marzipan, was originally served on Mothering Day, or, as it is now known, Mother's Day.

FOR THE MARZIPAN FILLING

12 ounces almond paste, crumbled	*2 egg yolks*
1 stick (½ cup) unsalted butter, well softened	
1 cup dried currants	*1 tablespoon all-purpose flour*
⅓ cup finely chopped mixed candied citrus peel	

FOR THE FRUITCAKE

2 sticks (1 cup) unsalted butter, softened	*¼ teaspoon freshly grated nutmeg*
1⅓ cups all-purpose flour	*¼ teaspoon salt*
1 teaspoon cinnamon	*4 large eggs*
¼ teaspoon ground allspice	*¾ cup sugar*
1 egg yolk	*1 tablespoon half-and-half or milk*

Make the marzipan filling:

In a bowl beat the almond paste with the butter and the egg yolks until well blended. Chill 2 level tablespoons of the mixture, wrapped in plastic wrap, for 30 minutes, or until it is firm, and divide it into 9 pieces. Roll each piece into a ball and chill the balls, covered. Transfer the remaining mixture to the pastry bag.

In a small bowl toss the currants and candied citrus peel with the flour.

Make the fruitcake:

Preheat the oven to 325° F. Butter the pan and dust it with flour.

In a large bowl with the mixer cream the butter. Beat in the flour, cinnamon, allspice, nutmeg, and salt. In another bowl with the mixer beat the whole eggs with the sugar. Set the bowl over a saucepan of simmering water and heat over low heat, stirring, until it is lukewarm (see illustration page 16). Remove the bowl from the pan and beat the mixture at high speed for 5 to 10 minutes, or until very light and almost triple in volume. Beat the mixture into the flour mixture until the batter is well blended.

Stir in the currant-candied peel combination. Spread half the batter evenly in the springform pan. Pipe half the marzipan filling over the batter and spread it evenly. Spread the remaining batter over the marzipan. Bake in the middle of the oven for 1⅓ hours, or until a cake tester inserted in the center comes out clean.

Remove the cake from the oven and increase the heat to 425° F. Pipe the remaining marzipan over the cake and spread it evenly. In a small bowl beat the egg yolk with the half-and-half or milk and brush some of the mixture over the top of the cake. With a knife score the marzipan in a crosshatch pattern. Arrange the chilled marzipan balls decoratively on the cake, pressing them down lightly. Brush them with egg yolk mixture and bake the cake for 15 minutes more, or until the top is golden. Let the cake cool on a rack for 30 minutes. Remove the sides of the pan and let the cake cool completely.

GROOM'S CAKE

Yield:
24 very thin slices

Equipment:
8-inch round straight-sided baking dish, 3 inches deep
hand-held electric mixer
kettle with lid
2 racks, one to fit kettle
pastry brush

Marion Cunningham, who devised this recipe, explains that the sprigs of rosemary used as garnish on this cake signify the warmth of affection.

2 sticks (1 cup) unsalted butter, softened
2¼ cups confectioners' sugar
5 large eggs
1½ cups all-purpose flour
2 teaspoons cinnamon
1 teaspoon ground allspice
1 teaspoon freshly grated nutmeg
½ teaspoon ground cloves
¼ cup fresh lemon juice

½ cup unsweetened bottled grape juice
1 tablespoon grated lemon rind
1½ cups raisins
1½ cups finely chopped glacéed citron
1½ cups coarsely chopped blanched almonds (for procedure page 549)
⅓ cup sieved apricot jam
sprigs of rosemary for garnish if desired

Butter the baking dish, line it with a round of wax paper, and butter the paper.

In a large bowl with the mixer cream the butter until light and fluffy, add 2 cups of the confectioners' sugar, ¼ cup at a time, beating, and beat the mixture until smooth. Add the eggs, one at a time, beating well after each addition. Sift together the flour, cinnamon, allspice, nutmeg, and cloves. Combine the lemon juice with the grape juice. Add the dry ingredients and the juices to the egg mixture alternately, one third at a time, beating well after each addition, and stir in the lemon rind, raisins, citron, and almonds. Turn the batter into the baking dish, cover the batter with a buttered round of wax paper, and cover the dish with a double layer of foil secured with kitchen string. Set the dish on the rack in the kettle and add enough simmering water to the kettle to reach halfway up the sides of the dish. Cover the kettle with the lid and steam the cake, adjusting the heat as necessary to keep the water at a simmer and adding more water as necessary, for 2½ to 3 hours, or until a cake tester inserted through the foil into the center of the cake comes out clean (see illustration page 326).

Remove the dish carefully from the kettle, remove the foil and wax paper, and let the cake stand on a rack for 30 minutes. Run a thin knife around the inside edge of the dish, invert the rack over the cake, and invert the cake onto it. Let the cake cool completely. Transfer the cake to a platter and sift the remaining ¼ cup confectioners' sugar over the top. Heat the apricot jam and brush it over the sides of the cake. Arrange a sprig of rosemary on the cake and garnish the platter with the remaining rosemary sprigs if desired.

BRIDE'S CAKE

Yield:
one 3-tier wedding
  cake, about 100
  servings

Equipment:
upright and hand-held
  electric mixers
one 5-inch round
  cake pan, 3 inches
  deep
three 8-inch round
  cake pans, 1½
  inches deep
one 12-inch round
  cake pan, 2 inches
  deep

Making your own wedding cake is certainly an ambitious undertaking, but one that is well worth the challenge should time allow. Marion Cunningham, who developed this recipe, suggests that much of the success in baking this lovely fourteen-layer creation lies in the organization. Be sure you have the proper equipment and enough refrigerator space to accommodate the finished cake.

FOR EACH BATCH OF BATTER

*1 stick (½ cup) unsalted butter,
  softened*
*¼ cup vegetable shortening at room
  temperature*
2 cups granulated sugar
3 large eggs

3 cups cake flour
*1 tablespoon double-acting baking
  powder*
1½ teaspoons salt
1 cup milk
1 tablespoon vanilla

FOR THE BUTTERCREAM

6 egg yolks
2½ cups confectioners' sugar
1½ cups milk
2 tablespoons grated orange rind

1 cup Grand Marnier

*7 sticks (3½ cups) unsalted butter,
  softened, plus 1 additional stick if
  needed*
¼ cup Grand Marnier

*¼ cup orange-flower water (available
  at specialty foods shops), or to taste*

FOR THE DECORATION

*12 cups Seven-Minute Icing
  (page 516)*

Royal Icing Flowers (page 515)

fresh mint leaves for garnish

Make the cakes:

In the large bowl of the upright mixer beat the butter and the shortening until light. Add the sugar, ½ cup at a time, beating, and beat the mixture, scraping down the sides of the bowl, until combined. Add the eggs, one at a time, beating well after each addition, and beat the mixture until it is pale and fluffy. Sift together the flour, baking powder, and salt and in a separate bowl combine the milk with the vanilla. Add the dry ingredients and the milk mixture alternately to the butter mixture, one third at a time, beating well after each addition and scraping down the sides of the bowl as necessary. Beat the batter until smooth.

Preheat the oven to 350° F.

Butter each cake pan and line it with a round of wax paper the same size as the bottom of the pan. Butter the paper and dust the pans with flour, shaking out the excess.

Pour ¾ cup of the batter into the 5-inch pan, smooth the top, and bake the cake in the middle of the oven for 15 to 20 minutes, or until a cake tester inserted in the center comes out clean. Let the cake cool in the pan on a rack for 5 minutes. Run a thin knife around the inside edge of the pan and invert the cake onto the rack. Peel off the paper and let the layer cool completely.

Pour the remaining batter into the 12-inch cake pan, smooth the top, and bake the cake in the middle of the oven for 35 to 40 minutes, or until a cake tester inserted in the center comes out clean. Let the cake cool in the pan on a large rack for 5 minutes. Run a thin knife around the inside edge of the pan and invert the cake onto the rack. Peel off the paper and let the layer cool completely.

Make a second batch of batter. Bake and cool a second 5-inch cake layer and a second 12-inch layer in the same manner.

Make a third batch of batter. Divide the batter among the three 8-inch cake pans, smooth the tops, and bake the cakes in the middle of the oven for 25 to 30 minutes, or until a cake tester inserted in the center comes out clean. Let the cakes cool in the pans on racks for 5 minutes, run a thin knife around the inside edges of the pans, and invert the cakes onto the racks. Peel off the paper and let the layers cool completely.

In the large bowl of the mixer beat the egg yolks with the confectioners' sugar until the mixture falls in a ribbon when the beater is lifted (see illustration page 16). In a large heavy stainless steel or enameled saucepan combine the milk with the orange rind, scald the mixture, and add it to the egg yolk mixture in a stream, stirring constantly with a wooden spoon. Pour the mixture back into the pan and cook it over moderately low heat without letting it boil, stirring constantly, for 5 minutes, or until it thickens slightly. Transfer the custard to the large bowl and beat it with the hand-held mixer until cool. Beat in the 3½ cups butter, one tablespoon at a time, making sure each piece is incorporated before adding the next, and beat the buttercream until soft and fluffy. Beat in the Grand Marnier, a few drops at a time.

(If frozen, thaw buttercream in the refrigerator overnight, let it stand at room temperature for 1 to 2 hours, or until it is soft, and beat it gently. Should the buttercream begin to separate, beat in an additional stick of softened unsalted butter, one tablespoon at a time, until the buttercream is smooth.)

In a small bowl combine the Grand Marnier and orange-flower water.

Using a long serrated knife, trim off horizontally the rounded top of each cake layer to make the layers level for stacking. Halve each layer horizontally and separate the halves (see illustration page 19). Arrange the

---

Keep the cake layers, wrapped individually in plastic wrap, at room temperature for 1 day before assembling the cake. The layers may be frozen, sealed in individual plastic bags or wrapped in foil, for 1 week. Thaw the layers at room temperature for several hours or overnight before assembling the cake.

Make the buttercream:

The buttercream may be chilled, covered, overnight or it may be frozen, covered, for up to 1 week.

To assemble the cake:

half-layers, cut sides up, on a work surface and brush the cut sides with the Grand Marnier mixture.

Set one of the 12-inch layer halves, brushed side up, on a large platter and spread it with a thin layer of the buttercream. Top the buttercream with another 12-inch layer, brushed side down, and spread the cake with a thin layer of the buttercream. Top the layers with the remaining 12-inch half-layers, spreading them with buttercream in the same manner. Stack the 8-inch half-layers, spreading them with buttercream in the same manner, on top of the 12-inch layers. Stack the 5-inch half-layers, spreading them with buttercream in the same manner on the 8-inch layers. Spread the remaining buttercream thinly over the layers, covering the cake completely, and chill the cake, uncovered, for at least 1 hour, or overnight if desired.

Decorate the cake:

The cake may stand in a cool, dark place for up to 2 hours before serving.

Using a long metal icing spatula, spread the seven-minute icing evenly over the cake, dipping the spatula in hot water occasionally to smooth the icing. Arrange the royal icing flowers carefully in tiers on the layers to create a cascading effect and garnish them with the mint leaves.

PUMPKIN CHEESECAKE

Yield:
16 to 20 servings

Equipment:
12-inch springform pan
food processor fitted with steel blade

FOR THE CRUST

1½ cups crushed gingersnap crumbs
¾ stick (6 tablespoons) unsalted
   butter, softened

¼ cup confectioners' sugar

FOR THE FILLING

3¼ cups granulated sugar
1½ cups pumpkin purée
10 egg yolks plus 3 large eggs
2 tablespoons cinnamon
3 pieces of crystallized ginger
   (available at specialty foods shops),
   minced

1 teaspoon mace
1 teaspoon salt
3 pounds cream cheese, softened
¼ cup heavy cream
2 tablespoons cornstarch
1 teaspoon lemon extract
1 teaspoon vanilla

Make the crust:

Generously butter the springform pan.

In the food processor or in a blender in batches blend the crushed gingersnap crumbs, the butter, and the confectioners' sugar. Press the mixture onto the bottom of the springform pan, tamping it down well, and chill the crust for 30 minutes.

Preheat the oven to 400° F. Bake the crust in the middle of the oven for 10 minutes. Transfer the pan to a rack and let the crust cool.

Make the filling:

Increase the oven temperature to 475° F.

In a bowl combine 2 cups of the granulated sugar with the the pumpkin purée. Lightly beat 6 of the egg yolks and stir them into the pumpkin mixture with the cinnamon, crystallized ginger, mace, and salt.

In a large bowl cream together the cream cheese and the remaining 1¼ cups granulated sugar. Add the whole eggs and the remaining 4 egg yolks, one at a time, beating well after each addition. Beat in the heavy cream, cornstarch, lemon extract, and vanilla and fold the pumpkin mixture into the cream cheese mixture.

Pour the filling into the springform pan and bake the cake in the middle of the oven for 10 minutes. Reduce the heat to 250° F. and bake the cake for 1½ hours more. (The center will be slightly soft.) Transfer the pan to a rack and let the cake cool for 1 hour. Chill the cake, lightly covered, for at least 3 hours. Remove the sides of the pan before serving.

RAISIN GINGERBREAD

Yield:
one 9-inch square cake

Made with molasses and sour cream, this gingerbread is moist and wonderfully spicy.

Equipment:
hand-held electric mixer
9-inch square cake pan
pastry brush

FOR THE GINGERBREAD

1 stick (½ cup) unsalted butter, cut into bits	2 teaspoons ground ginger
	1 teaspoon cinnamon
½ cup firmly packed light brown sugar	1 teaspoon baking soda
	½ teaspoon freshly grated nutmeg
2 large eggs, separated, at room temperature	½ teaspoon ground allspice
	½ teaspoon plus pinch of salt
¾ cup sour cream	pinch of cream of tartar
½ cup unsulfured molasses	2 tablespoons granulated sugar
1 cup raisins	½ cup apple jelly
3 tablespoons dark rum	sifted confectioners' sugar for garnish
2 cups all-purpose flour	

FOR THE APPLE CREAM

1½ cups well-chilled heavy cream	1½ cups Applesauce (page 473)

Make the gingerbread: In a large bowl with the mixer cream the butter, add the brown sugar, and beat the mixture until fluffy. Add the egg yolks and beat the mixture until combined well. Stir in the sour cream, molasses, raisins, and 2 tablespoons of the rum. Into a small bowl sift together the flour, ginger, cinnamon, baking soda, nutmeg, allspice, and the ½ teaspoon salt. Add the dry ingredients to the molasses mixture and stir the batter until just combined.

Preheat the oven to 350° F. Generously butter the cake pan.

In a bowl with the mixer beat the egg whites with the pinch of salt until frothy, add the cream of tartar, and beat the whites until they hold soft peaks. Add the granulated sugar and beat the whites until they hold stiff peaks (see illustrations page 238). Stir one third of the whites into the batter and fold in the remaining whites gently but thoroughly. Spoon the batter into the pan and bake the gingerbread in the middle of the oven for 30 to 35 minutes, or until a cake tester inserted in the center comes out clean. Let the cake cool in the pan on a rack for 5 minutes. Turn it out onto a cake plate and let it cool for 10 minutes.

In a small stainless steel or enameled saucepan melt the apple jelly with the remaining 1 tablespoon rum. Brush the glaze carefully over the gingerbread and let the cake cool completely. Hold a stencil over the gingerbread and sprinkle the surface with the confectioners' sugar.

Make the apple cream: In a chilled bowl with the mixer beat the cream until it hold soft peaks. Combine it with the applesauce. Makes about 2 cups.

Serve the gingerbread with the apple cream.

Photo on page 146.

Variation: BLUEBERRY GINGERBREAD: Omit the raisins from the above batter and fold in 1 cup blueberries, picked over, that have been tossed with 1 tablespoon flour. Bake as directed above and serve with lightly sweetened whipped cream.

HIGHLAND MOLASSES GINGER CAKE WITH GLACÉED FRUITS

Yield:
1 loaf cake, 9 by 5 by 3 inches

Equipment:
loaf pan, 9 by 5 by 3 inches

Here is another spicy ginger cake, this one slightly fancier than the one that precedes it because of the candied fruits and crystallized ginger in the batter.

3 cups sifted all-purpose flour
2 teaspoons baking soda
1½ teaspoons ground ginger
¼ teaspoon salt
½ cup dried currants
⅓ cup coarsely chopped Candied Orange Peel (page 522)
⅓ cup coarsely chopped glacéed mixed fruits
¼ cup minced crystallized ginger (available at specialty foods shops)

1 cup molasses
1½ sticks (¾ cup) unsalted butter
¼ cup firmly packed light brown sugar
3 large eggs, beaten lightly
¼ cup milk
fine dry bread crumbs (page 550) for dusting the loaf pan

Into a bowl sift together the flour, baking soda, ground ginger, and salt. Add the currants, candied orange peel, glacéed fruits, and the crystallized ginger and toss the mixture until the fruits are coated lightly with the flour mixture.

Preheat the oven to 325° F. and butter the loaf pan. Dust the loaf pan with the bread crumbs, shaking out the excess.

In a saucepan heat the molasses, butter, and brown sugar over low heat, stirring, until the butter is melted. Let the mixture cool for 10 minutes and beat in the eggs and the milk.

Make a well in the center of the flour mixture, pour in the molasses mixture, and stir the batter until just combined. Pour the batter into the pan and bake the cake for 1 to 1¼ hours, or until it pulls away from the sides of the pan. Let the cake cool in the pan on a rack for 10 minutes. Run a thin knife around the edge of the pan and invert the cake onto the rack. Let the cake cool before slicing it.

PANFORTE

Fruit and Nut Cake

Yield:
two 7-inch cakes

Equipment:
two 7-inch round cake pans, 1 inch deep
pastry brush
candy thermometer

Panforte, meaning literally strong bread, derives from Siena, Italy, and is a marvelous rich fruitcake that is served especially at Christmastime. Because it is so dense and confection–like, serve it in thin slices.

1 cup hazelnuts, toasted and skins removed (for procedure page 549)
1 cup blanched almonds (for procedure page 549), toasted lightly
1 cup diced glacéed mixed fruits
½ cup sifted all-purpose flour
1 tablespoon cinnamon

2 teaspoons diced glacéed citron
2 teaspoons diced candied lemon peel
2 teaspoons diced Candied Orange Peel (page 522)
½ cup granulated sugar
½ cup honey
sifted confectioners' sugar for dusting

Preheat the oven to 325° F. Butter the cake pans, dust them with flour, and knock out the excess flour.

In a bowl combine the hazelnuts, almonds, glacéed mixed fruits, flour, cinnamon, citron, lemon peel, and orange peel. In a heavy saucepan combine the granulated sugar and the honey and bring the syrup to a simmer over moderately low heat, stirring occasionally and washing down any sugar crystals clinging to the sides of the pan with the brush dipped in cold water until the sugar is dissolved. Cook the syrup, gently swirling the pan, until it reaches the soft-ball stage, or the candy thermometer registers 238° F. (For the stages of sugar syrup, see illustrations page 241.)

Pour the syrup into a large bowl, stir in the nut-and-fruit mixture, and combine the batter well. Divide the batter between the cake pans, smooth the tops with a spatula, and bake the cakes in the middle of the oven for 35 minutes. Transfer the cakes to racks and let them cool completely. Turn the cakes out onto serving plates and dust them heavily with the confectioners' sugar.

The cakes keep, wrapped in foil, in airtight containers for several weeks.

WHITE FRUITCAKE WITH ICING

Yield:
1 loaf cake, 12 by 4½
  by 3 inches

Equipment:
loaf pan, 12 by 4½ by
  3 inches
hand-held and upright
  electric mixers
candy thermometer

We all recognize dark fruitcakes, rich with dried fruits and doused in spirits. White fruitcakes by comparison are infinitely lighter, much more cake-like, and by all rights should be served at other times of the year besides the Christmas holidays. Try this appealing one in the spring.

FOR THE CAKE

½ cup sugar
½ stick (¼ cup) unsalted butter,
    softened
3 large eggs
3 cups all-purpose flour
1 tablespoon double-acting baking
    powder

½ teaspoon baking soda
½ teaspoon salt
1 cup buttermilk
2 cups diced glacéed mixed fruits

FOR THE ICING

2½ cups sugar
1½ cups water
3 tablespoons grated orange rind
3 egg whites at room temperature

pinch of cream of tartar
1½ teaspoons vanilla
1 to 2 teaspoons boiling water, if
    needed

Make the cake:

Butter the loaf pan, dust it with flour, and knock out the excess flour. Preheat the oven to 325° F.

In a large bowl with the mixer cream together the sugar and the butter until light and fluffy. Add the eggs, one at a time, beating well after each addition. Into a bowl sift together the flour, baking powder, baking soda, and salt. Stir the dry ingredients into the butter mixture alternately with the buttermilk. Fold in the glacéed fruits, combining the batter well. Pour the batter into the loaf pan and bake the cake in the middle of the oven for 1 to 1¼ hours, or until a cake tester inserted in the center comes out clean. Let the cake cool in the pan on a rack for 15 minutes, invert it onto the rack, and let it cool completely.

Make the icing:

In a saucepan combine the sugar, water, and grated orange rind. Bring the mixture to a boil over moderate heat, stirring until the sugar is dissolved, and cook the syrup until the candy thermometer registers 240° F.

In the large bowl of the upright mixer beat the egg whites with the cream of tartar until they hold soft peaks. Pour in the syrup in a stream, beating, and beat the mixture until the icing is fluffy and well combined. (For the stages of sugar syrup and how to pour it, see illustrations pages 240 and 241.) Stir in the vanilla.

Spread the sides and top of the cake with the icing, beating in the boiling water if the icing becomes too firm to spread, and let the cake stand until the icing is set.

Photo on page 400.

SPICED BLACK FRUITCAKE

Yield:
2 fruitcakes, 9 by 5 by
  3 inches

Equipment:
2 loaf pans, 9 by 5 by
  3 inches
cheesecloth
tightly covered
  containers for
  storage

This dense dark fruitcake requires at least a month to age. Plan ahead if you intend to give it as a Christmas present.

1 pound dried currants
12 ounces raisins
12 ounces golden raisins, chopped
12 ounces dried figs, chopped
8 ounces dried pitted prunes, stewed,
    drained, and chopped
8 ounces pitted dates, chopped
8 ounces slivered blanched almonds,
    toasted
6 ounces glacéed cherries, finely sliced
6 ounces citron, finely sliced
4 ounces Candied Orange Peel
    (page 522), finely shredded

3 cups dark rum plus rum for soaking
    the cheesecloth
2 sticks (1 cup) unsalted butter,
    softened
2 cups firmly packed dark brown sugar
1½ teaspoons cinnamon
1½ teaspoons freshly grated nutmeg
1½ teaspoons ground allspice
5 large eggs
2 cups sifted all-purpose flour
2 teaspoons double-acting baking
    powder
½ teaspoon salt

In a large bowl combine the currants, raisins, golden raisins, figs, prunes, dates, almonds, glacéed cherries, citron, and candied orange peel. Stir in the 3 cups dark rum and let the mixture macerate, covered, stirring it every other day, for 1 week.

Preheat the oven to 275° F. Butter the baking pans, line them with brown paper or wax paper, and butter the paper lightly.

In a bowl with the mixer cream the butter and gradually blend in the brown sugar, cinnamon, nutmeg, and allspice. Beat in 2 of the eggs. Into a large bowl sift the flour, baking powder, and salt. Blend 1 cup of the flour mixture into the creamed mixture and beat in the remaining 3 eggs. Stir in the fruits and the rum in which they macerated. Add the remaining flour mixture and combine the batter well.

Pour the batter into the pans, pressing it firmly into the corners. Put a shallow pan filled with hot water on the bottom of the oven under the cake pans and bake the cakes in the middle of the oven for 2½ hours, or until a cake tester inserted in the center comes out clean. Cool the cakes in the pans on racks for 1 hour.

While the cakes are cooling, soak cheesecloth in dark rum.

Transfer the cakes to racks, peel off the paper, and let the cakes cool completely. Wrap the cakes in the cheesecloth and store them in the containers. Moisten the cloths occasionally with the remaining dark rum and let the cakes age for at least 1 month.

DRIED FRUITS FRUITCAKE

Yield:
1 loaf cake, 9 by 5 by
  3 inches

Equipment:
loaf pan, 9 by 5 by 3
  inches
hand-held electric
  mixer

This unique fruitcake of various dried fruits and nuts employs no flour or sugar. Its mellow flavor improves by being aged for one month.

¾ cup dried apricots
½ cup dried peaches
1½ cups pitted dates, chopped
¾ cup chopped pitted prunes
¾ cup chopped dried figs
¾ cup raisins
⅔ cup chopped walnuts
⅔ cup blanched almonds
  (for procedure page 549), chopped
½ cup candied pineapple, coarsely
  chopped
½ cup glacéed cherries, coarsely
  chopped
1 cup graham cracker crumbs

½ teaspoon double-acting baking
  powder
½ teaspoon salt
½ teaspoon cinnamon
¼ teaspoon baking soda
¼ teaspoon freshly grated nutmeg
1 stick (½ cup) unsalted butter,
  softened
3 large eggs
⅓ cup honey
⅓ cup strawberry preserves
3 tablespoons fresh orange juice
½ teaspoon vanilla

Put the dried apricots and peaches in a large bowl, cover them with boiling water, and let them stand until they soften. Drain them well, chop them coarsely, and mix them with the dates, prunes, figs, raisins, walnuts, almonds, pineapple, and cherries. In a small bowl combine the graham cracker crumbs with the baking powder, salt, cinnamon, baking soda and nutmeg and stir into the fruit mixture.

Oil the loaf pan, line it with wax paper, and oil the paper. Preheat the oven to 300° F.

In a large bowl with the mixer cream the butter until smooth. Add the eggs, one at a time, beating well after each addition, and beat until the mixture is light and fluffy. Add the honey, strawberry preserves, orange juice, and vanilla and stir the mixture into the fruit mixture. Spoon the batter into the loaf pan and bake the fruitcake for 1½ to 2 hours, or until a cake tester inserted in the center comes out clean.

Let the cake rest in the pan on a rack until it is almost cool. Turn it out of the pan, peel off the paper gently, and let the cake cool completely. Store the fruitcake in an airtight container for about 1 month.

KUGELHUPF

Yield:
one 10-inch cake

Equipment:
10-inch *Kugelhupf* pan

This Austrian specialty made with yeast bakes in its own specially fluted mold. It is a pretty, subtle-tasting cake that is also very good sliced, toasted, and lightly buttered.

2 envelopes active dry yeast
1 cup warm milk
¾ cup plus 2 tablespoons granulated sugar
4 cups all-purpose flour plus additional for dusting
1 teaspoon salt

1 teaspoon vanilla
1 cup raisins
¾ cup sliced blanched almonds
grated rind of 1 lemon
4 large eggs, beaten
¾ cup unsalted butter, melted
confectioners' sugar for dusting

Dissolve the yeast in ½ cup of the warm milk with the 2 tablespoons granulated sugar. Let the mixture stand in a warm place for 15 minutes, or until the yeast is foamy.

Sift the flour into a warm bowl. Add the remaining ¾ cup granulated sugar, salt, vanilla, raisins, almonds, and grated lemon rind and toss the mixture to combine. Make a well in the center of the flour mixture, pour in the yeast mixture, and stir to incorporate as much flour as possible into the liquid. Stir in the beaten eggs and the melted butter, continuing to moisten the flour, and work in gradually the remaining ½ cup milk, or enough of it to form a smooth dough. Dust the dough with flour, cover it with a warm towel, and let it rise in a warm place for 2 hours, or until it is doubled in bulk.

Butter the *Kugelhupf* pan, dust it with flour, and knock out the excess flour.

Turn the dough out on a floured board, punch it down, and shape it quickly into a ring. Put the ring in the *Kugelhupf* pan, cover it with a warm towel, and let it rise in a warm place for 1 hour.

Preheat the oven to 375° F.

Bake the *Kugelhupf* for about 1 hour. (If the top browns too quickly, cover it with buttered paper.) Let the *Kugelhupf* cool in the pan on a rack. Turn the *Kugelhupf* out onto a rack and let cool completely. Dust the cake with confectioners' sugar and let it stand overnight before slicing.

BÛCHE DE NOËL

Yule Log

Yield:
one 15-inch rolled
  cake

Equipment:
jelly-roll pan, 15½ by
  10½ by 1 inches
upright and hand-held
  electric mixers
pastry brush
candy thermometer

FOR THE CAKE

4 large eggs, separated, plus 2 egg
  whites, at room temperature
½ cup granulated sugar
1 tablespoon eau-de-vie de
  framboise *(raspberry brandy)*
¼ teaspoon salt

¼ teaspoon cream of tartar
½ cup sifted all-purpose flour
¼ cup sifted unsweetened cocoa
  powder plus additional sifted cocoa
  powder for dusting the cake

FOR THE CHOCOLATE BUTTERCREAM

6 egg yolks
⅔ cup granulated sugar
¼ cup water
3 sticks (1½ cups) unsalted butter,
  softened

6 ounces semisweet chocolate, melted
  and cooled
1 tablespoon eau-de-vie de
  framboise

FOR THE MERINGUE

2 egg whites at room temperature
2 tablespoons granulated sugar
¼ cup confectioners' sugar, sifted

1 tablespoon eau-de-vie de
  framboise

FOR THE DECORATION

Meringue Mushrooms *(page 530)*
chocolate leaves *(page 546)*

2 tablespoons almond paste tinted with
  green food coloring

½ recipe Raspberry Sauce
  *(page 508), flavored with 4
  tablespoons* eau-de-vie de
  framboise, *or to taste*

¼ recipe (12) Chocolate Truffles
  (page 526), if desired
confectioners' sugar for sprinkling

Make the cake:

Preheat the oven to 425° F. Butter the jelly-roll pan and line it with wax paper, leaving a 2-inch overhang on each of the short ends. Butter the paper and dust it with flour, shaking out the excess.

In the large bowl of the upright mixer beat the egg yolks until smooth. Add 6 tablespoons of the granulated sugar, a little at a time, and beat the batter at medium speed for 3 to 4 minutes, or until creamy and light. Beat in the *framboise*. In another bowl with the hand-held mixer beat the egg whites with ⅛ teaspoon of the salt until frothy. Add the cream of tartar and beat the whites until they hold soft peaks. Add the remaining 2 tablespoons sugar, a little at a time, and beat the whites until they hold stiff peaks (see illustrations page 238). Fold the whites into the batter gently but thoroughly. Sift the flour, the ¼ cup cocoa powder, and the remaining ⅛ teaspoon salt over the batter, one third at a time, and fold in each addition until the batter is smooth.

Pour the batter into the jelly-roll pan, spread it evenly with a spatula, and bake the cake in the middle of the oven for 8 to 10 minutes, or until it pulls away from the sides of the pan and a cake tester inserted in the center comes out clean. Dust the cake lightly with cocoa powder, cover it with wax paper, and let it cool to warm. Pull the edges of the wax paper away from the pan, invert the cake onto a baking sheet, and carefully peel off the paper. Dust the cake lightly with the remaining cocoa powder, cover it with wax paper, and roll it up (see illustrations page 41). Let the cake cool completely.

Make the chocolate buttercream: In the bowl of the upright mixer beat the egg yolks until light and creamy. In a small heavy saucepan combine the sugar with the water. Bring the mixture to a boil and cook it over moderate heat, stirring and washing down any sugar crystals clinging to the sides of the pan with the brush dipped in cold water until the syrup reaches the soft-ball stage, or the candy thermometer registers 238° F. (For the stages of sugar syrup, see illustrations page 241.) With the mixer running, add the hot syrup to the yolks in a stream, beating, and beat the mixture until completely cool. Beat in the butter and the chocolate, a little at a time. Pour 2 cups of the buttercream into a bowl, beat in the *framboise*, and chill the buttercream, covered, until the cake is ready to be frosted. Transfer the remaining buttercream to a bowl and reserve it.

Make the meringue: In a bowl with the hand-held mixer beat the whites until they hold soft peaks. Add the granulated sugar and the confectioners' sugar, a little at a time, and beat the whites until they hold stiff peaks (see illustrations page 238). Fold the meringue into the reserved buttercream, stir in the *framboise*, and blend the mixture until smooth.

To assemble the cake: Have ready the meringue mushrooms, chocolate leaves, and the colored almond paste.

Unroll the cake, spoon the ½ cup raspberry sauce over it, letting the cake absorb the sauce, and spread the buttercream-meringue filling evenly over the cake, leaving a 1-inch border on each of the long sides. Halve the chocolate truffles and sprinkle them over the filling, if desired, and roll up the cake lengthwise.

Cut a 2-inch piece diagonally from each end of the cake and set the pieces aside. Transfer the cake to a serving tray and arrange the reserved end pieces on top of the cake to simulate sawed-off branches. Beat the chilled buttercream until smooth and with a spatula spread it over the cake. Gently pull the tines of a fork lengthwise over the buttercream to simulate bark and garnish the log with the meringue mushrooms and chocolate leaves. Force the green almond paste through a medium sieve and with the tip of a small knife attach it to the log around the mushrooms to simulate moss. Gently dust the log with sifted confectioners' sugar, simulating snow. Let the cake come to room temperature before serving. Cut the cake with a sharp serrated knife.

Photo on page 520.

CHOCOLATE RASPBERRY DOBOSTORTE

Yield:
one 8-inch-round
  9-layer cake,
  serving 12

Equipment:
three 8-inch round
  cake pans
hand-held and upright
  electric mixers
pastry brush
candy thermometer

One of the great Austrian specialties (although arriving via Hungary), Dobostorte is characterized by its caramel-coated top cake layer with individual slices marked while the caramel is still warm. The cake is made from sponge layers and is filled with chocolate buttercream and raspberry jam.

FOR THE CAKE LAYERS

6 large eggs, separated, the whites at
  room temperature
¾ cup plus 1 tablespoon sugar
1 teaspoon vanilla

1 cup cake flour (not self-rising)
¼ teaspoon plus pinch of salt
pinch of cream of tartar

FOR THE RASPBERRY FILLING

½ cup seedless raspberry jam
1 tablespoon eau-de-vie de
  framboise (raspberry brandy)

1 tablespoon fresh lemon juice, or to
  taste

1 recipe chocolate buttercream
  (page 114) made with 3 ounces
  semisweet chocolate, 2 ounces
  unsweetened chocolate, and 2
  tablespoons eau-de-vie de
  framboise

½ cup toasted and skinned hazelnuts
  (for procedure page 549), chopped
  fine

FOR THE CARAMEL

1 cup sugar
¼ teaspoon cream of tartar

½ cup water

13 hazelnuts, toasted and skinned, for garnish

Make the cake layers:

Invert the cake pans and butter and flour the undersides. Preheat the oven to 350° F.

    In a large bowl with the hand-held mixer beat the egg yolks until thick and pale, beat in ½ cup of the sugar, and beat the mixture for 5 minutes. Beat in the vanilla. Sift the flour and the ¼ teaspoon salt together over the yolk mixture and fold them in gently but thoroughly. In another bowl with the hand-held mixer beat the whites with the pinch of salt until frothy, add the cream of tartar, and beat the whites until they hold soft peaks. Add the remaining 5 tablespoons sugar, a little at a time, beating, and beat the whites until they just hold stiff peaks (see illustrations page 238). Stir one third of the whites into the batter and fold in the remaining whites gently but thoroughly.

    Spread a generous ½ cup of the batter with an icing spatula or a knife on each underside in an even layer and bake the cake layers on the same rack in

When the layers have cooled completely they may be stacked between sheets of wax paper, wrapped in plastic wrap, and chilled for 1 day. Remove the wax paper very carefully.

the middle of the oven for 7 to 9 minutes, or until pale golden. Let the cake layers cool for 2 minutes and loosen the edges with a thin-bladed knife. Transfer the layers to racks and let cool. Wipe the pans clean with paper towels and make 6 more layers in the same manner.

Make the raspberry filling:

In a small saucepan combine the jam, *eau-de-vie de framboise*, and the lemon juice, heat the mixture over moderately low heat, whisking, until smooth, and let cool to room temperature.

To assemble the cake:

Have ready the chocolate buttercream.

With a sharp knife trim the edges of the cake layers so that the layers are all the same size and shape, reserving the best layer, wrapped in plastic wrap, for the caramel top. Arrange one layer on a cake stand, using a small dab of the chocolate buttercream to anchor it to the stand, and spread it with 3 heaping tablespoons of the buttercream. Spread a second cake layer with 2 tablespoons of the raspberry filling, invert the layer, raspberry side down, onto the buttercream-spread layer, and spread the layer with 3 heaping tablespoons of buttercream. Continue to layer the remaining cake in the same manner. After spreading the eighth layer with the buttercream, spread the remaining buttercream around the sides of the cake. Chill the cake for 5 minutes to firm the buttercream slightly and press the chopped hazelnuts around the sides.

The cake may be prepared up to this point 2 days in advance and kept covered with an inverted bowl and chilled.

Make the caramel:

In a small saucepan combine the sugar, cream of tartar, and water, cook the mixture over moderate heat, stirring and washing down any sugar crystals clinging to the sides of the pan with the brush dipped in cold water until the sugar is dissolved, and bring the syrup to a boil. Boil the syrup, undisturbed, until it begins to turn a pale golden and swirl the pan gently until it is a golden brown caramel. While the syrup is boiling, put the reserved cake layer on a rack set over a few sheets of foil to protect the work surface and have ready a buttered knife. Pour enough of the caramel immediately over the cake layer to coat it with a thin layer, reserving the remaining caramel in the pan, and, working very quickly, draw the knife through the caramel glaze down to the cake, marking off 12 slices. (These lines decorate the cake and make it easier to slice without shattering the hardened caramel.) When the caramel has cooled completely, trim any caramel that has dripped around the edge with scissors.

Make the garnish:

Set a few sheets of foil over the work surface to protect it, invert a large sieve over the foil, and insert a wooden pick into the bottom of each whole hazelnut. Heat the reserved caramel over moderately low heat, swirling the pan, until it is melted. Dip the hazelnuts carefully into the caramel and insert the other end of the wooden picks into the sieve to allow the caramel to cool and harden. (Be very careful not to drip any caramel onto your hands or wear 2 pairs of rubber gloves to protect them from burns.) When the caramel-coated hazelnuts have cooled completely, press them onto the caramel-coated top cake layer, using some additional caramel, reheated, if necessary. Let the cake come to room temperature, arrange the caramel layer on top, and with a knife smooth the buttercream and chopped hazelnuts up around the edge of the the top layer.

PIES AND TARTS

*L*ife can be difficult, but a large wedge of chocolate cream or coconut custard pie, considered the ultimate indulgence, has a way of making everything just a little bit better. Perhaps this is a reason for the overwhelming popularity of pie in this country—not only as a dessert but also as a source for literary references. The expression, "As American as apple pie" rings true: Pie has always been and still is the favorite finale of memorable meals.

Making a truly great pie is considered an achievement; obtaining a flaky crust is considered "tricky," even difficult; and just exactly how long must you cook a custard or gel a chiffon filling? Successes are within everyone's grasp, however, and explicit instructions and, perhaps, just a little practice will help you achieve the "perfect" lemon meringue pie, guaranteed to clinch your reputation as a top-notch baker.

A perfect fruit tart, a tender pastry shell displaying decoratively arranged fruits enhanced by a shiny glaze, does not have to be reserved for a special occasion. While pie is the overwhelming American favorite, its French relation, the tart, has always been standard dessert fare at luncheon, dinner, or at those other times, composed, for example, to offer an unexpected guest. With a tart shell on hand, a neighbor's impromptu gift of fresh strawberries from his garden is transformed into a spectacular dessert when the shell is piled high with berries and glazed with red currant jelly.

Tarts come in so many guises from simple and unadorned, almost rustic, to elegant and sophisticated. Either way, with the basic pairing of free-standing pastry shell and filling, the results will be delicious.

Cranberry Maple
Pear Pie (page 133),
Pecan Pumpkin Pie
(page 143)

PIES

Pies are irresistible. They combine such elements as flaky crusts redolent with butter or with a satisfying crackle and crispness due to the addition of lard; fruit fillings with a magical balance of sweet and tart; custard fillings ranging from delicate and light to spicy and flavorful; light as air chiffon fillings; rich and creamy cream fillings; ethereal and always impressive meringue toppings; sweet and luscious nut fillings; and include turnovers and single-serving deep-dish pies for the individualist in all of us.

A homemade pie shows that the baker cares. Not only has he risen to what is often considered a challenge, but because a pie is baked for someone to make him happy (ask Billy Boy), it demonstrates a desire to please or even indulge. Eugene Field wrote, "The best of all physicians is apple pie and cheese." There must be a reason.

Pie can be simple and homey, like our Lemon Chess Pie (page 149), easily prepared from ingredients on hand or from seasonal specialties as in our Black Raspberry Pie (page 129). It can be prepared from local ingredients such as Key Lime Pie (page 148), ubiquitous, perhaps, in southern Florida, but an incredible treat throughout the rest of the country. Or a pie can be a fanciful combination but perfect marriage of ingredients as in our Eggnog Pie with Pecan Crust (page 152).

Any one of several pie doughs included here can be chosen to best enhance the pie filling or perhaps to best provide a contrast in texture or richness. Our lard pastry dough is used for Black Raspberry Pie. The crisp pastry holds up especially well to the juicy berry filling. Sour cream pastry, rich and tender, is paired with Deep-Dish Blueberry Peach Pie (page 138), but cream cheese pastry is certainly another wonderful option. Cheddar dough is used, appropriately, for Apple Cheddar Turnovers (page 140). We suggest serving them with additional Cheddar wedges— sometimes there is no such thing as gilding the lily.

PIE DOUGHS

A baker's reputation is often built upon that person's ability to make light, flaky pie crusts. Although not difficult to achieve, an understanding of the proper techniques is necessary before you begin.

When blending the dough, handle it as little as possible. The heat from your fingertips will soften the shortening. This hampers the goal of small particles melting and blending with the flour while baking, creating tiny puffs of steam and resulting in a light, flaky, layered crust. You can use either your fingertips to combine the dry ingredients and butter, rubbing the two together until the mixture resembles coarse meal, or you can cut the butter into the flour using two knives and a cutting motion to achieve small particles. (Another method, described on page 190 of the "Pastry" chapter, employs a pastry blender to cut in the butter.) Note that the shortening should be cold and ice water is added to form a soft, moist, but not sticky dough. It is advisable to chill the dough for about 30 minutes to allow the gluten in the flour to relax and to make the dough more manageable.

Dust a work surface lightly with flour, and, using a very lightly dusted rolling pin, roll out the dough from the center outward to the edges in all directions forming a circle (or whatever the shape of the baking form) ⅛ inch thick (or whatever the recipe indicates) and larger than the form to ensure that it will fit with sufficient overhang.

To transfer the pastry to the pie plate, simply roll it loosely around the rolling pin, hold the rolling pin over the plate, and unroll the pastry over the plate, as shown in the illustrations below. With your fingertips or knuckles, gently press the pastry against the sides.

With a fork, prick the shell to prevent it from buckling or shrinking. Sometimes the shell is brushed with beaten egg white for especially juicy fillings. When baked, the egg white glaze helps prevent the liquid of the filling from being absorbed into the crust.

Cutting in butter with fingertips/with two knives

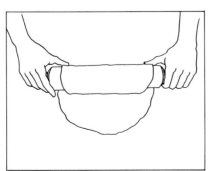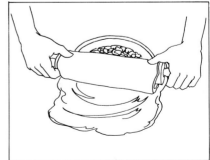

Rolling dough over rolling pin   Rolling dough off rolling pin

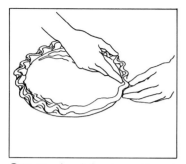  

Crimping dough for decorative edge: fluted edge; scalloped edge; rope edge

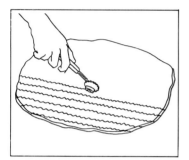 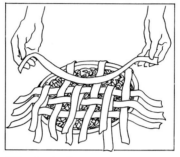 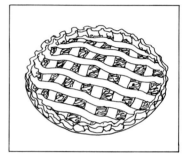

Cutting lattice strips   Weaving lattice crust   A simple lattice crust, a decorative
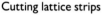   edge

A pie usually has a decorative edge as opposed to being trimmed flush with the rim like many a tart shell is. After fitting the dough snugly into the pie plate, trim the edge with kitchen shears or a sharp knife to allow a ½-inch overhang. For a single-crust pie, form a decorative edge using one of the methods illustrated above. For a double-crust pie, drape the top layer of dough with a 1-inch overhang over the filling. Fold the top crust under the bottom crust and crimp the edge decoratively. For a lattice crust, cut strips using a pastry wheel or sharp knife, and press the strips on in a lattice pattern (either woven or straight), firmly pressing the ends of the strips to the edge of the shell (see illustrations above).

Pie crusts can also be beautifully and amusingly garnished with pastry crust cutouts such as leaves scored to simulate veins and berries or a fruit, representative of the pie filling. The top crust, lattice crust, or pastry cutouts are sometimes brushed with an egg wash or sprinkled with sugar. An egg wash is a mixture of whole egg or egg yolk and water that is lightly beaten. When brushed on the top crust, it helps the pastry to brown and results in a shiny golden finish. When the egg is mixed with milk instead, it will result in a duller finish more suitable for a rustic look. Finally, steam vents may be cut in the top crust, allowing the steam from juicy fillings to escape, thereby preventing a possible soggy crust.

Recipes for crumb and nut crusts are included in this section. These crusts are particularly good with chiffon and cream fillings, their crunchy texture complementing the light creamy fillings. Our recipe for Apricot Chiffon Pie with a gingersnap crust is a splendid example.

FLAKY PIE PASTRY

Yield:
about 1 pound 2
  ounces dough
enough dough for 1
  double-crust 9-inch
  pie
or 2 single-crust
  9-inch pies

2¼ cups all-purpose flour
½ teaspoon salt
½ stick (¼ cup) cold unsalted butter,
  cut into bits

½ cup cold vegetable shortening, cut
  into bits
¼ cup ice water

The dough may be
rolled out
immediately or it may
be kept, wrapped in
wax paper and chilled,
for up to 2 days. The
dough may be frozen,
wrapped in plastic
wrap and foil, for up
to 1 month.

In a bowl combine the flour and salt, add the butter, and blend the mixture
with your fingertips or two knives until it resembles coarse meal (see illustrations page 121). Add the shortening and blend the mixture until it resembles meal. Add the ice water, tossing the mixture with a fork, and
adding more water if necessary to form a soft but not sticky dough. Shape
the dough into a ball. If making a double-crust pie, or one with a lattice
crust, divide the dough into 2 balls, one slightly larger than the other. If
making 2 single-crust pies, halve the dough.

LARD PASTRY DOUGH

Yield:
about 1¼ pounds
  dough
enough dough for 1
  double-crust 9-inch
  pie
or 2 single-crust
  9-inch pies

2½ cups all-purpose flour
1 teaspoon salt
½ cup cold lard, cut into bits
1 egg yolk, beaten lightly

1 tablespoon fresh lemon juice
¼ to ½ cup ice water
1 stick (½ cup) unsalted butter, cut
  into bits

Into a bowl sift together the flour and the salt and blend in the lard with
your fingertips or two knives until the mixture resembles coarse meal (see
illustrations page 121). Add the egg yolk, lemon juice, and enough of the
ice water to form a soft dough. Dust the dough with flour and roll it into a
16- by 7-inch rectangle. Dot the upper two thirds of the rectangle with the
butter, pressing the butter gently into the dough, fold the lower third of
the rectangle up to meet the center of the buttered portion, and fold the top
of the rectangle over the bottom. Chill the dough, covered, for 30 minutes. Sprinkle the dough with flour, turn it seam side down so that an open
side faces you, and roll it into a 16- by 7-inch rectangle. Fold the lower
third of the dough to meet the center of the rectangle, fold the upper third
to meet the center (so that both edges meet the center), and fold the top
half over the bottom half. Chill the dough, covered, for 15 minutes. Roll
out and fold the dough in the same manner one more time. Chill the
dough, covered, for 30 minutes, or until firm. If making 2 single-crust
pies, halve the dough.

The dough may be
kept, wrapped in wax
paper and chilled, for
up to 2 days. The
dough may be frozen,
wrapped in plastic
wrap and foil, for up
to 1 month.

SOUR CREAM PASTRY

Yield:
about 1¼ pounds
  dough
enough dough for 1
  double-crust 9-inch
  pie
or 2 single-crust 9-
  inch pies

Equipment:
food processor fitted
  with plastic or steel
  blade

The dough may be
kept, wrapped and
chilled, for up to 2
days. The dough may
be frozen, wrapped in
plastic wrap and foil,
for up to 1 month.

2¼ cups all-purpose flour
½ teaspoon salt
¾ stick (6 tablespoons) cold unsalted
  butter, cut into bits

6 tablespoons cold vegetable
  shortening, cut into bits
½ cup sour cream
1 to 2 tablespoons ice water

In the food processor combine the flour, salt, and butter and process the mixture until it resembles very coarse meal. (The butter should be the size of lima beans.) Add the vegetable shortening and process the mixture until it resembles coarse meal. Add the sour cream and 1 tablespoon of the water and process the mixture until it just holds together, adding more water if necessary to form the dough. Transfer the dough to plastic wrap, gather it together to form a ball using the plastic wrap, and chill it for at least 1 hour, or until firm. If making a double-crust pie, divide the dough into 2 balls, one slightly larger than the other. If making 2 single-crust pies, halve the dough.

CREAM CHEESE PASTRY

Yield:
about 1½ pounds
  dough
enough dough for 1
  double-crust 9-inch
  pie
or 2 single-crust
  9-inch pies

Equipment:
food processor fitted
  with plastic or steel
  blade

The dough may be
kept, wrapped and
chilled, for up to 2
days. The dough may
be frozen, wrapped in
plastic wrap and foil,
for up to 1 month.

2¼ cups all-purpose flour
½ teaspoon salt
¾ stick (6 tablespoons) cold unsalted
  butter, cut into bits

6 tablespoons cold vegetable
  shortening, cut into bits
8 ounces cream cheese, cut into
  tablespoons and softened
1 large egg, beaten lightly

In the food processor combine the flour, salt, and butter and process the mixture until it resembles very coarse meal. (The butter should be the size of lima beans.) Add the vegetable shortening and process the mixture until it resembles coarse meal. Add the cream cheese and the egg and process the mixture until it just holds together. Transfer the dough to plastic wrap, gather it together into a ball using the plastic wrap, and chill it for at least 1 hour.

CHEDDAR DOUGH

Yield:
about 1 pound dough (enough dough for 12 Apple Cheddar Turnovers [page 140]) or for 1 single-crust 9-inch pie

Equipment:
food processor fitted with steel blade

The dough keeps, wrapped and chilled, for 2 days. The dough may be frozen, wrapped in plastic wrap and foil, for up to 2 weeks.

1⅓ cups all-purpose flour
¼ teaspoon salt
¾ stick (6 tablespoons) cold unsalted butter, cut into bits
2 tablespoons cold vegetable shortening

2 ounces sharp Cheddar, grated fine and chilled well
1 egg yolk beaten lightly with 3 tablespoons cold water

In the food processor or in a bowl combine the flour and the salt, add the butter and the shortening, and blend the mixture, pulsing with the food processor, until it just resembles very coarse meal. Add the Cheddar and blend the mixture until it resembles coarse meal. If using the food processor, transfer the mixture to a bowl. Add the yolk mixture, tossing the mixture with a fork and adding more cold water if necessary, one tablespoon at a time, until the mixture forms a dough. Form the dough into a ball, flatten it slightly, and dust it with flour. Chill the dough, wrapped in wax paper, for at least 1 hour or overnight.

OTHER CRUSTS

GRAHAM CRACKER CRUST

Yield:
one 9-inch pie crust

Equipment:
9-inch pie plate

1½ cups graham cracker crumbs (about 11 crackers)
¼ cup sugar if desired

½ stick (¼ cup) unsalted butter, melted

Preheat the oven to 350° F.

In a bowl combine the crumbs, the sugar if desired, and the butter and press the mixture evenly onto the bottom and sides of the pie plate. Bake the shell on a baking sheet in the lower third of the oven for 5 minutes. Let the shell cool on a rack.

CHOCOLATE WAFER CRUMB CRUST

Yield:
one 9-inch pie crust

Equipment:
9-inch pie plate

2 cups chocolate wafer crumbs
⅓ cup sugar
¾ stick (6 tablespoons) unsalted
  butter, cut into bits and softened

2 egg whites
pinch of salt

Butter the pie plate lightly and preheat the oven to 300° F.

In a bowl combine the crumbs, sugar, and the butter and press the mixture onto the bottom and sides of the pie plate. Bake the shell on a baking sheet in the middle of the oven for 15 minutes and let it cool on a rack.

In a small bowl beat the egg whites with the salt until frothy and spoon them into the shell, spreading them gently with the back of a spoon to cover the bottom completely. Bake the shell on the baking sheet in the middle of the oven for 5 minutes and let it cool on a rack.

VANILLA WAFER ALMOND CRUST

Yield:
one 8-inch pie crust

Equipment:
8-inch pie plate

1¼ cups vanilla wafer crumbs
⅓ cup lightly toasted ground blanched
  almonds

½ stick (¼ cup) unsalted butter,
  melted

Preheat the oven to 350° F.

In a bowl combine the wafer crumbs, almonds, and butter and press the mixture onto the bottom and sides of the pie plate. Bake the shell on a baking sheet in the middle of the oven for 15 minutes, or until browned lightly, and let it cool on a rack.

NUT CRUST

Yield:
one 9-inch pie crust

Equipment:
9-inch pie plate

2 cups pecans or toasted and skins
  removed hazelnuts (for procedure
  page 549)

⅓ cup sugar
3 tablespoons unsalted butter, melted

Preheat the oven to 350° F.

In a blender pulverize the nuts and transfer them to a bowl. Combine the nuts well with the sugar and blend in the melted butter. Press the mixture evenly onto the bottom and sides of the pie plate and chill the shell for 30 minutes. Bake the shell on a baking sheet in the middle of the oven for 12 to 15 minutes, or until lightly browned around the edges. Let the shell cool on a rack.

FRUIT PIES

Fresh ripe fruits and seasoning to enhance each fruit's flavor are the important things to remember for a fruit filling. Apples, berries, pears, cherries, and even a mincemeat filling replete with raisins and dried currants are suggested here. We have even included several recipes for dried fruits, available all year round.

Deep-dish pies are made without bottom crusts in deep baking pans. Because of the greater amount of fruit, they are especially juicy and flavorful. We have even included an interesting recipe for individual deep-dish pies of cranberries and apples prepared in soufflé cups or ramekins and topped with a pastry crust. A wonderful pie topping is a streusel or crumb one and we use it to enhance the flavor of fresh peaches in our Streusel Peach Pie (page 136). Finally, we offer turnover recipes, one with a sweet crust and luscious dried fig filling; the other a Cheddar dough with an apple filling—a compelling variation of our opening recipe for the classic Apple Pie. From beginning to end, the apple reigns in the fruit pie section.

APPLE PIE

Yield:
one 9-inch pie

Equipment:
deep 9-inch pie plate

The traditional American favorite with an especially spicy and flavorful filling that includes golden raisins. Among the best varieties of apples to use for baking are: Greenings, Pippins, Golden Delicious, McIntosh, Rome Beauties, Jonathans, Staymans, Granny Smiths, and Winesaps.

1 recipe flaky pie pastry (page 123), divided into 2 balls, one slightly larger than the other

FOR THE FILLING
6 large Greening apples, peeled, cored, and thinly sliced
1 cup granulated sugar
2 tablespoons all-purpose flour
½ teaspoon cinnamon

½ teaspoon freshly grated nutmeg
pinch of salt
½ teaspoon grated lemon rind, or to taste
¾ cup golden raisins

1½ cups confectioners' sugar
2 tablespoons water
¼ teaspoon vanilla
heavy cream as an accompaniment if desired

Vanilla Ice Cream (page 349) as an accompaniment if desired

On a floured surface roll out the larger ball of dough ¹/₁₆ inch thick. Drape the dough over the rolling pin, unroll it over the plate, and fit it into the plate (see illustrations page 121). Trim the edge to form a ½-inch overhang. Chill the shell and remaining dough while preparing the filling.

Preheat the oven to 350° F.

Make the filling: Toss the apples with the granulated sugar, 1 tablespoon of the flour, the cinnamon, nutmeg, salt, and the lemon rind. Toss the raisins with the remaining 1 tablespoon flour.

Alternate layers of the apple mixture and the floured raisins in the chilled pie shell. Roll out the remaining ball of dough $1/16$ inch thick on the floured surface and drape it over the filling, trimming it to a ½-inch overhang. Fold the top crust under the bottom crust and crimp the edges decoratively (see illustrations page 122). Make decorative slits in the top crust for steam vents. Bake the pie in middle of the oven for for 60 to 70 minutes, or until the apples are tender and the crust is golden. Let the pie cool on a rack completely.

In a small bowl combine the confectioners' sugar, water, and the vanilla and mix until smooth. Spread the top crust with the glaze. The pie can be served slightly warm or at room temperature with heavy cream or ice cream as an accompaniment if desired.

STRAWBERRY RHUBARB PIE

Yield:
one 9-inch pie

1 recipe flaky pie pastry (page 123), divided into 2 balls, one slightly larger than the other

Equipment:
9-inch pie plate
pastry brush

FOR THE FILLING

2 cups (about 1 pint) hulled, sliced strawberries

1 cup sugar, or to taste, plus sugar for sprinkling the top crust

2 tablespoons cornstarch dissolved in 1 tablespoon cold water

8 ounces rhubarb, trimmed and cut into ¾-inch pieces to measure 2 cups

½ teaspoon grated lemon rind, or to taste

1 teaspoon fresh lemon juice

2 tablespoons unsalted butter, cut into bits

Chill the balls of dough, covered, for 1 hour. On a floured surface roll the larger ball into an 11-inch round. Drape the dough over the rolling pin, unroll it over the pie plate, and fit it into the plate (see illustrations page 121). Trim the edge to form a ½-inch overhang. Reserve the smaller ball, covered and chilled.

Make the filling: In a bowl combine the strawberries and the 1 cup sugar, let the mixture stand for 20 minutes, and stir in the cornstarch mixture. Add the rhubarb, lemon rind, and lemon juice and spoon the mixture into the pie shell. Dot the mixture with the butter.

Preheat the oven to 400° F.

On the floured surface roll the reserved ball of dough into a 10-inch round and drape the top crust over the filling. Trim the top crust, leaving a ½-inch overhang, fold it under the bottom crust to seal the pie, and crimp the edge decoratively (see illustrations page 122). Sprinkle the top of the pie with sugar and make decorative slits in the crust for steam vents. Bake in the middle of the oven for 40 to 50 minutes, or until the crust is golden. Let the pie cool on a rack.

BLACK RASPBERRY PIE

Yield:
one 9-inch pie

Equipment:
9-inch pie plate
baking sheet

Black raspberries are simply a slightly less sweet variety of red raspberries. This recipe also calls for plump, juicy, full-flavored blackberries, sweet but with a wonderful tartness, which are available wild or cultivated. Varieties of the blackberry that could be substituted are boysenberries, loganberries, and olallieberries.

1 recipe lard pastry dough (page 123), divided into 2 balls, one slightly larger than the other

FOR THE FILLING
1 cup sugar
3 to 4 tablespoons all-purpose flour
¼ teaspoon grated lemon rind
1 pint black raspberries, picked over

1½ cups blackberries, picked over
1 tablespoon fresh lemon juice
1 tablespoon unsalted butter, cut into bits

Vanilla Ice Cream (page 349) as an accompaniment if desired

Make the filling:

In a bowl combine well the sugar, 3 tablespoons of the flour, and the lemon rind. Add the black raspberries, the blackberries, and the lemon juice and toss the berries to coat them with the mixture. Add up to 1 tablespoon more flour if the berries are very juicy.

Preheat the oven to 425° F.

On a floured surface roll out the larger ball of dough ⅛ inch thick. Drape the dough over the rolling pin, unroll it over the pie plate, and fit it into the plate (see illustrations page 121). Trim the edge to form a ½-inch overhang. Spread the filling in the shell and dot it with the butter. Roll out the remaining ball of dough ⅛ inch thick on the floured surface and drape it over the filling. Trim the top crust, leaving a 1-inch overhang, and fold it under the bottom crust. Crimp the edge decoratively (see illustrations page 122) and make slits in the top crust for steam vents. Bake on the baking sheet in the lower third of the oven for 10 minutes. Reduce the oven temperature to 375° F. and bake the pie for 40 to 50 minutes more, or until the crust is golden and the filling is bubbly. Transfer to a rack and let cool. Serve the pie warm or at room temperature with the ice cream if desired.

GINGERED PEAR PIE

Yield:
one 9-inch pie

This is a perfect pie for the holidays, particularly when it is accompanied by Cranberry Swirl Ice Cream (page 350).

Equipment:
decorative cookie
  cutters
9-inch pie plate
pastry brush
baking sheet

1 recipe pâte brisée *(page 164)*

FOR THE FILLING

*3½ pounds very firm Bartlett pears
    (about 8 large pears), peeled,
    halved lengthwise, cored, and sliced
½ to ¾ cup sugar, or to taste
¼ cup all-purpose flour
¼ cup minced crystallized ginger
    (available at specialty foods shops)*

*3 tablespoons fresh lemon juice
2 teaspoons grated lemon rind
½ teaspoon cinnamon
2 tablespoons unsalted butter*

egg wash made by beating 1 egg with 1 tablespoon water

Pinch off one fourth of the dough, reserving the remaining dough, covered and chilled. Roll the dough $^1/_{16}$ inch thick on a floured surface and cut it into holly leaf and berry shapes using the cutters. Transfer the cutouts to a baking sheet and chill them, covered.

Preheat the oven to 450° F.

Make the filling:
In a large ceramic or glass bowl toss the pears with the sugar, flour, crystallized ginger, lemon juice, lemon rind, and cinnamon.

On a floured surface roll out half the reserved dough $^1/_{16}$ inch thick. Drape the dough over the rolling pin, unroll it over the pie plate, and fit it into the plate (see illustrations page 121). Trim the dough to form a ½-inch overhang. Fill the shell with the pear filling, mounding it slightly in the center, and dot the filling with the butter. Roll out the remaining dough $^1/_{16}$ inch thick and drape it over the filling. Trim the top crust, leaving a ½-inch overhang, fold it under the bottom crust, and crimp the edges decoratively (see illustrations page 122). Make slits in the top crust for steam vents and brush the dough with the egg wash. Arrange the holly leaf and berry cutouts decoratively on the pie and brush them with the egg wash. Bake the pie on the baking sheet on the lowest rack of the oven for 15 minutes. Reduce the heat to 375° F. and bake the pie for 40 minutes, or until the crust is golden and the filling is bubbly. Transfer to a rack and serve still slightly warm or at room temperature.

Photo opposite.

Gingered Pear Pie (above),
Cranberry Swirl Ice Cream (page 350)

DRIED FRUIT PIE

Yield:
one 11-inch pie

Equipment:
11-inch pie plate
pastry brush
fluted pastry wheel

This recipe calls for both *pâte brisée* and quick puff paste. The *pâte brisée* is used for the bottom crust and the puff paste is cut into strips to form a lattice top as well as a circular border. If time does not permit making the puff paste, a *pâte brisée* top crust could certainly be substituted for the lattice crust (simply double the amount of *pâte brisée* called for).

1½ recipes pâte brisée *(page 164),*
substituting 1 tablespoon sugar for
the salt

1 recipe quick puff paste (page 201)
1 large egg, beaten
cinnamon sugar (page 541)

FOR THE FILLING
2 cups pitted ready-to-eat prunes
2 cups dried apricots
1 cup golden raisins
½ cup dried apples

¾ cup sugar
½ cup chopped blanched almonds or
chopped walnuts
1 stick (½ cup) unsalted butter, melted

¼ cup apricot glaze (page 540)
sweetened whipped cream flavored
with vanilla or brandy to taste as
an accompaniment if desired

Maple Walnut Ice Cream (page 355)
or Ginger Ice Cream (page 349),
softened, as an accompaniment if
desired

On a lightly floured surface roll the *pâte brisée* ⅛ inch thick. Drape the dough over the rolling pin, unroll it over the pie plate, and fit it into the pan (see illustrations page 121). Trim the edge flush with the plate, prick the bottom of the shell with a fork, and chill the shell for 1 hour.

On a lightly floured surface roll the puff paste into a rectangle, at least 11 inches long and $^{3}/_{16}$ inch thick. Brush the dough lightly with the egg and sprinkle it with cinnamon sugar. With the pastry wheel cut eight ⅓-inch-wide lengthwise strips from the dough.

Make the filling: In a large saucepan cover the prunes, apricots, raisins, and apples with water, bring the water to a boil, and simmer the fruit for 10 minutes. Drain the fruit in a colander and chop it coarse. In a bowl combine the fruit with the sugar, nuts, and butter.

Preheat the oven to 425° F.

Fill the shell with the fruit mixture, mounding it in the center, moisten the edge of the shell with the beaten egg, and arrange the puff paste strips lattice-fashion over the fruit, pressing the ends onto the edge of the shell (see illustrations page 122). Cut one or two ½-inch-wide bands of the remaining puff paste long enough to fit around the circumference of the shell, reserving the remaining dough for another use. Brush the edge of the shell with the beaten egg and secure the puff paste border to the rim, crimping it decoratively. Bake the pie in the bottom third of the oven for 30 minutes. Reduce the heat to 375° F. and bake the pie for 20 to 30 minutes, or until the pastry is golden. Brush the fruit through the lattice with glaze. Serve the pie with the whipped cream or ice cream if desired.

CRANBERRY MAPLE PEAR PIE

Yield:
one 9-inch pie

Equipment:
9-inch pie plate
fluted pastry wheel
cardboard template in
the shape of a maple
leaf, about 3 inches
long and 2½ inches
wide

1 recipe flaky pie pastry (page 123)
divided into 2 balls, one larger than
the other; the larger ball rolled ⅛
inch thick, transferred to pie plate,
and fitted in (see illustrations page
121)
3 cups (a 12-ounce bag) fresh or
frozen cranberries, picked over

1 cup maple syrup
1 pound pears, peeled, cored, and cut
into ¼-inch pieces
4½ teaspoons cornstarch dissolved in 2
tablespoons cold water

In a saucepan combine the cranberries, syrup, and pears, bring the mixture to a boil, and simmer it, stirring occasionally, for 3 to 4 minutes, or until the cranberries have popped. Stir the cornstarch mixture, stir it into the cranberry mixture, and simmer the mixture, stirring, for 1 minute, or until thickened. Transfer the mixture to a bowl and let it cool.

Trim off the excess dough from the sides of the pie shell, leaving a 1-inch overhang and reserving the scraps. Fold the overhang over the rim and crimp the edges decoratively (see illustrations page 122). Prick the bottom of the shell with a fork and chill the shell for 30 minutes. Wrap the reserved scraps in plastic and chill while cutting the dough for the lattice crust.

On a floured surface roll out the other ball of dough ⅛ inch thick and with the pastry wheel or a sharp knife cut out ½-inch strips of the dough. Transfer the strips to a baking sheet and chill them for 10 minutes, or until they are just firm enough to work with. (If the strips get too cold they will become brittle and break.)

The cranberry mixture may be made up to 1 day in advance and kept covered and chilled.

The pie may be made up to 1 day in advance and kept, covered loosely, in a cool, dry place. If making the pie 1 day in advance reheat it in a preheated 350° F. oven for 10 to 15 minutes to crisp the crust.

On the lightly floured surface roll out the reserved scraps ⅛ inch thick and freeze the dough on a small baking sheet for 5 minutes, or until firm. Using the template cut out 2 maple leaves from the dough with scissors or a sharp knife and chill them on a flat surface.

Preheat the oven to 425° F.

Spoon the filling into the shell, spreading it evenly, and arrange the lattice strips on top (see illustrations page 122), twisting each strip corkscrew fashion. Trim the ends of the strips flush with the overhang of the shell, pressing them onto the shell, turn up the overhanging dough, and crimp the edge decoratively. Score the pastry maple leaves decoratively with a knife, arrange them on the lattice, and bake the pie in the upper third of the oven for 40 to 45 minutes, or until the pastry is golden and the filling is bubbling. Let the pie cool on a rack.

Photo on page 118.

CHERRY PIE WITH ALMOND CRUST

Yield:
one 9-inch pie

Equipment:
9-inch pie plate
pastry wheel

FOR THE CRUST

1 cup all-purpose flour
¾ cup plain cake flour
2 tablespoons sugar
¼ teaspoon salt
¾ stick (6 tablespoons) cold unsalted
　butter, cut into bits
¼ cup cold vegetable shortening, cut
　into bits

½ cup finely ground blanched almonds
1 large egg
2 tablespoons heavy cream
½ teaspoon almond extract
½ teaspoon vanilla

FOR THE FILLING

1 quart fresh sour red cherries, pitted
　(If fresh cherries are not available,
　use two 2-pound cans sour red
　pitted cherries with ¼ cup of the
　juice.)

1 cup sugar
2 tablespoons cornstarch
½ teaspoon grated lemon rind
¼ teaspoon almond extract
⅛ teaspoon salt

1 egg white beaten with 2 teaspoons sugar until frothy

Make the crust: Into a bowl sift together the all-purpose flour, the cake flour, sugar, and the salt. Blend the butter and shortening into the dry ingredients with your fingertips or two knives until the mixture resembles meal (see illustrations page 121). Mix in the almonds.

In a small bowl beat together the egg, the heavy cream, almond extract, and vanilla. Add just enough of the egg mixture to the dry ingredients to form a dough, toss it with a fork until it is incorporated, and form the dough into a ball. Wrap the dough in wax paper and chill it for at least 1 hour.

Cut off slightly more than half of the ball of dough and roll it into a round about 12 inches in diameter on a lightly floured surface. Lift the dough over the rolling pin and transfer it to the pie plate (see illustrations page 121), draping the excess dough loosely over the sides. Let the dough set for 10 minutes. Press the dough firmly into the plate and trim the excess, leaving a 1-inch overhang. Brush the shell with the egg mixture and reserve what remains. Chill the shell and the remaining dough for 30 minutes.

Make the filling: In a large bowl combine the cherries with the sugar, cornstarch, lemon rind, almond extract, and the salt. Let stand for 30 minutes. Drain the mixture into a bowl, measure the juices, and add water if needed to measure ¼ cup. Toss the filling lightly and pour it into the shell.

Preheat the oven to 425° F.

On a lightly floured surface roll out the remaining dough into a rectangle 10 inches long and ⅛ inch thick. With the pastry wheel or a large sharp knife cut out ten 10-inch strips about ⅓ inch wide. Moisten the rim of the shell with water and firmly press on the strips in a lattice pattern (see illustrations page 122). Crimp the overhanging dough into a decorative rim (see illustrations page 122). Brush the strips with the reserved egg mixture. Bake the pie in the lower third of the oven for 20 minutes. Reduce the heat to 375° F. and bake the pie for 30 minutes more, or until lightly browned. Transfer the pie to a rack and let it cool slightly.

MADEIRA MINCEMEAT PIE WITH CHEDDAR CRUST

Yield:
double-crust
  9-inch pie

Equipment:
9-inch pie plate
pastry brush

After making this recipe two cups Madeira mincemeat will remain. It can be used as the filling for Applejack Baked Apples (page 471).

2 recipes Cheddar dough (page 125), divided into 2 balls, one slightly larger than the other
egg wash made by beating 1 large egg with pinch of salt

1 recipe Madeira mincemeat (page 548)
sweetened whipped cream or Vanilla Ice Cream (page 349) as an accompaniment if desired

Preheat the oven to 425° F.

On a lightly floured surface roll out the smaller round of dough ⅛ inch thick, drape it over the rolling pin, and fit it into the pie plate (see illustrations page 121). Trim the edge to form a 1-inch overhang. Brush the bottom of the pie shell with some of the egg wash, reserving the excess. Fill the shell with the Madeira mincemeat.

Roll out the remaining ball of dough into a 10-inch round on the lightly floured surface and drape it over the filling. Trim the top crust, leaving a 1-inch overhang, fold it under the bottom crust, and crimp the edges decoratively (see illustrations page 122). Make slits in the top crust for steam vents and brush the dough with the remaining egg wash.

Bake the pie in the middle of the oven for 15 minutes. Reduce the oven temperature to 350° F. and bake the pie for 30 to 40 minutes, or until golden brown. Transfer the pie to a rack and let cool slightly. Serve warm with the whipped cream or ice cream as an accompaniment if desired.

STREUSEL PEACH PIE

Yield:
one 11-inch pie

Equipment:
11-inch pie plate, 1½ inches deep
pastry brush

1 recipe pâte brisée *(page 164), rolled ⅛ inch thick, transferred to pie plate, and fitted in (see illustrations page 121)*

FOR THE STREUSEL
⅔ cup firmly packed light brown sugar
3 tablespoons all-purpose flour

3 pounds peaches, peeled (for procedure page 548), pitted, and sliced

raw rice or dried beans for weighting the shell
1 egg white, beaten lightly

1 teaspoon cinnamon
½ stick (¼ cup) cold unsalted butter, cut into bits

1 tablespoon fresh lemon juice

Trim the edge of the dough to leave a ½-inch overhang. Crimp the edge of the shell decoratively (see illustrations page 122). Prick the bottom of the shell with a fork and chill for 30 minutes.

Preheat the oven to 425° F.

Line, weight, and blind-bake the shell (see illustrations page 163) in the lower third of the oven for 15 minutes. Carefully remove the rice and paper and bake the shell for 15 minutes. Brush the bottom and sides with the egg white and bake the shell for 5 minutes more, or until golden. Transfer the shell to a rack and let cool.

Make the streusel: In a small bowl combine the brown sugar, flour, and the cinnamon. Blend in the butter until the mixture resembles coarse meal. Sprinkle one third of the streusel into the bottom of the shell. Arrange half the peach slices, overlapping them slightly, in concentric circles over the streusel. Sprinkle the slices with half the remaining streusel and drizzle with some of the lemon juice. Top the streusel with the remaining slices, arranging them in the same manner, drizzle the slices with the remaining lemon juice, and sprinkle the remaining streusel over them.

Reduce the oven temperature to 375° F. Bake the pie in the middle of the oven for 45 to 55 minutes, or until the filling is bubbling and the peaches are tender. Transfer the pie to a rack to cool. Serve the pie at room temperature.

Photo opposite.

Streusel Peach Pie (above)

INDIVIDUAL CRANBERRY APPLE DEEP-DISH PIES

Yield:
twelve 1-cup
  individual pies

Equipment:
twelve 1-cup soufflé
  cups or ramekins

Individual deep-dish pies are a wonderful idea and can be frozen with such excellent results that they should be prepared to take advantage of seasonal fruits such as peaches and plums. These extremely homey desserts can be dressed up with pastry cutouts for a slightly fancier presentation.

1 recipe flaky pie pastry (page 123)

FOR THE FILLING
3 large eggs
2 cups sugar, or to taste
6 tablespoons all-purpose flour
18 ounces (1½ packages) cranberries (fresh or frozen), picked over and chopped coarse
2 pounds apples (about 5 medium-large), peeled, cored, and chopped coarse

½ cup coarsely chopped walnuts
½ cup raisins
¼ cup fresh orange juice
1 teaspoon grated orange rind

Make the filling:

Preheat the oven to 450° F.

In a bowl beat the eggs with the sugar until blended well. Gradually add the flour by tablespoons and beat well. Add the cranberries, apples, walnuts, raisins, orange juice, and the rind and toss gently. Divide the filling among the individual cups.

On a lightly floured board roll out the dough in a rectangle ⅛ inch thick. Cut out 12 rounds ⅓ inch larger than the soufflé cups. Put a pastry round on top of each cup and, pressing with the tines of a fork, seal the pastry to the rim of the cup.

Place the cups on a baking sheet and bake the pies in the middle of the oven for 15 minutes. Reduce the temperature to 400° F. and bake the pies for 10 minutes more, or until the crusts are golden. Serve warm or cool.

DEEP-DISH BLUEBERRY PEACH PIE

Yield:
one 2-quart
  deep-dish pie

Equipment:
2-quart round baking
  dish
pastry brush

1 recipe pâte brisée (page 164) or sour cream pastry (page 124)
2 pounds peaches, peeled (for procedure page 548), pitted, and sliced
1 pint blueberries, picked over
1 cup sugar
3 tablespoons quick-cooking tapioca

2 tablespoons fresh lemon juice
2 tablespoons unsalted butter, cut into bits
1½ teaspoons grated lemon rind
½ teaspoon cinnamon
egg wash made by beating 1 egg with 1 teaspoon water and pinch of salt

Butter the baking dish and preheat the oven to 375° F.

In a large bowl toss the peaches and the blueberries with the sugar, tapioca, lemon juice, butter, lemon rind, and the cinnamon.

On a lightly floured surface roll out the dough ⅛ inch thick. Spread the blueberry peach filling in the prepared dish. Drape the dough over the rolling pin, unroll it over the dish, and fit the dough over the dish. Crimp the edges decoratively (see illustrations page 122). Brush the top of the pie with the egg wash and cut slits in the top for steam vents. Bake the pie in the middle of the oven for 1 hour, or until the filling is bubbling and the top is golden. Serve the pie warm.

CAJUN SWEET DOUGH PIES

Fig Turnovers

Yield:
about 30 turnovers

Equipment:
hand-held electric mixer
4-inch round cutter
pastry brush

Cajun cooking with its French roots (via Nova Scotia) is the cooking of Louisiana. The people of Louisiana used local ingredients to develop and perfect their cuisine. Figs are common in Louisiana, where backyard fig trees are almost taken for granted and recipes for fresh figs or fig preserves abound. This recipe includes dried figs and spices for a luscious filling. You will notice that the procedure for rolling out the pastry is unusual; the dough is divided into small pieces that are prepared individually. We do not recommend taking any shortcuts with the dough. Be advised, too, that the figs must soak overnight.

FOR THE PASTRY

1½ sticks (¾ cup) unsalted butter, softened
1⅓ cups sugar
1 teaspoon vanilla
1 large egg

4⅔ cups all-purpose flour sifted with 2 teaspoons double-acting baking powder and 1 teaspoon salt
½ cup milk

FOR THE FILLING

1 pound dried figs, stemmed and chopped fine (preferably in a food processor)
2½ cups water
1 cup sugar

¼ teaspoon freshly grated nutmeg
¼ teaspoon ground allspice
1 tablespoon fresh lemon juice, or to taste

egg wash made by beating 1 egg with 1 tablespoon water

Make the pastry:
In a large bowl with the mixer cream the butter, beat in the sugar, a little at a time, and the vanilla, and beat the mixture until fluffy. Beat in the egg. Stir in the flour mixture in batches alternately with the milk. Chill the dough, dusted well with flour and wrapped in wax paper, for at least 1 hour or overnight.

Make the filling: In a heavy saucepan let the figs soak in the water overnight. Add the sugar, nutmeg, and the allspice, bring the mixture to a boil, stirring, and boil it, stirring frequently, for 20 minutes, or until thickened. Stir in the lemon juice, transfer the filling to a bowl, and let cool.

Butter baking sheets and preheat the oven to 375° F.

Cut the dough into 16 pieces. Working with one piece at a time and keeping the remaining pieces covered and chilled, roll out the piece ⅛ inch thick on a very well floured surface. With the cutter cut out one round from each piece, brush off any excess flour, and brush the round with the egg wash. Put 1 level tablespoon of the filling on the lower half of each round and fold over the top half to enclose it. Pinch the edges together to seal them, crimp them decoratively, and arrange the turnover on the baking sheet. Make turnovers with the remaining pieces of dough and filling in the same manner. Gather the scraps, chill the dough, and make more turnovers with the dough and the remaining filling. Bake the turnovers in the middle of the oven for 15 minutes, or until they are golden brown around the edges. Transfer to racks and let cool.

Photo on page 460.

APPLE CHEDDAR TURNOVERS

Yield:
12 turnovers

Equipment:
parchment paper
pastry brush

The pairing of a slice of apple pie with a wedge of Cheddar has become an American classic. The following recipe carries this combination to new heights with its use of a Cheddar turnover dough and spicy apple filling. Of course, there is no reason why an apple Cheddar turnover could not be accompanied by still another wedge of Cheddar!

1 recipe Cheddar dough (page 125)

FOR THE FILLING

¾ stick (6 tablespoons) unsalted butter
2 Golden Delicious apples, peeled, cored, and chopped
¼ cup firmly packed light brown sugar

2 tablespoons cider vinegar
1½ teaspoons quick-cooking tapioca
¼ teaspoon cinnamon
⅓ cup chopped walnuts

egg wash made by beating 1 egg with pinch of salt

Make the filling: Line a baking sheet with the parchment paper.

In a stainless steel skillet melt 2 tablespoons of the butter over moderately low heat, add the apples, sugar, vinegar, tapioca, and the cinnamon and bring the mixture to a boil, stirring. Simmer the mixture, covered, for 8 minutes, or until the apples are tender, transfer it to a bowl, and let cool.

Stir in the walnuts and chill the mixture, covered, for at least 1 hour or overnight.

On a floured surface roll out the dough ⅛ inch thick and cut it into 4-inch squares. Invert the squares onto a work surface, brush them with the egg wash, and put a rounded tablespoon of the apple mixture in the center of each square. Dot the apple mixture on each square with 1 teaspoon of the remaining butter, fold the squares in half diagonally to form triangles, and crimp the edges together with the tines of a fork. Transfer the turnovers to the baking sheet. Gather the scraps, reroll the dough, and make turnovers in the same manner with the remaining dough, apple mixture, and butter. Brush the tops of the turnovers with the remaining egg wash and cut 2 steam vents in each turnover. Chill the turnovers for 30 minutes.

Preheat the oven to 400° F.

Bake the turnovers in the middle of the oven for 15 to 20 minutes, or until golden. Let cool on racks.

CUSTARD AND CREAM PIES

Custard and cream pies, while basically composed of the same ingredients, use different cooking methods in combining them. The custard mixture bakes in the oven while the cream filling is cooked on top of the stove, thickened with cornstarch, and is poured into a prebaked shell. One exception is our recipe for Coconut Custard Pie (page 147). There, the custard and shell are cooked separately and the "slipped custard" method is employed to assemble the two.

A custard filling should be set but still slightly quivery when removed from the oven as it will continue baking while cooling. You want to be careful not to overbake or bake a custard filling at too high a temperature, as it will become too firm and dense. So check your oven with an oven thermometer if you suspect that your oven temperature may not be accurate.

Cream fillings must be stirred constantly while cooking over moderate heat. This will prevent undesirable lumps from forming and reduce the risk of scorching the cream. Like the custard filling, the cream filling will set up while chilling in the prepared pie shell.

Custard pies, though simple and often unassuming in appearance, are truly beloved. As the recipes included in our custard section indicate, these are the pies that have been embraced by Americans as part of their holiday feasts or family celebrations. What Thanksgiving dinner is considered complete without a pumpkin pie? And coconut custard has always been and remains a favorite at family gatherings.

Whether or not they admit it, almost everyone loves cream pies. Rich but not too rich, sweet but not too sweet, a creamy vanilla-flavored filling is poured into a flaky shell and the combination is superb. Even better when a layer of banana slices is added or when the filling is chocolate or butterscotch flavored and served in a crumb crust. We have included recipes for all of them.

PUMPKIN PIE

Yield:
one 11-inch pie

Equipment:
11-inch pie plate

1½ recipes pâte brisée (page 164), substituting 1½ teaspoons sugar for the salt; rolled ⅛ inch thick, transferred to pie plate, and fitted in (see illustrations page 121)

raw rice or dried beans for weighting the shell

FOR THE FILLING

¾ cup firmly packed dark brown sugar
¼ cup granulated sugar
1 tablespoon all-purpose flour
1 tablespoon unsulfured molasses
1½ teaspoons cinnamon
1 teaspoon ground ginger
¼ teaspoon freshly grated nutmeg

¼ teaspoon ground cloves
¼ teaspoon salt
2 cups canned pumpkin purée
3 large eggs, beaten lightly
1¾ cups light cream
2 tablespoons brandy

sweetened whipped cream flavored with vanilla or brandy as an accompaniment if desired

Trim off the excess dough from the sides of the pie shell, leaving a 1-inch overhang, fold the overhang over the rim, pressing it onto the sides of the shell, and crimp the edges decoratively (see illustrations page 122). Prick the bottom of the shell with a fork and chill the shell for 1 hour.

Preheat the oven to 400° F.

Line, weight, and blind-bake the shell (see illustrations page 163) in the middle of the oven for 10 minutes. Carefully remove the rice and paper and bake the shell for 10 to 15 minutes more, or until lightly colored. Let cool on a rack.

Reduce the oven temperature to 375° F.

Make the filling: In a bowl combine the brown sugar, granulated sugar, flour, molasses, cinnamon, ginger, nutmeg, cloves, and salt and stir in the pumpkin purée. In another bowl combine the eggs, light cream, and brandy and fold the mixture into the pumpkin mixture. Pour the filling into the shell.

Bake the pie in the middle of the oven for 35 to 40 minutes, or until the filling is set, and let it cool on a rack. Serve the pie with the whipped cream if desired.

PECAN PUMPKIN PIE

Yield:
one 9-inch pie

½ recipe flaky pie pastry (page 123)

Equipment:
9-inch pie plate

FOR THE PUMPKIN LAYER
¾ cup canned pumpkin purée   *2 tablespoons sour cream*
2 tablespoons firmly packed light   *⅛ teaspoon cinnamon*
  brown sugar   *⅛ teaspoon freshly grated nutmeg*
1 large egg, beaten lightly

FOR THE PECAN LAYER
¾ cup light corn syrup   *2 teaspoons vanilla*
½ cup firmly packed light brown   *¼ teaspoon freshly grated lemon rind*
  sugar   *1½ teaspoons fresh lemon juice*
3 large eggs, beaten lightly   *¼ teaspoon salt*
3 tablespoons unsalted butter, melted   *1⅓ cups pecans*
  and cooled

Preheat the oven to 425° F.

On a lightly floured surface roll out the dough ⅛ inch thick. Drape the dough over the rolling pin, unroll it over the plate, and fit it into the plate (see illustrations page 121). Trim the edge to form a ½-inch overhang. Crimp the edges decoratively (see illustrations page 122). Chill the shell while making the filling layers.

Make the pumpkin layer:

In a small bowl whisk together the pumpkin purée, brown sugar, egg, sour cream, cinnamon, and the nutmeg until the mixture is smooth.

Make the pecan layer:

In a small bowl combine well the corn syrup, brown sugar, eggs, butter, vanilla, rind, lemon juice, and the salt and stir in the pecans.

The pie may be made 1 day in advance and kept, covered loosely and chilled. If making the pie in advance, reheat it in a preheated 350° F. oven for 10 to 15 minutes, or until the crust is crisp.

Spread the pumpkin mixture evenly in the chilled pie shell and carefully spoon the pecan mixture over it. Bake the pie in the upper third of the oven for 20 minutes, reduce the heat to 350° F., and bake the pie for 20 to 30 minutes more, or until the filling is puffed slightly. (The center will appear to be not quite set.) Let the pie cool on a rack.

Photo on page 118.

PENNSYLVANIA DUTCH SHOOFLY PIE

Molasses Pie

Yield:
one 9-inch pie

Equipment:
9-inch pie plate

Shoofly pie is a Pennsylvania Dutch specialty. There are several explanations for its name. Some think it is so called because you have to "shoo away the flies" from the sweet molasses and brown sugar pie. Others say the pie was originally made to actually distract the flies from other foods! Shoofly pie can be made "wet" or "dry." Wet describes the state of the molasses filling as being a layer in and of itself at the bottom of the pie, and dry when the crumb layers are interspersed among the molasses layers. The following recipe combines the best of both.

*1 recipe pâte brisée (page 164),
   rolled ⅛ inch thick, transferred to
   pie plate, and fitted in (see
   illustrations page 121)
½ cup unsulfured molasses
½ cup dark corn syrup
¾ teaspoon baking soda*

*1 cup boiling water
1 large egg, beaten lightly
½ cup firmly packed light brown
   sugar
1 tablespoon cold lard
1 tablespoon cold unsalted butter
1 cup sifted unbleached flour*

Preheat the oven to 400° F.

Trim the edge of the dough leaving a 1-inch overhang. Fold the overhang up over the rim and crimp the edge decoratively (see illustrations page 122).

In a bowl combine the molasses, corn syrup, baking soda, and the boiling water. In another bowl whisk together the egg and ½ cup of the molasses mixture and whisk the egg mixture into the remaining molasses mixture. In another bowl blend together the sugar, lard, butter, and the flour until the mixture is fine and crumbly, stir 1 cup of the mixture into the molasses mixture, and pour the filling into the shell. Scatter the remaining flour mixture over the pie and bake the pie in the middle of the oven for 25 to 30 minutes, or until it is puffed and browned lightly. Let the pie cool on a rack.

MAPLE LEMON PIE

Yield:
one 8-inch pie

Equipment:
8-inch pie plate
pastry brush
9-inch fluted ring
baking sheet

The top crust of this pie is cut into a flower-like shape with the aid of a fluted flan ring. Although the forming of the top crust takes a little extra time, the extremely attractive and unique result is worth the effort. This makes an especially good holiday dessert.

1 recipe lard pastry dough (page 123),
half the dough rolled ⅛ inch thick,
transferred to pie plate, and fitted
in (see illustrations page 121)
3 lemons
½ cup sugar
⅓ cup maple syrup

egg wash made by beating 1 egg with
pinch of salt
3 large eggs
1 egg yolk
½ teaspoon vanilla
¼ teaspoon cinnamon

Grate the rind from the lemons, trim away the white pith, and cut the lemons crosswise into thin slices, seeding them. In a ceramic bowl layer the lemons with the sugar, maple syrup, and the lemon rind and chill the mixture, covered, for at least 2 hours or overnight.

Trim the edge of the dough flush with the edge of the plate. Brush the bottom of the shell with some of the egg wash, prick it with a fork, and let the shell stand for 5 minutes. In a bowl beat the whole eggs with the egg yolk, vanilla, and the cinnamon until the mixture is just combined. Fill the shell with the sliced lemon mixture and spoon the egg mixture over it.

Roll out the remaining dough ⅛ inch thick on a floured surface and, using the fluted ring as a guide, cut it into a decorative shape. Brush the edge of the bottom shell with some of the egg wash and arrange the top crust over the filling, pressing the dough gently to seal it to the edge of the bottom crust. (The top crust will extend about 1 inch over the edges of the pie plate.) Cut out 3 leaf shapes from the dough trimmings (see illustration), brush them with some of the egg wash, and arrange them decoratively on the crust. Brush the top of the pie with the remaining egg wash, make slits near the leaves for steam vents, and bake the pie on a baking sheet in the upper third of the oven for 15 minutes. Reduce the oven temperature to 400° F., bake the pie for 20 to 25 minutes more, or until a cake tester inserted in the center comes out clean and the pastry is golden. Let cool on a rack.

Photo on page 146.

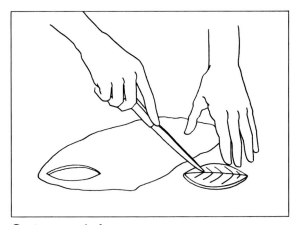

Cutting pastry leaf cutouts

COCONUT CUSTARD PIE

Yield:
one 9-inch pie

Equipment:
two 9-inch non-stick
  pie plates
food processor fitted
  with steel blade
cheesecloth
larger pan for
  waterbath

The custard and shell in this recipe are cooked separately to prevent the shell from becoming soggy—an unfortunate but not uncommon occurrence when the two are baked together. After cooling, the custard is simply slipped from the pie plate into the shell (explaining the name of this technique, "slipped custard"), and the pie can then sit at room temperature for several hours, or it can be chilled.

If you substitute sweetened flaked coconut for the fresh coconut, be sure to eliminate or reduce the sugar measurement in the custard.

½ recipe flaky pie pastry (page 123), rolled ⅛ inch thick, transferred to pie plate, and fitted in (see illustrations page 121)

raw rice or dried beans for weighting the shell

FOR THE FILLING

2½ cups half-and-half

3 cups grated fresh coconut (for procedure page 549), or sweetened flaked coconut

4 large eggs

½ cup sugar

2 teaspoons vanilla

pinch of salt

lightly whipped cream for garnish if desired

½ cup grated coconut, toasted, for garnish if desired

Trim the edge of the shell, leaving a ½-inch overhang. Crimp the edge of the shell decoratively (see illustrations page 121). Prick the dough with a fork and chill it for 30 minutes.

Preheat the oven to 400° F.

Line, weight, and blind-bake the shell (see illustrations page 163) in the lower third of the oven for 15 minutes. Remove the wax paper and rice. Reduce the oven temperature to 375° F. and bake the shell for 10 minutes more, or until golden. Transfer the shell to a rack and let it cool.

Reduce the oven temperature to 350° F. and butter the second pie plate.

Make the filling:

In a saucepan bring the half-and-half to a simmer, stir in 2 cups of the fresh coconut, and let the mixture stand for 20 minutes, or until it is room temperature. Transfer the coconut milk to the food processor and blend it for 1 minute. Strain the mixture through a sieve lined with the cheesecloth, squeezing the cheesecloth to extract all of the liquid, and add the eggs, sugar, vanilla, and salt. Stir in the remaining 1 cup coconut and pour the custard into the pie plate. Put the pie plate in the larger pan, add enough hot water to the pan to come halfway up the sides of the plate, and bake in the middle of the oven for for 30 to 35 minutes, or until the edges of the custard are set. (The center of the custard will still be a bit loose but will

Maple Lemon Pie (page 144), Apple Cream (page 107), Raisin Gingerbread (page 107)

set as it cools in the pan.) Transfer the pie plate to a rack and let it cool to room temperature. Using a plastic or rubber spatula, gently slide the custard into the shell and garnish the top of the pie with the whipped cream and toasted coconut, if desired.

KEY LIME PIE

Yield:
one 9-inch pie

Equipment:
9-inch pie plate
hand-held electric
    mixer

Key limes are indigenous to the Florida Keys and to parts of the Caribbean. If you are not fortunate enough to be able to obtain Key limes in Florida or from a particularly good specialty produce market, bottled Key lime juice may be substituted, or a combination of freshly squeezed lemon juice and Tahiti or Persian lime juice. Key lime pies can also be made with graham cracker crusts and may be topped with either sweetened whipped cream or meringue.

1 recipe pâte brisée *(page 164), rolled into an 11-inch round ⅛ inch thick, transferred to pie plate, and fitted in (see illustrations page 121)*

raw rice or dried beans for weighting the shell

FOR THE FILLING
3 egg yolks
½ cup freshly squeezed or bottled Key lime juice (see Shopping Sources page 555)
1 teaspoon grated lime rind

one 15-ounce can sweetened condensed milk
drop or two of green food coloring if desired

1 cup well-chilled heavy cream

3 tablespoons confectioners' sugar

Press the dough firmly into the pan, leaving a ½-inch overhang, and crimp the edges decoratively (see illustrations page 122). Prick the bottom of the shell with a fork and chill the shell for 30 minutes.

Preheat the oven to 400° F.

Line, weight, and blind-bake the shell (see illustrations page 163) in the lower third of the oven for 10 minutes. Remove the rice and paper and bake the shell for 10 to 15 minutes more, or until lightly colored. Transfer the shell to a rack and let it cool.

Make the filling: In a bowl with the mixer beat the egg yolks until light and lemon colored and add the lime juice and lime rind. Beat in the condensed milk and enough of the food coloring to attain a natural lime tint if desired. Pour the custard into the baked pie shell.

Reduce the oven temperature to 350° F.

Bake the pie in the middle of the oven for about 15 minutes, Transfer the pie to a rack and let it cool completely.

In a well-chilled bowl with the mixer beat the heavy cream until it holds soft peaks. Sift the confectioners' sugar over it and continue to beat the cream until it holds almost stiff peaks.

Spread the whipped cream with a metal spatula over the cooled pie filling, making decorative peaks. Serve the pie well chilled.

Variation:

KEY LIME PIE WITH MERINGUE TOPPING: Beat 4 egg whites until stiff but not dry and gradually beat in ½ cup superfine granulated sugar and 1 teaspoon lime juice. Spread the meringue generously over the filling, swirling it into irregular decorative peaks. Bake in a preheated 350° F. oven for about 15 minutes, or until the meringue is lightly browned.

LEMON CHESS PIE

Yield:
one 9-inch pie

Equipment:
9-inch pie plate

Of English origin, this pie, much loved in the South, contains cornmeal, rendering a subtle but sweet flavor. A perfect accompaniment to chicory coffee.

½ recipe lard pastry dough (page 123), rolled ⅛ inch thick, transferred to pie plate, and fitted in (see illustrations page 121)

FOR THE FILLING

4 large eggs, beaten lightly
8 tablespoons clarified butter (page 536)
1⅓ cups superfine granulated sugar

4 tablespoons fresh lemon juice
4 teaspoons yellow cornmeal
4 teaspoons grated lemon rind

Trim the dough, leaving a 1-inch overhang. Fold the overhang over the rim, pressing it onto the sides of the shell, and form a decorative edge (see illustrations page 122). Chill the shell for 1 hour.

Preheat the oven to 450° F.

Make the filling:

In a bowl combine the eggs, clarified butter, sugar, lemon juice, cornmeal, and the lemon rind and stir the mixture until it is blended. Pour the mixture in the prepared shell.

Bake the pie in the lower third of the oven for 15 minutes, reduce the oven temperature to 375° F., and bake the pie for 20 to 25 minutes more, or until the filling is set. Transfer the pie to a rack and let it cool.

VANILLA CREAM PIE

Yield:
one 9-inch pie

Equipment:
9-inch pie plate

The title of this recipe is a slight misnomer as the filling contains no cream. However, the consistency of the cornstarch-thickened filling is smooth and creamy enough to merit the name. For an even richer filling increase the amount of butter to six tablespoons.

½ recipe flaky pie pastry (page 123), rolled ⅛ inch thick, transferred to pie plate, and fitted in (see illustrations page 121)

raw rice or dried beans for weighting the shell

FOR THE FILLING
¾ cup sugar
⅓ cup cornstarch
¼ teaspoon salt
2¾ cups milk

4 egg yolks, beaten lightly
3 tablespoons unsalted butter
2½ teaspoons vanilla

Trim the dough, leaving a ½-inch overhang. Crimp the edge of the shell decoratively (see illustrations page 122). Prick the bottom of the shell with a fork and chill the shell for 30 minutes.

Preheat the oven to 400° F.

Line, weight, and blind-bake the shell (see illustrations page 163) in the lower third of the oven for 15 minutes. Carefully remove the rice and paper. Reduce the oven temperature to 375° F. and bake the shell for 10 minutes or until golden. Transfer the shell to a rack and let it cool.

Make the filling:

In saucepan but off the heat whisk together the sugar, cornstarch, and salt. Add the milk in a very slow stream, whisking constantly, whisk in the egg yolks gradually, and combine the filling well. Cook the filling over moderate heat, whisking constantly, until it reaches a full boil. Reduce the heat to low and, continuing to stir constantly, cook for 4 minutes. Remove the pan from the heat and stir in the butter and vanilla. Transfer the mixture to a bowl and cover the surface of the filling directly with a large round of buttered plastic wrap or wax paper to prevent a skin from forming. Let the filling cool to room temperature.

Pour the filling into the cooled pie shell and refrigerate the pie until completely set.

Variations:

CHOCOLATE CREAM PIE: Melt 3 ounces unsweetened chocolate and let cool. Add the melted chocolate to the milk and combine thoroughly. Proceed with the recipe as directed and pour the chocolate filling into a baked cooled Graham Cracker Crust (page 125). For a Double Chocolate Cream Pie replace the Graham Cracker Crust with a baked cooled Chocolate Wafer Crumb Crust (page 126).

BANANA CREAM PIE: Peel 3 bananas and cut them into ¼-inch slices. Arrange the slices in the bottom of the baked cooled pie shell and cover them with the cooled vanilla cream filling.

BUTTERSCOTCH CREAM PIE: Substitute 1 cup firmly packed dark brown sugar for the sugar, being careful to break up any lumps when combining it with the cornstarch and the salt. Reduce the amount of vanilla to 2 teaspoons. Proceed as directed above and pour the cooled filling into a baked cooled Graham Cracker Crust (page 125).

HAZELNUT PRALINE CREAM PIE: Reduce the amount of sugar to ½ cup and substitute 2½ teaspoons Frangelico (hazelnut liqueur), or to taste, for the vanilla. When incorporating the butter and Frangelico, fold in ½ cup finely ground hazelnut praline (page 544). Let the filling cool and pour it into a baked cooled Nut Crust (page 126) made with hazelnuts.

CHIFFON AND MERINGUE PIES

As chiffon is a fabric characterized by its gossamer, light nature, so its namesake shares those same ethereal qualities. Chiffon pies have a delicate texture, a sheerness achieved by the addition of whipped egg whites or heavy cream to the filling. Gelatin is often added, providing support for the airy structure.

The fillings are enhanced by slightly crunchy nut or crumb crusts, which also have the advantage of absorbing moisture less quickly from the fillings. Our Pumpkin Chiffon Pie (page 153) is the perfect solution when a traditional spicy and seasonal Thanksgiving dessert is required but an airier, less heavy one is desired. Likewise, Eggnog Pie with Pecan Crust (page 152) is a wonderful and authentic holiday dessert but lighter than the norm.

Meringue pies are also ethereal, but in a different way. They are topped with a tender egg white and sugar combination, stiffly beaten and lightly browned, or are made with a baked meringue shell, crisp but tender. Two dependable methods of making meringue are presented here, each ensuring wonderful results. Not only do we include recipes for the much loved lemon meringue and chocolate rum meringue or "angel" pies, but we offer Cranberry Meringue Pie (page 154), exquisite not only in its combination of flavors but also in its appearance. This pie is guaranteed to become a Christmas favorite.

EGGNOG PIE WITH PECAN CRUST

Yield:
one 9½-inch pie

Equipment:
9½-inch pie plate
hand-held electric
  mixer
pastry bag fitted with
  decorative tip

This glorious chiffon pie is flavored with both brandy and rum, resulting in a rich egg custard filling that is then lightened with whipped heavy cream and beaten egg whites. The pie has a pecan crust and is garnished with both rum-flavored whipped cream and chocolate curls. To make the eggnog flavoring even more authentic, dust the pie with nutmeg.

1 prebaked Nut Crust (page 126), made with 2½ cups ground pecans and an
    additional tablespoon unsalted butter

FOR THE FILLING

1½ tablespoons unflavored gelatin
3 tablespoons brandy
4 large eggs, separated, at room
    temperature
⅓ cup granulated sugar
1⅓ cups milk, scalded

¼ cup dark rum
1½ teaspoons vanilla
pinch of salt
¾ cup well-chilled heavy cream,
    lightly whipped

FOR THE TOPPING

1 cup well-chilled heavy cream
2 to 3 tablespoons sifted confectioners'
    sugar

1 to 2 tablespoons dark rum, or to
    taste

chocolate curls (page 545) for garnish

Make the filling:

In a small bowl sprinkle the gelatin over the brandy to soften for 10 minutes. In a bowl with the mixer beat the egg yolks with the sugar until the mixture falls in a ribbon when the beater is lifted (see illustration page 16). Add the scalded milk in a stream, stirring. Pour the mixture into a heavy saucepan and cook it over moderately low heat, stirring, with a wooden spoon, until it is thick enough to coat the spoon, but do not let it boil. Remove the pan from the heat and add the softened gelatin, rum, and vanilla, stirring until the gelatin is dissolved. Transfer the custard to a bowl set over a larger bowl of ice and cold water and let it cool, stirring occasionally, but do not let it set.

In a large bowl with the mixer beat the egg whites with the salt until they hold stiff peaks. Fold in the whipped heavy cream and the custard gently but thoroughly.

Pour enough of the filling into the prepared shell to fill the shell to the top and chill the pie for 20 minutes, or until the filling is set. Transfer the remaining filling to the shell, mounding it over the top, and chill the pie for 20 minutes more, or until set.

Make the topping:

In a chilled bowl with the mixer beat the heavy cream with the confectioners' sugar and the rum until it holds soft peaks.

Spread the whipped cream over the pie, mounding it slightly and reserving a small amount for garnish. With the pastry bag pipe the reserved whipped cream decoratively around the edge of the pie and decorate the center and sides with the chocolate curls. Sprinkle bits of broken chocolate curls over the whipped cream and chill the pie. Remove the pie from the refrigerator at least 30 minutes before serving.

PUMPKIN CHIFFON PIE

Yield:
one 9½-inch pie

Equipment:
9½-inch pie plate
hand-held electric
  mixer
pastry bag fitted with
  decorative tip

1 recipe pâte brisée (page 164), substituting 2 teaspoons sugar for the salt; rolled ⅛ inch thick, transferred to pie plate, and fitted in (see illustrations page 121)

raw rice or dried beans for weighting the shell

FOR THE FILLING

1 cup firmly packed dark brown sugar
5 large eggs, separated, at room temperature
1 teaspoon cinnamon
½ teaspoon freshly grated nutmeg
¼ teaspoon ground ginger

⅛ teaspoon ground allspice
2 cups canned pumpkin purée
½ cup heavy cream
5 tablespoons unsalted butter, melted
pinch of salt
¼ cup granulated sugar

sweetened whipped cream flavored with dark rum for garnish

12 Candied Pecan Halves (page 524) for garnish

Trim the excess dough from the sides of the shell, leaving a 1-inch overhang, fold the overhang over the rim, pressing it onto the sides of the shell, and crimp the edges decoratively (see illustrations page 122). Prick the bottom of the shell with a fork and chill the shell for 1 hour.

Preheat the oven to 400° F.

Line, weight, and blind-bake the shell (see illustrations page 163) in the middle of the oven for 10 minutes. Carefully remove the rice and paper and bake the shell for 10 to 15 minutes more, or until lightly colored. Let cool on a rack.

Reduce the oven temperature to 375° F.

Make the filling: In a bowl combine well the brown sugar, egg yolks, cinnamon, nutmeg, ginger, and allspice. In a large bowl combine the pumpkin purée, heavy cream, and butter, add the sugar mixture, and mix well. In another large bowl with the mixer beat the egg whites with the salt until they hold soft peaks. Sprinkle in the granulated sugar, one tablespoon at a time, beating, and continue to beat the whites until they hold stiff peaks. Fold the whites into the pumpkin mixture gently but thoroughly. Pour the filling into the shell.

Bake the pie in the middle of the oven for 40 to 45 minutes, or until the filling is puffed and set. Let cool on a rack. With the pastry bag garnish the pie with a border of whipped cream rosettes separated by candied pecan halves. (For detailed instructions on working with a pastry bag and piping rosettes, see pages 19 and 20.) Sprinkle 4 candied pecan halves, chopped, in the center of the pie and top them with a candied pecan half.

APRICOT CHIFFON PIE WITH GINGERSNAP CRUST

Yield:
one 9-inch pie

Equipment:
9-inch pie plate
food processor fitted
  with steel blade
hand-held electric
  mixer

FOR THE SHELL
1⅓ cups gingersnap crumbs
3 tablespoons confectioners' sugar

½ stick (¼ cup) unsalted butter,
  melted and cooled

FOR THE FILLING
1½ teaspoons unflavored gelatin
1 tablespoon fresh lime juice
¾ cup dried apricots
1 cup water
½ cup plus 3 tablespoons granulated
  sugar

½ cup apple juice
½ cup sour cream
3 egg whites at room temperature
pinch of salt
pinch of cream of tartar

1 gingersnap, crumbled, for garnish

Preheat the oven to 400° F.

Make the shell:
    In a bowl combine the gingersnap crumbs, the confectioners' sugar, and the butter. Press the mixture into the pie plate and bake it in the middle of the oven for 8 minutes. Let the shell cool on a rack.

Make the filling:
    In a small bowl sprinkle the gelatin over the lime juice and let it soften for 10 minutes. In a saucepan combine the apricots, water, and the ½ cup sugar, bring the mixture to a boil over moderate heat, and simmer it for 20 minutes. In the food processor purée the mixture, transfer it to a large bowl, and add the gelatin mixture, stirring until the gelatin is dissolved. Stir in the apple juice and let the mixture cool. Fold in the sour cream. In a bowl with the mixer beat the egg whites with the salt and the cream of tartar until frothy. Add the remaining 3 tablespoons sugar, one teaspoon at a time, beating, and beat the whites until they hold soft peaks. Fold the egg whites into the apricot mixture gently but thoroughly.
    Turn the filling into the shell and chill the pie for at least 6 hours. Just before serving, garnish the pie with the crumbled gingersnap.

CRANBERRY MERINGUE PIE

Yield:
one 9-inch pie

In this recipe the meringue mixture is warmed over simmering water until the sugar is dissolved and then beaten until the egg whites hold stiff peaks. This method ensures a light, airy, successful meringue. One word of warning: Be sure to allow the cranberry filling to cool completely before

Equipment:
9-inch pie plate
hand-held electric
mixer

spooning the meringue over it. If it is not cool, the meringue is likely to "weep," or separate, while being browned.

1 recipe pâte brisée *(page 164), rolled ⅛ inch thick, transferred to pie plate, and fitted in (see illustrations page 121)*

raw rice or beans for weighting the shell

FOR THE FILLING
⅔ cup sugar
4 tablespoons cornstarch
1 tablespoon fresh lemon juice
3 egg yolks, beaten lightly
1½ cups water

1½ cups cranberries, picked over and rinsed
2 tablespoons unsalted butter, cut into pieces

FOR THE MERINGUE
4 egg whites at room temperature
⅓ cup sugar

¼ teaspoon cream of tartar
pinch of salt

Trim the dough, leaving a ½-inch overhang. Crimp the edge of the shell decoratively (see illustrations page 122), prick the shell lightly with a fork, and chill it for 30 minutes, or freeze it for 15 minutes.

Preheat the oven to 425° F.

Line, weight, and blind-bake the shell (see illustrations page 163) in the lower third of the oven for 15 minutes. Remove the rice and foil carefully and bake the shell for 5 to 8 minutes more, or until golden. Let the shell cool in the pan on a rack.

Reduce the oven temperature to 350° F.

Make the filling: In a saucepan whisk together the sugar, cornstarch, lemon juice, egg yolks, and ½ cup of the water until the mixture is smooth. In another saucepan combine the cranberries and the remaining 1 cup water, bring the water to a boil, and simmer the mixture, covered, for 4 minutes. Purée the cranberry mixture in a blender and strain it through a fine sieve into a bowl, pressing hard on the solids. Stir the cranberry mixture into the yolk mixture, bring the mixture to a boil over moderate heat, whisking constantly, and cook it, whisking constantly, for 3 minutes. Remove the pan from the heat, add the butter, stirring until it is melted, and let the filling cool, stirring occasionally, for 15 minutes. Spread the filling in the shell and let it cool completely.

Make the meringue: In a metal bowl combine the egg whites, sugar, cream of tartar, and salt. Set the bowl over a pan of simmering water and stir the mixture until the sugar is dissolved. Remove the bowl from the pan and with the mixer beat the whites until they hold stiff, glossy peaks.

Spoon the meringue over the filling, smoothing it and covering the filling completely. Bake the pie in the middle of the oven for 8 to 10 minutes, or until the meringue is light golden. Let the pie cool in the pan on a rack and serve it at room temperature.

NORTH DAKOTA LEMON MERINGUE PIE

Yield:
one 9-inch pie

Equipment:
9-inch pie plate
hand-held electric
   mixer

Note the folding of this pie dough. First it is flattened into a round, spread with butter, folded in half, and folded again to form a pie-shaped wedge. The wedge is re-formed into a ball and rolled out to line the pie plate. This special handling provides an easy method of obtaining a dough with many layers—an extremely flaky "mock puff pastry" crust.

FOR THE SHELL
1¼ cups all-purpose flour
½ teaspoon salt
½ stick (¼ cup) cold unsalted butter,
   cut into bits, plus 1 tablespoon
   unsalted butter, softened

3 tablespoons cold lard, cut into bits
3 tablespoons ice water

FOR THE FILLING
1 cup sugar
¼ cup cornstarch
⅓ cup fresh lemon juice
2 tablespoons grated lemon rind

¼ teaspoon salt
3 egg yolks
1½ cups boiling water
1 tablespoon unsalted butter

FOR THE MERINGUE
3 egg whites at room temperature
½ teaspoon vanilla
¼ teaspoon cream of tartar

¼ teaspoon salt
¼ cup sugar

Preheat the oven to 400° F.

Make the shell:
   In a bowl combine the flour and the salt, add the cold butter and the lard, and blend the mixture until it resembles coarse meal. Add the ice water, toss the mixture until it is incorporated, and form the dough into a ball. Flatten the ball into a 6-inch round on a floured surface and spread it with the softened butter. Fold the dough in half and fold the halved dough again to form a pie-shaped wedge. Press the edges together and re-form the dough into a ball. Flatten the ball slightly and roll it into a round ⅛ inch thick on the floured surface. Fit the dough into the pie plate and crimp the edge decoratively (see illustrations page 122). Prick the shell lightly with a fork and bake it in the lower third of the oven for 15 to 20 minutes, or until it is puffed lightly and golden. Let the shell cool in the pan on a rack.

Make the filling:
   In a heavy stainless steel saucepan combine well the sugar, cornstarch, lemon juice, lemon rind, and the salt. Add the egg yolks, one at a time, beating well after each addition. Stir in the boiling water in a stream and the butter. Bring the mixture to a boil, stirring constantly, and simmer it, stirring, for 3 minutes, or until it is thickened, glossy, and translucent. Remove the pan from the heat and beat the mixture for 1 minute. Pour the filling into the shell, smoothing the top. Let the filling cool to room temperature. Reduce the oven temperature to 350° F.

North Dakota Lemon Meringue Pie (opposite)

Make the meringue: In a large bowl with the mixer beat the egg whites with the vanilla, cream of tartar, and the salt until they hold soft peaks, add the sugar, a little at a time, beating, and beat the meringue until it holds stiff peaks (see illustrations page 238). Spoon the meringue over the filling, covering the filling and the crust completely and drawing the meringue up into peaks over the surface of the pie, and bake the pie in the middle of the oven for 12 to 15 minutes, or until the meringue is golden. Let the pie cool on a rack.

Photo on page 157.

Variation: ORANGE MERINGUE PIE: Reduce the lemon juice in the filling to 1 tablespoon, add ⅓ cup fresh orange juice, and substitute 2 tablespoons grated orange rind for the lemon rind.

CHOCOLATE RUM MERINGUE PIE

Yield:
one 9-inch pie

Equipment:
9-inch metal pie plate
hand-held electric
  mixer

A pie made with a meringue shell is often called an angel pie. The shell can be baked ahead and kept crisp in a turned-off oven overnight. The shell can even be frozen, tightly wrapped. Fill the shell at least one hour before serving, which will allow the meringue to soften slightly.

FOR THE MERINGUE SHELL
2 egg whites at room temperature
pinch of salt
¼ teaspoon cream of tartar

½ cup superfine granulated sugar
½ teaspoon vanilla

FOR THE FILLING
6 ounces semisweet chocolate, chopped
  coarse
4 egg whites at room temperature
pinch of salt

¼ teaspoon cream of tartar
1 cup well-chilled heavy cream
2 tablespoons dark rum

sweetened whipped heavy cream for garnish

Butter the pie pan well and preheat the oven to 275° F.

Make the meringue shell: In a bowl with the mixer beat the egg whites with the salt until foamy, add the cream of tartar, and beat the whites until they hold soft peaks. Add the superfine sugar, one tablespoon at a time, and beat the meringue until it holds very stiff peaks (see illustrations page 238). Beat in the vanilla. Spoon the meringue into the pie plate, forming the sides of the shell with the back of the spoon. Bake the shell in the lower third of the oven for 1 hour. Turn off the heat, leave the oven door ajar, and let the shell dry in the oven for at least 1 hour.

Make the filling: In the top of a double boiler set over hot water melt the chocolate, stirring until smooth, and let it cool to lukewarm. In a bowl with the mixer beat the egg whites with the salt until foamy, add the cream of tartar, and continue to beat the whites until they hold stiff peaks.

In a large chilled bowl with the mixer beat the heavy cream with the dark rum until it holds stiff peaks. Fold the chocolate gently but thoroughly into the whipped cream and fold in the beaten egg whites.

Spoon the chocolate filling into the meringue shell and chill the pie for at least 1 hour. Garnish with large dollops of the whipped cream.

NUT PIES

What is it about nut pies that their fans love so? We think that it is the rather unlikely combination of a flaky pastry and a lustrous nut filling.

Pecan Pie (below), rich, sweet, and incredibly delicious, served warm with vanilla ice cream or whipped cream, is considered the ultimate pie by many. Peanut Butter Fudge Pie (page 160) is a type of candy pie especially popular with children. We've added espresso powder to the whipped cream accompaniment, however, for the adult in all of us. Note that these pies should be baked until puffed and just set. Like custard pies, the fillings will completely set while cooling, and, therefore, they must not be overbaked. They are both particularly good when served with whipped cream, which provides a welcome but toothsome relief from the sweetness of the fillings.

PECAN PIE

Yield:
one 11½-inch pie

Equipment:
11½-inch pie plate

1½ recipes pâte brisée *(page 164), substituting 1 tablespoon sugar for the salt; rolled ⅛ inch thick, transferred to pie plate, and fitted in (see illustrations page 121)*

raw rice or dried beans for weighting the shell

FOR THE FILLING

2 cups dark corn syrup
1 cup sugar
3 tablespoons unsalted butter, melted
3 tablespoons all-purpose flour

5 large eggs
1 tablespoon dark rum
½ teaspoon vanilla
2 cups pecan halves

sweetened whipped cream or Vanilla Ice Cream (page 349) as an accompaniment if desired

Trim excess dough from the sides of the shell, leaving a 1-inch overhang. Fold the overhang over the rim, pressing it onto the sides of the shell to form a decorative edge (see illustrations page 122). Prick the bottom of the shell with a fork and chill for 30 minutes.

Preheat the oven to 400° F.

Line, weight, and blind-bake the shell (see illustrations page 163) in the lower third of the oven for 15 minutes. Remove the rice and wax paper and bake the shell for 10 minutes more, or until lightly colored. Let the shell cool on a rack.

Reduce the oven temperature to 375° F.

Make the filling: In a large bowl combine the dark corn syrup, sugar, melted butter, and the flour. In a bowl lightly beat the eggs with the rum and the vanilla. Add the egg mixture to the sugar mixture and combine well. Arrange the pecans in the pastry shell and slowly pour in the filling.

Bake the pie in the middle of the oven for 40 minutes, or until it is puffed and set. Let the pie cool on a rack and serve it slightly warm with the whipped cream or ice cream.

PEANUT BUTTER FUDGE PIE

Yield:
9-inch pie

1 recipe pâte sucrée *(page 165), rolled ⅛ inch thick, transferred to pie plate, and fitted in (see illustrations page 163)*

Equipment:
9-inch ceramic or glass pie plate

FOR THE FILLING

4 ounces unsweetened chocolate, chopped coarse	*3 large eggs*
	1 cup dark corn syrup
3 tablespoons unsalted butter	*½ cup milk*
¼ cup smooth or chunky peanut butter	*⅔ cup coarsely chopped roasted*
1 teaspoon vanilla	*unsalted peanuts*
¾ cup plus 2 tablespoons granulated sugar	

1½ cups well-chilled heavy cream	*¼ cup confectioners' sugar*
1 tablespoon espresso powder	

Trim off the excess dough, leaving a 1-inch overhang. Fold the overhang back over the edge, form a decorative ¼-inch rim above the plate (see illustrations page 122), and chill the shell for 30 minutes.

Preheat the oven to 325° F.

Make the filling: In the top of a double boiler set over simmering water melt the chocolate with the butter, stirring. In a large bowl beat the peanut butter, vanilla, granulated sugar, and the eggs and add the corn syrup and the milk in a stream, beating. Beat in the chocolate mixture and stir in the peanuts.

Pour the filling into the shell and bake the pie in the lower third of the oven for 55 minutes to 1 hour, or until the filling is just set. Let the pie cool on a rack and chill it for 2 hours, or until the filling is set. (The filling will set fully when the pie has cooled completely.)

In a well-chilled bowl beat the cream with the espresso powder and the confectioners' sugar until it holds soft peaks, transfer it to a serving bowl, and serve it with the pie.

TARTS

The difference between pies and tarts is really quite simple. A tart is basically free standing and usually open faced. The dough is formed in a tart pan or flan form with a removable rim so that upon being baked the shell can be removed from the pan. Because of this, a different type of pastry is required; one that is less fragile or flaky than pie dough. And the shell is usually prebaked, filled with fruit alone—fresh, dried, poached, stewed, or even puréed; fruit with cream or almond fillings or a layer of whipped cream; nuts combined with rich, sweet caramel; or even a simple jam filling made even more flavorful with cinnamon, nutmeg, and cloves if desired.

Tarts lend themselves to creative interpretation. Even if a round tart pan has been called for, there is no reason why the tart cannot be prepared in whichever form you prefer or why it cannot be formed into any shape you desire. This is the beauty of a tart as opposed to a pie. A pie takes the shape of the pie plate. A tart, because it is free standing, takes the shape you create. Experiment with tart or flan shapes that coordinate with the arrangement of the fruit. If a pie plate or cake pan is the only thing available, however, a tart shell can even be fashioned over the bottom of the inverted plate or pan and can be carefully removed after baking.

A good pastry cream is often as essential part of a good tart. It must be made well to result in a smooth, creamy, and flavorful cream. (Follow the instructions for making pastry cream on page 537.)

Even the most rural *pâtisserie* in France has an extraordinarily varied selection of tarts in its window. The French certainly know that the combination of healthful fruit or nut fillings and pastry is a nutritionally sound dessert and not too worrisome calorically. Tarts are certainly good for your spirit and and a better understanding and serious consideration of tarts as a homemade dessert would be a wonderful thing in our country and a welcome addition to our baking repertoires. Tarts are not difficult to prepare and for as easy as they really are, they are not made often enough.

TART DOUGHS

There are different types of tart doughs but there is one that has been used by *Gourmet* throughout the years and has always given superb results. This dough is called *pâte brisée* and is a combination of flour and butter or shortening that is blended until the mixture resembles coarse meal like the standard pie pastry (see illustrations page 121). However, at that point *pâte brisée* is lightly kneaded with the heel of the hand against a work surface in a process called *fraisage*, to distribute the fat evenly. This results in a crust of substance, one that is crisp but tender, strong enough to be free-standing yet not tough. Butter is the principal fat used in *pâte brisée* for its excellent flavor, but a portion of vegetable shortening is also incorporated for flakiness. You will notice in our "Pies" section, this same *pâte brisée* dough is called for as a pie crust. Although not required to stand alone, this crust is especially appropriate for certain types of pie fillings.

Another classic tart pastry is *pâte sucrée*, a richer, sweeter, more cookie-like dough that employs only butter and to which egg and sugar are added. The egg makes the dough less fragile and permits more handling without fear of overworking the dough.

In this chapter we have also included a recipe for Rich Whole-Wheat Pastry Dough, made, as its name indicates, with whole-wheat flour. This produces a wholesome, more substantially textured crust and its slightly nutty flavor perfectly complements the spicy apple and pecan filling in the recipe for Apple Pecan Whole-Wheat Tart.

After chilling the dough it may be rolled out as described in the Pie Dough introduction (page 121). (You can also simply pat the buttery dough into the tart pan.) As illustrated, the dough is rolled out and transferred to the tart pan by rolling it over and off the rolling pin, laying it loosely onto the pan. Using your fingertips or knuckles, carefully press the dough into the pan, being careful to press the dough against the fluted sides and into the fluted edges of the tart pan or flan ring. Fold back some of the excess dough to create a sufficiently thick edge around the tart. The easiest way to trim the tart dough is to roll the rolling pin across the edge of the tart pan, trimming it flush with the edge of the pan and cutting it neatly against the pan's sharp top edge, letting the excess dough fall off. The result will be a neatly lined pan with an attractive edge. (If desired, a decorative edge could be formed, as described in the introduction to pie doughs.) To line tartlet tins, arrange the tins so they touch one another, lay the dough over the tins, and roll the pin over the dough as shown, lining the individual tins as you go. Prick the shell or tins and chill.

The term "blind-baking" is often interpreted to mean prebaking a tart shell. While it does mean this, it also means something far more literal. The term refers to baking the shell or tins with the bottom surface covered so that it is not visible. The surface is lined first with wax paper, then completely covered with raw rice or dried beans, being sure to weight the indents of the scalloped bottom rim of the tart tin. The weight of the rice or beans will prevent the dough from shrinking or blistering while baking. The shell is then transferred to a baking sheet and is baked as directed. "Blind-baking" is an essential part of tart-making because it allows for fillings which would otherwise render the tart's bottom crust soggy and fillings which could not have been baked simultaneously with the bottom crust.

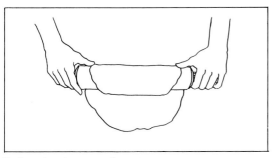

Rolling dough over rolling pin

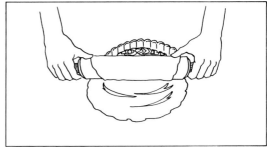

Rolling dough off rolling pin

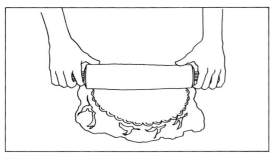

Trimming crust with pin

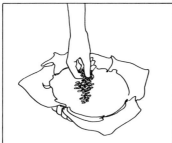

Pricking bottom of shell; weighting lined shell with raw rice; lined and weighted shell on baking sheet

PÂTE BRISÉE

Yield:
about 11 ounces
  dough
enough dough for one
  9- or 10-inch tart
  shell

Pâte brisée literally means "broken," or short, pastry in French. Short dough is light and has the discernible flavor of butter.

A specific technique, called *fraisage*, is used in making *pâte brisée*. By lightly smearing the dough across the work surface with the heel of the hand, the fat, in this case butter, is distributed throughout different layers of the pastry, thus rendering a tender yet firm crust. However, like all fine doughs, you do not want to overwork or overroll *pâte brisée*.

1¼ cups all-purpose flour
¾ stick (6 tablespoons) cold unsalted
*   butter, cut into bits*

2 tablespoons cold vegetable
*   shortening*
¼ teaspoon salt
3 tablespoons ice water

The dough may be
frozen, wrapped in
plastic and foil, for up
to 1 month. To
defrost, place in the
refrigerator
overnight.

In a large bowl with your fingertips or with two knives blend the flour, butter, vegetable shortening, and salt until the mixture resembles meal (see illustrations page 121). Add the ice water, toss the mixture until the water is incorporated, and form the dough into a ball. Knead the dough lightly with the heel of the hand against a smooth surface for a few seconds to distribute the fat evenly and re-form it into a ball. Dust the dough with flour and chill it, wrapped in wax paper, for at least 1 hour, or for up to 2 days.

Variation:

PÂTE BRISÉE: PROCESSOR METHOD: In a food processor fitted with the steel blade combine the flour, butter, vegetable shortening, and salt and process the mixture until it resembles coarse meal. Sprinkle the water over the mixture and process it until it comes together in large pieces about the size of pebbles. Transfer the dough to a work surface and if it is dry sprinkle it with 1 tablespoon more water. With the heel of your hand knead the dough against a smooth surface for a few seconds to distribute the fat evenly and form it into a ball. Dust the dough with flour and chill it, wrapped in wax paper, for at least 1 hour, or for up to 2 days.

PÂTE SUCRÉE

Yield:
about 15 ounces
    dough
enough dough for one
    10-inch shell

Pâte sucrée means sweet pastry in French and describes crumbly sweetened pastry dough similar in texture and flavor to cookie dough. The dough produces remarkable results when made into free-standing tarts as this firmer cookie-like dough, due to the addition of egg, holds up better as a free-form tart shell. The dough also withstands more handling because the natural oils of the egg help prevent the development of the gluten due to flour and moisture. The *fraisage* method, described in the recipe for *pâte brisée* is also used in making *pâte sucrée*. Of course, in most instances *pâte brisée* and *pâte sucrée* are interchangeable, and this sweetened dough can be substituted for *pâte brisée* with simply sweeter results.

1½ cups all-purpose flour
¼ cup sugar
¼ teaspoon salt
1 stick plus 1 tablespoon (½ cup plus
    1 tablespoon) cold unsalted butter,
    cut into bits

1 large egg, beaten lightly
1 to 2 tablespoons ice water

The dough may be frozen, wrapped in plastic and foil, for up to 1 month. To defrost, place in the refrigerator overnight.

Variation:

In a large bowl with your fingertips or with two knives blend the flour, sugar, salt, and the butter until the mixture resembles meal (see illustrations page 121). Add the egg and 1 tablespoon of the water, toss the mixture until the liquid is incorporated, adding 1 more tablespoon of water if the mixture is dry, and form the dough into a ball. Knead the dough lightly with the heel of your hand against a smooth surface for a few seconds to distribute the fat evenly and re-form it into a ball. Dust the dough with flour and chill it, wrapped in wax paper, for 1 hour.

PÂTE SUCRÉE: PROCESSOR METHOD: In a food processor fitted with the plastic or steel blade combine the flour, sugar, salt, and butter and process the mixture until it resembles coarse meal. In a bowl combine the egg with 1 tablespoon of the water and sprinkle it over the flour mixture. Process the mixture until it comes together in large pieces about the size of pebbles and transfer the dough to a work surface. If the mixture is dry, sprinkle it with 1 more tablespoon water. With the heel of your hand knead the dough against a smooth surface for a few seconds to distribute the fat evenly and form it into a ball. Dust the dough with flour and chill it, wrapped in wax paper, for at least 1 hour or for up to 2 days.

RICH WHOLE-WHEAT TART PASTRY

Yield:
about 12 ounces
dough
enough dough for one
9- or 10-inch tart
shell

½ cup all-purpose flour
½ cup whole-wheat flour
⅓ cup finely ground pecans
¾ stick (6 tablespoons) cold unsalted
   butter, cut into bits
2 tablespoons cold vegetable
   shortening, cut into bits
1½ teaspoons grated orange rind if
   desired

1 tablespoon sugar
½ teaspoon double-acting baking
   powder
⅛ teaspoon salt
3 to 4 tablespoons cold orange juice or
   ice water

The dough keeps
chilled, covered,
overnight. The dough
keeps frozen,
wrapped tightly in
plastic wrap and
aluminum foil, for up
to 2 weeks. To
defrost, place in the
refrigerator
overnight.

In a large bowl with your fingertips or with two knives blend the all-purpose flour, the whole-wheat flour, the pecans, butter, shortening, orange rind, if desired, sugar, baking powder, and the salt until the mixture resembles meal (see illustrations page 121). Add 3 tablespoons of the orange juice or ice water and toss the mixture until the liquid is incorporated, adding the additional tablespoon of liquid, or enough to form the dough into a ball. Knead the dough lightly with the heel of the hand against a smooth surface for a few seconds to distribute the fat evenly and re-form it into a ball. Dust the dough with flour and chill it, wrapped in wax paper, for 1 hour.

FRUIT TARTS

Fruit tarts are among the most impressive of desserts. While not difficult to execute, the combination of a buttery pastry or sugar cookie-like shell and ripe juicy fruits with, perhaps, a liqueur-flavored pastry cream or *crème fraîche* filling and a brilliant fruit glaze is too often reserved as a perfect dessert when dining out! In an attempt to bring the fruit tart back to its proper place, your dining table, we have included Mr. James Beard's classic recipe for Strawberry Tart. He provides the essential components and confidence and you provide the ripest fruit available. The result—perfect. Also included are recipes for tarts with chocolate-glazed shells, dried fruits, rhubarb, and even lemon slices. An especially appealing recipe is for Applesauce Tarts (page 168) using an applesauce made with green apples and with strips of vanilla-flavored hard sauce piped on top. Tartlets are simply small or individual tarts made in tartlet tins. A flan is a tart made in a flan form that has no bottom but which instead uses a baking sheet as the base. Flan forms come in varying shapes and sizes. Our Gooseberry Flan (page 173) is prepared in a circular form.

A simple tart of sliced apples is elevated to new heights with the addition of golden raisins, pecans, and orange liqueur, but retains its rustic nature by using a whole wheat (albeit rich) crust.

STRAWBERRY TART

Yield:
one 9-inch tart

Equipment:
9-inch round tart pan
  with removable rim
  or a flan ring with a
  baking sheet base
pastry brush

Developed by James Beard in 1972, this recipe provides the essential components of the perfectly textured and subtly flavored fruit tart. This classic dessert is comprised of a short *pâte brisée* (or *pâte sucrée*) tart shell and the finest quality and ripest fresh fruits. Combined just before serving to preserve the textures of all ingredients, the whole is glazed with red currant jelly. Served with kirsch-flavored whipped cream, it is truly a simple yet perfect dessert.

1 recipe pâte brisée (page 164), rolled ⅛ inch thick, transferred to tart pan, and fitted in (see illustrations page 163)
raw rice or dried beans for weighting the shell
1½ to 2 pints ripe strawberries, hulled

½ cup red currant glaze (page 541) made with 1 tablespoon kirsch, heated
kirsch-flavored whipped cream or Sabayon Sauce (page 494) flavored with kirsch as an accompaniment if desired

Trim the edge of the dough with the rolling pin. Prick the shell with a fork and chill the shell for 30 minutes.

Preheat the oven to 400° F.

Line, weight, and blind-bake the shell (see illustrations page 163) on a baking sheet in the lower third of the oven for 10 to 15 minutes. Carefully remove the rice and paper.

Reduce the oven temperature to 375° F.

Bake the shell for 5 to 10 minutes more, or until golden. Let cool on a rack.

Arrange the strawberries in the shell, building toward the center. You may make a double layer in the center. Brush the strawberries with the glaze and serve the tart with the flavored whipped cream or sabayon sauce.

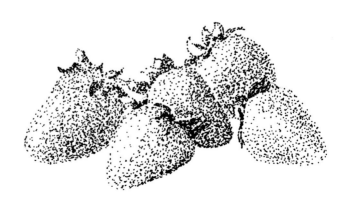

PEAR AND CHOCOLATE TART

Yield:
one 9-inch tart

Equipment:
9-inch round tart pan
with removable rim
or a flan ring with a
baking sheet base
pastry brush

1 recipe pâte brisée *(page 164),
rolled ⅛ inch thick, transferred to
tart pan, and fitted in (see
illustrations page 163)*
*raw rice or dried beans for weighting
the shell*
2 cups water
1 cup sugar
*a 1-inch piece of vanilla bean or
1 teaspoon vanilla*

4 to 6 pears, peeled, halved, and cored
*6 ounces semisweet chocolate, chopped
coarse*
2 tablespoons unsalted butter
*½ cup apricot glaze (page 540) made
with 2 tablespoons Cognac, heated*
*⅔ cup sliced blanched almonds,
toasted lightly*
*whipped cream as an accompaniment
if desired*

Trim the edge of the dough with the rolling pin. Prick the shell with a fork
and chill the shell for 30 minutes.

Preheat the oven to 400° F.

Line, weight, and blind-bake the shell (see illustrations page 163) on a
baking sheet in the lower third of the oven for 15 minutes. Remove the rice
and paper carefully. Reduce the oven temperature to 375° F. Bake the
shell for 10 to 15 minutes more, or until golden. Let cool on a rack.

In a large heavy skillet combine the water and the sugar and cook the
mixture until the sugar is dissolved. Add the vanilla bean and cook the syrup for 5 minutes. Add the pears and poach them for 15 to 25 minutes, depending on their degree of ripeness. Let the pears cool in the syrup and
drain them on paper towels. (The syrup may be reserved for poaching
other fruits, pages 466 to 470.)

In the top of a double boiler set over hot water melt the chocolate, stirring until smooth, and stir in the butter. Brush the bottom of the shell with
the chocolate and let set for 30 minutes. Arrange the poached pear halves
in the shell decoratively, brush them well with the apricot glaze, and garnish the tart with the almonds. Serve with the whipped cream.

APPLESAUCE TARTS

Yield:
twelve 2¾-inch tarts

Equipment:
twelve 2¾-inch tart
tins
food mill
pastry brush
pastry bag fitted with
small decorative tip

1 recipe pâte sucrée *(page 165)*
*12 large unpeeled Granny Smith
apples, quartered and cored*
½ cup water
sugar to taste

cinnamon to taste
freshly ground pepper to taste
apricot jam, melted and cooled
1 recipe Hard Sauce (page 495)

Roll the dough ⅛ inch thick on a lightly floured surface. Cut the dough
into 12 circles about an inch larger in diameter than the tart tins you are
using. Ease the circles into the tart tins and pinch them into place. Or ar-

range the tart tins together, touching one another, to approximate the shape of the rolled-out dough. Drape the dough over the rolling pin and unroll it over the tins. Roll the rolling pin over the dough to cut it (see illustrations page 163). Prick the shells with a fork and chill them for about 30 minutes.

In a large saucepan combine the apples with the water and cook them, covered tightly, over moderate heat for about 20 minutes, or until soft. Force the apples through the food mill into a bowl and stir in the sugar, cinnamon, and pepper. (You should have about 3 cups applesauce.)

Preheat the oven to 400° F.

Bake the shells on a baking sheet in the lower third of the oven for about 8 to 10 minutes, or until golden. Let the shells cool on a rack. When the tins are cool enough to handle, remove the shells from the tins and allow them to cool on the rack.

Brush the bottoms and sides of the shells with the apricot jam and fill each shell with about ¼ cup of the applesauce. Fill the pastry bag with the hard sauce and pipe 4 thin strips of it in a lattice pattern over the applesauce in each tart.

DRIED APRICOT TART

Yield:
one 14- by 4½-inch
  tart

Equipment:
14- by 4½-inch tart
  pan with removable
  rim
pastry brush

The shell of this tart is prepared with *pâte sucrée* and is only partially blind baked. The tart is then filled and is baked for another half hour. The partial blind-baking can be done ahead of time if desired.

1 recipe pâte sucrée *(page 165)*
raw rice or dried beans for weighting
  the shell
1 pound dried apricots
½ cup sugar
¾ stick (6 tablespoons) cold unsalted
  butter, cut into bits

¾ cup apricot glaze (page 540),
  heated
6 halved blanched almonds (for
  procedure page 549)
lightly sweetened whipped cream as
  an accompaniment if desired

On a lightly floured surface roll the dough into a ⅛-inch-thick rectangle, at least 17 by 8 inches. Drape the dough over the rolling pin and unroll it over the tart pan. Fit the dough firmly into the pan and trim the edge of the dough with the rolling pin. Prick the bottom of the shell with a fork and chill the shell for 1 hour.

Preheat the oven to 400° F.

Line, weight, and blind-bake the shell (see illustrations page 163) in the lower third of the oven for 10 to 15 minutes, or until it begins to set. Carefully remove the rice and wax paper and bake the shell for 5 minutes more, or until it is lightly colored. Carefully remove the shell from the pan, transfer it with a large spatula to a rack, and let it cool.

Reduce the oven temperature to 375° F.

In a saucepan combine the apricots with enough water to cover them by ½ inch and bring the water to a boil over moderately high heat. Reduce the heat to low, simmer the apricots for 20 minutes, and let them cool in the water.

Transfer the shell to a baking sheet, drain the apricots, and arrange them, slightly overlapping, in crosswise rows in the shell. Sprinkle the apricots with the sugar, dot them with the butter, and bake the tart in the upper third of the oven for 30 minutes. (If the apricots have not become richly colored, put the tart under a preheated broiler for about 3 minutes.) Brush the hot tart with the apricot glaze, transfer it to a rack, and let it cool slightly. Decorate the center of the tart with the almonds, transfer the tart to a serving board, and serve it slightly warm with the whipped cream.

RHUBARB TART

Yield:
one 9¾-inch tart

Equipment:
9¾-inch tart pan with
  removable rim
pastry brush

The shell of this tart is initially baked for thirty minutes, then filled with stewed rhubarb as well as ¾ cup of syrup. Because of the weight of the filling and the syrup, the tart continues baking on a rack set on a baking sheet to facilitate its handling.

1 recipe pâte brisée *(page 164)*
  substituting 2 teaspoons sugar for
  the salt; rolled ⅛ inch thick,
  transferred to tart pan, and fitted in
  (see illustrations page 163)

raw rice or dried beans for weighting
  the shell

FOR THE STEWED RHUBARB

2⅓ cups sugar
1 cup water

about 3 pounds rhubarb, cut into
  1¾-inch lengths (about 6 cups)

10 strawberries, hulled, with hulls
  reserved for garnish if desired

2 tablespoons brandy, or to taste

crème fraîche *(page 537) or lightly whipped cream as an accompaniment*
if desired

Trim the edge of the dough with the rolling pin. Prick the shell with a fork and chill the shell for 30 minutes.

Preheat the oven to 400° F.

Line, weight, and blind-bake the shell (see illustrations page 163) in the lower third of the oven for 10 to 15 minutes, or until it begins to set. Care-

Rhubarb Tart (opposite)

fully remove the rice and paper and bake the shell for 10 to 15 minutes more, or until lightly colored. Remove the shell from the pan, transfer it to a rack, and let it cool.

Make the stewed rhubarb:

In a skillet combine the sugar with the water and bring the mixture to a boil over moderately low heat, washing down any sugar crystals clinging to the sides of the pan with the brush dipped in cold water until the sugar is dissolved. Increase the heat to moderate and simmer the syrup for 5 minutes. Add half the rhubarb and simmer the mixture for 3 to 6 minutes, or until it is just soft, removing the pieces with a slotted spatula to a shallow dish. Simmer the remaining rhubarb in the syrup in the same manner, transferring it to the dish when it is just soft. Spoon the syrup over the rhubarb, let the mixture cool, and chill.

To assemble the tart:

Preheat the oven to 400° F.

As near to serving time as possible, with the shell still on the rack, transfer the rhubarb with a narrow metal slotted spatula to the shell, arrranging the fruit in slightly overlapping rows. Reserve the syrup. Arrange the strawberries around the shell.

In a skillet reduce the reserved syrup over moderately high heat to ¾ cup and stir in the brandy. Spoon the warm syrup over the rhubarb and strawberries. Heat a baking sheet. Set the tart with the rack on the baking sheet and bake it in the middle of the oven for 10 minutes. Let the tart cool on the rack for 10 minutes and transfer it to a serving plate. If desired, replace the strawberry hulls for decoration. Serve the tart with the *crème fraîche*.

Photo above.

APPLE AND PECAN TART IN WHOLE-WHEAT CRUST

Yield:
one 9½-inch tart

Equipment:
9½-inch tart pan with
  removable rim
pastry brush

*1 recipe rich whole-wheat tart pastry
  (page 166), rolled ⅛ inch thick,
  transferred to tart pan, and fitted in
  (see illustrations page 163)*
⅓ cup golden raisins
1 tablespoon orange-flavored liqueur
*3 large McIntosh apples (about
  1½ pounds), peeled, cored, and
  sliced*
½ cup finely chopped pecans
*¾ stick (6 tablespoons) unsalted
  butter, softened*

⅓ cup sugar
1 large egg, beaten lightly
1½ teaspoons grated orange rind
½ teaspoon vanilla
½ teaspoon cinnamon
⅛ teaspoon freshly grated nutmeg
*½ cup apricot glaze (page 540) made
  with 1 tablespoon orange-flavored
  liqueur, heated*

Trim the edge of the dough with the rolling pin. Prick the bottom of the shell with a fork and chill the shell for at least 30 minutes.

In a bowl toss the raisins with the liqueur and let them macerate for 30 minutes.

Preheat the oven to 375° F.

Arrange the apple slices, rounded side up (see illustration), in the tart pan and sprinkle them with the raisins, drained. In a bowl whisk together the pecans, butter, sugar, egg, orange rind, vanilla, cinnamon, and nut-meg until the mixture is combined. Spoon the filling over the apples, spreading it evenly. Bake the tart on a baking sheet in the lower third of the oven for 30 minutes. Transfer the tart to the middle of the oven and continue to bake it for 10 to 15 minutes longer, or until it is golden brown on top. Transfer to a rack.

While the tart is still warm spoon the glaze over the top. Let the tart cool on the rack. Serve the tart slightly warm or at room temperature.

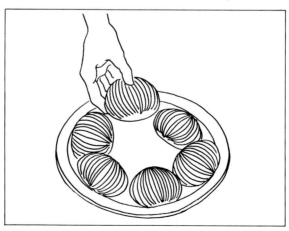

Arranging apple slices, rounded side up, in tart shell

GOOSEBERRY FLAN

Yield:
one 7-inch flan

Equipment:
7-inch tart pan with
  removable rim or a
  7-inch flan ring with
  a baking sheet base
pastry cutter

The word flan can be used interchangeably with the word tart to describe a pastry shell, usually with a short sweet crust, filled with fruit or a custard or both, but with no top crust. The bottomless round metal ring with straight sides that is placed on a baking sheet to form a flan or tart is called a flan ring and they are available in varying sizes at kitchenware shops. When the flan is baked, the ring is easily lifted off without breaking the pastry. A flan may also refer to a baked custard dessert similar to a *crème caramel*.

Gooseberries—aromatic, delicately sweet, and muscat-flavored—are available only in late spring and early summer. Gooseberries may be frozen whole or puréed and frozen during their short-lived season. They are also sold in cans and bottles in specialty foods shops.

FOR THE SHELL
1¼ cups all-purpose flour
1 stick (½ cup) cold unsalted butter,
  cut into bits
1 teaspoon granulated sugar
½ teaspoon salt
1 large egg, beaten lightly

FOR THE FILLING
1 pound fresh gooseberries, washed
  and picked over (or 3 cups drained
  canned gooseberries combined with
  the grated rind of 1 lemon and 2 to
  3 tablespoons granulated sugar, or
  to taste)
light brown sugar to taste
2 tablespoons water
grated rind of 1 lemon

Make the shell: In a bowl with your fingertips or two knives blend the flour with the butter, granulated sugar, and salt until the mixture resembles meal (see illustrations page 121). Toss the mixture with the egg until the egg is incorporated and form the dough into a ball. Wrap the dough in wax paper and chill it for 1 hour.

Cut off one third of the dough and return it to the refrigerator. Roll the remaining dough into an 8-inch round on a lightly floured surface. Drape the dough lightly over the rolling pin and transfer it to the tart pan (see illustrations page 163). Trim the edges, prick the shell, and chill the shell for 30 minutes.

Make the filling: In a saucepan combine the gooseberries, the brown sugar to taste, and the water and cook the mixture over moderately high heat until the berries are very soft. Stir in the lemon rind. Pour the filling into the shell.

Preheat the oven to 425° F.

Bake the tart in the lower third of the oven for 10 minutes. Transfer the tart to the middle of the oven, reduce the heat to 350° F., and bake for 30 minutes more. Remove the flan ring and bake the tart for 5 to 10 minutes more, or until golden. Transfer the tart to a rack and let it cool slightly.

PAPAYA TART WITH COCONUT PASTRY CREAM

Yield:
one 10-inch tart

Equipment:
10-inch tart pan with
  removable rim
hand-held electric
  mixer
pastry brush

1 recipe pâte sucrée *(page 165),
  rolled ⅛ inch thick, transferred to
  tart pan, and fitted in (see
  illustrations page 163)*

raw rice or dried beans for weighting
  the shell

FOR THE COCONUT PASTRY CREAM

1 cup milk
⅓ cup heavy cream
1 cup sweetened flaked coconut
3 egg yolks
⅓ cup sugar
2 tablespoons all-purpose flour

2 tablespoons cornstarch
2 tablespoons unsalted butter, cut into
  bits
1 tablespoon dark rum
½ teaspoon vanilla

½ cup apricot glaze *(page 540) made
  with 1 tablespoon dark rum*

1 papaya, peeled, halved, seeded, and
  cut into ⅛-inch-thick slices

Trim the edge of the dough with the rolling pin. Prick the shell with a fork
and chill the shell for 30 minutes.

Preheat the oven to 400° F.

Line, weight, and blind-bake the shell (see illustrations page 163) on a
baking sheet in the lower third of the oven for 15 minutes. Carefully remove the rice and paper. Reduce the oven temperature to 375° F. Bake the
shell for 10 to 15 minutes more, or until golden. Let the shell cool on a
rack.

**Make the coconut
pastry cream:**

In a heavy saucepan bring the milk and cream to a simmer, stir in the
coconut, and let the mixture stand for 15 minutes. In a large bowl with the
mixer beat the yolks until combined, add the sugar, a little at a time, beating, and beat the mixture until light and lemon colored. Add the flour and

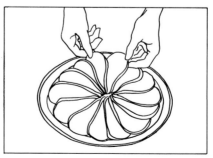

Arranging papaya slices decoratively in
tart shell

the cornstarch, a little at a time, beating, and beat the mixture until smooth. Add the milk mixture, in a stream, beating, and beat the mixture until well combined. Transfer the mixture to the saucepan, bring it to a boil, whisking constantly, and simmer it over low heat for 3 minutes, or until it is thick and custard-like. Remove the pan from the heat, beat in the butter, rum, and vanilla and transfer the cream to a plate. Let the pastry cream cool, covered with a buttered round of wax paper, and chill it for at least 1 hour, or until cold.

Brush the bottom of the pastry shell with some of the apricot glaze and spoon the pastry cream into the shell, smoothing it into an even layer. Arrange the papaya slices decoratively over the cream (see illustration) and brush the papaya with the remaining glaze. Keep the tart chilled until ready to serve. The tart is best served within 1 to 1½ hours after assembly.

SUMMER FRUIT TARTLETS

Yield:
12 tartlets

Equipment:
twelve 3-inch tartlet
   tins
pastry brush

½ recipe pâte sucrée *(page 165)*
*raw rice or dried beans for weighting
   the shells*
apricot glaze (page 540)
*¾ cup kirsch-flavored pastry cream
   (page 538)*

*assorted summer fruits, such as
   blueberries, sliced apricots, sliced
   unpeeled plums, sliced
   strawberries, honeydew melon
   balls, and mango balls*

On a floured surface roll the dough into a rectangle ⅛ inch thick. Arrange the tartlet tins close together in rows of 4. Drape the dough over the rolling pin and lay it loosely over the tins. Press the dough into the tins and roll the rolling pin, lightly floured, over the rims of the tins, trimming off the excess dough (see illustrations page 163). Prick the bottoms of the shells with a fork and chill the shells for at least 30 minutes.

Preheat the oven to 400° F.

Line, weight, and blind-bake the shells (or press the same size tins lightly into the shells) on a baking sheet in the middle of the oven for 10 minutes. Remove the rice and paper (or the tins) carefully and bake the shells for 5 minutes more, or until lightly colored. Transfer the tins to a rack and let the shells cool in the tins for 5 minutes. Turn the shells out onto the rack and let them cool completely.

With the pastry brush glaze each shell with the apricot glaze. Put 1 tablespoon pastry cream in each shell and top it with assorted fruit. Brush the fruits lightly with the additional apricot glaze.

Variation:

ASSORTED FRUIT WHIPPED CREAM TARTLETS: Substitute sweetened whipped cream flavored with vanilla for the pastry cream.

PLUM TART

Yield:
one 11-inch tart

Equipment:
11-inch round tart
pan with removable
rim

2 recipes pâte brisée *(page 164)*
*raw rice or dried beans for weighting
the shell*
*2 pounds ripe purple plums, halved or
quartered and pitted*
*⅔ cup sugar, or to taste, combined
with ½ teaspoon cinnamon*

*2 tablespoons unsalted butter, cut into
bits*
*1 tablespoon cornstarch dissolved in 2
tablespoons Tawny Port*

Nectarine Ice Cream (page 350) as an accompaniment if desired

On a lightly floured surface roll the dough into a ⅛-inch-thick round.
Drape the dough over the rolling pin and unroll it over the tart pan. Fit the
dough firmly into the pan. Trim off the excess dough, leaving a 1-inch
overhang, and fold the overhang over the rim, pressing it onto and ¼ inch
above the rim of the pan. Prick the bottom of the shell lightly with a fork
and chill the shell for 30 minutes.

Preheat the oven to 425° F.

Line, weight, and blind-bake the shell (see illustrations page 163) in the
lower third of the oven for 10 minutes. Carefully remove the rice and paper, bake the shell for 5 to 10 minutes more, or until it is pale golden, and
let it cool on a rack.

In a buttered stainless steel or enameled baking dish arrange the plums
skin side down in one layer, sprinkle them with the cinnamon sugar, and
dot them with the butter. Bake the plums in the oven for 30 minutes, or
until they are almost tender and have exuded their juices. Let the plums
cool for 10 minutes and with a slotted spoon arrange them skin side down
in the shell.

Reduce the oven temperature to 350° F.

Pour the cooking juice into a small stainless steel or enameled saucepan
and bring it to a boil. Stir the cornstarch mixture, add it in a stream to the
saucepan, stirring, and cook the mixture over moderate heat, stirring, for
1 minute, or until it is thickened. Spoon the glaze over the plums and bake
the tart on a baking sheet in the middle of the oven for 15 to 20 minutes, or
until the plums are tender. Let the tart cool in the pan on a rack, remove the
rim, and transfer the tart to a serving dish. Serve the tart with the nectarine
ice cream if desired.

Photo on page 354.

LEMON CURD TARTLETS

Yield:
ten 3-inch or
  fourteen to sixteen
  2-inch tartlets

1 recipe pâte brisée *(page 164) made*
  with an additional 1 tablespoon
  sugar; rolled ⅛ inch thick

raw rice or dried beans for weighting
  the shell

Equipment:
4-inch or 3-inch
  round fluted cutter
ten 3-inch or
  fourteen to sixteen
  2-inch tartlet tins
hand-held electric
  mixer

FOR THE LEMON CURD FILLING
4 egg yolks
½ cup sugar
½ stick (¼ cup) unsalted butter

juice of 2 lemons, strained
1 teaspoon grated lemon rind

½ cup well-chilled heavy cream

16 blanched almonds (for procedure
  page 549), toasted lightly

With the fluted cutter cut out rounds from the dough 1 inch larger than the tins. Press the rounds firmly into the tins, prick them with a fork, and chill them for 1 hour.

Preheat the oven to 400° F.

Line, weight, and blind-bake the shells (see illustrations page 163) on a baking sheet in the middle of the oven for 10 minutes. Carefully remove the rice and paper and bake the shells for 5 to 8 minutes more, or until lightly colored. Remove the shells from the tins and let them cool on a rack.

Make the lemon curd
filling:

In a heavy saucepan combine the egg yolks, sugar, butter, and the lemon juice. Cook the mixture over medium low heat, stirring, until the butter is melted and the custard is thick enough to coat a spoon. Do not let it boil. Transfer the custard to a bowl and stir in the lemon rind. Let the custard cool, cover it with a round of buttered wax paper, and chill it.

In a chilled bowl with the mixer beat the heavy cream until it forms soft peaks. Fold one fourth of the cream into the lemon curd, combine it well, and fold in the remaining cream. Just before serving, divide the filling among the shells and top each tartlet with a blanched almond.

Photo on page 302.

Variations:

BLOOD ORANGE AND LIME CURD TARTLETS: Substitute 1 recipe blood orange and lime curd (page 547) for the lemon curd filling.

PINK GRAPEFRUIT CURD TARTLETS: In a small saucepan boil ½ cup strained fresh pink grapefruit juice until it is reduced to about 2 tablespoons, add 2½ tablespoons sugar and ½ stick (¼ cup) unsalted butter, cut into bits, and simmer the mixture, stirring, until the sugar is dissolved. In a small bowl beat 1 large egg, add the hot liquid in a slow stream, whisking, and return the mixture to the pan. Cook the mixture over moderately low heat, stirring, until it is thickened to the consistency of hollandaise, but do not let it boil. Transfer the curd to a bowl and let it cool, covered with a lightly buttered round of wax paper.

ALSATIAN PEAR TART

Yield:
one 9-inch tart

Equipment:
9-inch flan pan with
   removable fluted
   rim
baking sheet

Alsatian in this instance refers to the combination of fruit and *crème fraîche* custard that has *eau-de-vie* distilled from the local fruits of the Alsace region of France added.

1 recipe thick crème fraîche *(page 537)*

FOR THE SWEET PASTRY DOUGH

1½ cups all-purpose flour
¼ cup sugar
pinch of salt
1 stick (½ cup) cold unsalted butter,
   cut into bits

1 egg yolk
about ¼ cup cold fresh orange juice if
   desired or ¼ cup ice water
raw rice or dried beans for weighting
   the shell

2 firm ripe pears

eau-de-vie de poire (pear brandy) or
   fresh lemon juice to taste

FOR THE CUSTARD

2 large eggs
1 large egg, separated
¼ cup milk

6 tablespoons sugar
¼ teaspoon grated lemon rind
¼ teaspoon vanilla

¾ cup sliced blanched almonds

3 tablespoons dried currants

Make the sweet pastry dough:

Into a bowl or a food processor sift together the flour, sugar, and the salt, add the butter, and blend the mixture until it resembles meal. If using the food processor, transfer the mixture to a bowl. In a small bowl whisk together the egg yolk and 1 tablespoon of the orange juice or ice water. Add the egg mixture to the flour mixture, stirring with a fork, and if necessary add enough of the remaining orange juice or ice water to form a dough. Form the dough into a ball, flatten it slightly, and chill it, wrapped in wax paper, for 30 minutes, or until just firm.

On a lightly floured surface roll the dough into a round ⅛ inch thick, fit it into the flan pan, and form an edge ¼ inch above the rim (see illustrations page 122). Prick the shell with a fork and chill it for 30 minutes.

Preheat the oven to 400° F.

Line, weight, and blind-bake the shell (see illustrations page 163) on the baking sheet in the lower third of the oven for 6 to 8 minutes, or until the sides have set. Remove the rice and paper carefully, bake the shell, pricking the air bubbles, for 6 minutes more, or until it is pale and golden, and let it cool in the pan on a rack.

Peel the pears, cut them into ¼-inch slices, and arrange the slices, overlapping slightly, decoratively in the shell. Sprinkle the pears with the *eau-de-vie de poire* and bake them in the shell on the baking sheet in the middle of the oven for 12 to 15 minutes, or until just tender.

Make the custard: In a bowl whisk together the eggs, egg yolk, ½ cup of the thick *crème fraîche* or sour cream, milk, 2 tablespoons of the sugar, lemon rind, and the vanilla. Ladle the custard over the pears.

Bake the tart for 17 to 20 minutes, or until the custard is barely set in the center, and transfer the tart to a rack.

In a bowl combine the almonds, currants, remaining 4 tablespoons sugar, and the egg white, beaten lightly, and stir the mixture to coat the almonds. Spoon the mixture carefully onto the tart, smoothing it gently, and bake the tart for 15 to 20 minutes, or until lightly golden. Serve the tart warm or at room temperature.

FRANGIPANE-FILLED AND NUT TARTS

Frangipane refers to an almond-flavored creamy filling combining eggs, sugar, butter, and ground almonds. When baked, the frangipane becomes almost cake-like in texture. Frangipane can be used as a separate layer in a tart, baked and then filled or the frangipane and filling can be baked together; as the frangipane bakes, it puffs up and sets around the fruit. In our recipes for Apricot Frangipane Tart (page 180) and Almond Cherry Tart (page 180), the almond cream is spread in the shell and topped with the fruits. After baking, the apricot halves and cherries are encircled by golden puffs of the frangipane, resulting in a rustic, pebbly appearance.

Apricot Frangipane Tart (page 180)   Pecan Caramel Tart (page 181) and Macadamia Nut Tartlets (page 182) are buttery, sweet, and luscious. Because of the richness of nut tarts, they are best served in small portions or as tartlets.

APRICOT FRANGIPANE TART

Yield:
1 tart, 11¼ by 8 by
  1 inches

Equipment:
rectangular tart pan
  with removable
  fluted rim, 11¼ by
  8 by 1 inches
baking sheet
hand-held electric
  mixer
pastry brush

Frangipane is an almond cream filling or a rich vanilla custard finished with crushed macaroons. When baked, frangipane takes on a cake-like texture.

*1½ recipes pâte brisée (page 164),
  rolled ⅛ inch thick, transferred to
  tart pan, and fitted in (see
  illustrations page 163)
1 stick (½ cup) unsalted butter, cut
  into bits and softened
⅓ cup plus 2 teaspoons sugar*

*2 large eggs
1 cup blanched almonds (for procedure
  page 549), ground
1 teaspoon vanilla
a 2-pound can apricot halves, drained
½ cup apricot glaze (page 540)*

Trim the edge of the dough with the rolling pin. Prick the shell with a fork and chill the shell for 30 minutes.

Preheat the oven to 350° F. and preheat the baking sheet.

In a bowl with the mixer cream the butter, add ⅓ cup of the sugar, and beat the mixture until fluffy. Add the eggs, one at a time, beating well after each addition, and beat in the almonds and the vanilla. Spread the frangipane mixture in the shell, top it with the apricot halves cut sides up, and bake the tart on the baking sheet in the lower third of the oven for 40 minutes, or until the filling is golden and set.

Preheat the broiler.

Sprinkle the tart with the remaining 2 teaspoons sugar and put it under the broiler about 6 inches from the heat for 2 to 3 minutes, or until the filling is browned. Brush the tart with the apricot glaze, let it cool, and remove the rim of the pan.

Photo on page 179.

ALMOND CHERRY TART

Yield:
one 10-inch tart

*1 recipe pâte brisée (page 164),
  rolled ⅛ inch thick, transferred to
  tart pan, and fitted in (see
  illustrations page 163)
1 large egg
1 egg yolk
½ cup granulated sugar
¾ stick (6 tablespoons) unsalted
  butter, softened*

*1 cup ground blanched almonds
½ teaspoon vanilla
3 cups pitted dark sweet cherries
½ cup red currant glaze (page 541)
  made with 1 to 2 tablespoons
  Amaretto, heated
sifted confectioners' sugar for garnish*

Equipment:
10-inch round tart
  pan with removable
  fluted rim
hand-held electric
  mixer
baking sheet
pastry brush

Trim the edge of the dough with the rolling pin. Prick the bottom of the shell with a fork and chill the shell for 30 minutes.

Preheat the oven to 375° F.

In a bowl with the mixer beat the egg, egg yolk, and granulated sugar until the mixture is thick and pale. Beat in the butter, almonds, and vanilla and spread the almond butter in the shell. Arrange the cherries decoratively on the almond butter and bake the tart on the baking sheet in the lower third of the oven for 30 minutes.

Reduce the oven temperature to 350° F. Bake the tart for 15 minutes more, or until a knife inserted in the center comes out clean. Let the tart cool on a rack for 30 minutes.

Spoon the red currant glaze over the tart. Just before serving, sprinkle the edge of the tart with the confectioners' sugar.

PECAN CARAMEL TART

Yield:
one 10-inch tart

This tart with its deliciously sweet filling that is cooked, not baked, is surprisingly confection-like in nature and should be served in thin wedges.

Equipment:
10-inch decorative
  flan form, 1 inch
  deep
baking sheet
candy thermometer

1 recipe pâte brisée (page 164), rolled ⅛ inch thick, transferred to flan form set on the baking sheet, and fitted in (see illustrations page 163)
raw rice or dried beans for weighting the shell
1 stick (½ cup) unsalted butter, cut into pieces

2 cups firmly packed light brown sugar
⅓ cup dark corn syrup
4 cups pecan halves
½ cup heavy cream
¼ teaspoon ground allspice
2 tablespoons dark rum

Trim the edge of the dough with the rolling pin. Prick the bottom of the shell with a fork and chill the shell for 30 minutes.

Preheat the oven to 425° F.

Line, weight, and blind-bake the shell (see illustrations page 163) in the lower third of the oven for 10 minutes. Remove the rice and paper carefully, bake the shell for 5 to 10 minutes more, or until it is golden, and let it cool on the baking sheet. Remove the shell from the flan form and arrange it on a serving plate.

In a heavy saucepan melt the butter, add the sugar and corn syrup, and cook the mixture over moderately low heat, stirring, with a wooden spoon, for 7 to 10 minutes, or until the candy thermometer registers 260° F. Remove the pan from the heat, add the pecan halves, heavy cream, and allspice, and stir the mixture until combined well. Cook the mixture over low heat, stirring, for 5 minutes, or until the candy thermometer registers 200° F. (For the stages of sugar syrup, see illustrations page 241.) Let the mixture cool for 5 minutes, stir in the rum, and spoon the mixture into the shell. Let the tart cool completely and chill it for at least 2 hours or overnight.

When it is cold, cut the tart into thin wedges or bite-size pieces with a knife dipped in hot water and let it stand at room temperature for 30 minutes.

MACADAMIA NUT TARTLETS

Yield:
6 tartlets

Equipment:
six 4-inch tartlet tins
5-inch round cutter
pastry brush

½ recipe pâte brisée *(page 164)*
⅔ cup sugar
3 tablespoons water
½ cup heavy cream, heated

1 cup whole macadamia nuts, chopped
   coarse and toasted
3 tablespoons unsalted butter, cut into
   tablespoons

Follow the directions for forming and baking tartlet shells as directed for Lemon Curd Tartlets (page 177).

In a heavy saucepan combine the sugar with the water and cook the mixture over moderate heat, washing down any sugar crystals clinging to the sides of the pan with the brush dipped in cold water until golden. Add the cream, a little at a time, and stir the mixture until smooth. Stir in the nuts and add the butter, one tablespoon at a time. Cook the mixture, stirring, for 3 minutes and let it cool for 5 minutes. Spoon the filling into the shells. Let the tartlets cool to room temperature before serving.

TARTS WITH DIFFERENT SHELLS

The two following recipes, one for Linzertorte (recipe opposite) and one for Pear, Port, and Saga Blue Tart (page 184) have nothing in common except for the fact that both are so undeniably fine that we consider them musts for this collection.

Linzertorte is a classic. Filled, simply, with red raspberry jam, it is the fragrant latticed nut crust that makes this tart so special. The dough is arranged diagonally across the jam in a lattice pattern forming the characteristic diamond shapes. This Linzer dough uses ground almonds and can be seasoned with the traditional spices cinnamon, cloves, and nutmeg if desired. Pear, Port, and Saga blue tart is a sophisticated combination of pears poached in port wine atop an irresistibly rich pastry crust made with the addition of Saga blue cheese, a fascinating combination of sweet and savory.

LINZERTORTE

Yield:
one 14- by 4½-inch tart, about 28 strips

Equipment:
14- by 4½-inch flan form with removable rim pastry brush

An Austrian specialty, named in honor of the city of Linz, where the torte was supposedly created, *Linzertorte* is a wonderful combination of a latticed nut crust and jam filling. Hazelnuts or walnuts can be substituted for the almonds in the crust, which can also be made spicier by the addition of cinnamon, nutmeg, and ground cloves.

As a longtime resident of Austria and an excellent baker in her own right, Lillian Langseth-Christensen suggests that the *Linzertorte* be made ahead of time as its flavor and consistency improve with keeping. In short, *Linzertorte* is a perfect example of a classic dessert that has no classic recipe—the crust, filling, and flavorings are at the discretion of the baker.

1⅓ cups all-purpose flour
⅓ cup confectioners' sugar plus additional confectioners' sugar for garnish if desired
pinch of salt
¾ cup blanched almonds (for procedure page 549), ground

1¼ sticks (½ cup plus 2 tablespoons) unsalted butter, cut into bits
3 egg yolks, beaten lightly
grated rind of ½ lemon
½ cup raspberry jam
1 tablespoon orange-flavored liqueur
egg wash of 1 egg, beaten lightly

Lightly butter the flan form.

Into a large bowl sift together the flour, the ⅓ cup confectioners' sugar, and salt. Stir in the almonds, add the butter with your fingertips or using two knives, and blend the mixture until well combined (see illustrations page 121). Add the egg yolks and lemon rind, toss the mixture until well combined, and form the dough into a ball. Dust the dough with flour and chill it, wrapped in wax paper, for 1½ hours.

Preheat the oven to 375° F.

On a floured surface roll half the dough into a 14- by 4½-inch rectangle and fit it into the flan form (see illustration page 163), pressing it in firmly. Force the jam through the sieve into a small bowl and stir in the liqueur. Spread the jam evenly over the dough, leaving a ½-inch border. Cut half the remaining dough into 14 pieces. With lightly floured hands roll each piece into a rope about ¼ inch in diameter. Halve each rope and arrange the ropes diagonally across the jam in a lattice pattern, pressing the ends onto the dough. Roll the remaining dough into 2 ropes, each about 20 inches long. Cut the ropes into 4 lengths to fit the sides and ends of the torte and fit them around the edge of the pastry, pressing them down firmly. Brush the lattice and edge with the egg wash.

Bake the pastry in the middle of the oven for 30 to 35 minutes, or until golden. Let the pastry cool in the flan form. Remove the tart from the form, wrap it in foil, and let it stand for at least 2 days.

With a sharp knife cut the pastry crosswise into ½-inch strips and halve each strip, if desired. Sprinkle the slices with the confectioners' sugar.

Photo on page 275.

Pear, Port, and Saga Blue Tart (below)

PEAR, PORT, AND SAGA BLUE TART

Yield:
one 9-inch tart

Equipment:
9-inch round tart pan
  with removable
  fluted rim
pastry brush

This recipe combines fruit and cheese in an especially inventive manner by encasing pears, first poached in Port wine syrup, in a pastry crust made from Saga blue cheese.

FOR THE SAGA BLUE PASTRY

1 cup all-purpose flour
1 tablespoon sugar
1 stick (½ cup) cold unsalted butter,
  cut into bits
¼ pound Saga blue cheese without the
  rind, cut into bits

2 tablespoons ice water
raw rice or dried beans for weighting
  the shell

2 cups dry red wine
1 cup Tawny Port
½ cup sugar
1 teaspoon black peppercorns
¼ teaspoon whole cloves
2 firm ripe pears, peeled and cored
    from the bottom, leaving the pears
    whole and the stems intact

½ cup apricot glaze (page 540)
    thinned with 2 tablespoons water,
    heated
mint sprig for garnish
sweetened whipped cream as an
    accompaniment if desired

Make the Saga blue pastry:

In a bowl blend the flour, sugar, butter, and the Saga blue until the mixture resembles coarse meal and stir in the 2 tablespoons ice water, or enough to form the dough into a ball. Knead the dough lightly with the heel of the hand against a smooth surface for a few seconds to distribute the fat evenly, re-form it into a ball, and flatten the ball slightly. Chill the dough, dusted with flour and wrapped in wax paper, for at least 2 hours or overnight.

The tart shell may be made 1 day ahead and kept covered and frozen.

On a floured surface roll out the dough ¼ inch thick and fit it into the tart pan (see illustrations page 163). Prick the shell all over with a fork and freeze it for at least 1 hour.

Preheat the oven to 400° F.

Line, weight, and blind-bake the shell (see illustrations page 163) in the middle of the oven for 15 minutes. Remove the rice and paper carefully and bake the shell for 5 minutes more, or until pale golden. Remove the shell from the pan and let it cool on a rack.

In a very deep saucepan combine the red wine, Port, sugar, peppercorns, and cloves, bring the liquid to a simmer, stirring, and cook the syrup over moderate heat for 5 minutes. Add the pears and simmer the mixture, turning the pears, for 10 to 20 minutes, or until the pears are just tender. Let the pears cool in the syrup.

The pears may be prepared 1 day ahead, kept covered and chilled in the syrup, and returned to room temperature.

Transfer the pears with a slotted spoon to a plate, strain the syrup, returning it to the saucepan, and reduce it over moderately high heat to about ¼ cup. Brush the pears with the glaze, halve them, and slice them lengthwise on the diagonal, leaving a few slices attached to one of the stems for the center of the tart. Arrange the slices in a circle on the tart shell, overlapping them, and fan the attached slices in the center to simulate a pear.

Brush the tart with the apricot glaze and garnish the tart with the mint sprig. Serve with the whipped cream if desired.

Photo opposite.

PASTRY

The pleasures of pastry are incalculable. From a simple combination of flour and butter, with a little liquid added, and maybe an egg but not always, and sometimes some yeast but that is infrequent, too, something remarkable happens. This earthbound mixture called dough encounters heat and suddenly is transformed into flaky crisp layers of marvelous light ethereal crumbs. It is magic and chemistry all in one, and unlike other wonders, like lightning or music, you can consume it.

We include six basic pastry doughs in this chapter, beginning with classic puff paste, that French *tour de force* of 1000 layers. The very cornerstone of French pastry-making, *pâte feuilletée,* or *feuilletage,* or *millefeuille,* as it is known, is a challenge for even the best bakers. The dough is formed in a specific manner and folded and "turned" to form multilayers of butter and dough. When baked, steam from the moisture in the butter rises, forcing the layers of dough to rise as well. Arithmetically it has been calculated that this occurs over 1000 times. Among the recipes for this captivating dough, you will find the classic Gâteau Pithiviers (page 198) and the splendid peekaboo jam tart Jalousie (page 197).

For those who like the pleasures of classic puff paste, but not necessarily the process of making it, we follow it with quick puff paste, turned in the same way as its sophisticated first cousin, but combined in an entirely different and quicker fashion. You will find a glorious recipe for Tarte Tatin (page 203) in this section and several very simple fine cookies.

Another contribution from the French to the world of pastry-making follows: brioche dough. And here begins a small collection of other yeasted doughs, including baba, or savarin, dough, and Danish pastry. Yeast pastry doughs and butter pastry doughs have only one thing in common: They are equally delicious, utterly unique.

Pâte à chou, cream puff pastry, follows Danish dough. Without yeast but with ample eggs, cooked over heat, and formed into shapes with a pastry bag, it too has no resemblance to the doughs that precede it. It is

Pineapple Savarin Chantilly (page 212)

perfectly wonderful, though, as *Profiteroles* (page 223), or Paris-Brest (page 224), or in the magnificent Gâteau Saint-Honoré (page 228).

We end this chapter with a short collection of recipes for *phyllo* and strudel dough, those paper-thin combinations that depend not at all on butter but on flour and liquid and on how the dough is stretched.

As puff paste rises into 1000 layers, the possibilities of these six singular pastry doughs are equally limitless.

CLASSIC PUFF PASTE

Classic puff paste, *pâte feuilletée, feuilletage classique*—three different terms meaning exactly the same thing. It is the pastry dough of all pastry doughs, the *succès fou,* contributed by the French to *haute cuisine* in the seventeenth century, and to date, despite our technical brilliance and scientific know-how, we have not been able to better it. There is really no need. *Pâte feuilletée* is rightfully named. It is classic and remains unrivaled.

What makes this dough so special? Its very name hints at the answer: the dough of many leaves, or layers, if you will. It begins, like most doughs, with flour and liquid combined to a paste. Onto this sheet of dough is placed a solid square of butter. The dough is folded around the butter, then rolled, folded, and turned in a fashion specific to puff paste. During this process the butter and dough are layered; when the dough is baked, steam from the moisture in the butter rises, forcing the layers of dough to rise with it—up to 1000 times. The texture of the layers is crisp and notably light and there is that exceptional flavor of butter throughout. It is an incredible occurrence when you think that *pâte brisée* (page 164) is made with essentially the same ingredients, in different proportions, of course, and that the remarkable difference in the way these doughs bake resides entirely in the way each of them is handled.

Making this dough is not easy, even for professional bakers. Moreover, it takes time; the dough is rolled and turned a total of six times, and each time it must be chilled to relax the gluten in the flour and to firm up the butter. In other words, when you make puff pastry, allow yourself enough time to do it well. It is also advisable to do it, particularly if it is for the first time, on a cool day. Butter melts, and this is precisely what you do not want to have happen when you are rolling the dough. A cool marble surface is the best one on which to work, but failing that, a stainless steel table. Also, if it is hot, chill your rolling pin.

As illustrated on page 190, you begin by preparing the dough mixture, also called the *détrempe.* We recommend using a pastry blender to do this, for uniformity of the size of the pieces of cut butter. You can also use two knives, or your fingertips, but they will provide heat, which is not necessarily desired. Form the dough into a ball and, unlike other doughs, with a large sharp knife or a pastry scraper, slash a deep cross right through the center of it. Wrap the dough carefully and chill it until firm, but not hard, as you will next need to roll it.

As the dough chills, prepare the square of butter: In a bowl combine the butter and the small amount of flour that is called for. Then transfer the mixture to the work surface and knead it as illustrated to soften it. Form it into a rough square and, between sheets of wax paper, then press it into a tidy 6-inch square. Flour the butter, rewrap it, and chill it. It is important to recognize at this point that you want the dough and the butter to be of equal consistency when you start rolling them out.

Next, lightly flour your work surface and on it roll the dough into a 9-inch square. As shown, then position the square of butter diagonally in the center of the dough. With the rolling pin, beginning at the center of the dough, roll the four corners of the dough evenly into 7-inch strips and fold each strip, without stretching it, over the butter to enclose the square completely. You want a compact package at this point.

You are now ready to start rolling and turning the dough—the first step in actually creating the layers of puff paste. Dust the work surface, dust the dough package, and with the rolling pin, always starting in the middle of the dough and always rolling gently away from you, roll the dough into a 16- by 10-inch rectangle, lifting and turning the dough occasionally to prevent it from sticking. Try to keep the sides as even as possible and if need be roll them lightly to make a tidy rectangle. As shown on page 190, fold the dough into thirds as you would a business letter; bring the top third of the dough down over the center and the bottom third up over the top. Then turn the dough seam side down so that an open side faces you. This is a most important step. If you forget to turn over the dough, you will be rolling it out the second time in the same direction you did the first, and there will be no layering effect. This constitutes your first "turn."

As described above, roll the dough again into a rectangle, fold it into thirds, and turn it seam side down. You have now executed turn 2, and the dough will most likely need to chill, wrapped in wax paper, for 30 minutes or so. You will make four more of these turns for a total of six, the usual number associated with the classic preparation, before rolling the dough out for final in the recipe.

■   ■   ■

The directions are straightforward, but the technique for making classic puff paste requires practice and skill. In undertaking it, there are two important considerations: first, the temperature of the butter. If it starts to melt or ooze into the dough from being overworked, you must chill the dough until the butter is firm. Two, the amount of pressure applied in rolling out this dough is directly related to its success. Less is more. In time you will acquire the confidence to work quickly and confidently with it. As the layers of puff paste increase exponentially, though, so will your delight when you can proceed to the glories of working with it, to fruit strips, and cornets, and that domed marvel Gâteau Pithiviers (page 198).

STEPS FOR MAKING PUFF PASTE:

 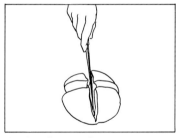 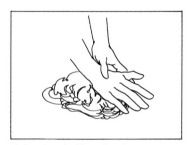

Blending flour and butter with pastry blender; Cutting deep cross in center of the dough; Kneading butter and flour together

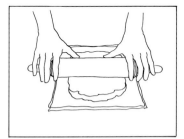  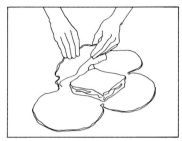

Rolling *détrempe* into rough square; Rolling corners of dough into strips; Folding strips of dough over butter to enclose butter completely

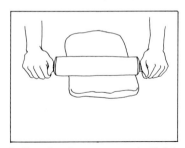 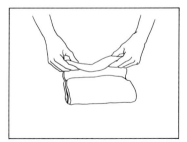 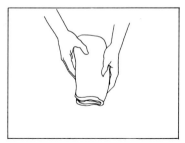

Rolling dough into rectangle; Folding top third of dough rectangle over center and bottom third over the top (first turn); Turning folded dough seam side down

CLASSIC PUFF PASTE

Yield:
1¾ pounds dough

Equipment:
pastry blender
 (optional)
pastry brush

Pâte feuilletée, puff paste, is one of the cornerstones of the classic French culinary repertoire. Rich in butter, the dough is folded and rolled in such a way that the butter is incorporated layer upon layer. As the dough bakes, steam from the butter rises, forcing the pastry into flaky heights, to a total of—believe it or not—over 1000 layers.

2½ cups all-purpose flour   *½ teaspoon salt*
3 sticks (1½ cups) cold unsalted butter   *⅔ to ¾ cup ice water*

In a bowl combine 2¼ cups of the flour, 4 tablespoons of the butter, cut into bits, and the salt and blend the mixture with your fingertips or the pastry blender until it resembles meal. Stir in ⅔ cup ice water and, if necessary, continue to add additional water by teaspoons until the mixture forms a soft dough. Gather the dough into a ball, cut a deep cross in the center, and form the dough into a 6-inch square. Dust the dough lightly with flour. Chill the dough, wrapped in wax paper, for 30 minutes, or until firm but not hard.

In a bowl combine the remaining 1¼ cups butter, cut into bits, with the remaining ¼ cup flour and toss the mixture to coat the butter. Knead the butter and flour together and form the mixture into a rough square. Put the square between sheets of wax paper and with a rolling pin press it into a 6-inch square. Remove the paper, dust the square well with flour, and wrap it in another sheet of wax paper. Chill the butter mixture until firm but not hard. (The dough and the floured butter should be of equal firmness.)

On a floured surface roll the dough into a 9-inch square. Lay the floured butter diagonally in the center of the square and roll the 4 visible corners of the dough into 7-inch strips. (The dough will form an X around the butter.) Fold each strip of dough over the butter to enclose the butter completely, making a package. Sprinkle the work surface with flour and turn the dough over into the flour. Sprinkle the dough with flour, with the rolling pin flatten the dough with uniform impressions, and roll it into a 16- by 10-inch rectangle. Turn the dough over, brush off any excess flour, and fold the top third of the rectangle over the center and the bottom third over the top.

Turn the folded dough seam side down so that an open side faces you (see illustrations opposite). With the rolling pin flatten the dough with uniform impressions. Roll the dough from the center away from you to within ½ inch of the end. Flatten the ends gently with uniform impressions. (Do not roll the pin over the end or the air and butter will be expelled.) Reverse the strip on the surface, flouring the surface as necessary, and again roll the dough from the center away from you to make a rectangle about 16 inches long. Turn the dough seam side up, brush any excess flour from it, and fold the rectangle in thirds as before. Chill the dough, wrapped in wax paper, for 30 minutes, or until firm but not hard. This completes 2 "turns."

Make 4 more turns, always starting with the seam side down and an open end facing you, chilling the dough after each turn or after every second turn depending upon the softness of the butter and the manageability of the dough. (You do not want the butter to become so soft that it seeps through the dough.) Chill the dough, wrapped in plastic wrap, for at least 2 hours and up to 3 days.

The dough may be frozen, wrapped in plastic wrap and foil, for up to 1 month.

Variation:

CLASSIC PUFF PASTE: PROCESSOR METHOD: Using the same measurements of ingredients as for handmade puff paste, in a processor fitted with the steel blade blend 2¼ cups flour, 4 tablespoons butter, cut into bits, and the salt until the mixture resembles meal. With the motor running, add the ⅔ cup ice water, adding more of the water if necessary, one teaspoon at a time, until the dough forms a ball. Knead the dough with the machine for 30 seconds and transfer it to a work surface. Dust the ball lightly with flour, cut a deep cross in the middle of it, and push each quarter outward to form the ball into a 6-inch square. Pat the dough until smooth and chill it, wrapped in wax paper, for 30 minutes, until firm but not hard.

Prepare the square of butter mixture, form the dough package, and roll and turn the dough as described in classic puff paste.

FREE-FORM SQUARE PUFF PASTE SHELL

Yield:
one 12-inch square
  pastry shell

Equipment:
pastry brush

½ recipe classic puff paste (page 190)
egg wash made by beating 1 egg with 1 teaspoon water and pinch of salt

On a lightly floured surface roll the classic puff paste into a 13-inch square ⅛ inch thick. Invert the pastry onto a moistened baking sheet and chill it for at least 1 hour, or until firm.

Fold the pastry square in half diagonally and trim the edges evenly. Cut a 1-inch border on the two open sides (not the folded side), being careful to leave the pastry attached at the right angle corner (see illustrations). Unfold the dough and moisten the edges with water. Fold the outer half of each border over onto the moistened edge of dough and press the border to the moistened dough. Trim the folded corners and with the back of a small knife decoratively scallop the sides of the tart, at the same time pressing the borders onto the base. Chill the shell, covered with plastic wrap, for at least 1 hour or overnight.

Preheat the oven to 425° F.

Brush the inside of the shell with the egg wash, being careful not to let any of the wash drip over the sides. Prick the base. Bake the shell in the lower third of the oven for 15 minutes. Reduce the heat to 350° F. and bake the shell for 12 to 15 minutes longer, or until golden brown. Let the shell

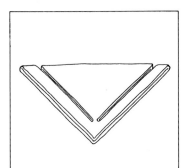 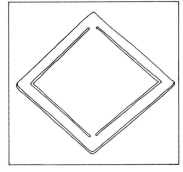 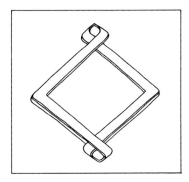

Forming free-form square puff paste shell

cool to warm on the baking sheet and transfer it to a rack to cool completely. The shell is now ready to be filled.

Note: Be sure to brush the inside of the baked shell with egg wash before filling the shell to prevent any sogginess.

FREE-FORM ROUND PUFF PASTE SHELL

Yield:
one 9½-inch round
  pastry shell

Equipment:
11-inch round guide
10-inch round guide
pastry brush

½ recipe classic puff paste (page 190)
egg wash made by beating 1 egg with 1 teaspoon water and pinch of salt

On a lightly floured surface roll the classic puff paste into a round ⅛ inch thick. Using the 11-inch guide cut the dough into a circle. Center the 10-inch guide on the dough and cut around it, forming a 1-inch band. Cut the band into 4 equal pieces. Invert the round onto a moistened baking sheet, brush the edges of it with water, and attach the bands onto the edge around the rim, trimming the ends of each band so that it overlaps the next by ½ inch. Moisten the ends of the bands with water and gently press them together to seal (see illustrations). With the back of a small knife decoratively scallop the sides of the shell. Chill the shell, covered with plastic wrap, for at least 1 hour or overnight.

Brush, prick, bake, and cool the shell as directed for free-form square puff paste shell (page 192).

Note: Be sure to brush the inside of the baked shell with egg wash before filling the shell to prevent any sogginess.

Forming free-form round puff paste shell

FREE-FORM PUFF PASTE STRIP

Yield:
one 12- by 5-inch
  pastry strip

Equipment:
pastry brush

You will note that this puff paste strip has sides only. No ends. Should you want an enclosed strip, cut 1-inch-wide pieces of dough at each end of the strip and simply attach them as you do the sides.

½ recipe classic puff paste (page 190)
egg wash made by beating 1 egg with 1 teaspoon water and pinch of salt

On a lightly floured surface roll the classic puff paste into a rectangle about 17 by 9 inches and ⅛ inch thick. Trim the edges and invert the dough onto a moistened baking sheet. Chill the dough for at least 1 hour, or until firm.

With a sharp knife cut 1-inch-wide bands from each long side, brush the long sides of the dough with water, and attach the bands, gently pressing them into the base (see illustration). With the back of a sharp knife scallop the sides of the strip and prick the center with a fork. Chill the strip, covered with plastic wrap, for at least 1 hour or overnight.

Brush, bake, and cool the strip as directed for free-form square puff paste shell (page 192).

Note: Be sure to brush the inside of the baked strip with egg wash before filling the shell to prevent any sogginess.

FILLINGS FOR BAKED PUFF PASTE SHELLS: Fillings include whipped cream, pastry cream, ice cream, or any custard or mousse-type preparation as a foundation. Top with fresh fruit and glaze the fruit with melted jelly or a liqueur-flavored glaze. For a very simple yet elegant filling gently fold melted jelly or sieved preserves into seasonal fresh fruit and arrange in the tart shell or strip.

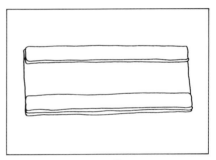

Forming free-form puff paste strip

STRAWBERRY FRUIT STRIP

Yield:
one 12- by 5-inch
strip, serving 6

Equipment:
pastry brush

Any fresh berry can be substituted for the strawberries in this strip—let the seasons dictate your choice. If desired, a layer of pastry cream or whipped cream can be used as a base for the fruit. In that case, however, do not assemble the strip more than an hour in advance of serving as the pastry may become slightly soggy from the cream.

*1 free-form puff paste strip, baked
  (page 193)
2 pints strawberries, hulled and
  halved if large
2 tablespoons orange-flavored liqueur*

*1 tablespoon sugar, or to taste
1 teaspoon fresh lemon juice
1 teaspoon grated orange rind
½ cup red currant jelly*

Arrange the puff paste shell on a serving tray.

In a bowl toss the strawberries with 1 tablespoon of the liqueur, the sugar, lemon juice, and grated orange rind and let stand, covered and chilled, for 1 hour.

In a small saucepan combine the remaining 1 tablespoon liqueur with the currant jelly and simmer the mixture until smooth. Brush the bottom of the strip with some of the currant glaze. Drain the strawberries, arrange them in the strip, mounding them in the center, and brush them with the glaze. The strip is best served within 1½ to 2 hours after assembly.

DRIED-FRUIT TURNOVERS

Yield:
8 to 10 turnovers

Equipment:
4-inch fluted cutter
pastry brush

Autumnal flavors—dried fruits, cider, cinnamon, and cloves—encased in puff pastry not as a tart nor as a strip, but rather as turnovers. This is yet another tempting reminder of the versatility of puff paste.

1 recipe classic puff paste (page 190)
8 ounces mixed dried fruits, minced
¾ stick (6 tablespoons) unsalted butter
½ cup apple cider
2 tablespoons honey
2 tablespoons brown sugar

1 tablespoon fresh lemon juice
½ teaspoon grated lemon rind
½ teaspoon cinnamon
¼ teaspoon ground cloves
egg wash made by beating 1 egg with
*   pinch of salt*

In a stainless steel saucepan cook the dried fruits and 4 tablespoons of the butter over moderate heat, stirring, for 5 minutes. Add the cider, honey, brown sugar, lemon juice, lemon rind, cinnamon, and cloves and cook, stirring, for 15 to 20 minutes, or until most of the liquid is evaporated. Stir in the remaining 2 tablespoons butter, transfer the mixture to a bowl, and let cool.

Roll the dough into a rectangle ⅛ inch thick on a floured surface and with the cutter cut it into rounds. Brush the rounds lightly with water and put 1 tablespoon of the dried-fruit mixture in the center of each round. Fold the rounds in half and press the edges together gently to seal in the filling. Invert the turnovers onto a moistened baking sheet and chill them for 30 minutes.

Preheat the oven to 425° F.

Brush the turnovers lightly with some egg wash and score them decoratively with the point of a sharp knife. Bake in the middle of the oven for 10 to 12 minutes, or until puffed and golden. Transfer the turnovers to racks to cool.

NESSELRODE CREAM CORNETS

Yield:
24 cornets

Equipment:
pastry brush
24 cornet molds
  (available at
  specialty
  kitchenware shops)
upright and hand-held
  electric mixers

Named after Count Nesselrode, a nineteenth-century Russian diplomat, these puff paste horns have an impressive filling, one with an Old-World feel, harkening back to times of grand combinations. Pastry cream is studded with glacéed fruits and chopped chestnuts, whipped cream is gently folded in, and the whole is spooned into delicate, crispy pastries. Here is a dessert to have by candlelight.

FOR THE CORNETS

1 recipe classic puff paste (page 190)

egg wash made by beating 1 egg lightly with 1 tablespoon heavy cream

FOR THE NESSELRODE CREAM

2 tablespoons halved glacéed red cherries
2 tablespoons halved glacéed green cherries
2 tablespoons coarsely chopped angelica (available at specialty foods shops)
2 tablespoons coarsely chopped cooked chestnuts (for procedure page 550)

¼ cup dark rum
6 egg yolks
½ cup granulated sugar
⅓ cup all-purpose flour, sifted
2 cups milk, scalded
1 teaspoon unflavored gelatin
3 tablespoons cold water
2 teaspoons vanilla
1 cup well-chilled heavy cream

confectioners' sugar for sifting

Make the cornets:

Butter the cornet molds.

On a lightly floured surface roll the dough into a rectangle 18 by 12 inches and ⅛ inch thick. With a sharp knife cut the dough into strips 12 by ¾ inches wide. Starting at the tip of one of the molds wrap a strip of the dough around it, without stretching the dough, slightly overlapping the edges. (The strip should cover about three fourths of the mold.) Wrap the remaining molds in the same manner. Lay the molds, dough ends underneath, on a moistened baking sheet and chill them for at least 30 minutes.

Preheat the oven to 350° F.

Brush the cornets with the egg wash and bake in the middle of the oven for 20 minutes, or until lightly browned. Carefully slip the cornets from the molds and let the pastries cool on a rack.

Make the nesselrode cream:

In a small bowl combine the red and green cherries, the angelica, and chestnuts. Add the rum and let the mixture macerate for at least 30 minutes.

In the bowl of the upright mixer beat the egg yolks with the sugar at medium speed until light and lemon colored. Gradually add the flour and beat until smooth. Add the hot milk in a stream. Transfer the mixture to a heavy saucepan, bring it to a simmer, and simmer it over low heat, stirring constantly, for 3 minutes. Remove the pan from the heat.

In a small bowl let the gelatin soften in the cold water for 5 minutes. Stir the gelatin into the yolk mixture with the vanilla. Strain the custard into a bowl set in a larger bowl of ice water and stir until completely cool and thickened. Chill the custard, covered, until cold.

In a chilled bowl with the hand-held mixer beat the cream until it holds soft peaks. Stir the custard to lighten it and stir in the glacéed fruit mixture. Fold in the whipped cream gently but thoroughly.

Fill the cornets generously with nesselrode cream and sift the confectioners' sugar over them. Serve at once.

JALOUSIE

Peekaboo Jam Tart

Yield:
one 15- by 5-inch tart,
serving 8 to 10

A lovely combination of buttery, flaky pastry and jam. The actual cutting of the dough for the peekaboo effect is not as difficult as one might at first think, and that, coupled with the simplicity of the filling, makes this a good dessert to remember once you have a supply of puff paste on hand.

½ recipe classic puff paste (page 190)
⅔ cup preserves or jam of choice or a
*   combination of jam and red currant*
*   jelly*

egg wash made by beating 1 egg with
*   1 teaspoon water and pinch of salt*
1 tablespoon sugar, or to taste
lightly whipped cream or ice cream as
*   an acompaniment if desired*

On a lightly floured surface roll the pastry into a rectangle 17 by 12 inches and ⅛ inch thick. With a sharp knife trim the edges to form a 15- by 10-inch rectangle and halve the dough lengthwise. Invert one half of the dough onto a moistened baking sheet and prick it with a fork. Smooth a layer of the jam down the center of the dough, leaving a 1-inch border on all sides, and brush the border with the egg wash. Fold the remaining dough in half lengthwise and cut ⅓-inch slits crosswise down the length of the folded side, cutting to within ⅔ inch from the edge of the dough. Unfold the dough on top of the jam, pressing the edges together to seal (see illustrations). Chill the tart for at least 1 hour.

Preheat the oven to 425° F.

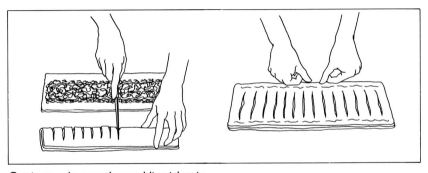

Cutting top layer and assembling jalousie

With the back of a small knife scallop the edges of the tart and brush the tart with the egg wash. Let stand for 5 minutes and brush the tart again with the egg wash. With the back of a fork score the sides of the tart. Bake in the lower third of the oven for 10 minutes. Reduce the heat to 375° F. and bake the tart for 15 minutes. Sprinkle the sugar over the tart and bake it for 5 to 10 minutes more, or until the pastry is crisp and golden brown. Let the tart cool for 10 minutes on the baking sheet and transfer it to a rack to cool. Serve the tart warm or at room temperature accompanied by the lightly whipped cream or ice cream if desired.

GÂTEAU PITHIVIERS

Almond-Filled Puff Pastry

Yield:
one 9-inch cake,
  serving about 8

Equipment:
9-inch round cake pan
10-inch round cake
  pan
pastry brush

From the town of Pithiviers, south of Paris, this famous pastry combines almond cream between layers of puff paste. Scored identifiably on top as only a *gâteau Pithiviers* should be, the dessert is best served at room temperature on the day it is made. Both the pastry and the almond cream can be made in advance, however.

2 recipes classic puff paste (page 190)   *egg wash made by beating 1 egg with*
1 recipe almond cream (page 539)   *1 tablespoon water*
                                       ¼ cup confectioners' sugar, sifted

On a floured surface roll the pastry into a rectangle 22 by 12 inches. Using the inverted 9-inch cake pan as a guide, cut a round of dough and, using the inverted 10-inch pan, cut another round of dough. Remove the excess dough and chill the scraps for another use (see pages 201 to 206). Drape the 9-inch round lightly over the rolling pin and transfer it to a moistened baking sheet. Spread the almond cream evenly on the round, mounding it slightly in the center and leaving a 1-inch border. Brush the border of the round with water. Drape the 10-inch round lightly over the rolling pin, unroll it over the almond cream, and press the edges of the 2 rounds together so that they are completely sealed. Chill the dough for 30 minutes. With the blunt edge of a small knife scallop the border. Cut an air vent in the center of the dough and chill the dough for at least 1 hour.

Three or four hours before serving, brush the dough well with the egg wash. With the point of a small sharp knife score the top of the cake about ⅛ inch deep in the Pithiviers design (see illustrations page 200).

Preheat the oven to 450° F.

Bake the pastry in the middle of the oven for 20 minutes. Reduce the heat to 400° F. and bake for 25 minutes more, or until the pastry has completely risen and is crisp. Remove the pastry from the oven and increase the heat to 500° F. Dredge the top of the pastry with the confectioners'

Gâteau Pithiviers (opposite)

sugar and bake in the upper third of the oven for 5 minutes, or until the sugar has melted into a glaze. Transfer the pastry with a large metal spatula to a rack to cool and serve at room temperature.

Photo on page 199.

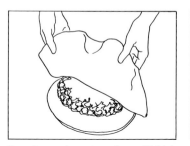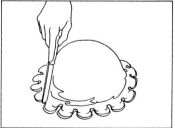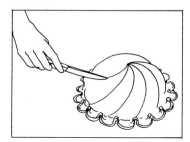

Forming and scoring gâteau Pithiviers

QUICK PUFF PASTE

At the beginning of this chapter we discussed the intricacies of classic puff paste, or *pâte feuilletée*, as it is called. With an elaborate flour and butter preparation and turned six times, classic puff paste might not be every cook's ideal recipe. For those dessert-makers who enjoy the pleasures of puff paste but not necessarily the challenge or time investment of making it, there is a splendid answer: quick puff paste. With a much easier dough preparation and turned at least two fewer times, quick puff paste still puffs into layers and is crisp and wonderfully ethereal when baked. Moreover, it can sometimes be used interchangeably with classic puff paste. For example, the recipe for Napoleon with Raspberry Sauce (page 202) calls for quick puff paste; there is no reason not to use the classic version, if you so desire.

To reiterate, the beauty of making quick puff paste is that the flour and butter are combined immediately in one bowl. There is no *détrempe*. You form the dough into a ball, you chill it, and in one hour, more or less, you are ready to roll the dough into turns. (For information and illustrations on this technique, see page 190.) Provided you have started with cold butter and the day is not an exceedingly hot one, you should be able to execute all four designated turns consecutively. Then chill the dough for 30 minutes to relax and solidify it, and the dough is ready to use.

In two of the recipes that appear in this section—Palmiers (page 205) and Walnut Twists (page 206)—you will see that we have called for either a recipe of quick puff paste or puff paste scraps, be they quick or classic. Saved carefully, stacked right on top of one another and never wadded into a dough ball, these scraps make absolutely glorious and quick cookies, which are also addictive on account of their lightness. One item to remember about puff paste cookies is that they do not keep. Susceptible to humidity, they are best made the day they are to be served and, ideally, not too far in advance of serving time.

We are not sure to whom credit should be given for the invention of quick puff paste. We owe that chef several *étoiles*, however. In this instance, a shortcut made one dough easier for us all.

QUICK PUFF PASTE

Yield:
1¼ pounds dough

Equipment:
pastry blender
(optional)

There are salient differences between quick puff paste and classic puff paste, not the least of which are implied by their titles. To begin with, while the ingredients for both doughs are exactly the same—flour, butter, salt, and ice water—the *way* they are combined is entirely specific. For quick puff paste, it occurs at one time, in one bowl, in just one step. There is no *détrempe* as in classic puff paste, and no preparation of a butter square. Further, while both doughs are turned, quick puff paste is turned at least two fewer times. As a consequence, quick puff paste is true to its name, is easier to make, and should take about half the amount of time to prepare.

2 cups all-purpose flour sifted with ½ teaspoon salt

2 sticks (1 cup) cold unsalted butter, cut into bits
½ cup ice water

In a large bowl with your fingertips or the pastry blender blend the flour mixture and the butter until the mixture resembles very coarse meal and the butter is the size of lima beans. Add the ice water and form the dough into a ball. Dust the dough with flour and chill it, wrapped in wax paper, for 1 hour.

On a floured surface roll the dough into a rectangle 12 by 6 inches, dusting it with flour if it sticks to the rolling pin. Fold the top third of the rectangle over the center and the bottom third over the top. Press down the top edge with the rolling pin so it adheres, turn the dough seam side down, and brush any excess flour from the dough. With an open side facing you roll the dough out again into a 12- by 6-inch rectangle and fold it into thirds as before. This completes 2 "turns." Make 2 more turns, always starting with the seam side down and an open end facing you. Chill the dough, wrapped in wax paper, for at least 30 minutes or for up to 3 days.

The dough may be frozen, wrapped in plastic wrap and foil, for up to 1 month.

Variation:

QUICK PUFF PASTE: PROCESSOR METHOD: Using the same measurements of ingredients as for handmade quick puff paste, in a processor fitted with the steel blade blend the flour mixture and butter for 5 seconds. Sprinkle the mixture with the water and process with on/off pulses until the mixture resembles very coarse meal and the butter is the size of lima beans. Transfer the mixture to plastic wrap, form it into a ball, and chill for 1 hour.

Roll, turn, and chill the dough as described in quick puff paste.

Napoleon with Raspberry Sauce (below)

NAPOLEON WITH RASPBERRY SAUCE

Yield:
12 by 5½-inch
  napoleon, serving 4

Equipment:
jelly-roll pan, 15½ by
  10½ inches
parchment paper
ruler

Somehow we all remember the first napoleon we ever tasted. It waited, surrounded by éclairs and tartlets, on a beautiful platter on a pastry cart in a French restaurant. Served by a waiter wearing white gloves, the dessert combined marvelous layers of pastry and custard and was topped with chocolate glaze. The following recipe again combines all those marvelous flaky layers and custard, but has the unexpected bonus of raspberry sauce.

1 recipe quick puff paste (page 201)
1 recipe pastry cream (page 537)
1 recipe Raspberry Sauce (page 508)

3 tablespoons confectioners' sugar
fresh raspberries and fresh mint sprigs
* for garnish*

Have ready the quick puff paste, pastry cream, and raspberry sauce.

Invert the jelly-roll pan and cover it with the parchment paper. Preheat the oven to 425° F.

Roll the dough into a rectangle ¹⁄₁₆ inch thick on a floured surface and trim the edges to measure 17 by 12 inches, reserving the trimmings for another use (see pages 205 and 206). Transfer the dough to the lined jelly-roll pan, letting the edges overhang, and prick it with a fork. Chill the dough for 20 minutes.

Bake the dough in the middle of the oven for 12 to 15 minutes, or until golden. Let the pastry cool on the pan on a rack. Turn the pastry over carefully and peel away the paper. Reduce the oven temperature to 350° F. and bake the pastry on the pan for 8 to 10 minutes, or until it is cooked through and crisp. Let the pastry cool on the rack and trim the edges to even them.

On a work surface cut the pastry crosswise vertically into 3 equal rectangles using the ruler and a very sharp knife. Put 1 layer of the pastry on a platter, spread it with half the pastry cream, and top the cream with a second pastry layer. Spread the remaining pastry cream over the pastry and top it with the remaining pastry layer. Sift the confectioners' sugar evenly over the top and garnish the napoleon with the raspberries and mint sprigs. Spoon some of the raspberry sauce around the dessert and serve the remaining sauce in a sauceboat. To serve, cut the napoleon crosswise with a serrated knife, using a gentle sawing motion.

Photo opposite.

TARTE TATIN

Upside-Down Apple Tart

Yield:
one 9-inch tart

Equipment:
jelly-roll pan
pastry brush
9-inch pie pan
9-inch plate

Another French perfection, this fruit tart is assembled in a pie pan. An amber caramel is made, apples are decoratively arranged in it, puff pastry is placed over the top, and the pan is set in the oven to bake. The tart is then reversed out of the pan, and the gloriously colored apple slices are again brushed with caramel before serving. Some dexterity, gained with practice, will facilitate the unmolding of this dessert. Your pastry may crack. No matter. Tarte Tatin remains a splendid creation and something even better to taste.

1 recipe quick puff paste (page 201)
1 stick (½ cup) unsalted butter
6 large apples such as McIntosh,
*   peeled, cored, and sliced thin*
1½ cups sugar
½ teaspoon grated lemon rind

6 tablespoons water
2 pinches cream of tartar
lightly whipped cream flavored with
*   dark rum or brandy as an*
*   accompaniment*

Have ready the quick puff paste.

In a large skillet melt the butter over moderate heat, add the apples, ½ cup of the sugar, and the lemon rind, and toss the apples until they are softened but still retain their shape. Transfer the mixture to the jelly-roll pan and let cool.

In a heavy skillet cook ½ cup of the sugar, 3 tablespoons of the water, and a pinch of the cream of tartar over moderately high heat, washing down any sugar crystals clinging to the sides of the pan with the brush dipped in cold water until it is a golden caramel. Pour the caramel into the pie pan, tilting the pan so that the caramel coats the bottom evenly, and let it set. Beginning at the outer rim of the pie pan arrange the apple slices, overlapping them slightly, in concentric circles, reversing the direction of the slices in each circle, until the bottom of the pan is entirely covered. Cover the layer with another layer of apple slices, arranging each circle of slices in the opposite direction from the corresponding bottom one. Fill the pan with the remaining apple slices, smoothing them out evenly.

Preheat the oven to 425° F.

On a floured surface roll the puff paste ⅛ inch thick. Using the plate as a guide cut out a 9-inch round from the pastry and lay it over the apples. Do not press the dough onto the sides of the pan. Heat a baking sheet in the middle of the oven until hot. Put the tart on it and bake for about 50 minutes, or until the crust is browned. Let the tart cool on a rack for 30 minutes and invert it onto a serving dish. The caramel will have been absorbed into the apples.

One to 2 hours before serving, with the remaining ½ cup sugar, 3 tablespoons water, and pinch of cream of tartar make a caramel as for lining the pie pan. Pour the caramel over the apples and with a metal spatula dipped in very hot water quickly spread it over them in one direction. Serve the tart with the whipped cream.

PUFF PASTE TARTLETS

Yield:
6 tartlets

Equipment:
pastry brush

Fill these tartlets with the fruit of your choice: whole raspberries, sliced strawberries, or nectarines arranged in a petal design, even miniature melon balls combined with lustrous grapes.

½ recipe quick puff paste (page 201)   *½ cup apricot preserves, sieved*
egg wash made by beating 1 egg with   *½ recipe pastry cream (page 537)*
* 1 teaspoon water and pinch of salt*   *assorted seasonal fruit*

Preheat the oven to 425° F.

On a lightly floured surface roll the dough ⅓ inch thick and cut it into six 6- by 3-inch rectangles. Invert the rectangles onto a moistened baking sheet and chill for 1 hour. Brush the rectangles with the egg wash, being careful not to let any drip down the sides of the dough, and with a small knife score the tops of the pastries in a crosshatch design. Bake the rectangles in the middle of the oven for 12 minutes. Reduce the oven temperature to 375° F. and bake the rectangles for 10 to 15 minutes more, or until crisp and golden brown. Let the rectangles cool for 5 minutes on the baking sheet and transfer them to a rack to cool completely.

In a small saucepan simmer the apricot preserves for 1 minute.

Cut the top third from each rectangle to make a lid and, if necessary, remove any uncooked dough from the center of each pastry case. Brush the bottom half of each case with some of the apricot preserves and spoon a thin layer of pastry cream over the preserves. Arrange the fruit decoratively over the pastry cream and brush it with the apricot preserves. Center each pastry case on a dessert plate and position its lid, slightly askew, over it.

PALMIERS

Yield:
1 recipe puff paste dough yields about 20 cookies

Another splendid French invention, these renowned cookies are rolled and cut in such a way that when baked they puff into palm leaf shapes. Crisp and caramelized and deliciously light, they are the perfect accompaniment to fresh fruit combinations, sherbet, or ice cream.

quick puff paste (page 201)　　　　　*granulated sugar for sprinkling*

Sprinkle the work surface generously with sugar. Roll the dough into a strip 5½ inches wide and ¼ inch thick. Fold over each long side to meet in the center, sprinkle the dough with sugar, and fold it to form a long 4-layered band about 1½ inches wide. Chill the dough, wrapped in plastic wrap, for 20 minutes.

Preheat the oven to 425° F.

Cut the dough crosswise into strips ½ inch wide. Put the strips cut side down about 2½ inches apart on an ungreased baking sheet and spread open the bottom half inch of each strip to form an inverted V (see illustrations). Bake in the middle of the oven for 10 minutes, or until the bottoms are caramelized. Turn the pastries, sprinkle them with sugar, and bake for 10 minutes more. Transfer the *palmiers* with a spatula to a rack and let cool.

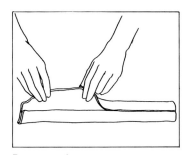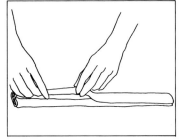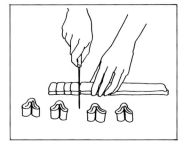

Forming palmiers

WALNUT TWISTS

Yield:
forty-eight 4-inch
  twists

Equipment:
pastry brush
plain pastry wheel

These lighter-than-air twists are nothing short of addictive. Easy to shape and quick to bake, they justify having a constant supply of puff pastry scraps on hand at any given moment.

½ recipe quick puff paste (page 201)
  or puff pastry scraps reserved from
  another use
egg wash made by beating 1 egg with
  pinch of salt

½ cup ground walnuts
¼ cup sifted confectioners' sugar
1 teaspoon cinnamon

Preheat the oven to 425° F.

Roll the dough into a 12- by 8-inch rectangle and brush it with some of the egg wash. In a bowl combine the walnuts, the ¼ cup sugar, and cinnamon, sprinkle the mixture over the dough, and press it into the dough lightly with a rolling pin. With the pastry wheel halve the dough lengthwise. Cut each half crosswise into 4- by ½-inch strips and twist each strip into a corkscrew. Arrange the twists ½ inch apart on a moistened baking sheet, pressing the ends onto the sheet to make them adhere, and bake in the middle of the oven for 8 to 10 minutes, or until puffed and golden. Transfer the twists to a rack and let cool.

Photo on page 29.

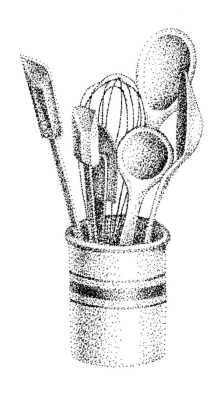

BRIOCHE DOUGH

Here begins our selection of pastry doughs that are made with yeast: brioche dough, Danish dough, and baba, or savarin, dough. Probably what most of us know about each of these, unless we are experienced bakers, is that we like the finished product immensely: those wonderful buttery morning pastries with the topknots; those flaky but light cheese envelopes; those heady, rum-soaked festive desserts. We particularly enjoy ordering them when we are out, but would we ever make them? The answer should be yes; each is easier than you think.

To begin with, yeast is not as perplexing as it might seem. Nor does it require the amount of guesswork often associated with it. Yeast is alive and is made active, proofed, when combined with lukewarm water and sugar. The yeast feeds on the sugar, which in turn begins to produce carbon dioxide and bubble. The foam that appears on top of the yeast mixture indicates that the yeast is indeed still alive, despite its packaging and unknowable shelf life, and is ready to work. The only way to damage yeast irrevocably is to kill it with the addition of too-hot water. Conversely, too-cool water will not activate it. The temperature you are after is comfortable to the wrist, about 105° F. to 115° F.

With that said, brioche dough begins with a sponge, the yeast mixture combined with a small amount of flour that is then left to rise until triple in bulk. This is a device to activate the yeast right from the start, and some cookbooks subscribe to it and others don't. We think it works.

Methodology aside, the remaining ingredients including a very healthy number of eggs, but not the butter, are stirred in. The dough is then kneaded in a manner specific to brioche. By handfuls you scoop it up and slap it, actually throw it back down, onto the work surface until the dough is smooth and elastic. There is nothing gentle about this process, unlike all the precautions one takes with other doughs. Next you cut in a splendid amount of butter, form the dough into a ball, and let it rise until triple in volume. The dough is then folded in three—as you would a letter—two times and chilled until ready to use.

Where are the pitfalls? There aren't many. Is it likely the yeast won't rise? Not very, because you have proofed it. Is the folding technique complicated as in classic puff pastry? The answer is definitely no. Does the dough freeze? Yes, for five days. Is it fun to make? Yes, and once you know how, what wonderful brioche recipes there are to try.

Begin with the recipes that follow. There is a remarkable Chocolate Brioche (page 209) that acts as the base of an equally splendid Chocolate Brioche Bread Pudding (page 325). Then there is a memorable brioche coffeecake that incorporates almond filling and mixed glacéed fruits. Finally there is a recipe for Brioche Doughnuts with Blueberry Jam (page 211). These jelly doughnuts you are not likely to forget either.

If there is a final postscript to be said about brioche dough it is this: If you are fond of butter, you must make homemade brioche dough.

CLASSIC BRIOCHE DOUGH

Yield:
1¼ pounds dough

Equipment:
pastry scraper

Brioche is a fine-textured sweet or savory yeast bread rich with butter and eggs. It is usually baked in the traditional fluted brioche mold and formed with a smaller knob or "topknot" on the top. The following recipes, however, suggest other methods for forming brioche, including coffeecakes, doughnuts, and loaf breads. Note the characteristic kneading method used for making brioche, which includes lifting the dough up and "slapping" it back down on a work surface until the dough is satiny and elastic and workable. Although slightly time-consuming to make, brioche is well worth the effort.

FOR THE SPONGE
2 teaspoons active dry yeast
1½ teaspoons sugar
3 tablespoons warm milk

1 large egg at room temperature
½ cup all-purpose flour

2 large eggs at room temperature,
    beaten lightly
1 tablespoon sugar
½ teaspoon salt

1½ cups all-purpose flour
1¼ sticks (10 tablespoons) unsalted
    butter, softened

Make the sponge:

In a large bowl proof the yeast with the sugar in the milk for 5 minutes, or until foamy. Add the egg and the ½ cup flour and beat the batter until smooth. Let the sponge rise, covered with plastic wrap and a towel, in a warm place for 1 to 1½ hours, or until it is almost triple in volume and it then deflates by itself.

Stir in the eggs, sugar, salt, and 1¼ cups of the flour until the mixture is combined (the dough will be wet and sticky). Transfer the dough to a smooth surface, knead it, adding the remaining ¼ cup flour, lifting the dough up and slapping it down for 6 to 8 minutes, or until satiny and elastic. Let it rest for 3 minutes.

With the pastry scraper begin adding the butter, one tablespoon at a time, spreading it into the dough, cutting the dough into pieces, and gathering it together again. Continue adding the butter until all of it is absorbed. The dough will be very sticky and ropy at first but will then become soft and fluffy. Knead just until all the butter is incorporated and try not to overwork the dough. Form the dough into a ball, put it into a buttered bowl, and let it rise in a warm place, covered with plastic wrap and a towel, for 1½ to 2 hours, or until almost triple in volume.

The dough may be kept, wrapped and weighted, in the refrigerator for up to 3 days.

Transfer the dough to a lightly floured surface, pat it into a 12- by 8-inch rectangle, and fold it into thirds as you would a letter. Turn the dough 90 degrees, pat it out into a rectangle again, and fold it again into thirds. Dust the dough with flour, wrap it in plastic wrap, and chill it, weighted down, for at least 2 hours or overnight.

Variation:

BRIOCHE DOUGH: PROCESSOR METHOD: In a bowl prepare the sponge as instructed in classic brioche dough.

In a food processor fitted with the steel blade combine the sponge, the remaining eggs, sugar, salt, and flour and process the mixture with on/off pulses, 5 to 10 seconds, or until combined. With the motor running, add the butter, one tablespoon at a time, until it is incorporated and the batter is smooth. Transfer the dough to a buttered bowl and let it rise in a warm place, covered with plastic wrap and a towel, for 1½ to 2 hours, or until almost triple in volume.

Fold and chill the dough as instructed in classic brioche dough.

CHOCOLATE BRIOCHE

Yield:
one 8-inch loaf

Equipment:
loaf pan, 8 by 4 by 2 inches
pastry scraper
pastry brush

This brioche forms the base for an irresistible chocolate bread pudding (page 325). On its own, the loaf is also wonderful topped with either of the flavored butters called for in the recipe.

1 envelope active dry yeast
3 tablespoons warm milk
3 tablespoons sugar
3 large eggs at room temperature
2 ounces semisweet chocolate, melted and cooled to warm
1 teaspoon vanilla
¼ teaspoon salt

2 to 2¼ cups all-purpose flour
1 stick (½ cup) unsalted butter, softened
egg wash made by beating 1 egg with 1 teaspoon water and pinch of salt
chocolate butter or cherry butter (both recipes page 536) as an accompaniment

In a bowl proof the yeast in the milk with 1 teaspoon of the sugar for 5 minutes, or until foamy. Add the eggs, the still warm chocolate, the remaining sugar, vanilla, and salt and beat the mixture until combined well. Stir in 2 cups of the flour, form the dough into a ball, and knead it, adding additional flour, if necessary, for 6 to 8 minutes, or until the dough is elastic. With the pastry scraper begin adding the butter, one tablespoon at a time, spreading it into the dough, cutting the dough, and gathering it together again until all the butter is absorbed and the dough is soft and fluffy. Transfer the dough to a buttered bowl and let it rise, covered with plastic wrap and a towel, in a warm place for 1½ hours, or until triple in volume.

Butter the loaf pan.

Transfer the dough to a lightly floured surface, pat it into a rectangle, and fold it into thirds as for a letter. Turn the dough 90 degrees and fold it into thirds again. Fit the dough seam side down into the loaf pan and let it rise, loosely covered with plastic wrap, in a warm place for 1 hour, or until the dough has risen 1 inch above the rim of the pan.

Preheat the oven to 350° F.

Brush the dough with the egg wash and bake it in the middle of the oven for 35 to 40 minutes, or until the loaf sounds hollow when tapped on the bottom. Let the loaf cool in the pan for 5 minutes, invert it onto a rack, and let cool completely. Serve with a flavored butter.

Variation: CHOCOLATE BRIOCHE: PROCESSOR METHOD: In a bowl proof the yeast in the milk with 1 teaspoon of the sugar for 5 minutes, or until foamy. Transfer the yeast mixture to a food processor fitted with the steel blade. Add the eggs, chocolate, the remaining sugar, vanilla, salt, and 2¼ cups of the flour and process the mixture, pulsing the machine on and off, for 5 to 10 seconds, or until combined. With the motor running, add the butter, one tablespoon at a time, until it is incorporated and the batter is smooth. Transfer the dough to a buttered bowl and let it rise in a warm place, covered with plastic wrap and a towel, for 1½ to 2 hours, or until almost triple in volume. Fold and chill the dough as described (page 209).

SWISS BRIOCHE

Brioche Coffeecake with Almond Filling and Candied Fruits

Yield:
one 8-inch cake

Equipment:
8-inch cake pan
pastry brush

Nut fillings are popular throughout Switzerland, which explains the title of this superb coffeecake of brioche dough, almonds, and rum-macerated candied fruits. Serve the cake while still slightly warm, if possible. Its flavors and texture are memorable.

1 recipe classic brioche dough (page 208)
½ cup mixed candied fruit

½ cup dried currants
1 tablespoon dark rum

FOR THE ALMOND FILLING
¾ stick (6 tablespoons) unsalted butter, softened
⅓ cup sugar
1 large egg, beaten lightly

½ cup whole blanched almonds (for procedure page 549), chopped fine
½ teaspoon vanilla
¼ teaspoon almond extract

egg wash made by beating 1 egg with 1 teaspoon water and pinch of salt

½ cup apricot glaze (page 540) made with 1 tablespoon dark rum

Butter the cake pan.

On a lightly floured surface roll one third of the dough into a round about ⅛ inch thick and fit it into the cake pan. Prick the bottom of the dough and chill it.

In a small bowl toss the candied fruit and the currants with the rum and let stand for 30 minutes.

Make the almond filling: In a bowl cream the butter, add the sugar a little at a time, and beat the mixture until it is light and fluffy. Slowly add the egg and beat the mixture until combined. Stir in the almonds, vanilla, and the almond extract.

On a lightly floured surface roll out the remaining dough into a 12- by 8-inch rectangle. Spread the dough with the almond filling, leaving a ¾-inch border on all sides. Drain the candied fruit mixture and spread it over the cream. Beginning with a long side, roll up the dough jelly-roll fashion. Put the dough seam side down on a cutting board and with a sharp knife, using a sawing motion, cut it into 8 slices. Arrange the slices, cut side down, in the cake pan, leaving equal space between them. Let the dough rise, covered with plastic wrap, in a warm place for 1 hour, or until puffed and almost double in volume.

Preheat the oven to 400° F.

Brush the slices with the egg wash. Bake the cake in the middle of the oven for 35 minutes, or until golden brown. Let the cake cool in the pan for 10 minutes, invert it onto a rack, and invert it right side up on the rack to cool completely.

In a small saucepan simmer the apricot preserves and the remaining tablespoon rum for 1 minute and brush the glaze over the cake. The cake is best served while it is still slightly warm.

BRIOCHE DOUGHNUTS WITH BLUEBERRY JAM

Yield:
8 doughnuts

Equipment:
4-inch round cutter
deep fryer

Doughnuts are made with yeast dough. The jelly doughnuts that follow are made with yeast dough as well, but brioche dough, rendering them particularly special—rich but airy. Any jam or preserve, as long as it has a certain density, may be substituted for the blueberry filling. Even though the dough is initially folded into half circles, it rises into wonderful individual rounds.

1 recipe classic brioche dough
  (page 208)
⅓ cup blueberry preserves

vegetable oil for deep frying
sifted confectioners' sugar for
  sprinkling

On a lightly floured surface roll the dough ⅓ inch thick and with the cutter stamp out rounds. Put 1 teaspoon of the preserves in the center of each round, moisten the edges of the dough with water, and pinch them together to seal. Reroll the scraps and stamp out doughnuts in the same manner. Let the doughnuts rise, covered loosely with plastic wrap, for 1 hour, or until puffed and almost double in volume.

In the deep fryer (or a deep skillet) heat enough oil to measure 3 inches to 375° F. and fry the doughnuts in batches for 1 to 2 minutes on each side, or until golden brown. Transfer the doughnuts to a tray lined with paper towels to drain and let cool. Before serving, sprinkle the doughnuts with the confectioners' sugar.

PINEAPPLE SAVARIN CHANTILLY

Yield:
one 8-inch savarin,
  serving 8 to 10

Equipment:
1½-quart savarin
  mold
jelly-roll pan
pastry brush
hand-held electric
  mixer
pastry bag fitted with
  large star tip

The only difference between a savarin and a baba is that the savarin is shaped in a ring mold while babas are baked in individual cups. Both employ the same rich, eggy yeast dough; both are wonderful foils for the liquor-flavored sugar syrup that is used to soak and flavor them. These are particularly festive desserts, especially the lovely Christmas babas on the following page.

2 slices Candied Pineapple (page 523), halved

dark rum as needed for steeping plus 2 tablespoons, plus additional to taste

FOR THE BABA DOUGH

1 envelope active dry yeast
½ cup lukewarm milk
3 tablespoons granulated sugar plus an additional pinch
2 cups all-purpose flour

½ teaspoon salt
4 large eggs, beaten lightly
1½ sticks (¾ cup) unsalted butter, softened

1 recipe rum syrup (page 542), still warm
½ cup apricot jam
1 cup well-chilled heavy cream

confectioners' sugar to taste
angelica leaves and a Candied Violet (page 524) for garnish

Cut each halved slice of pineapple crosswise into 4 thin slices. In a small bowl macerate the slices in dark rum to cover for several hours or overnight.

Butter well the savarin mold.

Make the baba dough:
In a small bowl proof the yeast in the milk with the pinch of sugar for 10 minutes. Into a large bowl sift the flour, the remaining 3 tablespoons granulated sugar, and the salt. Add the eggs and the yeast mixture and blend the mixture well with your hands for several minutes. With the fingers of one hand held together and slightly cupped knead the dough by lifting it, slapping it, and pulling it vigorously against the sides of the bowl for 3 minutes (the dough will be soft and sticky). Transfer the dough to a lightly buttered bowl and let it rise, covered with a dish towel, in a warm place for 1½ hours, or until double in bulk. Stir down the dough. Start adding the butter, 2 tablespoons at a time, kneading the dough with your hands as before for 4 minutes, or until all the butter is incorporated. Transfer the dough to the savarin mold and let it rise in a warm place until it reaches the top of the mold, about 1 to 1½ hours.

Preheat the oven to 450° F.

Bake the savarin in the middle of the oven for 10 minutes. Reduce the heat to 350° F. and bake for 25 to 30 minutes more, or until well browned. Remove the savarin from the oven and let it cool in the pan for 20 minutes.

Release the savarin from the sides of the mold with a knife and invert it onto a rack. Set the rack over the jelly-roll pan and spoon the rum syrup over the warm savarin, spooning the syrup that drips into the pan back over the cake until it is all absorbed.

In a small saucepan melt the apricot jam with the 2 tablespoons dark rum over moderate heat and boil for 1 minute. Strain the glaze and brush the savarin with it. Drain the pineapple slices, pat them dry, and arrange them cut edges down around the base of the savarin, pressing them against the cake so they adhere. Brush the pineapple slices with apricot glaze. In a chilled bowl with the mixer beat the heavy cream with confectioners' sugar and rum to taste until it holds soft peaks. Fill the pastry bag with the cream and fill the center of the savarin, piping the cream on top in a decorative manner. Decorate the cream with the angelica leaves and the candied violet. The savarin should be served barely warm and sprinkled with dark rum just before serving.

Photo on page 186.

BABAS AU RHUM NOËL

Yield:
12 small and 12 large babas

Equipment:
12 cylindrical baba tins, 2 inches deep and 2 inches in diameter, or *dariole* molds (available at specialty kitchenware shops)
12 cylindrical baba tins, 3 inches deep and 3 inches in diameter
large pastry bag fitted with number 9 plain tip
jelly-roll pan
pastry brush

¼ cup dried currants
¼ cup golden raisins
¼ cup minced mixed candied fruits
¼ cup plus 3 tablespoons dark rum plus additional rum to taste
1 recipe baba dough (recipe opposite) made through the step of incorporating the butter

all-purpose flour for dusting
1 recipe rum syrup (page 542), still warm
1 cup apricot jam
12 glacéed cherries, halved
pieces of angelica, cut into leaf shapes
1 cup well-chilled heavy cream
confectioners' sugar

In a small bowl macerate the currants, raisins, and candied fruit in the ¼ cup dark rum overnight.

Drain the currant mixture, pat the fruits dry with paper towels, and dust them with flour. Shake off the excess flour in a sieve and fold the fruit lightly into the baba dough.

Butter well the 24 baba tins and arrange them on a baking sheet.

Set the pastry bag over a tall wide-mouthed jar, fill it with the dough, and remove it from the jar.

Pipe the dough into the tins, filling the tins one third full. Let the dough rise in a warm place until it reaches the top of the tins. Put the babas on the baking sheet in the middle of the oven, reduce the heat to 425° F., and bake the babas for 15 minutes, or until well browned. Turn the babas out on a rack and let them cool for 20 minutes, or until just warm. Set the rack over the jelly-roll pan and spoon the rum syrup over the babas, spooning the syrup that collects in the pan back over the babas until they are moistened and spongy but not soggy.

Babas au Rhum Noël (page 213)

In a small saucepan melt the apricot jam with the remaining 3 table-spoons dark rum over moderate heat and boil for 1 minute. Strain the jam into a cup and brush the babas with the glaze. Decorate each baba with a cherry half and angelica leaves. Brush the babas with the remaining glaze and arrange them on their sides on a platter. In a chilled bowl beat the cream with the confectioners' sugar and the rum until it holds soft peaks and transfer it to the pastry bag. Pipe the whipped cream decoratively in the center of the platter.

Photo opposite.

DANISH PASTRY

We are often not clear on why we like something. All we know is that we like it. So it is, we suspect, with Danish pastries. We like them because they are sweet and pretty; they come in great variety, in different sizes and shapes; they are filled with wonderful combinations of fruit or cheese or nuts. They come one (or more) to a person and there is great appeal to that. We can look forward to them in the morning, or at any other time, for that matter, and that is good too. What we like about them specifically, though, is less obvious. We think it has much to do with the marvelous dough with which they are made.

Danish dough is a yeast dough rich with butter. You will note in our recipe for it a ratio of half the amount of butter to the amount of flour. Such a relationship is high by anyone's standards, but it is the norm and accounts for much of the wonderful texture and flavor of Danish dough. There is still another facet of this dough that accounts for its goodness: The yeast dough is made and rolled out; on it is placed a rectangle of butter. The dough is then folded and turned, like classic and quick puff pastry. Layer after layer of sweet butter is incorporated between layers of dough, which when baked rise and render those tender, flaky tiers. (For information and illustrations on this technique, see page 216.) Not even a filling is able to hold down a properly prepared and turned Danish dough.

When making this dough, there are several points to remember: The butter, once pounded into a rectangle, should be neither too soft nor too cold when placed on the dough. If it is too soft, it will seep into the dough when rolled; if it is too hard, you will have to push the rolling pin over it to soften it and risk shoving the dough as opposed to just rolling it. Either way the layers will not be nearly as flaky. If as you are rolling the dough out butter *does* come through, dust the area lightly with flour and chill the dough briefly, until the butter firms up. Continue rolling. Do not patch Danish dough, as you would strudel dough.

To make your first turn with the dough, roll it into an even rectangle as illustrated. Then fold it into thirds as you would a business letter: Bring the top third down over the center and the bottom third up over the top, pressing the top edge to seal it. Turn the dough so that a short side faces you. This constitutes your first turn. You will need to make three more turns, always chilling the dough between turns. After the final turn, the dough will need to rest in the refrigerator for at least two hours. One fact about Danish dough, that applies to all other turned doughs as well is that there is nothing instantaneous about it. You will need a minimum of at least four hours, not including the final chilling time. Nor does it freeze, nor should it remain in the refrigerator for more than twenty-four hours. Baked Danish pastries, however, freeze beautifully.

With the dough made, you can proceed to making Almond Bear Claws (page 218) or a superb variation on these, Hazelnut Bear Claws (page 218). Or consider Lemon Cheese Danish Envelopes (page 219) or their variation, which is filled with orange-apricot purée. The shaping of these two pastries is easy and illustrations of each accompany the recipes.

Earlier in this introduction we speculated on what we thought most people liked about Danish pastries and concluded that it was ineluctable. Now the speculation is over: People in general like Danish pastries, particularly homemade ones, for all the right reasons.

ROLLING DANISH PASTRY DOUGH:

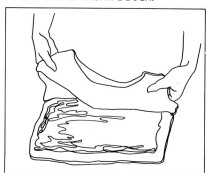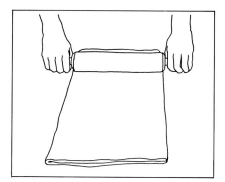

Arranging butter on bottom half of rectangle; rolling out dough

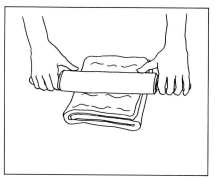

Rolling the first turn

DANISH PASTRY DOUGH

Yield:
2½ pounds dough

Danish dough, rich with butter, achieves its lovely layers of flakiness from its leavening by yeast and by virtue of the fact that the dough is rolled and "turned" like puff paste. The key, of course, is in the rolling. The butter should not become too soft, or it will break down and seep into the flour mixture, preventing the dough from rising properly. The butter cannot be too cold either, as you risk overworking the dough trying to soften it with the rolling pin, another way of collapsing the layers. A well-made *homemade* Danish is in a class by itself.

2 envelopes active dry yeast
¼ cup warm water
¾ cup milk
1 large egg
1 egg yolk

¼ cup sugar
1 teaspoon salt
3½ to 3¾ cups all-purpose flour
3 sticks (1½ cups) unsalted butter,
    softened

In a large bowl proof the yeast in the water for 5 minutes, or until frothy. Beat in the milk, egg, egg yolk, sugar, and salt until combined. Add 3¼ cups of the flour, one third at a time, stirring until the mixture forms a dough. Turn the dough out on a lightly floured surface, and knead it, adding all but 3 tablespoons of the remaining flour, for 2 to 3 minutes, or until it forms a soft and slightly sticky dough. Form the dough into a ball, dust it with flour, and chill it, covered with plastic wrap, for 20 minutes.

With a rolling pin pound the butter with the remaining 3 tablespoons flour until pliable and smooth. Shape the butter into a rough rectangle and put it between sheets of wax paper. Roll the butter into a rectangle about 12 by 8 inches. Chill the butter for 10 minutes, or until it is of the same consistency as the dough.

The dough can be refrigerated, wrapped in plastic wrap, for up to 24 hours, but should not be kept longer. Once baked, however, the pastries may be frozen, wrapped in plastic wrap and foil. To reheat, bake in a preheated 375° F. oven for 10 to 12 minutes, or until crisp.

On a lightly floured surface roll the dough into a rectangle about 18 by 15 inches. Arrange the butter on the bottom half of the dough, leaving a 1-inch border on three sides, and fold the top half of the dough over it, crimping the edges of the dough together to seal it. Turn the dough so that the short side faces you. Roll the dough into a 26- by 12-inch rectangle on the lightly floured surface, fold the top third of the rectangle over the center and the bottom third over the top, and press down the top edge with the rolling pin so it adheres. This constitutes 1 "turn" (see illustrations opposite). Turn the dough seam side down, dust with flour, and chill it, covered with plastic wrap, for 30 minutes. Make 3 more turns in the same manner, chilling the dough between turns, and let the dough rest, covered with plastic wrap, for at least 2 hours, or overnight.

ALMOND BEAR CLAWS

Yield:
12 pastries

Bear claws, only one of the forms Danish pastry can take, can be variously filled, but are particularly good with the following nut combinations.

Equipment:
pastry brush

½ recipe Danish pastry dough (page 217)

FOR THE FILLING

5⅓ tablespoons unsalted butter, softened
⅓ cup almond paste

⅔ cup confectioners' sugar
¼ teaspoon almond extract, if desired

½ cup sliced blanched almonds
1 tablespoon unsalted butter, melted
egg wash made by beating 1 egg with 1 teaspoon water and pinch of salt

1 to 2 tablespoons granulated sugar

Have ready the Danish pastry dough. Butter baking sheets.

Make the filling:
In a bowl cream the softened butter and the almond paste until fluffy. Gradually beat in the confectioners' sugar and almond extract if desired.

On a lightly floured surface roll the dough into a 16- by 12-inch rectangle. Cut the dough into twelve 4-inch squares and spread a tablespoon of the almond butter filling across the bottom half of each square, leaving a ½-inch border along three sides. Brush the border with the egg wash and fold the top of the dough over the filling, pressing the edges together to seal. With a sharp knife cut ¾-inch slits crosswise about ½ inch apart along the sealed edge of the dough of each pastry (see illustration opposite). Arrange the pastries about 2 inches apart on the baking sheets and gently curve each so that the "claws" open slightly. Let the pastries rise, covered loosely with plastic wrap, in a warm place for 45 minutes to 1 hour, or until they are puffed and have almost doubled in volume.

Preheat the oven to 400° F. In a small bowl toss the sliced almonds with the melted butter. Brush the pastries with the egg wash and sprinkle them with the almond mixture. Dust the pastries with granulated sugar to taste and bake in the middle of the oven for 12 to 15 minutes, or until crisp and golden. Let the pastries cool on the baking sheets for 5 minutes and transfer them to racks to cool completely.

Variation:
HAZELNUT FILLING FOR BEAR CLAWS: In a bowl combine ½ cup finely ground toasted and skins removed hazelnuts (for procedure page 549), ½ cup confectioners' sugar, ¾ stick (6 tablespoons) unsalted butter, softened, 1 egg yolk, and ¾ teaspoon cinnamon.

Roll, cut, fill, and bake pastries as instructed in almond bear claws, substituting ½ cup coarsely ground toasted and skinned hazelnuts for the sliced almonds in the topping.

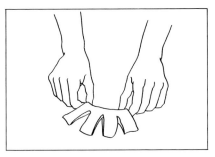 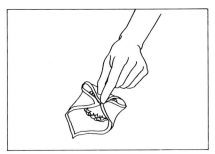

Forming Danish pastry bear claws and envelopes

LEMON CHEESE DANISH ENVELOPES

Yield:
12 pastries

Another way of shaping Danish dough, these envelopes are easy to make, as is the cheese or apricot combination that fills them.

Equipment:
pastry brush

½ recipe Danish pastry dough (page 217)

FOR THE FILLING
⅔ cup cream cheese, softened	*1 tablespoon all-purpose flour*
¼ cup sugar	*1 teaspoon grated lemon rind*
1 egg yolk	*½ teaspoon vanilla*

*egg wash made by beating 1 egg with
 1 teaspoon water and pinch of salt*   *1 to 2 tablespoons sugar*

Make the filling:

Have ready the Danish pastry dough. Butter baking sheets.

In a bowl combine the cream cheese, sugar, egg yolk, flour, lemon rind, and vanilla and beat the mixture until smooth.

On a lightly floured surface roll out the dough into a 16- by 12-inch rectangle. With a sharp knife cut the dough into twelve 4-inch squares. Put 1 tablespoon of the filling in the center of each square, brush the corners of the dough with the egg wash, and fold the corners of the dough over the filling, overlapping them slightly so that they meet one another in the center (see illustration above). Arrange the pastries about 2 inches apart on the baking sheets and let them rise, covered loosely with plastic wrap, in a warm place for 45 minutes to 1 hour, or until puffed and almost double in volume.

Preheat the oven to 400° F.

Brush the pastries with the egg wash, sprinkle them with sugar to taste, and bake them in the middle of the oven for 12 to 15 minutes, or until crisp and golden brown. Let the pastries cool on the baking sheets for 5 minutes and transfer them to racks to cool completely.

Variation:

ORANGE-APRICOT-FILLED DANISH ENVELOPES: In a saucepan simmer 1 cup dried apricots in water to cover for 10 minutes, or until tender. Drain the apricots, transfer them to a food processor fitted with the steel blade, and purée them. Add 5 tablespoons sugar, or to taste, 3 tablespoons unsalted butter, and 2 teaspoons grated orange rind and process the filling until smooth. Roll, cut, fill, and bake pastries as instructed in lemon cheese Danish envelopes.

PÂTE À CHOU

Pâte à chou—the pronunciation of this French dough even hints at its light-ness. It is cream puff pastry, and we know of it by the number of éclairs and *profiteroles* we have enjoyed in our lifetimes. Simultaneously crisp and light, *pâte à chou* is used most frequently as a container for pastry cream, whipped cream, ice cream, or custard. Like other pastry doughs, you could call it a vehicle, but a unique one in that this dough is actually cooked, like a sauce, over direct heat.

Considered by many to be the easiest of doughs to make, *pâte à chou* combines water and butter over heat. Flour is then added, all at one time, and the *panade,* the flour mixture, is vigorously stirred over the heat until

STEPS FOR MAKING PÂTE À CHOU

Adding flour all at once to butter mixture   Beating flour mixture until it forms a ball

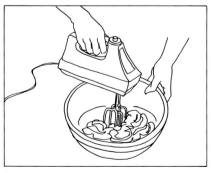

Incorporating eggs

it pulls away from the sides of the pan into a ball. The dough is transferred quickly to a bowl and while it is still warm, eggs are beaten in, one at a time, preferably with an electric mixer, or it may be done by hand (see illustrations opposite).

The process is extremely straightforward, and the only possible moment of hesitation might come when judging the consistency of the dough. It should stand in soft peaks, just as you would identify the soft peaks of beaten egg whites. If the dough is too thick, by all means beat in additional egg, a little at a time. The amount of liquid in the dough will depend upon the amount of water that evaporated when the pan was on the heat as well as the natural dryness of the flour you are using. In short, there is nothing untoward, or wrong, about needing to add extra eggs.

With a pastry bag you then pipe the dough into the desired shape: mounds for *choux*, elongated ovals for éclairs, large rounds for *gâteaux* such as Paris-Brest (page 224). In the oven something extraordinary happens: This dough, made without leavening of any kind, puffs! The eggs, beaten in whole as they are, are the catalyst. Crispy on the outside, with whatever uncooked dough removed from within, the *choux*, when cooled, are ready to be filled and quickly consumed.

No discussion of *pâte à chou* would be complete without mention of the remarkable *chef d'oeuvre*, Croquembouche (page 227). This dessert of filled cream puffs molded into a cone shape with amber caramel graces the head table as the centerpiece at many a French wedding and anniversary. It symbolizes many things, not the least of which is hope.

PÂTE À CHOU

Cream Puff Pastry

Yield:
2½ cups dough

Equipment:
wooden spoon
hand-held electric
   mixer

1 cup water
1 stick (½ cup) unsalted butter, cut
   into pieces

¼ teaspoon salt
1 cup all-purpose flour
3 to 5 large eggs

In a heavy saucepan bring the water to a boil with the butter and salt over high heat. Reduce the heat to moderate, add the flour all at once, and beat the mixture with the wooden spoon until it leaves the sides of the pan and forms a ball (see illustrations opposite). Transfer the mixture to a bowl and with the mixer on high speed beat in 3 eggs, one at a time, beating well after each addition (the batter should be stiff enough to just hold soft peaks). If the batter is too stiff, break 1 or 2 of the remaining eggs into a small bowl, beat lightly, and add just enough of it to the batter to thin it to the proper consistency. Proceed with one of the following recipes for *pâte à chou*. (If you are making *pâte à chou* in advance, rub the surface of the warm *pâte à chou* with butter, let the dough cool, and chill it, wrapped in plastic wrap. To use, warm the dough over very low heat, stirring constantly, until tepid.)

The *pâte à chou* may be kept for up to 3 days chilled, wrapped in plastic wrap.

PROFITEROLES WITH HOT CHOCOLATE SAUCE

Yield:
18 puffs, serving 6

Equipment:
pastry bag fitted with
  ½-inch pastry tip
pastry brush
small ice-cream scoop
hand-held electric
  mixer

Profiteroles are simply small cream puffs, which are filled with ice cream, as in the following recipe, or pastry cream.

½ recipe pâte à chou *(page 221)*
egg wash made by beating 1 egg with
  1 teaspoon water and pinch of salt
1 quart Vanilla Ice Cream (page
  349), softened slightly

1 recipe Hot Chocolate Sauce (page
  497)

Butter and flour a baking sheet and preheat the oven to 425° F.

Fill the pastry bag with the *pâte à chou* and pipe 18 puffs about 1½ inches in diameter and 1 inch high 2 inches apart on the baking sheet (see illustration). Brush the tops of the puffs with the egg wash, gently tapping down the "tails," and bake in the upper third of the oven for 10 minutes. Reduce the heat to 400° F. and bake the puffs for 15 to 20 minutes more, or until puffed and golden. Pierce the side of each puff with the tip of a sharp knife and let the puffs stand in the turned-off oven with the door ajar for 30 minutes. Transfer the puffs to a rack and let cool completely.

With the ice cream scoop make 18 ice-cream balls with the vanilla ice cream, put them on a baking sheet, and freeze them until solid.

To serve, carefully halve the puffs and fill the bottom of each puff with an ice-cream ball. Replace the tops, pressing them down slightly. Serve the *profiteroles* at once with the hot chocolate sauce.

Photo opposite.

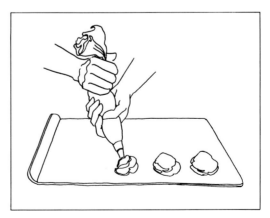

Piping pâte à chou puffs with pastry bag

Profiteroles with Hot
Chocolate Sauce
(above)

PARIS-BREST

Yield:
one 6-inch ring

Equipment:
6-inch plate or cake
  pan
large pastry bag fitted
  with large fluted or
  plain tip
pastry brush
hand-held electric
  mixer
medium fluted tip

This cream puff ring, a time-honored Parisian specialty, is often filled with praline-flavored pastry cream or buttercream. This version, filled with whipped cream only, is simpler, but no less tempting. (Note the small *choux* stashed in the filling.) If circumstances allow, assemble a Paris-Brest at the last minute to take full advantage of its lovely combination of crisp pastry and billowy cream.

1 recipe pâte à chou *(page 221)*   *3 tablespoons sliced blanched almonds*
egg wash made by beating 1 egg with
  2 tablespoons half-and-half

FOR THE FILLING
2 cups well-chilled heavy cream   *2 teaspoons vanilla*
½ cup confectioners' sugar plus
  additional for garnish

Butter and flour a large baking sheet. Preheat the oven to 425° F.

Mark a 6-inch circle on the baking sheet by pressing the rim of the dish or cake pan into the flour. Transfer the *pâte à chou* to the pastry bag and pipe a ring 1½ inches wide around the inside of the circle. Pipe another ring of the *pâte à chou* about 1 inch wide on top of the first ring. On the space remaining on the sheet pipe small puffs, about 1½ inches in diameter and 1 inch high, with the remaining *pâte à chou*. Brush the ring and the tops of the puffs with the egg wash and sprinkle the ring with the almonds. Bake in the middle of the oven for 10 minutes. Reduce the heat to 400° F. and bake for 20 minutes more, or until puffed and golden. Pierce the inside edge of the ring in several places with the tip of a sharp knife and let the pastry stand in the turned-off oven for 30 minutes. Transfer the ring and puffs to a rack and let cool. Cut off the top third of the ring carefully, setting it aside, and halve the puffs horizontally.

Make the filling: In a chilled bowl with the mixer beat the cream until it holds soft peaks, add the ½ cup confectioners' sugar and the vanilla, and beat the cream until it just holds stiff peaks.

Scoop out and discard any uncooked dough in the bottom part of the pastry ring, set the ring on a serving plate, and fill the ring with some of the whipped cream filling. Set the puff halves, cut side up, in the cream, pressing them in slightly, and fill the puffs with some of the remaining cream. Fit the pastry bag with the medium fluted tip and with the remaining whipped cream pipe rosettes over the small puffs and along the top edge of the ring. (For detailed instructions on working with a pastry bag and piping rosettes, see pages 19 and 20.) Replace the top of the ring and sift additional confectioners' sugar lightly over the dessert.

Photo opposite.

Paris-Brest (opposite)

MINIATURE ÉCLAIRS

Yield:
about 36 éclairs

Equipment:
pastry bag fitted with
⅓-inch plain tip
pastry brush
small metal skewer

These dainty miniature éclairs are perfect for the tea table. Should time be a factor, simply substitute flavored whipped cream for the pastry cream filling and ice the pastries not with fondant, which requires an hour to dry, but with a lustrous chocolate glaze. You could also, at that point, reverse the order of preparation: Fill them first, glaze them after.

½ recipe pâte à chou *(page 221)*
egg wash made by beating 1 egg with
   2 tablespoons milk
½ recipe fondant (page 540)
1 tablespoon instant espresso powder
   dissolved in 1 tablespoon dark rum

2 to 3 teaspoons unbeaten egg white,
   as needed
1 recipe coffee-flavored pastry cream
   (page 538)

Butter a baking sheet and preheat the oven to 425° F.

Fill the pastry bag with the *pâte à chou* and pipe out small éclairs about 1¾ inches long 2 inches apart onto the baking sheet (see illustration). Brush the tops of the éclairs with the egg wash and bake in the middle of the oven for 10 minutes. Reduce the heat to 375° F. and bake for 10 minutes more. Make a small hole with the skewer in one end of each éclair and let the éclairs stand in the turned-off oven for 10 minutes. Transfer to a rack and let cool.

Put the fondant in the top of a double boiler set over hot water and let it soften. Stir in the espresso mixture. Do not let the fondant get too warm or it will lose its shine. If it is too thick, stir in the egg white until it achieves the proper consistency. Dip the top of each éclair into the fondant and invert it onto a rack. Let the fondant set in a dry place for at least 1 hour.

Before serving, fill the pastry bag with the pastry cream. Pipe the cream into the hole in each éclair, filling it generously. Arrange the puffs on a platter and serve.

Variation:

MADELONS: Using a pastry bag fitted with a plain round tip, pipe small S shapes of the *pâte à chou* on a buttered baking sheet, sprinkle them with

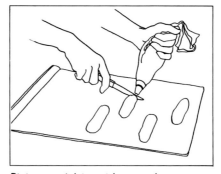

Piping out éclairs with pastry bag

vanilla sugar (page 541), and bake in the middle of a preheated 375° F. oven for 15 minutes, or until puffed. Let the pastries cool on a rack, split them horizontally with a sharp knife, and fill with red currant jelly. Serve with the tops slightly askew.

CROQUEMBOUCHE DE NOËL

Christmas Cream Puff Cake

Yield:
one 12-inch
  croquembouche

Equipment:
pastry bag fitted with
  ¼-inch tip
pastry brush
12-inch-high
  croquembouche
  mold (available at
  specialty
  kitchenware shops)

Served most frequently at weddings and similar celebrations in France, this gala creation combines cream puffs and caramel, but in a conical form. Meaning literally "crisp in mouth," this pastry, often used as a centerpiece, is best assembled on a cool, dry day. Take care working with the hot caramel and unmold this edifice carefully. You do not want all that labor to end up as a pancake on the serving plate!

1½ recipes pâte à chou (page 221)
egg wash made by beating 1 egg with
  1 teaspoon water and pinch of salt
2 recipes pastry cream (page 537)
4 cups sugar

1 cup water
¼ teaspoon cream of tartar
candied red and green cherries for
  garnish
flavorless vegetable oil

Butter and flour baking sheets. Preheat the oven to 425° F. Fill the pastry bag with the *pâte à chou* and pipe puffs about 1 inch in diameter and ¾ inch high 2 inches apart onto the baking sheets (see illustration page 223; you will need about 80 small puffs). Brush the tops of the puffs with the egg wash, gently tapping down the "tails," and bake the puffs in the upper third of the oven for 10 minutes. Reduce the heat to 400° F. and bake the puffs for 15 to 20 minutes more, or until puffed and golden. Pierce the side of each puff with the tip of a sharp knife and let the puffs stand in the turned-off oven with the door ajar for 30 minutes. Transfer the puffs to a rack and let cool completely. With a sharp knife cut a small slit in the side of each puff. Transfer the pastry cream to the pastry bag and fill the puffs.

In a heavy saucepan cook 2 cups of the sugar with ½ cup of the water and ⅛ teaspoon of the cream of tartar over moderately high heat, washing down any sugar crystals clinging to the sides of the pan with the brush dipped in cold water until the mixture is a light caramel. Dip the tops of the puffs, one at a time, into the hot caramel, being careful not to let it drip down on your fingers, and stand the puffs upright on a rack. Make a second batch of caramel with the remaining 2 cups sugar, ½ cup water, and ⅛ teaspoon cream of tartar.

Oil the inside of the *croquembouche* mold with vegetable oil and lay the mold on its side. Beginning with the smallest puffs, dip the bottoms and sides of the puffs, one at a time, into the hot caramel and arrange them closely together in a circle at the pointed end of the mold. Dip the bottom and sides of slightly larger puffs into the hot caramel and arrange a second layer of puffs on top of the first ring, filling in the center of the mold with additional puffs, fitting them as tightly as possible. Continue to build the pyramid, forming a solid cone of *chou* puffs, in the same manner. If the caramel in the pan should harden, reheat it over moderate heat, adding 1 to 2 tablespoons water and gently swirling the pan, until it has liquefied. When the caramel has set, invert the mold onto a serving plate and carefully remove it. If the caramel sticks when unmolding the mold, rotate the mold on its side over a very low flame to loosen the caramel. Then run a thin metal spatula around the inside of the mold. Carefully invert the mold onto a serving plate. Do not shake the mold to loosen the dessert.

For decoration, dip the red and green cherries into the remaining caramel and attach them to the *croquembouche*. The *croquembouche* may be assembled and stored in a cool, dry place until ready to serve.

GÂTEAU SAINT-HONORÉ

Yield:
one 9-inch pastry,
  serving 8 to 10

Equipment:
10-inch pie pan
9-inch pie pan
2 pastry bags
½-inch plain tip
pastry brush
small metal skewer
hand-held electric
  mixer
⅛-inch plain tip

Gâteau Saint-Honoré, another Parisian pastry *tour de force*, is actually named after the patron saint of pastry chefs and bakers. This remarkable flight of fancy combines two different kinds of pastry, a special pastry cream, caramel, whipped cream, and for garnish candied strawberries and, last but hardly least, spun sugar! As you will note from the photograph on page 230, it is a celebration cake, best made in stages, with ample time reserved for each step. The spun sugar, by the way, is a conceit—a glorious one, albeit—but in no way essential to the end result.

2 recipes pâte brisée *(page 164),*
  substituting 4 teaspoons sugar for
  the salt

1 recipe pâte à chou *(page 221)*
egg wash made by beating
  1 egg with 1 tablespoon cream

FOR THE CARAMEL
1 cup granulated sugar
¼ cup water

⅛ teaspoon cream of tartar

FOR THE CRÈME SAINT-HONORÉ
6 egg yolks
⅔ cup granulated sugar
⅓ cup all-purpose flour
1½ tablespoons unflavored gelatin
¼ cup cold water

2 cups milk, scalded
2 teaspoons vanilla
4 egg whites at room temperature
¼ cup orange-flavored liqueur
1 cup well-chilled heavy cream

FOR THE GARNISH
6 Candied Strawberries (page 523)
spun sugar (page 543)
1 cup well-chilled heavy cream

confectioners' sugar and orange-
  flavored liqueur to taste

Butter a baking sheet lightly. Preheat the oven to 400° F.

Roll the *pâte brisée* a bit thicker than ⅛ inch on a lightly floured surface. Drape the pastry over the rolling pin and unroll it on the baking sheet. Using the 10-inch pie pan, inverted, as a guide cut a round from the dough. Remove the excess dough and reserve it for another use. Prick the round at ½-inch intervals and bake it in the lower third of the oven for 15 to 20 minutes, or until lightly colored. Slide the round carefully onto a rack and let cool.

Butter another baking sheet and increase the oven temperature to 425° F. Using the 9-inch pie pan, inverted, as a guide mark a round in the butter. Fill one of the pastry bags, fitted with the ½-inch plain tip, with the *pâte à chou* and pipe a circle around the inner edge of the impression. Pipe puffs the size of walnuts within the circle and around the outer areas of the baking sheet and within the circle if necessary, leaving room for the puffs to expand (see illustration page 223). (You want a minimum of 13 puffs.) Brush the circle and the puffs with the egg wash and bake in the middle of the oven for 10 minutes. Reduce the heat to 400° F. and bake for 10 minutes. Reduce the heat to 350° F. and bake the pastry for 10 minutes more, or until it has completely risen and is well colored. With the skewer make a hole near the bottom in the side of each puff and make several holes in the inside edge of the ring to let the steam escape. Turn off the oven and return the pastry to it for 10 minutes. Transfer the ring and puffs to a rack to cool.

Make the caramel: In a heavy skillet cook the sugar with the water and cream of tartar over moderately high heat, washing down any sugar crystals clinging to the sides of the pan with the brush dipped in cold water until the mixture is a light caramel. Remove the pan from the heat.

To assemble the pastry: Transfer the *pâte brisée* round to a serving plate. Drizzle a ribbon of caramel around the edge of the round and set the ring of *pâte à chou* firmly on the caramel. Prop up one side of the caramel pan so that it is tilted and, working rapidly but carefully, dip the top of each puff into the caramel, putting the puffs on a buttered surface so that any drippings can be removed easily. If necessary, reheat the caramel to soften it, being careful not to let it burn. Or, make a second batch.

Dip the bottom of each puff in the caramel and set the puffs firmly on the *pâte à chou* ring with the hole in each puff facing in, leaving about ⅓ inch between the puffs. Let stand while you make the custard filling.

Make the *crème Saint-Honoré*: In a bowl with the mixer beat the egg yolks with the sugar until light and the mixture falls in a ribbon when the beater is lifted (see illustration page 16). Sift in the flour and combine well. In a small bowl let the gelatin soften in the water for 10 minutes. Whisk the hot milk in a stream into the yolk mixture, whisking constantly. Transfer the mixture to a heavy saucepan, bring it to a boil over moderate heat, stirring, for 2 minutes, and remove the pan from the heat. Stir the gelatin mixture to dissolve it and add it to the pan with the vanilla. In a bowl with the mixer beat the egg whites until they hold soft peaks. Stir the custard, strain it into a bowl, and while it is still hot beat in the egg whites and the liqueur. Chill the custard,

Gâteau Saint-Honoré (page 228)

covered with a buttered round of wax paper, until cool.

In a chilled bowl beat the heavy cream with the mixer until it holds soft peaks. Beat the custard with a whisk until smooth, then fold in the whipped cream. Chill the custard, covered, until ready to use.

To assemble the gâteau:

Have ready the candied strawberries and the spun sugar. In a chilled bowl with the mixer beat the remaining 1 cup heavy cream with the confectioners' sugar and liqueur until it holds stiff peaks.

Fill the second pastry bag, fitted with the ⅛-inch tip, with the *crème Saint-Honoré* and pipe the custard into the hole in each puff. Fill the center of the ring with the remaining custard. Fill another pastry bag with the liqueur-flavored whipped cream and pipe it over some or all of the *crème Saint-Honoré* and, if desired, pipe a whipped cream rosette between each of the puffs. Decorate the pastry with the candied strawberries and the spun sugar.

Photo opposite.

PHYLLO AND STRUDEL DOUGH

Phyllo and strudel dough share a similar paper thinness and, while we recommend making strudel dough not only because of the challenge of it but because it is also fun, we do not suggest making *phyllo* at home. In fact, we rarely see home recipes for *phyllo* and suspect the reason for this is because special equipment is needed to render the dough so exceptionally thin. Fortunately for all of us, *phyllo* is available at many supermarkets and specialty foods stores in packages in the frozen foods sections.

Unlike strudel dough, which is filled and rolled, *phyllo* is layered, and the key to layering it is to prevent it from drying out as you work. Remove only the number of leaves you need from the package and cover them with a damp dish cloth until ready to use. You will note in many dessert recipes that call for *phyllo,* including our own for Baklava (page 232), significant amounts of melted butter are used to keep the dough moist as it is layered. Because of their Greek and Middle Eastern origin, *phyllo* desserts are then usually soaked in a spiced honeyed syrup. The combination of crispy-flaky dough layers, butter, a filling most frequently made of nuts, and honey imbuing the whole is nothing short of heavenly.

Strudel is superb, too, in a completely different way. It is impossible to pass either an Austrian or German pastry shop and not marvel at the magnificent strudel in the window. They look so simple, those sugar-dusted rolls of apples or cherries, cheese or poppyseeds.

Lest we forget, appearances can be deceiving and someone, somewhere, worked very diligently and carefully to stretch that dough to its marvelous see-throughness. Unlike almost every other dough we can think of, you use the back of your hands—no rolling pin—to prepare stru-del, and over a table top! You then fill it and roll it and mark it with T (for triumphant!). Some things should be done at least once in life and making strudel is one of them.

BAKLAVA

Yield:
thirty 2-inch pastry
  diamonds

Equipment:
pastry brush
baking pan, 13 by 9 by
  2 inches

This Middle Eastern dessert of flaky pastry layered with walnuts is satu-rated with honey syrup redolent with spices. *Baklava*, undeniably sweet, is especially good served with strong black coffee.

*twenty-five 13- by 9-inch sheets of
  phyllo
3 sticks (1½ cups) unsalted butter,
  melted*

*1 pound shelled walnuts, chopped fine
5 tablespoons sugar
1 teaspoon cinnamon
ground cloves to taste*

FOR THE SYRUP
*3½ cups water
2 cups sugar
1 cup honey
1 teaspoon fresh lemon juice*

*3 slices of orange
3 slices of lemon
1 cinnamon stick
4 whole cloves*

Preheat the oven to 350° F.

Remove 10 of the *phyllo* sheets and keep the remaining sheets covered with a slightly dampened towel. With the brush carefully butter every other sheet and layer all of the sheets in the baking pan.

In a bowl combine the walnuts, the sugar, cinnamon, and ground cloves and spread one third of the mixture over the *phyllo*. Butter 5 more sheets of *phyllo* and lay them over the nut mixture. Sprinkle the *phyllo* with another one third of the nut mixture, butter 5 more *phyllo* sheets, and top them with the remaining nut mixture. Butter every other sheet of the remaining *phyllo* and arrange it over the nut mixture. With a sharp knife score the *baklava* into 2-inch diamond-shaped pieces. Heat the remaining butter (there should be about ½ cup) until it begins to brown and pour it evenly over the pastry. Sprinkle the top with a few drops of cold water.

Bake the *baklava* in the middle of the oven for 30 minutes. Reduce the temperature to 300° F. and bake the *baklava* for 1 hour more. Let the *bak-lava* cool on a rack.

Make the syrup:
In a saucepan combine the water, the sugar, lemon juice, orange and lemon slices, cinnamon stick, and the whole cloves, bring the mixture to a boil, and simmer it for 20 minutes. Strain the syrup into another saucepan and keep it hot.

Pour the hot syrup over the cooled *baklava*, cut the pastry into dia-monds, and serve with the syrup spooned over the diamonds.

PHYLLO NAPOLEONS WITH CHOCOLATE PASTRY CREAM

Yield:
6 napoleons

Equipment:
pastry brush
hand-held electric
  mixer
pastry bag fitted with
  star tip
small pastry bag fitted
  with $^1/_{16}$-inch plain
  tip

1 stick (½ cup) unsalted butter, melted
  and kept warm

twelve 17- by 12-inch sheets of
  phyllo *stacked between 2 sheets of
  wax paper and covered with
  a dampened kitchen towel*

FOR THE CHOCOLATE PASTRY CREAM

1 cup milk
¼ cup sugar
3 egg yolks
2 tablespoons all-purpose flour
3 ounces semisweet chocolate, chopped
  fine

1 ounce unsweetened chocolate,
  chopped fine
½ cup well-chilled heavy cream

FOR THE GLAZE

½ cup heavy cream

4 ounces bittersweet chocolate,
  chopped fine

1 cup confectioners' sugar

2 tablespoons water

Brush a baking sheet at least 17 inches long with some of the butter. Preheat the oven to 400° F.

Lay 1 sheet of the *phyllo* lengthwise on the baking sheet and brush it lightly with some of the remaining butter. Layer and butter 5 more sheets of the *phyllo* over the first sheet in the same manner. Using a ruler and a sharp knife, cut the *phyllo* into nine 5½- by 2½-inch rectangles, discarding the excess dough. Roll the edges over to form a ¼-inch border on the narrow ends of each rectangle and prick the rectangles all over with a knife. Bake the rectangles in the middle of the oven for 7 to 10 minutes, or until golden. Transfer to a rack to cool. Make 9 more pastry rectangles with the remaining *phyllo* sheets and the remaining butter in the same manner.

Make the chocolate pastry cream:

In a saucepan heat the milk with 2 tablespoons of the sugar over moderate heat, stirring, until the sugar is dissolved. In a bowl with the mixer beat the yolks with the remaining 2 tablespoons sugar until they are combined, add the flour, and beat the mixture until just combined. Add the heated milk in a stream, beating, and beat the mixture until it is combined well. Transfer the custard to a heavy saucepan, bring it to a boil, whisking constantly, and simmer it, stirring, for 3 minutes. Remove the pan from the heat and add the chocolate, stirring until it is melted. Transfer the pastry cream to a bowl, cover the surface directly with a buttered round of wax paper, and chill it, for 1 hour. In a chilled mixing bowl beat the cream until it holds soft peaks, fold the cream into the pastry cream, and keep the pastry cream chilled with the surface covered directly with a buttered round of wax paper for 45 minutes, of until firm enough to pipe. Transfer to the pastry bag fitted with the star tip.

Make the chocolate glaze:

In a small heavy saucepan bring the cream just to a simmer. Remove the pan from the heat, add the chocolate, and let the mixture stand, covered, for 5 minutes. Stir the chocolate glaze until smooth and tepid and strain it through a fine sieve into a small pitcher or bowl with a lip.

Arrange 6 of the *phyllo* rectangles, smooth side up, on a rack set over a jelly-roll pan, pour about one sixth of the glaze over each one, and chill for 5 minutes, or until the glaze is set. Arrange 6 of the remaining *phyllo* rectangles, smooth side down, on a platter, pipe 2 rows of the pastry cream lengthwise on top of each one, and gently press the remaining *phyllo* rectangles, smooth side down, on top of the pastry cream. Pipe 2 rows of the pastry cream lengthwise on top of each rectangle and press gently the chocolate-covered rectangles, chocolate side up, on top of the pastry cream. In a bowl whisk together the confectioners' sugar and the water, transfer the icing to the small pastry bag, and pipe the mixture in decorative patterns on the tops of the napoleons.

CHERRY STRUDEL

Yield:
12 to 14 servings

Equipment:
a tabletop more than 3 feet in diameter

There is simply no getting around it. The challenge of making strudel lies in the preparation of the dough, and your chances of success will markedly increase if you have extra hands on hand to stretch it. So, invite some friends over, have the appropriate-sized table, and then keep moving, cajoling the combination thinner and thinner. It is fun, and homemade strudel is incomparable.

FOR THE STRUDEL DOUGH

1 large egg	*pinch of salt*
²/₃ cup lukewarm water	*5 tablespoons unsalted butter, melted*
2 cups all-purpose flour	

FOR THE FILLING

1 cup fine fresh bread crumbs, toasted (for procedure page 550)	*1 cup slivered blanched almonds*
	1½ cups granulated sugar
3 cups pitted sweet black cherries	*1 teaspoon cinnamon*
1 cup golden raisins	*grated rind of 1 lemon*
2 sticks (1 cup) unsalted butter, melted	*sifted confectioners' sugar for sprinkling*

Make the strudel dough:

In a cup combine the egg and water well. Sift the flour onto a work surface. Make a well in the center and add the egg mixture, salt, and 1 tablespoon of the melted butter. Work the moist ingredients gradually into the flour, working from the inside of the well out until all the dry ingredients are incorporated and a dough forms. Knead the dough, pushing it away from you and turning it, until it comes away from the surface clean and silky and pliable. Shape the dough into a small loaf and let it rest on a floured surface, covered with a warm bowl, for 1 hour.

Cover the table top with a cloth and sprinkle the cloth with flour. On another floured surface roll out the dough as thin as possible and quickly transfer it on the back of your hands to the middle of the cloth. Now begin to stretch the dough. Reach under the dough with your fists, palms down, and draw them toward you, bending your wrists upward. Pull gently but steadily with the backs of your hands, stretching and working the dough while you walk around the table until the evenly pulled dough covers the table, with only a narrow thicker edge hanging down. The dough should be transparently thin (see illustration). Should the dough tear, patch the tear with a piece of dough taken from the edge. Attach it with a dab or two of butter. Drizzle the remaining 4 tablespoons butter over the dough.

Butter a baking sheet. Preheat the oven to 400° F.

Fill the strudel: Sprinkle the bread crumbs, cherries, raisins, and almonds over the dough. Dust the filling with the sugar, cinnamon, and lemon rind. Trim away the hanging edges of the dough. Gently lift the cloth from one end and roll the filling up jelly-roll fashion in the dough. Continue rolling until the strudel forms a cylinder. Slide the strudel onto the baking sheet, bend it into a horseshoe shape, and brush it generously with the 1 cup melted butter. Bake the strudel in the middle of the oven for 45 minutes to 1 hour, or until golden brown. Sprinkle generously with the confectioners' sugar and serve warm.

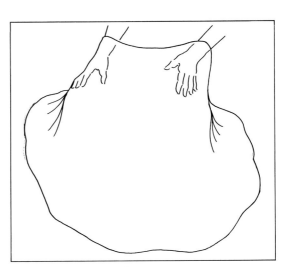

Stretching strudel dough

MERINGUES

amed after the town of Mehringyghen in what is today Switzerland, meringues were first made in 1720. They were so beloved by France's Queen Marie-Antoinette that, legend has it, she made them, herself, for the French court.

Although meringue is most often associated in our country with a frothy topping for lemon meringue pie, there are myriad other ways in which meringue may be used. We include recipes here for such superb presentations as floating island—flavored meringues baked in forms, unmolded, and floating on a sea of custard sauce; meringues shaped into shells, baked until dry and crisp, and filled with a wonderful variety of butters and creams; nutted meringues baked in crisp rounds that are layered with cake and buttercream to build towering and impressive desserts. Meringue layers are interspersed with vanilla ice cream and lemon curd, then frozen for our Frozen Lemon Meringue Cake (page 246). Another name for a cake formed from nut meringue layers (usually ground almonds) and various fillings is a *dacquoise*. Ours is filled with chocolate mousse and is even garnished with crumbled meringues; and our Orange Dacquoise (page 250) combines almond meringue layers and a rich orange buttercream. Baked Alaska may bring to mind a procession of white-gloved waiters weaving throughout a ship's dining room. In their hands they hold aloft flaming meringue-coated ice-cream cakes, in celebration of the last night at sea. You can easily re-create the fun and drama with our recipe. A *vacherin* is a large meringue shell or container filled with whatever you desire. Our beautiful *vacherin* holds ice cream and macerated fruits and is fancifully decorated with meringue rosettes. Finally, we include several recipes for little meringue cookies or kisses, studded with chocolate or flavored with a sweet coffee syrup.

Meringue combines beaten egg whites and sugar—an extremely

Vacherin aux Fruits
(page 254)

simple concept but one which is used as a foundation for so many other desserts. Beaten egg whites are basic to mousses, chilled soufflés, some Bavarian creams, sponge, angel food, and rolled cakes, ladyfingers, sponge puddings, and confections such as meringue mushrooms, besides the standard meringue desserts. They are even added to ice creams to retard the formation of ice crystals. Properly beaten, egg whites are the crucial element in baked soufflés, dessert omelets, and soufflé crêpes. Folded in immediately before baking, they provide the means for transforming the mixtures into airy puffs.

When egg whites are beaten, the incorporated air performs apparent magic. This dual process—beating and the added air—activates the proteins in the whites to bond them and form the structure we know as meringue foam. They further coagulate when baked giving the meringue its dry crisp texture.

There are two basic stages to beaten egg whites: (1) Egg whites beaten to the *soft peak stage*; they will not hold their shape but will slowly slide back on themselves lacking body. (2) Egg whites beaten to the *stiff peak stage*; they will hold their shape and stand rigid in actual points.

We suggest the following technique for beating egg whites: In a bowl with a mixer beat the egg whites with a pinch of salt until they are frothy, add a pinch of cream of tartar (cream of tartar acts not only as a stabilizing agent but it also helps increase the volume of the beaten whites), and beat until the whites hold soft peaks. Slowly add the sugar and continue beating until the whites hold stiff peaks. (For a comparison between soft and stiff peaks of beaten egg whites, see the illustration.) We call this combination of egg white and sugar a simple meringue. This method is quick, easy, and dependable provided the following rules are followed:

▪ Avoid making meringues on rainy or humid days. Humidity prevents meringue from hardening and, when baked, the meringue may absorb moisture from the air.

▪ Egg whites should be at room temperature as they are capable of absorbing the most air at that temperature and will therefore increase to maximum volume when beaten.

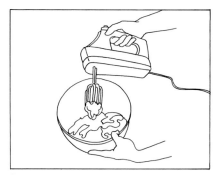 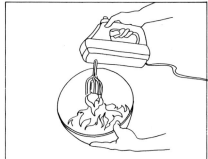

Egg whites at soft peak stage; egg whites and sugar at stiff peak stage

■ The bowl and beaters or whisk must be completely grease free. Likewise, the slightest bit of egg yolk present in the egg whites may retard the whites from becoming stiff when beating. (The fat inhibits coagulation of the egg proteins. The easiest and most foolproof way to remove yolk is to chase and scoop it up with a piece of egg shell.) Many feel that the traditional French method, now universal, of beating egg whites in a copper bowl and with a large balloon whisk is still the best. Indeed, beaten egg whites will be most stable if whisked in a copper bowl: The copper reacts chemically with the egg whites, creating volume and this stability, but most important, the copper helps to prevent the whites from being overbeaten. Overbeaten egg whites have gone past the stiff peak stage and look granular and actually broken down. They are past the point of being able to accept any more air and they are actually losing air when overbeaten. If this occurs, get a clean bowl and a brand new batch of egg whites and simply start all over again.

■ The sugar must be added very slowly, beating well after each addition so it dissolves fully. If not "beads" of syrup form on the baked meringues and in humid weather become even wetter.

■   ■   ■

Simple meringue will be, if made and baked properly, crisp but tender, light and fragile. It should not be held for very long before baking or the air will escape and the meringue will deflate.

Baking time determines, to great extent, the texture of the finished meringue. If the meringue is baked for a shorter amount of time, it will be crisp on the surface but soft and chewy in the center. The longer baked or allowed to dry overnight in a slow oven, the drier and crisper the center will be.

A meringue topping for a pie can be prepared with the standard simple meringue. Care should be taken to completely cover the surface of the pie, so that the meringue will not shrink and pull away from the sides after baking. An alternate method, as described in our Cranberry Meringue Pie (page 154), is to warm the egg whites and sugar over simmering water until the sugar is dissolved. The bowl is then removed from the pan and the mixture is beaten. This lengthier method results in a slightly denser meringue with better volume and stability, and the meringue is less likely to weep or bead when exposed to moisture. (This method is referred to by some as the Swiss meringue method, although we use the term to define the method described in the following paragraph.)

Aside from our simple meringue two other methods of preparing meringue are: the Swiss meringue method and the Italian meringue method. A Swiss meringue combines stiffly beaten egg whites with a portion of the sugar and the whites are then beaten until glossy. The remaining majority of the sugar is then folded into the whites by tablespoons. This method results in a very refined meringue because of the tenderizing effect of the sugar. It is slightly tricky to make, however; the meringue cannot be held for any longer than an hour because the mixture will separate.

Also, if overmixed after the final addition of sugar has been folded in, the baked meringue will have a slightly sticky center.

Italian meringue refers to the same ingredients but a different method of combining them. A boiled sugar syrup is made and is slowly beaten into stiffly beaten egg whites. Italian meringue should be used if the meringue has to stand for some time before baking. In its own way, Italian meringue is double fortified. It is denser than Swiss meringue because of the egg whites being partially cooked by the hot sugar syrup. Since the Italian meringue contains a sugar syrup which hardens, it is therefore more resilient than the Swiss meringue. Italian meringue will be harder and not as tender as the Swiss meringue type if baked, but because it is so stable, it is a better choice for the Vacherin aux Fruits (page 254). The *vacherin* demands a certain amount of time to pipe out the concentric circles of meringue and it requires careful stacking of the fragile layers.

Italian meringue is used for most frozen soufflés. The mixture is basically cooked by the hot sugar syrup, stiffly beaten whipped cream is added, and the whole is frozen. The sugar syrup must be poured in a thin, steady stream, and the whites must be beaten constantly (see illustration). If not, the syrup's weight will deflate the beaten whites and the mixture will not be as light.

Pouring hot sugar syrup into beaten egg whites

We've been talking about Italian meringue without really mentioning its second most important feature: the sugar syrup. A properly made sugar syrup is crucial not only for an Italian meringue but also for so many other desserts, either as an ingredient or as an actual foundation. Sugar syrups are integral parts of mousses, parfait custard mixtures, *appareil à bombe* mixtures, poaching syrups for fruits, fondant icings, candied fruits and nuts, toffees and penuche and caramel syrups for custards, puddings, and sauces.

An understanding of the basics of making sugar syrup is extremely important. When sugar and water are boiled together to form a sugar syrup, the water evaporates, and the concentration of sugar increases. The more concentrated the sugar (or the longer it's boiled), the harder the syrup will set when cooled; or the harder the mixture to which it is added will set. (We think of hard candies versus caramels as illustrations of this.) Therefore, by stopping the boiling process at different stages (by simply removing the syrup from the heat), you can produce syrups with varying sugar concentrations, resulting in syrups that will set in varying degrees when cool.

Concentrations of sugar syrups are normally described in the following manner as stages of sugar syrup: (You will note that a range of temperatures applies to each stage, and, in a recipe that calls for a specific temperature, as long as you are within that range your sugar syrup will be at the proper stage.)

Candy thermometer temperature	Explanations of illustrations
223-234° F.	Thread stage—sugar syrup forms a thin thread when dropped from a spoon.
234-240° F.	Soft-ball stage—sugar syrup after being dropped in cold water can be formed into a soft ball which flattens and loses its shape.
244-248° F.	Firm-ball stage—sugar syrup after being dropped in cold water can be formed into a firm but pliable ball that will hold it shape.
250-266° F.	Hard-ball stage—sugar syrup after being dropped in cold water can be formed into a hard non-pliable ball.
270-290° F.	Soft-crack stage—sugar syrup after being dropped in cold water can be stretched between your fingers, forming elastic or pliable strands.
300-310° F.	Hard-crack stage—sugar syrup after being dropped in cold water solidifies instantly and is brittle enough to be cracked.

SIX STAGES OF SUGAR SYRUP

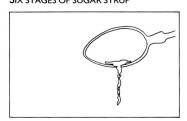

Thread

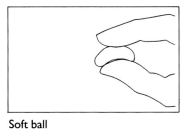

Soft ball

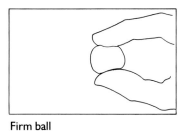

Firm ball

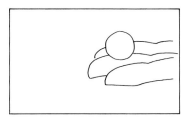

Hard ball

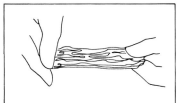

Soft crack

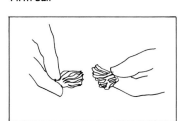

Hard crack

When boiling a sugar syrup it is essential that you prevent crystallization or small sugar crystals from forming on the sides of the pan and dropping back into the boiling sugar solution, causing the entire mass to crystallize or become gritty. This is done simply by washing down any sugar crystals clinging to the sides of the pan with a pastry brush dipped in cold water before they get a chance to crystallize. Furthermore, the sugar syrup should not be stirred after the sugar is dissolved.

MERINGUE SHELLS

Yield:
16 shells

6 egg whites at room temperature
pinch of cream of tartar
1½ cups granulated sugar

½ teaspoon vanilla sugar made with
  superfine granulated sugar (page
  541)

Equipment:
parchment paper
3-inch round cutter
upright electric mixer
pastry bag fitted with
  fluted tip

Cover 2 baking sheets with the parchment paper. Using the cutter as a guide, draw 16 circles on the paper.

In a large bowl with the mixer beat the egg whites at medium speed until foamy. Add the cream of tartar and continue to beat the whites until they hold soft peaks. Sprinkle in the granulated sugar, ¼ cup at a time, add the vanilla sugar, and continue to beat until the meringue holds very stiff peaks (see illustrations page 238).

Preheat the oven to 225° F.

Attach the parchment paper to the baking sheets by putting a dab of meringue on the underside of each corner. With a metal spatula spread a ¼-inch layer of the meringue within the perimeters of each of the circles, forming bases of the shells. Fill the pastry bag with the remaining meringue and pipe 1-inch borders of meringue around the edges of each base

Store in airtight containers.

to form shells. Bake the shells for 45 minutes, turn off the oven, and let the meringue shells stand in the oven to dry for at least 3 hours, or overnight.

Variation:

MERINGUE NESTS: Increase the oven temperature to 400° F. Spoon about 20 mounds of the meringue onto the parchment-lined baking sheets. With the back of the spoon make an indentation 3 inches in diameter in each mound. Put the meringue nests in the preheated oven and turn off the heat immediately. Let the meringues dry in the oven, without opening the oven door, for at least 12 hours.

FILLINGS FOR MERINGUE SHELLS OR NESTS: Fill with Chocolate Whipped Cream (page 496) and garnish with Chocolate Walnut Brittle Topping (page 501); fill with lemon butter (page 246) or Lemon Sherbet (page 371) and garnish with Candied Orange Peel (page 522); or, fill with Coconut Ice Cream (page 350), garnish with toasted coconut, and serve with a chocolate sauce of choice (pages 497 to 500).

ÎLE FLOTTANTE

Floating Island

Yield:
8 meringues,
   serving 8

Equipment:
eight ¾-cup charlotte
   molds or ramekins
hand-held electric
   mixer
large baking pan for
   waterbath
pastry brush

Île flottante is a dessert of meringue "islands" floating on a sea of vanilla custard. This version features almond praline meringues, vanilla custard, and hot caramel topping.

   This recipe departs from the traditional preparation insofar as the meringues are flavored with praline powder and are baked in charlotte molds or ramekins, as opposed to being poached freestanding in milk.

FOR THE MERINGUES

6 egg whites at room temperature
pinch of salt
¾ cup sugar plus additional sugar for
*   dusting the molds*

⅓ cup finely ground almond praline
*   (page 544)*

FOR THE CARAMEL

¾ cup sugar
3 tablespoons water

pinch of cream of tartar

1½ recipes Crème Anglaise (page
*   490), substituting milk for the*
*   half-and-half*

lightly toasted slivered blanched
*   almonds for topping*

Make the meringues:

Preheat the oven to 275° F. and butter and sugar the charlotte molds.

   In a bowl with the mixer beat the egg whites with the salt until they hold soft peaks. Add the sugar, one tablespoon at a time, beating, and continue to beat the meringue until it holds stiff peaks (see illustrations page 238). Fold in the praline powder gently but thoroughly. Fill the charlotte molds with the meringue, put the molds in the baking pan, and add enough hot water to the pan to reach halfway up the sides of the molds. Bake the meringues in the middle of the oven for 30 minutes. Allow the meringues to cool slightly in the molds but do not allow them to get too cold or they will be difficult to unmold.

Make the caramel:

   In a skillet combine the sugar, water, and cream of tartar and cook the mixture over moderately low heat, stirring, for a few seconds. Bring to a boil, washing down any sugar crystals clinging to the sides of the pan with the brush dipped in cold water until the sugar is dissolved, increase the heat to moderately high, and cook the syrup, gently swirling the pan, until the syrup turns a very light caramel color. Remove the pan from the heat and let the caramel stand for 1 minute to thicken. Makes ½ cup.

   Turn the meringues out onto a serving dish and fill the dish with the crème anglaise. Top the meringues with the toasted almonds and spoon the hot caramel over them. Serve at once.

   Photo on page 488.

HAZELNUT MERINGUE CAKE

Yield:
10 to 12 servings

Equipment:
pastry bag fitted with
  ¼-inch plain tip
hand-held and upright
  electric mixers
two 9-inch cake pans
pastry brush
candy thermometer
decorative tip for the
  pastry bag

This remarkably elegant meringue cake can easily be made ahead in stages: The meringue layers can be baked and stored in an airtight container, the chocolate cake may be made ahead and even frozen, and the coffee buttercream may be combined in advance and simply brought back to room temperature and rewhipped. The *crème ganache,* chocolate cream, however, should be made just before assembling; if left to stand, the mixture becomes difficult to spread. (For detailed instructions on the assembling and decorating of this cake and working with a pastry bag, see pages 19 and 20.)

Reserve this cake for a special occasion, such as New Year's Eve.

FOR THE MERINGUE LAYERS
4 egg whites at room temperature
pinch of salt
pinch of cream of tartar
1 cup granulated sugar
*1 cup confectioners' sugar, sifted, plus
  additional for sprinkling*

*¾ cup finely ground toasted and skins
  removed hazelnuts (for procedure
  page 549)*

FOR THE CHOCOLATE CAKE LAYER
4 large eggs, separated
⅓ cup sugar
pinch of salt
pinch of cream of tartar
1 tablespoon fresh orange juice

1 teaspoon grated orange rind
¼ cup all-purpose flour
*2 tablespoons unsweetened cocoa
  powder*

1 recipe coffee buttercream (page 23)
1 recipe crème ganache *(page 539)
  substituting orange-flavored liqueur
  for the Cognac or rum*

*¾ cup finely ground toasted and skins
  removed hazelnuts*
whole hazelnuts for garnish

Make the meringue layers:

Preheat the oven to 300° F. Butter and flour the cake pans.

In a large bowl with the hand-held mixer beat the egg whites with the salt until frothy, add the cream of tartar, and beat until the whites hold soft peaks. Gradually beat in the granulated sugar and beat the meringue until it holds stiff peaks (see illustrations page 238). Fold in the confectioners' sugar combined with the ground hazelnuts and spoon the meringue into the pastry bag. Pipe the meringue into the pans in a spiral design, starting at the center of each pan. Sift additional confectioners' sugar over the meringues, covering them, and bake in the middle of the oven for 1 hour, or until lightly browned. Let the meringues cool in the pans for 10 minutes, turn them out onto a rack, and let them cool completely.

Make the chocolate layer cake:

Preheat the oven to 350° F. Butter one of the cake pans , line it with wax paper, and butter and flour the paper.

In a bowl with the hand-held mixer combine the egg yolks, add the sugar, a little at a time, and beat the mixture until it falls in a ribbon when the beater is lifted (see illustration page 16). In another bowl with the mixer beat the egg whites with the salt until frothy, add the cream of tartar, and beat until the whites hold stiff peaks. Beat in the orange juice and orange rind. Stir one fourth of the whites into the egg yolk mixture. Pile the lightened yolk mixture on the remaining whites and sift the flour and cocoa over the top. Fold the mixtures together gently until no traces of white remain. Pour the batter into the pan and bake the cake in the middle of the oven for 15 minutes, or until a cake tester inserted in the center comes out clean. Let the cake cool in the pan, turn it out onto a rack, and peel off the paper.

Let the coffee buttercream come just to room temperature, or spreading consistency.

In a bowl combine the *crème ganache* and the hazelnuts, folding them in gently.

To assemble the cake: With a serrated knife trim the meringues into even flat rounds, reserving the trimmings. Halve the chocolate cake horizontally and spread the bottom layer with one third of the *crème ganache*. Top with a meringue, spread the meringue with another third of the *crème ganache*, and top the *crème ganache* with the remaining layer of chocolate cake. Spread the chocolate cake with the remaining *crème ganache* and top the cream with the other meringue, smooth side up. Cover the top and sides of the cake with two thirds of the coffee buttercream. Warm the blade of the serrated knife under running hot water, dry it, and run it in a zigzag motion over the top of the cake. Fill the pastry bag fitted with the decorative tip with the remaining coffee buttercream, pipe swirls around the top edge of the cake, and decorate the swirls with the whole hazelnuts. Finely grind the reserved meringue trimmings and press them around the sides of the cake. Chill the cake if desired and remove it from the refrigerator 30 minutes before serving.

FROZEN LEMON MERINGUE CAKE

Yield:
6 to 8 servings

Equipment:
parchment paper
hand-held electric
   mixer
7-inch cake pan

This light and lovely frozen cake incorporates lemon butter, or curd, and vanilla ice cream between layers of meringue. It is cooling and airy and the perfect finale to a summer supper. One note of caution: Soften the ice cream *only slightly*, and take the time to freeze each layer as instructed. If you don't, the layers have a way of sliding in the freezer and, while you will end up with a still wonderful-tasting dessert, its appearance may be a little less sublime.

FOR THE LEMON BUTTER
2 large eggs
2 egg yolks
1 cup sugar
¾ stick (6 tablespoons) unsalted butter, cut into bits

⅓ cup fresh lemon juice
1½ tablespoons grated lemon rind
⅛ teaspoon salt

FOR THE MERINGUES
3 egg whites at room temperature
⅜ teaspoon cream of tartar

⅓ cup sugar
¾ teaspoon vanilla

3 cups Vanilla Ice Cream (page 349), softened slightly

Make the lemon butter:

In a heavy saucepan combine the whole eggs, egg yolks, sugar, butter, lemon juice, lemon rind, and salt and cook the mixture over moderately low heat, stirring, until the butter is melted and the mixture is thick enough to coat a spoon. Do not let it boil. Transfer the mixture to a bowl, let it cool, and chill it, covered with a buttered round of wax paper. Makes about 2 cups.

Make the meringues:

Line a large baking sheet with the parchment paper and, using the cake pan, inverted, or a plate as a guide, trace 2 circles onto the paper. Preheat the oven to 250° F.

In a large bowl with the mixer beat the egg whites with the cream of tartar until they hold soft peaks. Beat in the sugar, one tablespoon at a time, and the vanilla and beat the meringue until it is shiny and very stiff (see illustrations page 238). Divide the meringue between the 2 circles, smooth it evenly with a spatula, and bake it in the middle of the oven for 1 hour. Turn off the oven and let the meringues stand in the oven for 2 hours, or until dry.

Place one of the meringues on a serving plate, spread it with 1 cup of the ice cream, leaving a ¼-inch border, and freeze it until the ice cream is firm. Spread the ice cream with half the lemon butter and freeze the meringue

Chocolate Mousse Dacquoise (page 248),
Iced Lemon Soufflé (page 398)

until the lemon butter is firm. Top with 1 cup of the remaining ice cream and freeze again until firm. Spread the ice cream with the remaining lemon butter and freeze. Top with the remaining ice cream and the remaining meringue and freeze the cake, covered, until firm. Serve the cake cut into wedges.

CHOCOLATE MOUSSE DACQUOISE

Yield:
18 to 20 servings

Equipment:
hand-held electric
  mixer
10- by 4½-inch
  rectangular flan
  form, or a similarly
  shaped tracing guide
food processor fitted
  with steel blade
pastry bag fitted with
  very small plain tip

A *dacquoise* is simply a cake that is made of nut meringue layers layered with various fillings. This *dacquoise* is made with hazelnut meringues, filled with chocolate mousse, glazed with chocolate, and decoratively iced. (For illustrations on how to glaze the cake and feather the icing, see pages 19 and 20.) It is a splendid and impressive dessert that, although requiring advance preparation, can be easily assembled the day of a party.

FOR THE CHOCOLATE MOUSSE

12 ounces semisweet chocolate, cut into bits
6 egg whites at room temperature
pinch of salt

pinch of cream of tartar
3 cups well-chilled heavy cream
1 teaspoon vanilla

FOR THE HAZELNUT MERINGUES

8 egg whites at room temperature
¼ teaspoon salt
¼ teaspoon cream of tartar
1½ cups granulated sugar
1½ cups toasted and skins removed hazelnuts (for procedure page 549), ground

2 tablespoons sifted cornstarch
1 teaspoon vanilla
sifted confectioners' sugar for sprinkling

8 ounces semisweet chocolate, cut into bits

1 cup heavy cream
1 tablespoon dark rum

½ cup confectioners' sugar, sifted
1 tablespoon lightly beaten egg white

¼ teaspoon fresh lemon juice

Make the chocolate mousse:

In the top of a double boiler set over hot water melt the chocolate, stirring. Let cool to lukewarm.

In a large bowl with the mixer beat the egg whites with the salt until frothy, add the cream of tartar, and beat until the whites hold stiff peaks. In a large chilled bowl with the mixer beat the heavy cream with the vanilla until it holds stiff peaks. Fold the chocolate gently but thoroughly into the beaten whites. Fold in the whipped cream. Makes 8 cups.

Make the hazelnut meringues:

Butter well and flour lightly 3 large baking sheets. Using the flan form or similar guide, trace with the point of a knife 2 outlines of the rectangular form onto each baking sheet for a total of 6 outlines. Keep the sheets chilled until ready to use.

Preheat oven to 300° F.

In a large bowl with the mixer beat the egg whites with the salt until frothy, add the cream of tartar, and beat until the whites hold soft peaks. Add ¼ cup of the granulated sugar, a little at a time, and beat the whites until they hold stiff peaks (see illustrations page 238). Fold in gently but thoroughly the remaining 1¼ cups granulated sugar, a little at a time, the ground hazelnuts, cornstarch, and vanilla. Divide the meringue evenly among the 6 rectangles, smoothing it with a spatula to fit within each form. Sprinkle the meringues lightly with the sifted confectioners' sugar and bake them in the middle of the oven for 1 hour, or until pale beige and crisp. Let the meringues cool for 3 minutes, transfer them carefully with a large spatula to racks, and let them cool completely.

To assemble the *dacquoise*:

With a serrated knife and the flan form or other guide used in making the meringues trim 4 of the meringues into neat rectangles. On a large rack set over a baking pan or jelly-roll pan arrange a meringue, spread it with a ½-inch layer of the chocolate mousse, and invert another meringue on the mousse. Spread the second meringue with a ½-inch layer of the mousse, invert another meringue on the mousse, and spread it with a ½-inch layer of the mousse. Invert the fourth meringue on top of the mousse, but do not spread the top layer with mousse. Smooth the sides of the cake with a spatula, using mousse, if necessary, to even out the sides. Chill the cake for 1 hour.

The mousse may be prepared I day in advance and stored, covered and chilled.

Crumble the remaining 2 meringues and in the food processor or in a blender grind them to a powder, transfer the powder to a bowl, and cover it loosely.

The meringues may be stored in airtight containers or in a cool oven for several hours or overnight.

In a heavy saucepan combine the semisweet chocolate, the heavy cream, and the rum. Heat the mixture, stirring, until the chocolate is melted and the mixture is smooth. Remove the pan from the heat and let the glaze cool until it is just warm, but do not let it become cold.

In a small bowl combine the confectioners' sugar, the egg white, and the lemon juice. Beat the mixture until it is thick and smooth and transfer the icing to the pastry bag.

The *dacquoise* may be assembled and chilled for several hours before serving.

Have ready a small thin-bladed knife; a piece of dampened paper towel; the warm chocolate glaze; and the pastry bag containing the icing. Pour all the chocolate glaze carefully over the cake, allowing it to run down the sides, and smooth it with a spatula until it covers the cake evenly. Before the glaze sets, position the cake with a long side facing you and pipe thin lines of the icing down the top of the cake at ½-inch intervals. Turn the cake so that a short side is facing you and with the tip of the knife draw four equidistant ⅟₁₆-inch-deep lines through the icing, pulling the tip of the knife through the icing toward you and wiping the knife with the paper towel after each draw. Turn the cake around so that the other short side is facing you, and draw the knife through the icing between each pair of lengthwise lines in the same manner, drawing the icing toward you (see illustrations page 20). Press the ground meringue around the sides of the cake. Chill the cake until the chocolate is set.

Photo on page 247.

ORANGE DACQUOISE

Yield:
one 10-inch cake

Equipment:
10-inch cake pan
upright electric mixer
pastry bag fitted with
 ¼-inch plain tip
star tip for the pastry
 bag
pastry brush
candy thermometer

FOR THE MERINGUES
7 egg whites at room temperature
pinch of salt
¾ cup plus 2 tablespoons granulated
 sugar

1 cup ground blanched almonds,
 toasted lightly

1 recipe orange buttercream (page 24)
sifted confectioners' sugar for
 sprinkling

1 recipe Candied Orange Peel (page
 522) for garnish

Make the meringues:

Butter and flour 2 baking sheets. Using the cake pan as a guide, draw a circle on each of the baking sheets with the tip of a thin-bladed knife. Preheat the oven to 250° F.

In the bowl of the upright mixer beat the egg whites with the salt until they hold soft peaks. Beat in the ¾ cup granulated sugar, a little at a time, and beat the meringue until stiff and glossy (see illustrations page 238). Combine the ground almonds with the remaining 2 tablespoons granulated sugar and fold the mixture gently but thoroughly into the meringue.

Fill the pastry bag with the meringue and pipe a continuous spiral starting in the middle of the circles until the outlines are filled (see illustration below). Smooth the top of the meringues with a metal spatula. Pipe the remaining meringue roughly on the uncovered areas of the baking sheets and bake for 45 minutes, or until crisp and dry but barely colored. Remove the meringues from the oven, let them cool, and transfer them carefully from the baking sheets to racks.

Transfer 1 cup of the orange buttercream to a small bowl. Break up the roughly shaped meringues into small pieces. Add them to the remaining buttercream. Chill both bowls of the buttercream, covered, until it is firm but still soft enough to spread.

To assemble the
dacquoise:

Put 1 teaspoon of the plain buttercream in the center of the inverted cake pan and set one of the meringue layers, smooth side down, on the pan. (The buttercream will secure it.) Spread the meringue-laced buttercream evenly over the layer to within ½ inch of the edge. Fit the star tip onto the pastry bag, fill the bag with the plain buttercream, and pipe a border around the edge of the filling. Top the filling with the remaining meringue layer, smooth side up, sprinkle it with confectioners' sugar, and decorate the center with the candied orange peel. With a spatula transfer the *dacquoise* to a cake plate and chill it for about 1 hour before serving.

Photo on page 252.

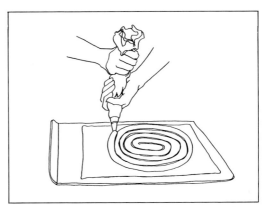

Piping out a continuous spiral of meringue to form
a layer

Ginger Walnut Roll with Molasses Cream (page 41), Orange Dacquoise (page 250)

BAKED ALASKA

Yield:
8 to 10 servings

Equipment:
9-inch cake pan
11½- by 7½-inch
  metal gratin dish or
  10-inch cake pan
upright electric mixer
wooden board 12
  inches in diameter
pastry bag fitted with
  large fluted tip

Often called *omelette à la norvégienne* in French, baked Alaska is a showy and fun dessert. It is made with cake and layers of ice cream, covered with meringue, and baked until browned. The meringue prevents the ice cream from melting during the browning and the resulting contrasting textures and temperatures are what make the dessert so special. Any type of cake or any flavor of ice cream may be substituted.

1 recipe vanilla génoise *batter (page 22)*
2 quarts Coffee Ice Cream (page 349) or 1 quart Coffee Ice Cream and 1 quart Dark Chocolate Ice Cream (page 349)
1 pint Vanilla Ice Cream (page 349)
6 egg whites at room temperature

pinch of salt
1 cup granulated sugar
2 tablespoons dark rum
1 recipe brandy syrup (page 542)
sifted confectioners' sugar for sprinkling
⅓ cup dark rum or Cognac, heated, if desired

Preheat the oven to 350° F. Butter and flour the gratin dish or 10-inch cake pan.

Pour the *génoise* batter into the prepared dish or 10-inch pan and bake it in the middle of the oven for 25 to 30 minutes, or until golden. Turn the cake out on a rack and let it cool completely. Chill the cake, wrapped in plastic wrap, but do not freeze it.

In the bowl of the mixer break up 1 quart of the coffee ice cream with a spoon and let it soften slightly. On low speed beat the ice cream briefly until smooth, but do not let it melt. Line the 9-inch cake pan or a shallow dish of the same shape but about 1 inch smaller than the cake with plastic wrap, pack the softened ice cream into it, and freeze for 1 hour, or until firm.

Break up and beat the vanilla ice cream in the same manner, spread it smoothly over the coffee layer, and freeze it for 1 hour, or until both layers are firm.

Break up and beat the remaining quart of coffee ice cream in the same manner and spread it smoothly over the vanilla layer. Freeze the ice cream, covered with plastic wrap, overnight.

In the bowl of the mixer beat the egg whites with the salt until they hold soft peaks. Beat in the sugar, a little at a time, beating, and beat the meringue until stiff and shiny (see illustrations page 238). Fold in the rum.

Preheat the oven to 450° F.

To assemble the baked Alaska:

Remove the plastic wrap from the cake, set the cake on the wooden board, and brush it well with the brandy syrup. Remove the plastic wrap from the ice cream and center the molded ice cream firmly on the cake. With a metal spatula spread a thick layer of the meringue over the ice cream and cake. Transfer the remaining meringue to the pastry bag and pipe it decoratively over the top and sides of the dessert and over the exposed section of the wooden base. Sprinkle the meringue with the confectioners' sugar, set the wooden board on a baking sheet, and bake the dessert in the upper third of the oven for 5 to 7 minutes, or until the meringue is golden. Put the baked Alaska on a platter, board and all, and serve it immediately. Or, if desired, pour the heated Cognac around the base of the dessert, ignite it, and serve the baked Alaska flaming.

VACHERIN AUX FRUITS

Meringue with Ice Cream and Macerated Fruits

Yield:
14 servings

Equipment:
upright electric mixer
pastry brush
candy thermometer
parchment paper
9-inch flower flan ring
   (available at specialty
   kitchenware stores)
pastry bag fitted with
   ¾-inch plain tip
decorative tip for the
   pastry bag
cake comb (optional)

A *vacherin* is a meringue ring or shell filled with ice cream, whipped cream, or fruits. It may be decorated with scrolls and rosettes of meringue for a more impressive presentation.

FOR 2 BATCHES OF ITALIAN MERINGUE
12 egg whites at room temperature
2 pinches of salt
2 pinches of cream of tartar
3 cups granulated sugar
1½ cups water
2 tablespoons eau-de-vie de
   framboise (raspberry brandy),
   or to taste

2 teaspoons vanilla
sifted confectioners' sugar for
   sprinkling

FOR THE FILLING
3 pints strawberries, hulled
3 pounds peaches, peeled (for
   procedure page 548), pitted and
   sliced
1 pint blueberries, picked over

¼ cup granulated sugar, or to taste
¼ cup fresh lemon juice, or to taste
3 tablespoons orange-flavored liqueur,
   or to taste

2 quarts Dark Chocolate Ice Cream
   (page 349), softened slightly

whipped cream flavored with brandy
   as an accompaniment if desired

Make the meringues:

In the bowl of the mixer beat 6 of the egg whites with a pinch of the salt until frothy, add a pinch of the cream of tartar, and beat until they hold soft peaks. Add ¼ cup of the granulated sugar and beat the whites until they hold stiff peaks (see illustrations page 238).

In a small saucepan combine 1¼ cups of the granulated sugar with ¾ cup of the water and bring the mixture to a boil. Boil over moderate heat, swirling the pan and washing down any sugar crystals clinging to the sides of the pan with the brush dipped in water until the mixture reaches the hard-ball stage, or the candy thermometer registers 250° F. With the mixer running, add the hot syrup to the egg whites in a stream, beating, and beat the meringue until cool. (For the stages of sugar syrup and how to pour it, see illustrations pages 240 and 241.) Beat in 1 tablespoon of the *eau-de-vie de framboise* and 1 teaspoon of the vanilla. Set the meringue aside.

Preheat the oven to 200° F.

Cover 2 large baking sheets with the parchment paper. Using the flower flan ring as a guide, draw firmly 2 outlines on each paper. Invert the paper onto the baking sheets and attach it by putting a dab of the meringue on the underside of each corner. Fill the pastry bag fitted with the plain tip with meringue and pipe a ring of the meringue just inside one of the outlines. Continue to pipe smaller concentric rings within the outer ring until the shape is completely filled. Pipe a single meringue ring just inside each of the remaining 3 outlines and sprinkle the meringues with the confectioners' sugar. Bake the meringues in the middle of the oven for 1½ hours, or until dry. Detach the meringues carefully from the parchment paper with the tip of a knife and with large metal spatulas transfer them carefully to racks to cool.

Make a second batch of Italian meringue in the same manner.

Line one of the baking sheets with clean parchment paper and put the meringue base on the paper. Fit the pastry bag with the decorative tip and transfer half of the second batch to the bag. Pipe a thin line of meringue along the rim of the base and on 2 of the rings. Stack the rimmed rings on the base, pressing them down lightly, and top the stack with the remaining meringue ring. With a metal spatula smooth a layer of the remaining meringue around the outside of the shell and along the top rim. Run the cake comb or a long serrated knife around the outside of the shell and along the top, forming decorative ridges. With the pastry bag pipe rosettes at intervals around the top of the shell. Pipe the remaining meringue in rosettes onto the baking sheet. (For detailed illustrations on working with a pastry bag, using a cake comb, and piping rosettes, see pages 19 and 20.) Bake the shell and the rosettes in the middle of the oven for 1½ hours, or until dry. Turn off the oven and let the meringues dry in the oven overnight.

The meringue shell and rosettes can be baked up to 1 week in advance and stored in airtight containers or in a cool oven.

Make the filling:

In a large glass bowl toss the strawberries, peaches, and blueberries with the sugar, lemon juice, and liqueur and chill, covered, for several hours or overnight. Drain the fruit.

Transfer the *vacherin* to a platter, fill it with some of the ice cream, and top the ice cream with the drained fruit. Decorate the platter with some of the meringue rosettes and serve the remaining rosettes and ice cream separately. Serve the *vacherin* with the whipped cream if desired.

Photo on page 236.

DOUBLE COFFEE KISSES

Yield:
18 meringue kisses

1 cup sugar
⅓ cup very strong coffee

3 egg whites at room temperature

Equipment:
candy thermometer
parchment paper
hand-held electric
    mixer

Preheat the oven to 300° F. and line baking sheets with the parchment paper.

In a heavy saucepan combine the sugar with the coffee. Bring the mixture to a boil and boil the syrup until the candy thermometer registers 248° F.

In a bowl with the mixer beat the egg whites until stiff. With the motor running gradually beat in the hot coffee syrup and continue to beat the meringue until stiff, glossy, and cool. (For the stages of sugar syrup and how to pour it, see illustrations pages 240 and 241.) Drop the meringue by teaspoonfuls 2 inches apart onto the paper and bake in the middle of the oven for about 40 minutes, or until dry. Remove the meringues from the paper in pairs and, while they are still warm, press the bottoms of each pair together.

Store in airtight
containers.

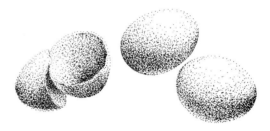

CHOCOLATE CHIP MERINGUE COOKIES

Yield:
about 45 meringue
    cookies

½ cup (about 4 large) egg whites at
*   room temperature*
¼ teaspoon salt
½ teaspoon cider vinegar

1 cup granulated sugar
2 teaspoons orange-flavored liqueur
1 cup semisweet chocolate morsels
1 tablespoon confectioners' sugar

Equipment:
hand-held electric
    mixer

Preheat the oven to 275° F. Line baking sheets with foil, shiny side down.

In a bowl with the mixer beat the egg whites with the salt until they are frothy, add the vinegar, and beat the whites until they hold soft peaks. Beat in the granulated sugar, a little at a time, and beat the meringue until it holds stiff, glossy peaks (see illustrations page 238). Beat in the liqueur. Fold in the chocolate chips. Spoon level tablespoons of the mixture 2 inches apart onto the baking sheets and sift the confectioners' sugar lightly over the meringues. Bake in the middle of the oven for 35 to 45 minutes, or until very lightly colored and firm to the touch. Transfer the meringues to racks and let them cool.

Store in airtight
containers.

MERINGUES AUX NOISETTES

Hazelnut Meringue Cookies

Yield:
about 24 meringue
cookies

An elegant cookie, perfect with fruit combinations such as Confetti Oranges with Glacéed Fruits (page 464) or Baked Pears Alicia (page 472), or your favorite ice cream or sherbet.

Equipment:
food processor fitted
with steel blade
hand-held electric
mixer
pastry bag fitted with
¼-inch plain tip

*¾ cup hazelnuts, toasted and skins
removed (for procedure
page 549)*
½ cup superfine granulated sugar
2½ teaspoons cornstarch
3 egg whites at room temperature

pinch of salt
⅛ teaspoon cream of tartar
2 tablespoons granulated sugar
½ teaspoon vanilla
⅛ teaspoon almond extract

Preheat the oven to 225° F. Butter and flour a baking sheet.

In the food processor or in a blender finely grind the hazelnuts. In a small bowl combine the nut powder with the superfine granulated sugar and sift in the cornstarch. In a bowl with the mixer beat the egg whites with the salt until frothy, add the cream of tartar, and beat until the whites hold soft peaks. Beat in the granulated sugar, one teaspoon at a time, and continue to beat the meringue until it holds stiff peaks (see illustrations page 238). Add the vanilla and almond extract and beat the meringue for 1 minute. Fold in one fourth of the nut mixture. Working quickly, fold in the remaining nut mixture, one fourth at a time. Transfer the meringue to the pastry bag and pipe 2-inch rounds (either in concentric circles or strong "squirts") about 1½ inches apart onto the prepared baking sheet. Bake in the middle of the oven for 1 hour, turn off the oven, and let the cookies dry in the oven for at least 3 hours.

**Store in airtight
containers.**

COOKIES

e don't think about it every day, but in truth there is a glorious variety to the *kinds* of cookie that can be made. And it is this very variety that explains the cookie's universal appeal. There is a cookie for everyone.

We begin with that great beginner's cookie—the drop—for some of us the first recipe we ever made and the one that started us on an irrevocable infatuation with all things baked. Imagine what life would be like without the chocolate chip cookie. Moreover, imagine what it would be like without the quest for the *perfect* chocolate chip cookie. Growing up without hermits or macaroons? Couldn't have been done.

Along these simple lines is the next type—the icebox, or refrigerator, cookie. You could describe it as a good friend, thin but reliable. Better yet, thanks to technology, icebox cookies can now be ever at the ready.

The basic cookie becomes more complex with the bar variety, an inspired combination of some sweet crust topped with a preserve, or toffee crunch, or a lemony curd. While bar cookies may never be confused with pastry, they can be employed to cast a similar spell. They are for many the hands' down all-out favorite, bar none.

Pressed cookies are entirely different. Buttery and pure, they are most frequently associated with the holidays, and rightfully so. We are reminded of them during the year, though, as we watch the grand old cookie presses in which they are made roll around in the back of a kitchen drawer. Most of those presses, like the recipes themselves, have been handed down from generation to generation.

Then there is a large group of cookies that we are choosing to call molded—specifically shaped—which include, to mention just a few, short, short nut balls, ladyfingers, and those French creations, *tuiles*, so cleverly conceived to resemble roof tiles.

Lastly, there are rolled cookies. They will require the same touch that is needed for dough-making in general. Cool hands, if you will.

"American-style" cookies: Chocolate Chip Cookies (page 260), Old-Fashioned Hermits with Lemon Glaze (page 264), Marbled Chocolate Butterscotch Brownies (page 259), Chocolate Almond Macaroons (page 262)

DROP COOKIES

We have called the drop cookie that great beginner's cookie, and it is just that. Drop cookies are simple, and no less good for it, satisfying, and easy to make. It is usually a one-bowl batter, requiring no elaborate kitchen equipment, using ingredients that most of us have on hand at any given moment, including a goodly assortment of various kinds of chocolate chips.

Three caveats apply when it comes to making drop cookies:

▪ The batters, which sometimes can be stiff, must be thoroughly combined.

▪ When dropping the batter by the spoonful onto the baking sheet, be sure to leave a sufficient amount of space between the mounds. Drop cookies spread during baking and too many's the time we have ended up with one giant cookie instead of the three dozen that were called for.

▪ If you are making a recipe for the first time, cool the baked cookies as suggested. After that you can adjust cooling times to achieve the texture you most prefer. Cookies tend to crisp as they cool.

Which leads us to that most pleasurable thought: Drop cookies can never be made just once. They must be tasted, tested and experimented with, remade, and perfected. They are best made on the spur of the moment. Their variety can be endlessly pleasing.

CHOCOLATE CHIP COOKIES

Yield:
about 55 cookies

Equipment:
hand-held electric
** mixer**

Everyone's idea of the "perfect" chocolate chip cookie is different. These have a delicious brown sugar flavor, and their texture will please both the chewy and crispy fans.

2 cups all-purpose flour
½ teaspoon salt
½ teaspoon baking soda
¼ teaspoon cinnamon
2 sticks (1 cup) unsalted butter,
*   softened*

¾ cup firmly packed dark brown sugar
¾ cup granulated sugar
1 large egg
1 teaspoon vanilla
1 package (12 ounces) semisweet
*   chocolate morsels*

Preheat the oven to 375° F.

In a bowl combine the flour, salt, baking soda, and the cinnamon.

In another bowl with the mixer cream the butter well. Gradually add the sugars, mixing well after each addition, and cream until light and fluffy. Add the egg and the vanilla and beat well.

Add the dry ingredients gradually to the butter mixture, combining well after each addition. Stir in the chocolate morsels.

Drop the dough by teaspoonfuls 2 inches apart onto ungreased baking sheets. (For a crisper cookie, flatten the cookie slightly with the back of a wet spoon.) Bake in the middle of the oven for 10 to 12 minutes. Transfer the cookies with a spatula to a rack and let cool. The cookies will become crisper as they cool. If you prefer the cookies softer, do not cool them on a rack.

Photo on page 258.

Variations:

PECAN CHOCOLATE CHIP COOKIES: Add 1 cup pecans, chopped and lightly toasted, to the cookie batter and bake as directed.

RAISIN CHOCOLATE CHIP COOKIES: Add 1 cup raisins to the cookie batter and bake as directed.

CHOCOLATE CHUNK COOKIES

Yield:
about 48 cookies

Equipment:
hand-held electric mixer

2 sticks (1 cup) unsalted butter, softened
1 cup firmly packed light brown sugar
½ cup granulated sugar
1 teaspoon vanilla
2 large eggs

2 ounces semisweet chocolate, melted and cooled, plus an additional 10 ounces semisweet chocolate, chopped coarse into ½-inch chunks
2 cups all-purpose flour
1 teaspoon salt
1 teaspoon baking soda

In a large bowl with the mixer cream the butter, add the brown sugar and granulated sugar, a little at a time, beating, and beat until fluffy. Stir in the vanilla and add the eggs, one at a time, beating well after each addition. Stir in the melted chocolate.

Into a bowl sift together the flour, salt, and baking soda. Beat the flour mixture into the batter in 3 batches, combining the mixture well, and stir in the coarsely chopped chocolate. Chill the dough, wrapped in plastic wrap, for 30 minutes, or until just firm.

Store in airtight containers with a slice of bread (to keep the cookies moist and chewy) for several days.

Preheat the oven to 375° F.

Put rounded teaspoons of the dough 3 inches apart on ungreased baking sheets. Bake the cookies in the middle of the oven for 8 minutes, or until the edges are golden, and transfer them with a spatula to racks to cool.

Variations:

RAISIN CHOCOLATE CHUNK COOKIES: Plump 1 cup raisins in boiling water to cover for 45 minutes and drain well. Reduce the amount of coarsely chopped chocolate to 8 ounces. Stir in raisins when adding the chopped chocolate.

WALNUT CHOCOLATE CHUNK COOKIES: Reduce the amount of coarsely chopped chocolate to 8 ounces and stir in 1 cup chopped walnuts with the chopped chocolate.

ALMOND MACAROONS

Yield:
about 36 macaroons

A chewy macaroon, rich in almond flavor.

Equipment:
parchment paper
food processor fitted
  with steel blade

*1 cup whole blanched almonds (for
    procedure page 549)*
1 cup sugar

¼ teaspoon almond extract
2 egg whites at room temperature

Line baking sheets with the parchment paper and preheat the oven to 300° F.
    In the food processor or in a blender grind the almonds with the sugar to a powder. Transfer the mixture to a bowl and blend in the almond extract and the egg whites, one at a time, until the mixture is combined well. Drop the batter by teaspoons 2 inches apart onto the baking sheets and bake in the middle of the oven for 20 to 25 minutes, or until lightly golden. Let the macaroons cool and peel them off the paper.

**Store in layers
separated by wax
paper in airtight
containers.**

COCONUT MACAROONS

Yield:
about 18 macaroons

3 egg whites at room temperature
1¼ cups sifted confectioners' sugar
1 teaspoon vanilla

*2 cups flaked sweetened coconut or
    2 cups grated fresh coconut
    (for procedure page 549)*
¼ cup sifted all-purpose flour

Equipment:
hand-held electric
  mixer

Butter and flour a baking sheet and preheat the oven to 325° F.
    In a bowl with the mixer beat the egg whites until frothy. Gradually beat in the confectioners' sugar and the vanilla and continue to beat the whites until very stiff. Combine the coconut with the flour and fold the mixture into the egg whites. Drop the batter by tablespoons 2 inches apart onto the baking sheet and bake in the middle of the oven for 20 minutes, or until lightly golden and slightly firm to the touch. Transfer immediately to racks and let cool completely.

**Store in layers
separated by wax
paper in an airtight
container.**

CHOCOLATE ALMOND MACAROONS

Yield:
about 20 macaroons

*3 ounces unsweetened chocolate,
    chopped coarse*
*1 cup whole blanched almonds (for
    procedure page 549)*
1 cup sugar

½ teaspoon almond extract
2 egg whites
*20 slivered blanched almonds for
    garnish*

Equipment:
parchment paper
food processor fitted
  with steel blade
pastry bag fitted with
  large star tip

Line a baking sheet with the parchment paper and preheat the oven to 300° F.

In a small saucepan melt the chocolate over low heat, stirring until the mixture is smooth, and let cool.

In the food processor or in a blender grind the almonds with the sugar to a powder. Transfer the mixture to a bowl and blend in the almond extract and the egg whites, one at a time, until the mixture is well combined. Add the melted chocolate and combine well. Using the pastry bag pipe out the batter in 1-inch diameter rosettes 2 inches apart onto the prepared baking sheet. (Or drop the batter by tablespoons 2 inches apart onto the sheet.) Garnish each macaroon with a slivered almond and bake in the middle of the oven for 20 to 25 minutes, or until the cookies are firm to the touch. Let the macaroons cool and peel them off the paper.

Store in layers
separated by wax
paper in airtight
containers.

Photo on page 258.

APPLESAUCE BRAN COOKIES

Yield:
about 48 cookies

Here is the classic soft and cakey applesauce spice cookie, with the healthful addition of bran.

Equipment:
hand-held electric
  mixer

¾ cup sifted all-purpose flour
¾ cup sifted whole-wheat flour
¾ cup bran flakes cereal
½ teaspoon baking soda
¼ teaspoon salt
1½ teaspoons cinnamon
¾ teaspoon ground ginger
¾ teaspoon freshly grated nutmeg
½ teaspoon ground cloves
1 stick (½ cup) unsalted butter,
  softened

½ cup solid vegetable shortening,
  softened
1 cup sugar
1 teaspoon vanilla
1 large egg
1 cup applesauce
1 cup raisins
¾ cup chopped walnuts, toasted
  lightly

Preheat the oven to 350° F.

In a bowl combine the all-purpose flour, whole-wheat flour, bran flakes, baking soda, salt, cinnamon, ginger, nutmeg, and the cloves.

In a large bowl with the mixer cream the butter and shortening well. Add the sugar, a little at a time, and cream the mixture until light and fluffy. Add the vanilla and the egg and combine well. Gradually add the dry ingredients alternately with the applesauce, beating well after each addition. Stir in the raisins and the walnuts. (The dough will be soft.)

Drop the dough by heaping teaspoonfuls about 2 inches apart onto ungreased baking sheets and bake in the middle of the oven for 8 to 10 minutes, or until lightly golden. Let the cookies cool on the baking sheets for 1 minute, transfer them with a spatula to racks, and let cool completely.

OLD-FASHIONED HERMITS WITH LEMON GLAZE

Yield:
about 48 cookies

Equipment:
hand-held electric
  mixer

A splendid interpretation of an American classic, these hermits are iced with lemon glaze. If time is short, however, they are equally delicious unglazed or sprinkled with confectioners' sugar.

1¾ cups sifted all-purpose flour
½ teaspoon baking soda
½ teaspoon salt
½ teaspoon cinnamon
½ teaspoon freshly grated nutmeg
½ teaspoon ground ginger
½ teaspoon ground cloves
½ cup solid vegetable shortening,
  softened

½ stick (¼ cup) unsalted butter,
  softened
1 cup firmly packed dark brown sugar
1 large egg
½ teaspoon vanilla
2 tablespoons water
1 cup raisins
1 cup coarsely chopped walnuts,
  lightly toasted

FOR THE LEMON GLAZE
1 cup sifted confectioners' sugar

2 tablespoons fresh lemon juice

Butter baking sheets and preheat the oven to 350° F.

In a bowl combine the flour, baking soda, salt, cinnamon, nutmeg, ginger, and the cloves and reserve.

In another bowl with the mixer cream together the shortening and the butter. Add the brown sugar and cream the mixture until light and fluffy. Add the egg, vanilla, and the water and beat well. Gradually add the dry ingredients to the mixture, mixing well after each addition, and beat until smooth. Stir in the raisins and the walnuts and combine well.

Drop the dough by teaspoonfuls 2 inches apart onto the baking sheets. Flatten the cookies slightly with the back of a spoon dipped in cold water and bake them in the middle of the oven for 15 minutes. With a metal spatula transfer the cookies to racks to cool slightly.

Make the lemon glaze:
Combine the confectioners' sugar and the lemon juice and mix well.

While the cookies are still warm, spread about ½ teaspoon glaze on each cookie or simply dip the top surface of the cookie into the glaze. Let cool on the racks.

Photo on page 258.

OATMEAL RAISIN COOKIES

Yield:
48 cookies

Equipment:
hand-held electric
mixer

1½ sticks (¾ cup) unsalted butter,
  softened
1 cup firmly packed dark brown sugar
¼ cup granulated sugar
2 large eggs
1 teaspoon vanilla
1 cup all-purpose flour

½ teaspoon baking soda
½ teaspoon cinnamon
¼ teaspoon salt
¼ teaspoon freshly grated nutmeg
2½ cups quick-cooking oats
1 cup raisins

Butter baking sheets and preheat the oven to 350° F.

In a bowl with the mixer cream the butter until fluffy. Add the dark brown sugar and granulated sugar and continue creaming until smooth. Add the eggs and the vanilla and blend well.

Combine the flour, baking soda, cinnamon, salt, and the nutmeg. Add the dry ingredients to the sugar mixture and blend well. Stir in the oats and the raisins and combine well.

Drop the dough by teaspoonfuls 2 inches apart onto the baking sheets. Flatten the cookies slightly with the back of a spoon dipped in cold water and bake them in the middle of the oven for 12 to 15 minutes, or until golden and slightly firm to the touch. With a metal spatula transfer the cookies immediately to a wire rack to cool.

Variation:

OATMEAL WALNUT COOKIES: Substitute 1 cup walnuts, toasted lightly and chopped coarse, for the raisins.

ICEBOX COOKIES

Icebox cookies, also known as refrigerator cookies, are singularly satisfying. Once the dough is made—and it is a very easy dough to combine and shape into a log—cookies can simply be sliced off the log and the log returned to the refrigerator. Or frozen, the dough will keep up to three months. The cookies can even be sliced extremely thin when the dough is still frozen for very crisp cookies. In short, cookies await, on demand, pending the mere preheating of the oven.

Icebox cookies are thin-cut and crispy when baked. Some are enhanced by spices such as cinnamon and cardamom and smell perfectly wonderful when baking. They are good accompaniments to fruit desserts, ice creams or sorbets, and some not-too-sweet puddings. You also might consider a tin of them and a festive package of the dough as a unique present during the holidays. There is very little to worry about, but lots to enjoy, when it comes to icebox cookies.

DANISH BUTTER COOKIES

Yield:
about 175 cookies

Equipment:
parchment paper

This meltingly tender butter cookie is an essential part of the traditional Danish Christmas baking repertoire. The recipe yields half sugared butter cookies and half plain cookies, and can be easily halved for a more manageable yield.

4 cups all-purpose flour
1⅓ cups granulated sugar
2 large eggs
2 teaspoons vanilla
3 sticks (1½ cups) cold unsalted
  butter, cut into bits

3 tablespoons coarse sugar crystals
  (available at specialty foods shops)
88 blanched almond halves (for
  procedure page 549)

Into a large bowl sift the flour and the sugar. Beat 1 of the eggs lightly with the vanilla and stir it into the flour mixture until combined. Cut in the butter until the mixture resembles coarse meal. Form the dough into a ball and chill it, wrapped in plastic wrap, for 20 minutes.

Halve the dough, roll each half into an 11-inch cylinder, and chill 1 of the cylinders, wrapped in wax paper, overnight. Brush the remaining cylinder with the remaining egg, beaten lightly, roll it in the sugar crystals, coating it well, and chill it, wrapped in plastic wrap, overnight. (At this point the dough may be frozen wrapped securely in plastic wrap and foil.)

Line baking sheets with the parchment paper and preheat the oven to 400° F.

Slice the cylinders ⅛ inch thick, arrange the rounds ½ inch apart on the baking sheets, and top each of the unsugared rounds with an almond half. Bake the cookies in the middle of the oven for 8 to 10 minutes, or until the edges are golden and the cookies are firm. Transfer the cookies to racks and let them cool.

Store in airtight containers. These cookies lend themselves to freezing in airtight containers for up to 3 months.

LEMON THINS

Yield:
about 50 cookies

Equipment:
hand-held electric
  mixer

These thins make a wonderful accompaniment to macerated fruit compotes or Lemon Sherbet (page 371).

1 cup sugar
1 stick (½ cup) unsalted butter,
  softened
1 large egg, beaten lightly
¼ cup diced candied lemon peel
2 tablespoons fresh lemon juice

2 teaspoons grated lemon rind
2½ cups all-purpose flour
1 teaspoon double-acting baking
  powder
¼ teaspoon salt

In a large bowl with the mixer cream together the sugar and the butter until light and lemon colored and stir in the egg, candied peel, lemon juice, and lemon rind.

Into a bowl sift together the flour, baking powder, and salt and stir the mixture into the sugar mixture. Form the dough into a 12-inch-long strip on a doubled sheet of wax paper, roll it tightly into a 12-inch-long roll, using the wax paper as a guide, and chill it, wrapped in the wax paper and aluminum foil, for at least 6 hours. (At this point the dough may be frozen.)

Butter the baking sheets and preheat the oven to 400° F.

Cut the roll into ¼-inch slices with a sharp knife, arrange the slices 2 inches apart on the baking sheets, and bake the cookies in the middle of the oven for 10 minutes. Transfer the cookies to racks to cool.

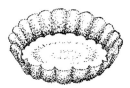

CARDAMOM COOKIES

Yield:
about 40 cookies

Equipment:
hand-held electric
**   mixer**

Cardamom, a member of the ginger family, is commonly used as an ingredient in Scandinavian baking. Its sweet yet tangy flavor is memorable in this butter cookie.

1½ sticks (¾ cup) unsalted butter,
*   softened*
⅔ cup firmly packed light brown
*   sugar*
¼ cup light cream

1½ cups sifted all-purpose flour
2 teaspoons ground cardamom
½ teaspoon baking soda
½ teaspoon salt
¼ cup granulated sugar

In a large bowl with the mixer cream together the butter and brown sugar until light and beat in the cream. Into a bowl sift together the flour, cardamom, baking soda, and salt. Stir the mixture into the butter mixture and chill the dough, covered, for 1 hour, or until firm enough to shape. Form the dough into a 10-inch log on a doubled sheet of wax paper. Using the paper as a guide, roll the dough tightly into a smooth 10-inch roll and chill it, wrapped in the paper and aluminum foil, in the freezing compartment of the refrigerator for at least 2 hours. (At this point the dough may be frozen.)

Preheat the oven to 375° F.

Cut the roll into ¼-inch slices with a sharp knife, arrange the slices 2 inches apart on ungreased baking sheets, and sprinkle each slice with a pinch of the granulated sugar. Bake the slices in the middle of the oven for 6 to 8 minutes, or until the edges are golden. Transfer the cookies to racks to cool.

ORANGE MELTAWAYS

Yield:
about 40 cookies

Equipment:
hand-held electric
  mixer

It is the combination of confectioners' sugar and cornstarch in this recipe that renders an extremely tender "meltaway" cookie.

1½ sticks (¾ cup) unsalted butter,
  softened
½ cup sifted confectioners' sugar
1 cup sifted all-purpose flour

½ cup cornstarch
4 teaspoons grated orange rind
1 teaspoon vanilla
¼ cup granulated sugar

In a large bowl with the mixer cream together the butter and confectioners' sugar until light and fluffy. Into a bowl sift together the flour and cornstarch and stir the mixture into the butter mixture. Stir in the orange rind and vanilla and chill the dough, covered, for 1 hour, or until firm enough to shape.

Form the dough into a 10-inch log on a doubled sheet of wax paper. Using the wax paper as a guide, roll the dough tightly into a smooth 10-inch roll. Chill, wrapped in the wax paper and aluminum foil, in the freezing compartment of the refrigerator for at least 2 hours. (At this point the dough may be frozen.)

Butter baking sheets lightly and preheat the oven to 375° F.

Onto a sheet of wax paper sprinkle the granulated sugar and in it roll the dough. Cut the dough into ¼-inch slices with a sharp knife. Arrange the slices 2 inches apart on the baking sheets and bake them in the middle of the oven for 10 minutes, or until the edges are golden. Transfer the cookies to racks to cool.

BUTTERSCOTCH COOKIES

Yield:
48 cookies

Equipment:
hand-held electric
  mixer

1¾ cups sifted all-purpose flour
½ teaspoon baking soda
¼ teaspoon salt
1 stick (½ cup) unsalted butter,
  softened

1¼ cups firmly packed light brown
  sugar
1 large egg
1 teaspoon vanilla

Into a bowl sift together the flour, baking soda, and the salt. In another bowl with the mixer cream together the butter and the sugar until fluffy. Add the egg and vanilla and beat until smooth. Add the flour mixture gradually, beating well after each addition, and blend the dough well.

On a piece of wax paper form the dough into a log 1½ inches in diameter, using the paper as a guide. Chill the log, wrapped in the wax paper and foil, in the freezing compartment of the refrigerator for 2 hours. (At this point the dough may be frozen.)

Preheat the oven to 375° F.

Cut the log into ⅛-inch slices with a sharp knife and arrange the cookies 2 inches apart on ungreased baking sheets. Bake in the middle of the oven for 10 to 12 minutes, or until the edges are golden. (Do not underbake the cookies.) Transfer the cookies with a metal spatula to racks to cool. The cookies will become very crisp as they cool.

Variation: BUTTERSCOTCH PECAN ICEBOX COOKIES: Add ¾ cup finely chopped pecans to the dough and bake as above.

BAR COOKIES

For many this variety of cookie is the *sine qua non* of sweets. Imagine combining a buttery dough, sometimes studded with nuts, sometimes not, with a topping like chocolate pecan toffee or brown-sugar-sweetened cranberries. The cookie bakes and you have two splendid layers—the best of all possible worlds—tender pastry covered with the combination of choice, be it raspberry jam (as in our splendid Linzer bars) or tart lemon curd. Easier than pie, baked in one pan, bar cookies are cut into pieces and are also sometimes known as squares.

In this category we are also including that all-time favorite: the brownie. We have the classic fudge brownie, made with unsweetened chocolate, butter, flour, eggs, and walnuts. This is what some of us remember as our first brownie; the simplest and the best. Then we have buttery fudge brownies, made with not only two kinds of chocolate but also twice the amount of butter, a dash of bourbon, and some pecans. Nontraditionalist are these and not for the faint of heart. We've also included a recipe for cream cheese brownies in which the chocolate batter is enlivened with cinnamony whipped cream cheese. These, too, are rich and luxurious and curiously savory. An assortment of brownies would not be complete without a recipe for blondies, non-chocolate brownies with lots of brown sugar, chocolate chips, and chopped nuts. And because there can never be enough brownie recipes we have appended one last—marbled chocolate butterscotch brownies—which encompasses just about everything, including whole-wheat flour, and not just for salutary effect.

In making bar cookies—and it is a pure pleasure to do so—there are several items to remember:

■ Should the bar have a pastry base, the less the dough is handled, the flakier it will be. Also, in lining the pan, remember to pat the dough in; do not force it. In our recipes there is usually enough butter involved to meld the base as it bakes. The dough should be evenly spread, but it does not have to be a perfectly conformed layer.

■ Lastly, let bar cookies cool as directed in the recipes. They can be difficult to cut if not allowed to come to the proper temperature.

A postscript: It is our experience that bar cookies do not store well, and some, like Lemon Squares (page 276), should not be refrigerated at all. We consider that all to the good. Once made, they should be eaten, and remade.

As to the whole issue of brownies—how long do they cook, do you like them chewy or cake-like, are they better frozen or just barely thawed—we leave all of those refinements to you. We have provided the takeoff points. As far as brownies and bar cookies go—and these tend to be highly personalized matters—we leave the destination of these grand recipes up to you.

CLASSIC FUDGE BROWNIES

Yield:
16 brownies

Equipment:
8-inch square baking pan
hand-held electric mixer

A traditional recipe for the American favorite.

3 ounces unsweetened chocolate, chopped coarse
1 stick (½ cup) unsalted butter, cut into bits
¾ cup sifted all-purpose flour
½ teaspoon double-acting baking powder

pinch of salt
2 large eggs
1¼ cups sugar
1 teaspoon vanilla
1 cup chopped walnuts

Butter and flour the baking pan and preheat the oven to 350° F.

In a small heavy saucepan melt the chocolate and butter over low heat, stirring until the mixture is smooth, and let the mixture cool completely. Into a bowl sift together the flour, baking powder, and salt. In a large bowl with the mixer beat the eggs, add the sugar, a little at a time, beating, and beat the mixture at high speed for 3 minutes, or until thick and pale. Stir in the chocolate mixture and the vanilla, add the flour mixture, stirring until the mixture is blended well, and stir in the walnuts. Pour the batter into the baking pan, smoothing the top, and bake it in the middle of the oven for 25 to 30 minutes, or until it pulls away slightly from the sides of the pan and a cake tester inserted in the center comes out with crumbs adhering to it. Let the brownies cool completely in the pan before cutting them into squares.

Variation:

CLASSIC FUDGE BROWNIES WITH CHOCOLATE FUDGE ICING: Have ready Chocolate Fudge Icing (page 513). Let brownies cool as above, spread them with frosting, and let the frosting set for 30 minutes.

CREAM CHEESE BROWNIES

Yield:
16 brownies

Equipment:
9-inch square baking
 pan
hand-held electric
 mixer

FOR THE CREAM CHEESE FILLING

5 ounces cream cheese at room
 temperature
2 tablespoons unsalted butter, softened
1/4 cup sugar

1 large egg
1/2 teaspoon vanilla
1/4 teaspoon cinnamon

FOR THE CHOCOLATE BATTER

4 ounces semisweet chocolate, chopped
 coarse
3 tablespoons unsalted butter, cut into
 bits
1/2 cup sifted all-purpose flour
1/2 teaspoon double-acting baking
 powder

1/4 teaspoon salt
2 large eggs
3/4 cup sugar
1 teaspoon vanilla
1/2 cup toasted and ground walnuts

Butter the baking pan and preheat the oven to 350° F.

Make the cream cheese filling:

In a bowl with the mixer cream the cream cheese with the butter until smooth. Gradually add the sugar, creaming until fluffy. Add the egg, vanilla, and cinnamon and beat the mixture well.

Make the chocolate batter:

In a saucepan melt the chocolate with the butter over very low heat. Cool and reserve. Combine the flour, baking powder, and salt.

In a bowl with the mixer beat the eggs until foamy. Gradually add the sugar, beating at high speed for 3 to 4 minutes, until pale yellow and thickened. Stir the flour mixture into the egg mixture, beating well. Blend in the reserved melted chocolate and stir in the vanilla and ground walnuts.

Spread half the chocolate batter evenly in the bottom of the baking pan. Spread the cheese mixture over the chocolate mixture. Drop the remaining chocolate batter in dollops over the cheese mixture. With a knife then swirl through the top two layers, creating a marbelized effect. Try not to disturb the bottom chocolate layer. Bake in the middle of the oven for 35 to 40 minutes, or until a cake tester inserted in the center comes out barely moist, with crumbs adhering to it. Let cool in the pan on a rack for at least 3 to 4 hours. Cut into sixteen 2¼-inch squares.

These brownies should be stored in the refrigerator and should not be frozen.

BUTTERY FUDGE BROWNIES

Yield:
30 brownies

Equipment:
baking pan, 13 by 9 by
   2 inches
hand-held electric
   mixer

This fudge brownie is twice as buttery and rich as our classic and contains both bourbon and pecans for a Southern touch.

*2 ounces unsweetened chocolate,
   chopped coarse*
*2 ounces semisweet chocolate, chopped
   coarse*
*2 sticks (1 cup) unsalted butter,
   softened*
1½ cups sugar

3 large eggs
1 teaspoon vanilla
1 cup sifted all-purpose flour
pinch of salt
1 cup chopped pecans
1½ tablespoons bourbon

Butter and flour the baking pan and preheat the oven to 350° F.

In a small heavy saucepan melt both chocolates with 1 stick of the butter, cut into pieces, over low heat, stirring until smooth, and let cool completely. In a large bowl with the mixer cream together the remaining 1 stick butter and the sugar and beat until light and fluffy. Add the eggs, one at a time, beating well after each addition, and stir in the vanilla and the chocolate mixture. Add the flour and the salt, stirring until the mixture is blended well, and stir in the pecans and bourbon. Pour the batter into the baking pan, smooth the top, and bake in the middle of the oven for 30 to 40 minutes, or until the cake pulls away slightly from the sides of the pan and a wooden pick inserted in the center comes out with crumbs adhering to it. Let the brownies cool completely in the pan on a rack before cutting into 2-inch bars.

BLONDIES

Yield:
30 blondies

Equipment:
baking pan, 13 by 9 by
   2 inches
hand-held electric
   mixer

Known as blondies or blonde brownies, these chewy bars are traditionally made with chocolate morsels and pecans or walnuts.

1¾ cups sifted all-purpose flour
*1¼ teaspoons double-acting baking
   powder*
pinch of salt
¾ teaspoon cinnamon
*1¼ sticks (½ cup plus 2 tablespoons)
   unsalted butter, softened*

*1½ cups firmly packed light brown
   sugar*
½ cup granulated sugar
2 large eggs
1½ teaspoons vanilla
*1 cup (a 6-ounce package) semisweet
   chocolate morsels*
¾ cup chopped pecans

Butter and flour the baking pan and preheat the oven to 350° F.

Into a bowl sift together the flour, baking powder, salt and the cinnamon. In a large bowl with the mixer cream together the butter, brown sugar, and the granulated sugar and beat the mixture until light and fluffy. Add the eggs, one at a time, beating well after each addition, and stir in the vanilla. Add the flour mixture, stirring until the batter is blended well, and stir in the chocolate morsels and the pecans.

Pour the batter into the baking pan, smooth the top, and bake in the middle of the oven for 30 to 35 minutes, or until the cake pulls away slightly from the sides of the pan and a wooden pick inserted in the center comes out with crumbs adhering to it. Let the blondies cool completely in the pan on a rack before cutting into serving pieces.

MARBLED CHOCOLATE BUTTERSCOTCH BROWNIES

Yield:
16 brownies

Equipment:
8-inch square
baking pan

A true butterscotch flavor is obtained by melting brown sugar with butter and cooking it slightly, which gives butterscotch its characteristic nutty, buttery flavor. The use of whole-wheat flour gives this brownie a hearty flavor and helps contribute to a more healthful dessert.

FOR THE BUTTERSCOTCH BATTER
½ stick (¼ cup) unsalted butter
¾ cup firmly packed dark brown sugar
1 large egg, beaten lightly
½ cup whole-wheat flour
1 teaspoon vanilla

¼ teaspoon salt
¼ teaspoon double-acting baking powder
½ cup chopped walnuts

FOR THE CHOCOLATE BATTER
2 ounces unsweetened chocolate, chopped coarse
½ stick (¼ cup) unsalted butter
½ cup firmly packed light brown sugar
1 egg, beaten lightly

¼ cup whole-wheat flour
1 teaspoon vanilla
¼ teaspoon salt
¼ teaspoon double-acting baking powder
½ cup chopped walnuts

Make the butter-scotch batter:

Make the chocolate batter:

Store in layers separated by wax paper in an airtight container.

Butter the baking pan and preheat the oven to 350° F.

In a saucepan melt the butter over moderately low heat, add the sugar, and bring the mixture to a boil, stirring, until the sugar is dissolved. Let the mixture cool. Beat in the egg, stir in the flour, vanilla, salt, and baking powder, and fold in the walnuts.

In the top of a double boiler set over hot water melt the chocolate with the butter and remove the pan from the heat. Stir in the sugar, beat in the egg, and stir in the flour, vanilla, salt, and the baking powder. Fold in the walnuts.

Pour the batters alternately in 2 batches into the baking pan and lightly swirl a knife through the mixture once to marbleize the batters. Bake in the middle of the oven for 25 to 30 minutes, or until a cake tester inserted in the center comes out clean. Transfer the dessert to a rack, let it cool, and cut it into 2-inch squares.

Photo on page 258.

LINZER BARS

Yield:
32 bar cookies

A cookie based on the famous Viennese *Linzertorte*. For a rendition of the tart see page 183.

Equipment:
hand-held electric mixer
8-inch square baking pan

FOR THE DOUGH

1 stick (½ cup) unsalted butter, softened
½ cup firmly packed light brown sugar
¼ cup granulated sugar
⅔ cup blanched almonds (for procedure page 549), toasted lightly and ground

1 large egg, beaten lightly
1½ cups all-purpose flour
¾ teaspoon double-acting baking powder
½ teaspoon cinnamon
¼ teaspoon salt

FOR THE FILLING

¾ cup raspberry jam

1 teaspoon grated lemon rind

confectioners' sugar for sifting

Preheat the oven to 375° F.

Make the dough:
In a large bowl with the mixer cream together the butter, brown sugar, and granulated sugar until the mixture is light and fluffy. Stir in the almonds and the egg.

Into a bowl sift together the flour, baking powder, cinnamon, and salt, stir the mixture into the almond mixture, and combine the dough well. Press two thirds of the dough into the baking pan. Roll out the remaining dough ⅛ inch thick between sheets of wax paper and chill it for 15 minutes, or until firm.

Make the filling:
In a small bowl combine the raspberry jam and lemon rind.

With a spatula spread the filling over the dough in the baking pan. Peel off the top sheet of paper from the chilled dough, cut the dough into ½-inch strips, and arrange the strips in a lattice pattern over the jam. Bake in the middle of the oven for 30 minutes, or until golden brown. Sift the confectioners' sugar evenly over the top of the dessert, let cool, and with a serrated knife cut it into 2- by 1-inch bars.

Variation:
APRICOT LINZER BARS: Replace the raspberry jam with ¾ cup apricot jam.

Clockwise from top left: Linzertorte (page 183), Filbert Balls (page 283), Rehrücken (page 68), Bavarian Apricot-Filled Almond Cookie (page 300), Sugar Pretzels (page 285), Bayrischer Nuss Stollen (page 81)

BUTTERSCOTCH CRANBERRY BARS

Yield:
30 bar cookies

Equipment:
baking pan, 13 by 9 by
2 inches

*1 cup cranberries, rinsed, picked over,
  and chopped*
*1¾ cups plus 2 tablespoons firmly
  packed dark brown sugar*
⅓ cup raisins
¼ cup dark rum
1 stick (½ cup) unsalted butter
2 large eggs, beaten lightly

1 teaspoon vanilla
1¾ cups all-purpose flour
*½ teaspoon double-acting baking
  powder*
½ teaspoon salt
*⅔ cup chopped walnuts, toasted
  lightly*

Butter the baking pan and preheat the oven to 350° F.

In a small bowl toss the cranberries with 2 tablespoons of the brown sugar and let the mixture stand for 15 minutes.

In a small saucepan combine the raisins and the rum, bring the liquid to a boil, and simmer the raisins, covered, for 5 minutes, or until they have absorbed the rum. Let cool.

In a saucepan melt the butter over moderately low heat, add the remaining 1¾ cups brown sugar, and cook the mixture, stirring, until it is just bubbly. Transfer the mixture to a heatproof bowl and let it cool for 15 minutes. Beat in the eggs and vanilla, add the flour, baking powder, and salt, and stir the batter until it is combined well. Fold in the cranberry mixture, walnuts, and raisins, turn the batter into the baking pan, spreading it evenly, and bake it in the middle of the oven for 35 to 45 minutes, or until a cake tester inserted in the center comes out clean. Let the dessert cool in the pan on a rack and cut it into bars about 2 by 1½ inches.

LEMON SQUARES

Yield:
16 squares

Equipment:
8-inch square pan
hand-held electric
  mixer

FOR THE BASE
1 cup sifted all-purpose flour
¼ cup sifted confectioners' sugar
½ teaspoon grated lemon rind

*1 stick (½ cup) cold unsalted butter,
  cut into bits*

FOR THE FILLING
2 large eggs
1 cup granulated sugar
6 tablespoons fresh lemon juice

2 tablespoons all-purpose flour
*½ teaspoon double-acting baking
  powder*

confectioners' sugar for garnish

Make the base:

Preheat the oven to 375° F.

In a bowl combine the flour, confectioners' sugar, and lemon rind. Cut in the butter until the mixture resembles coarse meal. Press the mixture evenly into the bottom of the ungreased baking pan. Transfer the pan to a baking sheet and bake the base in the lower third of the oven for 18 to 20 minutes, or until golden around the edges. (The base will be only partially baked at this point.)

Make the filling:

In a large bowl with the mixer combine the eggs and the sugar. Add the lemon juice and beat the mixture for 5 minutes, or until pale and smooth. Combine the flour and baking powder. Whisk the flour mixture into the egg mixture and combine well.

Store in an airtight container, but do not refrigerate as base will become soggy.

Pour the filling mixture over the partially baked base and continue baking the dessert on the baking sheet for 25 minutes. Sift confectioners' sugar over the dessert and let cool on a rack. Cut into 2-inch squares.

CHOCOLATE PECAN TOFFEE SQUARES

Yield:
16 squares

This bar cookie combines a crumbly shortbread base with a chewy chocolate pecan toffee topping.

Equipment:
8-inch square baking pan
candy thermometer

FOR THE BASE
1 cup sifted all-purpose flour
1/2 cup firmly packed light brown sugar

1 stick (1/2 cup) cold unsalted butter, cut into bits

FOR THE TOPPING
1 stick (1/2 cup) unsalted butter
2 tablespoons dark corn syrup
1 cup firmly packed light brown sugar
1/4 cup light cream

1 cup chopped pecans
1 teaspoon vanilla
2 ounces semisweet chocolate, chopped coarse

Make the base:

Preheat the oven to 350° F.

In a bowl combine the flour and the brown sugar. Cut in the butter until the mixture resembles coarse meal. Press the mixture evenly into the bottom of the baking pan and put the baking pan on a baking sheet. Bake the base in the lower third of the oven for 35 minutes, or until golden. Let the pan cool on a rack.

Make the topping:

In a heavy saucepan melt the butter, add the dark corn syrup and the brown sugar, and bring the mixture to a boil over moderate heat, stirring with a wooden spoon. Boil the mixture, stirring occasionally, until it reaches the hard-ball stage, or the candy thermometer registers 260° F. (For the stages of sugar syrup, see illustrations page 241.) Remove the pan from the heat and add the cream and the pecans, stirring gently. Return the pan to the heat, bring the mixture to a boil, and boil it until it reaches the soft-ball stage, or the candy thermometer registers 240° F. Remove the

Store in layers separated by wax paper in an airtight container.

pan from the heat and stir in the vanilla and the chocolate, stirring until the chocolate is completely melted.

Pour the topping over the cooled base, spreading it evenly. Let the dessert cool and chill it, covered with foil, for 2 hours, or until firm. Cut into 2-inch squares.

PRESSED COOKIES

Pressed cookies are loved for their subtle flavors, but also for the associations they bring to mind. They are the cookies of our childhood—those pale, delicate Christmas cookies so beautifully shaped to fit the season. We see wreaths and stars; we remember them as ornaments you could not only touch but also eat. They were made with those crazy contraptions called presses and if you were lucky enough, or awake at the time, you were given the chance to push the lever that forced the dough out of that metal tube into those lovely shapes. They never seemed to bake brown, those special cookies. It was as if they had been lifted out of new snow.

Nothing has changed. Our short collection of wonderful pressed cookies are all Christmas ones, two of the three having originated in Denmark, that land of butter and exceptional Yule baking. And these are buttery cookies, with a ratio of about one cup sweet butter to two cups flour. Add a little sugar and some flavoring, but not much, and all you need is the press or a pastry bag and a tip or two. Pressed cookies are deceptively understated. We have included a selection of pressed butter cookies of the first order.

SUGARED BUTTER STRIPS

Yield:
about 50 cookies

Equipment:
parchment paper
pastry bag fitted with
  ½-inch star tip
hand-held electric
  mixer

These German-inspired butter cookies, called *Strassburger*, are formed into strips resembling rows of shells that are then dusted with confectioners' sugar.

2 sticks (1 cup) unsalted butter,
  softened
¾ cup confectioners' sugar plus an
  additional ¼ cup for garnish

2 egg yolks
1 tablespoon vanilla
1¾ cups all-purpose flour, sifted

Line baking sheets with the parchment paper and preheat the oven to 425° F.

In a bowl with the mixer cream the butter with the ¾ cup sugar until light and fluffy. Add the egg yolks, one at a time, beating well after each addition, and the vanilla. Beat in the flour, ¼ cup at a time, and blend until a dough forms.

Put some of the dough into the pastry bag, reserving the remaining dough covered in plastic wrap, and pipe out 2¼-inch strips 1 inch apart onto the baking sheets, applying extra pressure in 4 separate spurts for each strip to make each look like a row of 4 shells. Pipe out the remaining dough in the same manner. Bake the cookies in the middle of the oven for 8 minutes, or until golden. Transfer the cookies to racks, sift the remaining confectioners' sugar over them, and let them cool.

Store in an airtight container.

VANILLA WREATHS

Yield:
about 125 cookies

Equipment:
parchment paper
metal cookie press
fitted with ½-inch
star plate

If you were to be baking these perfect little vanilla wreaths or *vanillekranse* authentically, as they are made in Denmark, you would be forming them with a disk that fits an electric meat grinder! A cookie press, however, can be substituted—with excellent results. These, too, are a traditional Danish Christmas cookie.

2¼ cups all-purpose flour
1¼ cups sugar
⅛ teaspoon double-acting baking
*   powder*
pinch of salt
2 sticks plus 2 tablespoons (1 cup plus
*   2 tablespoons) cold unsalted butter,*
*   cut into bits*

⅔ cup blanched whole almonds (for
*   procedure page 549), ground*
1 teaspoon vanilla

Onto a smooth surface sift together the flour, sugar, baking powder, and salt. Distribute the butter over the mixture and blend until it resembles meal. Sprinkle the almonds and vanilla over the mixture and blend until it forms a dough. Chill the dough, wrapped in foil, for 30 minutes.

Line baking sheets with the parchment paper.

Fill the cookie press with dough, reserving the remaining dough, wrapped and chilled, and press 2-inch strips ½ inch apart onto the sheets. Form each strip into a round, pressing the ends together gently, and chill the rounds for 15 minutes.

While the rounds are chilling, preheat the oven to 375° F.

Shape cookies with the reserved dough in the same manner and bake the rounds in batches in the middle of the oven for 8 minutes, or until golden. Transfer the cookies to racks and let them cool.

Store in airtight containers.

APRICOT JAM-FILLED STRIPS

Yield:
about 70 cookies

Equipment:
hand-held electric
  mixer
parchment paper
metal cookie press
  fitted with a
  1⅜-inch-wide
  opening disk, flat on
  one side and notched
  on the other
pastry brush

Most often prepared at Christmastime, these special, filled cookies are tra-ditionally served with Champagne or white wine, hence the name *Champagnebrød*.

½ cup apricot preserves
1 tablespoon apricot brandy
1¾ sticks (¾ cup plus 2 tablespoons)
  unsalted butter, softened
¾ cup sugar

1 large egg
the grated rind of 1 lemon
⅛ teaspoon salt
2 cups all-purpose flour

Strain the preserves into a small bowl, thin with the brandy, and reserve.

In a bowl with the mixer cream the butter with the sugar until light and fluffy and stir in the egg, lemon rind, and salt. Beat in the flour, ¼ cup at a time, and continue to blend the mixture until it forms a dough. Let the dough rest, covered, in a cool place for 10 minutes, but do not chill it.

Line a baking sheet with the parchment paper and preheat the oven to 375° F.

Fill the cookie press with dough, reserving the remaining dough, cov-ered. Press six 11½-inch long strips lengthwise and equidistantly apart onto the baking sheet and bake in the middle of the oven for 10 to 12 min-utes, or until just golden. With a long metal spatula invert every other strip. Spoon some of the reserved apricot preserves along each inverted strip and with the pastry brush spread it to the edges. Carefully top the preserves with the remaining strips, smooth sides down, and let soften in the oven for 2 to 3 minutes. With a sharp knife trim the ends and cut the strips into 1½-inch lengths. Transfer the cookies to a rack and let them cool. Form and bake cookies with the remaining dough in the same manner.

Store in airtight
containers.

MOLDED COOKIES

By molded cookies we mean those that are specifically shaped; not dropped, sliced, or pressed, but shaped in a distinctive manner. An obvi-ous example are the German sugar pretzels, formed by hand in both a large and small variety. Less obvious would be our miniature Florentines, those marvelous European creations, that actually have to be trimmed to control their glorious sugary batter. Another good example would be chocolate leaves, almond cookies actually formed into leaves with a leaf-shaped stencil. Then there are all those exceptional buttery nut cookies that are formed by hand into balls, like filbert balls and the Greek Christ-mas classic *kourabiedes*.

Among this varied and very international collection of cookies that follows we have acknowledged our debt to the French and have included a recipe for *langues de chat*, cats' tongues, as well as one for Madeleines, which might even make Proust proud. *Langues de chat* are, of course, made with a pastry bag. Madeleines are formed in a specific mold, those lovely fluted scallop-shaped containers in which nothing else should ever be baked.

And there is another French inspiration that is a molded cookie, too—*tuiles*—those super-thin rounds made to resemble the roof-top tiles of France by being simply molded around a rolling pin. You can also shape these wafers into cones, or cornets, if you will. Or by the aid of a mere custard cup or small glass bowl, you can transform these into *tulipes*, or tulip-shaped wafers.

The key to shaping a *tuile* is to mold the baked cookie while it is still basically warm yet cool enough to handle. Following the illustration on page 290, remove several pliable, still quite-warm rounds at a time from the baking sheet with a metal spatula. Return the baking sheet to a warm oven and leave the door ajar. Holding the rolling pin in your other hand just under the spatula, gently ease the cookies onto the pin. Quickly wrap the cookies around the rolling pin and let them set with the rolling pin in a horizontal position. When the cookies are cooled and curled, simply slip them off the pin and continue to make *tuiles* with the remaining rounds in the same manner. Needless to say, it would be very helpful to have several rolling pins.

To make a *tulipe,* as illustrated on page 288, you must also work with a still-warm round. Using a spatula, transfer the cookie to a custard cup and press it carefully into the bottom of the cup. With your thumb and index finger, pinch in the opposite sides of the cookie. Repeat with the remaining sides. Let the cookie cool in the cup and when cooled it should resemble the petal shape of a tulip. Fill with tangy lemon sherbet, as we did with another tulip-shaped invention, a Dessert Crêpe (page 434).

Molded cookies clearly exact some dexterity and thought. Note, for example on page 287, how to maximize the number of ladyfingers you can bake at one time by piping the batter not in equidistant rows on the baking sheet, but in staggered lines: a good solution, but one that is not immediately apparent. With ladyfingers so easy now to make in quantity, all the more reason to assemble on a frequent basis our splendid Rhubarb Raspberry Charlotte with Rhubarb Raspberry Sauce (page 474).

Making molded cookies can be captivating, and in this very diverse and wide array is a wonderful sampling of how many cultures have cleverly met that challenge.

ALMOND LOAF COOKIES

Yield:
about 65 cookies

Equipment:
parchment paper
hand-held electric
  mixer
pastry brush

This classic Danish Christmas cookie is known as *Finsk Brød* throughout Denmark.

2 sticks (1 cup) unsalted butter,
  softened
¾ cup confectioners' sugar, sifted
2 egg yolks
1 teaspoon almond extract
3¼ cups all-purpose flour

⅛ teaspoon double-acting baking
  powder
⅛ teaspoon salt
1 egg white, beaten until frothy
5 tablespoons sliced blanched almonds
2 tablespoons granulated sugar

Line 3 baking sheets with the parchment paper and preheat oven to 400° F.

In a bowl with the mixer cream the butter with the confectioners' sugar until light and fluffy. Add the egg yolks, one at a time, beating well after each addition, and stir in the almond extract. Into a bowl sift together the flour, baking powder, and the salt, add the mixture to the butter mixture, ¼ cup at a time, and blend until it forms a dough. Divide the dough into 13 pieces and roll each piece into a 10½-inch cylinder. Divide the cylinders among the baking sheets, leaving 1 inch between the cylinders, and trim the ends so that the cylinders measure exactly 10 inches. Cut the cylinders crosswise into five 2-inch pieces, making 65 cookies, and brush them with the egg white. Sprinkle the dough with the almonds, leaving the cut-lines uncovered, press the almonds lightly into the dough, and sprinkle them with the granulated sugar. Bake the strips in the middle of the oven for 20 minutes, or until golden. Transfer the cookies to racks, breaking them apart if necessary, and let them cool.

Store in airtight containers.

ARISTOCRATS

Yield:
about 72 cookies

Equipment:
hand-held electric
  mixer
parchment paper
pastry brush

These elegant butter cookie rounds are filled with chopped semisweet chocolate or walnuts and coated with coarse sugar crystals.

1¾ sticks (¾ cup plus 2 tablespoons)
  unsalted butter, softened
⅔ cup granulated sugar
2 large eggs
2½ cups all-purpose flour

⅓ cup finely chopped walnuts
1½ ounces semisweet chocolate,
  chopped finely
½ cup coarse sugar crystals (available
  at specialty foods shops)

In a bowl with the mixer cream the butter with the granulated sugar until fluffy. Beat in one of the eggs, beaten lightly, and add the flour, ¼ cup at a time, blending until the mixture forms a dough. Halve the dough and reserve one half, wrapped in foil and chilled for 30 minutes. Halve the remaining dough and knead the walnuts into it. Knead the chocolate into the remaining half and roll each piece of dough into a 10-inch cylinder.

Roll the reserved chilled dough into an 11- by 9-inch rectangle and halve the rectangle lengthwise. Brush the dough with the remaining egg, beaten lightly, and put 1 of the cylinders in the center of each half. Roll one of the rectangles around each cylinder to enclose the cylinder completely, smoothing the seams and pressing the ends together firmly. Brush the rolls with the egg, roll them in the sugar crystals, coating them well, and chill them, wrapped in foil, for at least 4 hours.

Line baking sheets with the parchment paper and preheat the oven to 400° F.

Store in airtight containers.

Slice each roll into 36 rounds, arrange the rounds ½ inch apart on the baking sheets, and bake in the middle of the oven for 10 minutes, or until golden. Transfer the cookies to racks and let them cool.

FILBERT BALLS

Yield:
about 60 balls

Equipment:
hand-held electric mixer
parchment paper

The hazelnut and the filbert are the same nut. The name hazelnut, however, refers to the wild nut, while the filbert is cultivated. Since the commercially marketed cultivated nuts are specified as filberts, it is this name one encounters more often, although hazelnut is widely used, too. In Germany these traditional Christmas cookies are called *Haselnuss Bällchen*.

3½ ounces semisweet chocolate
¾ stick (6 tablespoons) unsalted butter, softened
1 cup sifted confectioners' sugar

1¼ cups filberts, toasted and skins removed (for procedure page 549), ground

In the top of a double boiler set over hot water melt the chocolate and let cool. In a bowl with the mixer beat the butter with the sugar until fluffy. Stir in the chocolate and beat until very creamy and smooth. Stir in the filberts. Form the mixture into a ball and chill, wrapped in wax paper, for 30 minutes.

Line baking sheets with the parchment paper and preheat the oven to 300° F.

Pinch off 1 teaspoon of the dough at a time, rolling it between the palms of the hands into a ball. Arrange the balls ½ inch apart on the baking sheets and bake in the middle of the oven for 8 minutes, or until they have lost

Store in an airtight container.

their gloss. Let the balls cool on the baking sheets.

Photo on page 275.

Variation:

ALMOND BALLS (*Mandel Bällchen*): An interesting variation with an entirely different baking procedure. Use ¾ cup confectioners' sugar and ¾ cup blanched almonds, ground, and add ¼ teaspoon almond extract. Chill the dough, wrapped in wax paper, for 1 hour. Form balls and bake them in the middle of a preheated 175° F. oven for 50 minutes. Turn off the oven and let the balls stand in the oven for 1 hour, or until they are dry and can be easily removed from the paper. Makes about 40 balls.

KOURABIEDES

Yield:
about 60 cookies

Equipment:
hand-held electric
  mixer

Traditionally served in Greece at Christmas and the New Year, these rich, short, and buttery cookies are dusted heavily with confectioners' sugar and are garnished with whole cloves to recall the spices brought by the Wise Men to Bethlehem.

4 sticks (2 cups) unsalted butter,
  softened
¾ cup confectioners' sugar plus
  additional sifted for dusting

1 egg yolk
3 tablespoons Cognac
4½ cups sifted all-purpose flour
60 whole cloves

In a bowl with the mixer cream the butter until very light. Gradually add the ¾ cup sugar and continue beating until smooth and well blended. Add the egg yolk and the Cognac and beat the dough vigorously. Work in the flour, a little at a time, and beat the dough hard until smooth. Chill the dough for 1 hour, or until firm enough to handle easily.

Preheat the oven to 350° F.

With floured hands shape pieces of the dough into small balls about 1½ inches in diameter, put them on baking sheets, and stick a whole clove in the top of each. Bake the cookies in the middle of the oven for 15 minutes. Let the cookies cool on the baking sheets for several minutes and transfer them very gently to a wire rack. When the cookies are almost cool, sprinkle them generously with the sifted confectioners' sugar.

MINIATURE FLORENTINES

Yield:
about 80 cookies

Equipment:
parchment paper
2-inch round cutter
pastry brush

This classic lace cookie, studded with bits of almond and candied orange rind and brushed with melted sweet chocolate, is made even more elegant by its diminutive size.

½ cup sugar
3½ tablespoons unsalted butter
2½ tablespoons honey
2½ tablespoons heavy cream
⅔ cup sliced blanched almonds

3 tablespoons minced Candied Orange
  Peel (page 522)
8 ounces dark sweet chocolate,
  chopped coarse

Line baking sheets with the parchment paper and preheat oven to 400° F.

In a heavy saucepan combine the sugar, butter, honey, and cream, bring the mixture to a boil over moderate heat, stirring, and boil it, stirring constantly, for 5 minutes. Stir in the almonds and the orange peel and let the mixture cool for 5 minutes. (The mixture will be very thin.)

Spoon ½ teaspoons of the mixture 2 inches apart on the baking sheets and bake the cookies in the middle of the oven for 5 minutes. Dipping the cutter into cold water each time, trim the edges of the cookies and bake the cookies for 4 to 5 minutes more, or until they are golden and bubbly. (The cookies will look runny and underdone at this point.) Let the cookies cool on the sheets for 2 minutes, or until firm enough to be transferred. Transfer them carefully with a metal spatula to racks and let them cool completely. (If the cookies become too firm to remove from the baking sheets, return them to the oven to soften for about 1 minute.)

In the top of a double boiler set over hot water melt the chocolate and remove it from the heat. Brush a thin layer of the chocolate over the smooth undersides of the cookies and let it dry. Brush a second coat of chocolate on the undersides and with the tines of a fork make a zigzag pattern lightly across it. Let the chocolate cool.

Store in layers separated by wax paper in an airtight container.

SUGAR PRETZELS

Yield:
about 26 larger
   pretzels and about
   84 miniature
   pretzels

Equipment:
parchment paper
pastry brush

Pretzel-shaped almond-flavored cookies with a crunchy sugar topping, these are known throughout Germany as *Zucker Brezeln*. In this recipe the larger pretzels are sprinkled with the coarse sugar while the miniature ones are topped with crushed sugar.

1¾ cups all-purpose flour
⅓ cup confectioners' sugar
⅛ teaspoon salt
½ cup blanched almonds, ground
   coarsely
2 large eggs, each beaten lightly in a
   separate bowl

1½ sticks (¾ cup) cold unsalted
   butter, cut into bits
grated rind of 1 lemon
1 cup coarse sugar crystals or pearl
   sugar (available at specialty foods
   shops), ½ cup crushed

Into a large bowl sift together the flour, confectioners' sugar, and salt and stir in the almonds. Make a well in the center of the flour mixture and add 1 egg. Sprinkle the butter and the lemon rind over the mixture, then blend the mixture until it forms a dough. Chill, wrapped in wax paper, for 1½ hours, or until firm enough to handle. Halve the dough and reserve one half, wrapped and chilled.

Line baking sheets with the parchment paper and preheat the oven to 375° F.

Make the larger pretzels:	Roll 1 piece of the dough into a log 1 inch in diameter on a floured surface and cut it into 26 pieces. With lightly floured hands roll each piece into a 5½-inch rope, tapered at the ends, and form it into a pretzel shape. Arrange the pretzels on the baking sheets, brush them with some of the remaining egg, and sprinkle them with the ½ cup uncrushed coarse sugar. Bake in the middle of the oven for 12 to 15 minutes, or until golden. Transfer the pretzels to a rack and let them cool.
Make the smaller pretzels:	Halve the reserved dough and reserve one half, wrapped and chilled. On a floured surface roll the dough into a rope as thin as can be handled easily. Cut it into 4½-inch lengths and form it into miniature pretzel shapes. Arrange the pretzels on the baking sheets, brush them with the egg, and sprinkle them with the crushed coarse sugar. Bake in the middle of the oven for 8 to 10 minutes, or until golden. Let the pretzels cool on the baking sheets for 15 minutes, transfer them to racks, and let them cool completely. Roll, cut, shape, and bake the remaining dough in the same
Store in airtight containers.	manner. Photo on page 275.

LADYFINGERS

Yield:
about thirty 3½-inch
  ladyfingers or about
  fifteen 7-inch
  ladyfingers

These delicate sponge cookies are also used to line charlotte molds. Ladyfingers can be piped out to whatever length you desire, but for lining molds for charlottes or other chilled desserts, pipe them out ½ inch longer than the height of the mold.

Equipment:
upright electric mixer
parchment paper
large pastry bag fitted
  with large plain
  no. 9 tip

5 egg yolks
½ cup plus 2 tablespoons granulated
  sugar
1 teaspoon vanilla

¾ cup all-purpose flour
7 egg whites at room temperature
¼ cup confectioners' sugar

Preheat the oven to 350° F.

In the bowl of the mixer beat the egg yolks with ½ cup of the sugar and the vanilla at number 4 speed on the mixer for 5 minutes, or until the mixture is very thick and light. Sift in the flour in 4 batches, folding in each batch before adding the next. Transfer the mixture to a large bowl. In the bowl of the mixer beat the egg whites until they hold soft peaks, sprinkle in the remaining 2 tablespoons sugar, and continue to beat the whites until they hold stiff peaks (see illustrations page 238). Fold one fourth of the whites into the yolk mixture and fold in the remaining whites gently.

Put a dab of the batter on each corner of 2 baking sheets and cover the sheets with the parchment paper, pressing to make the corners adhere. Transfer the batter to the pastry bag and pipe it out in 3½-inch lengths at an angle across the length of the sheet (see illustration opposite). Sift confectioners' sugar over the ladyfingers, then rap the sheet and tilt to remove any excess sugar. Bake the ladyfingers in the middle of the oven for 15 minutes, or until lightly colored. Remove the ladyfingers from the paper with a metal spatula, transfer them to racks, and let them cool.

Variations: For orange- or lemon-flavored ladyfingers, add 2 teaspoons grated orange or lemon rind to the yolks. For crispy ladyfingers, sprinkle a few drops of water over the confectioners' sugar before baking the cookies. This will crystallize the sugar and result in a crunchier surface.

Piping ladyfingers at angles across length of baking sheet

CATS' TONGUES

Yield:
about 35 cookies

Equipment:
3 baking sheets
hand-held electric
  mixer
pastry bag fitted with
  ⅜-inch plain tip

These beloved long, thin, crisp butter cookies resembling a cat's tongue owe their texture to the low proportion of fat in the batter. Often referred to by their French name *langues de chat*, these cookies are the ideal accompaniment to a chilled soufflé or a frozen dessert.

½ stick (¼ cup) unsalted butter,
  softened
½ cup sugar

2 egg whites
5 tablespoons sifted cake flour (not the
  self-rising variety)

Butter heavily and flour the baking sheets and preheat the oven to 425° F.

In a bowl with the mixer cream the butter, add the sugar, and beat the mixture until light and fluffy. Add the egg whites and beat for 5 to 10 seconds, or until smooth but not frothy. (If the mixture appears curdled at this point, it is due simply to separation of the egg whites and is no cause for alarm. The batter will bind together with the addition of the flour.) Sift the cake flour over the mixture and fold it in.

Transfer the batter to the pastry bag and pipe 3-inch lengths 2 inches apart on the baking sheets, making the ends slightly wider than the middle. Rap the baking sheets on a hard surface several times to spread the batter slightly. Bake the cookies in the middle of the oven for 4 to 5 minutes, or until golden brown around the edges. Let the cookies stand on the sheets for 30 seconds, or until they are just firm enough to hold their shape, transfer them with a spatula to a rack, and let cool.

Store in layers separated by wax paper in an airtight container.

ALMOND TULIPES WITH STRAWBERRIES AND WHIPPED CREAM

Yield:
6 desserts

Equipment:
glass bowl 4 to 5
  inches in diameter

This recipe begins a series of molded cookies all based on a similar very thin batter that produces a soft pliable wafer, which can be shaped while warm into fanciful forms. Here the cookie is molded in a small bowl to resemble a tulip, hence its name, almond *tulipe*. Other forms for molding the wafers include rolling pins, wooden spoons, and cornets.

½ stick (¼ cup) unsalted butter,
  softened
½ cup confectioners' sugar
¾ teaspoon almond extract
¼ cup (about 2 large) egg whites at
  room temperature

¼ cup all-purpose flour
⅓ cup sliced blanched almonds,
  toasted lightly
3 cups sliced strawberries plus 6 small
  strawberries, sliced, for garnish
whipped cream

Butter baking sheets and preheat the oven to 425° F.

In a bowl cream the butter, beat in the sugar, and beat until fluffy. Add the almond extract and the egg whites and beat for 5 to 10 seconds, or until smooth but not frothy. Sift the flour over the mixture and fold it in with the almonds. (The batter will be a bit lumpy.)

Spoon 1½ tablespoons of the batter 2 inches apart onto the baking sheets and with the back of a spoon dipped in cold water spread the batter to form 5-inch rounds. Bake the cookies in the middle of the oven for 5 to 6 minutes, or until the edges are golden brown. Let the cookies stand on the baking sheets for 30 seconds, or until they are just firm enough to hold their shape, transfer them with a metal spatula to the glass bowl, and pinch in the 4 sides to make flower shapes (see illustration). If the *tulipes* become too firm to remove from the baking sheets, return them to the oven for a few seconds to soften. Let the *tulipes* cool on racks. Transfer the *tulipes* to dessert plates, divide the strawberries among them, and top each dessert with a dollop of the whipped cream and a sliced strawberry, fanned.

The *tulipes*, by virtue of their delicacy, cannot be filled in advance. Fill just before serving.

Photo opposite and on back jacket.

The *tulipes* can be made up to 2 days in advance. Store in an airtight container.

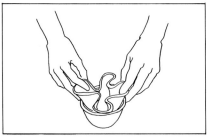

Shaping cookie wafers in bowl, pinching in sides to make *tulipe*

Almond Tulipes with Strawberries and Whipped Cream (opposite)

ALMOND CURL COOKIES

Yield:
about 60 cookies

Equipment:
rolling pin

This combination closely resembles the preceding one for Almond Tulipes. However these wafer cookies are shaped while still warm around a rolling pin and resemble the traditional French curved roof tiles called *tuiles*. Finely ground almonds are part of this batter and render these wafers crunchier than the *tulipes*.

1 stick (½ cup) unsalted butter,
   softened
1 cup sugar
4 egg whites at room temperature
1 teaspoon vanilla

¼ teaspoon almond extract
½ cup sifted all-purpose flour
⅔ cup blanched whole almonds (for
   procedure page 549), ground finely
2 cups toasted sliced almonds

Butter baking sheets and preheat the oven to 425° F.

In a bowl cream together the butter and the sugar until light and fluffy. Add the egg whites, vanilla, and almond extract and beat the mixture until it is just combined. Sift the flour over the mixture, fold it in, and fold in the ground almonds.

Working in batches, drop the batter by rounded teaspoons 4 inches apart onto the baking sheets, spread it into 3-inch rounds with the back of a spoon dipped in cold water, and sprinkle about 1½ teaspoons of the toasted almonds evenly over each round. Bake the cookies in batches in the middle of the oven for 4 to 5 minutes, or until golden brown around the edges. Working quickly, loosen the cookies, a few at a time, from the sheets with a metal spatula. Curl them around a rolling pin and let them cool until they hold their shape on the rolling pin (see illustration). Transfer the cookies as they harden to a rack to cool completely. (If the cookies become too hard to curl, return them to the hot oven for a few seconds to soften.)

Store in an airtight container.

Variation:

HAZELNUT TUILES: Substitute 1 cup lightly toasted and skins removed (for procedure page 549) finely chopped hazelnuts for the toasted sliced almonds.

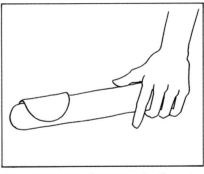

Curling cookie wafers around rolling pin

IRISH LACE COOKIES

Yield:
about 36 cookies

Equipment:
hand-held electric mixer

With the delicious crunchiness of rolled oats, this cookie is molded by hand into the shape of a cylinder.

¾ cup firmly packed light brown sugar
1 stick (½ cup) unsalted butter, softened

2 tablespoons all-purpose flour
2 tablespoons milk
1 teaspoon vanilla
1¼ cups old-fashioned rolled oats

Preheat the oven to 350° F.

In a bowl with the mixer cream together the brown sugar and the butter and beat in the flour, milk, and vanilla. Stir in the rolled oats and drop the mixture by teaspoons, 6 at a time, about 2 inches apart on an ungreased baking sheet. Bake in the middle of the oven for 10 minutes. Remove the cookies from the oven and let them stand on the sheet for 1 minute, or until they are just firm enough to turn with a spatula. Turn the cookies upside down on the sheet and, working quickly, roll them into cylinders on the sheet. (If the cookies become too hard to roll, return them to the oven for a few seconds to soften.) Continue to bake and roll cookies in the same manner with the remaining batter.

Store in layers separated by wax paper in an airtight container.

BROWN BUTTER AND NUTMEG MELTAWAYS

Yield:
about 80 cookies

Equipment:
hand-held electric mixer
parchment paper

The full rich flavor of butter in this recipe is further enhanced by cooking it until golden brown. Heat the butter slowly, however, as it burns quickly and turns very bitter.

2½ cups unbleached all-purpose flour
1 teaspoon freshly grated nutmeg
½ teaspoon double-acting baking powder
pinch of salt
2 sticks (1 cup) unsalted butter cooked over moderate heat until it is golden brown, cooled

½ cup confectioners' sugar, sifted
2 egg yolks
1 teaspoon vanilla
1½ cups chopped pecans
about ½ cup vanilla confectioners' sugar (page 541) for sifting

Into a bowl sift together the flour, nutmeg, baking powder, and the salt. In a large bowl with the mixer at low speed combine the butter and the confectioners' sugar add the egg yolks, one at a time, beating well after each addition, and the vanilla, and blend the mixture well. Add the flour mixture all at once and beat the mixture until it just forms a dough. Chill the dough, covered, for at least 2 hours or overnight.

Preheat the oven to 350° F. Line baking sheets with the parchment paper.

Roll level teaspoons of the dough into balls, arrange the balls 2 inches apart on the baking sheets, and flatten them slightly with the heel of the hand. Press a few pecan pieces into each round and bake the cookies in the middle of the oven for 10 minutes, or until they are set. Transfer the cookies to racks, let them cool for 5 minutes, and sift the vanilla confectioners' sugar lightly over them. Let the cookies cool completely.

Store in layers separated by wax paper in airtight containers.

PINE NUT PUFFS

Yield:
about 80 cookies

Equipment:
parchment paper
hand-held electric
*   mixer*

Pine nuts are actually the kernels of the seeds of certain members of the pine family. These sweet crunchy seeds, however, are commonly referred to as nuts. Nomenclature aside, they are perishable and are best kept in the refrigerator or freezer.

1½ cups pine nuts
2 cups unbleached all-purpose flour
¼ teaspoon double-acting baking
*   powder*
pinch of salt

2 sticks (1 cup) unsalted butter, melted
*   and cooled*
½ cup confectioners' sugar, sifted
2 teaspoons vanilla
about ½ cup vanilla confectioners'
*   sugar (page 541) for sifting*

Toast ½ cup of the pine nuts in a baking pan in the oven for 8 to 10 minutes, or until they are golden, let them cool, and chop them fine. Chop the remaining 1 cup pine nuts coarse and transfer them to a wide bowl.

Into a bowl sift together the flour, baking powder, and salt. In a large bowl with the electric mixer combine the butter and the confectioners' sugar at low speed and blend in the vanilla. Add the flour mixture in 2 batches, blending the mixture at low speed after each addition until just combined. Stir in the chopped toasted pine nuts and chill the dough, covered, for at least 2 hours or overnight.

Line baking sheets with the parchment paper. Preheat the oven to 350° F.

Roll level teaspoons of the dough into balls and roll the balls in the bowl of chopped pine nuts, pressing the nuts gently into the cookies. Arrange the balls 2 inches apart on the baking sheets and bake them in the middle of the oven for 10 to 12 minutes, or until they are set and lightly golden around the edges. Transfer the cookies to racks, let them cool for 5 minutes, and sift the vanilla confectioners' sugar lightly over them. Let the cookies cool completely.

Photo on page 299.

Store in layers separated by wax paper in airtight containers.

DATE NUGGETS

Yield:
about 95 cookies

Equipment:
hand-held electric
   mixer
parchment paper

2 cups unbleached all-purpose flour
1/4 teaspoon baking soda
pinch of salt
2 sticks (1 cup) unsalted butter,
   softened
3/4 cup granulated sugar combined with
   1/4 teaspoon cinnamon

1 1/2 teaspoons vanilla
1/2 cup pitted dates, finely chopped
1/2 cup pecans, toasted lightly and
   finely chopped
about 1/2 cup vanilla confectioners'
   sugar (page 541) for sifting

Into a bowl sift together the flour, baking soda, and salt. In a large bowl with the mixer cream the butter, add the granulated sugar mixture, a little at a time, beating, and beat for 1 minute. Beat in the vanilla and add the flour mixture in 2 batches, blending at low speed after each addition until the mixture is just combined. Stir in the dates and the pecans and chill the dough, covered, for at least 2 hours or overnight.

Line baking sheets with the parchment paper and preheat the oven to 350° F.

Store in layers
separated by wax
paper in airtight
containers.

Roll level teaspoons of the dough into balls, arrange the balls 2 inches apart on the baking sheets, and bake them in the middle of the oven for 10 to 12 minutes, or until they are set and lightly golden around the edges. Transfer the cookies with a spatula to racks, let them cool for 5 minutes, and sift the vanilla confectioners' sugar lightly over them. Let the cookies cool completely.

CURRANT CRISPS

Yield:
about 120 cookies

Equipment:
hand-held electric
   mixer
parchment paper

The combination of cornstarch and flour in this recipe results in a lovely textured butter cookie made even more flavorful by the addition of dried currants.

1 1/2 cups unbleached all-purpose flour
1 cup cornstarch
1 teaspoon double-acting baking
   powder
1/2 teaspoon salt

2 sticks (1 cup) unsalted butter,
   softened
1 cup sugar
1 large egg, beaten lightly
2 teaspoons vanilla
1 cup moist dried currants

Into a bowl sift together the flour, cornstarch, baking powder, and the salt. In a bowl with the mixer cream the butter, add the sugar, a little at a time, beating, and beat for 2 minutes. Add the egg and the vanilla and beat for 1 minute. Add the flour mixture in 2 batches, blending at low speed after each addition until it is just combined. Stir in the currants and chill the dough, covered, for at least 3 hours or overnight.

Line baking sheets with the parchment paper and preheat the oven to 375° F.

Roll level teaspoons of the dough into balls and arrange them 2 inches apart on the baking sheets. Flatten each ball with the tines of a fork, pressing the tines in one direction only to form an oval cookie with a ribbed design. Bake the cookies in the middle of the oven for 8 to 9 minutes, or until they are golden around the edges. Transfer the cookies to racks and

Store in airtight containers.

let them cool.

Photo on page 299.

WALNUT COOKIES

Yield:
about 45 cookies

Equipment:
food processor fitted
with steel blade
parchment paper

Because of the high proportion of butter to dry ingredients in this recipe, the result is a very crumbly or "short" cookie. This is the opposite of the crisp texture of Cats' Tongues (page 287), achieved by the low proportion of fat in that batter.

1¼ cups all-purpose flour
7 tablespoons cold unsalted butter, cut
    into bits
½ cup finely chopped walnuts
6 tablespoons confectioners' sugar,
    sifted

½ teaspoon vanilla
vanilla sugar (page 541) or additional
    confectioners' sugar for dusting

In the food processor blend the flour, butter, walnuts, confectioners' sugar, and the vanilla until the mixture just forms a dough. Form the dough into a ball, flatten it slightly, and chill it, wrapped in wax paper, for 20 minutes, or until it is firm.

Line baking sheets with the parchment paper and preheat the oven to 350° F.

Roll walnut-size pieces of the dough on a smooth surface into ropes about ⅓ inch thick, cut the ropes into 3-inch lengths, and bend the lengths to form crescent shapes. Arrange the crescents about 1 inch apart on the baking sheets and bake the cookies in the middle of the oven for 10 minutes, or until they are pale golden. Transfer the cookies to racks, while

Store in an airtight container.

they are still warm sift the vanilla sugar or confectioners' sugar over them, and let them cool.

NUT-FILLED CRESCENTS

Yield:
about 24 crescents

Equipment:
pastry wheel
pastry brush

These crescents are filled with a rich mixture of ground filberts, walnuts, and almonds and topped with a sugar icing. This recipe is unique in that the cookies are made with an actual flaky Danish pastry dough.

FOR THE DOUGH
1 recipe Danish Pastry Dough (page 217), halved; one half chilled

FOR THE FILLING
1 cup dry bread or cake crumbs
½ cup filberts, toasted and skins removed (for procedure page 549), ground
½ cup walnuts, ground
¼ cup blanched almonds, toasted lightly and ground

1 cup water
⅔ cup sugar
¼ cup minced Candied Orange Peel (page 522)
1 tablespoon unsalted butter, softened
cinnamon to taste

FOR THE ICING
1 cup confectioners' sugar, sifted
½ teaspoon vanilla

4 tablespoons milk

Make the dough:

On a lightly floured surface roll half the dough into a 20- by 15-inch rectangle. With the pastry wheel or a large sharp knife cut it into twelve 5-inch squares and cover the squares loosely with a dish towel.

Make the filling:

In a bowl combine the crumbs, filberts, walnuts, and almonds. In a small heavy saucepan combine the water with the sugar and cook the syrup over moderately low heat, stirring and washing down any sugar crystals clinging to the sides of the pan with the brush dipped in cold water until the sugar is dissolved. Increase the heat to moderately high and boil the syrup for 2 minutes. Remove the pan from the heat and add the orange peel, crumb mixture, butter, and the cinnamon. Stir the mixture until the crumbs have absorbed the syrup and the filling is thick and let it cool.

Make the icing:

In a small bowl combine the confectioners' sugar with the vanilla and add enough of the milk to make a thick icing.

To assemble:

Put 1½ tablespoons of the crumb filling diagonally across the center of each square, brush the edges of the squares lightly with water, and beginning at an unfilled corner, roll the squares diagonally. Bend the ends of the rolls inward to form crescents, moisten baking sheets with water, and put the crescents on the sheets, leaving 3 inches between. Let the crescents rise, covered loosely with a dish towel, in a warm place for 30 minutes.

Preheat the oven to 400° F.

Bake the crescents in the middle of the oven for 30 minutes, or until browned. Transfer the crescents to a rack. Brush the hot crescents with the icing. Make crescents with the reserved dough in the same manner.

MADELEINES

Yield:
12 *madeleines*

Equipment:
pastry brush
12 *madeleine* molds, 3
  by 2 inches
  (available at
  specialty kitchen-
  ware stores)
hand-held electric
  mixer

The *madeleine* was forever immortalized in French literature by Marcel Proust. Through the taste of tea and one of these delicate scallop-shaped butter cakes, Proust revived, unintentionally, a childhood memory that resulted in his writing of *Remembrance of Things Past.*

about 4½ tablespoons clarified butter
  (page 536)
2 large eggs at room temperature
¼ cup granulated sugar
1 tablespoon grated orange rind

1 tablespoon fresh orange juice
½ cup all-purpose flour
¼ cup confectioners' sugar if desired
  for sifting

Preheat the oven to 375° F.

With the pastry brush butter well the *madeleine* molds with some of the clarified butter, invert them to drain, and reserve the remaining butter.

In a bowl with the mixer beat the eggs with the granulated sugar for 5 to 10 minutes, or until the mixture is very light and falls in a ribbon when the beater is lifted (see illustration page 16). Stir in the orange rind and orange juice. Sift the flour over the mixture, one fourth at a time, and fold it in lightly with a rubber spatula. Add the reserved clarified butter in a stream, folding it in and making sure that no butter remains at the bottom of the bowl.

Spoon the batter into the molds, filling them two-thirds full, and arrange the molds on a baking sheet. Bake the *madeleines* in the lower third of the oven for 10 minutes, or until golden at the edges. Turn them onto a rack and let them cool. Sift the confectioners' sugar over them if desired.

Madeleines are best the day they are made, with a cup of tea.

Variation:

ALMOND MADELEINES: In place of the orange rind and orange juice, add 1 tablespoon milk and ½ teaspoon almond extract. After folding in the sifted flour, fold in ¼ cup ground blanched almonds.

BRANDY SNAPS WITH STRAWBERRIES

Yield:
about 10 brandy snaps

Equipment:
cannoli molds
  (available at
  specialty
  kitchenware stores)
or 1-inch-thick
  wooden dowels

FOR THE BRANDY SNAPS
½ stick (¼ cup) unsalted butter
¼ cup sugar
¼ cup unsulfured light molasses
1 teaspoon ground ginger

*1½ pints strawberries, hulled and
  sliced*
2½ tablespoons light rum, or to taste

⅛ teaspoon salt
½ cup all-purpose flour
2 teaspoons brandy

2½ tablespoons sugar, or to taste
*whipped cream or ice cream as an
  accompaniment if desired*

**Make the brandy
snaps:**

Butter baking sheets and preheat the oven to 325° F.

In a saucepan combine the butter, sugar, molasses, ginger, and the salt and cook the mixture over moderately low heat, stirring, until the sugar is dissolved. Remove the pan from the heat and stir in the flour and brandy.

Spoon tablespoons of the batter 6 inches apart onto the baking sheets and bake the brandy snaps in the middle of the oven for 12 to 15 minutes, or until they begin to darken. Let the brandy snaps stand on the baking sheets on a rack for 3 minutes, or until they are firm enough to roll. Wrap the brandy snaps around the *cannoli* molds or wooden dowels, let them stand until they have hardened completely, and slide them off the molds carefully. Make brandy snaps in batches with the remaining batter in the same manner, heating the batter each time if it has thickened.

The brandy snaps may be made 1 day in advance and kept in an airtight container.

In a bowl toss the strawberries with the rum and the sugar, fill each brandy snap with about ¼ cup of the mixture, and serve the brandy snaps with the whipped cream or ice cream if desired.

CHOCOLATE LEAVES

**Yield:
about 24 leaves**

These beautiful almond-flavored cookies are formed into leaves with a traditional leaf-shaped stencil, then coated with bittersweet chocolate.

**Equipment:
spice grinder
hand-held electric
  mixer
4¼-inch-long leaf-
  shaped metal stencil
  (available at
  specialty
  kitchenware stores)
  or a homemade
  heavy cardboard
  stencil**

6 tablespoons sliced blanched almonds
4½ tablespoons sugar
*4½ tablespoons unsalted butter,
  softened*
1 large egg, beaten lightly

½ teaspoon almond extract
¾ cup sifted all-purpose flour
*9 ounces bittersweet chocolate
  (preferably imported), chopped*

Butter a baking sheet and preheat the oven to 300° F.

In the spice grinder grind fine, in batches, the almonds with the sugar.

In a bowl with the mixer cream the butter, add the almond and sugar mixture, and beat the mixture until it is light and fluffy. Beat in the egg, almond extract, and flour and beat the dough until it is just combined.

Lay the stencil on the baking sheet. With a metal spatula spread a heaping tablespoon of the dough over the stencil and press the dough smoothly and evenly through the stencil onto the sheet, scraping off the excess dough. Lift the stencil straight up, leaving the leaf cookie on the sheet, wipe the stencil clean, and make leaves with the remaining dough in the same manner. Bake the cookies in the middle of the oven for 10 to 15 minutes, or until the edges are just golden. Transfer them to a rack and let them cool completely.

In a bowl set over barely simmering water melt the chocolate, stirring, and transfer it to a flat plate. Working with 1 cookie at a time, lay one side flat down on the chocolate, coating it, and holding the leaf near its pointed

The cookies may be
made up to 3 days in
advance and kept in a
cool place in an
airtight container.

top, lift the cookie out of the chocolate at an angle so that the chocolate
drips down to the base, forming ridges like the veins of a leaf. Transfer the
dipped cookies chocolate side up to a rack set on a baking sheet and chill
them for 30 minutes, or until the chocolate is hardened.

ROLLED COOKIES

What this final grouping of superb cookies has in common, aside from
their excellence, is that their doughs all require rolling out. These cookies
will not be dropped or shaped or sliced, although some of them probably
could be. Instead they will be stamped or cut out with special cutters and,
as in the case of our shortbreads, those doughs will be scored.

That said, these cookies have little else in common. They are a diver-
sified, fun lot. Among them are elegant high-style teatime cookies from
Austria and rough and tumble gingerbread men. There are cookies that
are leaf shaped, heart shaped, and cresent shaped. There are wonderful
American classics like sand tarts and sugar cookies and the German
Christmas classic *Lebkuchen*. There is a sensational almond butter cookie
filled with praline buttercream and an equally fine, though not so stylish,
Sherry finger reminiscent of those so preferred by the British.

Because we believe this set of cookies more complicated than any of
those that have preceded, a few words follow on the handling of short,
buttery doughs:

Always chill the dough as suggested. If you are in a hurry, hasten this
process by putting the dough in the freezer for a shorter amount of time,
but do not forget that it is there. What you are doing in chilling the dough
is (1) relaxing the gluten in the flour, which will make for a more tender
result, and (2) setting the butter to the proper consistency for rolling. If the
butter becomes too hard, you will have to work the dough, which will
toughen it.

■ As to the rolling-out process, flour the work surface and your cutter judiciously. Extra flour makes for a denser dough.

■ Know that the dough for some particularly short cookies, like
shortbread and honey spice cookies, requires being rolled between sheets
of wax paper or on a pastry cloth. If you don't have a pastry cloth, substitute wax paper. In short, don't just avoid the issue entirely and proceed to
roll the dough out on your board. That dough is too buttery to come up
successfully.

■ In using a cookie cutter, start from the outer edge of the dough and
work in. You'll have fewer scraps that way.

■ As to the rerolling of scraps, gather them into a ball of dough and

Chocolate Shortbread Hearts (page 308), Almond Leaves (page 306), Pine Nut Puffs (page 292),
Currant Crisps (page 293), Ginger Crescents (page 310)

roll it as gingerly as possible. At the risk of repeating ourselves, the more a dough is handled, the more it reacts negatively.

It would be inconceivable to think that you could not in this selection of cookies find the perfect cookie to fit the occasion. But who needs an occasion? A good cookie is an event in itself!

BAVARIAN APRICOT-FILLED ALMOND COOKIES

Yield:
about 24 cookies

Known as *Bayrische Mandelplatzchen,* these elegant Christmas cookies are a specialty of Bavaria, Germany.

Equipment:
hand-held electric
  mixer
parchment paper
2½-inch round cutter
1½-inch round cutter
pastry brush

1¾ sticks (¾ cup plus 2 tablespoons)
  unsalted butter, softened
⅔ cup confectioners' sugar, sifted
1 egg yolk
1¾ cups all-purpose flour
¼ teaspoon ground cloves

¼ teaspoon cinnamon
¾ cup blanched almonds (for
  procedure page 549), finely ground
1 egg white, beaten lightly
1 cup sliced blanched almonds
½ cup sieved apricot jam

In a bowl with the mixer cream together the butter and the sugar until light and fluffy. Add the egg yolk and beat the mixture until it is combined well. Sift the flour with the cloves and cinnamon and gradually add to the butter mixture. Add the ground almonds and blend until a dough forms. Chill the dough, wrapped in wax paper, for at least 1½ hours.

Line baking sheets with the parchment paper.

Quarter the dough, reserving three fourths wrapped and chilled. With a lightly floured rolling pin roll out one fourth of the dough ⅛ inch thick on a floured surface. With the larger cutter cut out rounds and with the smaller cutter cut out the centers from half the rounds, making rings. Re-roll the scraps and cut out more rounds and rings. Roll out and cut the reserved dough in the same manner. Arrange the rounds and rings on separate baking sheets and chill them for 1 hour.

Preheat the oven to 350° F.

Spread the sliced almonds on a plate. Brush the rings with the egg white. Turn each ring with a spatula onto the almonds and press the rings lightly onto the nuts. Return the rings almond side up to the baking sheet and bake for 10 to 12 minutes; bake the rounds for 10 to 15 minutes, or until lightly browned. Let the rings and rounds cool on the baking sheets for 20 minutes, or until they can be easily transferred to a rack, and let them cool completely. Spread the rounds with the apricot jam and top each one with a ring, pressing it down lightly.

Store in an airtight container.

Photo on page 275.

HONEY SPICE COOKIES

Yield:
25 cookies

Equipment:
jelly-roll pan, 15 by 10
  inches
pastry brush

These beloved spice cookies, known as *Lebkuchen* in Germany, are also formed into hearts and various other decorative shapes according to the season. Elaborate decoration and even inscription make the *Lebkuchen* of Nürnberg particular favorites.

3 cups all-purpose flour
1 tablespoon double-acting baking
  powder
¼ teaspoon salt
1¼ cups ground blanched almonds
½ cup minced orange peel
¼ cup minced glacéed citron plus diced
  citron for decoration
1 tablespoon grated lemon rind
1 tablespoon cinnamon
½ teaspoon ground cloves
½ teaspoon ground ginger
½ teaspoon ground allspice

½ teaspoon freshly grated nutmeg
¼ teaspoon ground cardamom
⅔ cup sugar
⅔ cup honey
¼ cup vegetable oil
1 tablespoon brandy
2 large eggs, beaten lightly
milk as needed
13 glacéed cherries, halved
100 blanched almond halves (for
  procedure page 549)
diced glacéed angelica (available at
  specialty foods shops) if desired

Into a bowl sift together the flour, baking powder, and salt. Add the ground almonds, orange peel, citron, lemon rind, and all the spices and combine well.

    In a saucepan combine the sugar, honey, and vegetable oil and bring the liquid to a boil over moderate heat, stirring constantly. Remove the pan from the heat, stir in the brandy, and let the mixture cool until lukewarm. Add the honey mixture to the flour mixture with the eggs and blend the dough until it forms a ball. Knead the dough on a floured surface for 1 minute, or until smooth and elastic, and chill it, wrapped in wax paper, for 1 hour, or until firm.

    Preheat the oven to 350° F.

    Roll the dough between sheets of wax paper into a 15- by 10-inch rectangle and transfer it with the paper to the jelly-roll pan, inverted. Remove the top piece of paper and with a sharp knife score the dough into 3- by 2-inch rectangles. Brush the dough with milk and arrange a cherry half in the center of each rectangle. Arrange 4 blanched almond halves on each rectangle, placing a half in each corner pointing toward the cherry, and arrange the diced citron or angelica decoratively between the almonds and the cherry on each rectangle. Bake the *Lebkuchen* in the middle of the oven for 20 to 30 minutes, or until glossy and golden brown. Let the *Lebkuchen* cool for 15 minutes, cut along the marks to separate the cookies into rectangles, and transfer the cookies to a rack to cool completely. Serve the *Lebkuchen* warm or at room temperature.

Store in an airtight
container.

Spice Cookie Hearts (below), Lemon Curd Tartlets (page 176)

SPICE COOKIE HEARTS

Yield:
about 80 cookies

Equipment:
heart-shaped 2½-inch
  cutter
pastry bag fitted with
  very small plain tip

FOR THE COOKIES
4½ cups all-purpose flour
¼ teaspoon salt
1 teaspoon cinnamon
½ teaspoon ground ginger
½ teaspoon ground allspice

1 cup dark corn syrup
¾ cup firmly packed dark brown sugar
1 stick (½ cup) plus 2 tablespoons
  unsalted butter, cut into bits

FOR THE ICING
1 egg white at room temperature
1 teaspoon fresh lemon juice, or to
  taste

about 1 cup confectioners' sugar, sifted

Make the cookies:
Line dampened baking sheets with foil and preheat the oven to 350° F.
   Into a large bowl sift together the flour, salt, cinnamon, ginger, and the allspice. In a saucepan combine the corn syrup, brown sugar, and the butter and cook over moderate heat, stirring, until the butter is melted. Stir into the flour mixture and combine the mixture well to form a soft dough. Halve the dough and on the baking sheets roll out each half ⅛ inch thick. Chill the dough on the sheets for 30 minutes.
   Flour the cutter and with it cut out cookies, leaving at least ½ inch be-

tween the cookies. Gather the scraps and reserve them. Bake the cookies in the middle of the oven for 10 to 12 minutes, or until colored lightly, and let cool completely on the baking sheets. Make more cookies in the same manner with the reserved dough scraps.

Make the icing: In a small bowl whisk the egg white with the lemon juice until frothy. Then whisk in the confectioners' sugar, a little at a time. If the icing seems too thick, thin it with a few drops of water, or, if too thin, whisk in some additional confectioners' sugar. Transfer the icing to the pastry bag and **Store in airtight containers.** pipe it decoratively onto the cooled cookies. Let the icing harden.

Photo opposite.

GINGERBREAD MEN

Yield:
about 50 gingerbread men

Equipment:
hand-held electric mixer
4-inch gingerbread-man cutter
pastry bag fitted with small decorative tip (optional)

2 sticks (1 cup) unsalted butter, softened
1 cup firmly packed light brown sugar
1 large egg
1 cup dark unsulfured molasses
2 tablespoons cider vinegar
5 cups all-purpose flour

2 teaspoons ground ginger
1½ teaspoons baking soda
1¼ teaspoons cinnamon
1 teaspoon ground cloves
½ teaspoon salt
1 recipe Sugar Icing (page 540) if desired

In a large bowl with the mixer cream the butter, add the sugar, and beat until fluffy. Beat in the egg, molassses, and vinegar. Into a bowl sift together the flour, ginger, baking soda, cinnamon, cloves, and the salt and stir the mixture into the butter mixture, a little at a time. (The dough will be soft.) Quarter the dough, dust it with flour, and wrap each piece in wax paper. Flatten the dough slightly and chill it for at least 3 hours or overnight.

Butter 2 baking sheets and preheat the oven to 375° F.

Roll out the dough, one piece at a time, ¼ inch thick on a floured surface. Flour the cookie cutter and cut out cookies. Transfer the cookies with a spatula to the baking sheets, arranging them 2 inches apart, and bake them in the middle of the oven for 6 to 8 minutes, or until no imprint remains when they are touched lightly with the fingertip. Transfer the cookies with the spatula to racks and let them cool. Make cookies with the dough scraps in the same manner. If desired, pipe the sugar icing decora-
Store in airtight containers. tively on the cookies using the pastry bag. Let the cookies stand for 20 minutes, or until the icing is set.

MORAVIAN CHRISTMAS COOKIES

Yield:
about 60 cookies

Equipment:
hand-held electric
  mixer
3-inch round cutter

The Moravians fled religious persecution in Europe and settled in the United States, primarily in Pennsylvania and in Winston-Salem, North Carolina. These wonderful thin molasses spice cookies are made from a traditional Moravian recipe and are especially popular at Christmastime.

4 cups sifted all-purpose flour
1¾ teaspoons ground ginger
1¾ teaspoons cinnamon
1½ teaspoons ground cloves
1¼ teaspoons ground mace
3 tablespoons lard

1 tablespoon unsalted butter, softened
½ cup firmly packed light brown
  sugar
1 cup unsulfured molasses
1½ teaspoons baking soda dissolved in
  1 tablespoon very hot water

Into a bowl sift together the flour, ginger, cinnamon, cloves, and the mace. In a large bowl with the mixer cream the lard and butter, add the sugar, and beat the mixture until light and fluffy. Add the molasses and baking soda mixture and combine. Stir in the flour mixture, a little at a time, and beat the mixture by hand until it forms a very stiff and crumbly dough.

Quarter the dough, form each quarter into a ball, and chill the balls, wrapped in plastic wrap, for 1 hour.

Lightly butter the baking sheets and preheat the oven to 300 ° F.

Roll out the dough, one ball at a time, ¹⁄₁₆ inch thick. Dipping the cutter in flour, cut out rounds and arrange them 1 inch apart on the baking sheets. Bake the cookies in the middle of the oven for 15 minutes, or until firm, and let them cool on the baking sheets for about 30 seconds. Transfer the cookies to racks and let them cool completely.

Store in airtight containers.

SUVAROFFS

Yield:
about 28 cookies

Equipment:
food processor fitted
  with steel blade
1½-inch round cutter
1-inch round cutter

An extremely short and elegant butter cookie filled with raspberry jam—a specialty in Austria.

1½ cups all-purpose flour
1½ sticks (¾ cup) cold unsalted
  butter, cut into bits

⅓ cup sugar
½ cup raspberry jam (preferably
  seedless)

In the food processor or in a bowl blend the flour and the butter until the mixture resembles coarse meal. Add the sugar and blend until a smooth dough forms. Form the dough into a ball, flatten it slightly, and chill it, wrapped in wax paper, for 1 hour.

Lightly butter baking sheets and preheat the oven to 325° F.

Roll out the dough ¼ inch thick between sheets of wax paper. Peel off the top layer of wax paper. Dipping the larger cutter in flour cut out as many rounds as possible. With the smaller cutter, floured, cut out the centers from half the rounds to form rings. Arrange the rings and the rounds carefully 1 inch apart on the baking sheets. Gather the scraps into a ball, reroll the dough, and cut out more rings and rounds in the same manner. (If the dough becomes too soft to work with, slide it with the wax paper onto a baking sheet and chill it in the freezing compartment of the refrigerator for 5 minutes, or until firm again.) Bake the cookies in the middle of the oven for 12 to 15 minutes, or until pale golden, transfer them carefully with a spatula to racks, and let them cool. Spread the flat side of each round evenly with a thin layer of the jam and top it with a ring flat side down. Fill the center of each ring with about ¼ teaspoon of the jam.

SUGAR COOKIES

Yield:
about 70 cookies

Equipment:
hand-held electric
   mixer
decorative cutters

2½ cups all-purpose flour
1 teaspoon cream of tartar
½ teaspoon baking soda
¼ teaspoon salt
¼ teaspoon freshly grated nutmeg if
   desired

2 sticks (1 cup) unsalted butter,
   softened
1 teaspoon vanilla
1¼ cups sugar
2 large eggs, beaten well
1 teaspoon grated lemon rind if desired

Into a bowl sift together the flour, cream of tartar, baking soda, salt, and nutmeg, if desired. In a bowl with the mixer cream the butter with the vanilla until light and fluffy and gradually beat in ¾ cup of the sugar to make a smooth mixture. Stir in the eggs. Add the dry ingredients gradually, combining the mixture well after each addition. Form the dough into 2 balls, dust the balls with flour, and chill them, wrapped in wax paper, for 2 hours.

Preheat the oven to 375° F.

Roll out one ball ¼ inch thick on a floured surface, cut out cookies with the cutters, and transfer the cookies with a spatula to baking sheets, arranging them 2 inches apart. Sprinkle each cookie with some of the remaining ½ cup sugar and bake in the middle of the oven for 8 to 10 minutes, or until lightly golden. Sprinkle the cookies lightly with sugar again while they are still warm. Transfer the cookies with the spatula to a rack to cool. Make cookies with the scraps and the remaining dough in the same manner.

Store in airtight
containers.

ALMOND LEAVES

Yield:
about 50 cookies

Equipment:
hand-held electric
  mixer
parchment paper
2¼-inch-long fluted
  or leaf-shaped
  cutter

You will note that unbleached all-purpose flour is called for in the following recipe. Available in most supermarkets, it combines a blend of hard-wheat flours, and is higher in gluten, rendering a crumblier texture when baked. Simple all-purpose flour is a ready substitute.

2 cups unbleached all-purpose flour
¼ teaspoon double-acting baking
  powder
¼ teaspoon salt
2 sticks (1 cup) unsalted butter,
  softened

½ cup plus 2 tablespoons
  confectioners' sugar, sifted
½ cup ground blanched almonds
1 teaspoon almond extract
sliced unblanched almonds for
  decoration

Into a bowl sift together the flour, baking powder, and salt. In a large bowl with the mixer cream the butter, add the confectioners' sugar, a little at a time, beating, and beat for 2 minutes. Add the ground almonds and almond extract and blend the mixture well. Add the flour mixture all at once and blend the mixture at low speed until a dough just forms. Transfer the dough to a large sheet of wax paper, cover it with wax paper, and roll it out gently ⅓ inch thick. Chill the dough between the sheets of paper on a baking sheet if it becomes too soft to roll out. Chill the dough between the sheets of paper on a baking sheet for 2 hours, or until very firm.

    Line baking sheets with the parchment paper. Preheat the oven to 325° F.

    Peel off the top sheet of wax paper, cut out leaves with the cutter, and arrange them 2 inches apart on the prepared baking sheets. Gather the scraps, reroll and chill the dough until firm, and cut out cookies in the same manner. Press an almond slice gently onto the top of each cookie and bake the cookies in the middle of the oven for 14 to 15 minutes, or until set and barely golden around the edges. Transfer the cookies to racks and let them cool.

Store in airtight containers.

    Photo on page 299.

SHORTBREAD

Yield:
16 wedges

Equipment:
hand-held electric
  mixer

1½ sticks (¾ cup) unsalted butter,
  softened
½ cup sugar plus 2 tablespoons, or to
  taste, for garnish

1½ cups all-purpose flour
½ cup cornstarch

Preheat the oven to 350° F.

    In a bowl with the mixer cream the butter well. Add the ½ cup sugar gradually and cream the mixture until light and fluffy. Combine the flour and the cornstarch. Add the dry mixture gradually to the creamed mixture, mixing well after each addition. Turn the dough out onto a lightly floured surface and knead it until smooth.

Divide the dough in half. Roll out each half into an 8-inch round between ¼ inch and ⅓ inch in thickness. With a large spatula put the rounds on an ungreased baking sheet and with a ruler or a sharp spatula mark each round into 8 wedges. Press the tines of a fork decoratively around the edges, sprinkle each round with 1 tablespoon of the remaining sugar, and bake in the lower third of the oven for 35 minutes, or until lightly golden and cooked through. While the shortbread is still warm cut it into wedges with a pastry wheel or large sharp knife. Transfer to racks to cool.

Store chilled in layers separated by wax paper in an airtight container.

Variation:

COCONUT SHORTBREAD: Reduce the ½ cup sugar to ¼ cup and add ½ cup sweetened flaked coconut to the dough. Knead the coconut into the dough and bake as directed above.

BROWN-SUGAR PECAN SHORTBREAD

Yield:
8 wedges

Equipment:
hand-held electric mixer

1 stick (½ cup) unsalted butter, softened
½ cup firmly packed light brown sugar
1 cup sifted all-purpose flour

¼ teaspoon salt
½ cup pecans, toasted lightly and chopped coarsely
1 tablespoon granulated sugar, or to taste, for garnish

Preheat the oven to 350° F.

In a bowl with the mixer cream the butter until light, add the brown sugar gradually, mixing well after each addition and leaving no lumps, and cream until light and fluffy. Combine the flour and salt. Add the dry ingredients gradually to the creamed mixture, mixing well after each addition. Stir the pecans into the dough.

Turn the dough out onto a lightly floured surface and knead until smooth. Roll the dough into a 9-inch round ⅓ inch thick. With a large spatula transfer the round to an ungreased baking sheet and with a ruler or sharp spatula mark it into 8 wedges. Press the tines of a fork decoratively around the edges, sprinkle the round with the granulated sugar, and bake in the lower third of the oven for 35 minutes, or until lightly golden and cooked through. While the shortbread is still warm cut it into wedges with a pastry wheel or large sharp knife. Transfer to a rack to cool.

Store chilled in layers separated by wax paper in an airtight container.

Variation:

BROWN-SUGAR WALNUT SHORTBREAD: Substitute ½ cup walnuts, toasted lightly and chopped coarsely, for the pecans.

CHOCOLATE SHORTBREAD HEARTS

Yield:
about 50 cookies

Equipment:
hand-held electric
  mixer
parchment paper
2½-inch-wide heart-
  shaped cutter

2 cups unbleached all-purpose flour
½ cup unsweetened cocoa powder
  (preferably Dutch process)
¼ teaspoon baking soda
¼ teaspoon salt

2½ sticks (1 cup plus 4 tablespoons)
  unsalted butter, softened
1¼ cups confectioners' sugar, sifted
1¼ teaspoons vanilla

Into a bowl sift together the flour, cocoa, baking soda, and salt. In a large bowl with the mixer cream the butter, add the confectioners' sugar, a little at a time, beating, and beat the mixture for 2 minutes. Beat in the vanilla and add the flour in 2 batches, blending the mixture at low speed after each addition until just combined.

Transfer the dough to a large sheet of wax paper, cover it with another large sheet of wax paper, and roll it out ⅓ inch thick. Chill the dough between the sheets of wax paper on a baking sheet for 2 hours, or until firm. (The dough may also be chilled, wrapped well in plastic wrap, for up to 2 days.)

Line baking sheets with the parchment paper and preheat the oven to 325° F.

Peel off the top sheet of wax paper, cut out hearts with the cutter, and arrange them 2 inches apart on the baking sheets. Bake the cookies in the middle of the oven for 16 to 18 minutes, or until set. Transfer the cookies to racks and let them cool. Gather the scraps, reroll and chill the dough until it is firm, and cut out and bake cookies in the same manner.

Store in airtight
containers.

Photo on page 299.

CREAM-FILLED ALMOND BUTTER COOKIES

Yield:
about 24 sandwich
  cookies

Equipment:
2-inch fluted round
  cutter
hand-held electric
  mixer

These tender and stylish almond butter cookies can be sandwiched together with almond butter cream or, for a more compelling texture, with almond praline cream.

FOR THE COOKIES
1 cup finely ground blanched almonds
2 cups sifted all-purpose flour
⅔ cup granulated sugar

2 sticks (1 cup) cold unsalted butter,
  cut into bits

FOR THE FILLING
2 sticks (1 cup) unsalted butter,
  softened
2 teaspoons almond extract

2 cups confectioners' sugar
1 cup almond praline powder if desired
  (page 544)

½ cup confectioners' sugar, sifted, for dusting

Make the cookies: In a large bowl combine well the almonds, flour, and granulated sugar. Cut in the butter until the mixture resembles coarse meal and turn it out onto a lightly floured surface. Divide the dough in half, kneading each half with the heel of your hand until smooth. Form the halves into balls, wrap them in wax paper, and chill for 2 hours.

Preheat the oven to 350° F.

Roll one of the balls of dough ⅛ inch thick between sheets of wax paper. Peel off the top sheet of wax paper. Cut out cookies with the cutter and transfer them with a spatula to baking sheets, arranging the cookies 2 inches apart. Bake in the middle of the oven for 13 to 15 minutes, or until lightly golden. Let the cookies cool on the baking sheets for 1 minute and with the spatula transfer them to a rack to cool. Make cookies with the remaining dough in the same manner.

Make the filling: In a bowl with the mixer cream the butter with the almond extract until soft. Gradually add the confectioners' sugar, beating well after each addition. Continue beating the mixture for 2 minutes, until very light and fluffy. Stir in the praline powder if desired.

Store chilled in layers separated by wax paper in an airtight container. When the cookies are completely cool, spread the flat sides, or bottoms, of half of them with about 1 teaspoon of the filling. Top the cookies with the remaining halves, flat sides down, forming sandwiches. Dust the cookies with the confectioners' sugar.

SHERRY FINGERS

Yield:
about 36 fingers

Sophisticated finger-shaped biscuits best accompanied by a glass of Sherry or any dessert wine.

Equipment:
pastry brush

1½ cups all-purpose flour
pinch of salt
1 stick (½ cup) cold unsalted butter, cut into bits
½ cup sugar plus additional for sprinkling

3 tablespoons cream Sherry or other medium-sweet blend Sherry
egg wash made by beating 1 egg lightly

Into a bowl sift together the flour and the salt. Cut in the butter until the mixture resembles coarse meal. Add the ½ cup sugar, stir in the Sherry, and form the dough into a ball. Wrap the dough in plastic wrap and chill for 30 minutes.

Butter baking sheets and preheat the the oven to 375° F.

Roll out the dough ⅛ inch thick on a lightly floured surface and cut it into 2½- by 1-inch fingers. Prick the fingers decoratively with the tines of a fork, brush them with the beaten egg, and sprinkle them with the additional granulated sugar. Transfer the fingers with a spatula to the baking sheets and bake for 15 minutes, or until lightly golden. Transfer immediately to a wire rack and let cool.

Store in an airtight container.

SAND TARTS

Yield:
about 48 cookies

Equipment:
hand-held electric
  mixer
2½-inch round cutter
pastry brush

The name for this classic American cookie is derived from the cinnamon-sugar topping that gives it its "sandy" appearance.

1 stick (½ cup) unsalted butter,
  softened
1 cup plus 3 tablespoons sugar
1 large egg
1 egg yolk
½ teaspoon vanilla
2 cups all-purpose flour

1 teaspoon double-acting baking
  powder
¼ teaspoon salt
milk as needed
1 teaspoon cinnamon
almond slivers if desired

In a bowl with the mixer cream the butter until light. Gradually add 1 cup of the sugar and continue to beat the mixture until as smooth as possible. Beat in the egg and the egg yolk thoroughly and add the vanilla. Sift together the flour, baking powder, and the salt and add to the butter mixture, blending until a dough forms. Chill the dough, wrapped in plastic wrap, for several hours or overnight.

Preheat the oven to 350° F.

Cut the dough into 4 pieces and working with one piece at a time roll it on a lightly floured surface as thinly as possible. Cut the dough with the cookie cutter, transfer the rounds to unbuttered baking sheets, and with the pastry brush brush the tops with a little milk. Combine the remaining sugar and cinnamon and sprinkle the cookies with the mixture, or top each cookie with an almond sliver. Bake the cookies for 8 to 10 minutes, or until the edges are a delicate brown. Transfer to racks to cool.

GINGER CRESCENTS

Yield:
about 60 cookies

Equipment:
hand-held electric
  mixer
parchment paper
2¼-inch-long
  crescent cutter

Dried gingerroot or ground ginger and crystallized ginger are combined to make this spectacular crescent cookie.

2¼ cups unbleached all-purpose flour
½ teaspoon baking soda
¼ teaspoon salt
2 sticks (1 cup) unsalted butter,
  softened
¾ cup firmly packed light brown
  sugar
¼ cup firmly packed dark brown sugar

1 tablespoon freshly grated dried
  Jamaican gingerroot (available at
  specialty foods shops and spice
  shops) or 1½ tablespoons ground
  ginger
1 teaspoon vanilla
crystallized ginger (available at
  specialty foods shops), sliced thin,
  for decoration if desired

Into a bowl sift together the flour, baking soda, and salt. In a large bowl with the mixer cream the butter, add the light and dark brown sugars, and beat the mixture for 3 minutes. Add the gingerroot or ground ginger and the vanilla and combine well. Add the flour mixture in 2 batches, blending the mixture at low speed after each addition until it is just combined. Transfer the dough to a large sheet of wax paper, cover it with another large sheet of wax paper, and roll it out gently ⅓ inch thick. Chill the dough between the sheets of wax paper on a baking sheet for 2 hours, or until firm, or chill the dough, wrapped well in plastic wrap, for up to 2 days.

Line baking sheets with the parchment paper and preheat oven to 325° F.

Peel off the top sheet of wax paper, cut out crescents with the cutter, and arrange them 2 inches apart on the baking sheets. Gather the scraps, reroll and chill the dough until it is firm, and cut out cookies in the same manner. Press a small piece of the crystallized ginger into each crescent if desired and bake the cookies in the middle of the oven for 14 to 15 minutes, or until set and barely golden around the edges. Transfer the cookies to racks and let them cool.

Photo on page 299.

Store in airtight containers.

PUDDINGS AND CUSTARDS

There are many kinds of pudding—cornstarch pudding (otherwise known as basic pudding), bread and butter pudding, rice pudding, steamed pudding, to name just a few—and what each of them has in common is not immediately apparent, aside from their obvious designation. Suffice it to say that a pudding is a dessert that has been thickened.

Custards can be more easily defined. They contain specific ingredients: eggs, milk or cream, sugar, and flavorings, which when cooked over heat thicken to a certain consistency because of the eggs. There is no such thing as an uncooked custard. This fundamental combination acts as the base of pastry cream and ice cream and any number of sauces. If you are in command of making custard, you are on your way to many a culinary delight.

Of course, custard—whether it is called vanilla sauce, crème anglaise, or English cream—acts as an ingredient in certain puddings. (The opposite cannot be said: Puddings do not participate in custards!) An example is Tipsy Parson (page 344), created by James Beard, with a rich crème anglaise that uses four or five egg yolks depending on the mood and passion of the cook. It is a classic for all the right reasons.

There are classics among our puddings too, indication of the importance they have had in our culinary heritage. Take Indian Pudding (page 317), rich with molasses and cornmeal and straight out of New England. Old-Fashioned Rice Pudding (page 319), which cooks for three hours, is a classic too, as is the ever-true Pearl Tapioca Pudding (page 316).

While puddings and custards may not generate the élan or excitement associated with other types of dessert like cakes and pastries and even ice creams, each in its own way plays a very significant role. There is nothing passé about puddings or custards. In fact, like all good things, they are once more coming into their own, reappreciated for their basic goodness.

Cabinet Pudding
(page 332)

313

PUDDINGS

There are cold puddings, there are hot puddings. There are old-fashioned puddings, there are new-fangled puddings. There are certain puddings we could not do without, like rice pudding, or Indian pudding, or bread and butter pudding. We remember these from our earliest days, from the nursery even, and while everything else in life has changed, they have remained wondrously the same. These are recipes we hold close to our hearts for they soothe in a singularly personal way.

There are puddings that comfort in other ways, as well: in celebration. What could be a more fitting finale to Christmas dinner than Steamed Cranberry Pudding with Grand Marnier Sauce (page 328)? Crowned with a glistening glaze of berries and served with a fragrant orange-flavored sauce, this dessert resembles a pretty package, at the first taste of which we suspect even Scrooge might have smiled.

BASIC PUDDINGS

While cornstarch puddings may sound quite inelegant, we've all had them, and, we dare say, liked them. They are, in fact, the basic puddings. They are also what many of us remember looking forward to, when as youngsters we came home from school and were greeted by a wonderful portion of pudding.

Indeed the ingredients of puddings are basic: milk, egg yolks, sugar, cornstarch, butter, and flavorings. The dry ingredients are combined, the milk and egg yolks are whisked in, and the pan is put over heat. Herein lies the success of a cornstarch pudding: As the base is brought to a boil, it must be whisked constantly to achieve its creamy, smooth texture. Simple and satisfying. But don't underestimate the potential of basic pudding. It takes on quite another dimension, elegant and compelling, when combined as Chocolate Butterscotch Pudding Parfaits (page 316).

Our second basic pudding is tapioca, a much-maligned combination that despite its reputation has nonetheless managed to assert itself as a classic. No mean feat, considering that pearl tapioca is often described as fisheye in appearance! The tapioca in this pudding needs to soak overnight, cook for three hours at the lowest possible heat, and then be baked in layers with meringue in between and on top. Its creamy texture, somewhat similar to that of a long-baked rice pudding, is soothing. Its color is pale and pretty. Tapioca pudding, quite obviously, involves a certain amount of planning in advance. Perhaps this is why we don't avail ourselves of it more often. A pity, for it is one of the puddings our parents probably grew up on.

Our final basic pudding is a curious one—a true American classic. It has an even longer baking time than tapioca pudding: four hours! We are talking about Indian pudding, that renowned New England combination of cornmeal, molasses, and milk. We suspect that like in many early recipes, the batter was made and while some other dish was taking up the direct heat of the fire, the pan of cornmeal pudding was waiting on the side, just barely warmed by the coals. It cooked slowly and true and when it was done was properly appreciated. As life has quickened, so has the cooking time in other versions of this recipe. You will see it in some sources reduced to one hour, with the cooking of the cornmeal finished for the most part on top of the stove. We believe that a classic is a classic, and that the texture of a pudding baked in a very slow oven for four hours is a remarkably good reminder of our roots.

VANILLA CORNSTARCH PUDDING

Yield:
4 servings

Equipment:
four 1-cup ramekins
 or serving dishes

Cornstarch is a fine white starch made from ground dried corn. Although it has greater thickening power than all-purpose flour, it may break down after thickening if overstirred or overcooked.

The eggs in this recipe are added merely for flavor and richness. Many a cornstarch pudding does not call for eggs at all—and the results are still very good indeed.

½ cup sugar
¼ cup cornstarch
⅛ teaspoon salt
2¾ cups milk

2 egg yolks, beaten lightly
2 tablespoons unsalted butter
1½ teaspoons vanilla

In a heavy saucepan off the heat whisk together the sugar, cornstarch, and salt. Gradually whisk in the milk and beat in the egg yolks, combining the mixture well. Put the pan over moderate heat, bring the mixture to a boil, stirring constantly with the whisk, and boil it for 1 minute, whisking constantly. Remove the pan from the heat and stir in the butter and vanilla.

Divide the pudding among the ramekins and cover with rounds of buttered wax paper or plastic wrap directly touching the surfaces. Chill the puddings until ready to serve.

Variations:

CHOCOLATE CORNSTARCH PUDDING: Increase the sugar to ¾ cup and add 3 ounces chopped semisweet chocolate to the milk mixture. (The chocolate will melt completely while the milk is heating.) Reduce the vanilla to ½ teaspoon.

BUTTERSCOTCH CORNSTARCH PUDDING: Substitute 1 cup firmly packed

Chocolate Butterscotch Pudding Parfaits (below)

light brown sugar for the sugar and reduce the vanilla to 1 teaspoon.
CHOCOLATE BUTTERSCOTCH PUDDING PARFAITS: Spoon the chocolate and butterscotch puddings in layers into 6 parfait glasses, beginning with chocolate and ending with butterscotch and a dollop of chocolate pudding. Chill the parfaits, covered, for at least 1 hour or up to 5 hours.
   Photo above.

PEARL TAPIOCA PUDDING

Yield:
8 servings

Equipment:
double boiler
1½-quart baking dish
hand-held electric
  mixer

Tapioca is actually a starch that is obtained from the root of the cassava plant. Although tapioca now comes in quick-cooking granular form, this recipe calls for the old-fashioned but time-honored method of soaking the pearl or "fish-eye" tapioca overnight and cooking it over low heat for several hours. Despite the unappetizing description of pearl tapioca, the result is truly a delicious, textured, lemon-flavored pudding.

1 cup pearl tapioca (not the quick-
  cooking variety)
4 cups milk
5 large eggs, separated, at room
  temperature

juice of ½ lemon
the grated rind of 1 lemon
¾ cup sugar
½ teaspoon salt

In a bowl let the tapioca soak overnight (or for at least 4 hours) in 1 cup of the milk in the refrigerator.

Transfer the mixture to the top of the double boiler, add the remaining 3 cups milk, and cook the tapioca and milk over hot water and the lowest possible heat for about 3 hours, or until the pearls are transparent and tender.

Butter the baking dish and preheat the oven to 325° F.

In bowl beat the egg yolks with the lemon juice, lemon rind, and sugar until combined. Add a small amount of the hot tapioca to the beaten egg yolk mixture, then gradually add the mixture to the tapioca and combine well. Cook the mixture over low heat until slightly thickened, or until it coats the back of a spoon, about 3 to 5 minutes. Spread half of the mixture in the bottom of the baking dish. In a bowl with the mixer beat the egg whites until they hold stiff but not dry peaks. Spread half the egg whites over the tapioca mixture, cover with the remaining tapioca mixture, and finish with the remaining egg whites. Bake the pudding in the middle of the oven for 15 minutes, or until the meringue is browned. Serve the tapioca pudding either warm or chilled.

INDIAN PUDDING

Yield:
6 to 8 servings

Equipment:
2-quart baking dish

Indian pudding is a true American classic—New England's oldest and most traditional dessert. Corn was called "Indian corn" by the early settlers, so the dessert's name refers to its major ingredient, cornmeal. Note the pudding's long baking time. The dessert requires a little planning in advance, but the results are well worth it.

2 large eggs
½ cup unsulfured molasses
¼ cup sugar
½ stick (¼ cup) unsalted butter, cut into bits
½ teaspoon salt

¼ teaspoon double-acting baking powder
6 cups milk
1 cup yellow cornmeal (preferably stone-ground)
heavy cream as an accompaniment if desired

Butter the baking dish and preheat the oven to 275° F.

In a heavy saucepan combine the eggs, molasses, sugar, butter, salt, and baking powder. Beat in 2 cups of the milk and bring the mixture to a simmer over moderate heat, stirring. In a bowl combine the cornmeal and 1 cup of the milk. Add the mixture to the saucepan in a stream, beating, and cook, stirring, for 2 to 3 minutes, or until thickened. In another saucepan heat the remaining 3 cups milk. Add the hot milk to the cornmeal mixture in a stream, stirring, and combine well. Pour the batter into the baking dish and bake the pudding in the middle of the oven for 4 hours, or until it is firm and pulls away slightly from the sides of the dish. Serve the pudding warm with the heavy cream if desired.

OLD-FASHIONED PUDDINGS

We could have easily expanded this short collection of old-fashioned puddings that follow to include others in this chapter; puddings, in general, *are* old-fashioned. We decided, however, to group types of pudding separately, and so have a mere handful here. But what a wonderful handful it is! Each pudding is different: There is a very traditional rice pudding and a not-so-traditional one made with maple syrup. There is a splendid summer pudding dependent upon the bounty of the season. Last, there is a lovely sponge pudding, which others might call a cake pudding for its curious but ever-so-appealing two-layer texture.

Rice pudding—the essential ingredients are so simple: rice, sugar, milk or cream, and flavoring. It achieves its creamy, luscious consistency by a long bake in a slow oven; three hours, as long as that might seem, in fact, is not too long. And at the end of that cooking time, you have tender grains of rice in a sweet milky sauce. Dusted with cinnamon or nutmeg, rice pudding is the quintessential pudding, one that we have liked from grade school days when dessert and recess were what we waited for each midday.

Maple Rice Pudding (page 319) is even sweeter. An American invention, our recipe depends exclusively on heavy cream, with eggs and maple syrup added. It is best served warm, with more maple syrup on the side.

Summer pudding relies upon another substance altogether for its wonderful texture—bread. Used to line a mold or bowl, the bread absorbs the juice of a summer berry filling. If you are fortunate enough to find a supply of fresh red currants as is called for in our recipe, by all means use them. Otherwise, and this is one of the beauties of this kind of dessert, substitute another fresh fruit—blueberries or blackberries, for example. The pudding is then covered, weighted, and left to chill overnight. What you unmold next day is a simple but particularly satisfying and beautiful cold pudding. It is simultaneously tart but sweet, light but substantial.

Sponge pudding relies upon something else entirely for its texture. Eggs. A pudding base is made that combines butter, sugar, egg yolks, flour, flavorings, and milk. In fact, this is a custard. Stiffly beaten egg whites are folded in, and when baked, something remarkable happens. The air in the egg whites forces its way to the top, creating a cake-like layer, with the custard layer remaining on the bottom. Sponge pudding dates way back to the earliest of American cookbooks, and it remains popular to this day for good reason. Its texture is fascinating, fun, and fine. Do not be surprised, though, when you remove this pudding from the oven. It will have puffed. Upon contact with the air, it will fall immediately. It can be served warm or chilled, and is perfectly delicious either way.

Three different puddings, each still very much in the current vernacular, and each for very good reason.

OLD-FASHIONED RICE PUDDING

Yield:
4 servings

Equipment:
shallow 1½-quart
baking dish

This is the rice pudding we all remember and love. Baked slowly for several hours, the dessert achieves a creamy consistency made even more luscious by the addition of a little heavy cream.

4 cups milk
¼ cup long-grain rice
⅓ cup sugar
¼ teaspoon salt

a 1-inch piece of vanilla bean
3 tablespoons heavy cream
⅛ teaspoon cinnamon or freshly grated
*   nutmeg for garnish if desired*

Preheat the oven to 300° F. and butter the baking dish.

In a bowl combine the milk, rice, sugar, salt, and the vanilla bean and pour into the baking dish. Bake in the middle of the oven, stirring occasionally, for 3 hours, or until the rice is creamy. Remove the vanilla bean and, using a wooden spoon, whip the pudding lightly. Chill the pudding, covered, until cold and stir in the heavy cream. Dust with the cinnamon or nutmeg if desired.

Variation:

OLD-FASHIONED RAISIN RICE PUDDING: Stir in ½ cup raisins 2 hours into the baking time.

MAPLE RICE PUDDING

Yield:
6 to 8 servings

Equipment:
shallow 1½-quart
baking dish

½ cup dried currants
¼ cup dark rum
⅔ cup long-grain rice
3⅙ cups heavy cream
grated rind of 1 lemon

⅔ cup maple syrup
2 large eggs, beaten lightly
lightly whipped cream or maple syrup
*   as an accompaniment*

Butter the baking dish.

In a small bowl soak the currants in the rum for at least 30 minutes. In a large saucepan cook the rice in boiling salted water to cover for 20 minutes. Drain the rice in a sieve and rinse it under running cold water. Return the rice to the pan, add ⅔ cup heavy cream and the lemon rind, and cook over moderate heat, stirring occasionally, for 10 minutes, or until the cream is absorbed.

Preheat the oven to 350° F.

Remove the pan from the heat and stir in the remaining 2½ cups heavy cream, the maple syrup, currant mixture, and the eggs. Transfer the mixture to the baking dish and bake it in the middle of the oven for 45 to 50 minutes, or until golden. Serve the pudding warm with the whipped cream or maple syrup.

SUMMER PUDDING

Yield:
8 to 10 servings

Equipment:
2-quart mold or bowl
2- or 3-pound weight

Fresh red currants are considered by some to be a crucial ingredient in summer puddings, reinforcing the flavor of the other fruits, in this case raspberries. In season from December through February, fresh currants are available in specialty produce markets.

Any seasonal fruit could be used for this summer pudding as long as it provides enough juice to color the bread. Simply substitute about two quarts of blackberries, cherries, or a mixture of fruits, including red currants or, if you are lucky, loganberries.

approximately 22 slices of very thin homemade-type white bread, crusts removed
3 pints raspberries
8 ounces (about 1¾ cups) red currants

¾ cup sugar
blueberries for garnish if desired
whipped cream as an accompaniment if desired

Line the sides of the mold or bowl with overlapping slices of bread, trimming as necessary. Cut a round of bread to fit the bottom of the mold and press it into the bottom. The bread should completely cover the mold.

In a saucepan combine the raspberries, red currants, and sugar and cook the mixture over moderately high heat for 4 minutes. Transfer the fruit to the bread-lined mold with a slotted spoon, pour in the juice, and cover with a layer of bread. Cover the mold with a round of wax paper cut to fit the inside of the mold and put a plate that fits the inside of the mold on the wax paper. Weight the pudding and chill overnight.

Remove the weight, plate, and wax paper, run a thin knife around the edge of the mold to loosen it, and invert a large chilled serving plate over the mold. Invert the pudding onto the plate, garnish with the fresh blueberries, and serve with whipped cream.

Variation:

BLUEBERRY SUMMER PUDDING: This variation uses a 1½-quart deep mold or bowl and yields 6 to 8 servings. Follow the same procedure for lining the mold with bread, using about 18 slices of bread, instead of 22. In a saucepan combine 1½ quarts blueberries and ¾ cup sugar. Cook the mixture, stirring, for about 4 minutes. Transfer the fruit to the bread-lined mold, pour in the juice, and cover the fruit with a layer of bread. Follow the same weighting, chilling, and serving directions above. Garnish the pudding with fresh berries—raspberries, blackberries, or blueberries—and serve with heavy cream.

LEMON SPONGE PUDDING

Yield:
6 servings

Equipment:
1½-quart glass soufflé dish
hand-held electric mixer
larger baking pan for waterbath

Sponge pudding, cake pudding, or pudding cake—different names for the same delicious, old-fashioned, and much sought-after dessert recipe. It is comfort food of the highest order, answering a host of pudding and cake needs. During baking this pudding separates, forming a custard-like sauce on the bottom and a spongecake layer on top.

½ stick (¼ cup) unsalted butter, softened
¾ cup granulated sugar
3 large eggs, separated
⅓ cup fresh lemon juice
⅓ cup all-purpose flour

1 tablespoon grated lemon rind
¼ teaspoon salt plus a pinch
1½ cups milk
pinch of cream of tartar
¼ cup confectioners' sugar for garnish if desired

Butter the soufflé dish and preheat the oven to 350° F.

In a large bowl with the mixer cream together the butter and sugar until light. Beat in the egg yolks, one at a time, beating well after each addition. Add the lemon juice, flour, lemon rind, and the ¼ teaspoon salt and combine well. Add the milk in a stream, beating, and combine the mixture well. In a bowl with the mixer beat the egg whites with the pinch of salt until frothy, add the cream of tartar, and beat until they hold stiff peaks (see illustrations page 238). Stir one fourth of the whites into the lemon mixture, fold in the remaining whites gently but thoroughly, and transfer the mixture to the soufflé dish. Put the dish in the larger pan, add enough boiling water to the pan to reach halfway up the sides of the dish, and bake the dessert in the middle of the oven for 50 minutes, or until the pudding is puffed and the top is golden. If desired sift the confectioners' sugar over the top. Serve the dessert warm or chilled.

BREAD AND BUTTER PUDDINGS

Bread and butter pudding is of English origin, but like many a good thing it has traveled elsewhere, been taken to other shores, and we all are the better for it. This simple, homey pudding couples two very gratifying components—buttered bread and custard. The bread soaks in the egg and milk or cream mixture, then the whole is baked, and there is this wonderful melding of flavors with a soft, soothing texture. It is comfort food of the first order and luckily for us comes in any number of varieties. Some bread puddings contain raisins and currants, such as the one we are calling Basic (page 322); others are made with French bread and are served with whiskey sauce, which we've named Creole (page 324); still others combine fruit, like Lemon and Blueberry Bread Pudding (page 323), which has an additional fillip: a glaze of tart orange marmalade.

Bread pudding becomes transcendental when made with chocolate brioche and chocolate custard as the one on page 325 is. No longer the easy, happy conclusion to a Sunday-night supper, this bread pudding is right for guests and would serve becomingly as the last course of an elegant dinner. Furthermore, it is accompanied by hot fudge sauce. Bread and butter puddings in general are very good. This last is nothing short of superb.

BASIC BREAD AND BUTTER PUDDING

Yield:
6 servings

Equipment:
8-inch square baking
  pan
deeper baking pan for
  waterbath

Bread pudding can be prepared with any type of bread—Italian, or French, as well as corn muffins, or even croutons. A homey, comforting, dessert, bread pudding can also be dressed up with remarkable results. See Chocolate Brioche Bread Pudding on page 325.

The versatility of bread pudding extends not only to its ingredients but also to its shape. The pudding given in our variation is prepared in a loaf pan and can actually be sliced and served with a topping or an accompanying sauce. The variation calls for Malmsey Madeira, the sweetest of all Madeira wines, full-bodied and fragrant.

12 slices of homemade-type day-old
  white bread, crusts removed
1 stick (½ cup) unsalted butter,
  softened
2 tablespoons golden raisins
2 tablespoons dried currants
1 tablespoon chopped Candied Orange
  Peel (page 522)

1 teaspoon cinnamon sugar
  (page 541)
5 large eggs
2 cups milk
2 cups heavy cream
½ cup sugar

Butter the baking pan.

Spread the bread with the butter, halve each slice diagonally, and arrange one third of the pieces in the pan. Sprinkle the bread with the golden raisins, currants, orange peel, and the cinnamon sugar. Continue making layers in the same manner, finishing with a layer of the bread.

In a bowl beat the eggs until they are combined. In a saucepan scald the milk and the cream with the sugar and pour it in a stream over the eggs, stirring. Pour the custard over the bread and let the mixture stand, covered loosely, at room temperature for at least 1 hour or chilled overnight.

Preheat the oven to 350° F.

Set the dish in the larger baking pan, add enough hot water to the larger pan to reach halfway up the sides of the baking pan, and bake the pudding in the middle of the oven for 1 hour, or until it is puffed and the top is crisp and browned. Serve the pudding warm.

Variation:

MADEIRA BREAD PUDDING: Butter a loaf pan, 9 by 5 by 2½ inches. Spread 9 bread slices, crusts removed, with ½ stick unsalted butter, softened. Cut the bread into ½-inch cubes and combine the cubes and 1 cup raisins in the loaf pan. In a bowl whisk together 2 cups milk, 3 large eggs, ¾ cup sugar, ⅓ to ½ cup Malmsey Madeira, or to taste, 1 teaspoon grated lemon rind, ½ teaspoon cinnamon, and ¼ teaspoon vanilla. Ladle the mixture over the bread and let the mixture stand, covered loosely, at room temperature for at least 1 hour or chilled overnight. Follow the same baking procedure, reducing the baking time to 45 minutes. Let stand in the pan on a rack for 10 minutes before serving.

LEMON AND BLUEBERRY BREAD AND BUTTER PUDDING

Yield:
6 servings

Equipment:
8-inch square baking
  pan
larger baking pan for
  waterbath
pastry brush

*12 slices of homemade-type white
  bread, crusts removed*
*½ stick (¼ cup) unsalted butter,
  softened*
1½ cups blueberries, picked over
2½ cups milk
⅓ cup strained fresh lemon juice

2 teaspoons grated lemon rind
3 large eggs, beaten lightly
¾ cup sugar
3 tablespoons Cointreau
pinch of salt
½ cup orange marmalade

Butter the baking pan.

Spread the bread with the butter and arrange 4 slices, buttered side down, in one layer in the baking pan. Sprinkle the bread with half the blueberries, arrange another layer of bread, buttered side down, over the berries, and sprinkle the remaining berries on top. Cover the berries with the remaining bread, buttered side down.

In a bowl whisk together the milk, lemon juice, lemon rind, eggs, sugar, 1 tablespoon of the Cointreau, and the salt and ladle the mixture over the bread. Let the mixture stand, covered loosely, at room temperature for at least 1 hour or chilled overnight.

Preheat the oven to 350° F.

In a small saucepan melt the marmalade with the remaining 2 tablespoons Cointreau and brush the top of the pudding with the mixture. Put the baking pan in the larger pan, add enough hot water to the larger pan to reach halfway up the sides of the baking pan, and bake the pudding in the middle of the oven for 40 minutes. Serve the pudding warm or at room temperature.

Creole Bread Pudding (below) with Whiskey Sauce (page 496)

CREOLE BREAD PUDDING

Yield:
8 to 10 servings

Equipment:
2½- to 2¾-quart soufflé dish

1⅓ cup raisins
⅔ cup whiskey
1¼ loaves of day-old French bread, cut into ½-inch cubes (enough cubes to measure 8 cups)
6 cups milk
5 large eggs

⅔ cup sugar
¾ stick (6 tablespoons) unsalted butter, melted and cooled
2 teaspoons vanilla
1 teaspoon salt
1 recipe Whiskey Sauce (page 496) as an accompaniment

Butter the soufflé dish.
In a bowl macerate the raisins in the whiskey. In a large bowl combine the bread cubes with the milk and let stand at room temperature, stirring occasionally, for at least 2 hours, or until the crusts are very soft. In a bowl beat together the eggs, sugar, melted butter, vanilla, and salt. Add the

mixture to the bread mixture with the raisins and whiskey and stir until well combined. Transfer the mixture to the soufflé dish and chill, covered, overnight.

Let the mixture come to room temperature. Preheat the oven to 375° F.

Stir the mixture and bake it in the middle of the oven for 1½ hours, or until the edge is puffed and golden brown. (The center will not have risen as much.) Serve the pudding warm or at room temperature with the whiskey sauce.

Photo opposite.

CHOCOLATE BRIOCHE BREAD PUDDING

Yield:
6 servings

Equipment:
8-inch square baking pan
larger baking pan for waterbath

This bread pudding is a superb combination of buttered chocolate brioche and chocolate custard and would make an excellent dessert to serve at a dinner party or as a birthday treat for a chocolate lover. The firm texture and rich eggy flavor of the brioche provide the perfect complement to the chocolate custard and elevate a simple bread pudding to a new height.

8 slices of Chocolate Brioche (about 8 ounces, page 209)
½ stick (¼ cup) unsalted butter, softened
2 cups milk
3 ounces semisweet chocolate, cut into bits
3 ounces unsweetened chocolate, cut into bits

1 tablespoon vanilla
3 large eggs
2 egg yolks
1 cup sugar
1 recipe Hot Fudge Sauce (page 500) or lightly whipped cream as an accompaniment

Butter the baking pan and preheat the oven to 350° F.

Spread the brioche slices with the butter and arrange the slices, buttered side down, in two layers in the baking pan.

In a saucepan scald the milk, add both the semisweet and unsweetened chocolate, and stir until the chocolate is melted and the mixture is smooth. Stir in the vanilla. In a bowl combine the whole eggs and egg yolks with the sugar and whisk in the chocolate mixture, whisking until the sugar is dissolved. Ladle the mixture over the brioche and let stand, covered loosely, at room temperature for at least 1 hour or chilled overnight.

Put the baking pan in the larger pan, add enough hot water to the larger pan to reach halfway up the sides of the baking pan, and bake the pudding in the middle of the oven for 30 to 35 minutes, or until a skewer inserted in the center comes out clean. Serve the pudding warm with the fudge sauce or whipped cream.

STEAMED PUDDINGS

Steamed puddings, inherited from our English forebears as possible variations on their much–beloved theme of Christmas pudding, harken back to another era. Slow to cook and festive in appearance, they are almost always reserved for the holidays, when only something Old World and reminiscent of times past will do. Moreover, many steamed puddings are accompanied by hard sauce, and it is not unusual for hard sauce and Christmas dinner to go hand in hand.

That association aside, steamed puddings should be served throughout the cold weather months. They are substantial and warming, perfect for any snowy or bleak winter eve. Furthermore, and this cannot be said often about desserts in general, steamed puddings are seasonal. No one should be considering turning on the back burner in 90 degree heat to ready a steamed pudding, not even with air-conditioning. Similarly, spring or the return of fair weather is not a time for steamed pudding, either, and the reason we say this has much to do with a steamed pudding's ingredients. Take, for example, our Steamed Cranberry Pudding with Grand Marnier Sauce (page 328). It is redolent with autumnal spices, contains three cups of bread crumbs, and is glazed and sauced. Decidedly delicious, but hardly the proper ending to a dinner of dandelion green salad, poached salmon, and asparagus.

Besides dropping temperatures, what you will need to make a successful steamed pudding is, to begin with, a pudding mold with a lid, available at specialty kitchenware stores. You will also need a heavy kettle fitted with a lid and a rack or two. Do not feel you have to buy a specific kettle. As the illustration below demonstrates, as long as the kettle is deep it will do: A canning kettle, for example, is ideal. A stockpot will also do. And if you do not have two racks, improvise one by removing the top and bottom of a used clean aluminum can. Use that ring as a rack.

You butter your mold well, you make your pudding batter, and you

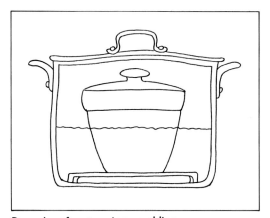

Procedure for steaming a pudding

spoon it into the mold. Know that the batter will fill only about two thirds of the container, the remaining space in the mold reserved for the expansion of the pudding as it steams. You cover the mold with its lid. So far, so good. Now on to the actual steaming process.

There is clearly a logical and careful progression to putting a pudding into a kettle for steaming. Otherwise you risk burning yourself rather badly. Place the rack in the kettle and add water to the kettle to reach approximately three inches up the sides of the mold. You will have to gauge this level by eye. Cover the kettle and bring the water to a boil.

Then gently stand the mold upright on the rack, the point here being that the pudding actually sits in the boiling water (see illustration opposite). When we think of other steaming processes, the Chinese method, for example, this is not the case: Water never touches what is going to be steamed. Cover the kettle and steam the pudding as directed, maintaining the water at a brisk boil. There should be bubbles rising but they should not be violent. Because of the length of time a steamed pudding actually cooks, you will need to check the level of the water in the kettle for evaporation. Therefore, as the pudding steams, keep a pan of hot water ready to replenish the kettle whenever necessary.

At the end of the suggested cooking time, remove the mold from the kettle to a second rack to cool. You will probably be best served in doing this by wearing a pair of pot-holder mittens. The kettle will be hot, the mold will be hot, and there will still be steam. At this point, if the pudding remains in the mold, it will stay warm for several hours—a useful bit of information if you are thinking about preparing the dessert ahead of time. You can, in fact, plan to serve the first course as well as the entrée and your steamed pudding will still be warm.

■　■　■

There is variety among the four steamed puddings we have included in this brief selection. Our Steamed Cranberry Pudding with Grand Marnier Sauce (page 328) is unique in that it contains bread crumbs as its base. Steamed Orange Pudding (page 329), fresh with orange juice and orange and lemon rind, contains flour as its main ingredient, as does Steamed Ginger Pudding (page 331), which has a startlingly large but correct amount of ground coriander in it. Finally, Cabinet Pudding (page 332) combines *génoise,* kumquats, and candied and dried fruits, these last arranged in a lovely decorative pattern around the sides of the mold.

Clearly, invention is part of the fun of steamed puddings. No two are alike. As we have mentioned, even though flour is the main ingredient in both the orange and ginger puddings, the orange pudding contains eggs, while the ginger pudding does not. Cabinet Pudding relies on cake as its base, while Cranberry Pudding boasts bread crumbs and ground nuts. What we are getting at is simple: While these are all steamed puddings, there is, in fact, great diversity among them, not only in flavor but in texture.

STEAMED CRANBERRY PUDDING WITH GRAND MARNIER SAUCE

Yield:
8 servings

Equipment:
2-quart steamed pudding mold with a tube and lid (available at specialty kitchenware stores), or a double layer of aluminum foil and kitchen string
food processor fitted with steel blade
heavy kettle fitted with lid
low rack to fit kettle
pastry brush
candy thermometer

This is a truly spectacular and festive steamed pudding beautifully garnished with cranberries and served with Grand Marnier sauce.

FOR THE PUDDING

3¾ cups cranberries, picked over
½ cup ground blanched almonds
1¾ cups plus 2 tablespoons sugar
3 tablespoons all-purpose flour
¾ teaspoon cinnamon
¼ teaspoon ground allspice
¼ teaspoon ground ginger
3 cups fine dry bread crumbs (for procedure page 550)

1½ sticks (¾ cup) unsalted butter, melted and cooled
⅔ cup milk
3 large eggs, beaten lightly
1 tablespoon double-acting baking powder
½ teaspoon salt

FOR THE GLAZE

1 cup cranberry juice
1 cup sugar

pinch of salt
1 cup cranberries, picked over

FOR THE SAUCE

1 cup sugar
1 cup heavy cream
1 stick (½ cup) unsalted butter, cut into bits

pinch of salt
1 tablespoon Grand Marnier
1 tablespoon fresh lemon juice, or to taste

a small sprig of ivy for decoration if desired

Make the pudding:

The pudding may be prepared 1 day in advance, chilled overnight, and reheated in the kettle in the same manner until it is heated through.

Butter the pudding mold, line the sides of the mold with wax paper, and butter and flour the inside of the mold.

In the food processor chop the cranberries coarse, transfer them to a bowl, and stir in the almonds. Sprinkle the mixture with 1 cup plus 2 tablespoons of the sugar, the flour, cinnamon, allspice, and the ginger and combine the mixture well. In another bowl combine the bread crumbs, butter, milk, eggs, baking powder, salt, and the remaining ¾ cup sugar and stir the mixture into the cranberry mixture.

Spoon the batter into the prepared mold, a little at a time, rapping the mold on a hard surface as it is filled to eliminate any air bubbles. (The mold will be about two thirds full.) Cover the mold tightly with the lid and tie the mold in a towel wrung out in cold water and floured. Tie a knot at the top of the towel to facilitate removal of the mold from the kettle.

Set the rack in the bottom of the kettle and add enough water to reach 3 inches up the side of the mold. Bring the water to a boil and keep it at a brisk but not rolling boil, covered with the lid of the kettle.

Place the mold on the rack and cover the kettle. Steam the pudding for 2 hours, checking occasionally to make certain the water is at a brisk but not rolling boil and adding more water if necessary (see illustration page 326). When a skewer inserted in the center of the pudding comes out with crumbs adhering to it, the pudding is done. Transfer the mold to a rack. (The pudding will stay warm in the mold, covered, for several hours.)

Make the glaze: In a deep heavy saucepan cook the cranberry juice, sugar, and the salt over moderate heat, stirring and washing down any sugar crystals clinging to the sides of the pan with the brush dipped in cold water until the sugar is dissolved. Bring the mixture to a boil and boil it, gently swirling the pan, until the candy thermometer registers 250° F. Add the cranberries, remove the pan from the heat, and let the glaze cool. Transfer the glaze to a small bowl and chill it, covered, until ready to serve.

Make the sauce: In a saucepan cook the sugar, cream, butter, and the salt over moderate heat, stirring, until the butter is melted and the mixture is smooth. Remove the pan from the heat, stir in the Grand Marnier and the lemon juice, and let the sauce cool. Transfer the sauce to a small bowl and chill it, covered, until it is thick.

The glaze and the sauce may be prepared several days in advance. Just before serving, unmold the warm pudding onto a serving plate, pour the cranberry glaze over it, and decorate it with the ivy sprig if desired. Serve the pudding, cut into slices, with the Grand Marnier sauce.

Photo on page 330.

STEAMED ORANGE PUDDING

Yield:
6 servings

Equipment:
1-quart steamed pudding mold with a lid (available at specialty kitchenware stores), or a double layer of aluminum foil and kitchen string
heavy kettle fitted with lid
2 racks, one to fit kettle

This beautifully molded pudding adds elegance as well as tradition to a holiday feast. The combination has a silkier texture than many other steamed puddings on account of the use of butter.

1 stick (½ cup) unsalted butter, softened
1 cup sugar
4 large eggs
2 cups all-purpose flour
2 teaspoons double-acting baking powder

½ cup fresh orange juice
1½ tablespoons grated orange rind
1½ tablespoons grated lemon rind
1 recipe Orange Hard Sauce (page 495) as an accompaniment

Butter the pudding mold well.

In a large bowl cream the butter, add the sugar, a little at a time, beating, and beat the mixture until fluffy. Add the eggs, one at a time, beating well after each addition. Into a bowl sift together the flour and baking powder and add the mixture to the butter mixture alternately with the orange juice. Stir in the orange and lemon rinds.

Set the rack in the bottom of the kettle and add enough water to reach 3

Steamed Cranberry Pudding with Grand Marnier Sauce (page 328)

inches up the side of the mold. Bring the water to a boil and keep it at a brisk but not rolling boil, covered with the lid of the kettle.

Spoon the batter into the mold and cover the mold with the lid. Place the mold in the kettle, cover the kettle, and steam the pudding for 2 hours, checking occasionally to make certain the water is at a brisk but not rolling boil and adding more water if necessary (see illustration page 326). Remove the mold from the kettle, remove the lid, and let the pudding stand in the mold on the second rack for 15 minutes. Turn the mold gently onto its side, rap it gently all around to loosen the pudding, and unmold the pudding carefully onto a serving plate. Serve the pudding warm with the orange hard sauce.

STEAMED GINGER PUDDING

Yield:
8 servings

Equipment:
2-quart steamed pudding mold with a lid (available at specialty kitchenware stores), or double layer of aluminum foil and kitchen string
2 racks, one to fit kettle
heavy kettle fitted with lid

The pudding may be made up to 1 month in advance and kept wrapped tightly in foil and frozen. Reheat the frozen pudding, wrapped in the foil, in a preheated 325° F. oven for 40 to 45 minutes, or until a metal tester inserted in the center for 5 minutes comes out warm.

1 stick (½ cup) unsalted butter, softened
½ cup unsulfured dark molasses
½ cup plus 2 tablespoons sugar
1 teaspoon baking soda dissolved in 2 tablespoons hot water
2 cups all-purpose flour

½ teaspoon salt
1½ tablespoons ground ginger
1 tablespoon ground coriander
¾ cup cold water
1 recipe Ginger Applesauce (page 473) and whipped cream as accompaniments if desired

Butter the mold well.

Set the rack for the kettle in the bottom of the kettle and add enough water to reach 3 inches up the side of the mold. Bring the water to a boil and keep it at a brisk but not rolling boil, covered with the lid of the kettle.

While the water is coming to a boil, in a bowl cream the butter, add the molasses, ½ cup of the sugar, and the baking soda mixture, and beat the mixture until it is combined well. In another bowl with a fork stir the flour, salt, ginger, and the coriander until the mixture is combined, add the mixture to the butter mixture in batches, beating, and beat the batter until it is combined well. Add the water and beat well.

Spoon the batter into the mold and cover the mold with the lid. Place the mold in the kettle, cover the kettle, and steam the pudding for 2 hours, checking occasionally to make certain the water is at a brisk but not rolling boil and adding more water if necessary (see illustration page 326). Remove the mold from the kettle, remove the lid, and let the pudding stand in the mold on the second rack for 10 minutes. Turn the mold gently onto its side, rap it gently all around to loosen the pudding, and slide the pudding carefully onto a serving plate. While the pudding is still warm pat the top and sides gently with the remaining 2 tablespoons sugar and let the pudding cool completely. Slice the pudding thin and serve it with the applesauce and the whipped cream if desired.

CABINET PUDDING

Yield:
6 servings

Equipment:
1½-quart charlotte
   mold
rack to fit kettle
heavy kettle fitted
   with lid

Gourmet's version of the traditional English cabinet pudding is a lovely combination of orange liqueur-soaked spongecake, custard, preserved kumquats, and candied fruits steamed in a charlotte mold.

⅓ cup thinly sliced candied cherries
3 tablespoons kirsch
⅓ cup dried currants
3 tablespoons orange-flavored liqueur
   plus an additional ¼ cup orange-
   flavored liqueur combined with
   2 tablespoons water
⅓ cup seeded and pithed preserved
   kumquats, sliced thin (available at
   specialty foods shops)

a 9-inch vanilla génoise layer (page
   22), made 24 hours in advance
3 large eggs
2 egg yolks
¼ cup sugar
1½ cups milk, scalded
½ cup heavy cream, scalded
Vanilla Ice Cream (page 349) as an
   accompaniment if desired

Butter the charlotte mold well and put a buttered round of wax paper cut to fit the bottom of the mold in place. Chill the mold.

In a small bowl combine the cherries with the kirsch. Put the currants in a small saucepan, add water to cover, and bring the water to a boil. Drain the currants and in another small bowl combine them with the 3 tablespoons orange-flavored liqueur. Drain the cherries and currants, reserving the kirsch and liqueur, pat them dry with paper towels, and press 1 tablespoon each of the cherries and currants onto the bottom and sides of the mold in a decorative pattern. Chill the mold.

Trim the brown edges from the *génoise*, slice enough cake to line the mold, plus some additional slices, and break the remaining cake into cubes. Put the cake on a rack and sprinkle it with the liqueur mixture.

In a bowl beat the eggs, egg yolks, and sugar until the mixture is very light and fluffy. Stir in the scalded milk, scalded cream, and the reserved kirsch and liqueur. Line the mold with the cake slices, spoon in ½ cup of the egg mixture, and sprinkle the mixture with some of the fruits and cake cubes. Add the remaining ingredients, layering them in the same manner, and cover the mold with a buttered round of foil, pressing the edges down well. Put a moistened dish towel, wrung out and dusted lightly with flour on one side, over the foil, floured side down. Secure the towel with kitchen string, running the string under the handles of the mold, and tie the diagonally opposite corners of the towel over the mold to form a handle. Put the mold on a rack in the kettle and add enough boiling water to reach two thirds of the way up the sides of the mold. Return the water to a boil, cover the kettle with the lid, and steam the pudding over very low heat for 1½ hours (see illustration page 326). Remove the mold from the kettle and remove the towel and foil. Let the pudding cool for 10 minutes, unmold it onto a serving dish, and serve it with the ice cream if desired.

Photo on page 312.

CUSTARDS

When we think of custard, most of us smile to ourselves and sigh, hmmn, *crème caramel*. Many's the occasion we have had it and loved it. It can truly be called the quintessential dessert.

Custard, however, has many other guises. This simple yet far from innocent combination of eggs, milk or cream, and sugar thickened over heat manifests itself as the basis of pastry cream, for one; ice cream, for another. On its own it can appear creamy, as in *pots de crème*; frothy, as in *zabaglione*; or complementary, as in tipsy parson.

A smooth custard is a successful custard, and, as a consequence, one caution should be taken when preparing it: Be sure to stir it as directed, otherwise the eggs will cook until firm. Secondly, many a custard bakes in a waterbath, a manner of consistently moderating the heat of the oven to the interior temperature of the custard. While this step might strike some as an inconvenience, it almost assures you the perfect texture.

BAKED CUSTARDS

Although there are recipes that call for the classic custard combination of eggs, milk, sugar, and flavorings to be made on top of the stove, we have confined our selection of custards to only those that are baked. Included among this grouping, besides several very basic and delicious ones, are caramel custards and *pots de crème*, or small custards.

Once again, we have the French to thank for a splendid idea: caramel custard, or *crème renversée au caramel*. The caramel lining the mold not only beautifully colors the custard when it is unmolded, but also adds a wonderful rich sugar flavor and glistening appearance to the dessert. Like any sugar syrup, the caramel should be heated to the proper point, designated in the recipes that follow by color, usually deep amber. If by chance you *do* go beyond this point with your syrup, know that it has burned and will be very bitter in flavor if you decide to use it, which is not recommended. (For information on the stages of sugar syrup, see "Meringues," page 241.) At that juncture you will want to line your molds quickly but very carefully, as the syrup will be over 300° F. We would advise wearing kitchen mittens while doing this. Our selection of caramel custards includes a basic one, an orange one, and pumpkin ginger, a superb finish to Thanksgiving dinner.

As you will notice in the recipes that follow, some baked custards are made with milk, others with half-and-half, and still others with heavy cream. The silkier the texture of the finished product, usually the higher the fat content in the liquid. Small Vanilla Custards (page 338), or *pots de crème,* are made with heavy cream. If you desire a less rich effect, by all means substitute milk.

BAKED CUSTARD

Yield:
6 servings

Equipment:
1-quart baking dish
larger baking pan for
 waterbath

Several of the following recipes were written by James Beard in 1970. As an accomplished cook, Mr. Beard had his own methods for doing things and often presented recipes in a simplified but always successful form. The recipes for Baked Custard, Caramel Custard, Pots de Crème, and Crème Brûlée are good examples. Note that in some instances we give alternative methods for the less experienced cook. Mr. Beard considered this recipe for baked custard, when properly made, one of the most perfect of desserts.

5 egg yolks
5 tablespoons sugar
the grated zest of 1 lemon
pinch of salt

2 cups milk
freshly grated nutmeg or mace if desired
whipped cream if desired

Preheat the oven to 325° F.

In a heavy enameled or stainless steel saucepan (or in a bowl) combine the egg yolks and sugar. Add the lemon zest and salt. In a saucepan heat the milk to the boiling point, stirring from time to time to prevent scorching. Drizzle the hot milk into the egg mixture, stirring vigorously with a whisk or wooden spatula until the mixture is well blended. Stir in the nutmeg or mace to taste. Pour the custard into the baking dish and put the dish in the larger pan half filled with hot water. (An easier method would be to place the baking dish in the larger pan and then add enough hot water to the pan to reach halfway up the sides of the dish.) Bake in the middle of the oven for 30 to 35 minutes. Do not overbake the custard. It will continue to cook after it is removed from the oven and on no account let the water in the pan boil. If it seems on the verge of boiling, add some cold water to it. Serve the custard chilled with the whipped cream if desired.

Variations:

VANILLA CUSTARD: If you wish, you may substitute vanilla flavor for the lemon flavor. In place of the lemon zest add a 1½-inch piece of vanilla bean to the milk as you heat it or stir in 2 teaspoons vanilla to the custard before it is baked.

If you wish to make a larger custard, you can double the recipe by using 10 egg yolks, 10 tablespoons sugar, and 4 cups milk, with the flavorings of your choice.

CARAMEL CUSTARD

Yield:
6 servings

Equipment:
1½-quart charlotte
   mold, or an
   earthenware,
   porcelain, or
   enameled metal
   baking dish
pastry brush
larger baking pan for
   waterbath

This dessert is more often referred to by its French name *crème renversée au caramel,* literally reversed caramel cream. It is a custard baked in a caramel-lined mold (either one large or several smaller individual molds), chilled, and inverted for serving. Note Mr. Beard's tempting variation of this recipe incorporating the syrup into the custard.

FOR THE CARAMEL

½ cup superfine granulated sugar   *2 to 3 tablespoons water*

FOR THE CUSTARD

2 large eggs   *pinch of salt*
4 egg yolks   *2¼ cups milk*
6 tablespoons granulated sugar   *a 1½-inch piece of vanilla bean*

Preheat the oven to 350° F. Heat the mold or the dish in which you will bake the caramel custard. (It may be kept warm in the pan of hot water in which you will bake the custard.)

Make the caramel: If you are using a charlotte mold for the caramel custard, make the syrup in the mold. If not, make it in a saucepan and transfer it to the baking dish. In a small heavy saucepan combine the superfine sugar and the water, cook the mixture over moderate heat, washing down any sugar crystals clinging to the sides of the pan with the brush dipped in cold water until the sugar is dissolved, and boil it, gently swirling the pan, until it is a pale golden caramel color. (Take care not to let the sugar syrup go beyond a deep caramel or amber color or it will begin to burn and become bitter. This is especially true when using superfine sugar as it caramelizes quickly.)

To line a mold or individual molds with caramel it is necessary to work rapidly but very carefully as the temperature of the caramel will be over 300° F. As soon as the sugar syrup reaches the desired color, remove the pan from the heat and carefully pour the syrup in a stream into the mold. Tip and swirl the mold to coat the bottom and sides evenly. (It is advisable to hold the mold with pot holders.) When the syrup stops running, turn the mold upside down onto a piece of wax paper to cool slightly and to let any excess syrup run out.

Make the custard: In a heavy saucepan or in a heatproof bowl combine the eggs, egg yolks, granulated sugar, and the salt. In another pan heat the milk with the vanilla bean until it comes to the boiling point, stirring occasionally to prevent scorching. Drizzle the hot milk into the egg mixture, whisking vigorously or stirring with a wooden spatula. Strain the custard into the caramelized mold or dish and put the dish in the pan half filled with hot water. (An easier method would be to place the mold in the larger pan and then add enough hot water to the pan to reach halfway up the sides of the mold.) Bake the custard in the middle of the oven for 35 minutes, or until a knife inserted in the center comes out clean, or the custard offers a very light resistance when you tap the top gently with your finger.

Caramel custard is usually served unmolded, either warm or chilled. To unmold it, loosen the edges with a sharp knife, put a serving plate over the top, invert the dish, and turn the custard out onto the plate. If there is a good deal of caramel left in the mold, add a small amount of hot water to the mold to soften the caramel and pour the remaining caramel over the custard.

Variation:

CARAMEL CUSTARD WITH CHESTNUT PURÉE: Instead of lining the mold with the caramel, incorporate it into the custard. Prepare the custard as above, stir in the caramel, and pour the mixture into a 1½-quart buttered and sugared ring mold. Bake in the waterbath as above. Chill, unmold, and fill the center with a purée of chestnuts topped with sweetened whipped cream flavored with 2 tablespoons Cognac. Use canned sweetened chestnut purée, or drain chestnuts in syrup and put them through a food mill or potato ricer.

ORANGE CUSTARDS

Yield:
12 servings

Equipment:
twelve ½-cup custard cups
large baking pan for waterbath

4 cups milk
1 cup sugar
the rind of 2 oranges
8 egg yolks

4 large eggs
¾ teaspoon salt
2 tablespoons orange-flavored liqueur

Preheat the oven to 325° F.

In a heavy stainless steel or enameled saucepan combine the milk, sugar, and the orange rind and bring the mixture just to the boiling point over moderately low heat, stirring until the sugar is dissolved. In a large bowl beat lightly the egg yolks and the eggs, strain the milk mixture over them, stirring, and stir the mixture until it is just combined. Stir in the salt and the liqueur and strain the custard into a large pitcher. Pour the custard into the custard cups, filling each three quarters full, and arrange the cups in the baking pan. Add enough hot water to the pan to reach halfway up the sides of the cups and bake the custards, covered with a baking sheet, in the middle of the oven for 25 minutes, or until they are just set. Remove the cups from the pan and let the custards cool. Serve the custards at room temperature or chilled.

Variation:

ORANGE CARAMEL CUSTARDS: In a heavy skillet combine 1½ cups sugar, ½ cup water, and a pinch of cream of tartar. Heat the mixture over moderately low heat, washing down any sugar crystals clinging to the sides of the pan with a brush dipped in cold water until the sugar is dissolved, and cook the mixture over moderate heat, gently swirling the pan, until it turns a deep caramel. Pour the caramel into the twelve ½-cup custard cups, tilting the cups to coat the bottoms evenly. Pour the custard mixture into the cups and bake the custards as above. Remove the custards from the baking pan, let them cool, and chill them, covered, overnight. Run a thin knife around the edge of each custard, invert a dessert plate over each cup, and invert the custards onto the plates. Garnish the custards with blanched julienne strips of orange peel.

PUMPKIN GINGER CARAMEL CUSTARDS

Yield:
8 servings

Equipment:
pastry brush
eight ¾-cup ramekins
baking pan for
  waterbath

A wonderful Thanksgiving offering—individual caramel custards with just the right blend of pumpkin and fresh gingerroot. For those not devoted to pumpkin pie, these may just be the answer.

FOR THE CARAMEL
1 cup sugar
½ cup water

¼ cup peeled and minced gingerroot

FOR THE CUSTARD
2 cups half-and-half
4 large eggs, beaten lightly
1½ cups canned pumpkin purée

½ cup sugar
¼ teaspoon salt

Make the caramel:
In a small heavy saucepan combine the sugar, water, and gingerroot, cook the mixture over moderate heat, washing down any sugar crystals clinging to the sides of the pan with the brush dipped in cold water until the sugar is dissolved, and boil it, gently swirling the pan, for 5 minutes. Strain the mixture into a bowl, reserving the gingerroot, and return the syrup to the saucepan. Cook the syrup over moderate heat, gently swirling the pan, until it is a deep caramel color. (Take care not to let the sugar syrup go beyond a deep caramel or amber color or it will begin to burn and become bitter.)

To line the ramekins with caramel it is necessary to work quickly but very carefully since the temperature of the caramel will be above 300° F. As soon as the sugar syrup reaches the desired color, remove the pan from the heat and carefully pour the syrup in a steam into the ramekins. Tip and swirl the ramekins to coat the bottom and sides of each evenly. (It is advisable to hold the ramekins with pot holders.) When the syrup stops running, turn the ramekins upside down onto a piece of wax paper to cool slightly and to let any excess syrup run out.

Make the custard:
Preheat the oven to 350° F.

In a saucepan scald the half-and-half with the reserved gingerroot. In a bowl combine the eggs, pumpkin purée, sugar, and the salt. Strain the half-and-half into the pumpkin mixture, whisking, and discard the gingerroot. Divide the custard among the prepared ramekins.

Put the ramekins in the baking pan, cover each with a piece of foil, and add enough hot water to the pan to reach halfway up the sides of the ramekins. Bake the custards in the middle of the oven for 40 to 45 minutes, or until they are just set. Remove the ramekins from the pan and let the custards cool until they are lukewarm. Run a thin knife around the edge of each ramekin and invert the custards onto a serving plate. Or chill the custards for at least 2 hours or overnight and invert them onto a serving plate.

Photo on page 89.

SMALL VANILLA CUSTARDS

Yield:
4 to 6 servings

Equipment:
6 small ½-cup *pots de crème* or ramekins
baking pan for waterbath

This custard dessert takes its French name *pots de crème vanille* from the little pots or *pots de crème* in which it is traditionally baked. It is customary, too, always to serve *pots de crème* with their lids.

5 egg yolks
5 tablespoons sugar

1 to 2 teaspoons vanilla
2 cups heavy cream

Preheat the oven to 350° F.

In a heavy enameled or stainless steel saucepan combine the egg yolks, sugar, and vanilla. In another pan heat the heavy cream until it almost reaches the boiling point. Drizzle the cream into the egg mixture, whisking vigorously. Strain the custard into the *pots de crème* and transfer to the baking pan. Add enough hot water to the baking pan to reach halfway up the sides of the dishes and bake the custards in the middle of the oven for 25 minutes, or until they are just cooked through. Do not let the water in the pan boil. If it seems on the verge of boiling, add some cold water to it. Let the custards cool.

Variation:

POTS DE CRÈME AU CHOCOLAT: Heat 6 ounces semisweet chocolate, finely chopped, with the cream until it is melted. For a stronger chocolate flavor, use 4 ounces unsweetened chocolate and 2 ounces semisweet.

COFFEE CUSTARDS

Yield:
8 servings

8 egg yolks
½ cup sugar
1 tablespoon vanilla
1 cup milk
1 cup strong brewed coffee

¾ cup heavy cream
8 candy coffee beans for garnish
   (available at specialty foods shops)
sweetened whipped cream flavored
   with vanilla for garnish

Equipment:
eight ½-cup *pots de
crème* or ramekins
large baking pan for
waterbath

Preheat the oven to 325° F.

In a bowl combine the egg yolks, sugar, and vanilla, beating the mixture with a fork until it is frothy. In a saucepan scald the milk with the coffee and add the mixture to the bowl in a stream, stirring. Stir in the heavy cream, let the mixture stand for 5 minutes, and skim the froth. Strain the mixture into the *pots de crème* and cover the custards with the lids or with foil. Set the dishes in the baking pan, add enough hot water to the pan to reach three fourths of the way up the sides of the dishes, and bake in the middle of the oven for 25 minutes, or until they are just set. Remove the dishes from the pan, let the custards cool, uncovered, and chill them, covered. Garnish each custard with a candy coffee bean and rosettes of the whipped cream.

Photo on page 340.

CRÈME BRÛLÉE

As everyone who has ever worked with sugar over heat knows, there is a point of no return, which can come upon you quickly. Before your very eyes, in a matter of minutes, what was once acceptable has turned into a molten mass.

It took an act of courage, therefore, on the part of the English to caramelize a sugar topping on custard. As we all know, though, the English are very fond of their sweets. If risking good custard meant achieving a double delight, why not chance it? Luckily for us, they succeeded, and we can all partake of the splendor known as *crème brûlée*.

The challenge of making *crème brûlée*, the custard of which is luxurious with heavy cream, is to caramelize the sugar topping without burning it. This usually means using a preheated broiler, or, if you are fortunate enough to have one, a salamander. This small circular iron is held by its long handle; is heated over a direct flame; and is applied directly to the sugar topping. What you are doing is melting the sugar, which will then harden when cooled. The advantage of using a salamander is that there is no need to worry about overcooking or curdling the custard while it is under the broiler.

Crème brûlée is an absolutely stellar dessert, sweet and silky and crunchy all at the same time. Raspberry Crème Brûlée (page 342) is even more special on account of the berries, and Eggnog Crème Brûlée (page 342) is a very fine alternative to the more traditional desserts of Christmas.

Coffee Custards (page 338)

CRÈME BRÛLÉE

Yield:
4 to 6 servings

Equipment:
4-cup baking dish of
  enameled metal,
  heatproof glass, or
  porcelain
larger baking pan for
  waterbath

Crème brûlée is actually of English origin. Known as "burnt cream," it became one of the great specialties of Corpus Christi College at Cambridge, where it eventually acquired the more elegant name of *crème brûlée*.

James Beard suggested that this dessert is even more delightful if the caramelized top is covered with Marrons Glacés (page 526) and is served with Cognac-flavored whipped cream. The dish can also be made just as deliciously with an equivalent amount of light brown sugar for the caramel topping. This recipe doubles successfully.

FOR THE CUSTARD
6 egg yolks
6 tablespoons sugar
pinch of salt

2¼ cups heavy cream
a 1-inch piece of vanilla bean

FOR THE CARAMEL TOPPING
approximately ½ cup sugar

whipped cream flavored with Cognac as an accompaniment if desired

Preheat the oven to 325° F.

Make the custard:
In a heavy enameled metal or stainless steel saucepan (or in a bowl) combine the egg yolks, sugar, and salt. In another saucepan heat the heavy cream with the vanilla bean, stirring occasionally so that the cream does not scorch, until it comes to the boiling point. Drizzle the cream into the egg mixture, stirring vigorously with a whisk or wooden spatula, until it is thoroughly mixed and remove the vanilla bean. Cook the mixture over moderate heat, stirring constantly, for 3 minutes. Strain the custard into the baking dish and put the dish into the baking pan half filled with hot water. (An easier method would be to place the baking dish in the larger pan and then add enough hot water to the pan to reach halfway up the sides of the dish.) Bake the custard in the middle of the oven for about 35 minutes, or until it is set but not overcooked. Do not let the water in the pan boil. Let the custard cool thoroughly, or chill it, if desired.

A few hours before serving, preheat the broiler and sift the sugar over the top of the custard to a thickness of about ¼ inch. Put the dish under the broiler and let the sugar caramelize, watching carefully to make sure it doesn't burn. The caramelized top should be hard and shiny and sound hollow when tapped. Chill the dessert thoroughly. Crack the crust as you serve the dessert and give each person a bit of the crust along with the custard. Serve it with the whipped cream if desired.

EGGNOG CRÈME BRÛLÉE

Yield:
8 servings

A festive and appropriate offering at a holiday buffet or dinner table.

Equipment:
hand-held electric
  mixer
eight ½-cup ramekins
baking pan

FOR THE CUSTARD
8 egg yolks
¼ cup sugar
2½ cups heavy cream, scalded

3 tablespoons bourbon
1 tablespoon dark rum
freshly grated nutmeg to taste

FOR THE CARAMEL TOPPING
¼ cup plus 2 tablespoons firmly
  packed light brown sugar

6 tablespoons granulated sugar

Make the custard:

In a bowl with the mixer beat the egg yolks with the sugar until the mixture is light and falls in a ribbon when the beater is lifted (see illustration page 16). Add the scalded heavy cream in a slow stream, beating. Transfer the mixture to a heavy saucepan and cook it over moderately low heat, stirring, preferably with a wooden spoon, for 5 to 10 minutes, or until it coats the spoon thickly, but do not let it boil. Remove the pan from the heat and stir in the bourbon, dark rum, and nutmeg. Divide the custard among the ramekins and chill the desserts for at least 2 hours, or until they are set.

Make the caramel topping:

Force the light brown sugar through a sieve into a bowl, add the granulated sugar, and combine the mixture well.

Preheat the broiler. Force the sugar mixture through a sieve over the chilled desserts and spread it gently to cover the custard completely in an even layer. Fill the baking pan with crushed ice, set the ramekins in the prepared pan, and put the pan under the broiler about 5 inches from the heat for 30 seconds, or until the sugar is melted and browned slightly. Chill the desserts for at least 1 hour before serving.

Variation:

RASPBERRY CRÈME BRÛLÉE: Divide 1 pint raspberries among the ramekins. Increase the scalded heavy cream to 3 cups and increase the cooking time for the custard to 10 to 15 minutes. Omit the bourbon and dark rum and replace it with 3 tablespoons *eau-de-vie de framboise* (raspberry brandy). Omit the nutmeg but add 2 teaspoons grated lemon rind. For the caramel topping use ¾ cup firmly packed light brown sugar only and force it through a sieve over the desserts as directed above.

SPECIALTY CUSTARDS

Zabaglione and Tipsy Parson (page 344) comprise our specialty custard collection, if we may be so bold as to call it that. Further, these two custard recipes could not be more dissimilar. *Zabaglione,* a marvelous Italian creation, is considered by some to be a wine sauce—based on egg yolks and sugar that are beaten until foamy with a generous shot of Marsala. The classic version is served warm, and it is akin to imbibing frothy aromatic custard, one that is slightly heavier than air, but only barely.

Tipsy Parson, on the other hand, utilizes crème anglaise as one of its wonderful ingredients that also include vanilla spongecake, macaroons, Sherry, and meringue. If you haven't already guessed, Tipsy Parson is a custard *and* pudding all in one. The cake is soaked with Sherry, topped with preserves and macaroons, and the whole is covered with crème anglaise. Just before serving, a meringue is made to top the dessert. It is not only the marrying of the flavors that makes this combination so memorable, but its lovely, soothing texture.

Tipsy Parson resembles another festive dessert—Christmas trifle—and each has graced many a holiday table. Unlike *zabaglione,* Tipsy Parson can be prepared in advance and actually improves in flavor as it stands. *Zabaglione* must be made at the very last minute, something you will not regret doing after you have had a first taste.

ZABAGLIONE WITH RASPBERRIES

Yield:
4 servings

Equipment:
hand-held electric mixer

This frothy mixture of egg yolks, sugar, and wine can be served as a hot custard dessert or as a chilled sauce. In Italian this classic dessert is called *zabaglione*; in French, *sabayon* refers to the identical combination.

The following recipe is a variation of the classic as it is made with the addition of balsamic vinegar and is served over fresh berries. It is also prepared with an electric mixer. If you are an absolute purist, *zabaglione* should be whipped with a whisk or rotary beater. Method of preparation aside, *zabaglione* should not be prepared in advance.

6 egg yolks
⅓ cup sugar
⅔ cup Marsala wine
1 tablespoon balsamic vinegar if desired

fresh raspberries or strawberries, hulled, as an accompaniment

In a large heatproof bowl with the mixer beat the egg yolks, beat in the sugar, a little at a time, and beat the mixture until pale and thick. Set the bowl over a pan of simmering water and beat the mixture for 1 minute.

Beat in the Marsala and the vinegar, if using, in a slow stream, and continue to beat the mixture at high speed for 6 to 10 minutes, or until very light and thickened and the beater leaves a pattern in its wake. Remove the bowl from the pan and beat the mixture for 1 minute more. Spoon the warm *zabaglione* over individual servings of raspberries.

Photo on frontispiece.

Variation: **CHILLED ZABAGLIONE:** In the top of a double boiler with a mixer beat 6 egg yolks with ⅔ cup superfine granulated sugar. Add ½ cup sweet Madeira wine and 2 tablespoons fresh lemon juice and beat 6 minutes. Transfer the mixture to a chilled large bowl and whisk until the mixture is completely cool. In another chilled bowl beat ½ cup well-chilled heavy cream until it holds stiff peaks and fold it into the chilled mixture.

JAMES BEARD'S TIPSY PARSON

Yield:
6 to 8 servings

Equipment:
decorative baking dish, 12 by 9 by 4 inches
hand-held electric mixer
pastry brush
pastry bag fitted with large fluted tip

This recipe, originally published in 1970, has been described by those who know it well as the best Tipsy Parson ever. Like Christmas trifle in ingredients, Tipsy Parson is a wonderful holiday dessert.

You will note in Mr. Beard's recipe for crème anglaise the option of using four or five egg yolks. The greater the number of yolks, the richer the sauce. We suspect Mr. Beard may well have opted for five.

FOR THE SPONGECAKE
4 large eggs, separated, at room temperature
¼ cup sugar

½ teaspoon vanilla
pinch of salt
⅓ cup all-purpose flour

FOR THE CRÈME ANGLAISE
4 or 5 egg yolks
6 tablespoons sugar
pinch of salt
2 cups heavy cream

1 teaspoon vanilla
2 tablespoons Cognac, or to taste
1 tablespoon unsalted butter, melted

¼ cup cream Sherry, or to taste
⅓ cup apricot preserves
½ recipe Almond Macaroons (page 262), crumbled
2 tablespoons Cognac, or to taste
3 egg whites at room temperature

5 tablespoons sugar
glacéed mixed fruits for garnish if desired
chopped unsalted pistachio nuts for garnish if desired

Make the spongecake: Butter and flour the baking dish and preheat the oven to 400° F.

Beat the egg yolks with the sugar and vanilla until they are thick. In a bowl with the mixer stiffly beat the egg whites with the salt. Fold one fourth of the whites thoroughly into the yolk mixture and pile the mixture on top of the remaining whites. Sift the flour over the top and fold the mixture together lightly but thoroughly. Pour the batter into the prepared pan and bake it in the middle of the oven for 12 to 15 minutes, or until the cake is lightly browned. Remove the cake from the pan and let it cool on a rack.

Make the crème anglaise:

In a bowl whisk together the egg yolks, sugar, and salt. In a saucepan heat the heavy cream over moderate heat until it is just at the boiling point, stirring to prevent it from scorching. Gradually pour the hot cream into the egg yolk mixture, very slowly at first, so the eggs are gradually heated. Do not stop stirring throughout this process. Transfer the custard to a heavy saucepan and cook it over moderate heat, stirring constantly with a wooden spatula, until the custard evenly coats the spatula. Remove the pan from the heat and stir in the vanilla and the Cognac. Rub the surface of the custard with the butter to prevent a skin from forming and let the custard cool.

To assemble:

In the baking dish arrange the spongecake layer. Sprinkle the cake generously with the Sherry, using enough of it to dampen and flavor the cake but not enough to make it soggy, and brush it with the apricot preserves. Top the preserves with the crumbled macaroons, sprinkle the crumbs lightly with the Cognac, and let the cake stand for 30 minutes to mellow. Pour the crème anglaise over the dessert and chill the dessert, covered, for several hours.

Preheat the oven to 350° F.

Just before serving, in a bowl with the mixer beat the egg whites until they hold soft peaks and gradually beat in the sugar to form a stiff meringue (see illustrations page 238). Transfer the meringue to the pastry bag and pipe mounds of it over the custard, being certain to cover it completely. Brown the dessert in the oven, garnish it with the candied fruits or chopped nuts, if desired, and serve at once.

ICE CREAMS AND OTHER FROZEN DESSERTS

O f the desserts that are most preferred by the greatest number of people, surely ice cream is either at the top of the list or very close to it. The reasons are self-evident. From our vantage point, ice cream is really a phenomenon. Take custard or custard and heavy cream and with cold and churning you arrive at *not* butter but ice cream. It can also be made with a meringue base or a whipped-cream base, to name only two. Ice cream assumes any number of wonderful flavors: ginger, molasses almond brittle, amaretto peach, vanilla, vanilla custard, and honey vanilla. We know more than a few people who after years of testing have decided that the very best dessert ever is a bowl of plain vanilla ice cream, and these people know of what they speak.

Combine ice cream with a topping or syrup and you have the best of all possible worlds—sundaes and sodas and parfaits. Combine it with cake and you've got that all-American favorite, ice-cream roll. On a more sophisticated note, simple ice cream can be fancied up with sugar work, as when it is topped with a lacy caramel cage.

And then there are the ices and sorbets, those perfect palate refreshers, so sublime in the summer when made with purées of seasonal fruits.

Many of those devoted to ice cream are almost but not quite equally smitten with frozen desserts, and by that we mean frozen soufflés and mousses and *bombes* and molds. It is easy to love our *bombes* and molds; they incorporate generous amounts of ice cream.

And as for our frozen soufflés and mousses, consider a few of those we have selected: Frozen Hazelnut Praline Soufflé (page 375), Frozen Dark Chocolate Mousse (page 377), and Espresso Tortoni with Chocolate-Covered Coffee Beans (page 378). We'll wager that if you are fond of ice creams and frozen desserts—mind you we only went so far as to say fond of—there isn't a recipe in this chapter you won't want to try at least once.

Amaretto Peach Ice Cream (page 355)

ICE CREAMS

Ice cream, there is really nothing like it in the world. It goes hand in hand with cake and the coupling is the *best* of all possible worlds. Birthday parties revolve around this age-old combination and for good reason. Singly, each of these desserts is grand; in unison, they are superb.

What is it about ice cream that makes it so special? It's not only that it is cold and refreshing and soothing. A tall glass of water can be so described and, as we all know, water does not hold a candle to ice cream. Much of the appeal, we think, lies in the creaminess of ice cream: There it is in the very word itself. When first invented, ice cream was made with dairy-fresh heavy cream—an entity entirely different from what we now buy, which is also called heavy cream. It was loaded with butterfat and had to be spooned out of the bottle. And contrary to our popular belief, it is interesting to note that that first ice cream was not invented in the United States. Frozen cream, as it was known, originated in England, where Charles I was so protective of the recipe that he paid his French chef hush money to keep the recipe secret! Like all good things, however, word got out and we are all the happier for it.

Americans commercialized ice cream into a national passion, and it was just a matter of time before this much-loved dessert would once again be made in the home kitchen, for homemade ice cream is utterly incomparable. In doing that, one appreciates anew the variety with which ice cream can be made. The recipes in this chapter celebrate this fact. You will note ice creams with the usual custard base; others with a custard base that is then heated and beaten to increase its volume; still others that start with an Italian meringue base. While the end product is glorious ice cream of one flavor or another, each of these differences affects the texture, and we have come full circle, back to one of the great appeals of ice cream.

Ice cream can be hand-churned, if you've the time, but you will have your ice cream sooner if you use an electric ice-cream maker or a new manual model. Available at kitchenware stores, these appliances differ in price and it is not always that the most expensive is the most reliable.

We are sure you will find many a favorite among the eighteen ice-cream recipes in this chapter. With ice cream made, you can then proceed to the second part of this collection—ice-cream creations—namely, sodas and sundaes, an ice-cream cake, and a pumpkin ice-cream pie. On a fancier note, ice cream is topped with caramel cages, a conceit of the French that to this day is a beautiful, festive contribution. Along this same line and on an even higher note, ice cream with caramel cages is presented in hand-made chocolate cups. And, lest we forget, remember dessert sauces on page 489.

VANILLA ICE CREAM

Yield:
I quart

Equipment:
food processor fitted
  with steel blade
hand-held electric
  mixer
ice-cream freezer

1 cup sugar
two 4-inch lengths of vanilla bean,
  chopped into small pieces

2 cups milk
2 cups heavy cream
6 egg yolks

In the food processor or in a blender blend the sugar with the vanilla bean until the bean is pulverized. In a heavy saucepan combine the sugar mixture with the milk and cream and scald the mixture, stirring. In a large bowl with the mixer, beat the egg yolks until they are light and lemon colored and pour the milk mixture through a fine sieve into the bowl in a stream, stirring. Transfer the mixture to another heavy saucepan and cook it over low heat, stirring, preferably with a wooden spoon, until it thickens and coats the back of the spoon, about 5 to 7 minutes. Transfer the custard to a metal bowl set in a bowl of ice and cold water and let it cool, covered with a round of wax paper or plastic wrap. Chill the custard for 2 hours and freeze it in the ice-cream freezer according to the manufacturer's instructions.

Variations:

DARK CHOCOLATE ICE CREAM: Omit the vanilla bean from the master recipe, increase the sugar to 1¼ cups, and add ⅔ cup unsweetened cocoa powder (preferably Dutch-process) to the milk and cream mixture before scalding. Make the custard as directed, chill, and stir in 1 teaspoon vanilla. Freeze the ice cream as directed.

RICH GRAND MARNIER ICE CREAM: Omit the vanilla bean from the master recipe and stir in ¼ cup Grand Marnier or other orange-flavored liqueur and 1 tablespoon grated orange rind pounded with an additional 1 teaspoon sugar in a mortar and pestle to the finished chilled custard. Freeze the ice cream as directed.

PISTACHIO ICE CREAM: Blanch and oven-dry ⅓ pound (about 1 cup) shelled unsalted pistachio nuts (for procedure page 549). Grind the nuts. Make 1½ recipes Vanilla Ice Cream as directed, substituting the ground nuts for the vanilla beans (do not remove the pistachios after infusing) and adding ¼ teaspoon almond extract and 3 or 4 drops of green food coloring to the cooked custard. Yields about 6 cups.

GINGER ICE CREAM: Omit the vanilla bean from the master recipe and add 1 teaspoon ground ginger to the milk and cream mixture before scalding. Make the custard as directed, chill, and stir in a 12-ounce jar of preserved ginger (available at specialty foods shops), drained and finely chopped, and ½ teaspoon vanilla. Freeze the ice cream as directed.

COFFEE ICE CREAM: Add ¼ cup instant espresso powder and an additional ¼ cup sugar to the milk and cream mixture before scalding. Make and freeze the ice cream as directed in the master recipe. For a more exotic combination, make coffee ice cream, let it soften slightly, then fold in a drained 13-ounce jar of chestnut pieces in syrup (available at specialty foods shops). Freeze the ice cream, covered tightly, in the freezing compartment of the refrigerator for at least 2 hours, or until set.

CRANBERRY SWIRL ICE CREAM: In a saucepan combine 2 cups rinsed and picked-over cranberries, ½ cup sugar, 2 tablespoons water, and a 2-inch strip of lemon rind. Bring to a boil, stirring, and boil over moderately high heat, stirring, for 10 minutes, or until the cranberries pop and the mixture is thick. Discard the lemon rind and transfer the cranberries to a bowl. Let cool, stirring occasionally, and chill until very cold. Swirl the cranberry mixture into 1 quart softened Vanilla Ice Cream, but do not combine it well. Freeze, covered tightly, in the freezing compartment of the refrigerator for at least 2 hours, or until set.

Photo on page 131.

NECTARINE ICE CREAM: Reduce the sugar in the master recipe to ¾ cup and the milk and cream to 1½ cups each. While the custard is chilling, make the nectarine purée: In a bowl toss 1½ pounds very ripe nectarines, peeled, pitted, and quartered, with ½ cup sugar and let the fruit stand for 30 minutes. In a food processor purée the nectarines, transfer the purée to the bowl, and chill it, covered, until very cold. Stir the purée into the chilled custard and freeze it in an ice-cream freezer according to the manufacturer's instructions.

Photo on page 354.

STRAWBERRY ICE CREAM: Omit the vanilla bean from the master recipe and reduce the milk and cream to 1½ cups each. While the custard is chilling make the strawberry purée: In a food processor or blender purée in batches 1 pound (about 1 pint) strawberries, hulled and sliced, and transfer the purée to a bowl. Stir in ½ cup superfine granulated sugar and 1 teaspoon fresh lemon juice and chill the mixture, covered, for 2 hours. Stir the purée into the chilled custard, add 1 teaspoon vanilla, and freeze as directed.

COCONUT ICE CREAM: Follow instructions for grating fresh coconut (for procedure page 549), reserving the liquid. Strain the reserved coconut liquid through a fine sieve into a measuring cup, reserving the grated coconut, and add enough milk to measure 2 cups liquid in all. Scald the coconut milk mixture with 2 cups heavy cream and transfer the mixture to a food processor or a blender. Blend the mixture with the reserved grated coconut in batches for 1 minute, transfer it to a bowl, and let it stand for 30 minutes. Strain the milk through a fine sieve lined with a double thickness of rinsed and squeezed cheesecloth, pressing hard on the solids. Proceed with the master recipe, omitting the vanilla bean and using the coconut milk mixture in place of the milk and cream. When the custard has cooled, stir in 1 teaspoon vanilla and freeze as directed.

VANILLA CUSTARD ICE CREAM

Yield:
about 1 quart

Equipment:
food processor fitted
with steel blade
hand-held electric
mixer
ice-cream freezer

In this recipe the custard is beaten over heat until it doubles in volume. Heavy cream is then added and the mixture is again beaten until double. This results in a greater percentage of air in the ice cream, making it lighter in weight and greater in volume, while the cream makes for rich tasting ice cream.

one 8-inch vanilla bean, chopped *½ cup milk*
¾ cup sugar *2 cups well-chilled heavy cream*
4 egg yolks *⅛ teaspoon salt*

In the food processor or in a blender grind the vanilla bean fine, add the sugar, and pulverize the mixture. In a metal bowl with the mixer beat well the egg yolks, milk, and the vanilla sugar and strain the mixture through a fine sieve into another bowl. Set the bowl over a pan of simmering water and with the mixer beat the mixture for 7 to 10 minutes, or until thickened and double in volume. Set the bowl in a bowl of ice and cold water and with the mixer beat the mixture until cold. Beat in the cream and salt and beat until thickened and almost double in volume. Transfer to the ice-cream freezer and freeze it according to the manufacturer's instructions.

Variations:

CHOCOLATE VELVET ICE CREAM: Substitute ¾ cup unsweetened cocoa powder (preferably Dutch-process) combined with 1 cup sugar for the vanilla sugar mixture in the master recipe. Add 2 teaspoons vanilla when beating in the cream and salt. Freeze as directed.

BUTTER PECAN CUSTARD ICE CREAM: In a skillet sauté ¾ cup chopped pecans in 2 tablespoons unsalted butter over moderately high heat, stirring, until golden brown and fragrant and transfer them with a slotted spoon to paper towels to drain.

Make the custard, omitting the vanilla bean and adding 2 tablespoons unsalted butter when beating the mixture over water. Let cool as directed, then beat in 1 cup of the cream, beating until the mixture is thickened and almost double in volume. Add the remaining 1 cup cream and ¼ teaspoon salt, beating, and beat for 30 seconds. Fold in the chopped pecans. Freeze as directed.

HONEY VANILLA ICE CREAM

Yield:
about 1 quart

Equipment:
hand-held electric
 mixer
ice-cream freezer

The ice-cream base in this recipe is whipped heavy cream to which gelatin has been added. The gelatin stabilizes and thickens the cream. Note that while there are no eggs in the base, the use of honey results in an exceptionally smooth-textured ice cream.

1½ teaspoons unflavored gelatin
2 tablespoons plus ¼ cup cold water
⅔ cup sugar
3 tablespoons honey

2½ cups well-chilled heavy cream
1½ tablespoons vanilla
⅛ teaspoon salt

In a small bowl sprinkle the gelatin over the 2 tablespoons cold water and let soften for 15 minutes. In a small heavy saucepan combine the sugar, honey, and the remaining ¼ cup water, bring the mixture to a boil over moderate heat, stirring until the sugar is dissolved, and remove the pan from the heat. Add the gelatin mixture and stir until the gelatin is dissolved. Transfer the mixture to a metal bowl set in a bowl of ice and cold water and stir until cool. Add 2 cups of the cream, stir the mixture until cold, and with the mixer beat it for 3 minutes, or until thickened and almost double in volume. Add the remaining ½ cup cream, the vanilla, and salt, beating, and beat the mixture for 30 seconds. Transfer to the ice-cream freezer and freeze according to the manufacturer's instructions.

HAZELNUT ICE CREAM

Yield:
about 1½ quarts

Equipment:
food processor fitted
 with steel blade
pastry brush
upright and hand-held
 electric mixers

This splendid ice cream is made with a base of beaten egg yolks and hot caramel syrup into which stiffly beaten whipped cream is folded. One of the best ice creams ever, this dessert is rich because of the number of egg yolks and the amount of cream that is added. Note that no ice-cream freezer is required.

6 ounces hazelnuts, toasted and skins
 removed (for procedure page 549)
¾ cup sugar
¼ cup water plus ½ cup boiling water

6 egg yolks
2 cups well-chilled heavy cream
2 teaspoons vanilla

In the food processor or in a blender grind the hazelnuts to a paste. In a small heavy saucepan combine the sugar with the ¼ cup water, cook the mixture over moderate heat, stirring and washing down any sugar crystals clinging to the sides of the pan with the brush dipped in cold water until the sugar is dissolved. Cook the syrup, swirling the pan and being careful not to let it burn, until the syrup is amber colored. Immediately add the boiling water in a slow stream, bring the mixture to a boil, stirring, and cook it, stirring, until the caramel is dissolved completely.

In the bowl of the upright mixer beat the egg yolks until lemon colored. With the mixer running, add the hot caramel in a stream and beat the mixture until cool. Transfer the mixture to a large bowl and stir in the hazelnut paste. In a chilled bowl with the hand-held mixer beat the cream until it holds stiff peaks and beat in the vanilla. Stir one fourth of the cream into the caramel mixture and fold in the remaining cream gently but thoroughly. Spoon the mixture into a bowl and freeze it, covered, until firm.

MOLASSES ALMOND BRITTLE ICE CREAM

Yield:
about 2 quarts

Equipment:
baking sheet
pastry brush
food processor fitted
  with steel blade
hand-held electric
  mixer
baking pan, 13 by 9 by
  2 inches

This recipe uses a meringue base combined with beaten egg yolks and whipped cream, which results in a very light, airy, yet rich-tasting ice cream. An additional bonus—the ice cream is frozen in a baking pan.

⅔ cup blanched whole almonds (for procedure page 549)
½ cup superfine granulated sugar
¼ cup cold water
6 large eggs, separated, at room temperature
pinch of cream of tartar
pinch of salt
1 cup confectioners' sugar
⅔ cup molasses
½ teaspoon vanilla
2 cups well-chilled heavy cream

Butter the baking sheet and preheat the oven to 300° F.

Toast the almonds in a shallow baking pan in the middle of the oven, stirring, for 20 to 30 minutes, or until pale golden, and let them cool. In a small heavy saucepan combine the superfine granulated sugar with the cold water, cook the mixture over moderate heat, washing down any sugar crystals clinging to the sides of the pan with the brush dipped in cold water, until the sugar is dissolved, and cook the syrup, undisturbed, until it is a light caramel. Stir in the almonds, pour the mixture onto the baking sheet, and let it cool. Break the almond brittle into small pieces and in the food processor grind it until it resembles coarse crumbs.

In a bowl with the mixer beat the egg whites with the salt until foamy, add the cream of tartar, and beat the whites until they hold soft peaks. Gradually beat in the confectioners' sugar and beat the whites until they hold stiff peaks (see illustrations page 238). Beat in the egg yolks, one at a time, the molasses, and vanilla. In a chilled bowl with the mixer beat the cream until it holds soft peaks and fold it into the egg mixture. Pour the mixture into the baking pan and freeze it until mushy. Fold in the almond brittle crumbs and freeze the ice cream in the pan until just firm.

Plum Tart (page 176), Nectarine Ice Cream (page 350)

MAPLE WALNUT ICE CREAM

Yield:
about 1 quart

Equipment:
hand-held electric
    mixer
2 refrigerator trays

This is actually the simplest of ice-cream combinations: An egg yolk custard is prepared with scalded cream, then whipped cream is folded in.

1½ cups light cream
4 egg yolks
½ cup maple syrup

pinch of salt
2 cups well-chilled heavy cream
1 cup coarsely chopped walnuts

In the top of a double boiler scald the light cream. In a bowl beat the egg yolks until combined and stir in the maple syrup and the salt. Gradually add the scalded light cream, stirring constantly, and return the mixture to the top of the double boiler. Cook over simmering water, stirring constantly, preferably with a wooden spoon, until it is thick enough to coat the back of the spoon, 5 to 7 minutes. Let the custard cool.

In a chilled bowl with the mixer beat the heavy cream until it holds soft peaks and fold it into the custard. Divide the mixture between the refrigerator trays and freeze until the custard begins to solidify. Stir ½ cup of walnuts into each tray and freeze the ice cream until firm.

AMARETTO PEACH ICE CREAM

Yield:
about 2 quarts

Equipment:
food processor fitted
    with steel blade
pastry brush
upright electric mixer
ice-cream freezer

1½ pounds peaches, peeled (for
    procedure page 548), pitted, and
    sliced
1 cup sugar
¼ cup water plus ½ cup boiling water
2 tablespoons fresh lemon juice

1 cup crumbled amaretti *(Italian*
    almond macaroon cookies,
    available at specialty foods shops)
3 tablespoons Amaretto
6 egg yolks
2 teaspoons vanilla
2 cups well-chilled heavy cream

In a bowl toss the peaches with ¼ cup of the sugar and the lemon juice and let the mixture stand for 30 minutes. Drain the peaches and purée them in the food processor. In a heavy saucepan combine the remaining ¾ cup sugar with the ¼ cup water, bring the mixture to a boil over moderate heat, washing down any sugar crystals clinging to the sides of the pan with the brush dipped in cold water, and simmer the syrup until it is a pale golden caramel. Add the ½ cup boiling water carefully (the mixture will bubble up) and simmer the syrup, stirring, until the caramel is dissolved.

In a small bowl sprinkle the cookies with the Amaretto and let stand for 5 minutes. In the large mixer bowl beat the egg yolks until they are thick and pale, add the syrup in a stream, beating, and beat the mixture until cool. Stir in the vanilla, peach purée, cookie mixture, and cream. Freeze mixture in the ice-cream freezer according to the manufacturer's instructions.

Photo on page 346.

TRIPLE CROWN
Mocha Soda

Yield:
1 serving

Equipment:
16-ounce ice-cream soda glass

2 tablespoons coffee syrup (page 542)
¼ cup cold milk
¾ cup chilled club soda or seltzer
dash of cinnamon

2 scoops Dark Chocolate Ice Cream (page 349) or Chocolate Velvet Ice Cream (page 351)

In the ice-cream soda glass combine the syrup and the milk, add the club soda or seltzer, and sprinkle the mixture with the cinnamon. Float the ice cream on top.
Photo opposite.

OOMPH GIRL À LA MODE
Cherry and Almond Sundae

Yield:
1 serving

Equipment:
sundae dish or stemmed dessert dish

This cherry sundae was named for Ann Sheridan, the red-haired actress and World War II pinup queen, whose nickname was "the oomph girl."

2 scoops Honey Vanilla Ice Cream (page 352) or Vanilla Custard Ice Cream (page 351)
2 heaping teaspoons Cherry Sauce (page 505)

unsweetened whipped cream for garnish
toasted sliced blanched almonds for garnish

In the sundae dish arrange the ice cream, top it with the cherry sauce, and garnish it with a dollop of the whipped cream and the almonds.
Photo opposite.

STRAWBERRY BLONDE
Strawberry and Ginger Ale Soda

Yield:
1 serving

Equipment:
16-ounce ice-cream soda glass

The Strawberry Blonde, a film that starred the beautiful Rita Hayworth, was the inspiration for this creation.

3 to 4 tablespoons strawberry syrup (page 543), or to taste
1 cup well-chilled ginger ale

2 scoops Honey Vanilla Ice Cream (page 352) or Vanilla Custard Ice Cream (page 351)

In the ice-cream soda glass combine the strawberry syrup and the ginger ale and float the ice cream on top.
Photo opposite.

Triple Crown, Oomph Girl à la Mode, Strawberry Blonde (opposite)

STRAWBERRY ICE-CREAM SODAS

Yield:
eight 16-ounce
  servings

Equipment:
eight 16-ounce ice-
  cream soda glasses

Here is the strawberry ice-cream soda we all fondly remember—the one we'd have on that hot, still summer day when our knees brushed the cool of the soda fountain counter and we'd have to stretch tall on the stool to reach the tip of the straw.

2 quarts Strawberry Ice Cream (page 350)
2 cups milk

2 cups strawberry syrup (page 543)
chilled club soda or seltzer
8 whole strawberries for garnish

Let the ice cream soften slightly.

In each glass combine ¼ cup each of the milk and strawberry syrup. Put 2 or 3 scoops of the ice cream into each glass and fill the glasses with the club soda or seltzer. Divide the remaining syrup among the sodas and garnish each soda with a strawberry.

INDEPENDENCE DAY ICE-CREAM CAKE

Yield:
8 servings

Equipment:
9-inch springform pan
hand-held and upright
  electric mixers
food processor fitted
  with steel blade
ice-cream freezer

This is a splendid and festive cake for grown-ups and children alike. Especially appropriate for a Fourth of July celebration, the cake is composed of layers of strawberry ice cream, white sour-cream-flavored cake, and blueberry ice cream.

FOR THE CAKE
1 stick (½ cup) unsalted butter,
  softened
1 cup sugar
2 large eggs at room temperature
½ cup sour cream

1¼ cups all-purpose flour
½ teaspoon double-acting baking
  powder
¼ teaspoon baking soda
¼ teaspoon salt

FOR THE ICE CREAMS
6 egg yolks
2 cups sugar
3 cups milk, scalded
1½ teaspoons vanilla

1½ cups well-chilled heavy cream
1¾ cups sliced strawberries
3 cups blueberries, picked over
½ teaspoon cinnamon

fresh whole strawberries for garnish

Make the cake:

Butter and flour the springform pan and preheat the oven to 350° F.

In a large bowl with the hand-held mixer cream the butter, add the sugar, and beat the mixture until light and fluffy. Add the eggs, one at a time, beating well after each addition, add the sour cream, and beat the mixture until it is just combined. Into a bowl sift together the flour, baking powder, baking soda, and salt, add the mixture to the butter mixture, and stir the batter until just combined. Pour the batter into the springform pan, smooth the top, and bake in the middle of the oven for 45 to 55 minutes, or until a tester comes out clean. Let the cake cool in the pan on a rack for 10 minutes, remove the sides and bottom of the pan, and let cool.

Make the ice creams: In the bowl of the upright mixer beat the egg yolks and the sugar for 5 minutes. Add the scalded milk in a stream, beating at low speed, transfer the custard to a heavy saucepan, and cook it over moderately low heat, stirring, preferably with a wooden spoon, until it thickens and coats the back of the spoon lightly, 5 to 7 minutes, but do not let the custard boil. Remove the pan from the heat and stir in the vanilla. Strain the custard through a fine sieve into a large metal bowl set over a bowl of ice and cold water and chill it, stirring occasionally, until it is very cold. Stir in the cream.

In the food processor purée the sliced strawberries. In a bowl combine the purée with 2 cups of the custard mixture and freeze in the ice-cream freezer according to the manufacturer's instructions.

In the food processor purée the blueberries with the cinnamon, add the remaining custard mixture, and freeze the mixture in the ice-cream freezer according to the manufacturer's instructions. Keep both ice creams frozen until it is time to assemble the cake.

To assemble the cake: Slice the cake horizontally into 4 layers (see illustration page 19) and put the top layer, cut side up, in the bottom of the springform pan. Soften the ice creams, if necessary, by beating them briefly in the bowl of the upright mixer (they should be just soft enough to spread). Spread half the blueberry ice cream with a large spoon on the cake layer and top it with the second cake layer, pressing the cake down gently to even out the ice cream. Spread all of the strawberry ice cream on top of the cake and top it with the third cake layer, pressing the cake down gently. Spread the remaining blueberry ice cream on top of the cake and top it with the last cake layer, cut side down, pressing the cake down gently. Freeze the cake, covered with plastic wrap or foil, for at least 3 hours or overnight. Cut the cake with a serrated knife, arrange the slices on a platter, and garnish them with the whole strawberries.

PUMPKIN ICE-CREAM PIE

Yield:
8 servings

Equipment:
9-inch glass pie plate
hand-held electric
 mixer
ice-cream freezer
pastry brush
9-inch round cake pan
pastry bag fitted with
 star tip

A perfect alternative to pumpkin pie as a classic Thanksgiving dessert, this pumpkin ice-cream pie sports an impressive caramel net topping. Unlike a caramel cage (page 363), which forms a dome, this net fits snugly over the pie and is rimmed with whipped cream.

FOR THE PUMPKIN ICE CREAM
¾ cup plus 2 tablespoons granulated
* sugar*
½ cup water
1 cup canned pumpkin purée

1 tablespoon dark rum
¼ teaspoon ground ginger
¼ teaspoon allspice
1 cup well-chilled heavy cream

FOR THE PIE SHELL
1 cup gingersnap crumbs
½ cup ground pecans
¼ cup sifted confectioners' sugar

¾ stick (6 tablespoons) unsalted
* butter, melted and cooled*

FOR THE CARAMEL NET
½ cup granulated sugar
¼ cup water

1 teaspoon honey
pinch of cream of tartar

1 cup well-chilled heavy cream

3 tablespoons sifted confectioners' sugar

Make the pumpkin ice cream:

In a saucepan combine the granulated sugar and water, bring the mixture to a boil over moderate heat, stirring until the sugar is dissolved, and boil the syrup, gently swirling the pan, for 6 minutes. In a bowl combine the pumpkin purée, rum, ginger, and allspice, add the syrup in a stream, beating, and let the mixture cool. In a chilled bowl with the mixer beat the heavy cream until it holds very soft peaks, fold it into the pumpkin mixture, and chill the mixture for 1 hour. Freeze the mixture in the ice-cream freezer according to the manufacturer's instructions.

Make the pie shell:

Lightly butter the pie plate and preheat the oven to 325° F.

In a bowl combine the gingersnap crumbs, the pecans, and the confectioners' sugar and stir in the butter. Press the mixture onto the bottom and sides of the pie plate. Bake the shell in the middle of the oven for 8 minutes, or until colored lightly but not browned. Let the shell cool in the pie plate on a rack.

Spoon the pumpkin ice cream into the shell, smooth the top and freeze the pie, wrapped tightly in foil, for at least 6 hours or up to 2 days.

Make the caramel net:

Oil the bottom of the cake pan, inverted, with flavorless vegetable oil.

In a heavy skillet combine the sugar, water, and honey and cook the mixture over low heat, stirring and washing down any sugar crystals clinging to the sides of the pan with the brush dipped in cold water until the sugar is dissolved. Increase the heat to moderately high, add the cream of tartar, and cook the syrup, swirling the skillet without stirring, until it

Nougatine Délices en Cage (page 362)

is a pale amber. Remove the skillet from the heat and prop it up so that the caramel runs to one side. Dip a fork into the caramel and drizzle the caramel in a grid-like pattern over the oiled pan. While it is still warm, slide the caramel net gently off the pan onto wax paper and let it harden.

To assemble the pie: In a chilled bowl with the mixer beat the remaining 1 cup heavy cream until it holds soft peaks, beat in the remaining confectioners' sugar, and beat the cream until it holds stiff peaks. Transfer the whipped cream to the pastry bag, arrange the caramel net carefully over the pie, and pipe the whipped cream around the edge.

NOUGATINE DÉLICES EN CAGE

Nougatine Shells with Ice Cream

Yield:
4 servings

Equipment:
marble or other non-
  porous surface
3½- by 1-inch tartlet
  tin
soup ladle, 3½ inches
  in diameter and 1
  inch deep
pastry brush
pastry bag fitted with
  decorative tip

Nougatine is a mixture of sugar syrup and almonds that is molded while warm into decorative shapes. In this recipe the nougatine is formed into small shells that serve as edible ice-cream bowls. The shells and ice cream are topped with lacy caramel cages for an even more dramatic presentation. This is a perfect dessert for a special occasion. You should, however, reserve making this dessert for a cool, dry day. Your chances of success, given the amount of sugar work, will improve radically with low humidity.

sweet almond oil

FOR THE NOUGATINE SHELLS
½ cup sugar
¼ cup water
pinch of cream of tartar

½ cup blanched almonds, (for
  procedure page 549), chopped and
  toasted

FOR THE CARAMEL CAGES
2 cups sugar
1 cup water

2 teaspoons honey
⅛ teaspoon cream of tartar

1 pint Vanilla Ice Cream (page 349)
  or Coffee Ice Cream (page 349)
whipped cream for garnish

4 Candied Violets (page 524) for
  garnish

Lightly oil with the sweet almond oil the marble or other nonporous surface, a rolling pin, the tartlet tin, the outside of the soup ladle, and a baking sheet.

Make the nougatine shells: In a heavy skillet combine the sugar with the water and cook the mixture over moderate heat, stirring and washing down any sugar crystals clinging to the sides of the pan with the brush dipped in cold water for 2 to 3 minutes, or until the sugar is dissolved. Increase the heat to moderately high, add the cream of tartar (to help prevent crystallization), and cook the syrup, gently swirling the pan, until it is a golden caramel. Stir in the almonds and remove the pan from the heat.

Pour the mixture onto the marble slab. (The nougatine will cool quickly, so you must work quickly.) When the mixture has begun to set but is still pliable, flip the nougatine over with a spatula so that it cools evenly on the other side. To even out the thickness, roll the sheet with the oiled rolling pin into a round ⅛ inch thick. Quickly cut out 4 rounds with a heavy, oiled knife. Place the rounds on the oiled baking sheet.

While the nougatine is still warm, fit 1 round into the tartlet tin and trim the edges with scissors. Let the shell cool completely and remove it from the tin. Make 3 more shells in the same manner and reserve any remaining nougatine for another use. If the nougatine rounds cool and harden before you can shape them, put the baking sheet in a preheated 225° F. oven for a moment to soften the rounds. Note that every time you reheat nougatine it darkens slightly.

Make the caramel cages:

In a heavy skillet combine the sugar, water, and honey and cook the mixture over low heat, washing down any sugar crystals clinging to the sides of the pan with the brush dipped in cold water until the sugar is dissolved. Increase the heat to moderately high, add the cream of tartar, and cook the syrup, gently swirling the pan, until it is a pale amber. Remove the pan from the heat and prop it up on one side so that the syrup accumulates on the other. Holding the inverted ladle over the pan of caramel, dip a fork into the caramel and drizzle the caramel over the ladle to form a web (see illustation). Gently release the caramel and refit it over the ladle. Drip additional caramel over the web until it is rather dense, remove the cage gently, and let it cool completely. Make 3 more cages with the remaining caramel in the same manner. (If the caramel begins to harden, place the pan over a very low flame until it softens.)

To assemble the desserts:

Fill each nougatine shell with 1 scoop of the ice cream and set a caramel cage over each scoop. Pipe a rosette of the whipped cream onto each cage and top the cream with a candied violet.

Photo on page 361.

Making caramel cage: Drizzling syrup with fork over ladle to form web

Ice Cream in Chocolate Cups with Caramel Cages (below)

ICE CREAM IN CHOCOLATE CUPS WITH CARAMEL CAGES

Yield:
serves 2

Equipment:
fluted cupcake papers

Cupcake papers are coated with melted chocolate and are then chilled. When the paper is peeled off, a chocolate cup remains, perfect for filling with scoops of ice cream. This wonderful presentation is made even more festive by the addition of caramel cages topping the ice cream. To break the cages, simply tap them with the back of a spoon.

2 caramel cages made with ½ the ingredients on page 362, according to the directions on page 363

FOR THE CHOCOLATE CUPS
4 ounces semisweet chocolate, broken into bits

½ pint Vanilla Ice Cream (page 349)   strawberries for garnish if desired

Make the chocolate cups:

Have ready the caramel cages.
    Melt the chocolate in a double boiler set over barely simmering water and with a small spoon spread it evenly on the inside bottom and sides of 2 double layers of the cupcake papers, spreading the papers open so that the sides are slanting outward. Put the chocolate cups in small bowls and chill them for 30 minutes.

Peel the papers carefully from the chocolate and chill the chocolate cups until they are needed.

Fill each chocolate cup with a scoop of the ice cream and set a caramel cage over each scoop. Arrange the desserts on a serving tray and garnish them with the strawberries if desired.

Photo opposite.

The cups may be made 1 day in advance and kept chilled.

PARFAITS

Parfait, the word has an Old World ring to it, summoning up an ice-cream dessert in a tall thin glass that our grandparents probably had liked, but which somehow never made it into today's fast lane. What we held on to were those lovely long glasses. Nothing could be farther from the truth. The parfait is alive and well—a most viable dessert, particularly when you want something a little more than ice cream, but not an ice-cream soda or a sundae. The parfait is ice cream layered with fruit, nuts, or syrup, and often topped with whipped cream.

Our first recipe brings vanilla parfait custard and crushed fresh raspberries together, an almost unsurpassable combination. Rum Raisin Parfait (page 366) serves as a variation on that theme, employing the same parfait custard, as does Pistachio Parfait with Caramel Sauce (page 367), a captivating concept. Chocolate Parfait Custard (page 367) follows these and is served as is, with no layering at all. It is curious that not one of these parfaits is served in a parfait glass, but rather in a shallow bowl or from one large serving bowl. The more the accoutrements change, the more the parfait remains marvelously the same.

VANILLA PARFAIT WITH RASPBERRIES

Yield:
about 5 cups,
  serving 4

Equipment:
upright and hand-held
  electric mixers
pastry brush
candy thermometer

"Parfait" originally referred to a coffee-flavored dessert made from beaten egg yolks, sugar syrup, and flavoring, finished with whipped cream, and frozen in a parfait glass. Today it has come to describe any layered frozen dessert made of ice cream and ribboned with syrups or sauces or fruit-and-nut fillings. This recipe, however, adheres to the classic interpretation, a rich but delicate and distinctive dessert. The following variations are all based on the same parfait custard.

FOR THE PARFAIT CUSTARD

3 large eggs
pinch of salt
¾ cup sugar

⅓ cup water
a 6-inch piece of vanilla bean, split

1½ cups well-chilled heavy cream
½ teaspoon fresh lemon juice

1½ cups fresh raspberries, crushed and
  sweetened with vanilla sugar (page
  541) to taste

Make the parfait custard:

In the bowl of the upright mixer beat the eggs with the salt until light and lemon colored. In a small heavy saucepan combine the sugar, the water, and the vanilla bean and cook the mixture over low heat, stirring and washing down any sugar crystals clinging to the sides of the pan with the brush dipped in cold water until the sugar is dissolved. Increase the heat to moderately high and boil the syrup, gently swirling the pan, until it reaches the thread stage, or the candy thermometer registers 230° F. (For the stages of sugar syrup, see illustrations page 241.) Remove and discard the vanilla bean.

With the upright mixer at high speed add the syrup in a stream to the eggs. Transfer the mixture to a heavy saucepan and cook it over moderately low heat, whisking, for 3 to 5 minutes, or until thick, but do not let it boil. Transfer the custard to a bowl set in a larger bowl of ice and water and stir until cool.

In a chilled bowl with the hand-held mixer beat the heavy cream until it holds soft peaks. Add the lemon juice to the custard and fold in the whipped cream. Transfer the custard to a glass bowl and freeze it, covered, for 4 hours, or until firm. Serve the parfait with the crushed fresh raspberries.

Variations:

RUM RAISIN PARFAIT: Make parfait custard as directed above. In a small bowl combine ⅓ cup raisins with ⅓ cup dark rum and let them macerate for 10 hours or overnight.

In a chilled bowl beat the heavy cream until it holds soft peaks. Add the raisin mixture, ¾ teaspoon fresh lemon juice, and ½ teaspoon vanilla to the custard and fold in the whipped cream. Transfer the parfait to a 1½-quart dish and freeze it, covered, for 4 hours, or until firm. Serve the parfait custard in chilled dessert dishes and top each serving with a generous dash of Angostura bitters, if desired. Makes about 6 cups.

PISTACHIO PARFAIT WITH CARAMEL SAUCE: Make parfait custard as directed in Vanilla Parfait with Raspberries, omitting the vanilla bean and adding 2 teaspoons pistachio flavor (available from Maid of Scandinavia, see Shopping Sources page 555), 1½ teaspoons vanilla, and ¾ teaspoon fresh lemon juice.

In a chilled bowl beat the heavy cream until it holds soft peaks. Fold the whipped cream into the parfait and add ¾ cup finely chopped blanched and oven-dried (for procedure page 549) pistachio nuts. Transfer the parfait custard to a bowl and freeze it, covered, for 4 hours, or until firm. Serve the parfait in chilled shallow dessert bowls with whipped cream, Caramel Sauce (page 502), and chopped pistachio nuts and strawberries for garnish, if desired.

CHOCOLATE PARFAIT CUSTARD

Yield:
about 3 cups, serving 3

Equipment:
upright and hand-held electric mixers
pastry brush
candy thermometer

2 ounces semisweet chocolate, cut into bits
½ ounce unsweetened chocolate, cut into bits
2 large eggs
pinch of salt

½ cup sugar
¼ cup water
2 tablespoons dark rum
½ teaspoon vanilla
1 cup well-chilled heavy cream

In a small bowl set in a pan of hot water melt the semisweet and unsweetened chocolates.

In the bowl of the upright mixer beat the eggs with the salt until they are light and lemon colored. In a small heavy saucepan combine the sugar and the water and cook the mixture over low heat, stirring and washing down any sugar crystals clinging to the sides of the pan with the brush dipped in cold water, until the sugar is dissolved. Increase the heat to moderately high and boil the syrup, gently swirling the pan, until it reaches the thread stage, or the candy thermometer registers 230° F. (For the stages of sugar syrup, see illustrations page 241.)

With the upright mixer on high speed add the syrup in a stream to the eggs. Transfer the mixture to a heavy saucepan and cook it over moderately low heat, whisking, for 3 to 5 minutes, or until thick, but do not let it boil. Stir in the melted chocolate, transfer the mixture to a bowl set in a larger bowl of ice water, and stir the custard until cool. Stir in the rum and the vanilla.

In a chilled bowl with the hand-held mixer beat the cream until it holds soft peaks. Fold the cream into the custard. Freeze the parfait custard, covered, for 4 hours, or until firm.

ICES

What one person calls ice, another frequently calls sorbet, while another shouts sherbet. There seems to be a certain murkiness to this whole area called ices, which we would like to clarify once and for all. An ice or a sorbet begins with a simple sugar syrup, which is then combined with fruit purée and frozen. Sherbet, and we have some clue of this when it is called milk sherbet, is sorbet with milk or cream or egg white added. As our recipes for Lemon Sherbet (page 371) and the heavenly Creamy Banana Sherbet (page 372) demonstrate, an ice-cream freezer is not needed to make sherbet. Granita, notably different in texture, also begins with a sugar syrup, but is frozen in such a way as to render a grainy, deliberately unsmooth texture.

An ice by any name is remarkably refreshing.

CITRUS SORBET

Yield:
about 2 quarts

Equipment:
pastry brush
ice-cream freezer

This sorbet is flavored with three different citrus-fruit rinds, as well as Sauternes, a sweet wine, and Aquavit, a Scandinavian spirit made from barley malt and grain or potatoes and caraway seeds. A lovely combination for a long hot summer's day.

4¼ cups water
1¾ cups granulated sugar
the grated rind of 3 thin-skinned
*   oranges, plus the juice of 6 oranges*
the grated rind and juice of 2 large
*   grapefruits*

the grated rind of 1 lemon, plus the
*   juice of 3 lemons*
1¾ cups light Sauternes
1½ cups superfine granulated sugar
3 tablespoons Aquavit
mint sprigs for garnish

In a saucepan combine the water with the granulated sugar and cook the mixture over low heat, stirring and washing down any sugar crystals clinging to the sides of the pan with the brush dipped in cold water until the sugar is dissolved. Increase the heat to moderately high and boil the syrup, gently swirling the pan, for 5 minutes. Let cool and chill.

In a bowl combine the grated orange, grapefruit, and lemon rinds, the orange, grapefruit, and lemon juices, the Sauternes, superfine sugar, and the Aquavit and stir in the syrup. Transfer the mixture to the ice-cream freezer and freeze it according to the manufacturer's instructions. (Or divide the mixture among refrigerator trays and freeze it until slushy. Transfer the sorbet to a chilled bowl and beat it with a fork, wire whisk, or rotary beater to break up the ice crystals. Return to the refrigerator trays and freeze until frozen but not solid.) Serve garnished with mint sprigs.

Variations:

CIDER SORBET: In a saucepan combine ¾ cup sugar with 1 cup water, bring the mixture to a boil, and boil it for 6 minutes. Remove the pan from the heat and let the syrup cool. Stir in 2 cups apple cider, ½ cup fresh orange juice, the juice of 1 lemon, and a pinch of salt. Transfer the mixture to an ice-cream freezer and freeze according to the manufacturer's instructions. Or freeze in refrigerator trays as instructed for Citrus Sorbet (recipe opposite). Makes about 1 quart, serving 4.

FRESH STRAWBERRY SORBET: In a saucepan combine 1 cup each of sugar and water, bring the mixture to a boil, and boil it for 6 minutes. Let cool slightly. Stir in 1½ cups fresh strawberry purée (page 547), the juice of ½ lemon and ½ orange, and a pinch of salt. Transfer the mixture to an ice-cream freezer and freeze according to the manufacturer's instructions. Or freeze in refrigerator trays as instructed for Citrus Sorbet (recipe opposite). Makes about 1 quart, serving 4.

RASPBERRY SORBET: In a saucepan combine 1⅓ cups each of granulated sugar and water, bring the water to a boil over moderate heat, stirring, and cook the mixture, stirring, until the sugar is dissolved. Pour the syrup into a bowl set in a bowl of ice and cold water and chill it for 1 hour. In the food processor purée a 1-pound package of frozen raspberries, thawed, and strain the purée through a fine sieve into the syrup. Add the lemon juice and combine. Chill the mixture for at least 2 hours and freeze it in the ice-cream freezer according to the manufacturer's instructions. Makes about 1 quart.

MANGO AND LIME SORBET: With a sharp stainless steel knife or vegetable peeler peel 2 pounds mangoes and dice the flesh, reserving the pits. (There should be about 3 cups diced mangoes.) In a heavy saucepan combine 1½ cups water with 1 cup sugar and bring the mixture to a boil over moderate heat, stirring until the sugar is dissolved. Add the reserved mango pits and simmer the mixture, covered, for 5 minutes. Remove the pits with a slotted spoon, scrape any remaining pulp into the syrup, and discard the pits. Pour the syrup into a bowl set in a bowl of ice and chill it for 1 hour. In a food processor fitted with the steel blade or in a blender in batches purée the diced mango with the syrup mixture. Transfer the mixture to a bowl and stir in 3 tablespoons fresh lime juice, or to taste. Chill the mixture for at least 2 hours and freeze it in an ice-cream freezer according to the manufacturer's instructions. Using a small ice-cream scoop, scoop out balls of the sorbet, dividing them among well-chilled dessert plates. Garnish each serving with a sprig of fresh mint. Makes about 1 quart.

PINK GRAPEFRUIT SORBET

Yield:
6 servings

Equipment:
ice-cream freezer

1⅓ cups sugar
1⅓ cups water
juice of 3 large pink grapefruits, or
    enough to make 2½ cups strained
    juice

1 tablespoon grenadine
⅓ cup tequila

In a saucepan combine the sugar and water, bring the mixture to a boil over moderate heat, stirring, and cook it, stirring, until the sugar is dissolved. Transfer the syrup to a bowl and chill it for 1 hour. Chill the grapefruit juice in another bowl for 1 hour. Add the syrup, the grenadine, and tequila to the juice and chill for at least 2 hours. Freeze the mixture in the ice-cream freezer according to the manufacturer's instructions. Arrange 2 scoops of the sorbet in each dessert glass.

ANANAS EN SURPRISE

Pineapple Ice with Meringue

Yield:
10 to 12 servings

Equipment:
food processor fitted
  with steel blade
2 ice-cube trays with
  dividers
hand-held electric
  mixer
pastry bag fitted with
  small star tip

This dessert is an extraordinary combination of hot and cold—a lightly browned meringue covering fresh pineapple ice, beautifully presented in a pineapple shell.

FOR THE PINEAPPLE ICE
one 3½-pound pineapple
¼ to ⅓ cup granulated sugar

¼ to ⅓ cup fresh lemon juice

FOR THE MERINGUE
3 egg whites at room temperature
pinch of salt
pinch of cream of tartar

¾ cup granulated sugar, ground to a
    powder in the food processor or
    blender

confectioners' sugar to taste

Make the pineapple
ice:

Halve the pineapple lengthwise. With a grapefruit or other small sharp knife cut around the inside edges and remove the pulp, leaving ¼-inch-thick shells. Pat the shells dry and freeze them, covered with plastic wrap.

Core the pineapple pulp and cut it into 1-inch pieces. In the food processor or in a blender purée the pulp until smooth, blend in the granulated sugar and the lemon juice to taste, and transfer the mixture to the ice-cube trays. Freeze the ice in the freezing compartment of the refrigerator until frozen, transfer the cubes to the food processor, and blend them until the ice is light and fluffy. Pack the ice into the pineapple shells, mounding it slightly, and freeze the shells, covered with plastic wrap, in the freezing compartment of the refrigerator until the ice is frozen.

Make the meringue:
Preheat the broiler.

In a bowl with the mixer beat the whites with the salt until foamy, add the cream of tartar, and beat the whites until they hold soft peaks. Add the pulverized granulated sugar, one tablespoon at a time, and beat the meringue until it holds stiff peaks (see illustrations page 238).

Transfer the meringue to the pastry bag and pipe it decoratively over the ice, covering the ice completely. Sift the confectioners' sugar over the meringue, arrange the shells on a baking sheet, and put them under the broiler about 6 inches from the heat for 30 seconds to 1 minute, or until the meringue is browned lightly. Serve the desserts immediately.

Photo on page 57.

LEMON SHERBET

Yield:
about 1 quart

Equipment:
hand-held mixer (optional)

Sherbet is nothing more than sorbet enriched with egg white or milk or cream. Cool and refreshing by itself, this sherbet takes on other lovely dimensions when used to fill Crêpe Tulipes with Raspberries (page 439).

3 cups milk
1 cup sugar
2 teaspoons unflavored gelatin

½ cup fresh lemon juice
2½ teaspoons grated lemon rind
1 egg white at room temperature

In a saucepan combine the milk, sugar, and gelatin and cook the mixture over moderate heat, stirring, until the sugar is just dissolved. Let cool. Stir the lemon juice and rind into the milk mixture (the mixture will appear curdled), transfer the mixture to a shallow pan, and freeze it, covered, until mushy. Transfer the mixture to a bowl and with the mixer beat it until fluffy. In a bowl with the mixer beat the egg white until it holds soft peaks and fold it into the sherbet base. Transfer the sherbet to a container and freeze it, covered.

Photo on page 432.

Variation:

ORANGE SHERBET: Substitute ⅔ cup fresh orange juice for the lemon juice and add it to the cooled milk-gelatin mixture with 2 tablespoons grated orange rind and 1 tablespoon grated lemon rind. Freeze and finish the sherbet as directed.

CREAMY BANANA SHERBET

Yield:
about 1 quart

Equipment:
ice-cream freezer or
  food processor
  fitted with steel
  blade

2 large ripe bananas, mashed
½ cup honey
3 cups half-and-half

1 tablespoon fresh lemon juice
½ teaspoon vanilla

In a large bowl combine all the ingredients, beating the mixture until smooth. Transfer the mixture to the ice-cream freezer and freeze it according to the manufacturer's instructions. Or purée the ingredients in the food processor, transfer the purée to a shallow pan, and freeze, covered with plastic wrap, until almost frozen. Spoon the mixture back into the processor and process it until smooth and fluffy. Freeze the sherbet, covered, until firm.

HERB TEA GRANITA

Yield:
4 servings

Equipment:
2 metal ice-cube trays
  without dividers

Granita is made from light sugar syrup combined with various flavorings. Ice crystals are allowed to form during the freezing process, resulting in an interesting granular texture.

3 cups cold water
3 Red Zinger herb tea bags or other
  hibiscus-flavored herb tea bags
2 mint herb tea bags

½ cup sugar
1 teaspoon fresh lemon juice, or to
  taste
4 mint sprigs for garnish

In a saucepan bring the cold water to a boil, add the tea bags, and remove from the heat. Let the mixture steep, covered, for 10 minutes. Remove the tea bags, squeezing as much liquid as possible into the tea, add the sugar and the lemon juice, and stir the mixture until the sugar is dissolved. Transfer the mixture to a metal bowl set in a larger bowl of ice and cold water and let it stand, stirring occasionally, until cold. Divide the mixture between the ice-cube trays or place in a shallow metal bowl and freeze it, stirring with a fork every 30 minutes, for 2 to 3 hours, or until firm but not frozen hard. Divide the granita among chilled dessert dishes and garnish each with a mint sprig.

OTHER FROZEN DESSERTS

As informal and fun and convenient and cooling as ice cream can be, our frozen desserts are formal and fancy and fascinating. There is nothing inelegant about any of them. They are on a grand scale, and by that we do not mean difficult to do. They are grand in that they create an effect.

We have included frozen soufflés and mousses and *trompe l'oeil bombes*. Some are spectacular and meant to astonish. Take, for example, Watermelon Bombe (page 384): It looks exactly like a sliced watermelon, right down to the seeds, some of which are made with chocolate, others with almonds. You will need to make two different ice creams and a raspberry sorbet, but when you are done not even you will believe your eyes.

Frozen desserts are best reserved for special occasions. In such a way do they retain their cachet. A marvelous selection from which to choose follows, including a recipe for that great favorite—*tortoni*.

FROZEN SOUFFLÉS AND MOUSSES

For purposes of clarity, we are defining frozen soufflés as light and airy desserts that are frozen in soufflé dishes made taller with the aid of paper collars. Frozen mousses, on the other hand, are similar in texture but are not frozen in soufflé dishes, favoring decorative molds or individual containers instead.

That said, frozen soufflés and frozen mousses start with either an Italian meringue or ribboned egg yolk base to which whipped cream or egg whites (or both) and flavorings are added. Frozen soufflés, mousses, and ice-cream creations are, interestingly, not interchangable, although many of the ingredients often repeat from one recipe to another. It is, of course, how they are combined that makes the difference. The end is to form a structure that accepts the maximum amount of air to produce a lovely and smooth but substantial frozen dessert. Frozen soufflés and mousses have more air in them than, say, a well-made ice cream, and this is as it should be; ice cream, after all, is churned; soufflés and mousses delicately folded.

Whether you are making or partaking of a frozen soufflé or mousse, you have a great deal of pleasure ahead of you. They are particularly pretty desserts, elegant and enchanting, and wonderful in the summer or for a festive occasion at any other time of the year.

FROZEN ORANGE SOUFFLÉ

Yield:
one 6-cup soufflé,
serving 6 to 8

One of James Beard's original recipes, this frozen soufflé is made with an Italian meringue base to which whipped cream and flavorings are added.

Equipment:
6-cup soufflé dish
candy thermometer
upright and hand-held
electric mixers

1 cup sugar
⅓ cup water
4 tablespoons grated orange rind
4 egg whites at room temperature
*¼ cup plus 1 tablespoon orange-
  flavored liqueur*

2½ cups well-chilled heavy cream
*orange sections or Candied Orange
  Peel (page 522), cut into long
  shreds, and Candied Violets (page
  524) for garnish*

Brush a 6-inch-wide doubled band of wax paper or foil long enough to fit around the soufflé dish with flavorless vegetable oil and fit the dish with a collar extending 3 inches above the rim. Secure it with string or tape (see illustration page 417). Put the dish in the freezer while making the filling.

Make the meringue:
In a saucepan cook the sugar and water, stirring, until the sugar is dissolved. Add 2 tablespoons of the grated orange rind, bring the syrup to a boil, and boil it until it reaches the soft-ball stage, or the candy thermometer registers 234° F. In the bowl of the upright mixer beat the egg whites until they hold soft peaks. Pour the hot syrup over them in a thin stream, beating constantly, and continue to beat the meringue until it holds firm peaks. (For the stages of sugar syrup and how to pour it, see illustrations pages 240 and 241.) Beat in the ¼ cup orange-flavored liqueur.

In a chilled bowl with the hand-held mixer whip the cream until it is firm. Fold in the remaining 2 tablespoons grated orange rind and the remaining 1 tablespoon orange-flavored liqueur. Fold the whipped cream into the meringue.

Fill the soufflé dish with the mixture, smoothing the top. Drape a piece of plastic wrap over the collar and dish and freeze the soufflé for about 6 hours, or until firm. Remove the plastic wrap and collar carefully and garnish the soufflé with the orange sections or candied orange peel and candied violets. Serve the soufflé with a delicate spongecake or with Madeleines (page 296).

FROZEN RASPBERRY SOUFFLÉ

Yield:
one 6-cup soufflé,
serving 6 to 8

*1¼ cups strained puréed fresh or
  frozen raspberries (about 14 ounces
  whole raspberries) plus 6 to 8
  whole raspberries for garnish*
1 tablespoon fresh lemon juice
*2 tablespoons eau-de-vie de
  framboise (raspberry brandy)*

⅔ cup plus 3 tablespoons sugar
3 tablespoons water
4 egg whites at room temperature
pinch of salt
1⅔ cups well-chilled heavy cream
*1 recipe Raspberry Sauce (page 508)
  as an accompaniment*

Equipment:
6-cup soufflé dish
pastry brush
candy thermometer
upright and hand-held
electric mixers

Brush a 6-inch-wide doubled band of wax paper or foil long enough to fit around the soufflé dish with flavorless vegetable oil and fit the dish with a collar extending 3 inches above the rim. Secure it with string or tape (see illustration page 417).

In a bowl combine the raspberry purée, lemon juice, and the *framboise.*

In a small heavy saucepan combine the ⅔ cup sugar with the water, bring the mixture to a boil, gently swirling the pan and washing down any sugar crystals clinging to the sides of the pan with the brush dipped in cold water, and boil the syrup until it reaches the soft-ball stage, or the candy thermometer reaches 238° F. In the bowl of the upright mixer beat the egg whites with the salt until they hold stiff peaks. With the mixer running, add the sugar syrup in a stream and beat the whites until cool. (For the stages of sugar syrup and how to pour it, see illustrations pages 240 and 241.)

In a chilled bowl with the hand-held mixer beat the cream with the remaining 3 tablespoons sugar until it holds soft peaks. Fold the whites into the raspberry purée gently but thoroughly and fold in the whipped cream. Spoon the mixture into the prepared dish, smooth the top, and freeze it for at least 6 hours, or overnight. Before serving, remove the wax paper collar carefully, garnish the top of the soufflé with the remaining whole raspberries, and serve with the raspberry sauce.

FROZEN HAZELNUT PRALINE SOUFFLÉ

Yield:
one 3-cup soufflé,
serving 3 to 4

Equipment:
3-cup soufflé dish
upright and hand-held
electric mixers

*½ recipe hazelnut praline (page 544),
    finely ground
6 egg yolks
½ cup sugar*

*1½ cups well-chilled heavy cream
3 to 4 tablespoons orange-flavored
    liqueur
unsweetened cocoa powder for dusting*

Brush a 6-inch-wide doubled band of wax paper or foil long enough to fit around the soufflé dish with flavorless vegetable oil and fit the dish with a collar extending 3 inches above the rim. Secure it with string or tape (see illustration page 417).

In the bowl of the upright mixer beat the egg yolks until combined and gradually add the sugar. Beat at high speed for 8 minutes, or until the mixture is pale and very thick and falls in a ribbon when the beater is lifted (see illustration page 16). (Or put the bowl over hot water and beat the mixture vigorously with a rotary beater.) In a chilled bowl with the hand-held mixer whip the heavy cream until it holds stiff peaks and fold it into the egg yolk mixture. Add the orange-flavored liqueur and stir in about ¾ cup of the praline. Pour the mixture into the soufflé dish and freeze for at least 4 hours. At serving time, transfer the dish to a cool place for about 5 minutes and carefully remove the collar. Press the remaining praline around the edges of the soufflé and sprinkle the top with the cocoa powder.

FROZEN MAPLE WALNUT SOUFFLÉ

Yield:
one 2-quart soufflé,
  serving 12

Equipment:
2-quart soufflé dish
upright and hand-held
  electric mixers
pastry brush
candy thermometer

*9 large eggs, separated, at room
  temperature*
1 cup sugar
⅓ cup water
⅓ cup dark rum
3 cups well-chilled heavy cream

1 cup maple syrup
pinch of salt
*2 cups ground walnuts, plus
  additional for garnish*
*walnut halves and rum-flavored
  whipped cream if desired*

Brush a 6-inch-wide doubled band of wax paper or foil long enough to fit around the soufflé dish with flavorless vegetable oil and fit the dish with a collar extending 3 inches above the rim. Secure it with string or tape (see illustration page 417).

In the large bowl of the upright mixer beat the egg yolks until they are thick and fall in a ribbon when the beater is lifted (see illustration page 16). In a small saucepan combine the sugar with the water, bring the liquid to a boil over moderately low heat, washing down any sugar crystals clinging to the sides of the pan with the brush dipped in cold water, and boil the syrup, gently swirling the pan, until it reaches the soft-ball stage, or the candy thermometer registers 234° F. (For the stages of sugar syrup, see illustrations page 241.) With the mixer on high speed, pour the syrup into the egg yolks in a stream and continue to beat the mixture for 10 minutes, or until thick and creamy. Beat in the rum.

In a large chilled bowl with the hand-held mixer beat the heavy cream until it holds soft peaks, add the maple syrup, and beat until the mixture holds stiff peaks. Fold the mixture into the egg yolk mixture. In another bowl with the upright mixer beat the egg whites with the salt until they hold stiff peaks and fold them into the egg yolk mixture with 2 cups ground walnuts. Transfer the mixture to the soufflé dish, smooth the top with a spatula, and freeze the soufflé overnight.

Remove the collar carefully, decorate the sides of the soufflé with walnut halves, and refreeze the soufflé. Before serving, decorate the top of the soufflé with a walnut half, rosettes of whipped cream if desired, and the remaining ground walnuts.

FROZEN DARK CHOCOLATE MOUSSE

Yield:
about 4 cups, serving
  4 to 6

Equipment:
1-quart mold
upright electric mixer
pastry brush
candy thermometer

8 ounces unsweetened chocolate,
  chopped coarse
4 large eggs, separated, at room
  temperature
1 cup sugar
¼ cup water
1 stick plus 2 tablespoons (10
  tablespoons) unsalted butter,
  softened

2 tablespoons coffee-flavored liqueur
  or dark rum
whipped cream for garnish
grated chocolate for garnish if desired

Brush the mold with flavorless vegetable oil.

In the top of a double boiler or in a bowl set in a pan of hot water melt the chocolate, stirring, and let cool.

In the bowl of the mixer beat the egg yolks until they are light and lemon colored. In a small heavy saucepan combine ¾ cup of the sugar and the water, bring the mixture to a boil, and boil it over moderate heat, washing down any sugar crystals clinging to the sides of the pan with the brush dipped in cold water, until it reaches the thread stage, or a candy thermometer registers 228° F. (For the stages of sugar syrup, see illustrations page 241.) With the mixer on high, add the hot syrup to the yolks in a stream and beat the mixture until cool. Add the butter, one tablespoon at a time, and beat the mixture until combined well. Add the chocolate and the liqueur or rum and beat the mixture until light and fluffy. Transfer the mixture to a large bowl.

In another bowl of the mixer beat the egg whites until they hold soft peaks. Gradually add the remaining ¼ cup sugar and beat the whites until they hold stiff peaks (see illustrations page 238). Stir one quarter of the whites into the chocolate mixture and fold in the remaining whites gently but thoroughly. Spoon the mousse into the mold, smooth the top, and freeze it, covered, for at least 4 hours, or until firm.

To serve, dip the mold into hot water for 1 minute and invert the mousse onto a plate. Garnish the mousse with the whipped cream and grated chocolate if desired.

Variation:

FROZEN WHITE AND DARK CHOCOLATE MOUSSE: Make 1 recipe each of unfrozen Frozen Dark Chocolate Mousse and unchilled White Chocolate Mousse (page 392). Pour the dark chocolate mixture into a 2-quart mold brushed with flavorless vegetable oil, add the white chocolate mixture, and with a knife swirl the mixtures together. Freeze the mousse, covered, for at least 4 hours, or until firm. Unmold and garnish as above. Serves 8 to 10.

FROZEN INDIVIDUAL COFFEE MOUSSES

Yield:
12 servings

Equipment:
hand-held and upright
   electric mixers
baking dish, 15 by 12
   by 3 inches
3-inch fluted cutter
   (optional)

10 large eggs, separated, at room
   temperature
½ cup plus 2 tablespoons granulated
   sugar
2 tablespoons plus 2 teaspoons instant
   espresso powder
½ teaspoon salt
½ teaspoon cream of tartar

2½ cups well-chilled heavy cream
⅓ cup confectioners' sugar
1½ teaspoons vanilla
12 chocolate coffee beans for garnish
   (available at specialty foods shops)
Almond Curl Cookies (page 290) as
   an accompaniment

In a large heatproof bowl set over a saucepan of simmering water with the hand-held mixer beat the egg yolks and the granulated sugar until the mixture falls in a ribbon when the beater is lifted (see illustration page 16). Add the instant espresso powder and beat until the powder is dissolved. Set the bowl in a large bowl of cracked ice and with the mixer beat the mixture until cool. In the bowl of the upright mixer beat the egg whites with the salt until frothy. Add the cream of tartar and beat until the whites hold soft peaks.

In a large chilled bowl with the hand-held mixer beat the cream with the confectioners' sugar and the vanilla until it holds stiff peaks. Fold the cream into the coffee mixture gently but thoroughly, fold in the egg whites gently but thoroughly, and transfer the mixture to the baking dish, smoothing the top. Freeze the mousse, covered with foil, for 6 hours or overnight.

Working quickly so that the mousse does not melt, score the top of the mousse in a crosshatch pattern with a knife, cut out 12 rounds with the cutter (or cut out squares if desired), and transfer them carefully with a chilled spatula to a chilled platter. Garnish each mousse with a chocolate coffee bean and freeze the mousses for at least 10 minutes, or until ready to serve. Serve with the cookies.

ESPRESSO TORTONI WITH CHOCOLATE-COVERED COFFEE BEANS

Yield:
6 servings

1 egg white at room temperature
pinch of cream of tartar
¼ cup granulated sugar
1 cup well-chilled heavy cream
1 tablespoon instant espresso powder
2 tablespoons Kahlúa

3 tablespoons finely chopped amaretti
   (Italian almond macaroons,
   available at specialty foods shops
   and some supermarkets)
2 ounces semisweet chocolate, chopped
about 24 espresso coffee beans
6 thin strips of lemon rind, tied in
   knots

Espresso Tortoni with Chocolate-Covered Coffee Beans (opposite)

Equipment:
hand-held electric
mixer
six ½-cup ramekins,
dishes, or espresso
cups
large-holed sieve
24 straight pins

In a bowl with the mixer beat the egg white until frothy, add the cream of tartar, and beat the white until it holds soft peaks. Add 1 tablespoon of the sugar, a little at a time, beating, and beat the white until it just holds stiff peaks (see illustrations page 238). In another chilled bowl with the mixer beat the cream with the espresso powder until it begins to thicken, add the remaining 3 tablespoons sugar and the Kahlúa, and beat the cream until it just holds stiff peaks. Stir one third of the whipped cream mixture into the egg white mixture and fold in the remaining whipped cream mixture with 2½ tablespoons of the *amaretti* crumbs gently but thoroughly. Spoon the mixture into the ramekins, smoothing the tops, sprinkle the tops with the remaining 1½ teaspoons *amaretti* crumbs, and freeze the tortonis, covered tightly, for at least 2 hours and up to 2 days.

In a small heatproof bowl set over barely simmering water melt the chocolate. Invert the sieve on a plate. Insert a pin into each coffee bean, dip the beans carefullly into the chocolate, coating them completely, and insert the heads of the pins at an angle into the sieve. (Reserve the remaining chocolate for another use.) Freeze the chocolate-covered coffee beans for at least 15 minutes or overnight and garnish each dessert with 3 or 4 of them and a lemon knot.

Photo above.

Cranberry Ice Mold (page 385)

BOMBES AND MOLDS

Unlike a frozen soufflé, which utilizes a simple soufflé dish in which to set, a *bombe* requires a mold, one that is spherically shaped, whence it derives its name. The mold is lined with one ice cream and customarily filled with a softer-textured filling, called an *appareil à bombe*. *Bombes* are part of the classic French cuisine and when you think of what it must have been like to prepare them, at the French court, for instance, with only ice blocks for refrigeration, you marvel once again at the splendid concept. They are dessert and astonishment all in one. Some of them also have the most marvelous names. For example, Bombe Joséphine (page 382) couples vanilla ice cream on the outside, a thin layer of orange sherbet within, with a creamy orange-liqueur-flavored mousse in the center. Bombe Adeline (page 381)—and we have to wonder who these legendary women were—boasts raspberry sorbet on the outside and a fragrant, wonderful, black currant mixture within. These are just two of the *bombes* we include.

The remaining molds in this collection are, admittedly, less dramatic but no less satisfying. Cranberry Ice Mold (page 385) makes a beautiful light dessert for the holidays and Spongecake Layered with Chocolate Ice Cream and Chocolate Mousse (page 386) is one of those wonderful desserts that everyone loves. We think it fair to say that *bombes* and molds are significantly more promising than their names might suggest.

PINEAPPLE STRAWBERRY BOMBE

Yield:
1-quart mold,
  serving 4

Equipment:
upright and hand-held
  electric mixers
1-quart mold

A *bombe* takes its name from the spherical mold in which the ice cream is frozen. They are made with layers of different flavored ice creams and garnishes, which in turn are made with an *appareil à bombe*—a custard-based ice-cream mixture that serves as the creamy center of this molded dessert. Bombe Adeline, a raspberry sorbet and black currant purée combination, and Bombe Joséphine, a vanilla ice cream, orange sherbet, and ground pistachio nuts combination, serve as splendid examples. The following recipe combines pineapple ice and strawberry purée and is garnished with candied strawberries.

*1 recipe pineapple ice (page 370),
    reserving half for another use*
½ cup sugar
⅓ cup water
3 egg yolks

½ pint strawberries, hulled and sliced
½ cup well-chilled heavy cream
*Candied Strawberries (page 523) and
    Candied Pineapple (page 523) for
    garnish if desired*

In a small saucepan combine the sugar and water and cook the mixture over low heat, stirring, until the sugar is dissolved. Bring the syrup just to a boil and let cool until lukewarm. In the bowl of the upright mixer beat the egg yolks until they are lemon colored and add the syrup in a stream, stirring. Transfer the mixture to the top of a double boiler and cook it over simmering water, stirring, preferably with a wooden spoon, for 15 to 20 minutes, or until it is thick enough to coat the spoon. Transfer the mixture to a bowl and beat it with the mixer until it is cool and falls in a ribbon when the beater is lifted (see illustration page 16). Chill the mixture, covered, for 1 hour.

In a heavy stainless steel saucepan cook the strawberries over moderate heat, stirring, for 15 minutes, or until they are reduced to a thick purée. Transfer the purée to a bowl and chill it, covered, for 1 hour.

Line the mold or bowl with a 1-inch layer of the pineapple ice, pressing the ice onto the bottom and sides, and freeze the ice until it is solid. In a chilled bowl with the hand-held mixer beat the cream until it holds soft peaks. Whisk the strawberry purée into the yolk mixture and fold in the whipped cream. Spoon the mixture into the lined mold and freeze the mold, covered with wax paper, for at least 6 hours or overnight. Remove the paper, dip the mold in warm water for several seconds to loosen it, and run a thin knife around the edge of the mold. Invert a chilled plate over the mold, invert the mold onto it, and decorate it with the candied strawberries and pineapple, if desired.

Variations:

BOMBE ADELINE: Oil a 2-quart melon mold and line it with a 1-inch-thick layer of Raspberry Sorbet (page 369). Freeze for 2 hours, or until the sorbet is hard.

Make the *appareil à bombe*:

In the bowl of the upright mixer beat 4 egg yolks until they are light and lemon colored and fall in a ribbon when the beater is lifted (see illustration page 16). In a saucepan bring 1 cup sugar and ½ cup water to a boil, stirring until the sugar is dissolved, and boil the syrup until it reaches the soft-ball stage, or a candy thermometer registers 234° F. (For the stages of sugar syrup, see illustrations page 241.) With the mixer running, drizzle the syrup into the egg yolks. Set the bowl over a bowl of ice and continue to beat the mixture for 5 to 10 minutes, or until cool. Fold in 1 cup black currant purée, made by sieving black currant preserves well and blending them with 3 tablespoons *crème de cassis* (black currant liqueur). In a chilled bowl whip 1 cup well-chilled heavy cream until stiff, fold it into the mixture, and fill the raspberry sorbet-lined *bombe* with it. Freeze for 2 hours. Cover the filling with a layer of the raspberry sorbet. Cover the *bombe* with the melon mold top or with foil and freeze it for 4 to 6 hours. Unmold the *bombe* onto a chilled platter, pipe vanilla-flavored whipped cream decoratively over it, and garnish it with fresh raspberries. Or serve the *bombe* with raspberry purée (page 546) and whipped cream. Serves 8.

BOMBE JOSÉPHINE: Oil a 3-quart mold, line it with a 1- to 1½-inch-thick layer of Vanilla Ice Cream (page 349), and sprinkle it very generously with finely ground unsalted pistachio nuts. Freeze the mold for 2 hours. Cover the ice cream with a thin layer of Orange Sherbet (page 371) and freeze it for 2 hours.

Make the *appareil à bombe*:

In the bowl of the upright mixer beat 8 egg yolks until they are light and lemon colored and fall in a ribbon when the beater is lifted (see illustration page 16). In a saucepan bring ¾ cup sugar and ½ cup water to a boil, stirring until the sugar is dissolved, and boil the syrup until it reaches the soft-ball stage, or a candy thermometer registers 234° F. (For the stages of sugar syrup, see illustrations page 241.) In the bowl of the upright mixer beat the syrup into the egg yolks in a thin stream and continue to beat the mixture until cool. Stir in ½ cup finely chopped Candied Orange Peel (page 522) and 3 tablespoons orange-flavored liqueur.

In a chilled bowl beat 2 cups well-chilled heavy cream until stiff and fold it into the egg mixture. Fill the *bombe* with the mixture, cover it with foil or plastic wrap, and freeze it for 3 hours. Cover the *bombe* with a layer of the vanilla ice cream, cover it with foil, and freeze for 6 to 8 hours. Unmold the *bombe* on a chilled platter and pipe rosettes of vanilla-flavored whipped cream over the surface. Decorate the dessert with Candied Violets (page 524). Serves 12.

ESPRESSO RUM BOMBE

Yield:
about 3 cups,
   serving 4

Equipment:
3-cup steamed
   pudding mold
   (available at
   specialty
   kitchenware stores)
food processor fitted
   with steel blade
hand-held electric
   mixer
ice-cream freezer
pastry bag fitted with
   decorative tip

While called a *bombe*, this dessert is actually formed in a steamed pudding mold, providing not only an interesting variation, but another use for this infrequently utilized piece of kitchen equipment.

¾ cup sugar
a 2-inch length of vanilla bean
1 cup milk
1 cup heavy cream
4 egg yolks
⅓ cup brewed espresso
2 tablespoons very finely ground
   espresso, plus additional ground
   espresso for sprinkling

1 cup Vanilla Ice Cream (page 349),
   softened slightly
2 tablespoons dark rum
sweetened rum-flavored whipped
   cream for garnish

Lightly oil the steamed pudding mold with flavorless vegetable oil.

In the food processor or in a blender blend the sugar with the vanilla bean until the bean is pulverized. In a heavy saucepan combine the sugar mixture with the milk and heavy cream and scald the mixture over moderate heat, stirring. In a bowl with the mixer beat the egg yolks until they are light and thick and, with the mixer running, pour the milk mixture through a fine sieve into the bowl in a stream. Transfer the custard to another heavy saucepan and cook it over moderately low heat, stirring, preferably with a wooden spoon, until it coats the back of the spoon, about 5 to 7 minutes. Stir in the brewed espresso. Transfer the custard to a metal bowl, set the bowl in a bowl of ice and cold water, and let the custard cool completely, covered with a round of wax paper or plastic wrap. Chill the custard for 2 hours, stir in the 2 tablespoons finely ground espresso, and freeze the custard in the ice-cream freezer according to the manufacturer's instructions.

Line the pudding mold with the espresso ice cream, making a layer about 1 inch thick. Freeze the ice cream, covered, until firm.

In a small bowl combine the vanilla ice cream and the rum and pack the mixture into the mold. Freeze the *bombe*, covered, until very hard. Loosen the edge with a sharp knife and invert the *bombe* onto a chilled serving plate, rubbing the mold with a dish towel rinsed in hot water and wrung out to loosen the ice cream from the mold, if necessary. Return the *bombe* to the freezer for a few minutes, if necessary, to keep it from melting. With the pastry bag pipe rosettes of the whipped cream in a pinwheel pattern onto the *bombe*. Sprinkle the top with the remaining ground espresso.

The *bombe* may be kept, decorated and frozen, for 24 hours.

Watermelon Bombe (below)

WATERMELON BOMBE

Yield:
serving 12 to 15

Equipment:
4-quart metal mixing
  bowl with a round
  bottom
ice-cream freezer
pastry brush

Two different kinds of ice cream and a sherbet are so constructed to re-semble a sliced watermelon; we've even simulated watermelon seeds. Here is *trompe l'oeil* dessert-making at it best.

custard mixture for 1½ recipes
  Pistachio Ice Cream (page 349),
  chilled but not frozen
custard mixture for 1½ recipes
  Vanilla Ice Cream (page 349),
  chilled but not frozen

mixture for 1½ recipes Raspberry
  Sorbet (page 369), chilled but not
  frozen
green food coloring
Chocolate Paillettes (page 529)
halved blanched almonds

Chill the metal mixing bowl.

Freeze the pistachio custard in the ice-cream freezer. Line the cold bowl with a ¾-inch layer of the ice cream, smoothing it with a metal spatula. Freeze the ice cream in the freezing compartment of the refrigerator for 1 hour. Freeze the vanilla custard in the ice-cream freezer. Spread a 1-inch layer of vanilla ice cream over the pistachio ice cream and freeze it for 1 hour. Freeze the raspberry mixture in the ice-cream freezer. Fill the bowl with the raspberry sorbet and freeze the *bombe*, well covered with plastic wrap, in the freezing compartment of the refrigerator for at least 8 hours or overnight.

Dip the bowl briefly into warm water, put a chilled dish over the bowl, and invert the *bombe* with a sharp rap onto the dish. To simulate watermelon skin, striate the pistachio ice cream with the brush dipped in green food coloring diluted with water. Cut the *bombe* into 1-inch-thick slices and quarter the slices. To simulate watermelon seeds, press 4 or 5 chocolate paillettes and 2 or 3 halved blanched almonds, trimmed a bit smaller, into each quarter slice. Arrange the slices and the remaining *bombe* on a platter and keep them frozen in the freezing compartment of the refrigerator, removing the platter 10 to 15 minutes before serving.

Photo opposite.

CRANBERRY ICE MOLD

Yield:
8 servings

Equipment:
1-quart decorative mold (preferably tin)
pastry brush
food processor fitted with steel blade or food mill
ice-cream freezer
2-pound weight

This is a magnificent dessert for the holidays—refreshing and simple to make. Consider serving it with Pumpkin Pie (page 142) to end the Thanksgiving feast on a high note.

4 cups cranberries, picked over and rinsed
5 cups water
½ cup superfine granulated sugar
2 cups granulated sugar

¾ cup fresh lemon juice
⅓ cup fresh orange juice
Frosted Cranberries (page 524) and candied mint leaves (available at specialty foods shops) for garnish

Chill the mold.

In a large enameled or stainless steel saucepan combine the cranberries and 2 cups of the water, bring the water to a boil over moderate heat, and stir in the superfine sugar. Simmer the mixture, washing down any sugar crystals clinging to the sides of the pan with the brush dipped in cold water, for 10 minutes. Purée the mixture in the processor or through the food mill into a bowl. Let the purée cool and chill it, covered, for at least 2 hours.

In a saucepan combine the remaining 3 cups water and the granulated sugar and cook the mixture over moderately low heat, stirring, until the sugar is dissolved. Bring the syrup to a boil, washing down any sugar crystals clinging to the sides of the pan with the brush dipped in cold water, and simmer for 3 minutes. Transfer the syrup to a large bowl, let it cool to room temperature, and chill it, covered, for at least 2 hours. Stir in the cranberry purée, lemon juice, and orange juice and freeze the mixture in the ice-cream freezer according to the manufacturer's instructions.

Fill the mold with the cranberry ice, packing it well, cover it with plastic wrap and a sheet of foil, and top it with the weight. Freeze for at least 6 hours or overnight. Run a thin knife around the rim of the mold, dip the mold in cool water for 2 or 3 seconds, and invert a chilled serving dish over it. Invert the mold with a sharp rap onto the serving dish. Garnish with the frosted cranberries and candied mint leaves.

Photo on page 380.

SPONGECAKE LAYERED WITH CHOCOLATE ICE CREAM AND CHOCOLATE MOUSSE

Yield:
8 servings

Equipment:
9-inch springform pan
upright electric mixer
pastry brush
2½-quart stainless
steel or glass mixing
bowl

This ice-cream creation fits almost any occasion. It is a glorious combination of spongecake, chocolate mousse, and chocolate ice cream served with whipped cream and garnished with grated chocolate.

FOR THE SPONGECAKE

6 large eggs, separated, at room temperature
pinch of salt
pinch of cream of tartar

1 cup sugar
1 tablespoon fresh lemon juice
1 cup all-purpose flour

FOR THE CHOCOLATE MOUSSE

4 egg yolks
⅔ cup sugar
2 teaspoons light corn syrup

3 tablespoons water
½ cup coarsely grated semisweet chocolate, melted and cooled

1 quart Dark Chocolate Ice Cream (page 349), softened
½ cup chopped toasted pecans
⅓ cup brandy combined with ⅓ cup orange-flavored liqueur
1½ cups well-chilled heavy cream

2 teaspoons vanilla
3 tablespoons grated semisweet chocolate for garnish
3 tablespoons unsweetened cocoa powder for garnish

Butter the pan, line the bottom with wax paper, and butter the paper. Dust the pan with flour and shaking out the excess. Preheat the oven to 350° F.

Make the spongecake:
In the bowl of the mixer beat the egg whites with the salt until frothy, add the cream of tartar, and beat until the whites hold soft peaks. Add ¼ cup of the sugar, a little at a time, beating, and beat the whites until they

hold stiff peaks (see illustrations page 238). In another bowl of the mixer beat the egg yolks with the lemon juice until they are lemon colored, beat in the remaining ¾ cup sugar, a little at a time, and beat the mixture until thick. Stir one fourth of the whites into the yolk mixture and fold in the remaining whites gently but thoroughly. Fold in the flour gently but thoroughly, ⅓ cup at a time. Spoon the batter into the pan and bake in the middle of the oven for 40 to 45 minutes, or until a cake tester inserted in the center comes out clean. Let the cake cool in the pan on a rack for 10 minutes, run a thin knife around the edge, and remove the sides of the pan. Let the cake cool on a rack.

Make the chocolate mousse: In the bowl of the mixer beat the egg yolks until lemon colored. In a small heavy saucepan combine the sugar and the corn syrup with the water, bring the mixture to a boil, and boil it over moderate heat, washing down any sugar crystals clinging to the sides of the pan with the brush dipped in cold water until it reaches the soft-ball stage, or the candy thermometer registers 238° F. (For the stages of sugar syrup, see illustrations page 241.) With the mixer running, add the hot syrup to the yolks in a stream and beat the mixture until completely cool. Transfer the mixture to a bowl, fold in the melted chocolate, and chill the mousse, covered, for 30 minutes.

To assemble the cake: In a bowl combine the ice cream and the pecans. Cut the spongecake horizontally into ½-inch-thick layers (see illustration page 19). Line the bottom and sides of the bowl with the cake, cut to fit, reserving 2 layers intact, and brush the cake with one third of the brandy mixture. Spoon the ice-cream mixture over the cake and cover it with one of the remaining layers of cake. Brush the cake with half the remaining brandy mixture, spoon the mousse over it, and cover it with the remaining cake layer. Sprinkle the remaining brandy mixture over the cake and freeze the mold, covered, until it is firm.

In a chilled bowl of the mixer beat the cream with the vanilla until it holds stiff peaks. Run a thin knife around the edge of the bowl, invert a chilled serving dish over the bowl, and invert the mold onto it. Sprinkle the mold with the grated chocolate and the cocoa powder and serve it with the whipped cream.

CHILLED DESSERTS

*I*f consuming ice cream amounts to almost a national pastime, transcending borders and good common sense, we suspect that eating chilled desserts could very probably attain the same popularity. It is just a matter of time, for in many cases we are only talking about differences of degrees between the two. A frozen dessert, such as ice cream, is simply colder than a chilled dessert. Take, for example, frozen versus chilled soufflés: The same ingredients, the difference is in the temperature.

In this burgeoning movement, therefore, we are first to extol the chilled dessert. We are including among them mousses—and there are many types—soufflés, Bavarian creams, and still other molded chilled desserts.

The variety of mousses alone is fascinating: To begin with, a mousse is a light, airy combination that can incorporate a variety of ingredients to render its texture. It is the texture that counts, however, and it should be somewhere between earth and moon, *sans* gravity. Sometimes this ethereal effect is rendered by mere stiffly beaten egg whites; sometimes by whipped cream; sometimes by gelatin in combination with the above; and sometimes by a sugar-syrup-based meringue and whipped cream. How it is achieved you will not forget once you have tasted it.

The other chilled desserts in this chapter are molded desserts, and are equally memorable. Take Raspberry Spiral Bavarian Cream (page 404), for example, or the no less classic cheese combination of Coeur à la Crème (page 408), or the grand Riz à l'Impératrice (page 410).

The fact that there are so many classic desserts in this chapter attests to the overall popularity of the chilled dessert. Mousses are very much in the popular vernacular again, and we would hope other chilled desserts to quickly follow suit.

Bavarois Rubané
(page 403)

CHILLED MOUSSES

A chilled mousse is distinguished by its texture, which should be light and airy and almost ethereal. This can be achieved in several different ways by adding to the base (1) stiffly beaten egg whites; (2) stiffly beaten egg whites and whipped heavy cream; (3) gelatin, stiffly beaten egg whites, and whipped cream; or (4) Italian meringue, sometimes combined with whipped heavy cream. While mousses might be light in texture, they are not, as the preceding descriptions attest, for those on a restricted regime! They are luxurious in texture—a wonderful summer dessert when made with fresh fruit purée and served in a hollowed-out citrus shell, for example, and an equally fine winter dessert when combined with chocolate, the perfect cold-weather antidote.

Chilled mousses are also beautiful to serve. They can be presented individually, with a favorite fruit sauce, perhaps. Or they can be served as one, in a lovely crystal bowl with the appropriate garnish.

Chilled mousses are also not difficult to prepare. The simple precautions of beating egg whites or cream or working with gelatin apply. The final incorporation of all the ingredients, however, should be done carefully. Your finished mousse should betray no signs of egg whites or traces of insufficiently folded-in whipped cream.

Lest we forget, chilled mousses also play another role: as the filling in layer cakes. For a remarkable example of this, see Chocolate Mousse Cake with Ganache Icing (page 64), the cake on the jacket of this volume.

ITALIAN ORANGE MOUSSE

Yield:
6 to 8 servings

Equipment:
hand-held electric mixer

7 large eggs, separated, at room temperature
¼ cup plus 7 tablespoons sugar

grated rind and juice of 1 orange
2 tablespoons Marsala
½ cup dry white wine

In a bowl with the mixer beat the egg yolks with the 7 tablespoons sugar until thick. Beat in the rind and juice of the orange and the Marsala. (The mixture will be thin.) Transfer the mixture to the top of a double boiler set over simmering but not boiling water, add the white wine, and beat the mixture constantly until it thickens and rises. Remove the pan from the heat and let cool.

In a bowl with the mixer beat the egg whites until they hold soft peaks. Beat in the remaining ¼ cup sugar, a little at a time, beating until stiff peaks form (see illustrations page 238) and fold the meringue gently but thoroughly into the yolk mixture. Transfer the mousse to a serving bowl and chill it, covered, for at least 2 hours.

CHOCOLATE ORANGE MOUSSE

Yield:
4 to 6 servings

Equipment:
hand-held electric
mixer

*4 ounces dark sweet chocolate,
chopped coarse
2 ounces bittersweet chocolate,
chopped coarse
5 tablespoons fresh orange juice*

*5 large eggs, separated, at room
temperature
1 tablespoon grated orange rind
2 tablespoons orange-flavored liqueur
if desired
whipped cream for garnish*

In a small heavy saucepan melt both chocolates with the orange juice over low heat, stirring constantly to prevent the chocolate from scorching. Remove the pan from the heat and beat in the egg yolks, one at a time. Stir in the orange rind and, if desired, the orange-flavored liqueur.

In a bowl with the mixer beat the egg whites until they hold stiff but not dry peaks and fold them gently but thoroughly into the yolk mixture. Pour the mousse into goblets and chill, covered, for at least 3 hours. Before serving, top each mousse with a dollop of whipped cream.

Variation:

CHOCOLATE MOUSSE À L'ORANGE: Cut the top third from 4 navel oranges, remove the pulp from the oranges, and reserve it for another use. Scrape the excess membrane from the orange shells with a spoon and chill the shells. Make Chocolate Orange Mousse, adding 3 tablespoons minced Candied Orange Peel (page 522) to the chocolate mixture. With a pastry bag fitted with a fluted tip pipe the mousse decoratively into the orange shells and chill the dessert, covered loosely, for 6 hours or overnight. Pipe a small rosette of lightly sweetened whipped cream onto each mousse before serving.

LEMON SYLLABUB

Yield:
6 servings

Equipment:
hand-held electric
mixer

This dessert, which may also be served as a thick luscious punch, dates back to the Elizabethan period. Its name is derived from "Sille," a wine popular long ago in England, and "bub," the Elizabethan colloquial term for frothy drink. An excellent accompaniment to syllabub would be Lemon Thins (page 266) or Ladyfingers (page 286).

*¼ cup fresh lemon juice
2 tablespoons superfine granulated
sugar*

*⅓ cup Champagne or brandy
1 tablespoon grated lemon rind
1½ cups well-chilled heavy cream*

In a ceramic or glass bowl combine the lemon juice, sugar, Champagne, and the lemon rind and chill until very cold. Add the cream and with the mixer beat until very thick. Spoon the syllabub into chilled Champagne glasses and chill the desserts until ready to serve.

WHITE CHOCOLATE MOUSSE WITH DARK CHOCOLATE SAUCE

Yield:
about 4 cups,
serving 6

Equipment:
hand-held mixer
  (optional)
1-quart serving dish

FOR THE MOUSSE

8 ounces white chocolate, cut into bits
1 cup well-chilled heavy cream
2 tablespoons unsalted butter, softened

1 to 2 tablespoons dark rum
2 egg whites at room temperature
1 tablespoon sugar

FOR THE DARK CHOCOLATE SAUCE

*6 ounces dark sweet chocolate, cut into
  bits*
½ cup heavy cream

1 tablespoon dark rum
1 tablespoon unsalted butter

Make the mousse:

In the top of a double boiler set over hot water combine the white chocolate, ⅓ cup of the cream, and the butter and stir the mixture until the chocolate just begins to melt. Remove the pan from the heat and continue stirring the mixture until smooth. Stir in the rum. Let the mixture cool to room temperature.

In a chilled bowl with the mixer beat the remaining cream until it holds soft peaks. In another bowl with the mixer beat the whites until they hold soft peaks. Gradually add the sugar and beat the whites until they hold stiff peaks (see illustrations page 238). Stir one quarter of the whites into the chocolate mixture and fold in the remaining whites gently but thoroughly. Fold in the whipped cream. Spoon the mousse into the serving dish and chill, covered, for at least 2 hours, or until firm.

Make the chocolate sauce:

In a small saucepan combine the dark chocolate and the cream and heat the mixture over moderate heat, stirring, until smooth. Add the rum and the butter and continue to stir the sauce until shiny. Serve the sauce warm with the mousse.

CHOCOLATE SWIRL MOUSSE

Yield:
6 servings

Equipment:
hand-held electric
  mixer

*12 ounces dark sweet chocolate,
  chopped coarse*
*2 tablespoons unsweetened cocoa
  powder*
½ cup heavy cream
1 tablespoon dark rum
*3 large eggs, separated, at room
  temperature*

pinch of salt
pinch of cream of tartar
¼ cup sugar
*2 tablespoons unsalted butter, cut into
  bits*
whipped cream for garnish if desired

In the top of a double boiler set over barely simmering water melt 4 ounces of the chocolate with the cocoa, cream, and rum, stirring, until smooth.

Stir in the egg yolks and cook the mixture, stirring, for 5 minutes, or until it thickens slightly. Remove the pan from the heat and let cool to room temperature.

In a large bowl with the mixer beat the egg whites with the salt until frothy, add the cream of tartar, and beat the whites until they hold soft peaks. Beat in the sugar, a little at a time, and beat the meringue until it holds stiff glossy peaks (see illustrations page 238). Stir one fourth of the meringue into the chocolate mixture and fold the chocolate mixture gently but thoroughly into the remaining meringue.

In the top of the double boiler set over barely simmering water melt the remaining 8 ounces chocolate with the butter, stirring. Let the mixture cool to the touch and fold it lightly into the mousse, swirling it in but being careful not to mix it in completely. Divide the mousse among goblets and chill it, covered, for 1 hour. Garnish each mousse with the whipped cream if desired.

LEMON ITALIAN MERINGUE MOUSSE

Yield:
4 to 6 servings

Equipment:
pastry brush
candy thermometer
hand-held electric
  mixer

1 cup sugar
⅓ cup fresh lemon juice
1 tablespoon grated lemon rind
2 egg whites at room temperature

pinch of salt
pinch of cream of tartar
1 cup well-chilled heavy cream

In a heavy saucepan combine the sugar, lemon juice, and grated lemon rind and bring the mixture to a boil over moderately high heat, stirring and washing down any sugar crystals clinging to the sides of the pan with the brush dipped in cold water until the sugar is dissolved. Boil the syrup, gently swirling the pan, until it reaches the soft-ball stage, or the candy thermometer registers 238° F.

While the syrup is cooking, in a bowl with the mixer beat the egg whites with the salt until frothy, add the cream of tartar, and continue to beat the whites until they hold soft peaks. Add the hot syrup in a stream, beating, and beat the meringue until it is stiff and cool. (For the stages of sugar syrup and how to pour it, see illustrations pages 240 and 241.)

In a chilled bowl with the mixer beat the heavy cream until it holds stiff peaks and fold the cream gently but thoroughly into the meringue. Transfer the mousse to a serving bowl and chill it, covered, for at least 1 hour.

CHOCOLATE MERINGUE MOUSSE

Yield:
4 to 6 servings

Equipment:
pastry brush
candy thermometer
hand-held electric
  mixer

4 ounces semisweet chocolate, cut into
  pieces
½ stick (¼ cup) unsalted butter, cut
  into pieces
2 egg yolks, beaten lightly

⅔ cup sugar
⅓ cup water
3 egg whites at room temperature
¼ teaspoon cream of tartar

In the top of a double boiler set over simmering water melt the chocolate with the butter, stirring until the mixture is smooth. Remove the pan from the heat, add the egg yolks in a stream, beating, and beat the mixture until well combined. Transfer to a large bowl and let cool.

In a small heavy saucepan combine the sugar with the water, bring the mixture to a boil over moderate heat, and boil it, stirring and washing down any sugar crystals clinging to the sides of the pan with the brush dipped in cold water until the sugar is dissolved. Boil the syrup, gently swirling the pan, until it reaches the soft-ball stage, or the candy thermometer registers 234° F. Remove the pan from the heat.

In a bowl with the mixer beat the egg whites until they are frothy, add the cream of tartar, and beat the whites until they hold soft peaks. With the mixer running add the hot syrup in a stream and beat the meringue until cool. (For the stages of sugar syrup and how to pour it, see illustrations pages 240 and 241.) Fold the meringue into the chocolate mixture in 3 batches, folding the mixture together gently but thoroughly after each addition. Spoon the mousse into a metal bowl and chill it, covered, for 1 hour.

Variation:

CHOCOLATE-MINT MERINGUE MOUSSE: Fold into the mousse 2 tablespoons *crème de menthe*, or to taste, or ⅛ teaspoon mint extract after folding in the meringue.

MANGO MOUSSE BARBADOS

Yield:
6 to 8 servings

Equipment:
food processor fitted
  with steel blade
hand-held electric
  mixer

5 pounds large ripe fleshy mangoes,
  peeled, pitted, and chopped coarse
½ cup fresh lime juice
½ cup superfine granulated sugar
1 envelope unflavored gelatin

¼ cup cold water
2 egg whites at room temperature
pinch of salt
½ cup well-chilled heavy cream

In the food processor or in a blender purée the mangoes with the lime juice. Pour the purée into a bowl and stir in the sugar.

In a small saucepan sprinkle the gelatin over the cold water and let it soften for 10 minutes. Stir the mixture over low heat until the gelatin is dissolved and let cool. Stir the gelatin mixture into the mango purée.

In a small bowl with the mixer beat the egg whites with the salt until they hold soft peaks. In a chilled bowl beat the cream until it holds stiff peaks, fold it into the egg whites, and fold the mixture gently into the mango purée. Divide the mousse among individual dishes and chill for 2 to 3 hours, or until set.

COFFEE AND MACAROON MOUSSES

Yield:
4 servings

Equipment:
hand-held electric
  mixer
four ¾-cup ramekins
pastry bag fitted with
  star tip

1 teaspoon unflavored gelatin
3 tablespoons dark rum
4 egg yolks
¼ cup plus 2 tablespoons sugar
2 pinches of salt
1 cup heavy cream
1½ tablespoons instant espresso
  powder

½ teaspoon vanilla
6 Almond Macaroons (page 262) plus
  macaroon crumbs for garnish
3 egg whites at room temperature
pinch of cream of tartar
whipped cream for garnish

In a small bowl sprinkle the gelatin over 1 tablespoon of the rum to soften for 10 minutes.

In a large bowl with the mixer beat the egg yolks, the ¼ cup sugar, and a pinch of the salt until the mixture is light and falls in a ribbon when the beater is lifted (see illustration page 16). In a heavy saucepan combine the heavy cream and the espresso powder, scald the mixture, and add it to the yolk mixture in a stream, beating. Transfer the custard to the saucepan and cook it over moderate heat, stirring constantly, until it thickens, but do not let it boil. Remove the pan from the heat, stir in the gelatin mixture and the vanilla, and stir the custard until the gelatin is completely dissolved. Strain the custard into a bowl set over a larger bowl of ice and cold water and let it cool, stirring, until it begins to thicken.

In a bowl crumble the 6 almond macaroons and sprinkle them with the remaining 2 tablespoons dark rum. In another bowl with the mixer beat the egg whites with the remaining pinch of salt until frothy, add the cream of tartar, and beat until the whites hold soft peaks. Gradually beat in the remaining 2 tablespoons sugar and beat the whites until they hold stiff peaks (see illustrations page 238). Fold the whites into the custard gently but thoroughly. Divide half the mousse among the ramekins, top the mousse with the macaroon-rum mixture, and top the crumbs with the remaining mousse. Chill the mousses for at least 1 hour. Spoon the whipped cream into the pastry bag, pipe a rosette of it on each mousse, and sprinkle the remaining macaroon crumbs over the tops.

CHILLED SOUFFLÉS

A chilled soufflé is not a soufflé at all, if what we mean by soufflé is a magical hot combination of flavored base leavened to dizzying heights by beaten egg whites, per our discussion on pages 416 and 417. Then what is a chilled soufflé? A lovely light combination of eggs and flavorings and whipped heavy cream, often with gelatin added, that is chilled in a soufflé dish. A chilled soufflé resembles a frozen soufflé because the soufflé dish in which a soufflé chills supports a collar, as does the dish or mold for a frozen soufflé.

Terminology aside, chilled soufflés, or individual chilled soufflés for that matter, create a splendid effect. They stand tall and regal, way above the edge of the dish. They also cut very tidily, a boon if you are serving a number of guests. Furthermore, they require no last-minute machinations as they have to be prepared entirely in advance in order to chill for a minimum of two hours or more. They come in wonderful combinations. See Chocolate Raspberry Soufflé (below), for instance, or Chilled Almond Praline Soufflés (page 397), which are accompanied by chocolate sauce. We think of chilled soufflés as the perfect finale for a dinner party. There is something clearly celebratory about them, which when you remove the paper collar you will know precisely of what we speak.

CHOCOLATE RASPBERRY SOUFFLÉ

Yield:
6 servings

Equipment:
1-quart soufflé dish
hand-held electric
  mixer

6 ounces imported bittersweet chocolate, chopped coarse
2 ounces unsweetened chocolate, chopped coarse
4 egg yolks

a 10-ounce package frozen raspberries in syrup, thawed and drained, reserving ½ cup of the syrup
6 egg whites at room temperature
¼ teaspoon cream of tartar
¼ cup sugar
1¼ cups well-chilled heavy cream

Fit the soufflé dish with a 6-inch-wide doubled band of foil, brushed with flavorless vegetable oil, to form a collar extending 3 inches above the rim (see illustration page 417).

In a large heatproof bowl over barely simmering water melt both chocolates, stirring occasionally, until smooth. In a bowl with the mixer beat the egg yolks until they are thick and pale. In a small saucepan bring the reserved raspberry syrup to a simmer, add it to the eggs yolks in a stream, beating constantly, and beat the mixture for 1 minute. Add the yolk mixture to the chocolate mixture in a stream, beating, and gently stir in the raspberries.

In a large bowl with the mixer beat the egg whites until frothy, add the cream of tartar, and beat the whites until they hold soft peaks. Add the sugar, a little at a time, and beat the whites until they hold stiff glossy peaks (see illustrations page 238). In a chilled bowl with the mixer beat the cream until it just holds stiff peaks. Stir one fourth of the whites into the chocolate mixture, fold in the remaining whites, and just before they are incorporated completely, fold in the whipped cream gently but thoroughly. Spoon the mixture into the prepared soufflé dish, smooth the top, and chill the dessert, covered loosely with plastic wrap, for at least 3 hours, or until set. Just before serving, remove the collar carefully.

The soufflé may be prepared 1 day in advance and kept covered and chilled with the foil collar in place.

CHILLED ALMOND PRALINE SOUFFLÉS

Yield:
8 servings

Equipment:
pastry brush
eight ¾-cup soufflé
  dishes or ramekins
hand-held electric
  mixer
food processor fitted
  with steel blade

1 envelope unflavored gelatin
1 cup milk
5 large eggs, separated, at room
  temperature
½ cup sugar
2 teaspoons vanilla

¼ teaspoon almond extract
½ recipe almond praline (page 544),
  coarsely ground
1 cup well-chilled heavy cream
1½ recipes Chocolate Sauce (page
  499) as an accompaniment

Brush the soufflé dishes or ramekins with flavorless vegetable oil. In a small bowl sprinkle the gelatin over ¼ cup of the milk and let it soften for 10 minutes. Put the bowl in a pan of hot water and heat the gelatin, stirring, until it is clear and completely dissolved.

In a bowl with the mixer beat the yolks until combined, gradually add all but 2 tablespoons of the sugar, and beat until the mixture is light and fluffy. Add the remaining milk, scalded, in a stream, transfer the mixture to a heavy saucepan, and cook it over moderately low heat, stirring, until it is thick enough to coat the back of a spoon. Add the gelatin mixture, vanilla, and almond extract and strain the mixture through a sieve into a bowl. Let cool to room temperature, stir in the almond praline, and chill the mixture, covered, until it is the consistency of raw egg whites.

In a bowl with the mixer beat the whites until they hold soft peaks. Add the remaining 2 tablespoons sugar and beat the whites until they hold stiff peaks (see illustrations page 238). In a chilled bowl beat the heavy cream until it holds soft peaks. Fold the whites into the almond praline mixture and fold in the cream gently but thoroughly. Spoon the mixture into the prepared dishes, rap them on a hard surface to expel any air bubbles, and chill them, covered, for at least 2 hours, or until they are set. To unmold, put each dish in a pan of hot water for 1 minute and invert the soufflés onto individual dessert plates. Before serving, spoon a pool of the chocolate sauce around each soufflé.

ICED LEMON SOUFFLÉ

Yield:
8 servings

Equipment:
1 ¼-quart soufflé dish
hand-held electric
    mixer
pastry bag fitted with
    star tip

The word "iced" here describes a soufflé mixture that is chilled but not frozen, as you will see from the procedure of this recipe.

1 envelope unflavored gelatin
¼ cup cold water
6 large eggs, separated, at room
    temperature
1¼ cups plus 2 tablespoons sugar
⅔ cup fresh lemon juice
3 tablespoons grated lemon rind

pinch of salt
pinch of cream of tartar
1½ cups well-chilled heavy cream
½ cup ground, blanched and oven-
    dried pistachios (for procedure page
    549)
whipped cream for garnish

Brush a 5-inch-wide doubled piece of foil or wax paper long enough to fit around the dish with flavorless vegetable oil. Fit the dish with the collar extending 2 inches above the rim (see illustration page 417).

In a small bowl sprinkle the gelatin over the cold water and let it soften for 10 minutes.

In the top of a double boiler set over simmering water or in a large bowl set in a pan of simmering water combine the egg yolks, the 1¼ cups sugar, the lemon juice, and the lemon rind and beat the mixture with the mixer over moderate heat for 15 minutes, or until it falls in a ribbon when the beater is lifted (see illustration page 16).

Set the bowl of gelatin mixture in a pan of hot water and stir the mixture until the gelatin is dissolved. Add it to the yolk mixture, beating until combined. Transfer the mixture to a ceramic bowl.

In a bowl with the mixer beat the egg whites with the salt until frothy, add the cream of tartar, and beat until they hold soft peaks. Add the remaining 2 tablespoons sugar and beat until the whites hold stiff peaks (see illustrations page 238). In a chilled bowl with the mixer beat the heavy cream until it holds stiff peaks.

Set the bowl of lemon mixture in a larger bowl of ice and cold water and stir the mixture until it is just cool, but do not let it set. Fold in the whipped cream and the egg whites gently but thoroughly and spoon the mixture into the soufflé dish. Smooth the top of the soufflé with the back of the spoon and chill for 3 hours, or until set.

Just before serving, remove the collar from the soufflé dish and garnish the outer rim of the soufflé with most of the pistachios. Pipe whipped cream rosettes on top of the soufflé and sprinkle them with the remaining pistachios.

Photo on page 247.

The soufflé can be chilled, covered loosely, overnight.

Variation:

ICED LIME SOUFFLÉ: Substitute the same amount of fresh lime juice for the lemon juice and reduce the amount of grated rind to 1½ to 2 teaspoons grated lime rind. Garnish with the pistachios, thin lime slices, and Candied Violets (page 524). Serve with whipped cream.

BAVARIAN CREAMS

We must again thank the French for having had the good sense and great taste to invent Bavarian cream, or as it is known there, *bavarois*. This splendid molded dessert has a custard base to which gelatin, flavorings and whipped cream, and sometimes beaten egg whites, are added. Bavarian creams are notably smooth and appealing in texture, and when unmolded are perfectly magnificent to look at as well as superb to taste.

Note the variety in the Bavarian creams that follow. One is based on chestnuts. Another employs ladyfingers to line a brioche mold that is then filled with orange Bavarian cream. Our third layers three differently flavored custards—vanilla, chocolate, and coffee—and our last incorporates jelly-roll slices to garnish a raspberry cream in a remarkable presentation. By description alone, these Bavarian creams might strike you as difficult to prepare. Granted, if you are making the ones that use ladyfingers or jelly-roll slices, you have an additional step ahead of you. In general, however, Bavarian creams are not meant to be taxing. They require a carefully prepared custard, which takes a certain awareness but not the practice, for instance, of a technique such as making puff pastry. Secondly, Bavarian creams depend upon the addition of a fully dissolved amount of gelatin; this, too, could hardly be described as complicated. Lastly, cream must be whipped to the appropriate stage and thoroughly folded in—a step that takes time but not courage. Once finished, in the mold, that is, most Bavarian creams can stand in the refrigerator overnight.

We would heartily recommend mastering Bavarian cream. From a presentation point of view, it is even more compelling than a chilled soufflé, and it subscribes to no seasonality whatsoever. A Bavarian cream is a special dessert anytime.

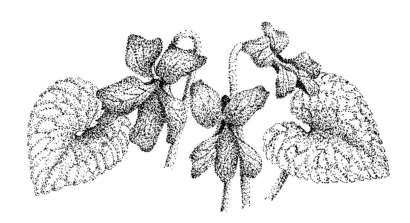

Bavarois Turinoise (opposite), White Fruitcake with Icing (page 110)

BAVAROIS TURINOISE

Molded Chestnut Bavarian Cream

Yield:
8 servings

Equipment:
hand-held electric
   mixer
4-cup decorative
   mold
pastry bag fitted with
   star tip

Bavarian cream, or *bavarois* as it is known in French, is a combination of custard or crème anglaise, whipped cream, and gelatin. Bavarian creams are usually set in decorative molds. The mold shown in the photograph of this recipe may be difficult to locate, and any four-cup mold can be used in its place.

1½ tablespoons unflavored gelatin
⅓ cup cold water
4 egg yolks
1 cup sugar
1 cup milk, scalded
1 teaspoon vanilla
1 cup chestnut purée (page 546)
½ ounce semisweet chocolate, melted
1½ cups well-chilled heavy cream
3 tablespoons dark rum or brandy

sweet almond oil for oiling the mold
sweetened whipped cream flavored
*   with dark rum or brandy for*
*   garnish*
Marrons Glacés (page 526) for
*   garnish*
grated chocolate for garnish
1 recipe Hot Chocolate Sauce (page
*   497) as an accompaniment*

In a small bowl sprinkle the gelatin over the cold water to soften for 10 minutes.

In a bowl with the mixer combine the egg yolks with the sugar and beat the mixture until it falls in a ribbon when the beater is lifted (see illustration page 16). Add the scalded milk in a stream, stirring, transfer the custard to a heavy saucepan, and cook it over moderate heat, stirring, until it thickens and coats the back of the spoon. Do not let the custard come to a simmer. Remove the pan from the heat, stir in the gelatin mixture and the vanilla, and stir the custard until the gelatin is completely dissolved. Add the chestnut purée and the melted chocolate and stir the custard until smooth. Strain the custard into a bowl and let it cool, stirring occasionally, until thick, but do not let it set.

In a chilled bowl with the mixer beat the heavy cream until it thickens, add the rum or brandy, and continue to beat the cream until it holds soft peaks. Stir one fourth of the whipped cream into the chestnut mixture and fold in the remaining whipped cream gently but thoroughly.

Rinse the mold with cold water but do not dry it and oil it lightly with the almond oil. Pour the Bavarian cream mixture into the mold, rap the mold lightly on a hard surface to fill any air spaces, and chill it overnight.

Run a sharp knife around the edge of the mold and dip the mold briefly into hot water. Invert a chilled serving dish over the mold and invert the Bavarian cream onto the dish. Spoon the liquor-flavored whipped cream into the pastry bag and pipe it around the dessert. Garnish the dish with the glacéed chestnuts, sprinkle the Bavarian cream with the grated chocolate, and serve it with the chocolate sauce.

Photo opposite.

ORANGE BAVARIAN CREAM

Yield:
8 servings

Equipment:
2-quart brioche mold
hand-held electric
  mixer

brandy syrup (page 542)
6 tablespoons orange-flavored liqueur
1 recipe Ladyfingers (page 286), each
  piped 7 inches long, for lining the
  mold
2 tablespoons unflavored gelatin
⅓ cup cold water
6 egg yolks
1 cup plus 2 tablespoons sugar

2 cups milk, scalded
3 tablespoons brandy
1 tablespoon grated orange rind
2 cups well-chilled heavy cream
Candied Violets (page 524) for
  garnish
orange sections for garnish
whipped cream as an accompaniment

Line the bottom of the brioche mold with a round of wax paper. In a shallow dish combine the brandy syrup with 3 tablespoons of the orange-flavored liqueur. Dip the flat sides of the ladyfingers into the syrup and put 1 ladyfinger in each fluted depression of the mold.

In a small bowl sprinkle the gelatin over the cold water and let it soften for 10 minutes. In a bowl with the mixer beat the egg yolks with the sugar until the mixture falls in a ribbon when the beater is lifted (see illustration page 16). Add the milk in a stream, stirring constantly. Transfer the custard to a heavy saucepan and cook it over moderately low heat, stirring constantly with a wooden spoon, until it thickens and begins to coat the spoon. Do not let the custard come to a simmer. Remove the pan from the heat, add the gelatin mixture, and stir the custard until the gelatin is dissolved. Strain the custard through a fine sieve into a metal bowl and stir in the brandy and the grated orange rind. Set the bowl in a larger bowl of ice cubes and water and let the custard cool, stirring occasionally, but do not let it set.

In a chilled bowl with the mixer beat the heavy cream until it thickens, add the remaining 3 tablespoons orange-flavored liqueur, and continue to beat the cream until it holds soft peaks. Fold the cream lightly but thoroughly into the custard. Pour the custard into the mold and rap the mold lightly on a hard surface to fill any air spaces. Chill the dessert, covered, for at least 4 hours or overnight.

Run the blade of a thin knife around the inside of the mold, invert a serving plate over the Bavarian cream, and invert the dessert onto the plate. Remove the paper, decorate the top of the dessert with the candied violets and orange sections, and serve with the whipped cream.

BAVAROIS RUBANÉ

Yield:
8 servings

Equipment:
hand-held electric
  mixer
8-cup decorative
  mold
pastry bag fitted with
  star tip

Bavarois rubané simply means striped Bavarian cream in French. Composed in layers, this dessert contains three tiers of variously colored and flavored custards: vanilla–rum, chocolate, and coffee–hazelnut. The result is a lovely, subtly ribboned mold.

1½ tablespoons unflavored gelatin
¼ cup cold water
6 egg yolks
¾ cup sugar
1½ cups milk, scalded
1½ teaspoons vanilla
3 ounces semisweet chocolate, chopped
  coarse
1½ tablespoons instant espresso
  powder

2 tablespoons hot water or coffee
¼ cup ground, lightly toasted and
  skinned hazelnuts (for procedure
  page 549)
1½ cups well-chilled heavy cream
3 tablespoons dark rum
sweet almond oil for oiling the mold
sweetened whipped cream flavored
  with rum for garnish
chocolate shavings for garnish

In a small bowl let the gelatin soak in the cold water for 10 minutes.

In a bowl with the mixer beat the egg yolks with the sugar until the mixture falls in a ribbon when the beater is lifted (see illustration page 16). Pour the scalded milk slowly into the egg mixture, stirring constantly. Transfer the custard to a heavy saucepan and cook it over moderately low heat, stirring constantly with a wooden spoon, until it thickens and begins to coat the spoon. Do not let the custard come to a simmer. Remove the pan from the heat and stir in the vanilla and the gelatin mixture. Stir the custard until the gelatin is completely dissolved and pour it through a sieve into a bowl. Divide the custard equally among 3 small bowls.

In a heavy saucepan melt the semisweet chocolate over low heat, let cool, and stir it well into the custard in one of the bowls. Dissolve the espresso powder in the 2 tablespoons hot water or coffee and stir the mixture into the custard in one of the remaining bowls. Stir the ground hazelnuts into the coffee-flavored custard.

In a chilled bowl with the mixer beat the heavy cream until it thickens. Add the rum and continue to beat the cream until it forms soft peaks. Put the remaining bowl of vanilla custard into a larger bowl of ice water and stir it occasionally until it is completely cool but not set. Fold in one third of the whipped cream.

Rinse the decorative mold with cold water but do not dry it and oil it lightly with the almond oil. Pour in the vanilla custard and chill it until it is completely set. Put the bowl of coffee custard into a larger bowl of ice water, stir it occasionally until it is cool but not set, and fold in half of the remaining whipped cream. Pour the mixture into the mold, forming a layer on top of the vanilla custard, and chill it until it is completely set.

If the chocolate custard is still warm, put the bowl into a larger bowl of ice water and stir it for a minute or two until it is cool but not set. Remove it from the ice water, fold in the remaining whipped cream, and pour it into the mold over the layer of coffee custard. Cover the dessert with foil and chill it for at least 4 hours.

Run a sharp knife around the mold and invert the dessert onto a serving dish. Spoon the rum-flavored whipped cream into the pastry bag and decorate the serving dish with rosettes of the cream. (For detailed instructions on working with a pastry bag and piping rosettes, see pages 19 and 20.) Garnish the Bavarian cream decoratively with the chocolate shavings.

Photo on page 388.

RASPBERRY SPIRAL BAVARIAN CREAM

Yield:
6 to 8 servings

Equipment:
hand-held electric mixer
2-quart metal charlotte mold

FOR THE JELLY ROLLS
1 vanilla génoise *sheet cake (page 22)*
½ cup raspberry jelly, melted and strained

2 tablespoons kirsch

FOR THE CUSTARD
*three 10-ounce packages frozen raspberries, thawed*ˀ STRAINED
1½ envelopes unflavored gelatin
⅓ cup kirsch
5 egg yolks
¾ cup sugar

1½ cups milk, scalded
2 teaspoons vanilla
3 egg whites at room temperature
pinch of salt
1 cup well-chilled heavy cream
sweet almond oil for oiling the mold

sweetened whipped cream as an accompaniment if desired

Raspberry Sauce (page 508) as an accompaniment if desired

Make the jelly rolls:

Make the custard:

Halve the *génoise* sheet cake crosswise. Combine the jelly and kirsch and spread each half with a thin layer of jelly. Beginning with a long side, roll up each half tightly, wrap the rolls snugly in foil, chill rolls for 1 hour.

Force the raspberries through a fine sieve into a bowl and reserve the purée.

In a small bowl sprinkle the gelatin over the kirsch to soften for 5 minutes. In a large bowl with the mixer beat the egg yolks until combined. Beat in the sugar, 2 tablespoons at a time, and continue to beat until the mixture falls in a ribbon when the beater is lifted (see illustration page 16). Add the hot milk in a stream, beating, transfer the mixture to a heavy saucepan, and cook it over low heat, stirring constantly, until it thickens and coats the back of a spoon. Do not let the custard come to a simmer. Remove the pan from the heat, stir in the gelatin mixture and the vanilla, and stir the custard until the gelatin is dissolved. Transfer the custard to a large metal bowl. In another bowl with the mixer beat the egg whites with the salt until they hold stiff peaks and fold them into the custard. Set the bowl of custard in a large bowl filled with ice and cold water and let it stand, stirring occasionally, until cool and thickened but do not let it set. Remove the bowl from the ice.

Cut the jelly rolls into ⅓-inch slices. In a chilled bowl with the mixer beat the heavy cream until it holds soft peaks. Fold in the reserved raspberry purée. Fold the raspberry mixture into the custard lightly.

Rinse the charlotte mold with cold water but do not dry it and oil it lightly with the sweet almond oil. Line the bottom of the mold with a round of wax paper. Arrange 5 or 6 jelly-roll slices in the bottom of the mold. Quickly pour a 1-inch layer of the custard mixture into the mold and cover it with jelly-roll slices, arranging them in the same manner. Continue to layer the custard mixture and jelly-roll slices in the same manner until all but 2½ inches of the mold has been filled. Arrange the remaining jelly-roll slices upright against the sides of the mold and fill the mold with the remaining custard mixture, being careful not to dislodge the slices around the mold. Chill the mold, covered, for at least 4 hours.

Run a thin knife around the edge of the mold, dip the mold in hot water for 2 or 3 seconds, and invert a chilled serving plate over it. Invert the Bavarian cream with a sharp rap onto the plate. Remove the wax paper and serve the Bavarian cream with the whipped cream and raspberry sauce if desired.

Raspberry Spiral Bavarian Cream (opposite)

Photo below.

MOLDED CHILLED DESSERTS

Our molded chilled desserts are a varied group. Among them we have classics of the first order: Blancmange, Mont-Blanc, Coeur à la Crème, Riz à l'Impératrice. And then we have some that are not so classic but equally good: Yogurt Cream Mold with Raspberry Sauce, for example, and two different jellies. What all these desserts have in common is that they are chilled and molded. With that said, we will address them individually, as each, in its own way, is unique.

History has it that the French combination of *blancmange*, or white food, was originally thickened with calf's foot or veal jelly, then with isinglass, then with gelatin, as it is today. A remarkably white, almond-flavored dessert, Blancmange (page 407) is a classic and has been described as pleasant by James Beard. We suspect that *blancmange* would best follow an elaborate dinner, one of complex flavors and textures, and act as counterpoint to what had preceded it.

Mont-Blanc and Coeur à la Crème also share French origin and that, we must admit, is all. Each could not be more different from the other. Mont-Blanc (page 408) consists of chestnut purée in a specific presentation. Coeur à la Crème (page 408) combines two different cheeses and heavy cream in a mold that is then served with fresh fruit and Melba sauce. Each of these is a classic, and rightfully so.

Riz à l'Impératrice (page 410) is also a classic and begins with a Bavarian cream to which elegant glacéed mixed fruits and lots of whipped cream are added. It is high-style rice pudding, and light-years away from the comforting Old-Fashioned Rice Pudding (page 319) of our youth. In its classic presentation it is almost always served with a brilliant fruit sauce.

On a more contemporary and lighter note, Yogurt Cream Mold with Raspberry Sauce (page 409) combines heavy cream, gelatin, and yogurt with simple vanilla flavoring. While this chilled dessert resembles *coeur à la crème* after a fashion, the yogurt renders the texture altogether different. The comparison is interesting.

Finally, we have included two jellies: a coffee one, fragrant with coffee-flavored liqueur, and a white wine one. What is it about dessert jellies that we find so appealing? To begin with, they are light and lovely, particularly for summer. The coffee jelly can be served with any number of variously flavored whipped creams, should you need to dress it up. The wine jelly lends itself to sweet thin cookies, such as Cats' Tongues (page 287). It is curious and gratifying to think that even the simplest, and in these we would include jellies, have a specific time, place and following in the remarkably rich and varied world of desserts.

BLANCMANGE

Yield:
4 to 6 servings

Equipment:
pastry brush
food processor fitted
  with steel blade
hand-held electric
  mixer
1-quart decorative
  mold

Blancmange dates back to medieval times and was originally made—before the arrival of unflavored gelatin, that is—with gelatinous veal stock. Today gelatin thickens the sweet almond cream mixture, resulting in a smooth and soothing dessert. The name *blancmange* describes the stark whiteness of the combination. A most appropriate accompaniment, and a wonderful contrast in texture, would be Almond Curl Cookies (page 290).

*1½ cups (12 ounces) blanched
  almonds (for procedure page 549),
  soaked in water to cover for 1 hour
1½ envelopes unflavored gelatin
1½ cups plus ⅓ cup cold water*

*1 cup sugar
1 cup well-chilled heavy cream
1 teaspoon vanilla
2 drops almond extract
sweet almond oil for oiling the mold*

In a small bowl sprinkle the gelatin over the ⅓ cup water to soften for 10 minutes.

In a small saucepan dissolve the sugar in ½ cup of the remaining water over moderate heat, stirring and washing down any sugar crystals clinging to the sides of the pan with the brush dipped in cold water, bring the syrup to a boil, and remove the pan from the heat. Stir in the softened gelatin mixture until it is dissolved and let cool.

Drain the almonds and in the food processor or in a blender grind them finely in 2 batches, adding ½ cup of the remaining cold water to each batch as the almonds are being ground. Line a large colander with a dampened dish towel, set the colander over a large bowl, and transfer the almonds to the colander. Twist the ends of the towel and squeeze the almonds gently but thoroughly until all the liquid is extracted. (There should be 1½ cups liquid.) Discard the squeezed almonds. Stir the gelatin mixture into the almond liquid. Set the almond mixture over a bowl filled with ice cubes and stir it until it is syrupy but not set. In a chilled bowl with the mixer beat the heavy cream with the vanilla and the almond extract until it holds soft peaks. Remove the bowl of almond mixture from the bowl of ice and fold in the cream.

Oil the decorative mold lightly with the almond oil. Pour the almond mixture into the prepared mold and chill the mold for at least 4 hours or overnight.

Dip the mold in hot water for 1 or 2 seconds and invert the *blancmange* onto a serving dish.

MONT-BLANC

Yield:
6 to 8 servings

Equipment:
pastry brush
4-cup ring mold
food mill fitted with
  fine disk

This dessert of sweetened puréed chestnuts in its most usual presentation is shaped into a mound and topped with whipped cream to resemble the snow-covered peaks of Mont Blanc in the French Alps. Extremely popular throughout Europe, this combination is known as *Monte Bianco* in Italy and *vermicelles aux marrons* in Switzerland, where the chestnut purée is piped through a pastry tube into a mound of strips resembling *vermicelli* pasta. In the following recipe the dessert is actually molded as opposed to being piped free-form. In any presentation it is equally enticing.

1½ pounds chestnuts, shelled and
  peeled (for procedure page 550)
a 2-inch piece of vanilla bean
1 cup milk
1¼ cups water
½ cup sugar

½ teaspoon vanilla
2 tablespoons unsalted butter, softened
2 tablespoons heavy cream
sweetened whipped cream flavored
  with vanilla as an accompaniment
chocolate shavings for garnish

In a saucepan combine the chestnuts, vanilla bean, milk, and 1 cup of the water and cook over moderate heat for 30 to 35 minutes, or until the chestnuts are very tender. Drain the chestnuts and in a shallow bowl mash them with a fork.

While the chestnuts are cooking, in a small saucepan dissolve the sugar in the remaining ¼ cup water and cook for 5 minutes, brushing down any sugar crystals clinging to the sides of the pan with the brush dipped in cold water. Stir the syrup and the vanilla into the chestnuts. Add the softened butter and cream and combine the mixture well.

Set the ring mold on a sheet of wax paper and purée the chestnut mixture in the food mill into the mold, letting it fall in naturally all around, until the mold is filled completely. Scoop up any purée that has fallen onto the wax paper and spoon it into the mold, pressing it in lightly. Cover the mold with foil and chill it for at least 2 hours.

Unmold the chestnut purée onto a serving dish, fill the center with the whipped cream, and garnish the cream with the chocolate shavings.

COEUR À LA CRÈME

Yield:
6 servings

Coeur à la Crème, a cheese dessert from France, combines heavy cream, cream cheese, and cottage cheese, which is then molded in the classic heart-shaped *coeur à la crème* mold or wicker basket. The mold contains tiny holes, allowing the whey to drain off and the desserts to become firm.

Equipment:
hand-held electric
 mixer
6 small *coeur à la
 crème* china molds
 or wicker molds
 (available at
 specialty
 kitchenware stores)
cheesecloth

Garnished with both Melba sauce and fresh berries, the dessert is rich and luxurious in its own way and requires a little preplanning as the molds must drain overnight.

4 ounces cream cheese, softened
4 ounces cottage cheese
pinch of salt
½ cup well-chilled heavy cream
3 tablespoons confectioners' sugar

1 teaspoon vanilla
*fresh strawberries, hulled and halved,
 as an accompaniment*
*1 recipe Melba Sauce (page 506) as
 an accompaniment*

In a bowl combine well the cream cheese, cottage cheese, and the salt. In a chilled bowl with the mixer beat the heavy cream with the confectioners' sugar and the vanilla until it holds soft peaks. Fold the whipped cream into the cheese mixture gently but thoroughly.

Line each *coeur à la crème* mold with a double layer of cheesecloth, rinsed and squeezed, letting the cloth overhang the sides of the molds. Fill the molds with the cheese mixture, doming it slightly, and cover the cheese mixture with the cheesecloth overhangs. Place the molds on a rack over a shallow pan, refrigerate them, and let the cheese drain overnight.

Unmold the hearts on individual dishes, peel off the cheesecloth, and surround each heart with some of the halved strawberries and a pool of the Melba sauce.

YOGURT CREAM MOLD WITH RASPBERRY SAUCE

Yield:
6 servings

Equipment:
1-quart decorative
 mold

4 teaspoons unflavored gelatin
¼ cup cold water
1½ cups heavy cream
½ cup sugar

2¼ cups plain yogurt
1 teaspoon vanilla
*Raspberry Sauce (page 508) as an
 accompaniment*

In a small bowl sprinkle the gelatin over the cold water and let it soften for 10 minutes. In a saucepan combine the heavy cream and the sugar and cook the mixture over moderate heat, stirring, for 5 minutes, or until the sugar is dissolved. Stir in the gelatin mixture, remove the pan from the heat, and stir the mixture until the gelatin is dissolved. Transfer the mixture to a bowl and let it cool for 5 minutes. Whisk in the yogurt and the vanilla and combine the mixture well.

Rinse the mold with cold water, but do not dry it. Pour in the yogurt mixture and chill it, covered loosely, for at least 2 hours.

Run a thin knife around the edge of the mold, dip the mold in warm water for a few seconds, and invert a serving plate over it. Invert the mold with a sharp rap onto the plate and serve it with the raspberry sauce.

MAPLE WALNUT SPONGE

Yield:
6 servings

Equipment:
hand-held electric
  mixer
1 ½-quart decorative
  mold

1 tablespoon unflavored gelatin
¼ cup cold water
1 cup maple syrup
1 egg white
pinch of cream of tartar

1½ cups well-chilled heavy cream
⅔ cup finely chopped walnuts
Maple Walnuts (page 525) for
  garnish

In a small bowl sprinkle the gelatin over the cold water to soften for 10 minutes. In a small saucepan combine the maple syrup and the gelatin mixture and heat over moderately low heat, stirring, until the gelatin is dissolved. Increase the heat to moderate and cook the mixture, stirring occasionally, until it is hot but not boiling.

In a bowl with the mixer beat the egg white with the cream of tartar until it holds stiff peaks. Add the hot maple syrup mixture in a slow stream, beating constantly, and continue to beat the meringue until it is cool and holds stiff, glossy peaks. In a chilled bowl with the mixer beat the heavy cream until it holds stiff peaks and fold it into the maple meringue with the chopped walnuts.

Oil the mold lightly with flavorless vegetable oil. Spoon the sponge into the mold, rap the mold sharply on a hard surface to remove any air bubbles, and chill the sponge, covered, for 4 hours, or until set.

Run a thin knife around the inside rim of the mold, dip the mold in hot water for a few seconds, and invert a chilled serving dish over it. Invert the mold with a sharp rap onto the serving dish and garnish the sponge with the maple walnuts.

RIZ À L'IMPÉRATRICE

Yield:
8 servings

Equipment:
hand-held electric
  mixer
2-quart mold

This classic French dessert, named for Empress Eugénie, consort of Napoléon III, is a molded rice custard flavored with kirsch, studded with glacéed fruits, and served with raspberry purée. Imperial best describes it.

½ cup diced glacéed mixed fruits
¼ cup plus 1 tablespoon kirsch
½ cup long-grain rice
1¾ cups plus 1¼ cups milk, scalded
½ cup plus ⅓ cup sugar
2 tablespoons unsalted butter
a ½-inch piece of vanilla bean
⅓ cup apricot jam
4 teaspoons unflavored gelatin

¼ cup water
4 egg yolks
1 cup well-chilled heavy cream
sweet almond oil for oiling the mold
cutouts of glacéed fruit for garnish
sweetened whipped cream for garnish
2 recipes raspberry purée (page 546)
  as an accompaniment

In a small bowl macerate the ½ cup glacéed fruits in the ¼ cup kirsch for at least 1 hour.

Preheat the oven to 325° F.

In a saucepan blanch the rice in boiling water to cover for 5 minutes. Drain the rice well and put it in a heavy ovenproof saucepan. Add the 1¾ cups milk, the ⅓ cup sugar, the butter, and the vanilla bean. Bring the mixture to a boil, transfer it to the oven, and bake it, tightly covered, for 1 hour. Transfer the rice to a large shallow dish, remove the vanilla bean, and let cool.

In a small saucepan melt the apricot jam with the remaining 1 tablespoon kirsch and strain the mixture into the rice. Add the glacéed fruits and the kirsch in which they have macerated and combine the mixture gently. In a small dish sprinkle the gelatin over the water to soften.

In a large bowl with the mixer beat the egg yolks with the remaining ½ cup sugar until light and the mixture falls in a ribbon when the beater is lifted (see illustration page 16). Pour in the 1¼ cups scalded milk in a thin stream, stirring. Transfer the mixture to a saucepan and cook it over low heat, stirring, until it is thick enough to coat the spoon. Do not let it boil. Remove the custard from the heat, add the gelatin mixture, and stir it until it is dissolved. Strain the custard into a bowl, set the bowl in a pan of ice cubes and water, and stir the custard until it is almost cool. Pour the custard into the rice, a little at a time, stirring to combine it. Let the mixture cool completely and thicken, but do not let it set.

In a chilled bowl with the mixer beat the cream until it holds soft peaks and fold it into the rice mixture. Rinse the mold and lightly oil it with the almond oil. Pour in the rice mixture and chill it for at least 6 hours.

Run the point of a sharp knife around the edge of the dessert, dip the mold in hot water for a few seconds, and invert it onto a serving dish. Decorate it with the cutouts of glacéed fruit and some of the sweetened whipped cream. Pour some of the raspberry purée around the mold and serve the remaining sauce and the remaining whipped cream separately.

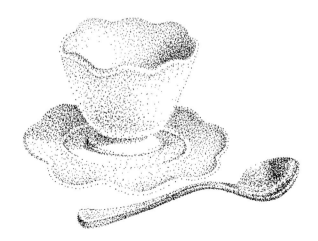

APRICOT RICE RING WITH APRICOT SAUCE

Yield:
12 servings

Equipment:
2½-quart ring mold

2 cups long-grain rice
5 cups milk
½ cup superfine granulated sugar
2 envelopes unflavored gelatin
1 cup cold water
1 teaspoon vanilla

2 cups well-chilled heavy cream
1 recipe Apricot Sauce (page 504)
Poached Apricots (page 466), left
    whole
chopped unsalted pistachios for garnish

In the top of a double boiler cook the rice in the milk over boiling water for 15 minutes. Stir in the sugar and continue to cook the mixture, stirring every 15 minutes, for about 40 minutes, or until almost all the liquid is absorbed and the rice is just tender.

In a small bowl let the gelatin soften in the cold water for 10 minutes.

Remove the rice from the heat, stir in the softened gelatin until it is dissolved, and add the vanilla. Transfer the rice mixture to a chilled bowl, set it in a pan of cold water, and let it cool, but do not let it set. In a large chilled bowl beat the cream until it holds soft peaks and fold it gently but thoroughly into the rice mixture. Rinse the ring mold with cold water but do not dry it, pour the rice into it, and chill the rice ring for at least 4 hours.

About 10 minutes before serving, dip the mold into warm water, invert a serving plate over it, and unmold the dessert. Pour the apricot sauce into the center and around the rice mold. Fill the center of the mold with the whole apricots and sprinkle them with the pistachios.

COFFEE JELLY

Yield:
8 servings

Equipment:
eight ½-cup gelatin
  molds
pastry bag fitted with
  star tip

2 envelopes unflavored gelatin
½ cup coffee-flavored liqueur
3 cups hot brewed coffee
¾ cup sugar
pinch of salt

lightly sweetened cinnamon-flavored
  whipped cream as an
  accompaniment if desired
Candied Violets (page 524) for
  garnish

In a bowl sprinkle the gelatin over the coffee liqueur and let it soften for 10 minutes. Add the hot coffee, sugar, and salt and stir the mixture until clear. Divide the liquid among the molds and chill until the jellies are set.

Spoon the whipped cream into the pastry bag and pipe a bed of it on a serving plate. Dip the molds into hot water for 2 to 3 seconds and turn the jellies out and onto the cream. Add a touch of whipped cream to each jelly and garnish the jellies with the candied violets.

Variation:

SHERRY COFFEE JELLY: Soften the gelatin in ½ cup cold water and dissolve it in 2 cups hot very strong brewed coffee for 10 minutes. Add ½ cup each of sugar and Sherry. Pour the liquid into a 3-cup decorative mold, rinsed with cold water, and chill the mixture until the jelly is set. Dip the mold into a bowl of hot water for several seconds and turn it out on a chilled dish, brushed with cold water. Serve the jelly with sweetened flavored whipped cream. Serves 6 to 8.

WHITE WINE JELLY

Yield:
6 to 8 servings

Equipment:
4-cup ring mold
cheesecloth

2 envelopes unflavored gelatin
1 bottle chilled dry white wine
1 cup sugar
½ cup brandy

grated rind of 1 lemon
juice of 1 lemon
sweetened whipped cream as an
*   accompaniment*

Soften the gelatin in ½ cup of the chilled wine. In an enameled saucepan combine the remaining wine with the sugar, brandy, and lemon rind. Bring the mixture almost to the boiling point, add the softened gelatin, and stir until the gelatin and sugar are dissolved. Remove the pan from the heat, let cool, and stir in the lemon juice.

Rinse the mold with cold water but do not dry it. Line a sieve with a double layer of the cheesecloth, pour the mixture through the cheesecloth into the mold, and chill the mold until the jelly is set. Dip the mold into a bowl of hot water for a few seconds and turn the jelly out onto a chilled platter. Fill the center with the whipped cream.

SOUFFLÉS AND DESSERT OMELETS

We have coupled soufflés and dessert omelets in one chapter because each, quite obviously, is made with eggs. With soufflés, we witness the absolutely extraordinary power of the beaten egg white in combination with a *béchamel,* or white sauce, base; custard base; or *bouilli*—milk, starch and sugar—base. With dessert or soufflé omelets, we observe how the same ingredient—the egg—combines with heat to produce an entirely different texture and configuration.

A soufflé is celebratory. It is magic and chemistry all in one. While a soufflé bakes, we have been told not to drop anything on the kitchen floor for fear that that sonic boom will affect the delicate balance in the oven, and woe be unto us if we open the oven door before the appointed hour. We anticipate, and our anticipation is well justified. Something that went into the oven as sauce-like and plain comes out tall—puffed and crowned—and at least twice its original height. As this lovely, airy hot dessert meets cooler air, it starts to fall before our very eyes. The soufflé's short-livedness contributes to its appeal, like the orchid's or the peony's.

If the soufflé, say, is a yellow diamond, the soufflé omelet is an opal, fiery but with fewer facets. Like soufflés, dessert omelets separate the yolks from the whites and then the whites, stiffly beaten, are folded in. Like soufflés, dessert omelets are baked. We cannot fault dessert omelets for not rising as soufflés do; they are not intended to. On a snowy Sunday evening after a day in the country, though, there is nothing better than a hearty vegetable soup with French bread and an Omelette Soufflée à la Normande (page 427), filled with apples, raisins, and Calvados. Or in the summer, see Marmalade Soufflé Omelet with Raspberries (page 429). All you really need to begin with is a good supply of fresh eggs.

In fact, let us begin with the egg, as in desserts.

Individual Chocolate Soufflé (page 423) with Hot Chocolate Sauce (page 497) and Whipped Cream

415

SOUFFLÉS

It is a perfectly blissful event in life to be asked in a restaurant before even tasting one's entrée if one wouldn't consider a soufflé for dessert. It brings it all out in the open, puts dessert in its proper perspective and appropriate place—first! How many other times in our lives have we (while pretending to cast a lingering last look over the menu) studied the dessert listings first and ordered an entrée on the basis of that last course?

Soufflés are undeniably special, considered by some to be the apogee of French dessert-making. They have their own times in space, however. They cannot be cajoled into cooking more quickly, and all the microwaving in the world will not produce a high-standing soufflé. A good dessert soufflé is worth every last minute of the wait. But why does it take so long?

Most of the soufflés we encounter start with a *roux* base—a combination of equal parts butter and flour whisked together over low heat. Into this paste liquid is stirred until the mixture forms a thick white sauce, also known as a *béchamel*. Egg yolks are added, flavorings stirred in, and the base is left to cool.

The most important part in making a soufflé occurs next. Egg whites, always at room temperature and always in a clean bowl, are beaten until stiff, preferably with a balloon whisk, but failing that with an electric mixer. These whites are then gently but thoroughly folded into the yolk base, and the whole is spooned into a prepared soufflé dish.

It is the whites that work the magic. In combination with heat, they continue to expand upward. When they have reached their summit, the soufflé should be at least twice its original height, its crown should be golden, and the soufflé should have puffed. It is extraordinary culinary architecture and transitory at best. While a soufflé must be allowed sufficient baking time to achieve its height, once ready it cannot wait to be served. In fact, the minute it is removed from the oven, it, alas, is on the wane.

The key, whether you are making a soufflé or in the happy position of being served one, resides in the successful beating of the egg whites. They should be stiffly beaten, but not dry. (For information on egg whites, see page 238.) They should also be carefully folded into the base. It is preferable to have occasional clumps of whites in your finished base rather than risk overworking and deflating the whites as you incorporate them.

The preparation of your souffle dish, which should always be straight sided, will assist in the success of your soufflé. To begin with, butter and sugar the dish in advance. Next, as illustrated opposite, form a collar of wax paper or foil to extend the sides of the dish. Butter the paper and as shown attach it to the dish with string or yarn. The *raison d'être* of the collar is simply to foster the continued upward mobility of the egg whites. While we have read of other sources that do not suggest the need

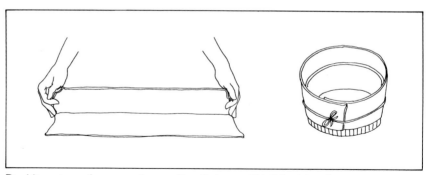

Doubling piece of paper to form collar; fitting soufflé dish with collar

for a paper collar, we believe only professionals can be that confident.

Be sure your oven is sufficiently preheated before you put in your soufflé. In most of the recipes that follow you will note that the oven starts off at one temperature, the soufflé is put in, and the oven temperature is lowered. The logic behind these two temperatures is simple. The egg whites are given extra heat, meaning help, in the beginning to get going. Once on their way, the temperature is then lowered for the slower cooking of the soufflé base. While we may jest about opening the oven door while a soufflé is baking, we advise against any drafts.

In our selection of soufflé recipes we begin with the most straightforward—Vanilla Soufflé. Variations on it ensue: one for that great French favorite, Grand Marnier soufflé. We've also included a recipe for Ginger Soufflé (page 419) that is made with fresh gingerroot. Then come our Individual Chocolate Soufflés accompanied by hot chocolate sauce (page 423).

Perhaps our dressiest choice among this offering is Chestnut Soufflé with Brandied Chocolate Sauce (page 424). Made with chestnut cream, the base has a marvelous surprise in the center of it—diced glacéed chestnuts. This combination would be the perfect finale to an elegant winter dinner, or perhaps even a small Christmas gathering. It is easier to accomplish than you think. Each of the soufflés we have included here can be partially prepared in advance. Make the respective base as instructed in the recipe and cover it tightly. If kept in a cool place, the base can be made three hours in advance. And if you decide to refrigerate the base, be sure to bring it back to room temperature before incorporating the egg whites. In this regard, there are some sources that advocate preparing the *entire* soufflé in advance, egg whites and all. While we do not recommend this, we do encourage experimentation. Depending upon how stiffly the egg whites were beaten and the length of the refrigeration, the soufflé might well rise to dizzying heights. Or it might not. If it doesn't, all you've lost is altitude and texture: You still have a very fine-tasting pudding-like dessert.

Begin, though, by making a soufflé as instructed. The joy, to say nothing of the pleasure of eating it, is worth those few minutes of final preparation. Moreover, it is a glorious feeling to leave the kitchen carrying a towering success.

VANILLA SOUFFLÉ

Yield:
4 to 6 servings

Equipment:
2-quart soufflé dish
upright or hand-held
electric mixer

There are three classic methods of making a sweet soufflé base to which stiffly beaten egg whites are added. The *bouilli* base combines milk, sugar and starch over heat, with egg yolks and flavorings added. The well-known and very reliable *roux* base method couples butter and flour over heat, with milk (either hot or cold) and flavorings added, and, finally, the pastry cream method that actually uses custard as the soufflé base. The following recipe exemplifies the *bouilli* method, the recipe for Individual Chocolate Soufflés (page 423) illustrates the *roux* base method, and the Gingered Pear Soufflé (page 421) demonstrates the pastry cream method. The flavored bases for all these methods can be prepared several hours in advance, and all that remains to be done before baking is to fold in stiffly beaten egg whites.

⅓ cup plus 3 tablespoons granulated
   sugar
¼ cup all-purpose flour
1 cup milk
2 tablespoons unsalted butter
4 egg yolks at room temperature

2 tablespoons vanilla
5 egg whites at room temperature
pinch of salt
⅛ teaspoon cream of tartar
sifted confectioners' sugar for dusting

Butter the soufflé dish and sprinkle it with granulated sugar, knocking out the excess. Butter and sugar a 6-inch-wide doubled piece of foil or wax paper long enough to fit around the dish. Fit the dish with the collar extending 2 inches above the rim (see illustration page 417).

In a bowl combine the ⅓ cup sugar, the flour, and ¼ cup of the milk and whisk the mixture until smooth. In a heavy saucepan bring the remaining ¾ cup milk to a simmer and add it, whisking, in a stream to the flour mixture. Return the mixture to the pan, bring it to a simmer, whisking, and cook it over moderately low heat, whisking, for 2 minutes. Remove the pan from the heat, beat in 1 tablespoon of the butter, and let the mixture cool for 2 minutes. Beat in the egg yolks, one at a time, beating well after each addition, and the vanilla. Strain the soufflé base into a bowl and dot the top with the remaining 1 tablespoon butter, cut into bits. (The base may be prepared in advance up to this point. Cover tightly with plastic wrap and keep in a cool place for up to 3 hours.)

Preheat the oven to 400° F.

In a bowl with the mixer beat the egg whites with the salt until frothy. Add the cream of tartar and beat the whites until they hold soft peaks. Add the remaining 3 tablespoons granulated sugar, a little at a time, and beat the whites until they hold stiff peaks (see illustrations page 238). Stir one fourth of the whites into the yolk mixture and fold in the remaining whites gently but thoroughly. Spoon the mixture into the prepared dish.

Put the soufflé in the middle of the oven, reduce the temperature to 375° F., and bake the soufflé for 30 to 35 minutes, or until the top is puffed and golden. Remove the collar carefully, dust the top of the soufflé with the confectioners' sugar, and serve at once.

Variations:

GRAND MARNIER SOUFFLÉ: For an orange-flavored soufflé, reduce the amount of vanilla to 1½ teaspoons and add 1½ tablespoons grated orange rind and 3 to 4 tablespoons Grand Marnier to the base.

COFFEE SOUFFLÉ: Dissolve 1 tablespoon instant espresso coffee powder in the heated milk, reduce the vanilla to 1 tablespoon, and add ½ teaspoon cinnamon to the base when adding the vanilla.

GINGER SOUFFLÉ

Yield:
4 to 6 servings

Equipment:
2-quart soufflé dish or charlotte mold
pastry brush
hand-held electric mixer

Fresh gingerroot brings to this soufflé a wonderfully aromatic spiciness.

¾ cup granulated sugar
½ cup peeled and grated fresh gingerroot
⅓ cup water
1 cup milk
2 tablespoons all-purpose flour
2 tablespoons cornstarch
6 large eggs, separated, at room temperature

3 tablespoons unsalted butter, cut into bits
pinch of salt
pinch of cream of tartar
sifted confectioners' sugar for dusting
small pieces of crystallized ginger (available at specialty foods shops) for garnish if desired

Butter the soufflé dish. Butter a 6-inch-wide doubled piece of foil or wax paper long enough to fit around the dish. Fit the dish with the collar extending 2 inches above the rim (see illustration page 417).

In a heavy saucepan combine ½ cup of the granulated sugar, the fresh gingerroot, and the water, bring to a boil, and simmer the mixture, washing down any sugar crystals clinging to the sides of the pan with the brush dipped in cold water, for 10 minutes. Let the syrup cool for 30 minutes.

In a saucepan combine the milk, the ginger syrup, flour, and cornstarch and cook the mixture over moderate heat, whisking, until thick. Remove the pan from the heat and beat in the egg yolks, one at a time, beating well after each addition. Strain the mixture into a large bowl and dot the top with the butter to prevent a skin from forming. (The base may be prepared in advance up to this point. Cover tightly with plastic wrap and keep in a cool place for up to 3 hours.)

Preheat the oven to 400° F.

In a bowl with the mixer beat the egg whites with the salt until frothy. Add the cream of tartar and beat until the whites hold soft peaks. Add the remaining ¼ cup granulated sugar, a little at a time, and beat the whites until they hold stiff peaks (see illustrations page 238). Stir one third of the whites into the yolk mixture and fold in the remaining whites gently but thoroughly. Spoon the mixture into the dish.

Put the soufflé in the middle of the oven, reduce the temperature to 375° F., and bake the soufflé for 35 minutes, or until the top is puffed and golden. Remove the collar carefully, dust the soufflé with the confectioners' sugar, and garnish it with pieces of the crystallized ginger if desired. Serve at once.

DRIED APRICOT SOUFFLÉ

Yield:
4 servings

Equipment:
1½-quart soufflé dish
food processor fitted
  with steel blade
hand-held electric
  mixer

Dried fruits make wonderful soufflés in the winter months, when fresh fruits are difficult to come by. This example combines puréed apricots and toasted almonds.

8 ounces dried apricots
1½ cups water
½ cup superfine granulated sugar
2 tablespoons kirsch or Cognac or
  1 tablespoon fresh lemon juice
4 egg whites at room temperature

½ cup granulated sugar
½ cup finely ground toasted blanched
  almonds
sweetened whipped cream flavored
  with vanilla as an accompaniment

Butter and sugar the soufflé dish, knocking out any excess sugar. Butter a 6-inch-wide doubled piece of wax paper long enough to fit around the dish. Fit the dish with the collar extending 2 inches above the rim (see illustration page 417).

In a small saucepan let the apricots soak in the water to cover for at least 2 hours. Bring the water to a boil and simmer the apricots for 10 minutes. In the food processor purée the apricots with the liquid, transfer the purée to a bowl, and stir in the superfine sugar and the liqueur or lemon juice. Combine well and let cool.

Preheat the oven to 375° F.

In a bowl with the mixer beat the egg whites until frothy. Add the granulated sugar, a little at a time, and beat until the whites hold stiff peaks (see illustrations page 238). Beat one fourth of the whites into the apricot purée, then fold the purée into the remaining whites gently but thoroughly. Fold in the almonds. Spoon the mixture into the dish and bake the soufflé in the middle of the oven for 30 to 35 minutes, or until the top is puffed and golden. Remove the collar and serve the soufflé at once with the whipped cream.

GINGERED PEAR SOUFFLÉ

Yield:
6 servings

Equipment:
2-quart soufflé dish
food processor fitted
  with steel blade
hand-held electric
  mixer

A ripe pear will yield slightly to pressure around its stem but should not be squashy. If fresh pears are not in season or the ones you have on hand are just not ready, canned pears, patted dry, work very well and can certainly be substituted in this recipe.

1 cup milk
¼ cup chopped crystallized ginger
  (available at specialty foods shops)
4 large eggs, separated, plus 1 egg
  white
½ cup granulated sugar
2 tablespoons cornstarch
2 tablespoons all-purpose flour
2 tablespoons unsalted butter

2 tablespoons dark rum
2 teaspoons vanilla
3 fresh ripe pears, peeled, cored, and
  sliced, or canned pears
3 tablespoons apricot jam, melted
½ teaspoon grated lemon rind
pinch of salt
sifted confectioners' sugar for garnish

Preheat the oven to 400° F. Butter and sugar the soufflé dish. Butter a 6-inch-wide double piece of wax paper long enough to fit around the dish. Fit the dish with the collar extending 3 inches about the rim (see illustration page 417).

In the food processor or in a blender combine the milk and the ginger and blend the mixture until combined well. Transfer the mixture to a heavy saucepan and bring it just to a simmer.

In a large bowl with the mixer beat the egg yolks until combined, add ¼ cup of the sugar, a little at a time, beating, and beat the mixture until light and lemon colored. Add the cornstarch and the flour, a little at a time, beating, and beat the mixture until smooth. Add the milk mixture in a stream, beating, and beat the mixture until combined well. Transfer the mixture to a heavy saucepan, bring it to a boil, whisking, and simmer it, whisking, for 3 minutes. The pastry cream will be thick and custard-like. Remove the pan from the heat and beat in the butter, rum, and the vanilla.

In a bowl toss the pear slices with the apricot jam and the grated lemon rind. Fold the pears into the pastry cream thoroughly.

In a large bowl with the mixer beat the egg whites until frothy. Add the salt and beat the whites until they hold soft peaks. Add the remaining sugar, a little at a time, and beat the whites until they hold stiff peaks but are not dry (see illustrations page 238). Stir one third of the whites into the pastry cream and fold in the remaining whites gently.

Spoon the mixture into the soufflé dish. Reduce the oven temperature to 375° F. Bake the soufflé in the middle of the oven for 35 to 40 minutes, or until the top is puffed and golden. Remove the collar carefully, sprinkle the soufflé with the confectioners' sugar, and serve at once.

PRALINE SOUFFLÉ

Yield:
8 servings

Equipment:
2½-quart soufflé dish
hand-held electric
  mixer

This soufflé, rich with praline powder, can be flambéed. At Hôtel des Frères Troisgros in Roanne, France, orange-flavored liqueur is poured over the crown and the whole is ignited. We recommend rum in the following recipe and suggest igniting it *before* pouring it over the top. Either way, the effect is dazzling.

½ *stick (¼ cup) plus 1 tablespoon*
  unsalted butter
¼ *cup all-purpose flour*
1 *cup milk*
½ *cup sugar*
6 *large eggs, separated, at room*
  temperature
2 *tablespoons plus 2 additional*
  tablespoons dark rum if desired

⅛ *teaspoon salt*
⅛ *teaspoon cream of tartar*
½ *recipe almond praline (page 544),*
  finely ground
sweetened whipped cream as an
  accompaniment

Butter and sugar the soufflé dish. Butter a 6-inch-wide doubled piece of wax paper long enough to fit around the dish. Fit the dish with the collar extending 3 inches above the rim (see illustration page 417).

In a saucepan melt the ½ stick butter over moderate heat, stir in the flour, and cook the *roux*, stirring, for 2 minutes. Add the milk and ¼ cup of the sugar and cook the mixture, whisking, until the sugar is melted and the mixture is thickened. Remove the pan from the heat and add the egg yolks, one at a time, beating well after each addition. Stir in 2 tablespoons of the dark rum. Dot the top with the remaining 1 tablespoon butter, cut into bits. (The base may be prepared in advance up to this point. Cover tightly with plastic wrap and keep in a cool place for up to 3 hours.)

Preheat the oven to 375° F.

In a bowl with the mixer beat the egg whites with the salt until frothy. Add the cream of tartar and beat until the whites hold soft peaks. Add the remaining ¼ cup of sugar, a little at a time, and beat the whites until they hold stiff peaks (see illustrations page 238).

Stir ⅔ cup of the praline powder into the yolk mixture and fold in one fourth of the whites gently but thoroughly. Pour the yolk mixture onto the remaining whites and fold the mixture until no traces of white remain. Spoon the mixture into the soufflé dish and smooth the top. Sprinkle the remaining ⅓ cup praline powder over the soufflé and bake the soufflé in the middle of the oven for 35 minutes, or until set. Remove the collar. Heat the remaining 2 tablespoons rum if desired, ignite it, and pour it over the soufflé. Serve the soufflé at once with the whipped cream.

INDIVIDUAL CHOCOLATE SOUFFLÉS

Yield:
4 servings

Equipment:
four 1-cup soufflé
 dishes
hand-held electric
 mixer
shallow baking pan for
 waterbath

These splendid per-person soufflés combine a wonderful crustiness on the outside while remaining still slightly moist within. If in doubt as to their doneness, you *can* test one by inserting a thin metal skewer into its center. Moist crumbs will adhere to the skewer if the soufflé is ready. We'd advise living dangerously though, and letting magic, also known as chemistry in this instance, take its course.

2 tablespoons plus 1 teaspoon unsalted
 butter
1 tablespoon all-purpose flour
½ cup milk, heated
5 ounces domestic semisweet chocolate,
 cut into bits
8 egg whites at room temperature
pinch of salt

pinch of cream of tartar
¼ cup granulated sugar
sifted confectioners' sugar for dusting
1 recipe Hot Chocolate Sauce (page
 497) as an accompaniment
whipped cream sprinkled with grated
 chocolate as an accompaniment

Butter and sugar the soufflé dishes, knocking out the excess sugar, and chill the dishes.

In a small saucepan melt the 2 tablespoons of butter over moderately low heat, stir in the flour, and cook the *roux*, stirring, for 3 minutes. Add the heated milk, whisking, and simmer the mixture, whisking, for 2 minutes. Remove the pan from the heat, add the chocolate, and stir the mixture until the chocolate is melted. Transfer the mixture to a bowl and dot the top with the remaining 1 teaspoon butter, cut into bits. (The base may be prepared in advance up to this point. Cover tightly with plastic wrap and keep in a cool place for up to 3 hours.)

Preheat the oven to 400° F.

In a bowl with the mixer beat the egg whites with the salt until frothy. Add the cream of tartar and beat until the whites hold soft peaks. Add the granulated sugar, a little at a time, beating, and beat the whites until they just hold stiff peaks (see illustrations page 238). Stir one fourth of the whites into the chocolate base and fold in the remaining whites gently but thoroughly. Spoon the mixture into the prepared dishes. If desired, form a topknot on the soufflés: Beginning at the edge of each soufflé dish, run a finger through the soufflé mixture in a spiral, lifting the finger in the center to form a peak. Set the dishes in the baking pan and add enough hot water to reach one third up the sides of the soufflé dishes.

Bake the soufflés in the middle of the oven for 18 to 20 minutes, or until they are puffed. Dust the tops of the soufflés with the confectioners' sugar and serve at once with the hot chocolate sauce and whipped cream.

Photo on page 414.

CHESTNUT SOUFFLÉ WITH BRANDIED CHOCOLATE SAUCE

Yield:
4 to 6 servings

Equipment:
**2-quart soufflé dish
hand-held electric
mixer**

5 tablespoons granulated sugar
2 tablespoons all-purpose flour
2 tablespoons cornstarch
1 cup milk
2 tablespoons unsalted butter
4 egg yolks at room temperature
2 tablespoons dark rum or Cognac
1 teaspoon vanilla
¾ cup chestnut cream (available at
   specialty foods shops)

5 egg whites at room temperature
pinch of salt
⅛ teaspoon cream of tartar
⅔ cup diced glacéed chestnuts
   (available at specialty foods shops)
sifted confectioners' sugar for garnish
1 recipe Brandied Chocolate Sauce as
   an accompaniment (page 498)

Butter the soufflé dish and sprinkle it with sugar, knocking out the excess. Butter and sugar a 6-inch-wide doubled piece of foil or wax paper long enough to fit around the dish. Fit the prepared dish with the collar extending 2 inches above the rim (see illustration page 417).

In a bowl combine 3 tablespoons of the granulated sugar, the flour, cornstarch, and ¼ cup of the milk and whisk until smooth.

In a heavy saucepan bring the remaining ¾ cup milk to a simmer and add it in a stream, whisking, to the flour mixture. Return the mixture to the pan, bring to a simmer, whisking, and cook it over moderately low heat, whisking, for 2 minutes. Remove the pan from the heat, beat in 1 tablespoon of the butter, and let the mixture cool for 2 minutes. Beat in the egg yolks, one at a time, beating well after each addition, the rum or Cognac, and the vanilla. Strain the mixture into a bowl, stir in the chestnut cream, and dot the top of the mixture with the remaining 1 tablespoon butter, cut into bits. (The base may be prepared in advance up to this point. Cover tightly with plastic wrap and keep in a cool place for up to 3 hours.)

Preheat the oven to 400° F.

In a bowl with the mixer beat the egg whites with the salt until frothy. Add the cream of tartar and beat the whites until they hold soft peaks. Add the remaining 2 tablespoons granulated sugar and beat the whites until they hold stiff peaks. Stir one fourth of the whites into the yolk mixture and fold in the remaining whites gently but thoroughly. Spoon half of the mixture into the prepared dish, arrange the glacéed chestnuts over the mixture, and cover them with the remaining soufflé mixture.

Put the soufflé in the middle of the oven, reduce the temperature to 375° F., and bake for 35 to 40 minutes, or until it is puffed and lightly golden. Remove the collar carefully, dust the top of the soufflé with the confectioners' sugar, and serve the soufflé at once with the chocolate sauce.

SALZBURGER NOCKERL

Yield:
4 servings

Equipment:
12-inch gratin dish
hand-held electric
  mixer

A time-honored Austrian specialty and the most famous local gastronomic creation of Salzburg, *Salzburger Nockerl* is a sweet airy soufflé, a lemony egg yolk mixture that is folded into meringue, then briefly baked.

1 tablespoon unsalted butter, softened
5 egg whites at room temperature
3 tablespoons granulated sugar
1 tablespoon all-purpose flour

3 egg yolks
grated rind of 1 lemon
sifted confectioners' sugar for dusting

Preheat the oven to 375° F. Heat the gratin dish slightly and coat it lightly with the butter.

In a bowl with the mixer beat the egg whites until they hold soft peaks. Gradually add the granulated sugar and beat the whites until they hold stiff peaks (see illustrations page 238). Sprinkle the flour over the whites and fold it in gently.

In another bowl with the mixer beat the egg yolks with the grated rind until thick and lemon colored and fold the mixture gently but thoroughly into the whites. Quickly divide the mixture into 4 large portions and arrange the portions in the prepared dish, smoothing the sides with the back of a spoon and shaping the mixture into mounds with the highest possible peaks. Bake in the middle of the oven for 15 minutes, or until lightly golden. Sprinkle with the confectioners' sugar and serve at once.

DESSERT OMELETS

The French, ever practical, were quick to recognize a sound idea, particularly when they had originally conceived it. If the soufflé, the omelet, and the crêpe each made a wonderful entrée, why wouldn't each make an equally marvelous dessert? Of course the French were right, they always were when it came to matters culinary. So were born three new categories of glorious combinations, each of which really only required a sweet as opposed to a savory filling or topping or garnish. The refinements and niceties would come later, and indeed they did.

Earlier in this chapter we discussed the wonders of dessert soufflés. Dessert omelets, which in the instances that follow are synonymous with soufflé omelets, are similar but ultimately different. For a dessert, or a soufflé, omelet the yolks are initially combined, then stiffly beaten egg whites are folded in, with flavorings. The whole is then baked. (There are, of course, other dessert omelets that can be made on the top of the stove which do not involve beaten egg whites.)

Like soufflés, dessert omelets can be made to serve one, as in Marmalade Soufflé Omelet with Raspberries (page 429), or many, like Omelette Soufflée à la Normande (recipe opposite). Unlike soufflés, they cook quickly, but cannot be made, even in part, in advance. Dessert omelets are infinitely easier to make from a technique point of view than soufflés and require no special equipment save an ovenproof omelet pan or sometimes a gratin dish. Why, then, you might ask, do we not think of dessert omelets more frequently?

We suspect that the last-minute preparation deters some. Perhaps it is the number of eggs for others. Or that in this meat-consuming country, a dessert of eggs seems slightly undesirable. Or a more likely reason could be that the egg quota of the day was spent on breakfast. To all of the above, we would seriously lobby every now and then for a lighter dinner and that the egg allowance be spent on dessert. Think of it: Scrambled eggs or Vanilla Lime Soufflé Omelet (page 430)? Eggs and bacon or Brown Sugar Soufflé Omelet (page 430), caramelized on the inside and flambéed with rum before it is served.

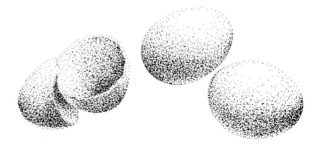

OMELETTE SOUFFLÉE À LA NORMANDE

Yield:
4 servings

Equipment:
12-inch oval gratin dish or oval metal platter
hand-held electric mixer

Normandy is the northern French province known especially for its apples and its local apple brandy, Calvados. Both of those ingredients are employed very tastefully in the following dessert omelet.

FOR THE FILLING
¼ cup raisins
1 tablespoon Calvados
2 cups peeled, cored, and sliced tart cooking apples
1 tablespoon granulated sugar
1 tablespoon fresh lemon juice
½ teaspoon grated lemon rind
⅛ teaspoon freshly grated nutmeg
½ stick (¼ cup) unsalted butter

FOR THE OMELET
5 large eggs, separated, at room temperature
5 tablespoons granulated sugar
2 tablespoons Calvados
1 teaspoon vanilla
pinch of salt
⅛ teaspoon cream of tartar
sifted confectioners' sugar for dusting

½ recipe Crème Anglaise (page 490), flavored with Calvados if desired

Butter and sugar the gratin dish or platter, knocking out the excess sugar.

Make the filling:
In a small bowl toss the raisins with the Calvados and let stand for 15 minutes. In another bowl toss the apples with the sugar, lemon juice, lemon rind, and nutmeg and let stand for 15 minutes.

In a skillet melt the butter over moderate heat, add the apple and raisin mixtures, tossing to coat them with the butter, and simmer, covered, for 3 minutes. Remove the lid, increase the heat to moderately high, and toss the mixture until it is thick and almost all the liquid has evaporated.

Make the omelet:
In a bowl with the mixer beat the yolks until combined. Add 4 tablespoons of the sugar, a little at a time, and beat the mixture until it falls in a ribbon when the beater is lifted. Beat in the Calvados and vanilla.

Preheat the oven to 325° F.

In a bowl with the mixer beat the whites with the salt until they are frothy. Add the cream of tartar and beat the whites until they hold soft peaks. Gradually add the remaining 1 tablespoon granulated sugar and beat the whites until stiff (see illustrations page 238). Stir one fourth of the whites into the yolk mixture and fold in the remaining whites gently but thoroughly. Spoon half of the mixture into the prepared dish, spoon the apple mixture over it, and top it with the remaining egg mixture. Smooth the top of the omelet decoratively and bake the omelet in the middle of the oven for 25 to 30 minutes, or until puffed and golden. Dust the omelet with the confectioners' sugar and serve it at once with the crème anglaise if desired.

MARMALADE SOUFFLÉ OMELET WITH RASPBERRIES

Yield:
2 omelets

Equipment:
hand-held electric mixer
small non-stick ovenproof skillet measuring 7½ inches across the top

4 large eggs, separated, at room temperature
6 tablespoons granulated sugar
1 tablespoon eau-de-vie de framboise *(raspberry brandy)*
4 tablespoons all-purpose flour
½ teaspoon double-acting baking powder
pinch of salt
2 tablespoons unsalted butter
¼ cup orange marmalade
½ pint fresh raspberries
sifted confectioners' sugar for dusting

Preheat the oven to 400° F.

In a bowl with the mixer beat the egg yolks with 2 tablespoons of the granulated sugar until the mixture is thick and pale. Add the *eau-de-vie de framboise*, the flour, and baking powder and beat until blended well.

In a bowl with the mixer beat the egg whites with the salt until they hold soft peaks, add the remaining 4 tablespoons granulated sugar, a little at a time, and beat the whites until they just hold stiff peaks (see illustrations page 238). Stir one fourth of the whites into the yolk mixture and fold in the remaining whites gently but thoroughly.

In the skillet heat 1 tablespoon of the butter over moderate heat until the foam subsides, add one half of the soufflé mixture, spreading it evenly in the pan, and cook for 30 seconds. Transfer the skillet to the oven and bake the omelet in the upper third of the oven for 5 to 6 minutes, or until puffed and set. Do not turn off the oven.

While the omelet is baking, heat the marmalade in a small saucepan. Spread half of it over the top of the omelet and heat the omelet in the oven for 1 minute more, or until the marmalade is just bubbling. Shake the pan to loosen the omelet, run a rubber spatula around the edge, and fold the omelet in half. Slide the omelet onto a heated plate and cover it loosely with foil. Make a second omelet with the remaining ingredients in the same manner.

To serve, divide the raspberries between the omelets, spooning them into the folded centers, and dust the omelets with confectioners' sugar.

Photo opposite.

Marmalade Soufflé
Omelet with
Raspberries (above)

VANILLA LIME SOUFFLÉ OMELET

Yield:
1 omelet, serving 6

Equipment:
hand-held electric
  mixer
1½-quart shallow
baking dish

4 egg yolks
1 cup granulated sugar
¼ cup plus 2 tablespoons heavy cream
1½ teaspoons grated lime rind
6 egg whites at room temperature
¼ teaspoon cream of tartar

1 tablespoon unsalted butter
1 tablespoon vanilla confectioners'
  sugar (page 541)
1½ tablespoons confectioners' sugar
  for dusting

Preheat the oven to 400° F.

In a large bowl with the mixer beat the egg yolks with ½ cup of the granulated sugar until the mixture falls in a ribbon when the beater is lifted (see illustration page 16). Beat in the ¼ cup heavy cream and continue to beat the mixture until it is thick and creamy. Stir in the grated rind.

In another large bowl with the mixer beat the egg whites with the cream of tartar until they hold soft peaks, beat in the remaining ½ cup granulated sugar, one tablespoon at a time, and continue to beat the meringue until it holds stiff peaks (see illustrations page 238). Stir one fourth of the meringue into the yolk mixture and fold in the remaining meringue.

Melt the butter in the baking dish in the oven and stir in the remaining 2 tablespoons heavy cream and the vanilla sugar. Pour the egg mixture into the baking dish, spreading it evenly and swirling the top with a rubber spatula. Dust the top with the confectioners' sugar and bake the omelet in the upper third of the oven for 10 to 12 minutes, or until puffed and golden but still creamy in the center. Serve at once.

BROWN SUGAR SOUFFLÉ OMELET

Yield:
1 omelet, serving 2

Equipment:
hand-held electric
  mixer
7-inch omelet pan

¼ cup firmly packed plus
  2 tablespoons light brown sugar
¼ cup finely chopped pecans
¼ teaspoon cinnamon
4 large eggs, separated, at room
  temperature

2 tablespoons heavy cream
pinch of cream of tartar
2 tablespoons granulated sugar
1 tablespoon unsalted butter
2 tablespoons dark rum

Preheat the broiler.

In a small bowl combine the ¼ cup brown sugar, the pecans, and the cinnamon.

In a bowl with the mixer beat the egg yolks until thick and lemon colored. Beat in the heavy cream.

In another bowl with the mixer beat the egg whites with the cream of tartar until they hold soft peaks, beat in the granulated sugar, one tablespoon at a time, and beat the meringue until it holds stiff peaks (see illustrations page 238). Stir one fourth of the meringue into the yolk mixture and fold in the remaining meringue gently but thoroughly.

Heat the omelet pan over moderately high heat until hot, add the butter, and heat it, tilting and rotating the pan to coat it with the butter, until the foam subsides. Pour in the egg mixture, spreading it evenly with a rubber spatula, and let it set for several seconds. Cook the omelet, shaking the pan, for 30 seconds to 1 minute, or until the bottom is golden brown. Remove the pan from the heat, sprinkle the top with the brown sugar mixture, then run the pan under the broiler about 4 inches from the heat for 1 minute, or until the sugar is caramelized and the omelet is puffed and golden. Shake the pan to loosen the omelet. With a rubber spatula fold the top third of the omelet, near the handle of the pan, over the middle third, tuck in the sides, and, tilting the pan forward, slide the omelet to the bottom of the pan. Fold over the bottom third and invert the omelet onto a heated platter. Force the remaining 2 tablespoons brown sugar through a sieve over the omelet.

In a small pan or in a ladle heat the dark rum, ignite it, and pour it over the omelet, basting the omelet with the rum until the flames go out. Serve the omelet at once.

CRÊPES, PANCAKES, AND FRITTERS

hat crêpes, pancakes, and fritters have in common is that each is made with batter—that combination of eggs, flour, and liquid. Crêpe batter contains more liquid in proportion to flour, rendering gossamer, tender rounds. Pancake batter contains more flour to produce denser, higher, and more toothsome results. Fritter batter must be substantial enough in consistency to adhere to whatever is being deep fried yet remain light. That is why it is usually made with beaten egg whites and beer.

The technicalities of the batters aside, crêpes, pancakes, and fritters share other characteristics as desserts. They are fun. Any one of them can be dressed up or down. Crêpes can be filled with something as simple as jam or appear flaming and dramatic as Crêpes Suzette Maison (page 436). By the addition of stiffly beaten egg whites, they can be made to puff up, as in soufflé crêpes. They can also be shaped into *tulipes* or ice-cream cones. They can even be layered to form a cake.

Dessert pancakes enjoy great popularity in Austria, where the simplest are made and filled with preserves and known as *Palatschinken* (page 444); the more elegant version is filled with a mixture of cottage cheese, sour cream, and raisins, and called *Topfenpalatschinken* (page 443). In our pancake grouping we are also including a recipe for Dessert Waffles with Blood Orange Sauce (page 444) and, last but not least, a recipe for *clafouti*, that splendid French creation which some consider a pudding, others a flan, and still others a cake.

A banana fritter is one thing; a strawberry fritter, dusted with confectioners' sugar and served while still very warm with a selection of sauces, is something altogether different. As fritters are deep fried, so is another type of dessert we are including in this section: doughnuts.

The quintessential truth about crêpes, pancakes, and fritters is that having just one is not nearly enough.

Lemon Sherbet in
Crêpe Tulipes with
Raspberries (page
439)

CRÊPES

We have the French to thank for the creation of crêpes, those thin, thin pancakes that can be variously filled and rolled, or folded and flambéed. Crêpes can be prepared simply or elegantly, but either way their quality depends upon the tenderness of the crêpe itself, which is brought about by allowing the batter to rest, or stand, after it has been combined. During this period the gluten, or protein, in the flour relaxes, resulting in additional air in the batter and, consequently, in the cooked crêpe.

A well-equipped kitchen includes among its *batterie* a well-seasoned crêpe pan, meaning that it has been adequately oiled over time and that it has never had anything other than crêpes cooked in it. And that is the only but essential piece of equipment you will need to make crêpes. They cook quickly and can be turned with just your fingertips. Stack the finished crêpes between sheets of wax paper, then wrap them in foil, and freeze in batches. Thaw frozen crêpes overnight in the refrigerator.

Crêpes are so easy to make and so enjoyable that we can't think of one reason not to have a good supply of them on hand all the time.

DESSERT CRÊPES

Yield:
about 12 crêpes

Equipment:
food processor fitted
  with steel blade
6- to 7-inch crêpe pan
  or non-stick pan
pastry brush

These crêpes are also known as *crêpes sucrées* because of the addition of sugar to the crêpe batter. The batter rests for 1 hour allowing the gluten to relax and the flour to absorb more liquid, resulting in a more tender crêpe. A crêpe that contains sugar like this one will brown more quickly, so watch it carefully as it cooks.

½ cup all-purpose flour
½ cup water
¼ cup milk
2 large eggs
1½ tablespoons unsalted butter,
* melted and cooled*

½ teaspoon sugar
pinch of salt
clarified butter (page 536), melted, for
* cooking the crêpes*

To make crêpes:

In the food processor or in a blender blend the flour, water, milk, eggs, butter, sugar, and salt for 5 seconds. Turn off the motor and with a rubber spatula scrape down the sides of the container. Blend the batter for 20 seconds more, transfer it to a bowl, and let it stand, covered with plastic wrap, for 1 hour.

Heat the pan over moderately high heat until hot. Brush the pan lightly with the clarified butter, heat the butter until it is hot but not smoking, and remove the pan from the heat. Stir the batter, half fill a ¼-cup measure with it, and off the heat pour the batter into the pan. Tilt and rotate the pan quickly to cover the bottom with a thin layer of the batter and pour any excess batter back into the bowl. Return the pan to the heat, loosen the edges of the crêpe with a metal spatula, and cook the crêpe until the underside is browned lightly. Turn the crêpe, brown the other side, and transfer the crêpe to a plate. Make crêpes with the remaining batter in the same manner, brushing the pan lightly with butter as necessary.

The crêpes may be prepared in advance, stacked, wrapped in plastic wrap, and refrigerated for up to 3 days or frozen.

CRÊPES À LA CONFITURE

Spread dessert crêpes with currant jelly or red raspberry, apricot, or black cherry preserves. Roll up the crêpes, arrange them side by side in a flameproof dish, and sprinkle them with granulated sugar. Put the dish in a preheated 450° F. oven or run it under a preheated broiler until the sugar is caramelized.

RUM-MARINATED MANGO CRÊPES

**Yield:
about 12 crêpes**

1 recipe Dessert Crêpes (recipe opposite)
1 tablespoon unsalted butter, melted
2 ripe mangoes, peeled and cut into
*   ¾-inch pieces*

2 tablespoons fresh lemon juice
1 tablespoon granulated sugar
⅓ cup dark rum
confectioners' sugar for dusting

Make dessert crêpes, fold them into quarters, and put them on a baking sheet. Preheat the oven to 400° F. Brush the tops of the crêpes with the butter and bake the crêpes for 10 minutes, or until browned lightly and slightly crisp.

In a bowl toss together the mangoes, lemon juice, granulated sugar, and rum. Stuff each crêpe with about ¼ cup of the mango mixture, transfer the crêpes to a platter, and dust them with the confectioners' sugar.

Photo on page 436.

Rum-Marinated Mango Crêpes (page 435)

CRÊPES FLAMBÉED

Dessert crêpes, like soufflés, lend themselves to being flambéed. To create this most dazzling effect, simply heat the liqueur being called for in the respective recipe until hot, pour it carefully over the assembled crêpes, then ignite it with a wooden kitchen match. Taking the necessary obvious precautions, like avoiding any billowing curtains or tripping over the family dog, serve the dish flaming. The presentation will indeed be impressive, and any concerns you may have about the risks of the device will vanish with the flames themselves, which extinguish rapidly, with the burning off of the alcohol.

CRÊPES SUZETTE MAISON

Yield:
about 24 crêpes

2 recipes Dessert Crêpes (page 434)
5 tablespoons sugar plus additional for
   sprinkling
½ stick (¼ cup) unsalted butter
¼ cup dark rum plus ½ cup heated

3 tablespoons water
juice of 2 oranges
zest of 1 orange
2 oranges, peeled and sectioned (for
   procedure page 548)

Make dessert crêpes. Fold the crêpes into quarters, arrange them in a shallow flameproof dish, and keep them warm.

In a saucepan combine the sugar, butter, the ¼ cup rum, the water, orange juice, and orange zest, bring the sauce to a boil over moderate heat, and cook it until it thickens slightly. Add the orange sections, pour the sauce over the crêpes, and sprinkle the crêpes with sugar and the remaining ½ cup rum. Ignite the rum and serve the crêpes flaming.

CRÊPES WITH STRAWBERRIES

Yield:
about 24 crêpes

2 recipes Dessert Crêpes (page 434)
2½ cups sliced strawberries
½ cup plus 6 tablespoons kirsch

sugar for sprinkling
heavy cream as an accompaniment

Make dessert crêpes and arrange them in one layer on a work surface. In a bowl let the strawberries macerate in the 6 tablespoons kirsch for 30 minutes.

Put about 2 tablespoons of the marinated strawberries in the center of each crêpe. Sprinkle the crêpes with sugar, roll them up, and arrange them side by side in a shallow flameproof dish. Heat the remaining ½ cup kirsch, ignite it, and pour it flaming over the crêpes. Serve the crêpes flaming, with the cream.

CRÊPES WITH RASPBERRIES

Yield:
about 12 crêpes

1 recipe Dessert Crêpes (page 434)
6 ounces cream cheese, softened
sour cream to taste
½ teaspoon crème de cassis (black currant liqueur), or to taste

1 pint raspberries
½ cup eau-de-vie de framboise (raspberry brandy)
¼ cup sugar
3 tablespoons brandy

Make dessert crêpes and keep them warm.

In a bowl blend the cream cheese with enough of the sour cream to make a smooth paste. Stir in the *crème de cassis*. Put 1 tablespoon of the mixture in the center of each crêpe, fold the crêpes in quarters, and arrange them side by side in a shallow flameproof dish.

In a small saucepan combine the raspberries, the *eau-de-vie de framboise,* and sugar and cook the mixture over moderate heat, stirring occasionally, until the raspberries are soft. Stir in the brandy, ignite the sauce and pour it over the crêpes.

CRÊPES WITH CHOCOLATE BUTTER CREAM

Yield:
about 24 crêpes

Equipment:
hand-held electric
mixer

2 recipes Dessert Crêpes (page 434)
3 large eggs
1¼ cups sugar
4 ounces unsweetened chocolate,
   melted

3 sticks (1½ cups) unsalted butter,
   softened
1 cup orange marmalade, heated
finely chopped walnuts for sprinkling
½ cup brandy, heated

Make dessert crêpes and keep them warm.

In a bowl combine well the eggs, sugar, and chocolate. Set the bowl in a larger bowl filled with cracked ice and beat the mixture with a whisk until it is light. With the mixer gradually beat in the softened butter by tablespoons and beat the mixture until thick and creamy. Put a generous tablespoon of the chocolate butter cream in the center of each crêpe, roll up the crêpes, and arrange them side by side in a shallow flameproof dish. Pour the heated marmalade over the crêpes and sprinkle the crêpes generously with the chopped walnuts. Sprinkle the heated brandy over the crêpes, ignite it, and serve the crêpes flaming.

ORANGE SOUFFLÉ CRÊPES

Yield:
4 crêpes

Equipment:
hand-held electric
mixer

For this light delectable dessert, dessert crêpes are filled with a mixture that causes them to puff up slightly during baking. Like a soufflé, soufflé crêpes should be served immediately, so timing is essential in their preparation. These crêpes may also be served with a garnish of Candied Orange Peel (page 522).

4 Dessert Crêpes (page 434)
2 tablespoons unsalted butter
2 tablespoons all-purpose flour
½ cup fresh orange juice
1 teaspoon grated orange rind
1 tablespoon Grand Marnier
1 egg yolk

2 egg whites at room temperature
pinch of salt
pinch of cream of tartar
¼ cup granulated sugar
sifted confectioners' sugar for
   sprinkling

Arrange the dessert crêpes on a baking sheet. Preheat the oven to 350° F.

In a small heavy saucepan melt the butter over moderately low heat, stir in the flour, and cook the *roux*, stirring, for 3 minutes. Whisk in the juice and the rind, bring the mixture to a boil, whisking, and simmer it, whisking, for 2 minutes. Transfer the mixture to a bowl and stir in the Grand Marnier and the egg yolk.

In another bowl with the mixer beat the egg whites with the salt until they are frothy, add the cream of tartar, and beat the whites until they hold soft peaks. Add the granulated sugar, a little at a time, beating constantly, and beat the whites until they just hold stiff peaks (see illustrations page 238). Stir one third of the whites into the yolk mixture, fold in the remaining whites, and spread the soufflé mixture ½ inch thick onto half of each crêpe. Fold the crêpes gently over the soufflé mixture and sprinkle them with some confectioners' sugar. Bake the crêpes in the middle of the oven for 10 minutes. Sprinkle the crêpes with additional confectioners' sugar and serve them immediately.

LEMON SHERBET IN CRÊPE TULIPES WITH RASPBERRIES

Yield:
8 *tulipes*

Equipment:
eight 1¼-cup glass custard cups

Tulipes are crisp wafer-thin cookies that are shaped while still warm and pliable in cups to resemble tulip flowers with ruffled edges (see recipe on page 288). In this recipe warm crêpes are fitted into molds to form that same tulip shape. Crêpe *tulipes* can, of course, be filled with any ice cream, sherbet, mousse, or seasonal fruit desired. This is a wonderful springtime or early summer dessert.

1 quart Lemon Sherbet (page 371)   *1 pint fresh raspberries*
8 Dessert Crêpes (page 434)   *mint sprigs for garnish*
2 recipes Raspberry Sauce (page 508)

Have ready the lemon sherbet and the dessert crêpes. Preheat the oven to 400° F.

Fit each crêpe into a custard cup and put a large ball of foil in the center of each crêpe to keep it open. Bake the *tulipes* on a jelly-roll pan for 5 minutes. Remove the foil and bake the *tulipes* for 2 to 3 minutes more, or until crisp and golden.

Spoon about 2 tablespoons of the raspberry sauce onto each of 8 dessert plates, set a *tulipe* on the sauce on each plate, and fill each *tulipe* with a scoop of the lemon sherbet. Sprinkle ¼ cup of the fresh raspberries over each *tulipe* and garnish the *tulipes* with the mint sprigs.

Photo on page 432.

CRÊPE ICE-CREAM CONES

Yield:
4 servings

Crêpes are shaped to resemble ice-cream cones and are filled with scoops of vanilla ice cream. A wonderful idea for a do-it-yourself ice-cream creation or for a children's party.

1 pint Vanilla Ice Cream (page 349)
4 Dessert Crêpes (page 434)
melted unsalted butter for brushing
2 large strawberries, hulled, halved lengthwise, and the halves sliced thin lengthwise

1 recipe Brown Sugar Chocolate Sauce (page 500) as an accompaniment if desired

Have ready the vanilla ice cream and the dessert crêpes. Preheat the oven to 400° F.

Arrange the crêpes browner side down on a work surface, fold them in half, and fold them in half again to form triangles. Lift the top flap of each triangle and put a large ball of foil inside to keep the cone open. Brush the crêpe cones with the butter and bake them on a baking sheet for 4 minutes, or until crisp. Remove the foil, fill each cone with a scoop of the ice cream, and garnish it with overlapping strawberry slices. Serve the crêpes with the chocolate sauce if desired.

HONEY PEAR CRÊPE CAKE

Yield:
one 8-inch crêpe cake

Equipment:
10-inch flameproof baking dish

Crêpes are layered with a delicious honey pear conserve, baked, carmelized, then served in wedges. The recipe for the conserve can easily be doubled and served as an accompaniment to ice cream or spread thickly on toasted brioche. Packaged beautifully, the conserve makes a wonderful and thoughtful homemade gift.

FOR THE HONEY PEAR CONSERVE
2 pounds Anjou Pears, peeled, cored, and cut into 1-inch pieces
¼ cup plus 1 tablespoon fresh lemon juice

½ cup honey, or to taste
¼ teaspoon ground cloves
1 tablespoon cinnamon
¼ cup dried currants

1 recipe Dessert Crêpes (page 434)
⅓ cup chopped walnuts
sugar for sprinkling
1 tablespoon unsalted butter, melted

Vanilla Ice Cream (page 349) or whipped cream as an accompaniment if desired

Make the honey pear conserve: In a large saucepan cook the pears, lemon juice, honey, cloves, and cinnamon over moderate heat, stirring, until the liquid begins to simmer, and simmer the mixture, stirring occasionally, for 35 to 45 minutes, or until it is thickened. Add the currants and simmer the mixture, covered partially, for 15 minutes. Transfer the conserve to a bowl, let it cool, and chill it, covered, overnight or for up to one week.

Have ready the dessert crêpes. Butter the baking dish well and preheat the oven to 400° F.

Arrange one of the crêpes in the bottom of the baking dish, smooth 2 tablespoons of the conserve over the crêpe, sprinkle with 1 tablespoon of the nuts, and top with another crêpe. Continue to layer the remaining crêpes, conserves, and nuts in the same manner, ending with a crêpe. Sprinkle the top of the crêpe cake with the sugar and drizzle the butter over it. Bake the cake in the upper third of the oven for 20 minutes, or until completely heated through. Put the cake under a preheated broiler for 1 to 2 minutes, or until the top is caramelized to a golden brown. Serve the cake with the vanilla ice cream or whipped cream and serve the remaining honey pear conserve as a garnish if desired.

To Can Honey Pear Conserve: If desired spoon the hot conserve into hot sterilized Mason-type jars (sterilizing procedure page 551), filling the jars to within ¼ inch of the top, and tap the jars on a hard surface to eliminate any air bubbles. Wipe the rims with a dampened cloth and seal the jars with the lids. Put the jars in a waterbath canner or on the rack in a kettle and add enough hot water to the canner to cover the jars by 2 inches. Cover the canner, bring the water to a boil, and process the jars for 10 minutes. Transfer the jars with tongs to a folded dish towel and let them cool. Store the conserve at room temperature. Makes about 2 cups.

PANCAKES

We think of pancakes or griddlecakes as breakfast fare, but in reality they have a whole other life. With the simple addition of a sweet topping or filling they are transformed into splendid desserts.

Among our selection of dessert pancakes is one that is actually baked until puffed and served in wedges. Another recipe calls for the pancakes to cook on the top of the stove, in the traditional manner. And a third takes conventionally prepared pancakes, fills them with a rich sour cream-raisin combination, covers them with a custard mixture, and bakes them until lightly browned. This last, an Austrian specialty called *Topfenpalatschinken*, would follow a very simple light meal, and almost act as a meal in itself. For such a small area in this fascinating but otherwise all-encompassing subject known as desserts, this constitutes quite some variety.

We are including in this section dessert and Belgian waffles as well. What differentiates waffles from pancakes in general is, one, obviously the shape. You cannot make waffles or even contemplate them, for that matter, without a waffle iron. Two, waffle batter is usually lightened by the addition of some type of leavener, either beaten egg white or baking powder. Belgian waffles, on the other hand, require an even more specific mold, available at specialty kitchenware stores.

Pancake and waffle batters, unlike crêpe batter, require no rest period. Pancakes and waffles, like crêpes, can be rolled or topped with fresh fruit, ice cream, or a wonderful chocolate or butterscotch sauce. Pancakes and waffles should be remembered and served more frequently as they make an informal yet very satisfying dessert.

PUFFED PANCAKE WITH STRAWBERRY ALMOND BUTTER

Yield:
4 servings

Equipment:
food processor fitted
  with steel blade
12-inch ovenproof
  skillet

This puffed pancake is served with a strawberry almond butter but could also be accompanied by ice cream, chocolate sauce, or raspberry or strawberry sauce and fresh fruit.

FOR THE STRAWBERRY ALMOND BUTTER

1 stick (½ cup) unsalted butter,
  softened
2½ cups sifted confectioners' sugar

1 pint strawberries, hulled
½ cup finely ground blanched almonds

3 large eggs
¾ cup milk
¾ cup sifted all-purpose flour
scant ¼ teaspoon almond extract

½ stick (¼ cup) unsalted butter
sugared sliced strawberries as an
  accompaniment

Make the strawberry almond butter:

In a bowl cream together the butter and confectioners' sugar. In the food processor or in a blender in batches purée the strawberries and force the purée through a fine sieve into the butter mixture. Beat the mixture until it is smooth and beat in the almonds. Chill the butter, covered, until firm.

Preheat the oven to 425° F.

In a bowl beat the eggs until they are thick and pale. Gradually add the milk and the sifted flour, beating the batter until it is very smooth, and stir in the almond extract. In the skillet melt the butter in the oven until it is bubbling. Pour the batter into the skillet and bake the pancake for 20 minutes, or until puffed and brown. Cut the pancake into wedges and serve it topped with the strawberry almond butter and the sliced strawberries.

COTTAGE CHEESE PANCAKES

Yield:
about 12 pancakes

Equipment:
7-inch omelet pan
ovenproof serving
   dish

These pancakes are known as *Topfenpalatschinken* throughout Austria and are an absolutely delicious, warm, homey dessert. The pancakes are filled with a sweetened cottage cheese-sour cream-and-raisin mixture and are baked in a rich cream sauce.

FOR THE PANCAKES

1½ cups milk
1 cup water
1½ cups all-purpose flour
¼ teaspoon salt

2 large eggs
1 egg yolk
unsalted butter for frying

FOR THE FILLING

1 stick (½ cup) unsalted butter,
   softened
¾ cup sugar
¼ teaspoon salt
1 teaspoon vanilla

the grated rind of 1 lemon
3 egg yolks
1½ cups well-drained cottage cheese
¾ cup raisins
¾ cup sour cream

3 cups milk
⅔ cup sugar

2 large eggs

Preheat the oven to 250° F.

Make the pancakes:
In a bowl combine the milk with the water, the flour, and the salt, stirring until the batter is smooth. Add the eggs and the egg yolk and beat the batter until it is smooth.

In the omelet pan heat just enough butter to cover the surface, pour in enough batter to make a large thin pancake, and cook the pancake over moderate heat, turning it once, until it is lightly browned on both sides. Transfer the pancake to a rack and continue making pancakes with the remaining batter, keeping the cooked *Palatschinken* warm in the oven.

Make the filling:
In another bowl cream the butter with the sugar, salt, the vanilla, and the grated lemon rind. Stir in the eggs, one at a time, combining the mixture well, add the cottage cheese, raisins, and sour cream, and reserve the filling.

Remove the pancakes from the oven and increase the oven temperature to 350° F. Spread one half of each pancake with the reserved cheese mixture, roll up the pancakes, and lay them side by side in the dish. In a bowl beat together the milk, sugar, and the eggs and pour the mixture over the pancakes. Bake the *Topfenpalatschinken* about 25 minutes, or until they are lightly browned and the sauce is thick and creamy. Serve at once.

PALATSCHINKEN

Yield:
about 8 pancakes

Equipment:
9-inch skillet

Although they are considered a Viennese specialty, these jam-filled pancakes are extremely popular throughout Austria. They are equally loved in Hungary, where they are known as *Palacsinta*.

1 tablespoon brandy
1 cup apricot or strawberry jam
1 cup all-purpose flour
pinch of salt
2 tablespoons granulated sugar

1 cup milk
2 large eggs
melted unsalted butter for frying
vanilla sugar (page 541) for dusting

Stir the brandy into the jam. Preheat the oven to 250° F.

Into a bowl sift the flour and salt. Stir in the granulated sugar and gradually add the milk to make a smooth batter. Add the eggs and stir the batter until smooth.

Heat the skillet and pour in just enough melted butter to cover the whole surface when the pan is tilted. Pour in enough batter to cover the pan thinly but completely. Cook the *Palatschinke* over moderate heat until the underside is lightly browned and the pancake is firm, turn the pancake with a spatula or wide knife, and brown it lightly on the other side. Transfer the *Palatschinke* to a warm plate, butter the pan again, and pour in the batter for the second *Palatschinke*. While it is browning, spread the surface of the first *Palatschinke* with a thin coating of the jam. Roll the pancake up neatly, place it on an ovenproof platter, and keep it warm in the oven. Continue making pancakes in the same manner, laying the *Palatschinken* side by side or stacking them like logs. Dust the finished *Palatschinken* generously with the vanilla sugar.

BLOOD ORANGE DESSERT WAFFLES WITH BLOOD ORANGE SAUCE

Yield:
6 servings

Equipment:
waffle iron
hand-held electric
  mixer

Blood oranges are a variety of orange grown mostly in Spain and Israel. California and Arizona produce the largest crops of blood oranges grown in the United States, but because the commercial output is still quite small there, the United States must import most of its supply.

The fruit of the blood orange ranges in color from deep burgundy to pale orange with only faint coloration. Besides their exquisite color, blood oranges are extremely sweet and have a faint berry-like flavor. They are available at specialty produce markets, usually starting mid-December through mid-May.

FOR THE WAFFLES

2 cups cake flour, sifted
2½ teaspoons double-acting baking
powder
2 tablespoons granulated sugar
½ teaspoon salt
½ teaspoon cinnamon

1 stick (½ cup) unsalted butter, melted
and cooled
4 large eggs, separated
1 cup milk
1 tablespoon grated blood orange rind

FOR THE SAUCE

9 to 12 blood oranges
1½ sticks (¾ cup) unsalted butter
⅔ cup granulated sugar

4 to 6 tablespoons orange-flavored
liqueur, or to taste

sifted confectioners' sugar for garnish

Vanilla Ice Cream (page 349) as an
accompaniment if desired

Make the waffles:

Butter and preheat the waffle iron. Preheat the oven to 250° F.
Into a bowl resift the flour with the baking powder, granulated sugar, salt, and cinnamon. In another bowl whisk together the butter, egg yolks, milk, and orange rind. In a bowl with the mixer beat the egg whites until they just hold stiff peaks. Whisk the milk mixture into the flour mixture until it is just combined and fold in the egg whites. Spoon 1 to 1¼ cups of the batter onto the waffle iron and cook the waffles according to the manufacturer's instructions. Continue to make waffles with the remaining batter in the same manner. Arrange the waffles on a baking sheet as they are done and keep them warm in the oven.

Make the sauce:

Holding the oranges over a bowl, with a serrated knife cut away the peel and pith from the oranges and section them between the membranes, using enough of the oranges to yield 3 cups segments. Reserve the segments with their juice in the bowl. In a skillet melt the butter over moderate heat, add the sugar and the juice that has accumulated from the oranges, and stir until the sugar is melted. Add the orange segments, cook them until they are heated through, and stir in the orange-flavored liqueur. Simmer the sauce for 1 minute (the sauce will be thin).

Arrange 2 waffles, halved diagonally, on each of 6 plates and sprinkle them with the confectioners' sugar. Spoon some of the sauce and oranges over the waffles and serve the remaining sauce separately. Serve with the ice cream as an accompaniment is desired.

Variation:

BELGIAN WAFFLES WITH STRAWBERRIES AND WHIPPED CREAM: Prepare waffle batter as directed but omit grated blood orange rind. Cook the waffles in an Electric Belgian Waffler (available from Maid of Scandinavia, see Shopping Sources, page 555) according to the manufacturer's instructions. Serve with fresh strawberries and sweetened whipped cream flavored with vanilla. Makes 6 Belgian waffles.

CHERRY CLAFOUTI

Yield:
4 to 6 servings

Equipment:
9½-inch pie plate

Clafouti is a difficult dessert to categorize. We have chosen to include it among fruit pancakes, but it could also rightly be considered a pudding, custard, flan, or even a batter cake. *Clafouti* is traditionally made with sweet black cherries, having originated in the Limousin province of France that is known for its cherries. A thick egg batter is poured over the fruit and the dessert is then baked until puffy. Since *clafouti* will fall quickly, it should be served immediately for full effect. A fallen *clafouti*, however, is still very palatable indeed.

¼ cup plus 1 tablespoon granulated sugar	*¾ cup all-purpose flour*
2 cups pitted sweet black cherries or canned cherries, drained	*2 large eggs*
	1 egg yolk
¾ cup milk	*⅛ teaspoon salt*
¾ cup light cream	*1 teaspoon vanilla*
	confectioners' sugar for sprinkling

Preheat the oven to 375° F. and butter the pie plate well.

Sprinkle the pie plate with the 1 tablespoon granulated sugar and distribute the cherries over the sugar. In a blender blend the milk, light cream, flour, eggs, egg yolk, and salt for 2 minutes. Add the ¼ cup granulated sugar and the vanilla, blend the mixture for a few seconds, and pour it over the cherries.

Bake the *clafouti* in the middle of the oven for 45 minutes, or until puffed and golden. Dust the *clafouti* generously with the confectioners' sugar and serve at once.

Variation:

PLUM CLAFOUTI: Substitute ¾ pound small purple plums, halved and pitted, for the sweet black cherries, arranging them skin side down in the pie plate. Bake as directed and dust the *clafouti* with vanilla sugar (page 541). Fresh peaches or fresh apricots, halved and pitted, could also be substituted.

FRITTERS

Fritters are deep fried, as are doughnuts. As a consequence, we have grouped both of these desserts together in this section.

Fritters and doughnuts are admittedly different, though. Most fritters are made with batter. Doughnuts begin with yeast dough. Both are deep fried in oil that must be heated to a specific temperature. Your success with these desserts is your ability to deep fry. How best to do that?

There are electric deep-fat fryers with built-in thermostats that tell you the temperature of the oil. These fryers, in combination with a deep-fat frying thermometer, take much of the guesswork out of deep frying, are safe, and with their high sides keep the kitchen free of oil spatters. Needless to say, a deep-fat thermometer is not interchangeable with a candy thermometer.

If you elect to deep fry in a pan, use a deep one and be sure to add enough oil to it to enable the fritter or doughnut to submerge. Use a frying thermometer and when you do check the temperature of the oil, do not touch the bottom of the pan with the thermometer. When the oil is hot enough, add only a few fritters or doughnuts at a time because neither will cook through if crowded, and it will be difficult to bring the oil back to the original cooking temperature if it is cooled down that precipitously. As the fritters or doughnuts are done, transfer them to paper towels to drain. A deep-fried dessert done well is magical, crispy on the outside, tender within. The desserts that follow attest to this.

BEER BATTER FOR FRITTERS

Yield:
about 2½ cups

This recipe calls for a 3-hour "resting" period for the fritter batter. This period allows fermentation to take place, which results in a very tender and light batter, especially so because of the addition of beer as well as beaten egg whites to the mixture. (There will be no taste of beer in the finished fritter—it is used simply for its leavening effect.) The rest also allows time for the gluten in the flour to relax. The batter may even be covered and refrigerated overnight to allow the gluten to relax. If there is no time to let the batter stand, do use as few strokes as possible in mixing the batter so that you activate the gluten as little as possible. This will help prevent any rubberiness.

1 cup all-purpose flour
¼ teaspoon salt
1 cup flat beer

2 teaspoons vegetable oil
2 medium egg whites, beaten until
    they hold stiff peaks

Into a bowl sift together the flour and salt. Make a well in the center, pour in the beer, and add the oil in a stream, stirring constantly until smooth. Strain the batter into another bowl and let it stand, covered with plastic wrap, for 3 hours or refrigerated overnight. Just before using, stir the batter and fold in the beaten egg whites.

Variation:

BLENDER BEER BATTER: Sift together the flour and salt. In a blender combine the flour mixture and the beer, blend the batter for 15 seconds, gradually adding the oil in a stream and stopping the motor once to scrape down the sides of the container with a rubber spatula. Strain the batter into a bowl and let it stand, covered with plastic wrap, for 3 hours. (The batter will be very effervescent.) Just before using, stir the batter and fold in the beaten egg whites.

BLENDER FRITTER BATTER

Yield:
about 3 cups

This dessert fritter batter is richer and sweeter than the preceding beer batter and contains milk and sugar as well as the spirit of your choice.

1 cup plus 1 tablespoon sifted all-
    purpose flour
1 cup hot milk
½ cup kirsch, Cognac, or rum

1 tablespoon unsalted butter, melted
1 tablespoon sugar
2 large eggs
pinch of salt

In the blender or in a food processor combine the flour, milk, kirsch, melted butter, sugar, eggs, and salt. Blend the batter for 15 seconds, stopping the motor once to scrape down the sides of the container with a rubber spatula. Pour the batter into a bowl and let it stand, covered, for 2 hours.

BANANA FRITTERS

Yield:
about 24 fritters

Equipment:
deep fryer

These fritters are prepared with a batter to which grated orange rind is added. They are especially delicious accompanied by Orange Marmalade Sauce (page 507).

1 recipe Beer Batter (page 447) or
    Blender Fritter Batter (recipe
    above), with 1 tablespoon grated
    orange rind added
3 bananas

2 tablespoons dark rum
1 tablespoon granulated sugar
vegetable shortening for deep frying
all-purpose flour for dredging
confectioners' sugar for sprinkling

Have ready the fritter batter of choice.

Cut the bananas into 1-inch pieces. In a bowl combine the rum and the granulated sugar, stir in the bananas, and let them macerate, tossing them occasionally, for 30 minutes.

In the deep fryer heat enough shortening to measure 3 inches to 375° F. In a bowl dredge the banana pieces in the flour, shaking off the excess. Working in batches, dip the bananas in the batter, let the excess drip off, and fry them in the shortening, turning them, for 1 to 2 minutes, or until they are golden. Remove the fritters with a slotted spoon and drain on paper towels. While the fritters are still warm, sift the confectioners' sugar over them and serve at once.

STRAWBERRY FRITTERS

Yield:
8 servings

Equipment:
deep fryer

When deep frying fruit fritters, the surface of the fruit should be as dry as possible so that the batter adheres and completely encases the fruit, thus preventing any loss of juice. In this recipe further precaution is taken by coating the strawberries with marmalade and crushed macaroons before dipping them into the batter.

1 recipe Beer Batter (page 447) or
  Blender Fritter Batter (recipe
  opposite)
2 pints large strawberries, hulled

½ cup orange marmalade
6 macaroons, crushed
vegetable shortening for deep frying
1 cup sugar

Have ready the fritter batter of choice.

Coat each strawberry with a thin layer of the orange marmalade, then roll the berries in the macaroons.

In the deep fryer heat enough shortening to measure 3 inches to 370° F. Working in batches, dip the strawberries into the batter, shaking off the excess, and fry them until they are golden brown and puffed. Remove the fritters with a slotted spoon and drain on paper towels. While the fritters are still warm, roll them in the sugar and serve at once.

APPLEJACK FRITTERS

Yield:
6 to 8 servings

Equipment:
deep fryer

For these fritters apple rings are macerated in applejack, or apple brandy, a distilled spirit made from fermented apple juice or hard cider. These fritters are very fine served while still warm with Ginger Ice Cream (page 349) or Cider Sorbet (page 369).

1 recipe Beer Batter (page 447)
6 large cooking apples such as Granny
  Smiths or Greenings
1 cup granulated sugar

3 tablespoons applejack
½ teaspoon cinnamon
vegetable oil for deep frying
confectioners' sugar for sprinkling

Have ready the beer batter.

Peel and core the apples and cut them into rings ⅓ inch thick. In a shallow dish combine the granulated sugar, applejack, and cinnamon. Add the apple rings and let them macerate, turning them once, for 1 hour.

In the deep fryer heat enough oil to measure 3 inches to 375° F. Working in batches, dip each apple ring in the batter, coating it completely. Fry the rings in the hot oil, turning them several times, for 4 minutes, or until puffed and browned. Drain the fritters on paper towels and while the fritters are still warm, sift the confectioners' sugar over them. Serve at once.

FRITTERS ARLÉSIENNE

Yield:
15 fritters

Equipment:
deep fryer

1½ cups all-purpose flour plus
    additional flour for sprinkling
⅓ cup granulated sugar
pinch of salt
3 egg yolks

½ cup dark rum
vegetable oil for deep frying
sifted confectioners' sugar for
    sprinkling

Into a bowl sift together the flour, the granulated sugar, and salt. Add the egg yolks and rum and blend the mixture until it forms a dough. Turn the dough out onto a lightly floured surface and knead it for 2 to 3 minutes, or until smooth. Form the dough into small egg shapes and flatten the shapes. On a floured surface roll the dough pieces into thin ovals about 6 inches long. Slash the ovals crosswise in the center with a sharp knife.

In the deep fryer heat enough oil to measure 3 inches to 375° F. Fry the ovals, a few at a time, until they are golden and remove them with a slotted spoon to paper towels to drain. Sprinkle the fritters with the confectioners' sugar and serve at once.

BEIGNETS

Yield:
about 32 beignets

Equipment:
deep fryer

Beignet is simply the French word for fritter. In the United States we associate it with the French Quarter of New Orleans, Louisiana, where *beignets* served with chicory coffee or *café au lait* have become the traditional way to end an evening on the town. You will note that no specific frying times are given in the following recipes. When the fritters are a deep golden color, they are done.

1 cup water
1 stick (½ cup) unsalted butter
1 teaspoon granulated sugar
¼ teaspoon salt
1 cup plus 2 tablespoons sifted all-
    purpose flour
4 large eggs

1 tablespoon orange flower water
    (available at pharmacies and
    specialty foods shops), rum, or
    1 teaspoon vanilla
vegetable shortening for deep frying
confectioners' sugar for sprinkling
1 recipe Apricot Sauce (page 504) or
    Orange Marmalade Sauce (page
    507) as an accompaniment

In a small saucepan combine the water, butter, granulated sugar, and salt and bring the mixture to a rapid boil. Remove the pan from the heat and add the flour all at once, stirring vigorously. Cook the mixture over low heat, beating briskly, until the ingredients are thoroughly combined and the dough cleanly leaves the sides of the pan and forms a ball (see illustrations page 220). Remove the pan from the heat. Add the eggs, one at a time, beating well after each addition. By hand or with an electric mixer set at medium speed beat the paste until it is smooth and glossy. Stir in the orange flower water, rum, or vanilla.

In the deep fryer heat enough shortening to measure 3 inches to 370° F. Drop the dough by teaspoonfuls into the shortening and fry the *beignets* in batches, turning them, until golden brown (about 3 minutes). With a slotted spoon remove to paper towels to drain. Sprinkle the *beignets* with the confectioners' sugar and serve them hot with the fruit sauce of choice.

Photo on page 452.

KRAPFEN

Yield:
about 24 *Krapfen*

Equipment:
2-inch round cutter
1½-inch round cutter
deep fryer

The word *Krapfen* means doughnut or fritter throughout Austria and Germany. These jam-filled doughnuts are particularly popular around *Fasching*, the pre-Lenten Carnival season when they are known as *Faschingkrapfen*, or carnival doughnuts.

two ¼-ounce packages (5 teaspoons
    total) active dry yeast or two
    .6-ounce cakes fresh yeast
¼ cup warm water
2 cups milk
¼ cup granulated sugar
1 teaspoon salt

7 cups sifted all-purpose flour
¼ cup vegetable oil
2 large eggs
¼ cup strawberry jam
vegetable shortening or lard for deep
    frying
confectioners' sugar for sprinkling

Dissolve the yeast in the warm water. In a saucepan scald the milk. Add the granulated sugar and the salt and let the milk cool to warm (90° F. on a meat thermometer). Pour the milk mixture into a large bowl, add the softened yeast, 4 cups of the flour, the oil, and the eggs, and stir the mixture with a wooden spoon, combining it well. Add the remaining 3 cups flour and beat the dough until it is smooth and comes away from the sides of the bowl. Cover the dough with a soft cloth and let it rise in a warm place until it doubles in bulk, about 1½ hours.

Turn the dough onto a well-floured surface, roll it out ½ inch thick, and cut it with the 2-inch cutter into rounds. Reroll the scraps of dough and cut them into rounds in the same manner. Place 1 teaspoon of the strawberry jam on half the rounds, cover them with the remaining rounds, and pinch the edges together. With the smaller cutter cut through the two rounds, sealing the edges. Lay the rounds on the soft cloth, dusted with flour, cover them with a warm cloth, and let them rise for 30 minutes.

In the deep fryer heat enough vegetable shortening or lard to measure 3 inches to 370° F. Fry the *Krapfen* until they are golden brown, turning them once. Drain on paper towels, sprinkle with the confectioners' sugar, and serve warm.

SPICED DOUGHNUTS

Yield:
18 doughnuts and
　18 holes

Equipment:
2½- to 3-inch
　doughnut cutter
deep fryer

The doughnut is probably one of the most popular American treats. Freshly made and rolled in vanilla sugar, they are especially satisfying. Remember, a doughnut cutter has a center hole, so doughnuts yield an equal number of equally delicious holes.

3¼ cups all-purpose flour plus
　additional flour for sprinkling
1½ teaspoons baking soda
1½ teaspoons double-acting baking
　powder
1 teaspoon salt
½ teaspoon cinnamon
⅛ teaspoon freshly grated nutmeg
⅛ teaspoon ground allspice

1 cup granulated sugar
2 large eggs, beaten well
2 tablespoons unsalted butter, melted
　and cooled
1 cup milk
vegetable oil for deep frying
confectioners' sugar for sifting or
　vanilla sugar (page 541) for rolling

Into a bowl sift together the 3¼ cups flour, the baking soda, baking powder, salt, cinnamon, nutmeg, and allspice. In a large bowl combine the granulated sugar, eggs, and melted butter. Add 1 cup of the flour mixture and ⅓ cup of the milk and combine the mixture well. Add the remaining flour mixture alternately with the remaining ⅔ cup milk, ⅓ cup at a time. Combine the mixture well and chill the dough, covered with a dish towel, for 1 hour.

Turn the dough out onto a lightly floured surface and incorporate just enough additional flour to form a soft dough that pulls away from the surface. Halve the dough and refrigerate half of it, wrapped in plastic wrap. Roll out the dough ⅓ inch thick and with the doughnut cutter, floured, cut out rounds.

In the deep fryer heat enough oil to measure 3 inches to 365° F. Fry the doughnuts and the holes in batches, turning them, until they are golden brown. Remove with a slotted spoon or tongs and drain on paper towels. Dust the doughnuts and the holes with the confectioners' sugar or roll them in the vanilla sugar. Make doughnuts and doughnut holes with the remaining dough and sugar them in the same manner.

Photo opposite.

Beignets (page 450),
Spiced Doughnuts
(above), Crullers
(page 454)

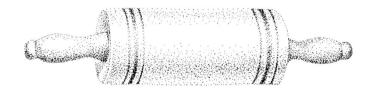

CRULLERS

Yield:
about 24 crullers

Equipment:
large pastry bag fitted
  with small star tip
deep fryer
wax paper cut into a
  round slightly
  smaller than
  the circumference
  of the deep fryer

Crullers are a type of doughnut made from a sweet dough especially rich in eggs. The name supposedly comes from the Dutch word *krullen*, meaning to curl. In our recipe the crullers are formed into strips. However, they can also be shaped into rounds.

2 cups all-purpose flour
2 teaspoons double-acting baking
*   powder*
½ teaspoon salt
¼ teaspoon freshly grated nutmeg
½ cup granulated sugar
3 tablespoons unsalted butter, softened

2 large eggs
¼ cup light cream
½ teaspoon vanilla
vegetable oil for deep frying
vanilla confectioners' sugar (page
*   541) for dusting if desired*

Into a bowl sift 1½ cups of the flour with the baking powder, salt, and nutmeg. In another bowl cream together the granulated sugar and the butter until light. Beat in the eggs, one at a time, half the flour mixture, the cream, and vanilla. Beat in the remaining flour mixture and combine the mixture. Turn the dough out onto a lightly floured surface. Sift the remaining ½ cup flour and knead in enough of it to form a soft dough that pulls away from the surface. Chill the dough in a bowl, covered, for 3 hours.

In the deep fryer heat enough oil to measure 3 inches to 370° F. Butter the wax paper round and fill the pastry bag with dough. Pipe out strips of the dough 4½ inches in length, a few at a time, onto the wax paper, invert the strips into the fryer, and fry them until golden brown. Remove the crullers with a slotted spoon and drain them on paper towels. Sift the vanilla sugar generously over them and serve.

To shape the crullers by hand: Cover the dough with plastic wrap and chill it overnight. Working with about one fourth of the dough at a time and keeping the rest covered and refrigerated, roll the dough out ¼ inch thick on a lightly floured surface. Cut the dough into 5- by 1-inch strips and twist the strips into coils, pinching each end firmly to retain the spiral shape. Fry the coils in the above manner. If desired, sift the vanilla sugar generously over them.

Photo on page 452.

BLUEBERRY BLINTZES

Yield:
15 blintzes

Equipment:
6-inch crêpe pan

A blintz is a type of crêpe associated with Jewish cooking. It is made with an egg batter, filled with either cheese or fruit, then rolled into a cylinder and sautéed in butter or baked. Because of this method of cooking, we have included this recipe here.

¾ cup all-purpose flour
½ cup milk
¼ cup water
3 large eggs
2 tablespoons unsalted butter, melted
   and cooled
¼ teaspoon salt

6 to 8 tablespoons clarified butter
   (page 536) plus additional, or oil,
   for brushing the pan
2 pints blueberries, picked over
½ cup granulated sugar
1 tablespoon fresh lemon juice
cinnamon sugar (page 541) for
   sprinkling
sour cream as an accompaniment

In a blender blend the flour, milk, water, eggs, melted unsalted butter, and salt for 5 seconds. Turn off the motor, scrape down the sides of the container with a rubber spatula, and blend the batter for 20 seconds more. Transfer the batter to a bowl and let it stand, covered with plastic wrap, for 1 hour.

Heat the crêpe pan over moderately high heat until it is hot and brush it lightly with the clarified butter or oil. Heat the butter or oil until it is hot but not smoking and remove the pan from the heat. Stir the batter, half fill a ¼-cup measure with it, and pour the batter into the pan. Quickly tilt and rotate the pan so that the batter covers the bottom in a thin layer and return any excess batter to the bowl. Return the pan to the heat, cook the crêpe until the underside is lightly browned, and loosen the edge of the crêpe with a metal spatula. Slide the crêpe onto a plate. Make crêpes with the remaining batter in the same manner, brushing the pan with clarified butter as needed and keeping the crêpes warm, covered with a dish towel.

In a saucepan combine the blueberries with the granulated sugar and lemon juice and cook the mixture, covered, over low heat for 5 minutes. Remove the lid, reduce the mixture over high heat for 10 to 15 minutes, or until it is thick, and let cool.

Put 2 tablespoons of the blueberry mixture 2 inches from one edge of the browned side of each crêpe and smooth it into a 3- by 1-inch strip. Fold in the sides of the crêpes to partially cover the filling and roll the blintzes into cylinders. In a skillet heat 6 tablespoons of the clarified butter over moderately high heat. Arrange 4 to 6 of the blintzes, seam sides down, in the pan, cook them, turning them with a spatula and adding more butter as needed, for 3 to 5 minutes on each side, or until they are browned, and transfer them to a heated platter. Cook the remaining blintzes in the same manner, adding clarified butter to the pan as needed. Sprinkle the blintzes with the cinnamon sugar and serve them with the sour cream.

FRUIT DESSERTS

*F*ruit and cheese combinations are classics and are always welcome, especially after a rather extravagant meal. However, often when a meal is meant to be festive or celebratory, something a bit more special is called for, showing a little more care and effort on the part of the cook.

Although fresh fruits are often at their best unadorned but at their peak of ripeness, there are also those fruits whose flavors actually improve or whose tartness or even astringency diminish when cooked. Fresh red currants are a perfect example, cooked and sugared in our recipe for Danish Currants with Cream (page 467). There are actually those who pass up dessert, however difficult this may be to believe. They would find it hard, though, to turn down the light, refreshing, healthful fruit desserts that we have included in this collection. (Besides, we all know that deep down everyone expects and anticipates an offer of dessert and even if one declines, at least he was given the choice!)

Fruit desserts can range from a simple poached fruit combination through elegant but very uncomplicated macerated fruits to impressive combinations of fruit, ladyfingers, flavored cream, and fruit purée sauce as in our Rhubarb Raspberry Charlotte with Rhubarb Raspberry Sauce (page 474).

Fruits that were once considered exotic are now commonplace, the result not only of our more sophisticated palates, due largely to travel, but of our insistence that these fruits be imported to our country. Included here are recipes that use litchi nuts, fresh figs, greengage plums, and mangoes, all of which are available now in the United States. Fruits are, for the most part, naturally sweet, so a minimum of sugar or other sweetener should be necessary. With our increased health and diet consciousness also, this is one more reason for the great interest in and appreciation of fruit desserts.

Baked Pears Alicia
(page 472)

457

MACERATED FRUITS

To macerate is to soak something in a liquid. Here we use the term to describe fruits that are macerated in liqueurs, wines, as well as in sugar syrups. Although as mentioned previously there are times when a simple, casual compote of cut fresh fruits fits the bill, there are other times when those same fruits deserve a little added attention. Perhaps just a splash of kirsch or *crème de cassis* and lemon juice, or a short steeping in a fragrant, warm, red wine syrup. Classic combinations get to be classics for good reasons. A classic is noted for a superior melding of flavors, each enhancing the others. Ambrosia is a perfect example—oranges macerated in a mixture of sweetened Sherry wine and layered with shredded coconut. Our version includes chunks of fresh pineapple as a luscious addition.

Chantilly is a garnish term that refers to sweetened or flavored whipped cream, also called *crème Chantilly*. Pineapple and strawberries are combined with kirsch in a classic combination and are topped with the whipped cream or *crème Chantilly* in our recipe for Pineapple and Strawberries Chantilly (page 459). Explicit instructions as well as a photo are given for constructing our wonderfully festive watermelon basket brimming with fresh summer fruits made particulary refreshing and potent with the addition of vermouth and anisette. Remember to modify this recipe when celebrating a child's summer birthday or last day of the school year! Finally we present raspberries with melon, perfect for ending a summer dinner party on an elegant note, and Confetti Oranges with Glacéed Fruits (page 464), an impressive but light dessert appropriate during the holidays.

LITCHI NUT AND PINEAPPLE COMPOTE

Yield:
4 servings

James Beard's interest in and knowledge of exotic foods even before they became fashionable is legendary. This original recipe, calling for litchi nuts, was published in 1971.

Fresh litchi nuts, cultivated in Florida, are available only during the summer months—from the end of June to the end of August. Their superior taste, however, is worth the wait. Failing finding the fresh, canned litchi nuts, drained of any syrup, can be used with excellent results.

16 litchi nuts
2 cups fresh pineapple chunks

3 tablespoons kirsch or orange-
flavored liqueur

Crack the pods and peel the litchi nuts and combine the litchis with the pineapple chunks in a large bowl. Flavor the compote with the kirsch or orange-flavored liqueur and chill the fruit, covered, for 2 hours.

THE BERRIES

Yield:
4 servings

1 cup raspberries
1 cup strawberries, hulled
1 cup blueberries, picked over
1½ cups black raspberries
4½ tablespoons sugar

2 tablespoons crème de cassis (black currant liqueur)
juice of 1 lemon
crème fraîche (page 537) as an accompaniment

In a bowl combine the raspberries, strawberries, blueberries, and the black raspberries, sprinkle the berries with the sugar, crème de cassis, and the lemon juice to taste, and toss the mixture. Let the berries macerate, covered and chilled, for 1 hour. Serve the fruit compote, chilled, with the crème fraîche.

FIGS IN PORT

Yield:
4 servings

12 fresh ripe figs, stemmed
Port to cover the figs

honey thinned with fresh lemon juice to taste, or lightly sweetened whipped cream as an accompaniment

Rinse and dry the figs and pierce each one 4 or 5 times with a pin. Put the figs in a deep bowl and add enough Port to cover them. Chill the figs, covered, for 1 to 2 hours. Divide the figs and Port among glass bowls and top them with the honey or whipped cream.

PINEAPPLE AND STRAWBERRIES CHANTILLY

Yield:
4 to 6 servings

1 large pineapple
1 pint strawberries, hulled
sugar to taste

kirsch to taste
1 cup well-chilled heavy cream, whipped and sweetened

Halve the pineapple lengthwise, leaves and all, and scoop out the fruit, leaving a shell about ¾ inch thick. Set the shells aside. Cut the pineapple into small chunks, discarding the core, and in a bowl combine it with the strawberries, halved if they are large, reserving 2 large berries for the garnish. Sprinkle the fruit with sugar, add kirsch, and toss gently. Chill the mixture thoroughly. Pile the fruit into the pineapple shells and top it with the sweetened whipped cream. Garnish each half with a reserved strawberry, quartered.

PINEAPPLE AND ORANGE AMBROSIA

Yield:
20 servings

Ambrosia was the food of the gods in Greek mythology. Today the name is given to a sweet compote containing oranges and coconut. Compotes are popular throughout the United States, but especially so in the South.

2 pineapples, peeled, quartered lengthwise, and cored
12 navel oranges, peel and pith removed, but not sectioned (for procedure page 548)

⅔ cup sugar
⅓ cup medium-dry Sherry
2 cups grated fresh coconut (for procedure page 549) or packaged shredded coconut

Cut three fourths of the pineapple into ½-inch chunks and put the chunks in a large serving bowl. Cut 9 of the oranges into ½-inch chunks and add the chunks to the bowl. Sprinkle ½ cup of the sugar, ¼ cup of the Sherry, and 1½ cups of the coconut over the fruit, toss the mixture gently, and spread it to form a relatively flat surface.

Cut the remaining pineapple crosswise into ¼-inch slices and halve the slices. Cut the remaining oranges crosswise into ¼-inch slices and quarter the slices. Arrange the pineapple and orange slices decoratively on the fruit, sprinkle the remaining sugar, Sherry, and coconut over the fruit, and chill the ambrosia, covered, for 2 to 4 hours.

Photo opposite.

ORANGES IN RED WINE SYRUP

Yield:
6 to 8 servings

6 navel oranges, peel and pith removed, but not sectioned (for procedure page 548)
½ cup sugar
½ cup water
1½ cups dry red wine

4 thin slices of lemon
a 3-inch cinnamon stick
4 whole cloves
2 tablespoons Cognac

Pineapple and Orange Ambrosia (above), Cajun Sweet Dough Pies (page 139), Praline Nuggets (page 525)

Cut the oranges crosswise into ¼-inch slices and arrange the slices decoratively in a shallow serving dish.

In a stainless steel or enameled saucepan combine the sugar and water, bring the mixture to a boil over moderate heat, stirring, and cook it, stirring, until the sugar is dissolved. Add the wine, lemon slices, cinnamon stick, and cloves, bring the syrup to a boil, and simmer it for 15 minutes. Remove the pan from the heat, stir in the Cognac, and pour the syrup over the orange slices. Chill the dessert, covered, for at least 3 hours.

WATERMELON BASKET

Yield:
20 to 30 servings

Equipment:
cardboard guide for
  cutting scalloped
  edge
melon-ball cutter
pastry brush

A watermelon basket—the perfect ending to a summer picnic luncheon or an *alfresco* supper. Serve several varieties of cookies such as Lemon Thins and Danish Butter Cookies (both recipes page 266) as accompaniments.

1 medium-sized watermelon
2 cups mixed melon balls, such as
  cantaloupe or honeydew
2 cups strawberries, hulled
2 cups raspberries
1 cup blueberries, picked over
1 cup seedless grapes

1 orange, peeled and pith removed and
  sectioned (for procedure page 548)
1 cup sugar
¾ cup water
2 cups dry vermouth
¾ cup anisette
2 bananas, sliced

Make a watermelon basket: With the tip of a sharp knife score a 2-inch-wide band across the center of the width of the watermelon, stopping about one third of the way down from the top. (This will be the handle of the basket.) Place the cardboard guide flat against the side of the melon about one third of the way down from the top and score the rind into scallops all the way around. Using the scoring marks as guides, cut through the rind of the melon along the handle and the scalloped edges. Cut away the sections and hollow out the melon in large pieces.

With the melon-ball cutter scoop out balls from the melon pieces, seeding them when possible, and put them in a large bowl. Add the mixed melon balls, strawberries, raspberries, blueberries, grapes, and orange sections.

In a saucepan combine the sugar and water over moderate heat, washing down any sugar crystals clinging to the sides of the pan with the brush dipped in cold water. Increase the heat to moderately high and boil the syrup for 5 minutes. Remove the pan from the heat, let the syrup cool, and add the vermouth and ½ cup of the anisette. Pour the syrup over the fruits and toss the mixture lightly. Transfer the fruits to the watermelon basket and chill the basket, covered with foil, overnight. Before serving, add the banana slices and sprinkle the fruits with the remaining ¼ cup anisette.

Photo opposite.

Watermelon Basket (above)

RASPBERRIES WITH MELON

Yield:
4 to 6 servings

1 Persian or Crenshaw melon
1½ pints raspberries
3 tablespoons sugar
2 or 3 tablespoons eau-de-vie de
    framboise *(raspberry brandy)*,
    heated to evaporate the alcohol

1 pint Vanilla Ice Cream *(page 349)*
    or Raspberry Sorbet *(page 369)*

Cut a slice from one end of the melon so that the pulp can be scooped out for serving; reserve the slice. Cut a thin slice from the opposite end so that the melon will stand. Remove the seeds from the melon.

Toss the berries with the sugar and *eau-de-vie de framboise*. Fill the melon with the berry mixture and replace the top slice. Pack the melon in ice for 3 hours. To serve, scoop out pieces of melon with some of the raspberries and serve over the ice cream or sherbet in footed glasses.

CONFETTI ORANGES WITH GLACÉED FRUITS

Yield:
6 servings

Equipment:
lemon zester
pastry brush

½ cup chopped glacéed mixed fruits
3 tablespoons Cognac
6 navel oranges or tangelos
1½ cups sugar

⅔ cup water
pinch of cream of tartar
1½ cups boiling water

In a bowl let the chopped glacéed fruits macerate in the Cognac overnight.

With the lemon zester remove the rinds from 2 of the navel oranges or tangelos, reserving the fruit. In a saucepan blanch the strips of rind in boiling water to cover for 5 minutes. Drain the strips in a sieve, refresh them under running cold water, and pat them dry with paper towels. Remove the pith from the reserved oranges (for procedure page 548). Peel and pith the remaining 4 oranges and chill all the oranges in a serving dish, covered, for 1 hour.

In a heavy saucepan combine the sugar, ⅔ cup water, and cream of tartar and bring the mixture to a boil over moderately low heat, stirring and washing down any sugar crystals clinging to the sides of the pan with the brush dipped in cold water. Increase the heat to high and boil the syrup,

Confetti Oranges with Glacéed Fruits (opposite)

gently swirling the pan, until the syrup turns a golden caramel color. Remove the pan from the heat and add the 1½ cups boiling water in a stream, stirring. Simmer the sauce over low heat, stirring, for 3 minutes, transfer it to a metal bowl, and let it cool.

Garnish the oranges with the glacéed fruit mixture, sprinkle them with the strips of rind, and pour the sauce over the oranges.

Photo above.

POACHED FRUITS

The verb "stew" can be used interchangeably with poach, although stewing is normally used to describe the cooking method for dried fruits. Both indicate the process of cooking slowly or at a simmer. Basic poached fruits are poached in a sugar syrup that can then be served chilled or still warm as a sauce for the fruit. Examples are our recipes for poached apricots or greengage plums, delicious served either simply on their own or accompanied by heavy cream or as an ice-cream topping. Other poaching syrups, however, can be used for different fruits, including fruit juice, wines, and even combinations of caramel and fruit purées.

Currants are poached until tender and are then puréed, flavored, and thickened, resulting in a delicious fruit pudding, a specialty throughout Scandinavia. Another foreign specialty, *pesche arrossite,* an Italian fruit dessert, combines peaches poached in a mixture of caramel, raspberry purée, and orange juice, which also serves as a warm sauce. Our recipe for brandied peaches features peaches poached in a ginger-flavored sugar syrup. Brandy is added to the syrup and detailed instructions are given for canning the peaches and brandy syrup to be used as a sweet and luscious accompaniment to cakes and ice creams. Finally, the normally mundane stewed prune is practically exalted when poached in red wine and brandy and served with cider sorbet. Our interpretation may improve the lowly reputation of stewed prunes once and for all.

POACHED APRICOTS

Yield:
12 servings

24 apricots
3 cups water
1½ cups sugar
1 small piece of vanilla bean or 1
    teaspoon vanilla

sweetened whipped cream flavored
    with Cognac or apricot liqueur as
    an accompaniment

Blanch the apricots in boiling water for 10 seconds, drain immediately, and let cool. Peel the apricots and halve and pit them.

In a large saucepan combine the water, sugar, and vanilla bean or vanilla. Bring the mixture to a boil and boil the syrup for 4 or 5 minutes. Add the apricots and poach them for 15 to 25 minutes, or until they are just tender. Let the apricots cool in the syrup. Serve chilled with the syrup and flavored whipped cream.

POACHED GREENGAGE PLUMS

Yield:
4 servings

The green-gold-skinned greengage plum is considered by many to be the finest flavored plum. Mild and sweet, its flavor is further enhanced by being poached in a full-bodied vanilla sugar syrup.

1½ cups sugar
1½ cups water
a 1-inch piece of vanilla bean

8 greengage plums, halved and pitted
heavy or light cream for topping
pinch of cinnamon if desired

In a large saucepan combine the sugar, water, and vanilla bean, bring the liquid to a boil, and simmer the syrup for 5 minutes. Add the plums and poach them very gently until they are just tender, about 10 minutes. Do not let them overcook. Serve the plums warm with the syrup and heavy cream or chilled with the syrup and light cream. Dust lightly with the cinnamon if desired.

DANISH CURRANTS WITH CREAM

Yield:
8 to 10 servings

Denmark is famous for its refreshing red fruit puddings served with rich whipped or heavy cream. Fresh red currants are called for in this recipe, which is called *rødgrød med fløde* in Danish.

In season from December through February, fresh currants may be found in specialty produce markets. Because of their numerous seeds, the currants must be rubbed through a fine sieve before being thickened.

2 pints red currants, stemmed and
    washed
1 pint red raspberries
2 cups water
¾ cup sugar

½ cup quick-cooking tapioca
pinch of salt
1 teaspoon vanilla
whipped cream as accompaniment if
    desired

In a stainless steel saucepan cook the currants and raspberries in the water for about 10 minutes. Force the mixture through a sieve into another saucepan and combine the fruit purée with the sugar, tapioca, and salt. Cook the mixture over low heat, stirring constantly, for about 10 minutes, or until thickened. Stir in the vanilla and let the mixture cool. Chill the dessert for several hours and serve it with whipped cream if desired.

POACHED PEACHES WITH RASPBERRY SAUCE

Yield:
12 servings

Equipment:
chafing dish

An Italian dessert, *pesche arrossite,* or blushing peaches, is prepared with an Italian brandy and can be accompanied by *amaretti* biscuits.

1 cup sugar
1 stick (½ cup) unsalted butter
½ recipe raspberry purée (page 546)
juice of 2 oranges
grated rind of 1 orange

12 peaches, peeled (for procedure page 548)
½ cup Italian brandy (such as grappa), warmed

In the blazer of the chafing dish heat together the sugar and 2 tablespoons of the butter and cook the mixture over low heat until it caramelizes. Blend the remaining 6 tablespoons butter into the caramel and stir in the raspberry purée, the orange juice, and grated rind. Bring the sauce to a simmer, add the peaches, and poach them in the sauce until they acquire a blush and are heated through.

Ignite the warmed brandy and pour it over the peaches. Baste the peaches with the sauce until the flames expire. Serve the peaches with the sauce poured over them.

ORANGE SPICED RHUBARB

Yield:
4 servings

1 cup fresh orange juice
1 cup sugar
½ cup water
2 tablespoons grated orange rind
½ teaspoon cinnamon
¼ teaspoon ground cloves
¼ teaspoon ground ginger

1 pound rhubarb, trimmed and cut into 1-inch pieces (about 4 cups)
3 tablespoons cornstarch
¼ cup Tawny Port
blanched julienne strips of orange rind for garnish
sour cream and brown sugar as accompaniments if desired

In a stainless steel saucepan combine the orange juice with the sugar, water, grated orange rind, cinnamon, cloves, and ginger and bring the mixture to a boil over moderate heat, stirring. Add the rhubarb and simmer, stirring occasionally, until the rhubarb is tender but retains its shape. Increase the heat to moderately high and bring the syrup to a boil.

In a small cup dissolve the cornstarch in the Port and add the mixture to the pan, stirring. Cook over moderate heat, stirring, for 1 minute. Transfer the rhubarb mixture to a bowl and let cool. Garnish with the julienne orange rind and serve with the sour cream and brown sugar if desired.

Photo on page 57.

BRANDIED PEACHES

Yield:
3 quarts

Equipment:
3 sterilized 1-quart
  Mason-type jars (for
  procedure page
  551)
candy thermometer
waterbath canner or
  deep kettle with
  rack
canning tongs

4 cups sugar
4 cups water
a 2-inch piece of gingerroot, peeled
  and cut into 15 paper-thin slices

2 pounds firm-ripe peaches, peeled
  (for procedure page 548)
1½ cups brandy

In a saucepan bring the sugar and water to a boil with the gingerroot, stirring until the sugar is dissolved. Add the peaches and simmer them in batches in the syrup for 5 minutes, or until tender when pierced with a skewer. Remove the peaches as they are cooked and divide them equally among the prepared jars. Set the jars, uncovered, aside.

Boil the syrup, undisturbed, until the candy thermometer registers 220° F. and let it cool for 5 minutes. In a bowl combine 4 cups of the syrup with the brandy and pour the mixture over the peaches, filling the jars to within ½ inch of the tops. (If more liquid is needed, add equal amounts of the syrup and brandy.) Wipe the rims of the jars with a dampened cloth and seal the jars with the lids.

Put the jars in the waterbath canner or on a rack in a deep kettle and add enough hot water to the canner to cover the jars by 2 inches. Bring the water to a boil and process the jars, covered, for 15 minutes. Transfer the jars with the tongs to a folded dish towel and let them cool. Let the peaches stand in a cool, dark place for 4 weeks. Serve as is or as an accompaniment to Vanilla Ice Cream (page 349) or Sand Torte (page 72).

PRUNES IN WINE AND ARMAGNAC

Yield:
8 to 10 servings

Equipment:
1½-quart ceramic or
  glass container with
  cover

Armagnac is a type of brandy produced in specific areas of Gascony, France. While Armagnac is considered drier and more pungent than Cognac, the difference between the two brandies is simply a matter of taste, and Cognac can easily be substituted.

2 cups dry red wine
¾ cup sugar
two 12-ounce boxes pitted prunes
1 cup Armagnac

Vanilla Ice Cream (page 349)
  or Cider Sorbet (page 369)
  as an accompaniment

In a stainless steel saucepan combine the wine and the sugar, bring the mixture to a boil, stirring until the sugar is dissolved, and boil it for 1 minute. Add the prunes and the Armagnac and simmer the mixture, covered, for 15 minutes. Let the mixture cool, covered, for 15 minutes and spoon it into the container. Let the mixture cool completely, covered. The prunes will keep, covered and chilled, for up to 4 weeks. Serve the prunes with the ice cream or sorbet.

Variation: **PRUNES IN RED WINE AND MADEIRA:** In a heavy casserole let two 12-ounce boxes pitted prunes steep in 2 cups Madeira for 12 hours. Add 2 cups dry red wine, 1 cup sugar, and the peel of 1 lemon and'cook the mixture over moderate heat for about 20 minutes, or until the prunes are tender. Let the prunes cool in the liquid. Pour the prunes and the liquid into a serving bowl and chill them, covered. Serve the dessert with whipped cream.

OLD-FASHIONED FRUIT DESSERTS

Baked fruit combinations comprise an especially appealing and satisfying group. Included are spicy baked apples with mincemeat or dried fruit and nut fillings and baked pears served with a Port wine sauce. A charlotte can refer to either a simple baked dessert prepared in a bread-lined charlotte mold and filled with a fruit purée or to a more elegant interpretation of a ladyfinger-lined mold with a fruit-flavored Bavarian cream filling. We have chosen the latter but have made the filling even lighter by omitting the egg yolks in our recipe for Rhubarb Raspberry Charlotte with Rhubarb Raspberry Sauce (page 474).

Baked fruit desserts are truly representative of early American cooking that has survived over hundreds of years. These simple and homey desserts are still being prepared at home with the same types of ingredient favored by the original settlers who created them.

The differences among these hearty baked fruit and pastry desserts are often determined by the thicknesses of the crust which vary or which may even be cut into the fruit after baking or, in some instances, may even be replaced by a combination of crumbs or streusel as a topping instead of a top crust.

The following types of dessert are represented: crumbles, baked fruit with a crumb or streusel topping; crisps, fruit fillings generously covered with a crisp and crunchy topping; and bettys, layered desserts of fruits and buttered and spiced crumbs. Also included is a slump, a stewed fruit with a dumpling-like batter topping. When the dumpling batter is placed beneath and on top of the fruit layer and baked, the top becomes crisp while the bottom layer remains moist; pandowdy, fruit covered with a crust which, after baking, is cut back into the fruit filling; and cobblers, fruit fillings with a thick crust either whole or dropped by round sections forming a cobbled surface.

These desserts are usually served warm with accompanying heavy cream, ice cream, or delectable cream sauces.

APPLEJACK BAKED APPLES

Yield:
6 servings

Equipment:
10-inch shallow
  baking dish

*6 Rome Beauties or other baking
  apples, rinsed
½ cup firmly packed brown sugar
½ teaspoon cinnamon
6 teaspoons unsalted butter, softened*

*⅓ cup water
⅓ cup applejack
¾ cup Madeira mincemeat (page 548)
  for filling
heavy cream as an accompaniment*

Preheat the oven to 400° F.

Core the apples and peel a strip one third of the way down from the top around each apple. Arrange the apples in the baking dish. Combine the brown sugar with the cinnamon and fill the cavities of the apples with the mixture. Seal each cavity with 1 teaspoon of the butter. Pour the water and the applejack into the dish and bake the apples in the middle of the oven, basting them every 5 minutes, for 30 minutes. Fill the cavities with the mincemeat and bake the apples, basting them every 5 minutes, for 10 to 15 minutes more, or until tender. Serve the apples warm with the heavy cream.

Variation:

BAKED APPLES WITH DRIED FRUIT AND NUTS: Prepare and bake the apples as above, using Calvados for the applejack, and replace the mincemeat filling with the following: Let ⅓ cup raisins and ⅓ cup chopped dried apricots macerate in 3 tablespoons Calvados for at least 1 hour. In a small saucepan combine ¾ cup strained apricot jam, 1 tablespoon fresh lemon juice, 3 tablespoons Calvados, or to taste, and 1½ tablespoons grated lemon rind and heat the glaze over low heat, stirring, until hot. Brush the apples generously with the glaze and divide the fruit filling among the cavities. Continue baking the apples, basting them every 5 minutes, for 10 to 15 minutes more, or until tender. Sprinkle the tops with ¾ cup finely chopped walnuts. Serve the apples warm with the heavy cream.

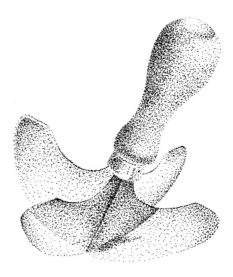

CARAMEL PEACHES

Yield:
6 servings

Equipment:
10-inch gratin dish

*6 large ripe peaches, peeled (for
    procedure page 548), halved and
    pitted*
½ cup light corn syrup
*½ cup firmly packed light brown
    sugar*

1 teaspoon vanilla
½ cup heavy cream
½ cup lightly toasted sliced almonds
*1 cup lightly whipped cream flavored
    with rum or brandy to taste as an
    accompaniment*

Preheat the oven to 375° F. and butter the gratin dish.

In a saucepan combine the corn syrup, brown sugar, and vanilla and cook the mixture over low heat for 2 to 3 minutes, or until the sugar has melted and the syrup has thinned.

Arrange the peaches cut side down in one layer in the dish. Pour the syrup over them and bake, covered with foil, for 15 minutes. Remove the foil, baste the peaches with the syrup, and bake, basting them twice, for 10 to 15 minutes longer, or until tender. Remove the dish from the oven and preheat the broiler.

Put the gratin dish over moderately high heat and cook for 5 minutes, or until the syrup is quite thick. Add the heavy cream, a little at a time, stirring and basting the peaches with the caramel until it thickens again.

Put the dish under the broiler for 5 minutes, or until the tops of the peaches are browned. Sprinkle the peaches with the toasted almonds, spoon the caramel over the nuts, and serve the peaches with the rum- or brandy-flavored whipped cream.

BAKED PEARS ALICIA

Yield:
24 servings

Equipment:
flameproof baking
    dish, 14 by 10 by 2
    inches

Who Alicia is we don't know, but this dessert lives on in her memory. This preparation should not be confused with the classic fruit dessert Poires Alma, which also calls for poaching the pears in Port wine.

24 Bosc pears
juice of 1 lemon
3 cups water
1¼ cups sugar
2 cups white Port
1 cup orange-flavored liqueur

*3 wide strips of freshly peeled orange
    rind*
½ cup brandy, or to taste
*sweetened whipped cream flavored
    with brandy or orange-flavored
    liqueur as an accompaniment*

Carefully peel the pears, leaving the stems intact and dropping the pears as they are peeled into a bowl of cold water acidulated with the lemon juice.

Preheat the oven to 375° F.

In a saucepan bring the water and the sugar to a boil over moderate heat and simmer the syrup for 5 minutes. Arrange the pears on their sides in one layer in the baking dish and pour over them the Port, liqueur, and the syrup. Add the orange rind to the mixture. Bring the liquid to a simmer on top of the stove, cover the dish with aluminum foil, and bake the pears in the middle of the oven for 30 minutes. Remove the foil and turn the pears onto their other sides, lifting them carefully by the stems. Replace the foil and bake the pears for 20 to 30 minutes more, or until tender. Carefully transfer the pears by the stems to a deep dish, add the brandy, and ladle the cooking juices over them. Let the pears cool and chill them, covered, overnight. Serve them with their syrup and the whipped cream.

Photo on page 456.

APPLESAUCE

Yield:
about 1½ cups

A unique recipe, this applesauce is sweetened with an apricot-flavored sugar syrup. If a greater yield is desired, the recipe can be doubled or tripled successfully.

⅓ cup water
¼ cup sugar
2 tablespoons apricot jam
1 tablespoon fresh lemon juice

3 apples, peeled, cored, halved, and
*   thickly sliced*
heavy cream as an accompaniment if
*   desired*

In a heavy saucepan combine the water, sugar, apricot jam, and lemon juice and cook the mixture over moderate heat, stirring until the sugar is dissolved. Bring the syrup to a boil and simmer it, undisturbed, for 5 minutes. Add the apples and simmer the mixture for 10 to 15 minutes, or until the apples are softened. Transfer the apples with a slotted spoon to a bowl and purée by beating them with a spoon. Reduce the syrup over high heat until it thickens and blend it into the apples. Chill the applesauce and, if desired, serve it with the cream.

Variation:

GINGER APPLESAUCE: Eliminate the apricot jam from the sugar syrup. To the finished applesauce add ¼ teaspoon each of ground ginger and crystallized ginger, chopped fine, if desired.

RHUBARB RASPBERRY CHARLOTTE WITH RHUBARB RASPBERRY SAUCE

Yield:
6 to 8 servings

Equipment:
9-cup charlotte mold,
   measuring 6 inches
   across the bottom
   and 4 inches deep
food processor fitted
   with steel blade
hand-held electric
   mixer
pastry bag fitted with
   star tip

*confectioners' sugar for sprinkling the
   mold and dusting the charlotte*
*1½ recipes Ladyfingers (page 286),
   each piped 4½ inches long*
6 cups sliced rhubarb (about 2 pounds)
¾ cup granulated sugar
2 tablespoons fresh lemon juice
1¾ cups water plus ½ cup cold water
*2 envelopes plus 1½ teaspoons
   unflavored gelatin*
*1 pint raspberries plus about ⅓ cup for
   decoration*
1¼ cups well-chilled heavy cream

Oil lightly the charlotte mold, line the bottom and sides of it with wide strips of plastic wrap, and sprinkle the plastic wrap with some of the confectioners' sugar, sifted. Trim enough ladyfingers to fit snugly and cover the bottom of the mold, lay them sugared side down in the mold, and stand the remaining ladyfingers sugared side outward around the sides of the mold, trimming them if necessary to fit snugly.

In a large saucepan combine the rhubarb, granulated sugar, lemon juice, and 1½ cups of the water, bring the mixture to a boil, covered, and simmer it, covered, stirring occasionally, for 30 minutes, or until the rhubarb is very soft. While the rhubarb is cooking, in a small saucepan sprinkle the gelatin over the ½ cup cold water and let it soften for 10 minutes. Heat the gelatin mixture over low heat, stirring occasionally, until the gelatin is dissolved.

In the food processor purée the pint of raspberries and strain the purée through a fine sieve set over a bowl, pressing hard on the solids. Add the purée to the rhubarb mixture and combine the mixture well. Reserve 2 cups of the rhubarb raspberry mixture, covered and chilled, purée the remaining mixture, and in a bowl combine it with the gelatin. Set the bowl in a larger bowl of ice and cold water and stir until cold and very thick.

In a chilled bowl with the mixer beat 1 cup of the cream until it just holds stiff peaks and fold it into the rhubarb gelatin mixture. Spoon the mixture into the charlotte mold and chill the charlotte, covered, for 4 hours, or until set.

Invert the charlotte onto a plate and remove the mold carefully. In another chilled bowl with the mixer beat the remaining ¼ cup cream until it just holds stiff peaks, transfer it to the pastry bag, and pipe rosettes around the base of the charlotte. (For detailed illustrations on working with a pastry bag and piping rosettes, see page 20.) Decorate the charlotte with the remaining ⅓ cup raspberries and dust it with the remaining confectioners' sugar, sifted. Thin the reserved rhubarb raspberry mixture with the remaining ¼ cup water and serve the sauce with the charlotte.

Photo opposite.

The charlotte, ungarnished, may be made 1 day in advance and kept covered and chilled.

Rhubarb Raspberry Charlotte with Rhubarb Raspberry Sauce (above)

BLUEBERRY CRUMBLE

Yield:
6 servings

Equipment:
baking dish, 11 by 8 inches

A crumble is a baked fruit dessert with a crumb topping made of flour, butter, sugar, and nuts or spices, which is sometimes also called a streusel. Any fruit could be substituted in this recipe.

1½ pints blueberries, rinsed and
   picked over
¾ cup sugar
juice of 1 lemon
¼ teaspoon cinnamon
¾ cup all-purpose flour

¾ stick (6 tablespoons) unsalted
   butter, cut into bits
½ teaspoon salt
heavy cream or Vanilla Ice Cream
   (page 349) as an accompaniment

Butter the baking dish and preheat the oven to 350° F.

Put the blueberries in the baking dish and sprinkle them with 6 tablespoons of the sugar, the lemon juice, and the cinnamon. In a bowl combine the flour, butter, remaining 6 tablespoons sugar, and salt and work the mixture to a crumbly consistency. Sprinkle the mixture over the blueberries and bake in the middle of the oven for about 40 minutes. Serve with the cream or ice cream.

GINGERED PECAN PEACH CRUMBLE

Yield:
6 to 8 servings

Equipment:
baking dish, 11 by 8 inches

The additions of crystallized ginger and chopped pecans transform this crumble recipe from a traditionally simple and homey dessert to a special and sophisticated one.

3 pounds peaches, peeled (for
   procedure page 548), pitted and
   sliced
¼ cup firmly packed light brown
   sugar
¼ cup minced crystallized ginger
   (available at specialty foods shops)

2 tablespoons unsalted butter, cut into
   bits
2 tablespoons fresh lemon juice
1 tablespoon all-purpose flour
¼ teaspoon freshly grated nutmeg

FOR THE TOPPING
¾ cup all-purpose flour
¾ cup sugar
¾ cup chopped pecans

¾ stick (6 tablespoons) cold unsalted
   butter, cut into bits
pinch of salt

Butter the baking dish and preheat the oven to 375° F.

In a large bowl toss the peaches with the brown sugar, ginger, butter, lemon juice, flour, and nutmeg and spread the mixture in the baking dish.

Make the topping:
In a bowl combine the flour, sugar, pecans, butter, and salt and blend until the mixture resembles coarse meal.

Sprinkle the topping over the peach mixture, spreading it evenly, and bake the crumble in the middle of the oven for 50 minutes to 1 hour, or until it is bubbling and the top is golden.

RHUBARB CRISP

Yield:
6 servings

Equipment:
glass baking dish, 8 by 8 by 2 inches

1 pound rhubarb, trimmed and cut into ¾-inch pieces (about 4 cups)
1 cup granulated sugar
1¼ cups all-purpose flour
½ teaspoon cinnamon
1 cup firmly packed dark brown sugar

½ cup old-fashioned rolled oats
1 stick (½ cup) unsalted butter, melted and cooled
Vanilla Ice Cream (page 349) or crème fraîche (page 537) as an accompaniment

Preheat the oven to 375° F. and butter the baking dish.

In a large bowl combine the rhubarb with the granulated sugar, ¼ cup of the flour, and the cinnamon and transfer the mixture to the baking dish.

In a bowl thoroughly combine the remaining 1 cup flour, the brown sugar, rolled oats, and melted butter. Sprinkle the streusel over the rhubarb mixture and bake in the middle of the oven for 35 minutes. Let the dessert cool and serve it with the ice cream or *crème fraîche*.

APPLE CURRANT CRISP

Yield:
6 servings

Equipment:
9-inch square baking dish

1 cup boiling water
1 cup dried currants

FOR THE STREUSEL
1 cup chopped pecans
¾ cup all-purpose flour
⅓ cup granulated sugar
⅓ cup firmly packed light brown sugar

5 Golden Delicious apples, peeled, cored, and chopped coarse

1 stick (½ cup) cold unsalted butter, cut into bits
½ teaspoon cinnamon

lightly sweetened whipped cream as an accompaniment

In a small heatproof bowl pour the boiling water over the currants and let the currants plump for 10 minutes.

Butter the baking dish and preheat the oven to 375° F.

Put the apples in the baking dish, drain the currants, and toss them with the apples.

Make the streusel: In a bowl combine the pecans, flour, granulated sugar, brown sugar, butter, and cinnamon and blend until the mixture resembles meal.

Sprinkle the streusel over the apple mixture and bake the crisp in the middle of the oven for 40 minutes, or until the topping is browned and the apples are tender. Serve the crisp with the whipped cream.

APPLE AND PEAR MAPLE BROWN BETTY

Yield:
6 to 8 servings

Equipment:
2-quart ceramic or
glass baking dish

A betty is simply a dessert of layered fruit and buttered bread crumbs that is baked and served warm. Our version also contains maple syrup.

3 apples, such as McIntosh, peeled, halved, cored, and cut into ¼-inch slices
3 pears, such as Bartlett or Bosc, peeled, halved, cored, and cut into ¼-inch slices
juice of ½ lemon
¾ cup firmly packed light brown sugar
1 teaspoon cinnnamon
¼ teaspoon freshly grated nutmeg
¼ teaspoon ground cloves
¼ teaspoon ground ginger
1 teaspoon grated lemon rind
1½ cups fine fresh bread crumbs (for procedure page 550), toasted lightly
¾ stick (6 tablespoons) unsalted butter, cut into bits
5 tablespoons fresh orange juice
½ cup maple syrup
light cream as an accompaniment

Butter the baking dish and preheat the oven to 375° F.

Drop the apple and pear slices into a bowl of cold water acidulated with the lemon juice. In a small bowl combine the brown sugar, cinnamon, nutmeg, cloves, ginger, and lemon rind. In the baking dish arrange a layer of bread crumbs and sprinkle it with 1 tablespoon butter. Add a layer of sliced fruit, drained, and sprinkle it with some of the sugar mixture, 1 tablespoon orange juice, and some of the maple syrup. Repeat alternating layers about 5 times, ending with a layer of bread crumbs and butter.

Bake the dessert in the middle of the oven for about 50 minutes, or until the pears and apples are tender and the mixture is bubbling. Serve the dessert with the cream.

PLUM SLUMP

Yield:
6 to 8 servings

Equipment:
deep 9-inch round
baking dish

Italian plums are also called "prune" plums. They are small and firm and blue-black in color. Because Italian plums do not yield as much juice as other plum varieties, they are especially appropriate for many baked fruit desserts.

4 cups pitted and quartered Italian plums
½ cup firmly packed light brown sugar
1 tablespoon fresh lemon juice
1½ cups all-purpose flour
5 tablespoons granulated sugar
2½ teaspoons double-acting baking powder
½ teaspoon salt
½ stick plus 1 tablespoon (5 tablespoons) unsalted butter, cut into bits
½ cup milk
½ cup light cream

In a saucepan combine the plums with the brown sugar and lemon juice and simmer the mixture, stirring, for 3 minutes.

Butter the baking dish and preheat the oven to 425° F.

Into a bowl sift together the flour, 3 tablespoons of the granulated sugar, the baking powder, and the salt. Add the butter and blend the mixture until it is well combined. Combine the milk and light cream and add enough of it, stirring, to the flour mixture to make a batter that forms soft mounds when it is dropped from a spoon. Drop half of the batter by tablespoons into the baking dish. Pour the plum mixture over the batter and spoon the remaining batter over it. Sprinkle the slump with the remaining 2 tablespoons granulated sugar and bake it in the middle of the oven for 25 minutes, or until the top is golden. Serve warm.

APPLE PANDOWDY WITH MAPLE CREAM SAUCE

Yield:
6 to 8 servings

Equipment:
8-inch round
  baking dish

The origin of the name "pandowdy" is obscure. We know that the English verb "dowl" means to mix dough in a hurry and the word possibly stems from that verb, describing the dessert's easy preparation. Or perhaps the name "pandowdy" simply describes the dessert's "dowdy" although delicious appearance. This recipe calls for salt fatback, which is fatback that is cured with salt and not smoked. The small amount provides additional richness as well as flavor.

*1¼ cups plus 1 tablespoon all-purpose
  flour*
¼ teaspoon salt
3 tablespoons cold lard, cut into bits
*3 tablespoons unsalted butter, cut into
  bits*
3 tablespoons ice water

1 ounce salt fatback
*5 large tart apples, such as Granny
  Smiths or Greenings*
⅓ cup maple syrup
*1 recipe Maple Cream Sauce (page
  492)*

In a large bowl combine the 1¼ cups flour with the salt, lard, and butter and blend the mixture until it is well combined. Add the ice water, toss the mixture until the water is incorporated, and form the dough into a ball. Chill the dough, wrapped in plastic wrap, for 1 hour.

Cut the salt fatback into ¼-inch cubes and blanch the cubes in boiling water for 2 minutes. Drain well.

Peel the apples and cut them into ½-inch slices to measure 6 cups. In the baking dish toss them with the maple syrup and the remaining tablespoon flour. Stir in the fatback.

Preheat the oven to 450° F.

Roll the dough into a 10-inch circle on a lightly floured surface, fit it over the apple mixture, crimping the edges decoratively, and make several slits in the dough. Bake the pandowdy in the middle of the oven for 15 minutes, reduce the heat to 300° F., and bake for 3 hours more. Cut the crust into 1–inch squares with a sharp knife and mix it into the apples. Bake the pandowdy at 400° F. for 10 minutes more and serve it hot with the maple cream sauce.

SOUR CHERRY COBBLER

Yield:
6 to 8 servings

Equipment:
shallow 3-quart
baking dish

two 1-pound cans pitted sour cherries, drained, reserving ¼ cup of the juice
1 cup sugar
1½ tablespoons cornstarch
1 tablespoon fresh lemon juice

½ teaspoon cinnamon
½ teaspoon grated lemon rind
pinch of ground cloves
freshly grated nutmeg to taste
3 tablespoons unsalted butter, cut into bits

FOR THE BISCUIT DOUGH
2 cups unbleached all-purpose flour
1 tablespoon sugar
2½ teaspoons double-acting baking powder
1 teaspoon salt
½ stick (¼ cup) cold unsalted butter, cut into bits

2 tablespoons cold vegetable shortening
1 cup plus about 2 tablespoons heavy cream

1 recipe Brown Sugar Sour Cream Sauce (page 492) as an accompaniment if desired

Butter the baking dish and preheat the oven to 425° F.

In a large bowl toss together gently the cherries, the reserved cherry juice, sugar, cornstarch, lemon juice, cinnamon, lemon rind, cloves, and nutmeg and let the mixture stand for 15 minutes. Arrange the mixture in the baking dish and dot it with the butter.

Make the biscuit dough:

Into a bowl sift together the flour, sugar, baking powder, and salt. Add the butter and the shortening and blend the mixture until it resembles coarse meal. Stir in 1 cup of the cream and form the dough into a ball. On a floured surface press the dough gently or roll it into a round just large enough to cover the cherry mixture. Arrange it over the cherry mixture, crimping the edge decoratively. Brush the dough with the remaining cream, cut steam vents in the center with the point of a knife, and bake the cobbler in the middle of the oven for 30 minutes, or until the pastry is pale golden and the filling is bubbling. Serve the cobbler warm with the brown sugar sour cream sauce if desired.

CRANBERRY COBBLER WITH ORANGE SAUCE

Yield:
6 to 8 servings

Equipment:
9-inch square
baking pan

This cobbler makes interesting use of cornmeal in its crust and is accompanied by a delicious orange sauce. Both the cornmeal and orange sauce serve as perfect complements to the cranberry flavor.

4 cups cranberries, picked over and
    rinsed
1 cup plus 1 tablespoon granulated
    sugar
1 cup strained fresh orange juice
½ cup firmly packed light brown
    sugar
2 tablespoons cornstarch
3 tablespoons unsalted butter
¾ cup all-purpose flour

1 teaspoon double-acting baking
    powder
½ teaspoon baking soda
½ teaspoon salt
⅔ cup stone-ground yellow cornmeal
1 cup buttermilk
1 large egg
1 recipe Orange Sauce (page 507) as
    an accompaniment

Butter the baking pan and preheat the oven to 425° F.

In a heavy saucepan combine the cranberries, the 1 cup sugar, the orange juice, brown sugar, and cornstarch and simmer the mixture, stirring, for 10 minutes. Add 1 tablespoon of the butter, cut into bits, and transfer the mixture to the baking pan.

Into a bowl sift together the flour, the remaining tablespoon sugar, the baking powder, baking soda, and the salt and add the cornmeal. Melt the remaining 2 tablespoons butter. In another bowl beat the buttermilk with the egg and the melted butter and stir the mixture into the flour mixture. Drop the batter by heaping tablespoons on the cranberry mixture and bake the cobbler in the middle of the oven for 25 to 30 minutes, or until the top is browned. Serve the cobbler warm or at room temperature with the orange sauce.

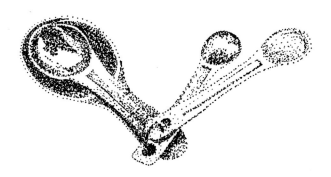

SNOWS, FOOLS, AND WHIPS

What's in a name? That which we call a snow, fool, or whip by any other name would taste as sweet. The three names refer to basically the same fruit dessert. Sweet purées of fruits, either cooked or uncooked, are combined with whipped heavy cream or with whipped cream and stiffly beaten egg whites to form light, creamy, lovely looking desserts, which can be beautifully presented in glass goblets.

Prune whip, unfortunately, is too often identified with nursery cooking—a lumpy "good for you" dessert—two strikes against it without even having been tasted! Our prune whip, however, is different. While still wonderfully good for you, the prunes are simmered gently with lemons, orange rind, and cinnamon, then puréed, free from lumps, in a food processor or blender, and combined with beaten cream and egg white for a particularly gossamer rendition. Likewise mango fool and apple snow are especially appealing.

APPLE SNOW

Yield:
8 servings

Equipment:
**food mill fitted with
  coarse disk**
**hand-held electric
  mixer**

*2 pounds tart apples, such as Granny
    Smiths, peeled, cored, and
    quartered*
1½ cups sugar plus sugar to taste
a 3½-inch cinnamon stick
two 2- by 1-inch strips of lemon rind
4 egg whites at room temperature

pinch of cream of tartar
pinch of salt
*½ cup chilled heavy cream, whipped
    until it holds stiff peaks*
chocolate shavings for garnish

In a heavy stainless steel saucepan combine the apples, 1 cup of the sugar, the cinnamon stick, and the strips of lemon rind. Cook the mixture, covered, over low heat, stirring occasionally, for 25 to 30 minutes, or until the apples are soft. Mash the apples with a fork and cook them over high heat, stirring, for 10 minutes, or until the liquid is evaporated. Discard the cinnamon stick and the lemon rind and purée the mixture through the coarse disk of the food mill (or in a food processor fitted with steel blade) into a bowl. While the purée is still hot add sugar to taste. Chill the apple purée, covered.

In a bowl with the mixer beat the egg whites with the cream of tartar and salt until they hold soft peaks. Add the remaining ½ cup sugar, a little at a time, beating, and beat the meringue until it holds stiff peaks (see illustrations page 238). Fold the meringue into the apple purée gently but thoroughly and fold in the whipped cream. Transfer the mixture to a serving dish and garnish it with the chocolate shavings.

MANGO FOOL BARBADOS

Yield:
6 to 8 servings

Equipment:
food processor fitted
  with steel blade

A ripe mango will yield to gentle pressure. A small amount of green is acceptable and does not indicate unripeness. Very green and hard mangoes, however, have been picked prematurely and will not ripen. If the mango is only slightly green, fresh smelling, and firm but not hard, the fruit may be softened by keeping it in a brown paper bag at room temperature for several days.

*3 very ripe mangoes, peeled and
    chopped coarse*
½ cup sugar

1 tablespoon fresh lime juice
*3 cups stiffly whipped cream flavored
    with 1½ ounces light rum if desired*

In the food processor purée the mangoes and force the purée through a fine sieve. Measure 3 cups purée and combine it with the sugar and lime juice. Chill the mixture thoroughly. Fold in the whipped cream, flavored with the rum if desired, and blend the mixture lightly so that it has discernible streaks of cream and mango. Serve in glass goblets.

PRUNE WHIP

Yield:
6 servings

Equipment:
food processor fitted
  with steel blade
hand-held electric
  mixer

1¼ cups pitted prunes
a ½-inch lemon slice, seeded
a 2-inch strip of orange rind
a 1-inch cinnamon stick
2 tablespoons sugar

1 cup well-chilled heavy cream
1 egg white at room temperature
pinch of cream of tartar
pinch of salt

In a stainless steel or enameled saucepan soak the prunes in hot water to cover for 2 hours. Add the lemon slice, orange peel, and cinnamon stick, bring the water to a boil over moderate heat, stirring occasionally, and simmer the mixture, stirring occasionally, for 25 minutes. Stir in the sugar and cook the mixture, stirring occasionally, for 20 minutes. Discard the lemon slice, orange rind, and cinnamon stick and purée the mixture in the food processor or in a blender. Transfer the purée to a large bowl and let it cool.

In a chilled large bowl beat the cream with the mixer until it holds soft peaks and fold it into the purée. In a small bowl with the mixer beat the egg white with the cream of tartar and salt until it holds stiff peaks and fold it into the prune mixture. Spoon the prune whip into dessert glasses and chill it, covered, for at least 1 hour.

COUPES AND CLASSIC FRUIT DESSERTS

A *coupe* is simply an ice cream and fruit dessert—the ice cream is served in a *coupe*, or decorative dish or glass and garnished with a fruit topping. Our peach *coupe*, a slight variation on *pêche Melba*, takes this fabulous dessert even one step farther and adds both sweetened whipped cream and chopped pistachios. Another recipe features poached apricots layered with crumbled almond macaroons and pineapple ice. Although prepared here in a large serving dish, individual *coupes* could certainly be used instead if desired.

A classic is noted for a superior but subtle melding of flavors, textures, and even colors, each complementing, even enhancing the others. At one point each of these classic fruit desserts was an inspired creation; today they have become standards of excellence, proven with time. We conclude with three classics—all proven through the years and still popular today. A brunch ending with Bananas Foster (page 486) is still part of the traditional New Orleans dining experience and Cherries Jubilee (page 486) will still elicit "oohs" and "aahs" from the most sophisticated or jaded gourmet. Figs with Mascarpone (page 487) is simply a perfect example of a classic pairing of luscious foods, both in taste and texture.

Peach Coupes
(opposite)

PEACH COUPES

Yield:
4 servings

Equipment:
pastry brush
pastry bag fitted with
star tip

Coupe is the French word for dish or glass and specifically refers to an ice-cream dessert served in such a glass.

4 cups water
1½ cups sugar
rind of 2 lemons, cut into long strips
1 vanilla bean, split lengthwise
4 firm-ripe peaches
1 cup strawberry purée (page 546)

4 scoops Vanilla Ice Cream
  (page 349) or Nectarine Ice Cream
  (page 350)
sweetened whipped cream for garnish
chopped unsalted pistachios for garnish

In a saucepan combine the water, sugar, lemon rind strips, and vanilla bean. Bring the water to a boil over moderately high heat, stirring and washing down any sugar crystals clinging to the sides of the pan with the brush dipped in cold water until the sugar is dissolved. Simmer the syrup for 5 minutes. Drop the peaches into the syrup and poach them at a bare simmer for 8 minutes. Let the peaches cool in the syrup, slip off the skins, and slice the peaches.

Spoon ¼ cup of raspberry purée into each of 4 chilled coupes or stemmed glasses. Top the purée in each glass with a scoop of ice cream, surround the ice cream with the peaches, and nap it with more purée. Pipe the sweetened whipped cream decoratively over the top of each *coupe* and sprinkle it with the chopped pistachios.

Photo opposite.

POACHED APRICOTS WITH PINEAPPLE ICE

Yield:
12 servings

24 apricots
1½ to 2 cups apricot preserves, forced
  through a sieve
apricot liqueur or Cognac to taste
½ recipe Almond Macaroons (page
  262), crushed to crumbs (about 1½
  cups)

12 scoops Pineapple Ice
  (page 370)
¾ cup chopped unsalted pistachios
sweetened whipped cream as an
  accompaniment

Poach apricots (see page 466) and transfer them to a serving dish. Increase the heat under the saucepan to moderately high and boil the syrup down for 4 to 5 minutes. Add the sieved jam to the syrup and reduce the mixture for 5 minutes more. Flavor the syrup with the liqueur. Let the syrup cool.

Line a large serving dish with the macaroon crumbs and drizzle them with spoonfuls of the apricot syrup. Add the ice and top it with the poached apricots. Pour the syrup over the dessert and garnish it with the chopped pistachios. Serve with the sweetened whipped cream.

BANANAS FOSTER

Yield:
4 servings

The classic bananas Foster recipe is said to have been created at Brennan's Restaurant in New Orleans, Louisiana, in honor of one of their regular customers, Mr. Richard Foster. Below is our rendition of the dessert, which can also be served over the richer Vanilla Custard Ice Cream (page 351) or Honey Vanilla Ice Cream (page 352).

1 stick (½ cup) unsalted butter
½ cup firmly packed light brown
* sugar*
4 ripe bananas, peeled and halved
* lengthwise and crosswise*

½ teaspoon cinnamon
½ cup light or dark rum, or to taste,
* warmed*
4 scoops Vanilla Ice Cream (page
* 349)*

Melt the butter in a skillet, add the brown sugar, and heat the mixture, stirring, until the sugar is completely dissolved. Add the bananas and sauté them 3 to 4 minutes on each side, until tender. Sprinkle the bananas with the cinnamon. Pour the warmed rum over the bananas, ignite it, and baste the bananas with the sauce until the flames are extinguished. Divide the ice cream among dessert plates, top each portion with a banana, and baste with the sauce.

CHERRIES JUBILEE

Yield:
6 servings

1½ pints Vanilla Ice Cream
* (page 349)*
1½ pounds fresh black cherries, pitted

2 cups sugar syrup (page 542)
½ cup kirsch, heated

Spoon the ice cream into a dessert bowl or divide it among individual bowls. Put the ice cream in the freezing compartment of the refrigerator.

In a skillet cook the cherries in the sugar syrup for 6 minutes. Add the heated kirsch and ignite it. Spoon the flaming cherry sauce over the ice cream. Serve at once.

FIGS WITH MASCARPONE

Yield:
6 servings

Mascarpone is an extremely rich fresh whipped Italian cream cheese and its pairing with ripe figs is truly luscious. Fresh figs are in season from June through October. A sophisticated dessert like this is best served after an equally sophisticated Italian dinner.

18 fresh ripe figs, stemmed and cut in half lengthwise

3 cups fresh Mascarpone cheese, softened to room temperature

Arrange 6 fig halves per plate in a decorative pattern. Spoon about ½ cup cheese in a dollop in the middle of the plate or spoon small dollops over the fig halves.

DESSERT SAUCES

e sometimes think of a sauce as an afterthought, something that is not always essential to the dish at hand, but once made—if there is the time, that is—as basically beneficial to the whole. Nothing could be farther from the truth. Imagine a hot fudge sundae without the hot fudge sauce. That's like trying to play baseball without the ball.

Our dessert sauces fall into categories. We begin with the custard sauces and that great classic Crème Anglaise (page 490), as superb on fruit combinations as it is on steamed puddings. Sauces, rich with eggs and wine, follow and remind us of *zabaglione*. From there we move on to butter sauces and in particular to a selection of hard sauces, for many the only reason to eat plum pudding! Whipped creams round out that section.

We believe that the more chocolate sauce options you have the happier you will be and therefore have included nine different possibilities. There are hot ones, cold ones, flambéed ones, nutted ones. There is even one made with milk chocolate. There is certainly more than one to your liking.

Sugar sauces follow—butterscotch, caramel, and marshmallow, to name just a few. We conclude the chapter with a little level-headedness—fruit sauces—as handsome as many of them are healthful. See our fresh pineapple sauce, for example, or our cherry sauce, or our superb hot tangerine sauce.

There is hardly a chapter in this book that does not in some way allude to certain recipes being enhanced by one of the following sauces. Our napoleon sits in a shimmering pool of raspberry sauce; a three-layer devil's food cake calls for rhubarb sauce; a cherry cobbler is topped with brown sugar sour cream sauce. To say that the dessert sauce is versatile is an understatement. To add that a dessert sauce is an essential part of the dessert is not far from the truth. The sauce can even become the dessert's *raison d'être*.

Île Flottante
(page 243)

CRÈME ANGLAISE
Vanilla Custard Sauce

Yield:
3 cups

Equipment:
hand-held electric
  mixer

Crème Anglaise is a classic dessert sauce basic to many other classic desserts, including Bavarians and ice creams. If you want to serve the sauce warm, reheat it over very low heat, stirring, and under no circumstances let it come to a boil.

6 egg yolks
3 tablespoons sugar

2 cups half-and-half, scalded
1 teaspoon vanilla

In a bowl with the mixer beat the egg yolks with the sugar until the mixture is light and falls in a ribbon when the beater is lifted (see illustration page 16). Add the half-and-half in a stream, stirring, transfer the custard to a heavy saucepan, and cook it over moderately low heat, stirring, until it thickens, but do not let it boil. Remove the pan from the heat and stir in the vanilla. Strain the custard into a metal bowl set in a bowl of ice and water, let it cool, stirring occasionally, and chill it, covered.

Variation:

CARAMEL CUSTARD SAUCE: In a heavy skillet combine ⅓ cup sugar, ⅓ cup water, and a pinch of cream of tartar and cook the sugar mixture, washing down any sugar crystals clinging to the sides of the pan with a pastry brush dipped in cold water, until it caramelizes to a light golden color. Remove the skillet from the heat and pour in the crème anglaise, stirring constantly with a whisk until the caramel is dissolved and the mixture is well blended. Strain the caramel custard into a sauceboat and let it cool to room temperature or chill it, covered with a buttered round of wax paper directly touching the surface.

ALMOND CUSTARD SAUCE

Yield:
about 1½ cups

2 egg yolks
1 large egg
⅓ cup vanilla sugar (page 541)

1 cup light cream, scalded
2 tablespoons almond-flavored liqueur
¼ cup chopped lightly toasted almonds

In a bowl beat the egg yolks and whole egg with the vanilla sugar until light. Pour in the hot cream in a stream, stirring constantly. Transfer the mixture to a heavy saucepan and cook it over moderate heat, stirring with a wooden spatula, until it is thickened and lightly coats the spatula. Do not let it boil. Remove the pan from the heat, stir in the liqueur, and strain the custard into a bowl. Cover the sauce with a buttered round of wax paper directly touching the surface, let it cool, and stir in the almonds.

BRANDIED COFFEE CUSTARD SAUCE

Yield:
about 1⅓ cups

3 egg yolks
¼ cup sugar
1 cup heavy cream, scalded

2 teaspoons instant espresso dissolved
    in 1 teaspoon boiling water
3 tablespoons brandy

In a bowl beat the egg yolks with the sugar until light. Pour in the cream in a stream, stirring constantly. Transfer the mixture to a heavy saucepan and cook it over moderate heat, stirring with a wooden spatula, until it is thickened and lightly coats the spatula. Do not let it boil. Remove the pan from the heat and strain the custard into a bowl. Stir in the dissolved espresso and the brandy. Cover the sauce with a buttered round of wax paper directly touching the surface and let it cool to room temperature.

GINGERED CUSTARD SAUCE

Yield:
about 1⅓ cups

Equipment:
pastry brush

A sauce of this nature nicely complements any poached fruit compote.

½ cup sugar
½ cup water
1½ teaspoons ground ginger
1 teaspoon unsalted butter
1 cup light cream

3 egg yolks
¼ cup finely chopped crystallized
    ginger (available at specialty foods
    shops)

In a small saucepan combine the sugar and water, bring the mixture to a boil over moderate heat, and boil it, washing down any sugar crystals clinging to the sides of the pan with the brush dipped in cold water for 10 minutes. Add the ground ginger and the butter and simmer the mixture for 2 minutes. Let the syrup cool for 10 minutes.

In a saucepan combine the light cream with the syrup and scald the mixture over low heat. In a bowl beat the egg yolks until light. Pour in the cream mixture in a stream, stirring constantly. Transfer the mixture to a heavy saucepan and cook it over moderate heat, stirring with a wooden spatula, until it is thickened and lightly coats the spatula. Do not let it boil.

Remove the pan from the heat and strain the custard into a sauceboat. Stir in the crystallized ginger. Serve the sauce warm.

BROWN SUGAR SOUR CREAM SAUCE

Yield:
about 1½ cups

This recipe is served with Sour Cherry Cobbler (page 480).

*⅓ cup firmly packed light brown
    sugar*
1 cup sour cream

*1 to 2 tablespoons Cognac or dark
    rum, or to taste*

Into a bowl crumble the brown sugar, beat in the sour cream, a little at a time, and the Cognac, and beat the sauce until it is just combined.

MAPLE CREAM SAUCE

Yield:
1 cup

This sauce accompanies Apple Pandowdy (page 479).

1½ cups heavy cream
¼ cup maple syrup

¼ cup light corn syrup

In a small heavy saucepan combine the heavy cream with the maple syrup and the light corn syrup and cook the mixture over moderate heat, stirring, for 5 minutes, or until it is thickened and reduced by one third. Transfer the sauce to a bowl and chill it.

EGGNOG SAUCE

Yield:
about 2½ cups

Although eggnog is traditionally served at Christmastime, this eggnog sauce is a delightful accompaniment to Sand Torte (page 72) or Dessert Crêpes (page 434) at any time of the year.

2 cups light cream, scalded
½ cup sugar
4 egg yolks

½ teaspoon vanilla
pinch of salt
2 tablespoons bourbon

In a saucepan combine the hot cream and sugar, stirring until the sugar is dissolved. In the top of a double boiler beat the egg yolks with the vanilla and the salt until light. Gradually stir in the hot cream mixture and cook the sauce over hot water, stirring constantly, preferably with a wooden spoon, until it is thick enough to coat the spoon. Stir in the bourbon.

RUM SAUCE

Yield:
about 3 cups

Equipment:
hand-held electric
    mixer

Serve this sauce with chilled fruit desserts.

2 cups milk
4 egg yolks
1/2 cup sugar

6 tablespoons dark rum
1/2 cup well-chilled heavy cream,
    whipped

In the top of a double boiler over direct heat scald the milk. In a bowl with
the mixer beat the egg yolks with the sugar and gradually add the mixture
to the scalded milk, stirring constantly. Return the pan to the top of the
double boiler and over simmering water cook the sauce, stirring constantly with a wooden spoon, until it coats the spoon. Strain the sauce into a
bowl and let it cool. Stir in the rum and fold in the whipped cream. Chill
the sauce until ready to serve.

VANILLA SAUCE

Yield:
2 cups

Equipment:
hand-held electric
    mixer

Serve this sauce warm over steamed or baked puddings or poached fruits.

1 cup well-chilled heavy cream
2/3 cup confectioners' sugar

1 stick (1/2 cup) unsalted butter, cut
    into pieces
1 teaspoon vanilla

In a chilled bowl with the mixer beat the cream until it holds soft peaks.
    In a small saucepan combine the confectioners' sugar and the butter and
cook the mixture over low heat, stirring, until smooth and thick. Remove
the pan from the heat and fold the mixture gently but thoroughly into the
whipped cream. Fold in the vanilla. Serve the sauce warm.

RUM RAISIN SAUCE

Yield:
about 1 1/2 cups

Equipment:
pastry brush

1/2 cup raisins
1/2 cup dark rum, or to taste
1 cup sugar

1/4 cup water
pinch of cream of tartar
1/2 cup heavy cream

In a small bowl let the raisins macerate in 1/4 cup of the dark rum for 2
hours, or until they are plump. In a heavy saucepan combine the sugar
with the water and the cream of tartar and bring the mixture to a boil over
moderate heat, stirring and washing down any sugar crystals clinging to
the sides of the pan with the brush dipped in cold water until the sugar is

dissolved. Cook the syrup over moderately high heat, gently swirling the pan, until it is a golden caramel. Remove the pan from the heat and pour in the heavy cream and the remaining ¼ cup dark rum, or to taste, swirling the pan to combine the sauce. Stir in the raisin mixture and serve the sauce warm over ice cream.

SABAYON SAUCE

Yield:
about 1½ cups

Equipment:
hand-held electric
   mixer

The kirsch variation of this recipe is the suggested accompaniment to James Beard's Strawberry Tart (page 167). The sauce would work very nicely with poached fruit combinations as well.

8 egg yolks
½ cup sugar

½ cup Marsala, Sherry, or Madeira
wine

In the top of a double boiler with the mixer beat the egg yolks with the sugar until light. Beat in the wine. Set the pan over cold water and cook the mixture over medium heat, stirring constantly, until the water reaches the boiling point and the sauce is smooth and creamy. Remove the pan from the heat and cool the sauce slightly by beating it for several minutes. Transfer the sauce to a sauceboat and serve it either warm or at room temperature.

Variation:

KIRSCH SABAYON SAUCE: Substitute ½ cup kirsch for the Marsala, Sherry, or Madeira wine.

RED WINE CHERRY SAUCE

Yield:
about 2 cups

Serve this sauce warm with custards, ice creams, or pastries.

⅓ cup sugar
¾ cup dry red wine
2 cups pitted sour red cherries
1 teaspoon cornstarch mixed with 1
   tablespoon cold water

1 tablespoon brandy or cherry brandy
3 tablespoons chopped blanched
   almonds

In a stainless steel saucepan combine the sugar and the wine, bring the mixture to a boil, and boil it for 5 minutes. Add the cherries and cook the mixture for 5 minutes. Stir in the cornstarch mixture and cook the sauce until it is clear and slightly thickened. Let the sauce cool slightly and stir in the brandy and the almonds. Serve the sauce while still warm.

HARD SAUCE

Yield:
about 1 cup

Hard sauce is actually a sweetened, flavored butter and is especially good served over rich hot steamed puddings or warm fruit desserts. Despite its name, hard sauce should be served soft enough to spread.

2 sticks (1 cup) unsalted butter,
*   softened*
1 cup confectioners' sugar, sifted

3 tablespoons amber rum
3 tablespoon brandy

In a bowl cream together the butter and the confectioners' sugar until the mixture is fluffy and beat in the rum and brandy, one tablespoon at a time. Transfer the sauce to a serving bowl. Chill until firm but let the sauce come to room temperature before serving.

ORANGE HARD SAUCE

Yield:
about 1 cup

This sauce is the accompaniment to Steamed Orange Pudding (page 329).

¾ stick (6 tablespoons) unsalted
*   butter, softened*
1 cup sifted confectioners' sugar

1 tablespoon grated orange rind
2 teaspoons fresh orange juice

In a bowl cream the butter. Add the confectioners' sugar, a little at a time, beating, and beat in the orange rind and the orange juice. Beat the mixture until it is fluffy and transfer it to a serving bowl.

RUM BUTTER

Yield:
about 2 cups

This recipe would accompany Steamed Ginger Pudding (page 331) very nicely.

2 sticks (1 cup) unsalted butter,
*   softened*
1 cup Demerara sugar (available at
*   specialty foods shops)*

¼ cup dark rum
2 tablespoons grated orange rind
freshly grated nutmeg to taste

In a warm bowl cream together the butter and the Demerara sugar. Beat in the dark rum, one tablespoon at a time, the orange rind, and the nutmeg and beat the mixture until light and fluffy. Transfer the rum butter to a small serving bowl.

WHISKEY SAUCE

Yield:
about 1¾ cups

Creole Bread Pudding (page 324) is enhanced by the silkiness of this fragrant sauce.

1 stick (½ cup) unsalted butter,
   softened
½ cup sugar

2 large eggs
1 cup whiskey, or to taste

In a bowl cream together the butter and sugar until fluffy. Beat in the eggs, one at a time. Transfer the mixture to the top of a double boiler set over simmering water, stir in the whiskey, and cook the mixture, stirring, until it is thickened slightly. Transfer the sauce to a pitcher and serve it hot.

WHIPPED CREAM

Yield:
about 1½ cups

Equipment:
hand-held electric
  mixer

Note that heavy cream doubles in volume when whipped and can easily be flavored with any liqueur, extract, or instant coffee or espresso powder.

¾ cup well-chilled heavy cream
2 teaspoons sugar, or to taste

½ teaspoon vanilla, or to taste

In a chilled bowl with the mixer beat the heavy cream with the sugar and the vanilla until it holds soft peaks.

CHOCOLATE WHIPPED CREAM

Yield:
about 1½ cups

Equipment:
hand-held electric
  mixer

1 ounce unsweetened chocolate,
   chopped coarse
¾ cup well-chilled heavy cream

1 tablespoon sugar, or to taste
¼ teaspoon vanilla

In the top of a double boiler or in a small metal bowl set over barely simmering water melt the chocolate, stirring, until smooth, remove from the heat, and let cool.

In a chilled bowl with the mixer beat the heavy cream with the sugar and the vanilla until it holds soft peaks. Fold the cooled chocolate into the whipped cream gently but thoroughly.

COCOA WHIPPED CREAM

Yield:
about 1½ cups

Equipment:
hand-held electric
    mixer

¾ cup well-chilled heavy cream
2 tablespoons sugar
1 tablespoon unsweetened cocoa
    powder

¼ teaspoon vanilla

In a chilled bowl with the mixer beat the heavy cream with the sugar, cocoa, and the vanilla until it holds soft peaks.

WHIPPED CREAM FRUIT SAUCE

Yield:
2¼ cups

Serve this sauce with ice cream or fruit desserts.

Equipment:
hand-held electric
    mixer

1 cup well-chilled heavy cream
pinch of salt
¼ cup fresh fruit of choice, such as
    berries or chopped peeled peaches or
    nectarines

eau-de-vie de framboise (raspberry
    brandy) or kirsch if desired

In a chilled bowl with the mixer beat the cream with the salt until it holds soft peaks. Gently but thoroughly fold in the fruit of choice and the liqueur if desired.

HOT CHOCOLATE SAUCE

Yield:
about 1 cup

This all-purpose chocolate sauce is the perfect accompaniment to Bavarois Turinoise (page 401) and Profiteroles (page 223).

8 ounces semisweet chocolate, cut into
    bits

½ cup strong brewed coffee
Cognac to taste

In the top of a double boiler set over hot water melt the chocolate with the coffee. Keep the sauce warm over hot water until serving time. If the sauce becomes too thick, add more coffee or Cognac to taste or water.
    Photo on page 222.

FLAMBÉED CHOCOLATE SAUCE

Yield:
about 1 ½ cups

Serve this flaming sauce with poached pears, ice cream, or cream puffs.

4 ounces semisweet chocolate, cut into
 bits
¼ cup water
½ cup confectioners' sugar

¼ cup orange-flavored liqueur plus an
 additional ¼ cup, heated
¼ cup light cream

In the top of a double boiler set over hot water melt the chocolate with the water, stirring. Stir in the confectioners' sugar, ¼ cup of the orange-flavored liqueur, and the light cream. Transfer the sauce to a sauceboat, gently pour over it the remaining heated liqueur, and ignite it. Serve the sauce flaming.

RUM-FLAVORED CHOCOLATE SAUCE

Yield:
about 2 cups

This sauce would be very appropriate with *profiteroles* (page 223).

¾ cup heavy cream
8 ounces dark sweet chocolate, cut into
 bits
2 tablespoons sugar, or to taste

2 tablespoons dark rum
2 tablespoons cold unsalted butter, cut
 into bits

In a saucepan combine the cream and the chocolate and heat the mixture over moderately low heat, stirring, until the chocolate is just melted. Stir in the sugar and the rum and cook the sauce, stirring, until the sugar is just dissolved. Stir in the butter and heat the sauce, stirring, until it is smooth and shiny. Transfer the sauce to a sauceboat and serve it while still warm.

BRANDIED CHOCOLATE SAUCE

Yield:
about 1½ cups

¾ cup sugar
½ cup heavy cream
1½ tablespoons unsalted butter
2 ounces unsweetened chocolate, cut
 into bits

3 tablespoons brandy
½ teaspoon vanilla

In a saucepan combine the sugar, heavy cream, butter, and chocolate and cook the mixture over low heat, stirring, until the butter and chocolate are melted. Increase the heat to moderate, bring the mixture to a simmer, stirring, and simmer it, undisturbed, for 5 minutes. Remove the pan from the heat and stir in the brandy and vanilla. Let the sauce cool for 5 minutes and serve it warm.

CHOCOLATE SAUCE

Yield:
about 1¼ cups

8 ounces dark sweet chocolate, chopped into bits
1 cup water

pinch of salt
Cognac or orange-flavored liqueur to taste

In the top of a double boiler melt the chocolate with the water and the salt, stirring frequently, until smooth. Flavor the sauce with the liqueur of choice, transfer the sauce to a sauceboat, and serve warm.

CHOCOLATE PRALINE SAUCE

Yield:
about 1½ cups

8 ounces milk chocolate, chopped into bits
1 cup light cream

½ cup coarsely chopped almond praline (page 544)
brandy or rum to taste if desired

In a small saucepan melt the chocolate with the cream and bring the mixture to a boil over moderately high heat. Reduce the heat to low and simmer the sauce until thickened. Stir in the praline and the brandy or rum to taste. Transfer the sauce to a sauceboat and serve it warm.

CHOCOLATE HONEY ALMOND SAUCE

Yield:
1 cup

4 ounces unsweetened chocolate, chopped coarse
1 tablespoon orange-flavored liqueur
pinch of salt

⅔ cup honey, strained
⅓ cup blanched slivered toasted almonds

In the top of a double boiler melt the chocolate with the liqueur, stirring until smooth. Add the salt and stir in the honey. Continue to cook, stirring frequently, until the mixture is thoroughly blended and smooth. Stir in the almonds. Cover the pan, remove it from the heat, and let the sauce stand for 15 minutes, stirring occasionally to keep it smooth.

HOT FUDGE SAUCE

Yield:
about 1 ½ cups

Here is the ultimate chocolate dessert sauce and the crucial ingredient in a hot fudge sundae.

3 ounces unsweetened chocolate, cut into bits
3 tablespoons unsalted butter
½ cup water

1 cup sugar
3 tablespoons light corn syrup
¼ teaspoon salt
2 teaspoons vanilla

The sauce keeps, covered and chilled, for up to 1 month and should be reheated in a bowl set over simmering water.

In a small heavy saucepan melt the chocolate and the butter with the water over moderately low heat, stirring, until the mixture is smooth. Add the sugar and the corn syrup and bring the mixture to a boil over moderate heat, stirring until the sugar is dissolved. Cook the mixture at a slow boil for 8 minutes, remove the pan from the heat, and stir in the salt and the vanilla. Let the sauce cool until it is warm before spooning it over ice cream. (The sauce will harden on the ice cream.)

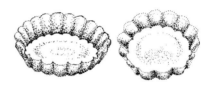

BROWN SUGAR CHOCOLATE SAUCE

Yield:
about 1 ½ cups

This recipe accompanies Crêpe Ice-Cream Cones (page 440).

2 ounces semisweet chocolate, cut into bits
⅔ cup heavy cream
½ cup unsweetened cocoa powder

⅓ cup firmly packed dark brown sugar
¼ cup water
⅛ teaspoon salt
1 teaspoon vanilla

The sauce keeps, covered and chilled, for up to 2 weeks.

In a heavy saucepan heat the chocolate and the cream over moderately low heat, stirring, until the chocolate is melted, but do not let the mixture boil. In a small bowl combine the cocoa powder with the brown sugar. In a small heavy saucepan bring the water to a simmer, add the cocoa powder mixture, a little at a time, stirring, and cook the mixture over moderately low heat, stirring until the sugar is dissolved and the mixture is smooth. Add the chocolate cream mixture and the salt and cook the mixture, stirring, until it is smooth, but do not let it boil. Remove the pan from the heat, stir in the vanilla, and transfer the sauce to a bowl. Let the sauce cool and chill it, covered, for at least 2 hours, or until cold.

CHOCOLATE WALNUT BRITTLE TOPPING

Yield:
about 2 cups

1 stick (½ cup) unsalted butter
½ cup sugar

½ cup chopped walnuts
3 ounces semisweet chocolate bits

Equipment:
pastry brush
candy thermometer

In a heavy saucepan combine the butter and the sugar and bring the mixture to a boil over moderate heat, stirring and washing down any sugar crystals clinging to the sides of the pan with the brush dipped in cold water until the sugar is dissolved. Cook the syrup over moderately high heat, gently swirling the pan, until the candy thermometer registers 290° F. (For the stages of sugar syrup, see illustrations page 241.) Remove the pan from the heat, stir in the walnuts, and pour the mixture onto a lightly oiled marble surface or a lightly oiled jelly-roll pan. Sprinkle the chocolate bits over the top of the mixture and let the brittle cool until it is hard. Transfer the brittle to a cutting board and chop it.

Store the brittle in an airtight container at room temperature.

BUTTERSCOTCH SAUCE

Yield:
about 1⅔ cups

Equipment:
pastry brush
candy thermometer

Butterscotch sauce is similar to a caramel sauce, however, it is enriched with butter and heavy cream, which give the sauce its characteristic luscious taste and texture. Serve the sauce with ice cream or baked apples.

1 cup firmly packed light brown sugar
¼ cup light corn syrup
½ stick (¼ cup) unsalted butter, cut
*   into bits*

½ cup water
½ cup heavy cream
1 teaspoon vanilla

In a large, heavy saucepan combine the sugar, corn syrup, butter, and ¼ cup of the water, cook the mixture over moderate heat, stirring and washing down any sugar crystals clinging to the sides of the pan with the brush dipped in cold water until the sugar is dissolved, and boil it, undisturbed, over moderately high heat until the candy thermometer registers 290° F. (For the stages of sugar syrup, see illustrations page 241.) Remove the pan from the heat, add carefully the remaining ¼ cup water, and return the mixture to a boil over moderate heat, stirring until the caramel is dissolved. Add the cream and boil the mixture for 2 minutes. Remove the pan from the heat and stir in the vanilla. Transfer the sauce to a bowl and let it cool to room temperature.

The sauce keeps, covered and chilled, for up to 1 month.

CARAMEL SAUCE

Yield:
I cup

This caramel sauce accompanies Pistachio Parfait (page 367) and is a perfect topping for ice cream.

Equipment:
pastry brush

1 cup granulated sugar   *⅓ cup water plus 1 cup boiling water*

In a heavy skillet combine the sugar and the ⅓ cup water and cook the mixture over low heat, stirring and washing down any sugar crystals clinging to the sides of the pan with the brush dipped in cold water until the sugar is dissolved. Increase the heat to high and boil the syrup, swirling the pan occasionally, until the syrup is a deep caramel color. Remove the pan from the heat and add the boiling water in a stream. Bring the mixture to a boil, stirring, and simmer the sauce for 5 minutes, or until thickened. Let the sauce cool to room temperature.

HONEY SAUCE

Yield:
about I cup

3 tablespoons unsalted butter, melted   *⅔ cup honey, strained*
2 teaspoons cornstarch

In a saucepan blend together the butter and cornstarch, add the honey, and cook the mixture over low heat, stirring constantly, for 5 minutes. Serve warm or cold.

Variation:

HONEY CINNAMON SAUCE: Add ½ teaspoon cinnamon to the mixture.

GINGER SAUCE

Yield:
about I cup

This sauce makes a splendid and unusual ice-cream topping.

Equipment:
pastry brush
candy thermometer

1 cup water   *¼ cup chopped crystallized ginger*
¾ cup sugar   *(available at specialty foods shops)*
juice of 1 lemon

In a saucepan combine the water, sugar, and the lemon juice, bring the mixture to a boil over moderate heat, stirring and washing down any sugar crystals clinging to the sides of the pan with the brush dipped in cold water until the sugar is dissolved, and boil it, over moderately high heat to the thread stage or until the candy thermometer registers 230° F. (For the stages of sugar syrup, see illustrations page 241.) Remove the syrup from the heat and stir in the ginger. Pour into a sauceboat and serve warm.

MAPLE PECAN SAUCE

Yield:
about 1 cup

This sauce is especially good served over Vanilla Ice Cream or Coffee Ice Cream (both recipes page 349).

Equipment:
candy thermometer

¾ cup maple syrup
½ cup heavy cream

½ cup coarsely chopped pecans

In a saucepan combine the maple syrup with the heavy cream and cook the mixture over low heat for 8 to 10 minutes, or until it thickens slightly and the candy thermometer registers 220° F. Remove the pan from the heat and beat the mixture for 1 minute. Stir in the pecans. Let the sauce cool before serving.

Variation:

MAPLE WALNUT SAUCE: Substitute ½ cup coarsely chopped walnuts for the pecans.

MARSHMALLOW SAUCE

Yield:
about 2½ cups

Equipment:
hand-held electric
  mixer
pastry brush
candy thermometer

1 tablespoon unflavored gelatin
1½ teaspoons cornstarch
½ cup half-and-half
2 egg whites at room temperature
pinch of cream of tartar

1 cup sugar
½ cup light corn syrup
½ cup water
1 teaspoon vanilla

In a small heavy saucepan combine the gelatin, cornstarch, and half-and-half and let the mixture stand for 15 minutes. Heat the mixture over moderately low heat, stirring, until the gelatin is dissolved, but do not let it boil. Keep the mixture warm.

In a large bowl with the mixer beat the egg whites with the cream of tartar and the salt until they hold soft peaks. In a saucepan combine the sugar, corn syrup, and the water, bring the mixture to a boil over moderate heat, stirring and washing down any sugar crystals clinging to the sides of the pan with the brush dipped in cold water until the sugar is dissolved, and boil it, gently swirling the pan, over moderately high heat until the candy thermometer registers 240° F. Add the syrup to the egg whites in a stream, beating, add the half-and-half mixture in a stream, beating, and beat the mixture until it is room temperature. (For the stages of sugar syrup and how to pour it, see illustrations pages 240 and 241.) Beat in the vanilla and chill the sauce, covered, for at least 2 hours or up to 3 days. (The sauce will gel.) Before using it, beat the sauce with the mixer for 1 to 2 minutes, or until it is of pouring consistency.

The sauce may be chilled, covered, and beaten again in the same manner for up to 3 days.

APRICOT SAUCE

Yield:
about 1¼ cups

This sauce accompanies Apricot Rice Ring (page 412).

1 pound dried apricots
1 cup sugar, or to taste
canned apricot nectar as needed
¼ cup apricot brandy

2 tablespoons brandy
¼ to ½ teaspoon vanilla or almond
  extract

In a saucepan soak the apricots in cold water just to cover for 24 hours.
   Bring the apricots to a boil in the same water and boil them, stirring occasionally, for 30 minutes. Stir in the sugar and simmer the apricots, stirring frequently, for about 1 hour, or until soft. (Add a little nectar if the apricots become too dry.) Force the apricots through a sieve into a bowl or purée them in a blender. In a bowl combine the purée with the apricot brandy, brandy, and the extract. Chill the sauce, covered, and thin it, if necessary, with apricot nectar to taste.

APRICOT RUM SAUCE

Yield:
about 1 cup

1 cup pure apricot jam without pectin
  added
¼ cup plus an additional 3 to 4
  tablespoons dark rum

2 tablespoons water

In a heavy saucepan melt the apricot jam with the ¼ cup rum and the water over moderate heat, stirring. Force the mixture through a fine sieve into a serving bowl and stir in the remaining rum.

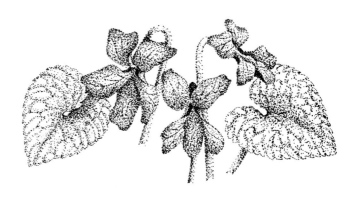

BLUEBERRY SAUCE

Yield:
about 2 cups

This hot sauce should be served with warm puddings, pound cake, or even Dessert Crêpes (page 434).

¼ cup sugar
1 tablespoon all-purpose flour
pinch of salt
1 cup water

1 teaspoon fresh lemon juice
1 cup blueberries, picked over
3 tablespoons unsalted butter
¼ teaspoon ground cinnamon

In a saucepan combine the sugar, flour, and salt. Add the water and lemon juice and cook the mixture until thickened. Add the blueberries and cook over moderate heat, stirring occasionally for 1 minute. Remove the pan from the heat and add the butter and cinnamon. Stir until the butter is melted and serve the sauce hot.

CHERRY SAUCE

Yield:
about 3 cups

This sauce is a wonderful topping for ice cream and is an ingredient in Oomph Girl à la Mode—cherry and almond sundae—on page 356.

2 pounds sweet cherries (thawed if
frozen), pitted, reserving any juice
¾ cup sugar
2 teaspoons cornstarch dissolved in 2
tablespoons cold water

1 tablespoon fresh lemon juice, or to
taste

In a stainless steel or enameled saucepan combine the cherries, the reserved juice, and sugar, cook the mixture over moderately low heat, stirring, until the cherries give off their liquid and the sugar is dissolved, and simmer the mixture, stirring, for 3 minutes. Stir the cornstarch mixture, add it to the cherry mixture, stirring, and simmer the mixture for 2 minutes, or until it is thickened slightly. Transfer the sauce to a bowl, stir in the lemon juice, and let the sauce cool. Chill the sauce, covered, for at least 2 hours, or until cold.

The sauce keeps,
covered and chilled,
for up to 1 week.

Photo on page 357.

GLACÉED FRUIT SAUCE

Yield:
about 2½ cups

This sauce is particularly good during the holidays as an ice cream or gingerbread topping.

¾ cup chopped glacéed mixed fruits
½ cup kirsch
3 tablespoons unsalted butter
3 tablespoons all-purpose flour

1½ cups light cream
¼ cup sugar
½ cup well-chilled heavy cream,
  whipped

In a bowl let the mixed fruits macerate in the kirsch for 2 hours. In a saucepan melt the butter over low heat, remove the pan from the heat, and blend in the flour. Stir in the light cream, add the fruit mixture, and bring the sauce to a boil over low heat, stirring constantly. Stir in the sugar until dissolved and simmer the sauce, stirring, for 5 minutes. Quickly fold in the whipped cream, transfer the sauce to a serving bowl, and serve at once.

LEMON SAUCE

Yield:
about 1½ cups

½ cup sugar
2 tablespoons cornstarch
1 cup water

juice of 1 lemon
2 tablespoons unsalted butter
2 teaspoons grated lemon rind

In a saucepan combine the sugar with the cornstarch, add the water, and simmer the mixture until clear and thickened. Remove the pan from the heat and stir in the lemon juice, butter, and the grated rind. Transfer the sauce to a serving bowl and serve it warm.

MELBA SAUCE

Yield
2 cups

Melba sauce was created by Georges Auguste Escoffier in honor of Dame Nellie Melba, the great Australian-born soprano. Although the sauce is usually made with raspberries only, we have added strawberries. Serve this sauce with Coeur à la Crème (page 408), cheesecake, or rice pudding.

1 pint fresh strawberries, hulled
1 pint fresh raspberries, picked over

½ cup sugar, or to taste
2 tablespoons fresh lemon juice

Rub the strawberries and the raspberries through a sieve into a bowl. Transfer the purée to a blender, add the sugar and the lemon juice, and blend the mixture for 1 minute. Chill the sauce until ready to serve.

ORANGE SAUCE

Yield:
about 2 cups

This sauce accompanies Cranberry Cobbler (page 481) and is a perfect complement as well to Banana Fritters (page 448).

¼ cup strained fresh orange juice plus 1⅓ cups additional strained orange juice
2 tablespoons cornstarch

½ cup sugar
⅓ cup light cream
1 tablespoon dark rum, or to taste
½ teaspoon grated lemon rind

In a saucepan combine the ¼ cup orange juice with the cornstarch and stir in the additional 1⅓ cups orange juice in a stream. Add the sugar and cook the mixture over low heat, stirring, for 5 minutes, or until it is clear. Stir in the light cream, rum, and lemon rind, transfer the sauce to a bowl, and serve warm.

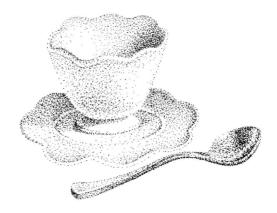

ORANGE MARMALADE SAUCE

Yield:
about 1⅓ cups

This sauce can accompany any of the fruit fritters (pages 448 and 449).

1 cup orange marmalade
⅓ cup orange-flavored liqueur

2 tablespoons fresh lemon juice

In a saucepan combine the marmalade with the liqueur and the lemon juice, heat the mixture over moderately low heat until the marmalade is melted, and transfer the sauce to a small pitcher.

FRESH PINEAPPLE SAUCE

Yield:
about 3 cups

Equipment:
food processor fitted
  with steel blade

The sauce keeps,
covered and chilled,
for up to 5 days.

This sauce makes a wonderful topping for ice cream.

*a 3-pound pineapple, peeled, cored,
  and chopped*

½ cup sugar

Reserve 2 cups of the pineapple. In the food processor or in a blender in batches purée the remaining chopped pineapple and transfer the purée to a stainless steel or enameled saucepan. Add the sugar, bring the mixture to a boil over moderate heat, stirring, and simmer it, stirring occasionally, for 10 minutes. Strain the mixture through a fine sieve into a bowl, pressing hard on the solids, and skim the froth. Add the reserved pineapple, combine the sauce well, and let it cool. Chill the sauce, covered, for at least 1 hour, or until it is cold.

RASPBERRY SAUCE

Yield:
about 1 cup

Equipment:
food processor fitted
  with steel blade

This versatile sauce accompanies Yogurt Cream Mold (page 409), our Napoleon (page 202), or any Bavarian cream (pages 399 to 405). It is the ideal dessert sauce to include in your repertoire.

*two 10-ounce packages frozen
  raspberries, thawed and drained*
*1 tablespoon fresh lemon juice, or to
  taste*

*2 tablespoons superfine granulated
  sugar, or to taste*

In the food processor or in a blender purée the raspberries with the lemon juice and strain the sauce through a fine sieve into a bowl, pressing hard on the solids. Stir in the sugar to taste.
　Photo on page 202.

RHUBARB SAUCE

Yield:
about 3 cups

*4 cups thinly sliced fresh rhubarb or 2
  pounds frozen chopped rhubarb,
  thawed and drained*

1 cup sugar, or to taste
¼ cup water

In a stainless steel or enameled saucepan combine the rhubarb, sugar, and the water, bring the mixture to a boil over moderate heat, stirring until the

The sauce keeps, covered and chilled, for I week. sugar is dissolved, and simmer it, stirring occasionally, for 10 to 15 minutes, or until the rhubarb is soft. Transfer the sauce to a serving bowl and let it cool.

STRAWBERRY SAUCE

Yield: about 2½ cups

½ cup sugar
½ cup water

2 cups sliced ripe strawberries
kirsch to taste

In a saucepan combine the sugar and water and bring the mixture to a boil over moderately high heat. Simmer the syrup for 5 minutes, remove the pan from the heat, add the strawberries and the kirsch to taste.

TANGERINE SAUCE

Yield: 2 cups

This sauce can accompany Beignets (page 450) or Banana Fritters (page 448) and could be readily used as a topping for Dessert Crêpes (page 434) or as a substitute for the sauce in the recipe for Blood Orange Dessert Waffles with Blood Orange Sauce (page 444).

1 cup fresh tangerine juice
½ cup water
¼ cup sugar

1½ tablespoons cornstarch
1 cup tangerine sections, cut into
* pieces*

In a small saucepan combine the tangerine juice, water, sugar, and the cornstarch and simmer the mixture, stirring constantly, for 5 minutes. Add the tangerine pieces and serve the sauce hot in a sauceboat.

ICINGS AND BUTTERCREAMS

An icing is not a frosting, and neither an icing nor a frosting is a buttercream, but, luckily for us all, each performs in the same wonderful way. They cover cakes or pastries and sometimes cookies—an icing less thickly than a frosting, and a frosting with fewer specific ingredients than a buttercream.

Buttercream, or *crème au beurre*, is a classic preparation in the French repertoire that combines hot sugar syrup, egg yolks (or whites, see page 517), butter, and flavorings into a light, fluffy emulsification. There are different ways of preparing buttercream: poaching the egg yolks, for example, and mixing the egg yolk/syrup mixture into the butter. We beat the yolks (or whites) first, pour hot syrup into them, and then add butter. Other buttercreams are totally uncooked. No matter the method, the intent is the same—a delicate, smooth, and lustrous combination.

You will see that we have included two recipes for vanilla buttercream: one, made as described above; the other substituting egg whites for egg yolks. This change renders an even lighter, whiter buttercream, better suited, we think, for citrus flavorings. Know that this buttercream made with egg whites has been specifically created to let those worried about cholesterol in egg yolks nonetheless enjoy buttercream.

As a lighter buttercream is more appropriate for certain types of cake and oftentimes during the warmer months of the year, so are some combinations of cake and frosting much more irresistible than others. It is for good reason that we do not see pound cakes, rich with butter, iced with buttercream. Nor do we see angel food cakes topped with buttercream. Armagnac Chocolate Cake with Prunes (page 63) would also never sport a chocolate buttercream, regardless of how much you might love chocolate! In short, when choosing an icing or a buttercream for a cake, remember it is mutual admiration—one complements the other.

Chocolate Mousse
Cake with Ganache
Icing (page 64)

BUTTERMILK FROSTING

Yield:
about 3 cups

Equipment:
pastry brush
candy thermometer
hand-held electric
  mixer

This frosting, especially good on chocolate layer cakes, has just the right tanginess. You might also consider it as a very appropriate topping for Buttermilk Spice Cake (page 52).

2 cups sugar
1 cup buttermilk
1 stick (½ cup) unsalted butter, cut
  into bits

2 teaspoons light corn syrup
1 teaspoon baking soda
1 teaspoon vanilla

In a large heavy saucepan combine the sugar, buttermilk, butter, corn syrup, and the baking soda. Bring the mixture to a boil over moderate heat, stirring and washing down any sugar crystals clinging to the sides of the pan with the brush dipped in cold water until the sugar is dissolved. Boil the syrup, stirring, until it reaches the soft-ball stage, or the candy thermometer registers 235° F. (For the stages of sugar syrup, see illustrations page 241.) Let the syrup cool slightly and stir in the vanilla. With the mixer beat the frosting until it is thick enough to spread.

CHOCOLATE ICING WITH COGNAC

Yield:
about 3 cups, enough
  to ice a 3-layer 8-
  inch cake

Equipment:
hand-held electric
  mixer

3 ounces unsweetened chocolate
1¾ cups confectioners' sugar
1 tablespoon Cognac mixed with
  2 tablespoons hot water

3 egg yolks
½ stick (¼ cup) unsalted butter,
  softened

In the top of a double boiler set over hot water melt the chocolate. Remove the pan from the heat and stir in the confectioners' sugar and the Cognac mixture until smooth. Transfer the mixture to a bowl. Add the egg yolks, one at a time, beating hard after each addition. With the mixer beat in the butter, one tablespoon at a time, and beat the icing until very smooth and shiny.

CHOCOLATE MINT ICING

Yield:
about 3 cups, enough
  to ice a 3-layer 8-
  inch cake

3 ounces unsweetened chocolate,
  chopped coarse
¾ cup evaporated milk
¼ cup water
1 cup sugar

1 large egg
a 3-ounce package of after-dinner
  mints, chopped coarse, reserving
  ¼ cup for garnish

Equipment:
rotary or hand-held
electric mixer

In the top of a double boiler over hot water melt the chocolate, stirring. In a bowl combine the evaporated milk, water, sugar, and the egg. Stir the mixture into the melted chocolate and cook over the hot water, stirring frequently, for about 30 minutes. Remove the icing from the heat and beat it with the mixer until very smooth. Stir in the mints until smooth. Chill the icing, covered, for about 2 hours. Use the reserved chopped mints to garnish the surface of the iced cake.

CHOCOLATE FUDGE ICING

Yield:
about 3½ cups

Equipment:
candy thermometer

A good fudge icing recipe is like an heirloom. It keeps being handed down, lovingly, from one generation to the next. Here is another one to add to your collection.

3 cups sugar
1 cup milk
3½ tablespoons light corn syrup

2 ounces unsweetened chocolate, cut
into bits
½ stick (¼ cup) unsalted butter

In a heavy saucepan combine the sugar, milk, corn syrup, and the chocolate. Bring the mixture slowly to a boil and cook it over low heat until the sugar is dissolved. Cook the icing until a small drop forms a soft ball when dropped into cold water, or the candy thermometer registers 235° F. (For the stages of sugar syrup, see illustrations page 241.) Remove the pan from the heat and beat in the butter, one tablespoon at a time. Pour the icing into a cool bowl and let it cool until just hot to the touch, or the candy thermometer registers 112° F. Beat the icing with a wooden spoon until it is of spreading consistency.

CREAM CHEESE CHOCOLATE ICING

Yield:
about 3 cups

Equipment:
hand-held electric
mixer

As cream cheese frosting can be enriched with butter (page 51), so can it be made with cream—and the additional bonus of melted chocolate.

2 ounces unsweetened chocolate,
chopped coarse
¼ cup heavy cream
3 ounces cream cheese, softened

2 cups confectioners' sugar
pinch of salt
1 teaspoon vanilla

In the top of a double boiler over hot water melt the chocolate, stirring until smooth, and set aside. In a bowl with the mixer beat the heavy cream with the cream cheese until light and fluffy. Beat in the confectioners' sugar, a little at a time, until the mixture is of good spreading consistency. Stir in the melted chocolate, salt, and the vanilla. If necessary, continue to beat the icing to the desired consistency.

MOCHA ICING

Yield:
about 1½ cups

Equipment:
candy thermometer

3 ounces German sweet chocolate or imported dark sweet chocolate, chopped coarse

1 teaspoon unsalted butter, softened
6 tablespoons strong black coffee
¾ cup granulated sugar

In the top of a double boiler over hot water melt the chocolate and add the butter, stirring until smooth. Set the mixture aside. In a heavy saucepan combine the coffee and the sugar, bring the mixture to a boil, and boil it for 15 minutes, or until the syrup spins a fine thread. (For the stages of sugar syrup, see illustrations page 241.) Slowly pour the boiling syrup into the chocolate, stirring constantly. Pour the icing over the cake at once.

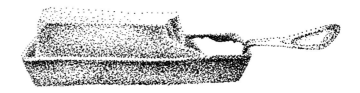

PENUCHE ICING

Yield:
about 3 cups

Equipment:
hand-held electric
  mixer

The dictionary defines penuche as fudge, usually made of brown sugar, butter, cream or milk, and nuts. The candy is popular in the South, where it is sometimes spelled penoche. Our penuche icing has all the above ingredients except the nuts, which you could easily add, and is remarkably fine on devil's food cake.

1 stick (½ cup) unsalted butter
1 cup firmly packed light brown sugar

¼ cup milk
2 cups sifted confectioners' sugar

In a heavy saucepan melt the butter over moderate heat, stir in the brown sugar, and bring the mixture to a boil. Cook the syrup over low heat, stirring, for 2 minutes. Add the milk and cook the mixture over moderate heat, stirring, until it comes to a boil. Transfer the syrup to a bowl and let it cool. With the mixer beat in the confectioners' sugar, a little at a time, and beat the icing until smooth. Stir in more milk, if necessary, to thin the icing to the desired consistency.

ROYAL ICING

Yield:
enough for 72 flowers

Equipment:
hand-held electric
    mixer

This royal icing is used to make the flowers that adorn Bride's Cake (page 104) and, if you prefer, can be made without the addition of food coloring. For instructions on how to pipe flowers see the following recipe.

1⅓ cups vegetable shortening at room
    temperature
¼ cup hot water
5 cups confectioners' sugar, sifted

1 teaspoon vanilla
1 drop of yellow food coloring
1 drop of red food coloring

In a bowl with the mixer beat the shortening until light and fluffy and beat in the hot water, one tablespoon at a time. Beat in the sugar, one cup at a time, beating well after each addition, and beat in the vanilla. Transfer ⅓ cup of the icing to a small bowl and beat in the yellow food coloring. Transfer one fourth of the remaining icing to another small bowl and beat in the red food coloring to form a pale pink icing.

TO MAKE ROYAL ICING FLOWERS

Yield:
about 72 flowers

Equipment:
large pastry bag
rose petal tip (#127)
rose nail
stack of seventy-two
    2-inch squares wax
    paper
small pastry bag
very small plain tip
    (#2)
⅓-cup muffin tin
    (optional)

If you have never made icing flowers before, you should practice. Know, too, that these flowers are fragile. Extras would be helpful.

1 recipe Royal Icing (recipe above)

Fit the large pastry bag with the rose petal tip and fold down the top half of the bag. Using a knife, fill the narrow end only of the tip with some of the pink icing and spread the icing in a strip 5 inches up the same side of the bag. Using a clean knife, fill the pastry bag with about 1 cup of the white icing, being careful not to dislodge the strip of pink icing. (The bag should be about half full.) Gather the sides of the bag together, twist the bag to close it, and push the icing down toward the tip, eliminating any air pockets. Holding the pastry bag in one hand and the rose nail in the other, pipe a dab of the icing onto the nail head and invert the nail head onto the stack of wax paper squares. Turn the nail head right side up with the wax paper square in place. Holding the pastry bag with the narrow end of the tip down and at the center of the nail head, pipe 1 petal onto the wax paper by moving the tip in a half-moon arc and turning the nail at the same time counterclockwise a quarter turn. Begin the next petal slightly underneath the furled edge of the previous one and pipe it in the same manner, turning the nail a quarter turn each time, to form a flower. Transfer the flower on the wax paper square carefully to a baking sheet and let it dry to form a flat flower or put the flower on the wax paper square in the muffin tin to form

The flowers may be stored in 1 layer in airtight containers for up to 1 week.

a flower with petals that curl up at the ends. Continue to make flowers, refilling the pastry bag as necessary, in the same manner and dry them as desired.

Transfer the yellow icing to the small pastry bag fitted with the very small plain tip, pipe 3 dots in the center of each flower, and let the flowers dry, uncovered, overnight.

SEVEN-MINUTE ICING

Yield:
about 12 cups

Equipment:
4½-quart heatproof
  bowl
hand-held electric
  mixer

The yield of this recipe was specifically created to accommodate the amount of icing needed to top the orange buttercream on Bride's Cake (page 104). Marion Cunningham advises that the icing cannot be made more than several hours in advance or it will become sticky. The recipe can be halved, and halved again.

2¼ cups granulated sugar
1½ teaspoons cream of tartar
½ teaspoon salt

6 egg whites at room temperature
¾ cup cold water
2 tablespoons vanilla

In the bowl set over a large saucepan of simmering water beat the sugar, cream of tartar, salt, egg whites, and the water with the mixer for 5 to 7 minutes, or until the mixture holds stiff peaks. Remove the bowl from the pan, beat the icing for 2 to 3 minutes more, or until it is cool, and beat in the vanilla.

SOUR CREAM NUT FROSTING

Yield:
about 2 cups

Equipment:
hand-held electric
  mixer

This frosting is particularly successful on spice cakes or even gingerbread.

1 cup sugar
½ cup sour cream
2 tablespoons unsalted butter

¾ teaspoon vanilla
½ chopped walnuts
½ chopped raisins

In a small saucepan combine the sugar, sour cream, and the butter. Cook the mixture over moderate heat, stirring, until it is the consistency of heavy cream. Let it cool slightly and add the vanilla. With the mixer beat the frosting until it is of spreading consistency. Stir in the chopped walnuts and raisins.

VANILLA BUTTERCREAM #1

Yield:
about 2 cups

Equipment:
pastry brush

1 cup sugar
¾ cup water
6 egg yolks

2 sticks (1 cup) unsalted butter
1 teaspoon vanilla

In a small saucepan dissolve the sugar in the water over moderate heat, stirring and washing down any sugar crystals clinging to the sides of the pan with the brush dipped in cold water until the sugar dissolves, and cook the syrup until it reaches the soft-ball stage, or a candy thermometer registers 236° F. (For the stages of sugar syrup, see illustrations page 241.) In the top of a double boiler set over simmering water beat the egg yolks until frothy. Add the hot syrup in a stream, beating, and continue to beat the mixture until it is smooth. Remove the pan from the water and beat the mixture until thick and completely cool. Beat in the butter, one tablespoon at a time, stir in the vanilla, and chill the buttercream, covered, until firm but still of spreading consistency.

VANILLA BUTTERCREAM #2

Yield:
about 3 cups

Equipment:
pastry brush
candy thermometer
upright electric mixer

This recipe for buttercream, unlike the classic one above, is made with egg whites to which hot sugar syrup is added. Lighter in texture than an egg-yolk-based buttercream, it is obviously lower in cholesterol and a very good alternative for those keeping watch on such counts.

1¼ cups sugar
⅓ cup water
5 egg whites at room temperature
pinch of salt

⅛ teaspoon cream of tartar
3 sticks (1½ cups) unsalted butter,
    softened

In a small heavy saucepan combine the sugar with the water. Bring the mixture to a boil and boil it over moderate heat, stirring and washing down any sugar crystals clinging to the sides of the pan with the brush dipped in cold water until it reaches the hard-ball stage, or the candy thermometer reaches 248° F.

In the bowl of the mixer beat the egg whites with the salt until foamy. Add the cream of tartar and beat the whites until they hold stiff but not dry peaks (see illustrations page 238). With the mixer running, add the hot syrup to the whites in a stream, beating, and beat the mixture until completely cool. (For the stages of sugar syrup and how to pour it, see illustrations pages 240 and 241.) Beat in the butter, a little at a time. Chill the buttercream, covered, until firm but still soft enough to spread.

CHESTNUT BUTTERCREAM

Yield:
about 2 or 3 cups

Consider layering meringue rounds with this superb combination or using it as the filling for a chocolate *génoise* jelly roll.

1 recipe vanilla buttercream #1 or #2　　　*2 tablespoons dark rum, or to taste*
　(page 517)
1 cup finely chopped Marrons Glacés,
　drained (page 526)

In a bowl combine well the buttercream and the chestnuts. Stir in the rum.

PRALINE BUTTERCREAM

Yield:
about 2 or 3 cups

This makes a wonderful topping for either a chocolate *génoise* or devil's food layer cake.

1 recipe vanilla buttercream #1 or #2　　　*½ cup hazelnut praline powder (page*
　(page 517)　　　　　　　　　　　　　　　*544)*

In a bowl combine the buttercream and praline powder gently but thoroughly.

STRAWBERRY BUTTERCREAM

Yield:
about 2 or 3 cups

For a lovely summer cake, consider this for the covering on simple vanilla *génoise* layers. Add a few sliced strawberries to a portion of the buttercream and use as the filling.

1 recipe vanilla buttercream #1 or #2　　　*2 tablespoons crème de cassis (black*
　(page 517)　　　　　　　　　　　　　　　*currant liqueur), or to taste*
2 tablespoons strawberry purée (page
　547)

In a bowl combine well the buttercream and the strawberry purée. Stir in the *crème de cassis*.

LEMON BUTTERCREAM

Yield:
about 3 cups

1 recipe vanilla buttercream #2
  (page 517)
3 tablespoons grated lemon rind

1½ tablespoons fresh lemon juice
1½ tablespoons dark rum, or to taste

In a bowl combine the buttercream with the grated rind, lemon juice, and
the dark rum.

FRIANDISES

friandises have been described as petits fours or small confections and candies. They are those lovely little delicacies that appear after dinner, and while they may come as a delightful surprise, they are anything but an afterthought. They are always small and choice and are best enjoyed slowly.

We can only surmise on how the *friandise* came into being. Imagine a pleasing dinner's having ended. The gentlemen retire to the smoking room; the women disappear upstairs. Later, the men and women regroup in another parlor. It is the small of the evening, and to send everyone on their way, silver trays appear. On each is an assortment of sweets: a chocolate, a nut, a fruit, a pastry, perhaps.

In our selection of *friandises* chocolates include truffles, one creamy, another studded with hazelnuts. There are bourbon-flavored praline nuggets and spiced almonds, pecans, and walnuts, a combination that would be appropriate with a glass of Sherry. *Marrons glacés*, chestnuts preserved in vanilla syrup, are a famous French delicacy. They are considered a luxury throughout France but a staple in Parisian specialty foods stores. We offer a recipe for *marrons glacés* so that you can offer them as they do in France. There are brandied cherries in need of steeping for thirty days that will eventually reside in handmade chocolate cases. There are chocolate-covered strawberries. We even suggest how to candy your own violets or rose petals.

Meringue mushrooms, those traditional *trompe l'oeil* confections that adorn Yule logs, fall among this grouping of *friandises*. Filled with chocolate cream that is piped to resemble the underside of a mushroom cap, these mushrooms are not likely to fool a mycologist, but will prove very captivating when artfully arranged on a Majolica platter.

We should add here that there is nothing to prevent you from including among a *friandise* selection cookies, but in miniature version. Any of the *tuile* cookies (pages 288 to 290) would be fitting.

Bûche de Noël
(page 114)

CANDIED ORANGE PEEL

Yield:
about 6 cups

Equipment:
4-quart kettle
pastry brush

The peel of citrus fruits is especially good for candying in a sugar syrup. Pink or white grapefruit or lemon peel can easily be substituted for the orange as desired. The candied peels can be served on their own, dipped in melted chocolate, or rolled in cocoa powder.

5 large navel oranges   *1¼ cups water*
3½ cups sugar   *3 tablespoons light corn syrup*

Quarter the oranges lengthwise and remove the pulp, reserving it for another use. With a spoon remove as much of the white pith as possible and cut the peel lengthwise into ½-inch strips. In the kettle cover the peel with cold water, bring the water to a boil, and simmer the peel for 10 minutes. Drain the peel, repeat the process 2 more times, and pat the peel dry with paper towels.

Line 2 jelly-roll pans with wax paper and sprinkle the paper with 1 cup of the sugar.

In the kettle combine the remaining 2½ cups sugar, the 1¼ cups water, and the corn syrup. Bring the mixture to a boil and boil it, washing down any sugar crystals clinging to the sides of the pan with the brush dipped in cold water for 20 minutes. Stir in the peel and simmer the mixture, stirring occasionally, for 15 minutes, or until the syrup is thickened. Continue to simmer the mixture, stirring constantly and being very careful not to let the syrup burn, until almost all the syrup is absorbed. Transfer the peel with tongs to the jelly-roll pans, roll each strip in the sugar to coat it well, and let the peel dry in one layer overnight.

Store in layers separated by wax paper in an airtight container in a cool, dry place. The peel keeps for up to 2 weeks.

GLAZED STRAWBERRIES

Yield:
about 24 small glazed
  strawberries

one 12-ounce jar red currant jelly   *1 pint strawberries with stems intact*

Line a jelly-roll pan or platter with wax paper.

In a saucepan melt the jelly over moderate heat, whisking, and whisk it until smooth. Holding each strawberry by its stem, dip it in the jelly, let the excess drip off, and put the strawberry on the jelly-roll pan. Continue to glaze the remaining berries in the same manner, reheating the jelly over low heat, stirring, if it becomes too thick.

Chill the strawberries for 1 hour, or until the glaze is set. If desired, arrange the strawberries in small fluted paper cups and serve them with liqueurs or coffee.

CANDIED STRAWBERRIES

Yield:
24 small or 16
  medium to large
  candied
  strawberries

Equipment:
pastry brush
candy thermometer
  (optional)
marble slab lightly
  coated with sweet
  almond oil

1 cup sugar
¼ cup water
2 or 3 drops red food coloring if desired

pinch of cream of tartar
1 pint strawberries with hulls and
  stems intact

In a heavy saucepan combine the sugar, water, food coloring, if desired, and cream of tartar and bring the mixture to a boil, washing down any sugar crystals clinging to the sides of the pan with the brush dipped in cold water until the sugar is dissolved. Boil the syrup to the hard-crack stage, or until the candy thermometer registers 300° F., and set the pan at once in a shallow pan of hot water to prevent the syrup from hardening too fast. (For the stages of sugar syrup, see illustrations page 241.)

Holding each strawberry by its stem, carefully but quickly dip it into the syrup. Let the excess syrup drip off for a moment and put each berry on the oiled marble slab or on an oiled sheet of wax paper. Transfer the candied berries to a dish and put the dish in a cool, dry place. Use the berries within 2 to 4 hours, or before the glaze begins to moisturize. Decorate cakes and other desserts with the berries or serve them in fluted paper cups as confections.

CANDIED PINEAPPLE

Yield:
10 candied pineapple
  rings

Equipment:
ten 8-inch wooden
  skewers
pastry brush
candy thermometer

The rings will keep
for 30 minutes to 1
hour in a cool, dry
place.

2 cups sugar
1 cup water

10 rings fresh pineapple, patted dry

Thread each skewer horizontally through the middle of each pineapple ring. In a small deep saucepan combine the sugar and water and bring the mixture to a boil over moderate heat, washing down any sugar crystals clinging to the sides of the pan with the brush dipped in cold water until the sugar is dissolved. Boil the syrup, gently swirling the pan, until it reaches the hard-crack stage, or the candy thermometer register 300° F. (For the stages of sugar syrup, see illustrations page 241.) Remove the pan from the heat and, working quickly but very carefully, first dip one half of the ring into the syrup and then the other coating the ring completely. Transfer each skewer to a rack to cool.

CANDIED VIOLETS

Equipment:
small pastry brush or
  small paint brush

There is a piece of candy-making equipment that is not easily obtainable and, unfortunately, quite expensive called a *candissoire*. It is used for candying violets with multiple treatments of sugar syrup. Although this is an extremely interesting technique, we have provided an alternate and simpler, yet just as effective method.

heavily perfumed violets   *granulated sugar*
egg whites, beaten lightly

**Store in layers
separated by wax
paper in airtight
containers in a cool,
dry place.**

Remove the stems from the violets. Wash and dry the blossoms thoroughly. Line a baking sheet or tray with wax paper.

    With the brush carefully paint the violet blossoms with the egg white and sprinkle well with the sugar. Transfer the blossoms to the baking sheets and let dry completely.

Variation:

CANDIED ROSE PETALS: Follow the same directions as above, using petals from highly perfumed roses.

FROSTED CRANBERRIES

Yield:
2 cups

4 egg whites   *1 cup sugar*
2 cups cranberries, picked over

In a small bowl beat one of the egg whites until foamy. Add ½ cup of the cranberries and coat them with the egg white. Spread the cranberries on a sheet of wax paper. Sift ¼ cup of the sugar, or to taste, through a fine sieve over the cranberries and roll the cranberries in the sugar. Repeat the procedure with the remaining cranberries, ½ cup at a time. Let the cranberries dry in a cool place for at least 2 hours.

CANDIED PECAN HALVES

Yield:
about 16 halves

¼ cup water   *pinch of cream of tartar*
¼ cup sugar   *pecan halves*

Equipment:
pastry brush
candy thermometer
thin metal skewer

In a small heavy saucepan bring the water to a boil with the sugar and the cream of tartar and cook the mixture over moderately high heat, washing down any sugar crystals clinging to the sides of the pan with the brush dipped in cold water until the syrup reaches the hard-crack stage, or the candy thermometer registers 300° F. (For the stages of sugar syrup, see illustrations page 241.) With the skewer gently pierce each pecan half and dip it into the syrup, coating it completely. Transfer the pecans to wax paper and let them dry. Continue to candy the remaining pecans and syrup in the same manner.

Store in airtight containers for in a cool, dry place.

PRALINE NUGGETS

Yield: about 100 nuggets

Equipment: hand-held electric mixer

Pecan halves with a bourbon-flavored praline coating are baked until puffed and crispy.

1 cup firmly packed light brown sugar, sieved
2 tablespoons ground pecans
1 tablespoon cornstarch
1 tablespoon bourbon or dark rum

1 egg white at room temperature
pinch of cream of tartar
pinch of salt
2 cups pecan halves

Butter 2 baking sheets and preheat the oven to 300° F.

In a bowl whisk together the brown sugar, ground pecans, and cornstarch. Add the bourbon and whisk until well blended.

In another bowl with the mixer beat the egg white with the cream of tartar and salt until it holds stiff peaks. Stir one third of the egg white into the sugar mixture and fold in the remaining white. (The mixture will become more liquid.) Add the pecan halves, stirring to coat them well. Arrange the pecan halves, rounded sides up, 2 inches apart on the baking sheets, and bake them in batches in the middle of the oven for 12 minutes, or until puffed and golden brown. Let the nuggets cool on the sheets for 1 minute, transfer them to racks, and let them cool completely.

Photo on page 460.

Store in airtight containers in a cool place for up to 5 days.

MAPLE WALNUTS

Yield: about 16 walnut halves (about ½ cup)

Equipment: pastry brush candy thermometer thin metal skewer

2 ounces walnut halves   *1 cup maple syrup*

Oil a baking sheet.

In a saucepan bring the maple syrup to a boil over moderately high heat and cook it, washing down any sugar crystals clinging to the sides of the pan with the brush dipped in cold water until it reaches the soft-crack stage, or the candy thermometer registers 270°F. (For the stages of sugar syrup, see illustrations page 241.) Remove the pan from the heat and,

Store in layers
separated by wax
paper in an airtight
container in a cool
place.

working quickly, pierce each walnut half with the skewer, dip it into the maple syrup, and transfer the coated walnut to the baking sheet. Continue to pierce and dip the remaining walnuts in the same manner. Let the walnuts cool completely.

MARRONS GLACÉS

Yield:
4 cups

Equipment:
pastry brush
sterilized 1-quart
  Mason-type jar (for
  procedure page
  551) with a lid or
  two 1-pint jars

Whole peeled chestnuts are poached in sugar syrup until tender and are then glazed. They can be used in dessert sauces or as a superb layer in parfaits, for example Chocolate Parfait Custard (page 367). Liqueur can be substituted for the dark rum if desired.

1½ pounds chestnuts, shelled and
  peeled (for procedure page 550)
1½ cups water
1½ cups sugar

vanilla beans
piece of lemon peel
3 to 4 tablespoons dark rum

In a saucepan simmer the shelled and peeled chestnuts in enough water to cover them by 1 inch for 30 minutes, or until they are just tender. Drain thoroughly.

In a heavy saucepan combine the sugar, the water, 1 vanilla bean, and the lemon peel and bring the liquid to a boil over moderately low heat, washing down any sugar crystals clinging to the sides of the pan with the brush dipped in cold water until the sugar is dissolved. Add the chestnuts and simmer them for 10 minutes. Transfer the chestnuts with a slotted spoon to the sterilized jars and add a piece of vanilla bean to the jar or to each jar.

Sealed, the chestnuts
in syrup keep
indefinitely.

Boil the syrup for 10 minutes, or until it thickens, and stir in the rum. Pour the syrup over the chestnuts and seal the jars.

CHOCOLATE TRUFFLES

Yield:
about 50 truffles

Bourbon or dark rum could be substituted for the *eau-de-vie de framboise* called for in this recipe with equally delicious results.

12 ounces dark sweet chocolate,
  chopped coarse
4 egg yolks, beaten lightly
¼ cup heavy cream
1 stick (½ cup) unsalted butter, cut
  into bits and softened

3 tablespoons eau-de-vie de
  framboise (raspberry brandy)
⅓ cup unsweetened cocoa powder for
  rolling

In the top of a double boiler set over hot water melt the chocolate, stirring until smooth, and remove the pan from the heat. In a heavy saucepan combine the egg yolks and the cream and cook the mixture over low heat, stirring constantly, until thickened, but do not let it boil. Remove the pan from the heat and add the chocolate, stirring. Beat in the butter, piece by piece, and beat the mixture until thick and smooth. In a bowl combine the chocolate mixture with the *eau-de-vie de framboise* and chill the mixture, covered, for 4 hours, or until firm.

Line a jelly-roll pan with wax paper.

Scoop out a heaping teaspoon of the chocolate mixture, roll it into a ball, and roll the ball in the cocoa, coating it completely. Transfer the truffle to the jelly-roll pan. Make truffles with the remaining chocolate mixture and cocoa in the same manner. Chill the truffles in one layer for 2 hours, or until firm. Transfer the truffles to an airtight container and chill them until ready to serve.

The truffles keep, chilled, in an airtight container for up to 3 days.

CHOCOLATE HAZELNUT TRUFFLES

Yield:
40 truffles

This superb truffle is made with a brandy-flavored chocolate mixture that encases a whole hazelnut, all of which is then rolled in chopped hazelnuts.

3 tablespoons unsalted butter, softened
½ cup confectioners' sugar
1 egg yolk
2 tablespoons brandy
6 ounces semisweet chocolate, broken
* into pieces*

1 cup hazelnuts, toasted and skins
* removed (for procedure page 549),*
* reserving 40 of them whole and*
* chopping the remaining ones fine*

In a bowl cream the butter and beat in the sugar, a little at a time, until the mixture is light and fluffy. Beat the egg yolk and the brandy and combine the mixture well. In the top of a double boiler set over barely simmering water melt the chocolate, stirring, until smooth. Add the chocolate to the butter mixture, combine well, and chill the mixture, covered, for 1 hour, or until firm.

Line a tray with wax paper.

Shape level teaspoons of the mixture into balls around the whole hazelnuts, enclosing the nuts completely, and roll the balls in the chopped hazelnuts. Chill the truffles in one layer on the tray until firm.

Store in layers separated by wax paper in an airtight container in the refrigerator. The truffles keep for up to I week.

CHOCOLATE CASHEW TOFFEE

Yield:
about 1½ pounds

Equipment:
metal baking pan, 13
  by 9 inches
pastry brush
candy thermometer

1¼ cups firmly packed light brown
  sugar
¼ cup light corn syrup
5 tablespoons unsalted butter, cut into
  bits
1 tablespoon cider vinegar

¼ cup water
1 teaspoon vanilla
1 cup semisweet chocolate bits
¾ cup finely chopped roasted and
  salted cashews

Butter the baking pan.

In a heavy 2-quart saucepan combine the brown sugar, corn syrup, butter, vinegar, and the water, bring the mixture to a boil over moderate heat, washing down any sugar crystals clinging to the sides of the pan with the brush dipped in cold water until the sugar is dissolved, and boil the syrup, gently swirling the pan, until it is deep golden and the candy thermometer registers 290° F. (For the stages of sugar syrup, see illustrations page 241.) Stir in the vanilla, pour the toffee into the baking pan, tilting the pan and spreading the toffee with the back of a wooden spoon, and let it cool completely.

Store in layers
separated by wax
paper in an airtight
container in a cool,
dry place. The toffee
keeps for up to 1
week.

In the top of a double boiler set over barely simmering water melt the chocolate bits, stirring until smooth, and spread the chocolate evenly over the toffee. Sprinkle the cashews evenly over the chocolate, pressing them gently into it, and chill the confection for 30 minutes, or until the chocolate is firm. With a thin knife loosen the confection from the pan and using the knife as a lever remove it in one piece from the pan. On a chopping board cut the confection into serving pieces.

CHOCOLATE-COVERED STRAWBERRIES

Yield:
16 large or about 24
  medium
  strawberries

These splendid berries can be made even more special by being injected with liqueur. It is done with a flavoring injector or syringe, available at better kitchenware stores (see Shopping Sources page 555). We suggest using large long-stemmed strawberries for a particularly effective presentation.

6 ounces imported dark sweet
  chocolate, cut into pieces
2 to 3 tablespoons heavy cream
2 teaspoons orange-flavored liqueur

1 tablespoon unsalted butter, softened
1½ pints preferably large or medium
  strawberries with long stems intact

Line a baking sheet or tray with foil or wax paper.

In the top of a double boiler set over hot water melt the chocolate, stirring. Add 2 tablespoons of the cream, the liqueur, and butter and heat the mixture, stirring, until smooth. Holding each strawberry by its stem, dip it into the chocolate mixture, coating the lower two thirds and letting the excess drip back into the pan. (If the chocolate becomes too thick, return the pan to the heat and beat in the remaining cream, one teaspoon at a time, as necessary to thin the mixture to coating consistency.) As the strawberries are coated transfer them to the baking sheet. Let the chocolate cool and chill the strawberries for 15 to 20 minutes, or until the chocolate is set.

The strawberries keep, uncovered, at room temperature for 2 to 6 hours.

CHOCOLATE-COVERED APRICOTS

Yield:
3 cups

2½ cups dried apricots

½ pound imported dark sweet chocolate, chopped coarse

Line a baking sheet with wax paper.

In the top of a double boiler set over hot water melt the chocolate, stirring until smooth. Holding the apricot by one end, dip half of it into the melted chocolate, letting the excess drip off. Place the dipped apricot on the baking sheet and let the chocolate set. Continue to dip the remaining apricots in the melted chocolate in the same manner. The apricots are best served the day they are made.

CHOCOLATE PAILLETTES

Yield:
about 75

Equipment:
cake pans
½-inch oval metal
  cutter

We know of paillettes as spangles, sequins, or beads—adornments to eveningware. In this instance, they adorn too, as a garnish, simulating seeds for the Watermelon Bombe (page 384).

2 ounces semisweet chocolate, chopped coarse

In the top of a double boiler set over hot water melt the chocolate, stirring until smooth. With a metal spatula spread the chocolate in a $\frac{1}{16}$-inch layer on the bottom of the cake pans, inverted. Chill the chocolate for 30 minutes, or until hardened. With the cutter cut out ½-inch ovals and transfer them with the metal spatula to a sheet of foil. Keep the paillettes chilled until needed.

CHOCOLATE CASES

Yield:
12 cases

Equipment:
finely meshed rack
shallow pan
twelve 1-inch metal
   petit four tins
   (available at
   specialty
   kitchenware shops)
pastry brush

3 ounces semisweet chocolate, cut into bits
1½ tablespoons unsalted butter, softened
½ teaspoon oil plus additional for brushing

On the rack set over the pan invert the petit four tins, brush them with oil, and lay pieces of plastic wrap, each slightly larger than the tins, over each one, molding the plastic wrap to adhere to the tin. In a double boiler set over barely simmering water melt the chocolate and stir in the butter and the oil. Spoon the chocolate mixture generously onto the plastic over the tins, coating the tins completely, and chill the tins for 20 minutes, or until the chocolate is firm but not hard. With scissors trim the chocolate flush with the edge of the tins. Put the tins in the freezing compartment of the refrigerator for at least 1 hour. Lift the chocolate cases off the tins and remove the plastic wrap just before filling the cases.

Photo on page 29.

MERINGUE MUSHROOMS

Yield:
66 confections

Equipment:
pastry brush
candy thermometer
hand-held electric
   mixer
parchment paper
pastry bag fitted with
   ⅓-inch plain tip
small star tip

Meringue mushrooms are the traditional garnish on Yule logs. See the photo of our festive Bûche de Noël on page 520.

1 cup plus 1 tablespoon sugar
¼ cup water
2 large egg whites
pinch of salt
⅛ teaspoon cream of tartar

unsweetened cocoa powder for sprinkling if desired
1 recipe chocolate cream (page 539) at room temperature

In a heavy saucepan combine the 1 cup sugar with the water and bring the mixture to a boil over low heat, washing down any sugar crystals clinging to the sides of the pan with the brush dipped in cold water until the sugar is dissolved. Boil the syrup until it reaches the soft-ball stage, or until the candy thermometer registers 240° F.

While the syrup is cooking, in a bowl with the mixer beat the egg whites with the salt until foamy. Add the cream of tartar and beat the whites for 30 seconds. Sprinkle in the remaining 1 tablespoon sugar and beat the whites until they hold stiff peaks. Add the syrup in a stream, beating, and beat the meringue for 10 minutes, or until cool. (For the stages of sugar syrup and how to pour it, see illustrations pages 240 and 241.)

Preheat the oven to 200° F. Line baking sheets with the parchment paper. Fill the pastry bag fitted with the plain tip with the meringue and pipe out 66 mounds, each about 1 inch in diameter, 1 inch apart onto the baking sheets. Sift a bit of the cocoa over each cap, if desired, to simulate sand. Holding the pastry bag straight up, pipe out 66 medium-wide lengths onto the baking sheets, to resemble mushroom stems. Bake the meringues in the middle of the oven for 2 hours. Remove the baking sheet from the oven and with your fingertip push in the underside of each mushroom cap. Return the meringues to the oven and bake them for 30 minutes more. Turn off the oven and let the meringues stand in the oven overnight.

Store chilled in layers separated by wax paper in an airtight container.

Fill the pastry bag fitted with the star tip with the chocolate cream and pipe it into the undersides of the caps to simulate gills. Push a stem into each cap and chill the caps until the filling is firm.

BOURBON BALLS

Yield:
36 balls

Bourbon, a whiskey distilled from corn, is a spirit indigenous to the United States and especially the South. Besides being the essential ingredient in mint juleps, it is also widely used in desserts and confections. Bourbon balls are not only incredibly tasty but are incredibly easy to make, as they require no cooking. Note, however, that they should be made a week in advance to allow the flavors to meld. Vanilla wafers or gingersnaps could be used in place of the chocolate wafer crumbs if desired.

½ cup chopped raisins
¼ cup bourbon
2 cups chocolate wafer crumbs
½ cup firmly packed dark brown sugar
1 cup finely chopped pecans

¼ cup unsulfured molasses
½ teaspoon cinnamon
½ teaspoon ground ginger
½ teaspoon ground cloves

Store in an airtight container in a cool dark place for at least 1 week before serving.

In a small bowl let the raisins macerate in the bourbon for 15 minutes. In a large bowl combine well the wafer crumbs, brown sugar, ½ cup of the chopped pecans, the raisin mixture, molasses, cinnamon, ginger, and cloves. Form the mixture into 1-inch balls and roll the balls in the remaining ½ cup finely chopped pecans.

FONDANT BRANDIED CHERRIES IN CHOCOLATE CASES

Yield:
12 confections

This fanciful combination involves a three-step process. The chocolate cases have to be made, as well as the brandied cherries, which are then dipped in a mock fondant. The cherries themselves need to be aged for at least thirty days. This is clearly a recipe which requires advance preparation and is best reserved for a very special occasion.

*12 Brandied Cherries (recipe
　follows), patted dry
1¼ cups sifted confectioners' sugar*

*2 egg whites
2 tablespoons kirsch
12 Chocolate Cases (page 530)*

Set a rack over a sheet of wax paper.

In a bowl beat the confectioners' sugar with the egg whites and the kirsch until smooth. Holding each cherry by its stem, dip it into the sugar mixture and transfer it to the rack. Continue to dip the remaining cherries in the same manner. Let the cherries dry for 30 minutes. Dip the cherries into the sugar mixture a second time and let them stand on the rack for 1 hour, or until dry. Put 1 cherry in each of the chocolate cases.

Photo on page 29.

BRANDIED CHERRIES

Yield:
1 quart

Equipment:
needle
pastry brush
sterilized 1-quart
　Mason-type jar (for
　procedure page
　551) with a lid

*1 pound firm sweet cherries, with
　stems trimmed about 1 inch long
1 cup sugar*

*¼ cup cold water
1½ cups brandy plus additional
　brandy to cover*

Rinse the cherries and with the needle prick each cherry in 5 or 6 places. In a saucepan cover the cherries with water, bring the water to a boil over low heat, and simmer the cherries for 2 minutes. Transfer the cherries with a skimmer to a bowl of cold water, let them cool, and drain them. In the saucepan cover the cherries with cold water, bring the water to a boil, and simmer the cherries for 2 minutes more. Refresh under running cold water and repeat the process a third time.

In another saucepan combine the sugar with the water, bring the mixture to a boil over low heat, washing down any sugar crystals clinging to the sides of the pan with the brush dipped in cold water, and simmer the syrup for 3 minutes. Remove the pan from the heat, add ½ cup of the brandy, 2 tablespoons at a time, stirring, and let the mixture cool completely. Stir in 1 cup more brandy. Drain the cherries well, transfer them, holding them by their stems, to the Mason-type jar, and pour the syrup over them, adding more brandy if necessary to cover the cherries completely. Seal the jar with the lid and store the cherries in a cool place for at least 1 month.

SPICED NUTS

Yield:
about 5 cups

4 ounces blanched whole almonds (for
   procedure page 549)
4 ounces walnuts
4 ounces pecans
3 egg whites, beaten lightly

1 cup sugar
2½ teaspoons cinnamon
1½ teaspoons freshly grated nutmeg
½ teaspoon ground allspice
½ teaspoon ground ginger

Store in an airtight container in a cool, dry place.

Lightly oil baking sheets and preheat the oven to 350° F. In a bowl combine the almonds, walnuts, and pecans with the egg whites and stir the mixture until the nuts are well coated. In another bowl combine the sugar, cinnamon, nutmeg, allspice, and the ginger. Transfer the nuts with a slotted spoon to the sugar mixture and toss them to coat them thoroughly. Arrange the nuts ½ inch apart on the baking sheets and bake them in the middle of the oven for 8 to 10 minutes, or until they are browned and crisp Let the nuts cool on the baking sheets for 1 minute, transfer them with a spatula to a rack, and let them cool completely.

WALNUT PENUCHE

Yield:
forty-nine 1-inch
  squares

Equipment:
pastry brush
candy thermometer
7-inch square shallow
  pan

Penuche is a fudge-like confection made with brown sugar and cream and, in this recipe, it is made even more delicious with the additions of walnuts and rum.

1 cup granulated sugar
1 cup light cream
1 cup firmly packed light brown sugar

1 tablespoon dark rum
2 cups broken or halved walnuts

Butter the baking pan.

    In a heavy saucepan combine the granulated sugar, light cream, and the light brown sugar. Bring the mixture to a boil over moderate heat, stirring constantly and washing down any sugar crystals clinging to the sides of the pan with the brush dipped in cold water. Reduce the heat and simmer the mixture, undisturbed, until it reaches the soft-ball stage, or the candy thermometer registers 238° F. (For the stages of sugar syrup, see illustrations page 241.) Remove the pan from the heat and let the mixture cool for 5 minutes. Add the rum and beat the mixture until it thickens. Sprinkle the walnuts into the baking pan, pour in the fudge mixture, and shake the pan until the mixture is evenly distributed. Let the penuche cool to room temperature and cut it into 1-inch squares.

ESSENTIAL PREPARATIONS

*I*n this final chapter of *Gourmet's Best Desserts* we have collected recipes integral to other recipes in the volume, as well as a handful of procedural instructions. The recipes make for a very varied grouping: There are butters and custards, icings and glazes, syrups for soaks and sugars, fruit purées, and, lastly, several chocolate preparations that serve as decorations, a marzipan recipe, and even one mincemeat. The procedural instructions include such basics as how to toast and skin hazelnuts, blanch almonds, peel oranges, grate fresh coconut, and sterilize Mason-type canning jars.

Some of these recipes are clearly more essential to your mastering the many aspects of dessert-making than are others. Being able to turn out a silky-smooth pastry cream is crucial to the success of a number of desserts—fruit tarts, for example, or Boston cream pie—and all of the principles of preparing a cooked custard (see the introduction to "Custards," page 333) apply. Similarly, think of the number of recipes that rely on something as simple as perfectly whipped heavy cream. There are pies and tarts, mousse cakes, pastries, ice creams, and the list could go on and on.

Alternatively, there are recipes in this chapter that are clearly less essential to other preparations elsewhere in the book, but which are interesting in their own right and will act to increase your culinary expertise. *Crème fraîche*, for instance. We have actually included two different preparations for this recipe—one that is heated and one that is not.

And there are recipes herein that would never be defined as essential except as they act as an *important* ingredient in another recipe. There is no pie without the mincemeat in Madeira Mincemeat Pie with Cheddar Crust (page 135). Among these non-essentials we would even include marzipan, unless, of course, you are a dedicated cake decorator.

To review this chapter is to appreciate anew the diversity of components that comprise the glorious world of desserts.

CLARIFIED BUTTER

Yield:
about ¾ cup

Equipment:
cheesecloth
jar or crock

The butter keeps,
covered and chilled,
indefinitely.

2 sticks (1 cup) unsalted butter, cut into 1-inch pieces

In a heavy saucepan melt the butter over low heat. Remove the pan from the heat, let the butter stand for 3 minutes, and skim the froth. Strain the butter through a sieve lined with a double thickness of rinsed and squeezed cheesecloth into a bowl, leaving the milky solids in the bottom of the pan. When clarified, butter loses about one fourth of its volume.

Pour the clarified butter into the jar or crock and store it, covered, in the refrigerator.

CHOCOLATE BUTTER

Yield:
about 1 cup

*1 stick (½ cup) unsalted butter,
   softened*
1 cup sifted confectioners' sugar

*1 ounce unsweetened chocolate, melted
   and cooled*
2 teaspoons vanilla
⅛ teaspoon salt

In a bowl cream the butter, add the confectioners' sugar, a little at a time, the chocolate, vanilla, and the salt, beating, and beat the mixture until it is smooth and blended well. Transfer the butter to a crock and chill it for 30 minutes, or until it is firm enough to spread.

CHERRY BUTTER

Yield:
about 1½ cups

Equipment:
food processor fitted
  with steel blade

The butter keeps,
covered and chilled,
for up to 2 weeks.

½ cup pitted dark sweet cherries
*½ cup firmly packed light brown
   sugar*

*1 stick (½ cup) unsalted butter, cut
   into bits and softened*
1 tablespoon fresh lemon juice

In the food processor blend the cherries, brown sugar, butter, and the lemon juice until combined well. Transfer the mixture to a ramekin and chill it, covered. Let the cherry butter soften slightly at room temperature before serving it.

CRÈME FRAÎCHE

Yield:
about 1 cup

1 cup heavy cream

1 tablespoon buttermilk

The *crème fraîche* keeps, covered and chilled, for 2 to 4 weeks.

In a jar combine the cream and the buttermilk and shake the mixture, covered tightly, for at least 1 minute. Let stand at room temperature for at least 8 hours, or until thick.

THICK CRÈME FRAÎCHE

Yield:
about 2⅓ cups

2 cups heavy cream (not ultra-pasteurized)

⅓ cup buttermilk

The *crème fraîche* keeps, covered and chilled, for up to 2 weeks.

In a saucepan combine the cream and buttermilk and heat the mixture over moderate heat until it is just warm (99° F.). Do not let the mixture become hot. Pour the mixture into a plastic or glass container and put the container, covered, in a larger container. Add enough warm water to the larger container to come up to the level of the cream and let the mixture stand in a warm place for 12 to 36 hours, or until thickened, adding more warm water to the container as necessary to keep it warm. Store the *crème fraîche*, covered and chilled. (It will become thicker as it chills.)

PASTRY CREAM

Yield:
1 cup

Equipment:
hand-held electric mixer

3 egg yolks
⅓ cup sugar
2 tablespoons cornstarch

2 tablespoons all-purpose flour
1 cup milk, scalded
1 teaspoon vanilla

In a large bowl with the mixer beat the egg yolks until combined, add the sugar, a little at a time, beating, and beat the mixture until light and lemon colored. Add the cornstarch and the flour, a little at a time, beating, and beat the mixture until smooth. Add the hot milk in a stream, beating, and beat the mixture until combined well. Transfer the mixture to a heavy saucepan and bring it to a boil, stirring. Simmer the mixture, stirring, for 3 minutes. The mixture will be thick and custard-like. Remove the pan from the heat and stir in the vanilla. Strain the pastry cream into a bowl and chill it, covered with a buttered round of wax paper, for 1 hour, or until chilled well.

KIRSCH-FLAVORED PASTRY CREAM

Yield:
1¾ to 2 cups

Equipment:
hand-held electric
  mixer

2 egg yolks
¼ cup sugar
2 tablespoons all-purpose flour, sifted
⅔ cup milk, scalded

½ teaspoon unflavored gelatin
4 teaspoons cold water
2 tablespoons kirsch
⅓ cup well-chilled heavy cream

In a bowl with the mixer beat the egg yolks and sugar until light and lemon colored. Gradually add the flour and beat the mixture until smooth. Add the hot milk in a stream, stirring. Transfer the mixture to a heavy saucepan and boil it over moderate heat, stirring, for 2 minutes. Remove the pan from the heat.

Sprinkle the gelatin over the water to soften and stir it into the cream with the kirsch. Strain the pastry cream into a bowl, cover it with a buttered round of wax paper, and let it cool.

In a chilled bowl with the mixer beat the cream until it holds soft peaks. Stir the chilled pastry cream briskly with a whisk until soft and smooth and fold in the whipped cream.

Variation:

COFFEE-FLAVORED PASTRY CREAM: Substitute 1 tablespoon instant espresso dissolved in 1 tablespoon dark rum for the kirsch and proceed as above.

ALMOND PASTRY CREAM

Yield:
about 2½ cups

Equipment:
hand-held electric
  mixer

4 egg yolks
1 large egg
⅓ cup sugar
⅓ cup all-purpose flour, sifted
1½ cups milk, scalded
3 tablespoons unsalted butter, softened
  and cut in pieces

⅓ cup pulverized amaretti (Italian
  almond macaroon cookies,
  available at specialty foods shops)
3 tablespoons Cognac
1 teaspoon vanilla
¼ teaspoon almond extract
1 cup whipped heavy cream

In a bowl with the mixer combine the egg yolks, egg, and sugar and beat the mixture until light and lemon colored. Add the flour gradually and beat until smooth. Add the scalded milk in a stream, beating. Transfer the mixture to a heavy saucepan and boil it over moderately low heat, stirring with a wooden paddle, for 2 minutes. Remove the pan from the heat and beat in the butter. Stir in the *amaretti*, Cognac, vanilla, and almond extract. Transfer the pastry cream to a bowl and let the cream cool, covered with a buttered round of wax paper. Fold the whipped cream into the pastry cream gently but thoroughly.

ALMOND CREAM

1 cup ground lightly toasted almonds
¼ cup ground Almond Macaroons
   (page 262)
1 large egg, beaten lightly
1 egg yolk

⅓ cup sugar
1 stick (½ cup) unsalted butter, cut
   into pieces and softened
2 tablespoons dark rum
1 tablespoon lemon rind

Into a bowl sift the ground almonds and macaroons. Stir in the egg, egg yolk, sugar, butter, rum, and lemon rind and combine the mixture well. Form the almond cream into a cake about 6 inches in diameter and chill it for several hours, or until completely firm.

CHESTNUT CREAM

Yield:
about 4 cups

Equipment:
hand-held electric
  mixer

1 cup Marrons Glacés (page 526)
1½ cups well-chilled heavy cream

2 tablespoons brandy

Drain the chestnuts, reserving the syrup, and chop them coarse. In a chilled bowl with the mixer beat the cream until it holds stiff peaks. Fold in 3 tablespoons of the reserved syrup, the brandy, and the chestnuts. Use the cream to fill Chocolate Cases (page 530).

CHOCOLATE CREAM

Crème Ganache

Yield:
about 2½ cups

Equipment:
hand-held electric
  mixer

8 ounces semisweet chocolate, chopped
  coarse

⅔ cup heavy cream
¼ cup orange-flavored liqueur

In the top of a double boiler set over hot water melt the chocolate with the heavy cream and the liqueur, stirring until smooth. Transfer the mixture to a metal bowl, let it cool, and chill it, stirring occasionally, for 30 minutes. With the mixer beat the chocolate until it just holds soft peaks.

FONDANT

Yield:
about 2 cups

2 cups sugar
¾ cup water

1 tablespoon light corn syrup

Equipment:
pastry brush
candy thermometer
moistened smooth
  surface, preferably a
  marble slab

In a saucepan combine the sugar with the water and corn syrup and cook over low heat, washing down any sugar crystals clinging to the sides of the pan with the brush dipped in cold water until the sugar is dissolved. Increase the heat to moderately high and cook the syrup, gently swirling the pan, until the candy thermometer registers 240° F. (For the stages of sugar syrup, see illustrations page 241.) Pour the syrup onto the moistened smooth surface and let it cool for 1 to 2 minutes. With a metal or wooden scraper work the syrup from the edges toward the center until it is white and creamy. Scrape the fondant into a ball and, when it is cool enough to handle, knead it as you would dough until smooth.

The fondant keeps,
wrapped and chilled,
indefinitely.

SUGAR ICING

Yield:
enough icing for
  about fifty 4-inch
  cookies

2 egg whites
pinch of cream of tartar
pinch of salt

2 teaspoons water
3 cups confectioners' sugar, sifted
food coloring if desired

Equipment:
hand-held electric
  mixer

In a large bowl with the mixer beat the egg whites with the cream of tartar, salt, and water until frothy. Beat in the sugar, a little at a time, and beat until the mixture holds stiff peaks (see illustrations page 238). Beat in the food coloring if desired. Decorate baked cookies with the icing, using a spatula or a pastry bag fitted with a small decorative tip, and let the cookies stand for 20 minutes, or until the icing is set.

APRICOT GLAZE

Yield:
½ cup

½ cup apricot preserves, strained

1 tablespoon Cognac if desired

In a small saucepan combine the preserves and the Cognac, if desired. Bring the mixture to a boil, stirring, and simmer it, stirring, for 1 minute.

Variation:

RUM-FLAVORED APRICOT GLAZE: Substitute 1 tablespoon dark rum for the Cognac.

RED CURRANT GLAZE

Yield:
I cup

1 cup red currant jelly

1 tablespoon kirsch, or to taste

In a stainless steel or enameled saucepan melt the jelly with the kirsch over moderately low heat, stirring. Bring the mixture to a boil, stirring, and simmer it for 1 minute.

VANILLA SUGAR

Yield:
3 cups

3 cups granulated sugar

one 8-inch vanilla bean, split lengthwise

The sugar keeps, covered tightly, indefinitely.

Pour the sugar into a jar, bury the vanilla bean in it, and let the mixture stand, covered tightly, shaking the jar several times, for 2 weeks. The used vanilla beans, rinsed and dried, may be reused.

VANILLA CONFECTIONERS' SUGAR

Yield:
3 cups

3 cups confectioners' sugar, sifted

one 8-inch vanilla bean, split lengthwise

The confectioners' sugar keeps, covered tightly, indefinitely.

Pour the confectioners' sugar into a jar, bury the vanilla bean in it, and let the mixture stand, covered tightly, shaking the jar several times, for 10 days. The used vanilla beans, rinsed and dried, may be reused.

CINNAMON SUGAR

Yield:
about I cup

1 teaspoon cinnamon

1 cup granulated sugar

The sugar keeps, covered tightly, indefinitely.

In a bowl combine the cinnamon with the sugar.

SUGAR SYRUP

Yield:
2½ cups

Equipment:
pastry brush

The syrup keeps,
chilled, in a sealed jar
indefinitely.

1 cup sugar   *2 cups water*

In a saucepan combine the sugar and water and bring the mixture to a boil, stirring and washing down any sugar crystals clinging to the sides of the pan with the brush dipped in cold water until the sugar is dissolved. Cook the syrup over moderate heat, undisturbed, for 5 minutes and let it cool.

BRANDY SYRUP

Yield: 1½ cups

½ cup sugar   *¼ cup brandy*
1 cup water

In a heavy saucepan dissolve the sugar in the water over moderate heat and cook the syrup for 10 minutes. Remove the pan from the heat and stir in the brandy.

RUM SYRUP

Yield:
3 cups

1 cup sugar   *½ cup dark rum*
2 cups water

In a heavy saucepan dissolve the sugar in the water over moderate heat and cook the syrup for 10 minutes. Remove the pan from the heat and stir in the dark rum.

COFFEE SYRUP

Yield:
about ¾ cup

The syrup keeps,
covered and chilled,
for up to 1 month.

½ cup firmly packed light brown   *½ cup water*
     sugar   *¼ cup instant coffee powder*
2 tablespoons dark corn syrup

In a small heavy saucepan combine the sugar, corn syrup, and water, bring the mixture to a boil over moderate heat, stirring until the sugar is dissolved, and remove the pan from the heat. Add the coffee powder, stirring until dissolved, skim the froth, and let the syrup cool. Transfer the syrup to a bowl and chill it, covered, for at least 1 hour, or until cold.

STRAWBERRY SYRUP

Yield:
about 3 cups

3 cups hulled and thinly sliced
*   strawberries*

⅔ cup sugar
⅔ cup water

Equipment:
food processor fitted
    with steel blade

The syrup keeps,
covered and chilled,
for at least I week.

In the food processor or in a blender in batches purée the strawberries, transfer the purée to a stainless steel or enameled saucepan, and stir in the sugar and water. Bring the mixture to a boil over moderate heat, stirring, and simmer it for 1 minute. Force the mixture through a fine sieve set over a bowl and chill the syrup, covered, for at least 3 hours.

SPUN SUGAR

Equipment:
candy thermometer
pastry brush

2 cups sugar
¼ teaspoon cream of tartar

1 cup water

Tape 2 wooden spoons parallel to each other 10 inches apart on a kitchen counter so that the handles project 8 inches out from the counter. Lightly oil the handles. Spread newspapers around the area where the sugar will be spun. With a wire clipper cut off the bottom of a fairly large whisk so that the wires hang free.

Remove the spun
sugar from the
handles gently and
store it in a cool, dry
place until ready to
use. Spun sugar
should not be made
more than several
hours in advance of
serving.

In a small heavy saucepan dissolve the sugar and cream of tartar in the water and cook the syrup over high heat, washing down any sugar crystals clinging to the sides of the pan with the brush dipped in cold water until the candy thermometer registers 290° F. (For the stages of sugar syrup, see illustrations page 241.) Remove the pan from the heat and let the syrup stand for 30 seconds. Dip the whisk in the syrup, let the syrup drip off for a moment, and shake the whisk back and forth across the two wooden handles so that the sugar threads accumulate between the handles (see illustration). Continue to spin the sugar until the desired amount has been made.

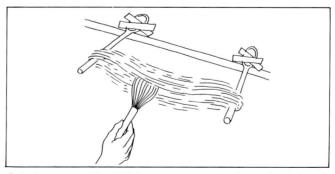

Spinning sugar with whisk between spoon handles to form threads

ALMOND PRALINE

Yield:
about 2 cups

Equipment:
marble slab or jelly-
  roll pan
pastry brush

A wonderful dessert staple to have on hand, almond praline, ground to a powder, can also be used as a topping for ice creams, puddings, or mousses.

1½ cups sugar
¼ cup water

1 cup whole blanched almonds (for procedure page 549)

Oil the marble slab or jelly-roll pan well.

In a heavy saucepan bring the sugar and water to a boil over moderately high heat, stirring and washing down any sugar crystals clinging to the sides of the pan with the brush dipped in cold water until the sugar is dissolved. Cook the syrup, gently swirling the pan, until it turns a light caramel. Add the almonds and swirl the pan until the nuts are coated with the caramel and begin to make a popping sound. Boil the syrup until it is a slightly darker caramel color. Pour the praline onto the marble slab and let it cool until hard. Transfer the praline to a cutting board and chop it coarse.

The praline keeps,
covered and chilled,
in a glass jar
indefinitely.

HAZELNUT PRALINE

Yield:
about 3 cups

Equipment:
well-oiled marble slab
  or baking sheet
pastry brush

2 cups sugar
⅓ cup water

1½ cups hazelnuts, toasted and skins removed (for procedure see page 549)

Oil the marble slab or baking sheet well.

In a heavy saucepan bring the sugar and water to a boil over moderately high heat, stirring and washing down any sugar crystals clinging to the sides of the pan with the brush dipped in cold water until the sugar is dissolved. Cook the syrup, gently swirling the pan, until it turns a light caramel. Stir in the hazelnuts, return the syrup to a boil, and boil it until it is a slightly darker caramel. Pour the praline immediately onto the marble slab and let it cool completely. Break the praline into pieces. If praline powder is required, grind it fine in batches in a food processor fitted with the steel blade.

The praline keeps,
covered and chilled,
in a glass jar
indefinitely.

MARZIPAN DECORATIONS

Equipment:
small fine-tipped paint
  brush

The following marzipan decorations enliven the top of Carrot Cake with Cream Cheese Frosting (page 51). Of course, marzipan can be fashioned into any shape of choice.

FOR THE MARZIPAN
one 8-ounce can almond paste, grated,
1⅔ to 2 cups confectioners' sugar,
  sifted

1 tablespoon vanilla
1 tablespoon lightly beaten egg white

1 tablespoon unsweetened cocoa
  powder combined with 1 tablespoon
  water
2 drops of red food coloring combined
  with 1 tablespoon evaporated milk
4 drops of yellow food coloring
  combined with 2 drops of red food
  coloring

3 drops of green food coloring
  combined with 2 drops of yellow
  food coloring

Make the marzipan:

In a bowl combine the almond paste, 1⅔ cups of the confectioners' sugar, the vanilla, and the egg white and knead the mixture, adding more of the confectioners' sugar if the marzipan is too sticky, until smooth.

Form one third of the marzipan into 8 small rabbits and let the rabbits dry on wax paper overnight. Chill the remaining marzipan in an airtight container. Using the brush, paint the rabbits and their eyes carefully with the cocoa mixture and color their noses with the evaporated milk mixture. Knead the combined yellow and red food coloring into a small amount of the remaining marzipan and form carrots with it. Knead the combined green and yellow food coloring into a small amount of the remaining marzipan, form leaves for the carrots with some of it, and force the remaining green marzipan through a fine sieve to form grass. Transfer the grass with a small knife from the sieve to wax paper to dry for 1 hour.

CHOCOLATE CURLS

Equipment:
2 or 3 cake tins

3 ounces semisweet chocolate, chopped coarse

In the top of a double boiler set over hot water melt the chocolate, stirring until smooth. With a metal spatula spread the chocolate in a very thin layer onto the surface of the inverted cake tins. Chill the chocolate for 10 to 15 minutes, or until it loses its shine and is solid but still pliable. Removing one pan from the refrigerator at a time, put a metal spatula under an edge of the chocolate and push it firmly away from you along the pan so that the chocolate curls as it is pushed.

Chill the chocolate for several minutes more if it becomes too soft. Transfer the curls to a sheet of wax paper and chill them as they are made.

CHOCOLATE LEAVES

Yield:
24 leaves

3 ounces imported bittersweet chocolate, cut into bits

twenty-four 2-inch lemon leaves or other decorative non-poisonous leaves (available at florists)

Line a jelly-roll pan with wax paper.

In the top of a double boiler set over barely simmering water melt the chocolate, stirring until smooth. With a spoon coat the back (non-shiny) side of each leaf with the chocolate, being careful not to let the chocolate drip onto the shiny side. Put the leaves, chocolate side up, on the jelly-roll pan. Prop the edges of the leaves with pieces of foil or paper towel to allow the edges to curl. Chill the leaves for 20 minutes, or until the chocolate has hardened, and, working quickly, peel off the lemon leaves. (If the chocolate gets too soft, chill the leaves for 5 minutes more, or until the chocolate has hardened.) Keep the chocolate leaves chilled until just before serving.

CHESTNUT PURÉE

Yield:
about 1 cup

Equipment:
food mill fitted with medium disk

¾ pound chestnuts, shelled and peeled (for procedure page 550)
one 2-inch piece of vanilla bean

milk
water

In a saucepan simmer the chestnuts with the vanilla bean in equal parts milk and water to cover for 40 minutes, or until soft. Drain the chestnuts and purée them through the food mill into a bowl.

RASPBERRY PURÉE

Yield:
about 2 cups

1½ pints fresh raspberries or two 10-ounce packages frozen raspberries, thawed and drained

½ cup superfine granulated sugar, or to taste
2 tablespoons kirsch

Force the fresh raspberries through a fine sieve into a bowl. (Or purée the frozen raspberries in a food processor fitted with the steel blade and strain the purée through a fine sieve into a bowl.) Stir in the sugar and the kirsch. Chill the purée, covered.

STRAWBERRY PURÉE

Yield:
about 2 cups

Equipment:
food processor fitted
   with steel blade

1 pound (about 1 pint) strawberries, hulled and sliced
½ cup superfine granulated sugar

1 teaspoon fresh lemon juice
1 tablespoon eau-de-vie de framboise (raspberry brandy)

In the food processor or in a blender purée in batches the strawberries and transfer the purée to a bowl. Stir in the sugar, lemon juice, and the *eau-de-vie de framboise*, and chill the mixture, covered, for 2 hours.

BLOOD ORANGE AND LIME CURD

Yield:
about 2 cups

6 egg yolks
¾ cup blood orange juice (about 1 pound blood oranges), half the peel grated and the other half cut into strips

¼ cup fresh lime juice (about 2 limes), the peel from one cut into strips
½ cup sugar
1 stick (½ cup) unsalted butter, cut into pieces

In the top of a double boiler combine the egg yolks, orange juice, strips of orange peel, lime juice, strips of lime peel, and the sugar and whisk the mixture over simmering water until wisps of steam appear and it comes just to a simmer. Remove the pan from the heat and beat in the butter, one tablespoon at a time. Strain the curd into a bowl and stir in the grated orange rind. Cover the curd with a buttered round of wax paper and let it cool. Chill the curd in a covered container until ready to use.

MADEIRA MINCEMEAT

Yield:
about 6 cups

Equipment:
food grinder
2 sterilized 1-quart
  Mason-type jars (for
  procedure page
  551)

1 pound lean boiled beef
8 ounces beef suet
2 cups firmly packed light brown
  sugar
2 cups raisins
2 cups dried currants
½ cup chopped walnuts or almonds
½ cup glacéed citron
¼ cup Candied Orange Peel (page
  522), chopped

¼ cup candied lemon peel, chopped
½ tablespoon salt
½ tablespoon freshly grated nutmeg
½ tablespoon cinnamon
1 teaspoon mace
1 teaspoon ground cloves
1 teaspoon ground ginger
½ cup minus 2 tablespoons brandy
1½ cups Sercial or Verdelho Madeira

Put the beef and the suet through the food grinder onto a sheet of wax paper. In a large bowl combine well the meat mixture, sugar, raisins, currants, nuts, citron, orange peel, lemon peel, salt, nutmeg, cinnamon, mace, cloves, and ginger.

Pack the mixture into the sterilized Mason-type jars, divide the brandy and the Madeira between the jars, and seal the jars with the lids. Let the mincemeat ripen in the refrigerator for at least 2 weeks.

PROCEDURES

TO PEEL AND SECTION ORANGES

With a sharp stainless steel paring knife slice off enough skin from both ends of the orange to expose the flesh. Working on a board to catch any juices, stand the orange upright and with the knife cut downward along the contours of the orange, removing strips of the skin with the white pith attached to expose the flesh of the orange completely.

To section the orange, hold it over a bowl to collect additional juices. Slice down to the core on either side of each segment, separating the sections from the membranes and letting the segments and juices fall into the bowl.

TO PEEL PEACHES

In a kettle of boiling water blanch the peaches for 30 seconds, transfer them to a bowl of ice and cold water, and slip off the skins.

TO GRATE FRESH COCONUT

Yield:
about 4 cups

Equipment:
food processor fitted
  with steel blade

1 large coconut without any cracks and containing liquid

Preheat the oven to 400° F.

    Pierce the eyes of the coconut with an ice pick or a skewer, drain the liquid, and reserve it for another use. Bake the coconut for 15 minutes. Break it with a hammer and remove the flesh from the shell, levering it out carefully with the point of a strong knife. Peel off the brown membrane with a vegetable peeler and cut the coconut meat into small pieces. Grind the pieces a few at a time in the food processor or in a blender. (Or grate the meat on the fine side of a grater.)

TO BLANCH ALMONDS

Into a large saucepan of boiling water drop the almonds. Boil them for 1 minute, or until the skins wrinkle, and drain them in a colander. Refresh the almonds under cold water, slip off the skins by squeezing the almonds between two fingers, and pat the almonds dry. Let the almonds stand in one layer on a baking sheet for 2 hours, or until they are completely dry. Do not dry the almonds in the oven.

TO TOAST AND SKIN HAZELNUTS (OR FILBERTS)

Preheat the oven to 350° F.

    Toast the hazelnuts in one layer in a jelly-roll pan for 10 to 15 minutes, or until they are colored lightly and the skins blister. Wrap the nuts in a dish towel and let them steam for 1 minute. Rub the nuts in the towel to remove the skins and let them cool. Note that some of the hazelnuts will not be completely skinned; they can be used nonetheless.

TO BLANCH AND OVEN-DRY PISTACHIO NUTS

Preheat the oven to 300° F.

    In a heatproof bowl pour boiling water to cover the pistachio nuts and let the nuts stand for 1 minute. Drain the nuts, turn them out onto a dish towel, and rub off the skins. Spread the nuts on a baking sheet and let them dry in the oven for 15 minutes.

TO ROAST AND PEEL CHESTNUTS

Preheat the oven to 400° F.

    With a sharp knife score each chestnut ¼ inch deep all around. Spread the chestnuts, no more than 1 pound at a time, in one layer in a jelly-roll pan and roast them for 20 minutes, or until the shells are just opened. Holding the chestnuts in a pot holder or a thick towel, peel off both layers of skin with a knife while the chestnuts are still hot.

TO COOK CHESTNUTS

In a deep skillet arrange shelled and peeled chestnuts in one layer, add water to cover, and simmer the chestnuts for 45 minutes, or until tender. Drain and pat the chestnuts dry.

TO MAKE FINE FRESH BREAD CRUMBS

Yield:
about 4½ cups

Equipment:
food processor fitted
  with steel blade

a 1-pound loaf of homemade-type white bread, sliced

Tear the bread slices into 1-inch pieces and grind them fine in batches in the food processor or in a blender. Store the crumbs, covered and chilled.

TO MAKE FINE DRY BREAD CRUMBS

Yield:
about 3½ cups

Equipment:
food processor fitted
  with steel blade

a 1-pound loaf of homemade-type white bread, sliced

Put the bread slices on a rack to dry overnight. Or, preheat the oven to 250° F. and dry the slices on a baking sheet in the oven, turning them, for 25 to 30 minutes, or until they are crisp but not colored. Break the bread into 1-inch pieces and grind it fine in batches in the food processor or in a blender. Store the crumbs in a cool, dry place.

TO STERILIZE JARS AND GLASSES

Wash the jars in hot suds and rinse them in scalding water. Put the jars in a kettle and cover them with hot water. Bring the water to a boil, covered, and boil the jars for 15 minutes from the time that steam emerges from the kettle. Turn off the heat and let the jars stand in the hot water. Just before they are to be filled invert the jars onto a dish towel to dry. The jars should be filled while they are still hot. Sterilize the jar lids for 5 minutes, or according to the manufacturer's instructions.

TO SEAL JARS OR GLASSES WITH PARAFFIN

Jars or glasses should be filled to within ¼ inch of the top with jelly or jam and the remaining headspace should be filled with a double layer of melted paraffin.

To prepare the paraffin, shave the bar into the top of a double boiler set over simmering water and melt it. When ready to seal the jar, wipe off any jelly that may have stuck to the rim. Pour a ⅛-inch layer of the melted paraffin over the jelly, swirling it to cover the jelly completely, and let it set. Pour another layer of paraffin in the same manner and let it set.

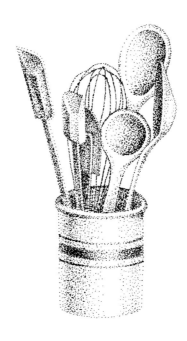

RECIPE ACKNOWLEDGMENTS

JEAN ANDERSON Highland Molasses Ginger Cake with Glacéed Fruits, page 108; Pennsylvania Dutch Shoofly Pie, page 144; Moravian Christmas Cookies, page 304; Molasses Almond Brittle Ice Cream, page 353

JAMES BEARD Strawberry Tart, page 167; Baked Custard, page 334; Caramel Custard, page 335; Small Vanilla Custards, page 340; Crème Brûlée, page 341; James Beard's Tipsy Parson, page 344; Frozen Orange Soufflé, page 374; Bombe Adeline, page 381; Bombe Joséphine, page 382; Poached Apricots, page 466

LILLIAN LANGSETH-CHRISTENSEN Wachauer Torte, page 31; Walnut Cake with Coffee Buttercream, page 56; Rehrücken, page 68; Bayrischer Nuss Stollen, page 81; Marillenkuchen, page 86, Linzertorte, page 183; Cherry Strudel, page 234; Sugared Butter Strips, page 278; Vanilla Wreaths, page 279; Apricot Jam-Filled Strips, page 280; Aristocrats, page 282; Almond Loaf Cookies, page 282; Filbert Balls, page 283; Sugar Pretzels, page 285; Bavarian Apricot-Filled Almond Cookies, page 300; Honey Spice Cookies, page 301; Lemon Syllabub, page 391; Salzburger Nockerl, page 425; Palatschinken, page 444; Krapfen, page 451

MARION CUNNINGHAM Groom's Cake, page 103; Bride's Cake, page 104; Steamed Ginger Pudding, page 331; Chocolate Butter, page 536

GEORGIA CHAN DOWNARD Deep-Dish Blueberry Peach Pie, page 138; Almond Cherry Tart, page 180; Madeira Bread Pudding, page 323; Amaretto Peach Ice Cream, page 355; Gingered Pecan Peach Crumble, page 476; Sour Cherry Cobbler, page 480; Cherry Butter, page 536; Madeira Mincemeat, 548

MIMI ELDER Maple Rice Pudding, page 319

MIREILLE GUILIANO Galette des Rois, page 100

BARBARA KAROFF Orange Steamed Pudding, page 329

MARGARET H. KOEHLER New York Cheesecake, page 93; Chocolate Cheesecake, page 94

ELISABETH LAMBERT ORTIZ Coffee Custards, page 338; Mango Mousse Barbados, page 394; Mango Fool Barbados, page 483

(MRS.) LOU SIEBERT PAPPAS Rich Grand Marnier Ice Cream, page 349; Spongecake Layered with Chocolate Ice Cream and Chocolate Mousse, page 386; Praline Soufflé, page 422

SHIRLEY SARVIS Banana Cream Layer Cake, page 50; Orange Pecan Cake, page 73; Frozen Lemon Meringue Cake, page 246; Parfait Custard, page 366; Rum Raisin Parfait, page 366; Vanilla Parfait with Raspberries, page 366; Chocolate Parfait Custard, page 367; Pistachio Parfait with Caramel Sauce, page 367; Brown Sugar Soufflé Omelet, page 430; Vanilla Lime Soufflé Omelet, page 430

IRENE SAX Lemon and Blueberry Bread and Butter Pudding, page 323

RICHARD SAX Alsatian Pear Tart, page 178

MARGARET SHAKESPEARE Chocolate Meringue Mousse, page 394

ELIZABETH SCHNEIDER Indian Pudding, page 317; Plum Slump, page 478; Apple Pandowdy with Maple Cream Sauce, page 479; Cranberry Cobbler with Orange Sauce, page 481

NADIA STANCHIOFF Queen of Sheba Soul Cake, page 66

KATHRYN STEWART Rhubarb Crisp, page 477

SALLY TAGER Lemon Roll, page 42

LISA YOCKELSON Brown Butter and Nutmeg Meltaways, page 291; Pine Nut Puffs, page 292; Currant Crisps, page 293; Date Nuggets, page 293; Almond Leaves, page 306; Chocolate Shortbread Hearts, page 308; Ginger Crescents, page 310

CARRIE YOUNG Devil's Food Cake with Rhubarb Sauce, page 60; North Dakota Lemon Meringue Pie, page 156

TABLESETTING ACKNOWLEDGMENTS

The editors have not listed below any photographs in which the properties are privately owned. All addresses unless otherwise indicated are in New York City. Duplicate addresses for sources are not given.

Back Jacket and page 288: French tole tray, circa 1790—Pierre Deux Antiques, 369 Bleecker Street. Val St. Lambert "Balmoral" crystal plates—Cardel, Ltd., 621 Madison Avenue.

Frontispiece: Georg Jensen "Bernadotte" sterling dessert spoon, Royal Copenhagen/Georg Jensen Silversmiths, 683 Madison Avenue. Orrefors "Casino Royale" crystal coupes—Orrefors Crystal Gallery, 58 East 57th Street.

Page 12: Ginori "Rapallo" china platter—Cardel, Ltd., Gorham Historic Charleston Reproductions "King Charles" sterling cake server; Mottahedeh Charleston Reproductions "Blue Canton" vase—B. Altman & Company, Fifth Avenue and Thirty-fourth Street.

Page 25: Iron Mountain "Pond Mountain" stoneware dinner plate—Royal Copenhagen Porcelain, 683 Madison Avenue.

Page 29: English silver tray; Caughley-Coalport porcelain cups and saucers, circa 1800 (three of a set of nine); English sterling coffeepot, sugar bowl, and sugar tongs—James Robinson, 15 East 57th Street. "Quirinale" handmade sterling demitasse spoons—Buccellati, Inc., 46 East 57th Street. English papier-mâché tray, circa 1820, on wooden stand—Stair & Company, Inc., 942 Madison Avenue. Rumanian handwoven wool rug—Coury Rugs, Inc., 515 Madison Avenue.

Page 37: Organdy tablecloth—Léron, Inc., 745 Fifth Avenue.

Page 57: Italian silver-plate tray; silver-plate tray—S. Wyler, Inc., 713 Madison Avenue. Peill "Florida" crystal bowl—Cardel, Ltd.

Page 89: Glass cake stand—Mayhew, 507 Park Avenue. "Navarre" sterling tray by Wilcox & Wagoner, New York City, circa 1900—F. Gorevic & Son, Inc., 635 Madison Avenue. English engraved cut-glass plates, circa 1850—Bardith Ltd., 901 Madison Avenue. English "Queen Anne" hand-forged sterling serving pieces—James Robinson.

Page 118: Spode china dessert plates (from a set of 8), circa 1820—James II Galleries, Ltd., 15 East 57th Street. Handmade tassel—Alberto Pirini, Borgo Ognissanti, 22, Florence, Italy.

Page 131: French glass bowl—Pampered Kitchens★, 21 East 10th Street.

Page 137: "Dover" sterling dessert forks and pie server—Oneida Silversmiths, Oneida, New York. "Naomi" bone china dessert plates—Waterford-/Wedgwood, 41 Madison Avenue. English cut-glass jug, circa 1810—Bardith Ltd. "Colleen" crystal iced-tea glasses—Waterford/Wedgwood.

Page 157: Villeroy & Boch "Basket" porcelain dessert plates—Mayhew. "Thaxton" sterling dessert fork—Thaxton & Company, 780 Madison Avenue. Nineteenth-century cotton tea cloth; linen napkins—Cherchez, 864 Lexington Avenue.

Page 171: Victorian Sheffield tray, circa 1870—S. Wyler, Inc.

Page 179: Silver-plate tray—F. Gorevic & Son, Inc.

Page 184: Old American coin silver tray by L. Forbes & Co., Saint Louis, 1857—F. Gorevic & Son, Inc.

Page 186: "Torchon" hand-forged sterling cake knife—Buccellati, Inc. Handmade sterling basket—Cartier, Inc., 653 Fifth Avenue. Hand-appliquéd organdy tablecloth—Bergdorf Goodman, 754 Fifth Avenue.

Page 199: Haviland "Imperatrice Eugenie" china dessert plate and sugar bowl—Lord & Taylor, Fifth Avenue and Thirty-eighth Street. Rosenthal "Tivoli" crystal tumblers; St. Louis "Cerdagne" crystal pitcher; "Queen Anne" silver iced-tea spoons—Cardel, Ltd. "Old French" (Encore Collection) sterling cake server; "Old English Tipt" sterling lemon fork—The Gorham Company, Providence, Rhode Island. "Lily of the Valley" organdy napkins—Léron, Inc. Wicker table—Mayhew. Victorian bamboo table with tiles—The Very Thing★, 149 East 72nd Street. Folding screen (one of a kind); plants—Stephen Barany★, 149 East 72nd Street.

Page 202: Limoges cake plate—Mayhew.

Page 214: "Stanton Hall" sterling cake server—Oneida Silversmiths. "Snowflakes" hand-embroidered organza and linen tablecloth—Léron, Inc. "Eckespoint" poinsettias—Paul Ecke Poinsettia Ranch, Encinitas, California.

Page 222: Minton china compote and dessert plate, circa 1840, English cut glass jar, circa 1830—Bardith Ltd.

Page 225: English silverplate salver, circa 1870; set of 6 flashed and cut glass plates, circa 1865—James II Galleries, Ltd.

Page 230: Sterling serving dish; "Column" sterling cake server—Cartier. "Chinese" natural straw basket—The JoJo Shop★, 145 East 72nd Street. Flower arrangement—Stephen Barany★. "Copa" cotton table fabric (available through decorator)—Quadrille Wallpapers and Fabrics, Inc., 979 Third Avenue. Rattan side chair—Walters Wicker Wonderland, 991 Second Avenue.

Page 236: English silver-plate waiter—S. Wyler, Inc.

Page 247: Bernardaud "Aries" Limoges porcelain cake plate—Mayhew. "Queen Anne" hand-forged sterling serving spoon and caker server—James Robinson. French Apilco 1¼-quart porcelain soufflé dish—Bazaar de la Cuisine, Inc.★, 1003 Second Avenue.

Page 252: Giraud Limoges "Cheverney" porcelain tart tray; Chamart "Tahiti Gold" porcelain cake plate—Mayhew. "Scroll" sterling cake server—James Robinson. English china dessert plates, circa 1850, James II Galleries, Ltd.

Page 258: Wedgwood china dessert plates, circa 1810, James II Galleries, Ltd.

Page 299: French porcelain biscuit boxes, circa 1900—Howard Kaplan's French Country Store, 35 East 10th Street.

Page 302: Sterling basket, circa 1920; sterling platter by Reed & Barton, circa 1920—F. Gorevic & Son, Inc. Nineteenth-century English decoupage screen—Trevor Potts Antiques, 1011 Lexington Avenue.

Page 312: Mansion House pewter sconce—Oneida Silversmiths.

Page 316: Parfait glasses—Cardel. Cotton canvas table cover—Cherchez.

Page 324: Kimax glass soufflé—Manhattan Ad Hoc Housewares★, 842 Lexington Avenue.

Page 330: Delft charger, circa 1760—Bardith, Ltd.

Page 340: "Moustiers Berain Bleu" French faïence *pots de crème* with matching tray—The Mediterranean Shop, 876 Madison Avenue.

Page 354: Arzberg German porcelain cake stand—Mayhew.

Page 357: Ice-cream soda and sundae glasses; stainless steel sundae spoon—Bridge Kitchenware Corporation, 214 East 52nd Street. Stainless steel ice-cream soda spoons—Manhattan Ad Hoc Housewares★. Tablescapes "Candy Stripes" cotton napkins with polyester and cotton lace—Wolfman ● Gold & Good Company, 484 Broome Street. Wurlitzer jukebox (model 1015), 1947; Carrara glass table top with cast-iron base, circa 1900—Urban Archaeology, 135 Spring Street.

Page 361: Waterford crystal cake stand—Bloomingdale's, 1000 Third Avenue.

Page 364: Gorham sterling tray, circa 1850—F. Gorevic & Son, Inc.

Page 379: Italian "New Wave Geometric" hand-painted earthenware espresso cups and saucers designed by Rosanna Imports—Panache, 1015 Western Avenue, Seattle, Washington.

Page 384: Rosenthal "Romance White" porcelain platter—Cardel, Ltd.

Page 388: Sterling tray—Cartier. Hand-embroidered organdy tablecloth—Bergdorf Goodman.

Page 400: Victorian silver waiter; Victorian silver tray; English footed glass bowl, circa 1830—James II Galleries, Ltd.

Page 405: Lalique "Honfleur" crystal serving plate—Cardel, Ltd.

Page 414: Hand-painted Louis XV Style "faux bois" wood table (available through decorator)—Yale R. Burge, 305 East 63rd Street. Pillivuyt soufflé dish, Bridge Kitchenware Corporation.

Page 428: Nineteenth-century Rorstrand china dessert plates, Christofle "Vendome" silverplate flatware, Linen napkins—Bergdorf Goodman.

Page 432: "George Sand" hand-painted porcelain dessert plate (special order only)—Céralene, Inc., 55 East 57th Street. English sterling tray, Sheffield, circa 1925—James Robinson.

Page 436: Ungaro glass platter—Cardel, Ltd.

Page 456: "Plateau" crystal plate—Baccarat, Inc., 55 East 57th Street. Norwegian crystal bowl (ladle not shown)—Plummer McCutcheon★, 145 East 57th Street.

Page 460: Ironstone bowl; Spanish painted wire baskets—Wolfman ● Gold & Good Company.

Page 465: "Malmaison" silver-plate dish—Christofle Silver at Baccarat, Inc.

Page 475: English silver-plate waiter, circa 1870; set of 6 flashed and cut engraved glass plates, circa 1865—James II Galleries, Ltd.

Page 484: Avitra Hungarian crystal coupes—Mayhew.

Page 488: Stuart crystal bowl—Cardel, Ltd. St. Louis glass vases, circa 1830—James II Galleries, Ltd. "Bedford Quilt" cotton fabric (available through decorator)—Brunschwig & Fils, Inc., 979 Third Avenue. Philippine rattan chairs with cushions; Chinese woven straw rug—Bloomingdale's. Antique wicker fernery—The Gazebo of New York, 660 Madison Avenue. "Regine" vinyl wallpaper and matching cotton fabric (available through decorator)—Carleton V Ltd., 979 Third Avenue.

Page 520: English lustre glass vase, circa 1850—James II Galleries, Ltd. Tiffany sterling tray, circa 1925; Tiffany

"Atlantis" sterling cake server, circa 1900—Fortunoff, 681 Fifth Avenue. Italian nineteenth-century drawn-work cloth—Françoise Nunnallé Fine Arts, 105 West 55th Street (by appointment only).

(*★ indicates that the business is no longer in existence*)

SHOPPING SOURCES

Most of the ingredients and equipment used in the recipes throughout this book are readily available in supermarkets or in local kitchenware shops. However, if you are unable to locate a specific ingredient such as chocolate coffee beans or crystallized ginger or specific equipment such as *coeur à la crème* or *croquembouche* molds, we suggest the following mail-order sources:

Madame Chocolate
1940-C Lehigh Avenue
Glenview, Illinois 60025
312-729-3330 (chocolate)

Bridge Kitchenware Corporation
214 East 52nd Street
New York, New York 10022
212-688-4220 (equipment)

The Chef's Catalog
3915 Commercial Avenue
Northbrook, Illinois 60062
312-480-9400 (equipment and some foodstuffs)

Maid of Scandinavia
3244 Raleigh Avenue
Minneapolis, Minnesota 55416
800-328-6722 (equipment and foodstuffs)

Maison Glass
52 East 58th Street
New York, New York 10022
212-755-3316 (equipment and some foodstuffs)

Williams-Sonoma
Mail-Order Department
P.O. Box 7456
San Francisco, California 94120-7456
415-421-4242 (equipment and some foodstuffs)

Key West Lime Juice
Nellie & Joe's, Inc.
P.O. Box 2368
Key West, Florida 33045
305-296-5566 (key lime juice)

GENERAL INDEX

RECIPE TITLE INDEX